Vietnam Handbook

Published by Footprint Handbooks
6 Riverside Court
Lower Bristol Road
Bath BA2 3DZ. England
T +44 (0)1225 469141
F +44 (0)1225 469461
Email handbooks@footprint.cix.co.uk
Web www.footprint-handbooks.co.uk

ISBN 1 900949 36 9
CIP DATA: A catalogue record for this
book is available from the British Library.

In USA, published by
Passport Books, a division of
NTC/Contemporary Publishing Group
4255 West Touhy Avenue, Lincolnwood
(Chicago), Illinois 60646-1975, USA
T 847 679 5500 F 847 679 24941
Email NTCPUB2@AOL.COM

ISBN 0 8442-2193-7
Library of Congress Catalog Card
Number on file

© Footprint Handbooks Ltd 1999
Second edition

Footprint Handbooks and the Footprint
mark are a registered trademark of
Footprint Handbooks Ltd.

Credits

Series editor
Patrick Dawson
Editorial
Senior editor: Sarah Thorowgood
Maps: Alex Nott and Jo Williams
Production
Pre-Press Manager: Jo Morgan
Typesetting: Ann Griffiths and
Emma Bryers
Maps: Kevin Feeney, Richard Ponsford,
Robert Lunn and Claire Benison
Proof reading: Howard David and
John Work

Marketing
MBargo, Singapore

Design
Mytton Williams

Photography
Front cover: Tony Stone Images.
Back cover: Impact Photos.
Inside colour section: Impact Photos;
John Wright; Dan White; Duncan
MacArthur; Jayawardene Travel
Photography.

Printed and bound
in Italy by LEGOPRINT.

Every effort has been made to ensure
that the facts in this Handbook are
accurate. However, travellers should still
obtain advice from consulates, airlines
etc about current travel and visa
requirements before travelling. The
authors and publishers cannot accept
responsibility for any loss, injury or
inconvenience however caused.

Neither the black and white nor
coloured maps are intended to have any
political significance.

Vietnam

Footprint

Handbook

John Colet and Joshua Eliot

Mariners '... took such an Affection to that Country [of Vietnam] that not a Man of them would go away; so that the Captian of the Ship was forc'd to drive them abroad with many Blows and Cuts ...'

Borri, Christoforo (1633) *Cochin China*, London: Richard Clutterbuck

Contents

Left: *smoky incense coils and sticks in the Pagoda of the Jade Emperor, one of Saigon's most popular and attractive temples.*

6

Right: *pigs on sale in the market town of Vinh Long, in the Mekong Delta.*

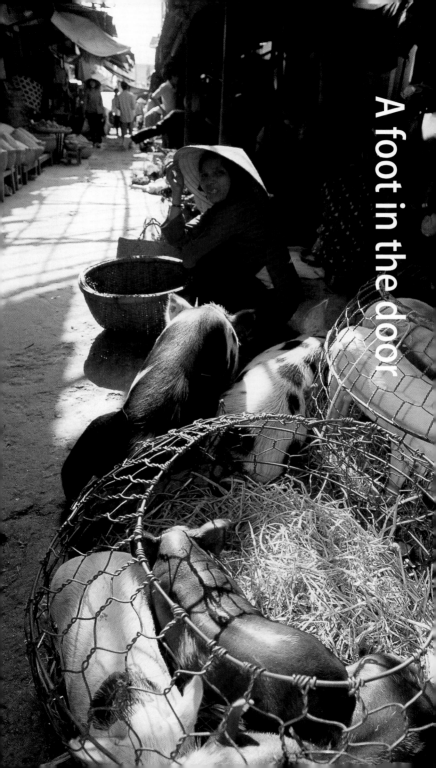

A foot in the door

Below: downtown Saigon on a Sunday night. *Right*: the colonial bricks of Saigon's Notredame Cathedral reflected in the glass of the city's new office towers. *Centre*: Halong Bay, In the north of the country, with its thousands of islets. *Bottom*: threshing rice in the Mekong Delta.

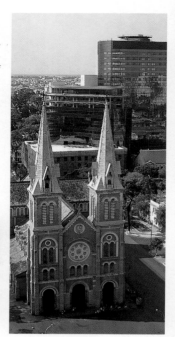

Highlights

Anyone arriving in Vietnam for the first time will have his or her own private collection of emotions and expectations. Vietnam conjures up strong, and often conflicting, images - grim jungle warfare, cloudy pagodas, dour communism, beautiful ao dai-clad women. For some, these expectations are confirmed by experience but most find that Vietnam is nothing like the place they imagined and they leave with broadened horizons and new perceptions of this extraordinary country.

Hanoi: ancient and modern

With a wonderful natural setting on the Red River, Hanoi is an elegant and refined city of lakes and parks connected by well ordered, tree-lined streets. Not yet fully a capital city in the modern sense (thankfully), Hanoi is making rapid strides and has acquired, in the space of ten short years, restaurants to quicken the heart of the most demanding of gourmets, hotels to delight the sternest of critics, and cafés and shops to cheer the most jaded of diplomat's wives. And herein lies Hanoi's real charm and delight: it manages to combine ancient with modern - cyclos with limos, noodle carts with nouvelle cuisine and, most importantly, every gradation in between.

Saigon nightlife

At just 300 years old, Saigon is a relative youngster compared with Hanoi and this seems to show in the boundless energy of the southern city. Having shrugged off wartime and Communist curfews, the Saigonese seem determined that their city should never sleep. Few people realize Vietnam has nightlife of any sophistication but Saigon has a range of bars of international, as well as ill, repute. Discos, night-clubs, pleasure-domes and dens – it has them all. If you return home bleary-eyed at four o'clock in the morning after slurping that much needed bowl of pho, expect to be greeted by fresh, newly-risen joggers out stretching their legs and grannies practising tai chi.

Vietnam's two rice baskets

Any country with as queer a shape as Vietnam might be expected to offer some interesting landscapes and scenery. The country has been likened to a bamboo carrying-pole with rice baskets at either end: the Red River Delta in the north and the Mekong Delta in the south. The narrow central provinces provide the slender connection between these two (literal and metaphorical) baskets.

Backbone of the country

Around the Red River Delta are ranged the mountains of the north culminating in Fan Si Pan, Vietnam's highest peak. Further south they form a knobbly backbone to the country and a barrier to cultural influences from the Indianised states to the west. Not only have the mountains proved an effective screen to alien cultures, they have also nurtured in their isolated pockets small but vibrant ethnic minorities of diverse traditions. The villages and human landscapes of the Tay, Thai, Ba'na and Hmong tribes reflect their differing beliefs, farming methods, history, crops and technologies: the Thai with their assiduously sculpted rice terraces, the vertiginous fields that the Hmong cultivate and the compact, walled villages of the Ba'na.

Beaches and coastline

Vietnam's sinuous coastline threads its way around 3,000 kilometres of rocky headlands and mountainous promontories, through muddy deltas and argillaceous swamps, across parched salt pans, sandy dunes and sunny beaches. Along its compass there are some wonderfully exciting and very lovely stretches.

The coast features strongly in almost all visits to Vietnam and a boat trip or two is almost mandatory. Many find great pleasure drifting among the thousand islets of Halong Bay; others prefer the quiet of Phu Quoc's coves. Nha Trang's golden miles are busy with tourist traffic, but far fewer make it to Ho Coc's pleasantly isolated shores.

Historical sights

Hué: 19th century capital Hué was made capital in 1802 and served as the seat of the Nguyen dynasty until 1945. Its architecture was consciously modelled on that of imperial China and is grand in conception, massive in scale and far more ambitious than anything else in Vietnam. The vast imperial palace was largely destroyed in the Tet offensive of 1968 but a number of pavilions and temples survive. Each emperor, and many leading courtiers, built himself a tomb in the surrounding countryside using court geomancers to select the perfect setting - and these came through the conflict largely undamaged. Today, the tombs are either neglected, or sprucely maintained, depending upon the popularity of the buildings with tourists and the light in which the emperor's life is portrayed by Party historians. Some slide into deeper obscurity obliterated by weeds and decay, while the less fortunate ones are 'restored' somewhat insensitively.

Growing old gracefully Hoi An, a charming town just south of Danang, is a wonderfully preserved slice of history. Hoi An's port silted up two hundred years ago and little has changed since then. Most of its buildings date from between the 16th to 19th centuries and the town has retained its compact nature and diminutive scale. The people of Hoi An have also maintained a poise, grace and tranquility which makes the town a glorious place to relax and visit temples, clan houses and burghers' homes.

Hanoi's heritage Capital for a thousand years, Hanoi has collected the architecture, artefacts and atmosphere you would expect from such a history. Generations of monarchs, monks, mandarins and merchants have left their mark on Hanoi's citadels, temples, and artisans' quarters. The pressures of being a capital city in a country frantic to become an economic tiger do show, but Hanoi none the less remains a fair and refined city with a rich artistic heritage.

The war remembered Most people are more familiar with Vietnam's modern history than its ancient history. Indeed, the image of Vietnam carried by some newly arrived visitors is shaped solely by 'The Vietnam War'. Thankfully, there are not many visible reminders of those terrible times and those there are tend to be visually disappointing. But to anyone with even the skimpiest understanding of the events of 1945 - 1975, the war sites are invested with strong historical symbolism. Cu Chi, outside Saigon, is one of the more visited war sites and although much has been reconstructed, visitors familiar with the story of the men and women who lived and fought in the tunnels cannot fail to be moved by the experience.

Ancient Champa ruins In the plastic arts of sculpture and architecture the Vietnamese rarely displayed the virtuosity or creativity of some of their neighbours. It was left, therefore, to the artistically accomplished Cham, occupants of the kingdom of Champa, in what is now central Vietnam, to produce Vietnam's most lovely architecture and her finest sculpture. The Cham derived their inspiration from the ancient Khmer kingdoms and flourished artistically between the seventh and the twelfth centuries. Hindu and Sivaists, the Cham ornamented their temples with images of Vishnu, Siva and Ganesh. Cham temples take the form of small but beautifully proportioned towers. The finest examples of Cham building are to be seen at My Son (outside Danang) and Nha Trang, with another distinguished collection at Phan Rang. There is also a museum of Cham sculpture in Danang, which shows the scuptor's art at its very finest.

Left: renovated 13th century Cham ruins of Po Klaung-garai, near Phan Rang; **Below**: Cham temple ruins from the seventh century at My Son; **Centre**: detail from the Hein Nhon gate in the thick outer walls of the Imperial City at Hué. Emperor Gia Long commenced construction in 1804 and it took 20,000 men just to build the walls.
Bottom: everyday scene, cycling past the Vietnamese flag in Hanoi.

XAM - ĐEC CHIA XIM
CHỦ TỊCH QUỐC HỘI
QUYỀN QUỐC TRƯỞNG
VƯƠNG QUỐC CAM - PU - C
THĂM HỮU NGHỊ CHÍNH T
NƯỚC C.H.X.H.C.N VIỆT N

Cuisine

What do you get if you cross a corpulent Chinese cook sweating in his string vest and wielding a razor-sharp chopper with a skinny, irate French chef wringing his hands over a deflated soufflé? Answer: Vietnamese cooking. Sprinkle in a good dose of *nuoc mam*; add lots of green leaves, chillies, innovative flair; leave to mature for several centuries and the result is some of the most exciting, original and tasty food available anywhere between Paris and Peking.

Culinary culs-de-sac
Unfortunately, those staying in predominantly tourist hotels may leave the country thinking that Vietnamese cuisine consists of a monotonous diet of spring rolls, crab soup, chicken in lemon grass and steamed rice – and that hardy perennial of the backpacker café, the banana pancake. If you want to break out of this dead end cuisine and be a bit more adventurous, then the best plan of attack is to get friendly with a couple of locals – easy enough in Vietnam – and ask them to introduce you to the local fare.

A national favourite
A particular delight that should not be missed is *pho*. Pho is a bowl of white, flat noodle soup served with chicken or beef. The soup is made from stock flavoured with star anise, ginger and other spices and herbs but precise, individual recipies often remain a closely guarded secret. Pho is usually eaten in the morning, often in the evening but rarely at lunchtime, when Vietnamese require a more filling meal accompanied by rice. On each table of a pho restaurant sits a plate of fresh green leaves: mint, cinnamon basil and the spiky looking *ngo gai*, together with bean sprouts, chopped red chillies, barbecue sauce and sliced lemons enabling patrons to produce their own variations on a theme.

Roll your own
There are many types of roll: the most common are deep fried spring rolls (confusingly, *cha gio* in the south and *nem ranh* in the north) but if these appear on your table too frequently, look for the fresh or do-it-yourself types, such as *bi cuon* or *bo bia*. Essentially, these are salads with prawns or grilled meats wrapped in rice paper. Customers who roll their own cigarettes are at a distinct advantage while innocents abroad are liable to produce sagging Camberwell Carrots that collapse in the lap.

Seafood
It would be invidious to isolate a particular seafood dish when there are so many to chose from. Prawns are prawns – the bigger and the less adulterated the better. But a marvellous dish that does deserve commendation is crab in tamarind sauce. This glorious fusion of flavours, bitter tamarind, garlic, piquant spring onion and fresh crab is quite delicious. To the Vietnamese, part of the fun of eating crab is the fiddly process of extracting meat from the furthest recesses of its claws and legs. A willingness to crack, crunch, poke and suck is required to do it justice, not a task for the squeamish but great for those who aren't.

Gastronomic priority
When it comes to food, Vietnamese do not stand on ceremony and (perhaps rather like the French) regard peripherals such as furniture, service and ambience as mere distractions to the task of ploughing through plates, crocks, casseroles and tureens charged with piping hot meats, vegetables and soups. Do not expect good service, courses to arrive in the right order, or to eat at the same time as your companions but do expect the freshest and tastiest food you will find anywhere. And as a rule of thumb: if you are not enjoying the food you are eating in the wrong type of place – not in the wrong country.

Left: crêpe stall in Saigon. French influence has pervaded cuisine in Saigon at both the 'haute' and the 'bass' level. **Below**: beans at a stall in Buon Ma Thuot's market, Dak Lak province. **Centre**: Dalat's market, where exotic fruit and vegetables grown in the temperate climate of the surrounding area are sold. **Bottom**: the ubiquitous pho noodle soup, eaten daily by Vietnamese up and down the country.

Ethnic minorities

The population of Vietnam is estimated at 75 million people. Of these, around 90 percent are ethnic Vietnamese or *kinh*. Chinese form a large segment of the urban population, especially in Saigon's Chinatown, Cholon and the remaining minorities, often referred to as *montagnards*, tend to live in the highland areas of north and central Vietnam. Separated from the majority by language, custom, religion and habit, the hill tribes are 'Vietnamese' only in the sense that they occupy the modern territorial space recognised as Vietnam. Having said that, things are changing: ethnic minorities of today are just as likely to wear jeans as sarongs; most speak Vietnamese; many minority children are educated in government schools; in some instances minority girls take Vietnamese husbands, a milestone in the process of ethnic assimilation. Historically, the sentiments of the minorities have not been as resolutely pro-Vietnamese as government propaganda would have us believe. The anti-colonial struggle was nobly supported by hill tribes, but competition between montagnard and kinh for land and political supremacy is still a problem.

Human landscapes The people of the hill tribes take a bit of finding but diversions into the Central Highlands, excursions from Dalat or a trip up to Sapa will reveal a wholly different Vietnam. Their culture is rich and varied; their beliefs and customs are remarkable; their resourcefulness and utilisation of marginal land is a marvel and their scenic assemblages of fields, costume, villages and houses represent some of the most breath-takingly beautiful sights in the country.

Black Hmong Visitors to Vietnam are most likely to meet people from the Black Hmong or the Thai tribes. The Black Hmong are concentrated in the northwest of Vietnam at higher elevations, usually over 1,500 metres. Living at such altitudes in the forested hills, high above the rivers and alluvial plains, they make their living by shifting cultivation. They clear steep slopes and plant maize, sweet potatoes, dry rice, bananas and traditionally opium, a valuable cash crop. The Hmong are among the more retiring and retiscent of the hill-tribes. Their houses and fields are often surrounded by barricades of thorn bushes to deter visitors. Ironically, however, most visitors to Vietnam will meet the Hmong traders of Sapa, who are some of the more gregarious of all the minorities. Being from higher altitudes where temperatures are lower, the Hmong typically dress in heavy clothing. Not surprisingly, the dress of the Black Hmong is predominantly black. The younger girls wear an indigo skirt but graduate to a black, above the knee skirt with black leggings at the onset of puberty. The Hmong, like many of the other minorities, are fond of heavy silver jewellery: necklaces, earrings and bracelets.

Thai In sharp contrast to the Hmong, the Thai live on the valley floors where they cultivate rice in paddy fields just like the Vietnamese. Unlike the Vietnamese, however, the Thai have taken the very sensible precaution of building their houses on stilts to keep themselves and their possessions dry during the annual flood. The space beneath the stilt houses is an ideal place for keeping chickens, pigs, bicycles and so on and where the young children often play. Being lowland folk, their lives are inextricably linked with water. The children splash and swim at all times of day but especially in the evening when they drive the buffaloes down for a well earned wallow. The Thai are excellent weavers and produce hand-loomed fabrics of great intricacy and beauty. Found all over Northwest Vietnam there are thought to be about one million Thai in total but such is their integration into Vietnamese society that it can be difficult to distinguish them from kinh. However, in the remote country and in small villages their traditions, culture and costumes are still clearly distinctive.

Left: men of the Black Hmong hill tribe at Sapa market. Inevitably it is the men who first abandon their traditional garb as the North Vietnamese army helmets suggest. **Below**: portrait of Thai girls. **Centre**: buffalos (used to pull ploughs) and rice terraces in the Sapa Valley. **Bottom**: children of the Meo hill tribe engrossed in their noodle soup. **Next page**: street scene from the bustling Cholon district, Saigon's Chinatown, in the southwest of the city.

Essentials

2

Essentials

Planning your trip

Where to start

Vietnam is a long thin country with a distinctive and curvaceous S-shaped coastline. Having a capital in the north and its largest city in the south makes it easy for the traveller to fly in at one end of the country and depart from the other without having to double back. So where should you land: Hanoi or Saigon?

For a list of tour operators worldwide, see page 59.

For those intending to fly in to one city and out at the other there really is now no clear advantage one way or the other. Saigon still has the edge over Hanoi in terms of the variety and choice of tour operators and Saigonese are, perhaps, a more gregarious and less xenophobic bunch than the Hanoians and they speak better English which might make acclimatization easier. On the other hand Hanoi and surrounds are infinitely more interesting than Saigon; Hanoi retains more that is distinctively and indisputably Vietnamese than Saigon, which is rapidly becoming a bland synthesis of Asian styles and values. But that is perhaps really only relevant to the Saigon *or* Hanoi argument which short stay visitors must debate.

Where to go

Particular highlights which any visitor to Vietnam would do well not to miss are: (from north to south) the hill station of **Sapa** for its stunning scenery and hill-tribes (for those who don't mind roughing it a tour of North West or North East Vietnam should be given careful consideration); **Hanoi**, which itself is historical, beautiful and cultured, lies at the heart of a vast range of architectural and scenic treasures (which can be done on day trips out); time permitting, **Cat Ba Island** and **Halong Bay** should be included for their coastal scenery. Moving south there then follows a yawning gulf of mediocrity so it is not until **Hué** that the next stop should be made. Hué's palaces and mausoleums deserve two days but most visitors give them only one (it does rather depend on the weather). The splendid train journey from Hué to Danang should not be missed but Danang itself has little to commend it (apart from the Cham Museum) which is why most travellers head straight for nearby **Hoi An**, an enchanting 17th century mercantile town. Between here and Saigon the seaside town of **Nha Trang** is the main attraction but the sleepy resort of **Phan Thiet** should be considered as a more tranquil alternative. **Saigon**, although a city of six million, is really a small town: no sensible tourist will stray far from the colonial core which, containing as it does all anyone could possibly need in the way of hedonistic pleasures (and with scarcely any intellectual or cultural distractions), is the most popular destination in the country. The six million are jammed into suburbs, an indescribable density of bodies living out their days in an inferno of noise, sewage and motorbikes. While the **Mekong Delta** has its attractions it would be hard to justify its inclusion on the 'must-see' list.

When to go

Despite its historic and cultural resonance Tet, Vietnamese new year, is not really a good time to visit. This movable feast usually falls between late January and March and with aftershocks lasts for about a fortnight. It is the only holiday most people get in the year. Popular destinations are packed, roads are jammed and for a couple of days almost all hotels and restaurants are shut.

During the school summer holidays some resorts get busier, Cat Ba, Do Son, Phan Thiet and Long Hai, for example: prices rise, there is a severe squeeze on rooms and weekends will be worse.

Most of Vietnam is hot and wet for much of the year. In the north and highland areas the winter months, December to March, can be chilly. Travel in the south and Mekong Delta can be difficult at the height of the Monsoon (particularly September, October and November). The central regions and north sometimes suffer typhoons and tropical storms from May to November. Hué is at its wettest wet from September to January. Climatatically the best time to see Vietnam is around December to March. With luck it should be dry. In the south it is warm but not too hot with lovely cool evenings. Admittedly the north and the highlands will be a bit chilly but they should be dry with clear blue skies.

What to take

Cash Take some small denomination US dollars for incidental expenses and large denomination bills (US$100) for changing into the local currency (dong). Make sure bills are 'clean'/unmarked. **Money belt. Travellers' cheques** together with proof of purchase. (See Money section page 22.)

Passport photographs A stock of at least four and completed Visa Application Form.

A small first aid kit Including medicine for stomach disorders/diarrhoea (can be hard to find outside Saigon/Hanoi).

Torch Can be useful for viewing caves, dark pagodas and during power cuts.

Penknife

Photocopies Of passport and visa (and entry permit, issued on arrival).

Clothes Long-sleeved shirts for cool evenings, severely air-conditioned restaurants and to prevent sunburn. Long trousers and socks to keep mosquitoes from biting in the evening. Warm clothing is necessary for upland areas in winter. Women might consider wearing dresses rather than jeans when travelling, for easier access to squat toilets.

Shampoo With screw-on top (Body Shop is the only supplier of travel proof shampoo and creams).

Reading material Little available, and journeys are long.

Slide film Available in Saigon and Hanoi but rarely elsewhere; print film is more widely sold. Do not get slides processed in Vietnam – chemicals tend to be stale, poor results.

Insect repellent

Strong padlock For locking bags in hotel rooms and while travelling.

What not to take

Maps Cheap ones are available in Saigon and Hanoi.

Dictionaries Many cheap ones on sale in larger towns.

Foreign cigarettes They can be bought in Vietnam.

Waterproof/umbrella For wet season: ubiquitous and cheap in Vietnam.

Video tapes (See Customs, page 21), although small VCR tapes are fine.

Too many clothes Cheap in Vietnam.

Travel light   Many travellers take too much. T-shirts and shorts etc can be bought cheaply in Vietnam. Good quality underwear and socks cannot, however. Bottled water is widely available. There is no need to bring water filters unless trekking in remote areas. Books are very scarce, so bring plenty. Print film can be bought everywhere, slide film only in Hanoi and Saigon. Most young people sensibly carry all their worldly goods in rucksacks and are referred to by the Vietnamese as *tay ba lo,* a term which has acquired derogatory overtones. Hotels, even those at the bottom end of the market, usually provide mosquito nets so it should not be necessary to bring your own.

Vietnamese embassies and consulates

Australia, 6 Timbara Crest, O'Malley, Canberra ACT, T62866059.

Cambodia, 436 Blvd Preach, Phnoṃ Penh, T25481.

Canada, 226 Maclaren Street, Ottawa, Ontario, K2P OL9, T613-2360772.

China, 34 Guanghua Lu, Jianguo Dang Nghiem Hoanh, Menwai, Beijing, T5321125.

CIS, UL Nolshaia Piragovxkaia, 13 Nguyen Manh Cam, Moscow, T2450925.

France, 62-66 Rue Boileau, Paris 16e, T 452-45063.

Germany, Konstantin Strasse 37, 5300-Bonn 2, T357021.

India, 42 F South Extension, New Delhi, T624586.

Indonesia, 25 Jalan Teuku Umar, Jakarta, T325347.

Italy, 000187 Roman Piazza, Barberini 12, T4755286.

Japan, 50-11 Motoyoyogi-Cho, Shibuya-ku, Tokyo 151, T446311.

Laos, No 1, That Luang, Vientiane, T5578.

Malaysia, 4 Persisan Stonor, Kuala Lumpur, T2484036.

Myanmar (Burma), 40 Komin Kochin Rd, Yangon (Rangoon), T50361.

New Zealand see Australia.

Philippines, 54 Victor Cruz, Malate, Manila, T500364.

Sweden, Orbyslotsvag 26, 12578 Alvsjo, Stockholm, T861214, F010-468 995713.

Switzerland, 34 Chemin Francois Lehman, 1218 Grand Sacconnex, Geneva.

Thailand, 83/1 Wireless Rd, Bangkok 10501, T2517201.

UK, 12-14 Victoria Rd, London W8 5RD, T0171-937 1912, 0900-1200, 1400-1800.

USA, Liaison Office, 1233, 20th St NW, Washington DC 20036, T202-8610737, F202-8611397.

For details of foreign embassies in Vietnam, see the directory under individual town listings.

Essentials

Before you travel

Getting in

Valid passports with visas issued by a Vietnamese embassy are required by all visitors, irrespective of citizenship. Visas are not available on arrival in Vietnam. Time needed to process a visa varies from country to country and according to type of visa required. Tourist visas generally take two to three days. Bangkok is regarded as the easiest and quickest place to get a visa.

Visas are normally valid only for arrival by air, Noi Bai (Hanoi airport) and Tan Son Nhat (Saigon airport). The standard tourist visa is valid for one month for one entry (*mot lan*) only. Business visas are valid for three or six months and usually enable multiple entry (*nhieu lan*). Those wishing to enter or leave Vietnam by land must specify the border crossing when applying. It is possible to alter point of departure at immigration offices in Hanoi and Saigon. Visa regulations are ever changing: usually it is possible to extend visas within Vietnam but not during Party Congresses. Check your visa carefully: Vietnamese embassies are notoriously sloppy in getting the details right, Vietnamese immigration is famously eagle eyed in picking up its comrades' errors. And very costly it can prove too.

All visitors must present the duplicate copy of the Visa Application Form (together with photograph) to the immigration officer on arrival.

All luggage entering and leaving Vietnam is x-rayed. Gold and currency must be declared on arrival. The purpose of the x-ray is to identify video tapes. Incoming tapes will probably be confiscated and can be collected a few days later after screening by culture and information department. This gives them time to duplicate porn and Western movies which are then sold on to video rental shops.

Visas

Customs

Export of wood products or antiques (ie anything that appears to be more than 20 years old) is banned, thus allowing customs to confiscate most anything that tickles their fancy.

Duty free allowance 200 cigarettes, two litres of spirits. Perfume and jewellery for personal use. In practice the officers are pretty lenient.

Vaccinations No vaccination is required but recommended innoculations include:

Children Diphtheria, Tetanus, Whooping cough, Polio, Typhoid, Hepatitis A, Hepatitis B, Rabies, Japanese Encephalitis, TB, HIB, Measles, Mumps, Rubella.

Adults Diphtheria, Tetanus, Polio, Typhoid, Hepatitis A, Hepatitis B, Rabies, Japanese Encephalitis, TB, Rubella.

The advisability of these vaccinations varies according to the length of your stay and whether you will be spending prolonged spells in rural areas. Check with your GP. Similarly, check with your GP for his recommendation on malaria prophylaxis. For itineraries that are predominantly urban, malaria tablets are generally not advised.

Money

Cash
See individual town directories for bank listings.
Outside Hanoi and Saigon it is best to take US$ cash. Clean (ie unmarked) US$100 bills receive the best rates. Small US$ bills receive slightly lower rates. US$ can be changed in banks, in larger hotels and in gold shops or jewellers. Do not change money in the street or if approached by strangers. Banks in the main centres will also change other major currencies including Sterling, HK$, Thai baht, French francs, Swiss francs, A$, S$, C$, Yen and Deutschmarks. If possible, try to pay for everything in dong, not in US$; prices are usually less in dong, and in more remote areas people may be unaware of the latest exchange rate. Also, to ordinary Vietnamese 14,000d is a lot of money, while US$1 means nothing.

Currency The unit of currency is the **dong**. Notes in circulation are in denominations of 200, 500, 1,000, 2,000, 5,000, 10,000, 20,000 and 50,000 dong (beware, 20,000 and 5,000 dong notes look very similar). The exchange rate at the time of going to press was US$1 = 13,900d; £1 = 22,440d. 1998 saw wild gyrations in the currency market, a widening of the black market versus official exchange rate and severe restrictions on the use of the former enemy's currency.

Airlines flying to Vietnam

Airline (From)	Via	To
Aeroflot (UK)	Moscow	Hanoi, Saigon
Air France (UK)	Paris	Hanoi, Saigon
Asiana (USA, CAN)	Seoul	Saigon
Cathay Pacific (UK, USA, CAN)	Hong Kong	Hanoi, Saigon
China Southern (UK)	Nanning	Hanoi
China Airlines (USA)	Taipei, Anchorage	Saigon
Eva (USA)	Taipei	Saigon
Japan Airlines (UK, USA, CAN)	Tokyo/Osaka	Saigon
KLM Royal Dutch Airlines (UK)	Amsterdam	Saigon
Korean Air (USA, CAN)	Seoul	Saigon
Lauda Air (UK)	Vienna/Bankok	Saigon
Lufthansa (UK)	Frankfurt	Saigon
Malaysia Airlines (USA, AUS)	Kuala Lumpur	Hanoi, Saigon
Philippine Airlines (AUS)	Manila	Saigon
Qantas (AUS, NZ)	Sydney/Melbourne	Saigon
Singapore Airlines (UK, USA, CAN, AUS, NZ)	Singapore	Hanoi, Saigon
Swissair (UK)	Zurich	Saigon
Thai International (UK, USA, CAN, AUS, NZ)	Bankok	Hanoi, Saigon
Vietnam Airlines (UK, USA, AUS)	most of the above	Hanoi, Saigon

Essentials

Any amount of foreign currency can be taken into or out of Vietnam, although amounts of over US$3,000 must be declared on the customs form. Do not take dong out of the country as it cannot be converted overseas. In fact it is jolly difficult to convert dong back into serious currencies even inside Vietnam.

Cash point machines ATM cash dispensers are available at ANZ Bank in Hanoi and Saigon and at HongKong Bank in Saigon.

Credit cards Credit cards are not widely accepted. Large hotels, expensive restaurants and medical centres are the exceptions. A surcharge of three percent is often added.

Travellers' cheques Best denominated in US$, can only be cashed in banks in the major towns. Commission of two to four percent payable on encashment, the higher rates apply on cashing into dollars. When cashing TCs it is necessary to take proof of purchase and passport to the bank.

Getting there

Air

There was a period when international connections with Vietnam were improving rapidly. That situation seems to have run its course (for the time being at least) leaving Vietnam relatively isolated in comparison with the regional hubs. While there are several direct flights weekly from Europe none is non-stop and there are, at the time of writing, no direct flights from the US. Saigon, and to a lesser extent Hanoi, is pretty well connected with other Southeast Asian countries which remain the source of most foreign visitors.

The best deals from Europe tend to involve getting to Bangkok as cheaply as possible and flying in from there. There are numerous airlines with direct connections

Essentials

from Europe, the west coast of the US, Australia and New Zealand, as well as cities in Asia. From the States the quickest route is via Japan or Taiwan.

Train

International rail connections with Vietnam only exist with China. There are connections with Peking via Nanning to Hanoi and from Kunming to Hanoi. The lines are slow and distances are great.

Road

There is a road crossing at Moc Bai connecting Phnom Penh in Cambodia with Saigon and there is one through bus service daily. Similarly, there is a road crossing open at Lao Bao, north of Hué, which enables travel through to Savannakhet in Laos.

Touching down

Airport information

Both Noi Bai (Hanoi) and Tan Son Nhat (Saigon) airports have a limited range of facilities including duty free shops (both on arrival and departure). Banks and Post Offices (both for mailing and local and international calls) are there but cannot be relied upon to be open, particularly the banks.

At both airports passengers are driven from the aeroplane to the terminal by bus. There then follows a frantic scramble for the immigration desks and a long queue while passport, visa and visa application form are scrutinized for possible inconsistencies. Luggage is then collected (do lock suitcases as thefts are not uncommon at this stage) and customs broached. All luggage is x-rayed in a valiant search to protect the Vietnamese from culturally unsuitable items.

You are then free to face the country although it will appear that a large proportion of the population has come to meet you: many are taxi drivers anxious to grab your bags. Keep calm and keep a close eye and firm hand on your possessions. It is only at this stage that money can be changed. There are two options: either have a few small dollar bills with which to pay for your taxi or change a small amount here. The latter is quite a challenge given the mental gymnastics required to keep accounts of a currency which makes one an instant millionaire, especially for a lone traveller with lots of luggage to guard.

Emergency and essential numbers

Police: T113.	**IDD code for Vietnam**: T84.
Fire: T114.	**Official time**: GMT + 7.
Ambulance: T115.	**Business hours**: 0800-1130, 1200-1600.
Directory enquiries: T108 or T116.	**Weights and measures**: metric

On departure: US$10 (for domestic flights it is 20,000d). **Airport tax**

In Saigon there is only one way into town: taxi. To anywhere central, the fare should not **Transport** be more than about US$5 (70,000d). In Hanoi there is an airport bus which charges **to town** foreigners US$4 and locals US$2 (which gets many visitors off to a pretty huffy start). The taxi to central Hanoi is about US$7 (100,000d). The Hanoi airport bus delivers passengers to the Vietnam Airlines office at 1 Quang Trung St and departs from there. Taxis out to Noi Bai airport cost double the incoming fare (ie 200,000d). Passengers going to Tan Son Nhat have to pay a road toll of an additional 7,000d.

Tourist information

The national tourist authorities are light years behind Thailand's. They have not yet grasped the simple fact that travellers want accurate, up-to-date information and maps and are happy to let foreign publishers of guide books relieve them of that burden. Too many comrades in tourism departments are still stuck in the Marxist groove: foreigners are bad; more customers mean more work.

There are no specific discounts for student travellers in Vietnam. However, the **Student** backpacker trail which most young people follow offers the best prices available. **travellers**

Considering the proportion of the Vietnamese population that are seriously disabled **Disabled** foreigners might expect better facilities and allowances for the immobile: expect **travellers** none. Unless users of wheelchairs wish to tussle for road space with unsympathetic truck drivers a wheelchair is useless: a wheelchair cannot proceed 20 metres down a city pavement. But in general expect restaurant and hotel staff to be accommodating and helpful.

There are several well-known bars in central Saigon where gay boys can be picked up. **Gay/lesbian** Cruising in dark streets is not advised. The gay lifestyle is nothing like as well **travellers** developed as in Thailand where the gay traveller will have a far better time. As with exotic religions Vietnamese are more likely to be curious than intolerant.

Rules, customs and etiquette

Vietnam is remarkably relaxed and easy going with regard to conventions. The people, especially in small towns and rural areas, are of course pretty old-fashioned, but it is difficult to cause offence unwittingly. The main complaint Vietnamese have of foreigners is their fondness for dirty and torn clothing. Backpackers, who are the main exponents of grunge, come in for particularly severe criticism and the term *tay ba lo* (literally Western backpacker) is a contemptuous one reflecting the low priority many budget travellers seem to allocate to personal hygiene and the antiquity and inadequacy of their shorts and vests.

Shoes should be removed before entering temples and before going into most people's houses. Modesty should be preserved and excessive displays of bare flesh are not considered good form, particularly in temples and private houses. (Not that the Vietnamese are unduly prudish they just like things to be kept in their proper place.) Shorts are fine for the beach and travellers' cafés but not for smart restaurants (old, knee-length colonial administrator style shorts are, of course, perfectly OK).

Kissing and canoodling in public are likely to draw wide attention, not much of it favourable. But walking hand in hand is now accepted as a common if slightly eccentric Western habit. Hand shaking among men is a standard greeting (often with both hands for added cordiality) and although Vietnamese women will consent to the process it is often clear that they would prefer not to. The head is held by some to be sacred and people would rather you didn't pat them on it, which amazingly some visitors do, but the Vietnamese do not have the hang-ups which the Thais have about someone's feet being higher than their head. In short, the Vietnamese are pragmatic and tolerant and only the most unfeeling behaviour is likely to trouble them.

Dinner table etiquette (which fast food and television have abolished in all but the best homes in Europe and America) happily still survives in Vietnam. But being Vietnam it is pretty informal and again only the least sensitive will cause offence. The obvious things like not starting until everyone has been served their rice apply, and not hogging all the prawns. Dishes are set in the middle of the table for all to dip into with their chopsticks. Take one or two pieces only at a time. Spoon soup into your bowl and eat it with your spoon or put your bowl to your lips. The latter method together with shovelling chopsticks is a perfectly acceptable method for getting rice into the mouth. Nose-blowing is considered unhygienic: if you must, turn away from the table. Meals are generally a family occasion and an opportunity for conversation.

Tipping Rare but appreciated. Perhaps leave the small change unless the service has been particularly charming or helpful in which case 5,000-10,000d will be ample. Big hotels already add 10 percent.

Religion The Vietnamese are open to religious experiences of all kinds. Unlike in Islamic countries it is not possible to cause a religious offence unwittingly in Vietnam. The Vietnamese government is hostile to proselytising – particularly by Christians. But the Roman Catholic church is more vital than in many European countries and foreigners are perfectly free to attend services. Vietnam is predominantly a Buddhist country. Following Chinese tradition ancestor worship is widely practiced and animism (the belief in and worship of spiritis of inanimate objects such as venerable trees, the land, mountains and so on) is widespread.

Drugs Are common and cheap. Attitudes towards users tend to be relaxed but use is ill-advised. Many healthy, young male visitors to Vietnam just keel over and die as a result of drink and drug cocktails. Partly as a result of increasing demand cremation in Vietnam is now much cheaper than it was; a few years ago foreigners' bodies were sent to Bangkok to be burned. Attitudes to traffickers are harsh although the death penalty is usually reserved for Vietnamese and other Asians whose governments are less likely to kick up a fuss.

Safety This is our most strongly worded warning ever. Bag and jewellery snatching is a common and serious problem. Do not take valuables on to the streets of Saigon. Possessions are safer in all but the most disreputable hotels than on the streets. Do not wear expensive jewellery or watches: they will be stolen. Wallets in back pockets will vanish. Women should never carry handbags. Thieves work in teams in central Saigon often with beggar women carrying babies as a decoy. Beware people who obstruct your path (pushing a bicycle across the pavement is a common ruse), your pockets are being emptied from behind. The situation in other cities is not so bad, but take care in Nha Trang and Hanoi.

Young men on fast motorbikes cruise the central streets of Saigon waiting to pounce in an unguarded moment. They snatch at bags, chains and watches often causing serious injury. Despite multiple warnings it is quite extraordinary how casual many tourists are, flashing their video cameras and necklaces around. Just imagine that one or two pairs of eyes in central Saigon are sizing you up. Consulates in Saigon are faced with an endless string of refugees who have lost all their valuables and papers. Such a loss will ruin your holiday but is easy to avoid.

Stick to tried and trusted cyclo drivers after dark or, better still, go by taxi which is cheaper in any case. Never go by cyclo in a strange part of town after dark.

If you are robbed report the incident to the police (for your insurance claim). Otherwise the police are of no use whatsoever. They will do little or nothing. Some suspect that the bag snatchers are well known to the police. Bribes have been known to result in the miraculous return of property.

Stand on every street corner collecting bribes ... er ... sorry, fines for supposed breaches of traffic law. If you are invited to make a contribution to the police widows and orphans fund but clearly you have committed no offence, refuse point blank. Feign total ignorance of English. If this does not work and your motorbike keys have been confiscated try to negotiate the size of your donation downwards. **Traffic police**

Lone women travellers have fewer problems in Vietnam than in many other Asian countries. The most common form of harassment usually consists of comic and harmless displays of macho behaviour with the odd lewd suggestion thrown in for good measure. Expect such comments as 'you are very beautiful' and 'you have a beautiful body', which are intended to be flattering. In other words nothing that the average woman has not met before or is not able to laugh off. At night observe the rules given above, apply common sense and you will find Vietnam is safer than Britain or America. **Women travelling alone**

Almost all visitors to Vietnam have a great time. But it would be misleading to pretend there are no problems. Apart from theft and the dual-pricing system the two most common complaints are noise and traffic. **Unavoidable problems**

This is a passion of the Vietnamese. Can ever a people have fallen so helpless a victim to aural excitement as the Vietnamese? While the invention of the metal-tipped plough is regarded as 'quite a useful thing' it pales into insignificance in the annals of popular Vietnamese history by comparison with the invention of the amplifier and microphone. Yes, that funny little box with a tail which has the power to make even the most insignificant and anonymous of mice into a dictator. **Noise**

There are three main sources of noise: vehicles, home electronics and people and all three are to a large extent unavoidable. Road noise comes principally from car and truck horns, a branch of applied technology in which Vietnam can proudly claim world leadership. Boys in Cholon are taught from the age of five how to wire a motorbike horn directly to the ignition and by the age of 10 they are able to boost the decibel rating of the humblest hooter by several hundred percent. In their teen years they graduate to cars then trucks while a few of the most gifted finally emerge in noise heaven where they are given bus horns to tinker with. These are the air horns which screech and wail with vicious ferocity almost without interruption from 0500 to 2200 every day on every major road in the country in the heroic task of sweeping lesser vehicles, people and animals into the ditch.

Television and karaoke fall into the home electronics category. It is possible that owners of such devices genuinely believe they are providing a community service by adjusting the volume setting to levels at which the entire street can listen in. And in the bad old days when few people had sets of their own perhaps that was the case.

Essentials

Unfortunately, now that everyone has their own machine (just a bit bigger than their neighbours') they still all feel the same noble instincts in regard to community broadcasting. Noise of this sort was used by the Americans to flush General Noriega of Panama out of his den – it is easy to understand why.

For centuries children have grown up living with the fact that in a family of 16 there is only one way to make your feelings known. And in the ensuing competition to make oneself heard presumably a bit of Darwinesque natural selection crept in. The result: poor hearing but vocal powers of which an Italian tenor would be proud. Family banter pertaining to whose turn it is to cook the rice or which TV channel to watch sound, to the untutored ear, like violent arguments, while mild family disagreements are sometimes mistaken by foreigners for street riots.

All in all therefore, Vietnam is a noisy place. It may sound amusing but it is not. Those staying in budget accommodation in densely packed poorer quarters will quickly need to develop noise tolerance. And adjust to the Vietnamese clock.

Traffic Traffic is to physical health what noise is to mental health. In short, a threat. We describe (see box Crossing the road, page 256) how to cross a city street safely, a feature of this book to which authors of grateful letters attribute their being able to write said letter.

Perhaps 'drivers' would be a more accurate heading than 'traffic' because it is they who are the root of the problem. The driving habits of a nation reveal its secrets. They reveal to the outsider how courteous or selfish, how forgiving or how heedless its people instinctively are, shielded behind the anonymity of their vehicle. And in this respect, it has reluctantly to be admitted, Vietnam is found wanting.

How else to explain the conduct of the apparently benign Mrs Bich on her Honda Spacey which resulted in the hospitalisation of two 13-year old school girls? How else do we account for the recklessly selfish behaviour of taxi driver and himself father of four, Mr Hung, to the weeping parents of the once adorable little boy now reduced to jam sponge? For a people of historical patience who thought one thousand years not too long a wait before evicting the hated Chinese; for a people to whom a decades-long occupation by French and Americans was over in 'next to no time' it has to be said that the modern Vietnamese are extraordinarily impatient. Impatient and (as drivers) wholly deficient in manners and courtesy.

Haste, to the taxi driver racing to pick up a fare, is a living. It is death and injury to pedestrians and cyclists. The speed with which Vietnam has developed in the last decade means that men who three years ago were sitting on the back of trundling buffalo carts are now driving 30 ton trucks down Highway 1. The technology is different but quickly mastered. What has not had time to evolve is the common sense, decency, manners and courtesy that prevent European roads from being blood baths.

Interestingly, debates in the Vietnamese press on road carnage concentrate exclusively on technical short-comings – old cars, antique trucks – and neatly sidestep the true cause – a total absence of respect for other road users. It is hard to avoid the feeling that Vietnamese drivers regard every journey as a race. A race in which there are no winners and no winning post but in which every vehicle in front represents a loss of face and personal injury. 'How *dare* you block my way?' is what the horn says. 'Just who do you think you are using *my* road space?'

Sadly, until the Vietnamese come to a mature understanding of the lethal nature of cars, trucks and buses children, pedestrians and cyclists will continue to be mown down by the children behind the steering wheels.

Hotel classification

L US$200+ **Luxury**.
A+ US$100-200 **First class plus**: a
number of newly built and refurbished
hotels in these categories. Competition
means that prices may be discounted –
certainly for long-staying guests.
A US$50-100 **First class**: the hotels in
the country that can be considered first
class are chiefly found in Saigon and
Hanoi. Hotels in this category should offer
reasonable business services, and a range
of recreational facilities, restaurants and
bars. A 10 % service charge will be added
to the bill.
B US$25-50 **Tourist class**: all rooms will
have air-conditioning and an attached
bathroom with hot water. Other services
should include one or more restaurants, a
bar, and room service. Breakfast will often
be included in the price. A 10 % service
may be added to the bill.

C US$15-25 **Economy**: rooms should be
a/c and have attached bathrooms with
hot water and 'western' toilets. A
restaurant and room service will probably
be available.
D US$8-15 **Budget**: air-conditioning
unlikely although they should have an
attached bathroom. Toilets should be
Western-style. Bed linen will be provided,
towels perhaps. There may be a
restaurant. No service charge.
E US$4-8 and **F** less than
US$4 **Vietnamese**: fan-cooled rooms,
often dirty, and in many cases with
shared bathroom facilities. Toilets are
likely to be of the 'squat' Asian variety.
Bed linen should be provided, towels
probably not. These hotels are geared to
Vietnamese travellers; staff are
unlikely to speak much English. No
service charge.

For quick reference, a less detailed version of this hotel price information appears on the inside front cover of the book.

Essentials

Where to stay

There are far fewer decent hotels in Vietnam than in Thailand. The range and quality is poor by comparison. And, indeed, until recently the prices in Vietnam were far too high. Fortunately for the traveller, the decline in tourist numbers has compelled hotels to cut their prices to realistic levels. It always pays to bargain no matter what standard or type of hotel: from family hotel to state guesthouse to foreign owned resort: bargain.

Hotels are represented on the maps in this book by a ■ symbol.

   There are a couple of five star hotels in Hanoi and a clutch of decent four star hotels in Hanoi and Saigon. There are a couple of good beach resorts. The best hotels tend to be newly built joint ventures with foreign management. Remarkably they are not always the most expensive being familiar with the judicious arts of 'promotions' and 'packages' in order to keep occupancy at fair levels.

   Some older hotels, particularly the Metropole in Hanoi, the Palace in Dalat and the Continental in Saigon have been well renovated and exude colonial charm and a sense of history as well as offering good service and a comfortable bed.

   In all the largest cities there is a range of accommodation from the comfiest and priciest, down to the most spartan and cheap but with a tendency towards the latter end. It is possible to find a/c rooms with hot water, fridge, IDD and satellite TV in towns of any size.

   Maintenance is not something the Vietnamese are good at so hotels (especially state run hotels) tend to lapse into disrepair fairly quickly. State run hotels are often not the cleanest, but family guesthouses are usually spick and span. More expensive hotels have safe deposit boxes; in cheaper hotels do not leave valuables lying around where they can be the source of temptation. Lock them into suitcases rather than taking them on to the street.

Getting around

Air

Vietnam Airlines is Vietnam's domestic carrier. The two main hubs are Hanoi in the north and Saigon (Ho Chi Minh City) in the south. There are air connections to: Hanoi, Haiphong, Na San and Dien Bien in the north; Vinh, Hué, Danang, Play Ku, Qui Nhon, Buon Ma Thuot, Dalat and Nha Trang in the central region; and Saigon, Phu Quoc and Rach Gia in the south. See the map for more details.

Tickets should be booked for all flights as soon as possible after arrival. Flights can subsequently be altered at no cost at Vietnam Airlines booking offices in larger towns along the way, seat availability permitting. Following the Phnom Penh Tupolev crash in 1997 the infamous fleet of Soviet aircraft has been largely replaced by airworthy Airbuses and capitalist Boeings. But at times of high demand the old aircraft are still used.

A few points to consider:
● Nearly all embassies and multinational companies have policies that forbid their staff to fly on the old Soviet aircraft.
● Vietnam Airlines now maintains and repairs its own Boeings and Airbuses.
● Airbuses and Boeings are now flown by Vietnamese pilots retrained from the old aircraft.
● Since 1998, Vietnam Airlines has plunged heavily into debt so has had to cut back dramatically on all areas of expenditure.
● More than 100 people die on Vietnam's roads every day.
● Despite the poor safety record of Vietnam Airlines it is quicker, and probably a safer way to travel than going by road. Until the financial crisis of 1998, Vietnam Airlines was developing quite well. It invested heavily in new aircraft and staff but with the collapse in demand which accompanied the Asian crisis came virtual bankruptcy. The government refused to allow the national carrier to raise its prices for Vietnamese passengers while its prices for foreigners already make it one of the most expensive domestic airlines in the world.
● The main frustration air travellers are likely to face is cancellation of their flight. The need to economize means that flights between Hanoi and Saigon do not operate unless the aircraft is full. No prior warning is given so take plenty of reading material and don't cut international connections too fine. Services to a number of towns have been reduced to a couple of flights per week. In-flight service has been cancelled on short flights while on longer flights it never was never much to boast of: 'Rather good chilli sauce' was the verdict of one seasoned traveller.

Some generalizations you are free to dispute or agree with: distances are great; trains and buses are slow; journeys are uncomfortable; roads are dangerous; prices for foreigners are too high.

Nevertheless, the majority of travellers go overland. It is perfectly possible to travel the length of the country in this way although those staying a fortnight or less should consider travelling at least part of the way by air. The Hanoi to Hué sector is the least interesting leg on the north-south Mandarin Route and is best flown. The scenic Hué to Danang sector should not be missed, both road and rail journeys offer fabulous views. Hué to Saigon is full of interest and although some points are far apart, the journey can be done well either by train, public bus or tourist bus (using the open ticket, for example).

Vietnam Airlines Domestic Routes

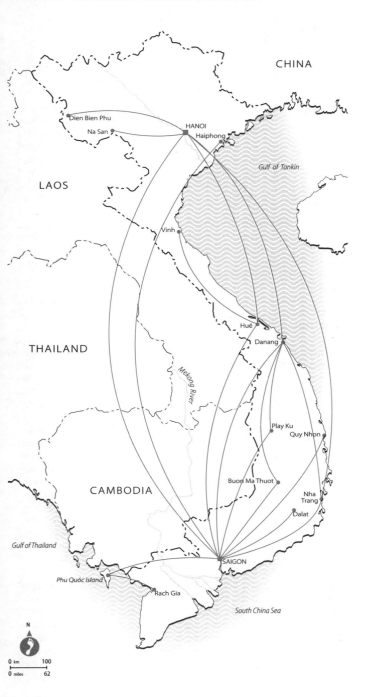

Essentials

 Vietnam Airlines Booking Offices

Ban Me Thuot	25 Nguyen Chi Thanh St	T050-855055
Dalat	40 Ho Tung Mau St	T063-822895
Danang	35 Tran Phu St	T0511-821130
Dien Bien Phu	Dien Bien Phu Airport	T023-824411
Hanoi	1 Quang Trung St	T04-83208320
Haiphong	30 Tran Phu St	T031-849242
Hué	7 Nguyen Tri Phuong St	T054-824709
Nha Trang	91 Nguyen Thien Thuan St	T058-826768
Phu Quoc	Phu Quoc Airport	T077-846086
Pleiku	89 Hung Vuong St	T059-824680
Quy Nhon	2 Ly Thuong Kiet St	T056-823125
Rach Gia	180 Nguyen Trung Truc St	T077-861848
Saigon	116 Nguyen Hue Blvd	T08-8320320
Son La	Na San Airport	T022-845107
Vinh	41 Le Loi St	T038-840637

Sample one way fares (foreigner and Viet Kieu prices)
Hanoi to Saigon US$137 ; Hanoi to Hue US$72 ; Hanoi to Danang US$72 ; Hanoi to Nha Trang US$105 ; Hanoi to Dien Bien Phu US$47 ; Saigon to Nha Trang US$47 ; Saigon to Danang US$72 ; Saigon to Hué US$72 ; Saigon to Phu Quoc US$51 ; Saigon to Dalat US$33 ; Saigon to Pleiku US$51 ; Danang to Ban Me Thuot US$36 ; Danang to Nha Trang US$36

Overland

Train A railway line links Hanoi with Saigon, passing through many of the towns and cities worth visiting, including Hué, Danang and Nha Trang. Other than going by air, the train is the most comfortable way to travel. *But*, this only applies to first class. Fares are not cheap. Locals pay about 25 percent of the price that foreigners are charged. The difference in price between first and second class is small and it is worth paying the extra. The express trains plying the Saigon-Hanoi route take between 36 and 46 hours to make the full journey. First class travel is civilized; second class acceptable; for those in other classes it can be a nightmare – the sort of journey to tell one's grandchildren about. The slow local trains are entertaining if you have the time and want to enjoy the local people's company. The kitchen on the Hanoi-Saigon service serves soups and simple, but adequate, rice dishes (it is a good idea to take additional food and drink on long journeys though). First class long distance tickets include the price of meals. With overnight stays at hotels along the way to see the sights, a rail sight-seeing tour from Hanoi to Saigon, or vice versa, should take a minimum of 10 days. For some routes sleepers need to be booked three days in advance, although it is always worth checking on availability. It is possible to book bicycles onto trains, but this must be done at least two days ahead (example of cost, Nha Trang to Danang US$4).

Bus Buses, in general, are slow, old and cramped, but they usually arrive at their destination. The most common roadside enterprises are car (and bicycle) repair outfits. This is indicative of the appalling state of many of the roads and vehicles. It is not uncommon to see buses being totally disassembled at the side of the road and it is rare to travel through the country by public transport without experiencing several breakdowns or punctures. Speeds average no more than 35 kilometres per hour; public road transport can be a long and tiresome (sometimes excruciating) business but it is also fascinating and the best way to meet Vietnamese people. A bewildering array of

Every man and his pig

"Vietnam is great ... except for the transport." This commonly voiced sentiment reflects the views of many visitors to Vietnam. The problem is a reflection of the run-down and underfunded public transport system and the large numbers of people needing to travel. It may be of some consolation to the modern day traveller to know that discomfort and overcrowding on Vietnam's buses is nothing new, the following account was written in 1928:

"The bus was licensed for six first class passengers and sixteen second. We started with five of the former and 22 of the latter, discarded nobody and picked up every suppliant. Besides the passengers was their luggage, and this did not mean a modest hand-bag apiece. It meant sleeping-mats, boxes, sacks, bales, furniture, crates of merchandise and poultry. In addition we carried a live pig and a bicycle, the latter hung outboard over the side like a life-boat in a steamer's davits. The second-class sufferers sat on each other, on the floor, on the piled-up luggage. The overflow mounted the already overburdened roof. One youth rode all day clinging to the running-boards, another to the step. How the topheavy vehicle contrived to keep its feet when hurtling round corners at top speed was nothing short of miraculous.

We passed out of cultivated country into desolate heaths again and climbing a hill beheld a strange procession racing along the sky-line to cut us off. It consisted of an Annamite and three French priests, skirts and umbrellas tucked up under their arms, mighty beards streaming in the breeze, galloping like colts, whooping like Cherokees. The native convert, being young and slender, reached the road first and executed a sort of war-dance in front of the oncoming bus. It stopped. The three missionaries arrived panting brokenly, sponging their foreheads. One was evidently fresh to the job. He was young, wore a cassock, and his beard was a mere tuft of struggling fluff, but the other two were old stagers, wearing native dress and beards of true tropical exuberance.

The bus by this time contained seven first class passengers and thirty second. It was unthinkable that it would take in any more. But the driver never hesitated. The convert went up to join the throng (and the pig) on the roof. With a modesty commensurate with his beard, the young priest relegated himself to the second-class and the two elders hove their vast carcasses in on top of us. On top of us literally. With a sunny smile, but without any warning or by your leave, the vaster of the pair sank ponderously and devastatingly upon my knees, apparently prepared to stop there all the way to Quang-Tri."

Extract taken from Crosbie Garstin (1928) The voyage from London to Indochina, Heinemann.

---

contraptions pass for buses, from old French jalopies, Chevrolet, Ford and DMC vans, to Soviet buses. Many (and this includes lorries) have ingenious cooling systems in which water is fed into the radiator from barrels strapped to the roof; along the route there are water stations to replenish depleted barrels (look for the sign *nuoc mui* or *do nuoc*).

As American humourist PJ O'Rourke remarked after his visit: "In America they drive on the right side of the road, in England they drive on the left side, and in Vietnam they drive on both sides ..." Roads in Vietnam are notoriously dangerous.

Most bus stations are on the outskirts of town; in bigger centres there may be several stations. Long-distance buses invariably leave very early in the morning (0400-0500). Less comfortable but quicker are the minibus services (some are a/c) which ply the more popular routes. These are usually grossly overladen and driven by maniacs. Buses are the cheapest form of transport, although sometimes foreigners find they are being asked two to three times the correct price. Prices are normally prominently displayed at bus stations. It helps avoid being overcharged if you can find out what the correct fare should be.

Essentials

Example of fares by minibus Saigon-Dalat, US$7; **Saigon-Nha Trang**, US$15; **Saigon-Hué**, US$35; **Hanoi-Hué**, US$22.

Car hire   Self-drive car hire is not available. Cars with drivers can be hired for around US$20-50 per day depending on distance travelled and who the car is hired from. It pays to shop around.

Bicycle and   In cities and towns often the best (and cheapest) way to get around is to hire a bicycle
motorbike   or motorbike. Take time to familiarise yourself with road conditions and ride slowly. Most towns are small enough for bicycles to be an attractive option but if taking in a sweep of the surrounding countryside (touring around the Central Highlands, for example) then a motorbike will mean you can see more. Bicycles are pretty hard work in Dalat and Kon Tum too.

Hotels often have bicycles for hire and there is usually someone willing to lend their machine for a small charge (8,000-15,000d per day). Many travellers' cafés rent out bicycles and motorbikes, the latter for 70,000d- 90,000d per day. Some longer stay visitors buy bicycles (around US$50) which, if it hasn't been stolen by the time they leave, they sell on or give to Vietnamese friends.

Always park your bicycle or motorbike in a guarded parking place (*gui xe*). Ask for a ticket. The 2,000d this costs is worth every ..., well, every dong even if you are just popping in to the Post Office to post a letter.

Motorcycle taxi   *Ôm* means to cuddle. This means of transport is ubiquitous and cheap. You will find
(Honda ôm or   them on most street corners, outside hotels or in the street. With their uniform baseball
xe ôm)   caps and dangling cigarette, *xe ôm* drivers are readily recognizable. In the north and upland areas the Honda is replaced with the Minsk, that Russian workhorse of the hills.

Cyclo   Tourists, housewives and young school children like them but no one else does. They are, to be blunt, a bloody nuisance. Slow moving, obstructive and driven by elderly gangsters who cannot afford motorbikes they should be scrapped. Cyclo operators, like horse carriage drivers before them, cling obstinately to their obsolete technology and archaic work practices and, with as much prescience as dinosaurs, unwittingly add their names to the list of endangered species.

For a start they charge double a *xe ôm*. Which, when multiplied by the rich-foreigner-premium (a touching belief all cyclo drivers hold as a sacred creed) makes a slow and hazardous journey by cyclo more expensive than a nice a/c taxi ride – especially if there are two or three of you. Hence, while the *xe ôm* drivers are doing brisk business the local cyclo drivers will be snoozing on the street corner dreaming of the crisp dollar bills (cyclo drivers always dream in dollars) today will surely bring.

Adding to the cyclo drivers' woes is the fact that a number of streets in the centres of Saigon and Hanoi are one-way or out of bounds to cyclos, necessitating lengthy detours which add to the time and cost. Do not go by cyclo after dark unless the driver is well known to you or you know the route.

Not infrequently, ithough, visitors encounter a cyclo driver who regales them with stories of flying Hueys with the Yanks, life in re-education camp and who gives a potted history of all the pagodas he takes them to and then peddles to a fantastic little diner which does brilliant veggie noodles very cheaply. Taxi drivers never do that.

Taxi   Taxis ply the streets of Hanoi and Saigon. They are now also to be found in virtually every large town in the country but normally need to be summoned by telephone. They are cheap, around 10,000d per kilometre or less and the drivers generally know their way around and are better English speakers than cyclo drivers. But too many are reckless, dangerous and off their heads on drugs, and have an annoying tendency not to carry change.

Vietnamese addresses

Unlike the systems of some neighbouring countries, addresses in Vietnam do, in general, follow quite a logical pattern. A few points to note:

Odd numbers usually run consecutively on one side of the street, evens on the other.

bis after a number, as in 16bis Hai Ba Trung St, means there is more than one number 16, probably a considerable distance apart.

Large buildings with a single street number are usually subdivided 21A, 21B, 21C etc; some buildings may be further subdivided 21C1, 21C2, 21C3 and so on.

An oblique (/ – sec or tren in Vietnamese) in a number, as in 23/16 Dinh Tien Hoang St, means that the address is to be found in a small side street (hem) – in this case running off Dinh Tien Hoang St by the side of no 23: the house in question will probably be signed 23/16 rather than just 16. Usually, but by no means always, a

hem will be quieter than the main street and it may be worth looking at a guesthouse with an oblique number for that reason (especially in the Pham Ngu Lao area of Saigon).

An address will sometimes contain the letter F followed by a number, as in F6; this is short for phuong (ward, a small administrative area); its inclusion in an address is a reflection of the tidy, bureaucratic nature of the Vietnamese mind not an aid to finding one's destination.

Q in an address stands for quân or district; this points you in the right general direction and will be important in locating your destination as a long street in Hanoi or Saigon may run through several quan. In suburban and rural areas districts are known as huyên, Huyên Nha Be in Saigon, for instance.

There are no post codes or zip codes in Vietnam.

Keeping in touch

Language

Outside Saigon, Hanoi, Hué, Hoi An, Nha Trang, Dalat and other tourist centres language can be a problem for those who have no knowledge of Vietnamese. Vietnamese is not easy to pick up and pronunciation presents enormous difficulties. The Vietnamese language uses six tones and has 12 vowels and 27 consonants. Like other tonal languages, one word can mean many things depending upon the tone used: 'ma', for example, can mean horse, cheek, ghost, grave and rice seedling. But it is worth making an effort and the Vietnamese are delighted when foreigners try to communicate in their language. Thanks to Alexandre de Rhodes, Vietnamese is written in a Roman alphabet making life much easier: place and street names are instantly recognizable. Vietnamese–English and English–Vietnamese dictionaries are cheap and widely available in Saigon and Hanoi.

For a list of useful words and phrases, see inside the back cover.

English is much the most useful foreign language despite the vast subsidies the French government pours into French language training. Spoken English is taught badly in secondary schools hence any Vietnamese who wants to learn must enrol at a private language centre if they are to make progress in communication, and enrol they do – in their countless thousands. Visitors will not uncommonly find themselves being asked by bashful students to distinguish between the pronunciation of 'thirst' and 'first' or even to elucidate on some complex point of grammar (probably something to do with gerunds or syntax) with which, unfortunately, the Vietnamese education system is obsessed.

Essentials

French is still spoken and often very nicely by the more elderly and educated. Nevertheless, in the world of modern trade patterns and competition for jobs it is studied by far fewer students than are the Chinese and Japanese languages.

Postal services

Generally these are pretty good. International aerograms take about two weeks in each direction. Every town has a Post Office as does every district in every city. And such is the nature of Vietnamese bureaucracy that provincial capitals have two General Post Offices: for the province and for the town. Post Offices tend to keep long opening hours: 0700-1900 seven days a week, smaller ones closing for lunch.

General Post Offices in the major cities are geared up for sending parcels overseas and usually offer packing services as well for a small additional fee. Receiving parcels can be a tedious process. Packages are rarely delivered to the door but a note is sent to your address inviting you to the Post Office. After a long wait at two or three wrong counters, the checking of your passport and the payment of a fee, the parcel is produced and opened by customs officers. If you are Vietnamese they will pocket what they fancy and you will say thank you. If you are a foreigner they may simply ask you to pay a customs due. All the major international courier companies have offices near the big General Post Offices.

Post Offices offer domestic telegram services which can be very useful for getting messages to places which are not on the telephone. There is an express mail service, EMS, which will deliver letters or small packages the length of the country the following day.

Post Offices in Saigon, Hanoi, Hué, Hoi An, Nha Trang, Dalat and Danang provide Poste Restante facilities, ask your family and friends to print your surname. For example: Chris ARNOLD, c/o Poste Restante, GPO, Hanoi.

Telephone and fax services

For a list of telephone codes see the inside front cover of this book.

All Post Offices provide international telephone and fax services. The cost of calls is exorbitant (US$4-5 per minute to Europe or the States) and some Post Offices and hotels still insist on charging a minimum of three minutes. Hotels then add their own surcharge. It is advisable, therefore, to make arrangements to be called from abroad. Call back services were banned for a long time but are just beginning to appear. Check with the General Post Office for current details.

Long distance domestic calls are quite pricey but local calls are cheap or even free of charge. Most shops or cafés will let you call a local number for 2,000d: look for the blue sign *dien thoai cong cong*, public telephone.

Email

Owing to government paranoia, Vietnam has a long way to go to catch up with neighbouring countries in terms of internet communication. All of the first wave of cyber cafés were closed down and their computers confiscated by officials fearful of the effects of a free flow of information on a closed society. Although emailing is now usually easy enough, access to the internet from within Vietnam is restricted as the authorities battle vainly to fire-wall Vietnam-related topics.

Many travellers' cafés in Hanoi and Saigon provide email access; in Hoi An the tailors' shops do. Rates for receiving, sending and printing have fallen as competition has spread and given the cost of telephoning abroad it is not surprising that if visitors do not have a hotmail address when they arrive in Vietnam they very soon get one. Rates are currently around 400d per minute on-line plus 1,000d per page printed.

Cyber cafés

Hanoi
Handspan travel, 116 Hang Bac St, T04-8281996, F04-8257171, tfhandspn@hn.vnn.vn
Queen Café, 65 Hang Bac St, T04-8260860, F04-8260300, queenaz@fpt.vn
Vinhpat III, 26 Le Thai To St, T04-8285799/8289033, F04-8285799/8283705, vinhphat@fpt.vn, everco3@hotmail.com

Saigon
Tin Café, 2A Le Duan St, T08-8229786, Tincafe@tlnet.com.vn
Internet Service, 110 Bui Thi Xuan Street, T08-8300317, vmax.110@hcm.vnn.vn
Hong Hoa Internet Service, 250 De Tham St and 185/28 Pham Ngu Lao, T08-8361915, honhoarr@hcm.vnn.vn
NGOCHUE, 171\22 Co Bac St, T08-8360089, nghue@kst.cinetvn.com Price/minute VND800
Cafe "333", 1 De Tham St, hue@netnam2.org.vn
Saigon Net, 220 De Tham St, T08-8372573, tiendat@Saigonnet.vn

Hoi An
Thu Thao, 32 Tran Phu St, T0510-61815
Nha Trang Internet Service, 45 Quang Trung St, T058-810881, vmaxnt@dng.vnn.vn

Media

For a directory of 2,000 cybercafés in 113 countries, plus a discussion forum for travellers, see www.netcafe.com/.

Newspapers

One or two day-old editions of the *Financial Times, International Tribune, USA Today, Figaro* and some weeklies, such as the *Economist* are available in Saigon and Hanoi, sometimes with the thick, black felt-tip pen of the censor in evidence.

The English language daily *Vietnam News* is widely available and covers Vietnamese and foreign news selectively but not badly. It has especially good sports pages and covers English football thoroughly. The Sunday edition is worth reading for its cultural stories, and is particularly good on the traditions of ethnic minorities. Unlike Western newspapers Vietnamese papers are less about what has happened (that is, news) and more about what will happen or what should happen: 'Output of fertilizer to grow 200 percent' or 'Youth Volunteers to eradicate illiteracy in Central Highlands by 2000', for example. Inside the back page of *Vietnam News* is an excellent 'What's on' which is highly recommended for visitors interested in cultural events or concerts in Hanoi and Saigon.

The *Saigon Times Daily* is more business oriented and a bit dry. There are several weeklies of which the *Vietnam Investment Review* is the best but somewhat cringeing and not a patch on what it used to be and the monthly *Vietnam Economic Times* which is very thorough and remains forthright in its views.

Food and drink

As we made clear in the opening pages food is a major attraction of Vietnam and it is one of the paradoxes of this enigmatic country that so much food should be so readily and deliciously available. Eating out is so cheap that practically every meal will be taken in a restaurant or café. Saigon and Hanoi offer a wide range of cuisines besides Vietnamese so that only Congolese, Icelandic and English tourists will be deprived of home cooking, a fate they are no doubt resigned to.

Distinctive fruits

Custard apple (or sugar apple) Scaly green skin, squeeze the skin to open the fruit and scoop out the flesh with a spoon.

Durian (Durio zibethinus) A large prickly fruit, with yellow flesh, about the size of a football. Infamous for its pungent smell. While it is today regarded by many visitors as simply revolting, early Europeans (16th-18th centuries) raved about it, possibly because it was similar in taste to western delicacies of the period. Borri (1744) thought that "God himself, who had produc'd that fruit." But by 1880 Burbridge was writing: "Its odour – one scarcely feels justified in using the word `perfume' – is so potent, so vague, but withal so insinuating, that it can scarcely be tolerated inside the house". Banned from public transport in Singapore and hotel rooms throughout the region, and beloved by most Southeast Asians (where prize specimens can cost a week's salary), it has an alluring taste if the odour can be overcome (it has been described as like eating blancmange on the toilet). Some maintain it is an addiction. Durian-flavoured chewing gum, ice cream and jams are all available.

Jackfruit Similar in appearance to durian but not so spiky. Yellow flesh, tasting slightly like custard.

Mango (Mangifera indica) A rainforest fruit which is now cultivated. Widely available in the West; in Southeast Asia there are hundreds of different varieties with subtle variations in flavour. Delicious eaten with sticky rice and a sweet sauce (in Thailand). The best mangoes in the region are considered to be those from South Thailand.

Mangosteen (Garcinia mangostana) An aubergine-coloured hard shell covers this small fruit which is about the size of a tennis ball. Cut or squeeze the purple shell to reach its sweet white flesh which is prized by many visitors above all others. In 1898, an American resident of Java wrote, erotically and in obvious ecstasy: "The five white segments separate easily, and they melt on the tongue with a touch of tart and a touch of sweet; one moment a memory of the juiciest, most fragrant apple, at another a remembrance of the smoothest cream ice, the most exquisite and delicately flavoured fruit-acid known – all of the delights of nature's laboratory condensed in that ball of neige parfumée". Southeast Asians believe it should be eaten as a chaser to durian.

Papaya (Carica papaya) A New World Fruit that was not introduced into Southeast Asia until the 16th century. Large, round or oval in shape, yellow or green-skinned, with bright orange flesh and a mass of round, black seeds in the middle. The flesh, in texture and taste, is somewhere between a mango and a melon. Some maintain that it tastes `soapy'.

Pomelo A large round fruit the size of anything from an ostrich egg to a football, with thick, green skin, thick pith, and flesh not unlike that of the grapefruit, but less acidic.

Rambutan (Nephelium lappaceum) The bright red and hairy rambutan – rambut is the Malay word for `hair' – with its slightly rubbery but sweet flesh is a close relative of the lychee of southern China and tastes similar. The Thai word for rambutan is ngoh, which is the nickname given by Thais to the fuzzy-haired Negrito aboriginals in the southern jungles.

Salak (Salacca edulis) A small pear-shaped fruit about the size of a large plum with a rough, brown, scaly skin (somewhat like a miniature pangolin) and yellow-white, crisp flesh. It is related to the sago and rattan trees.

Tamarind (Tamarindus indicus) Brown seedpods with dry brittle skins and a brown tart-sweet fruit which grow on a tree introduced into Southeast Asia from India. The name is Arabic for `Indian date'. The flesh has a high tartaric acid content and is used to flavour curries, jams, jellies and chutneys as well as for cleaning brass and copper. Elephants have a predilection for tamarind balls.

Eating: useful words and phrases

Can I have the menu, please? *Xin cho tôi xem thực đơn?*

I'm a vegetarian *Tôi ăn chay*

No chilli, please *Xin đừng cho ớt*

MSG *bột ngọt/ mì chính (N)*

chilli *ớt*

I'd like some rice *Tôi muốn một ít cơm*

spring rolls *chả giò*

noodles *mì; hủ tiếu; bún*

bread *bánh mì*

fish sauce *nước nắm*

soya sauce *nước tương*

meat *thịt*

pork *thịt heo*

beef *thịt bò*

chicken *thịt gà*

duck *thịt vịt*

goat *thịt dê*

fish *cá*

crab *cua*

eel *lươn*

lobster *tôm hùm*

shrimp *tôm*

squid *mực*

egg *trứng*

vegetable *rau cải*

tofu *đậu hũ*

spinach *rau muống*

bamboo shoot *măng*

bean sprouts *giá*

beans *đậu*

cauliflower *bông cải*

green pepper *ớt Đà Lạt*

corn *bắp/ ngô*

tomato *cà chua*

carrot *cà rốt*

cucumber *dưa leo*

lettuce *rau sà lách*

onion *hành tây*

potato *khoai tây*

mushroom *nấm*

soup *canh/xúp*

boiled *luộc*

steamed *hấp*

fried *chiên/ rán*

roasted *quay*

grilled *nướng*

fruits *trái cây*

avocado *trái/quả bơ*

banana *trái/quả chuối*

grapefruit *trái/quả bưởi*

lemon *trái/quả chanh*

longan *trái/quả nhãn*

lychee *trái/quả vải*

mandarin *trái/quả quýt*

orange *trái/quả cam*

papaya *trái/quả đu đủ*

peach *trái/quả đào*

pineapple *trái/quả thơm/dứa*

plum *trái/quả mận/roi*

rambutan *trái/quả chôm chôm*

watermelon *trái/quả dưa hấu*

Do you have traditional food? *Có món ăn truyền thống không?*

Do you have any special dishes? *Món nào là đặc sản của quán?*

It's delicious *Rất ngon*

I'm thirsty *Tôi khát nước*

Cold water please *Cho tôi xin một cốc nước lạnh*

no sugar *không đường*

no ice *không đá*

black coffee *cà phê đen*

iced coffee *cà phê đá*

iced coffee with milk *Cà phê sữa đá*

tea *trà/chè (N)*

a bottle of beer *Một chai bia*

a can of beer *Một lon bia*

a bottle of mineral water *Một chai nước suối*

Is the water safe to drink? *Nước uống có sạch không?*

lemon juice *nước chanh*

orange juice *cam vắt*

coconut *nước dừa*

pineapple shake *sinh tố thơm*

rice wine *rượu đế*

Note that there may be variations in the language between north and south Vietnam. Some north/ south alternatives are given here.
N = north

Essentials

For day trips, an early morning visit to the markets will produce a picnic fit for a king. **Markets** Hard-boiled quails' eggs, thinly sliced garlic sausage and salami, pickled vegetables, beef tomatoes, cucumber, pâté, cheese and, of course, warm baguette and fresh fruit. And far from costing a king's ransom it will feed four for around a dollar a head.

Essentials

 Bird's nest soup

The tiny nests of the brown-rumped swift (Collocalia esculenta), also known as the edible-nest swiftlet or sea swallow, are collected for bird's nest soup, a Chinese delicacy, throughout Southeast Asia. The semi-oval nests are made of silk-like strands of saliva secreted by the birds which, when cooked in broth, softens and becomes a little like noodles. Like so many Chinese delicacies, the nests are believed to have aphrodisiac qualities, and the soup has even been suggested as a cure for AIDS. The red nests are the most highly valued, and the Vietnamese Emperor Minh Mang (1820-1840) is said to have owed his extraordinary vitality to his inordinate consumption of bird's nest soup. This may explain why restaurants serving it are sometimes also associated with a plethora of massage parlours. Collecting the nests is a precarious but profitable business and in some areas mafias of concessionaires vigorously guard and protect their assets. The men who collect the nests on a piecework basis risk serious injury climbing rickety ladders to cave roofs in sometimes almost total darkness, save for a candle strapped to their heads.

Restaurants While it is possible to eat very cheaply in Vietnam (especially outside Hanoi and Saigon) the higher class of restaurant, particularly those serving foreign cuisine, can prove quite expensive, especially with wine. But with judicious shopping around it is not hard to find excellent value for money, particularly in the small, family restaurants. In the listing sections we describe a range of diners which should satisfy every palate and every pocket.

Bars Bars as we know them tend not to exist far from the tourist or ex-pat populations. Cold beer, rock music and pool are easy to find in the main centres but are virtually non-existent elsewhere. Which is not to say the Vietnamese don't know how to enjoy themselves it is just that they do things differently.

A common type of Vietnamese bar is the *bia hoi*. *Bia hoi* is draught beer (fairly weak) but fresh and thirst-quenching. At just four thousand dong a litre it is also remarkably good value. Bia hoi outlets often sell simple food dishes, *bo luc lac* (diced steak with frites), for example.

Bia ôm is altogether a different kettle of fish. *Bia ôm* bars are girly bars and another integral part of Vietnamese social fabric. In a Vietnamese *bia ôm* the girls drink beer with the men. There may be a certain amount of touchy feely but nothing too overt and usually the girls go home to their own beds. It is a form of geisha tea house but without the etiquette and without the tea. In seedier city quarters *bia ôm* bars are almost brothels.

Shopping

Vietnam is not a haven for shoppers in the same way that other countries in the region are. Locally produced goods are usually rather shoddy, although they can make novel gifts (for example the North Vietnamese Army helmet). Handicrafts and traditionally woven fabrics are good buys. Tailors are cheap and can produce skirts, shirts and jackets from patterns and photographs. And ladies, remember the ao dai is a most unforgiving garment, exquisite on a slender frame but unsuited to the Western build. Most fabrics tend to be synthetic but in the bigger markets there is now a lot of excellent coarse Vietnamese silk. Antiques and authentic reproductions are available in most tourist centres, the latter often at reasonable prices. There is a ban on the export of antiques, however, and visitors should get a licence from the customs department, a tedious and time-consuming process.

Words and phrases for shopping

I'd like to buy some clothes	*Tôi muốn mua một ít quần áo*
shoes	*giày*
sandals	*dép*
socks	*vớ*
hat	*nón*
rucksack	*ba lô*
bag	*giỏ xách*
pottery	*đồ gốm*
handicaft	*đồ thủ công*
paintings	*tranh*
How much is it?	*Giá bao nhiêu?*
It's too expensive	*Mắc quá*
Can you lower the price?	*Có bớt không?*
Oh, it's still very expensive	*Ồ, vẫn còn mắc lắm*
Is 10,000 dong OK?	*10,000 đồng, được không?*
Can I have a look?	*Tôi có thể xem dược không?*
Sorry, I don't like it	*Rất tiếc, tôi không thích*
Do you have another one?	*Ông/bà có cái khác không?*
I will take this one	*Tôi sẽ mua cái này*
They don't/ It doesn't fit me	*Nó không vừa với tôi*
It's too small	*Nó nhỏ quá*
Do you have one in a bigger size?	*Ông/ bà có cỡ lớn hơn không?*
smaller/bigger	*nhỏ hơn/lớn hơn*
longer/ shorter	*dài hơn/ngắn hơn*
tighter/ looser	*chật hơn/ rộng hơn*

Lacquerware Lacquerware is plentiful and cheap. Lacquer pictures are heavy to carry about and should be bought (if at all) near the end of a trip. Small lacquer trinkets such as boxes and trays are more portable and make nice presents. Ethnic products, fabrics, wickerware and jewellery is of course best bought (and cheapest) in the uplands but plenty is available in the two main cities. Cham fabrics, for example, are available in Saigon while those of the Thai and Hmông minorities can be widely seen in Hanoi.

Junk Junk collectors will have a field-day in Saigon and Hanoi – many trinkets were left behind by French, Americans and Russians: old cameras, watches, cigarette lighters (most Zippos are fake), 1960s Coca Cola signs and Pernod ashtrays.

Manufacturers of outdoor wear, rucksacks, boots and training shoes have located factories in Vietnam. A considerable amount of genuine branded stock finds its way into the shops of Hanoi and Saigon at prices as little as 100 percent of European shop prices.

Holidays and festivals

January *New Year's Day* (1st: public holiday).

February *Tet*, traditional new year (movable, 1st to the 7th day of the new lunar year – late January/March: public holiday). The big celebration of the year, the word Tet is the shortened version of *tet nguyen dan* ('first morning of the new period'). Tet is the time to forgive and forget, and to pay off debts. It is also everyone's birthday – the

For details of local festivals, see individual town headings. Vietnamese do not celebrate each individual's birthday, everyone is one year older on Tet. Enormous quantities of food are consumed (this is not the time to worry about money), new clothes are bought, houses painted and repaired, and firecrackers lit to welcome in the new year, at least they were until the government ban. As a Vietnamese saying has it: 'Hungry all year but Tet three days full'. It is believed that before Tet the spirit of the hearth, Ong Tao, leaves on a journey to visit the palace of the Jade Emperor where he must report on family affairs. To ensure that Ong Tao sets off in good cheer, a ceremony is held before Tet, Le Tao Quan, and during his absence a shrine is constructed (Cay Neu) to keep evil spirits at bay until his return. On the afternoon before Tet, Tat Nien, a sacrifice is offered at the family altar to dead relatives who are invited back to join in the festivities. Great attention is paid to preparations for Tet, because it is believed that the first week of the new year dictates the fortunes for the rest of the year. The first visitor to the house on New Year's morning should be an influential, wealthy and happy person, so families take care to arrange a suitable caller.

Founding anniversary of the Communist Party of Vietnam (3rd: public holiday).

March *Hai Ba Trung Day* (movable, 6th day of 2nd lunar month). Celebrates the famous Trung sisters who led a revolt against the Chinese in 41 AD (see page 82).

April *Liberation Day of South Vietnam and Saigon* (30th: public holiday).

Thanh Minh, New Year of the Dead (5th or 6th, 3rd lunar month), or Feast of the Pure Light. People are supposed to walk outdoors to evoke the spirit of the dead and family shrines and tombs are cleaned and decorated.

May *International Labour Day* (1st: public holiday); *Anniversary of the Birth of Ho Chi Minh* (19th: public holiday); *Celebration of the birth, death and enlightenment of the Buddha* (15th day of the 4th lunar month) not a public holiday but one marked by Buddhists.

August *Trung Nguyen* or Wandering Souls Day (movable, 15th day of the 7th lunar month). One of the most important festivals. During this time, prayers can absolve the sins of the dead who leave hell and return, hungry and naked, to their relatives. The Wandering Souls are those with no homes to go to. There are celebrations in Buddhist temples and homes, food is placed out on tables, and money is burned.

September *National Day* (2nd: public holiday).
President Ho's Anniversary (3rd: public holiday).
Tet Trung Thu or Mid Autumn Festival (movable, 15th day of the 8th month). Particularly celebrated by children. Moon cakes are baked, lanterns made and painted, and children parade through towns with music and lanterns.

November *Confucius' Birthday* (movable, 28th day of the 9th month).

Health

Hospitals and medical facilities are listed in the directory under individual towns. Staying healthy in Vietnam is straightforward. With the following advice and precautions you should keep as healthy as you do at home. Most visitors return home having experienced no problems at all beyond an upset stomach. However in Vietnam the health risks, especially in the tropical areas, are different from those encountered in Europe or the USA. It also depends on how you travel and where. The country has a mainly tropical climate; nevertheless the acquisition of true tropical disease by the visitor is probably conditioned as much by the rural nature and standard of hygiene of the surroundings than by the climate. There is an obvious difference in health risks between the business traveller who tends to stay in international class hotels in the large cities and the backpacker trekking through the rural areas. There are no hard and fast rules to follow; you will often have to make your own judgement on the healthiness or otherwise of your surroundings.

Medical facilities

There are French or English speaking doctors in the major cities who have particular experience in dealing with locally occurring diseases. Your Embassy representative will often be able to give you the name of local reputable doctors and most of the better hotels have a doctor on standby. If you do fall ill and cannot find a recommended doctor, try the outpatient department of a hospital – private hospitals are usually less crowded and offer a more acceptable standard to foreigners. The likelihood of finding good medical care diminishes very rapidly as you move away from the big cities. Especially in the rural areas there are systems and traditions of medicine wholly different from the western model and you be will confronted with less orthodox forms of treatment such as herbal medicines and acupuncture, not that these are unfamiliar to most western travellers.

There is very little control on the sale of drugs and medicines in Vietnam. You may be able to buy any and every drug in pharmacies without a prescription. Be wary of this because pharmacists can be poorly trained and might sell you drugs that are unsuitable, dangerous or old. Many drugs and medicines are manufactured under licence from American or European companies, so the trade names may be familiar to you. This means you do not have to carry a whole chest of medicines with you, but remember that the shelf life of some items, especially vaccines and antibiotics, is markedly reduced in hot conditions. Buy your supplies at the better outlets where there are more refrigerators, even though they are more expensive and check the expiry date of all preparations you buy. Immigration officials occasionally confiscate scheduled drugs (Lomotil is an example) if they are not accompanied by a doctor's prescription. **Medicines**

Before travelling

Take out medical insurance. Make sure it covers all eventualities especially evacuation to your home country by a medically equipped plane, if necessary. You should have a dental check up, obtain a spare glasses prescription, a spare oral contraceptive prescription (or enough pills to last) and, if you suffer from a chronic illness (such as diabetes, high blood pressure, ear or sinus troubles, cardio-pulmonary disease or nervous disorder) arrange for a check up with your doctor, who can at the same time provide you with a letter explaining the details of your disability in English and French. Check the current practice in countries you are visiting for malaria prophylaxis (prevention). If you are on regular medication, make sure you have enough to cover the period of your travel.

More preparation is probably necessary for babies and children than for an adult and perhaps a little more care should be taken when travelling to remote areas where health services are primitive. This is because children can be become more rapidly ill than adults (on the other hand they often recover more quickly). Diarrhoea and vomiting are the most common problems, so take the usual precautions, but more intensively. Breast-feeding is best and most convenient for babies, but powdered milk **Children** is available in the cities, as are a few baby foods. Bananas and other fruits are all nutritious and can be cleanly prepared. The treatment of diarrhoea is the same for adults, except that it should start earlier and be continued with more persistence. Children get dehydrated very quickly in hot countries and can become drowsy and uncooperative unless cajoled to drink water or juice plus salts. Upper respiratory infections, such as colds, catarrh and middle ear infections are also common and if your child suffers from these normally take some antibiotics against the possibility. Outer ear infections after swimming are also common and antibiotic eardrops will help. Wet wipes are always useful and difficult to find in Vietnam as are disposable nappies.

Medical supplies You may like to take some of the following items with you from home:

Sunglasses – ones designed for intense sunlight
Earplugs – for sleeping on aeroplanes and in noisy hotels
Suntan cream – with a high protection factor
Insect repellent – containing DET for preference
Mosquito net – lightweight, permethrin-impregnated for choice
Tablets – for travel sickness
Tampons – can be expensive in some countries in South East Asia
Condoms
Contraceptives
Water sterilizing tablets
Anti-malarial tablets
Anti-infective ointment for example Cetrimide
Dusting powder for feet etc – containing fungicide
Antacid tablets – for indigestion
Sachets of rehydration salts plus anti-diarrhoea preparations
Painkillers such as Paracetamol or Aspirin
Antibiotics – for diarrhoea etc
First Aid Kit – Small pack containing a few sterile syringes and needles and disposable gloves. The risk of catching hepatitis etc from a dirty needle used for injection is very low in Vietnam, but some may be reassured by carrying their own supplies – available from camping shops and airport shops.

Vaccination and immunization

Smallpox vaccination is no longer required anywhere in the world and cholera vaccination is no longer recognized as necessary for international travel by the World Health Organization – it is not very effective either. Yellow fever vaccination is not required either although you may be asked for a certificate if you have been in a country affected by yellow fever immediately before travelling to South East Asia. Vaccination against the following diseases are recommended.

Typhoid A disease spread by the insanitary preparation of food. A number of new vaccines against this condition are now available; the older TAB and monovalent typhoid vaccines are being phased out. The newer, for example Typhim Vi, cause less side effects, but are more expensive. For those who do not like injections, there are now oral vaccines.

Poliomyelitis Despite its decline in the world this remains a serious disease if caught and is easy to protect against. There are live oral vaccines and in some countries injected vaccines. Whichever one you choose it is a good idea to have a booster every 3-5 years if visiting developing countries regularly.

One dose should be given with a booster at six weeks and another at six months and **Tetanus**
10 yearly boosters thereafter are recommended. Children should already be properly
protected against diphtheria, poliomyelitis and pertussis (whooping cough), measles
and HIB all of which can be more serious infections in South East Asia than at home.
Measles, mumps and rubella vaccine is also given to children throughout the world,
but those teenage girls who have not had rubella (German measles) should be tested
and vaccinated. Hepatitis B vaccination for babies is now routine in some countries.
Consult your doctor for advice on tuberculosis inoculation: the disease is still
widespread in South East Asia.

Is less of a problem for travellers than it used to be because of the development of two **Infectious**
extremely effective vaccines against the A and B form of the disease. It remains **hepatitis**
common, however, in South East Asia. A combined hepatitis A & B vaccine is now
licensed and has been available since 1997 – one jab covers both diseases.

These might be considered in the case of epidemics for example meningitis. **Other**
Meningococcal meningitis and Japanese B encephalitis (JVE): there is an extremely **vaccinations**
small risk of these rather serious diseases. Both are seasonal and vary according to
region. Meningitis can occur in epidemic form. JVE is a viral disease transmitted from
pigs to man by mosquitoes. For details of the vaccinations consult a travel clinic.

Further information

Further information on health risks abroad, vaccinations etc may be available from a
local travel clinic. If you wish to take specific drugs with you such as antibiotics these
are best prescribed by your own doctor. Beware, however, that not all doctors can be
experts on the health problems of remote countries. More detailed or more
up-to-date information than local doctors can provide are available from various
sources. In the UK there are hospital departments specializing in tropical diseases in
London, Liverpool, Birmingham and Glasgow and the Malaria Reference Laboratory at
the London School of Hygiene and Tropical Medicine provides free advice about
malaria, T0891-600350. In the USA the local Public Health Services can give such
information and information is available centrally from the Centres for Disease Control
(CDC) in Atlanta, T404-3324559.

There are in addition computerized data bases which can be accessed for
destination – specific up-to-the-minute information. In the UK there is MASTA
(Medical Advisory Service to Travellers Abroad) T0171-6314408, Tx8953473,
F0171-4365389 and Travax (Glasgow, T0141-9467120 extension 247). Other
information on medical problems overseas can be obtained from the book by Richard
Dawood (Editor) – Travellers' Health, How to Stay Healthy Abroad, Oxford University
Press 1992 £7.99 (new edition imminent). We strongly recommend this revised and
updated edition, especially to the intrepid traveller heading for the more out of the
way places. General advice is also available in the UK in 'Health Information for
Overseas Travel' published by the Department of Health and available from HMSO and
'International Travel and Health' published by WHO Handbooks on First Aid are
produced by the British & American Red Cross and by St. John's Ambulance (UK).

On the way

For most travellers a trip to South East Asia means a long air flight. If this crosses time
zones then jetlag can be a problem where your body's biological clock gets out of
synchrony with the real time at your destination. The main symptoms are tiredness
and sleepiness at inconvenient times and, conversely, a tendency to wake up in the
middle of the night feeling like you want your breakfast. Most find that the problem is

worse when flying in an easterly direction. The best way to get over jetlag is probably to try to force yourself into the new time zone as strictly as possible which may involve, on a westward flight, trying to stay awake until your normal bedtime and on an eastward flight forgetting that you have lost some sleep on the way out and going to bed relatively early but near your normal time the evening after you arrive. The symptoms of jetlag may be helped by keeping up your fluid intake on the journey, but not with alcohol. The hormone melatonin seems to reduce the symptoms of jetlag but is not presently licensed in most of Europe although can be obtained from health food stores in the USA.

On long-haul flights it is also important to stretch your legs at least every hour to prevent slowing of the circulation and the possible development of blood clots. Drinking plenty of non-alcoholic fluids will also help.

If travelling by boat then sea sickness can be a problem – dealt with in the usual way by taking anti-motion sickness pills.

Staying healthy

Intestinal upsets

The thought of catching a stomach bug worries visitors to South East Asia but there have been great improvements in food hygiene and most such infections are preventable. Travellers' diarrhoea and vomiting is due, most of the time, to food poisoning, usually passed on by the insanitary habits of food handlers. As a general rule the cleaner your surroundings and the smarter the restaurant, the less likely you are to suffer.

Foods to avoid: uncooked, undercooked, partially cooked or reheated meat, fish, eggs, raw vegetables and salads, especially when they have been left out exposed to flies. Stick to fresh food that has been cooked from raw just before eating and make sure you peel fruit yourself. Wash and dry your hands before eating – disposable wet-wipe tissues are useful for this.

Shellfish eaten raw are risky and at certain times of the year some fish and shellfish concentrate toxins from their environment and cause various kinds of food poisoning. Liver fluke can also be transmitted The local authorities notify the public not to eat these foods. Do not ignore the warning.

Heat treated milk (UHT pasteurized or sterilized) is becoming more available in South East Asia as is pasteurized cheese. On the whole matured or processed cheeses are safer than the fresh varieties. Fresh unpasteurized milk from whatever animal can be a source of food poisoning germs, tuberculosis and brucellosis. This applies equally to ice-cream, yoghurt and cheese made from unpasteurized milk, so avoid these home-made products - the factory made ones are probably safer.

Tap water is rarely safe outside the major cities, especially in the rainy season. Stream water, if you are in the countryside, is often contaminated by local communities. Filtered or bottled water is usually available and safe, although you must make sure that somebody is not filling bottles from the tap and hammering on a new crown cap. If your hotel has a central hot water supply this water is safe to drink after cooling. Ice for drinks should be made from boiled water, but rarely is so stand your glass on the ice cubes, rather than putting them in the drink. The better hotels have water purifying systems.

Travellers' diarrhoea

This is usually caused by eating food which has been contaminated by food poisoning germs. Drinking water is rarely the culprit. Sea water or river water is more likely to be contaminated by sewage and so swimming in such dilute effluent can also be a cause.

Infection with various organisms can give rise to travellers' diarrhoea. They may be viruses, bacteria, for example Escherichia coli (probably the most common cause world-wide), protozoa (such as amoebas and giardia), salmonella and cholera. The diarrhoea may come on suddenly or rather slowly. It may or may not be accompanied by vomiting or by severe abdominal pain and the passage of blood or mucus when it is called dysentery.

How do you know which type you have caught and how to treat it?
If you can time the onset of the diarrhoea to the minute ('acute') then it is probably due to a virus or a bacterium and/or the onset of dysentery. The treatment in addition to rehydration is Ciprofloxacin 500 milligrams every 12 hours; the drug is now widely available and there are many similar ones.

If the diarrhoea comes on slowly or intermittently ('sub-acute') then it is more likely to be protozoal, that is caused by an amoeba or giardia. Antibiotics such as Ciprofloxacin will have little effect. These cases are best treated by a doctor as is any outbreak of diarrhoea continuing for more than three days. Sometimes blood is passed in amoebic dysentery and for this you should certainly seek medical help. If this is not available then the best treatment is probably Tinidazole (Fasigyn) one tablet four times a day for three days. If there are severe stomach cramps, the following drugs may help but are not very useful in the management of acute diarrhoea: Loperamide (Imodium) and Diphenoxylate with Atropine (Lomotil). They should not be given to children.

Any kind of diarrhoea, whether or not accompanied by vomiting, responds well to the replacement of water and salts, taken as frequent small sips, of some kind of rehydration solution. There are proprietary preparations consisting of sachets of powder which you dissolve in boiled water or you can make your own by adding half a teaspoonful of salt (3.5 grams) and four tablespoonful of sugar (40 grams) to a litre of boiled water.

Thus the lynch pins of treatment for diarrhoea are rest, fluid and salt replacement, antibiotics such as Ciprofloxacin for the bacterial types and special diagnostic tests and medical treatment for the Amoeba and Giardia infections. Salmonella infections and cholera, although rare, can be devastating diseases and it would be wise to get to a hospital as soon as possible if these were suspected.

Fasting, peculiar diets and the consumption of large quantities of yoghurt have not been found useful in calming travellers' diarrhoea or in rehabilitating inflamed bowels. Oral rehydration has on the other hand, especially in children, been a life saving technique and should always be practised, whatever other treatment you use. As there is some evidence that alcohol and milk might prolong diarrhoea they should be avoided during and immediately after an attack. So should chillies!

Diarrhoea occurring day after day for long periods of time (chronic diarrhoea) is notoriously resistant to amateur attempts at treatment and warrants proper diagnostic tests (cities with reasonable sized hospitals have laboratories for stool samples). There are ways of preventing travellers' diarrhoea for short periods of time by taking antibiotics, but this is not a foolproof technique and should not be used other than in exceptional circumstances. Doxycycline is possibly the best drug. Some preventatives such as Enterovioform can have serious side effects if taken for long periods.

Paradoxically **constipation** is also common, probably induced by dietary change, inadequate fluid intake in hot places and long bus journeys. Simple laxatives are useful in the short-term and bulky foods such as rice, beans and plenty of fruit are also useful.

There are a number of ways of purifying water in order to make it safe to drink. Dirty water should first be strained through a filter bag (camping shops) and then boiled or treated. Bringing water to a rolling boil at sea level is sufficient to make the water safe for drinking, but at higher altitudes you have to boil the water for longer to ensure that all the microbes are killed.

Essentials

Purifying water

There are sterilizing methods that can be used and there are proprietary preparations containing chlorine (for example Puritabs) or iodine (for example Pota Aqua) compounds. Chlorine compounds generally do not kill protozoa (for example Giardia).

There are a number of water filters now on the market available in personal and expedition size. They work either on mechanical or chemical principles, or may do both. Make sure you take the spare parts or spare chemicals with you and do not believe everything the manufacturers say.

Heat and cold Full acclimatization to high temperatures takes about two weeks. During this period it is normal to feel a bit apathetic, especially if the relative humidity is high. Drink plenty of water (up to 15 litres a day are required when working physically hard in the tropics), use salt on your food and avoid extreme exertion. Tepid showers are more cooling than hot or cold ones. Large hats do not cool you down, but do prevent sunburn. Remember that, especially in the highlands, there can be a large and sudden drop in temperature between sun and shade and between night and day, so dress accordingly. Warm jackets or woollens are essential after dark at high altitude. Loose cotton is still the best material when the weather is hot.

Air pollution With the rapid growth of traffic in the large cities air pollution will become an increasing problem. Expect sore throats and itchy eyes. Sufferers from asthma or bronchitis may have to increase their regular maintenance treatment.

Insects These are mostly more of a nuisance than a serious hazard and if you try, you can prevent yourself entirely from being bitten. Some, such as mosquitoes are, of course, carriers of potentially serious diseases, so it is sensible to avoid being bitten as much as possible. Sleep off the ground and use a mosquito net or some kind of insecticide. Preparations containing pyrethrum or synthetic pyrethroids are safe. They are available as aerosols or pumps and the best way to use these is to spray the room thoroughly in all areas (follow the instructions rather than the insects) and then shut the door for a while, re-entering when the smell has dispersed. Mosquito coils release insecticide as they burn slowly. They are widely available and useful out of doors. Tablets of insecticide which are placed on a heated mat plugged into a wall socket are probably the most effective. They fill the room with insecticidal fumes in the same way as aerosols or coils.

You can also use insect repellents, most of which are effective against a wide range of pests. The most common and effective is diethyl metatoluamide (DET). DET liquid is best for arms and face (care around eyes and with spectacles – DET dissolves plastic). Aerosol spray is good for clothes and ankles and liquid DET can be dissolved in water and used to impregnate cotton clothes and mosquito nets. Some repellents now contain DET and permethrin, an insecticide. Impregnated wrist and ankle bands can also be useful.

If you are bitten or stung, itching may be relieved by cool baths, antihistamine tablets (care with alcohol or driving) or mild corticosteriod creams, e.g. hydrocortisone (great care: never use if any hint of infection). Careful scratching of all your bites once a day can be surprisingly effective. Calamine lotion and cream have limited effectiveness and antihistamine creams are not recommended – they can cause allergies themselves.

Bites which become infected should be treated with a local antiseptic or antibiotic cream such as Cetrimide, as should any infected sores or scratches.

When living rough, skin infestations with body lice (crabs) and scabies are easy to pick up. Use whatever local commercial preparation is recommended for lice and scabies.

Crotamiton cream (Eurax) alleviates itching and also kills a number of skin parasites. Malathion lotion 5 percent (Prioderm) kills lice effectively, but avoid the use of the toxic agricultural preparation of Malathion, more often used to commit suicide.

Usually attach themselves to the lower parts of the body often after walking in areas **Ticks** where cattle have grazed. They take a while to attach themselves strongly, but swell up as they start to suck blood. The important thing is to remove them gently, so that they do not leave their head parts in your skin because this can cause a nasty allergic reaction some days later. Do not use petrol, vaseline, lighted cigarettes etc to remove the tick, but, with a pair of tweezers remove the beast gently by gripping it at the attached (head) end and rock it out in very much the same way that a tooth is extracted. Certain tropical flies which lay their eggs under the skin of sheep and cattle also occasionally do the same thing to humans with the unpleasant result that a maggot grows under the skin and pops up as a boil or pimple. The best way to remove these is to cover the boil with oil, vaseline or nail varnish so as to stop the maggot breathing, then to squeeze it out gently the next day.

The burning power of the tropical sun, especially at high altitude, is phenomenal. **Sunburn**
Always wear a wide brimmed hat and use some form of suncream or lotion on untanned skin. Normal temperate zone suntan lotions (protection factor up to seven) are not much good; you need to use the types designed specifically for the tropics or for mountaineers or skiers with protection factors up to 15 or above. These are often not available in Vietnam. Glare from the sun can cause conjunctivitis, so wear sunglasses especially on tropical beaches, where high protection factor sunscreen should also be used.

This very common, intensely itchy rash is avoided by frequent washing and by **Prickly heat** wearing loose clothing. It is cured by allowing skin to dry off through use of powder or by spending two nights in an air conditioned hotel!

This and other fungal skin infections are best treated with Tolnaftate or Clotrimazole. **Athlete's Foot**

Other risks and more serious diseases

Remember that rabies is endemic throughout South East Asia, so avoid dogs and cover your toes at night from vampire bats, which also carry the disease. If you are bitten by a domestic or wild animal, do not leave things to chance: scrub the wound with soap and water and/or disinfectant, try to have the animal captured (within limits) or at least determine its ownership, where possible, and seek medical assistance at once. The course of treatment depends on whether you have already been satisfactorily vaccinated against rabies. If you have (this is worthwhile if you are spending lengths of time in developing countries) then some further doses of vaccine are all that is required. Human diploid vaccine is the best, but expensive: other, older kinds of vaccine, such as that derived from duck embryos may be the only types available. These are effective, much cheaper and interchangeable generally with the human derived types. If not already vaccinated then anti rabies serum (immunoglobulin) may be required in addition. It is important to finish the course of treatment whether the animal survives or not.

Aids is increasing its prevalence in South East Asia. It is not wholly confined to the well **AIDS** known high risk sections of the population i.e. homosexual men, intravenous drug abusers, prostitutes and the children of infected mothers. Heterosexual transmission is now the dominant mode of infection and so the main risk to travellers is from casual sex. The same precautions should be taken as when encountering any sexually

Essentials

☞ *Modelling AIDS in Southeast Asia*

There has been a tendency to assume that there is a single AIDS 'pandemic'. However in reality it seems that there are possibly 3 different patterns to the spread of AIDS – 1 is characteristic of Europe and North America, the 2nd of Sub-Saharan Africa, and a 3rd of Asia. This 3rd pattern, described by Tim Brown and Peter Xenos of the East-West Population Institute in Hawaii, is different in a number of important respects. Furthermore, they argue that these differences are likely to make the disease both more serious and more intractable. The pattern is based on the experience of Thailand, and it is assumed that the Thai experience will soon be seen reflected in other countries in Asia.

It seems that the possibility of transmission per exposure, whether that be through sexual relations or needle sharing, is higher in Asia than in Europe and North America because of the high incidence of sexually transmitted diseases, especially among sex workers. Furthermore, a significant proportion of the male population of the countries of the region visit prostitutes for sex, meaning that the population 'at risk' is also very high. Therefore, in Thailand – and by implication also soon in many other countries of Asia – AIDS quickly made the cross-over from the homosexual and drug-using populations, to the

heterosexual population. Thailand's first AIDS case was reported in 1984. By the end of 1988, 30 percent of addicts visiting methodone treatment centres were HIV positive. 5 years later, by the end of 1993, levels of infection among sex workers had similarly reached 30 percent. Now, nearly 2 percent of women visiting pre-natal clinics are testing HIV positive. Thus, in the space of less than 10 years – far faster than in Europe and North America, and even faster than in Africa – AIDS has spread from homosexuals and drug addicts to the wives and babies of heterosexual men.

In August 1994, at a major international conference on AIDS in Asia, James Allen of the American Medical Association likened – to considerable anger it should be added – AIDS to the Black Death in Europe. The costs to Asia of the disease are likely to be truly staggering: McGraw-Hill have put a figure of US$38-52bn on the social and economic costs of AIDS in the region.

Southeast Asia: potential for the spread of AIDS/HIV

Rapidly increasing: Myanmar; Cambodia; Thailand
Potential for rapid increase: Indonesia; Laos; Malaysia; Vietnam
Increasing: Singapore
Not classified: Brunei

transmitted disease. The disease has not yet had the impact on Vietnam and Cambodia as it has on Thailand. The AIDS virus (HIV) can be passed via unsterile needles which have been previously used to inject an HIV positive patient, but the risk of this is very small indeed. It would, however, be sensible to check that needles have been properly sterilized or disposable needles are used. The chance of picking up Hepatitis B in this way is more of a danger. Be wary of carrying disposable needles. Customs officials may find them suspicious. The risk of receiving a blood transfusion with blood infected with the HIV virus is greater than from dirty needles because of the amount of fluid exchanged. Supplies of blood for transfusion are supposed to be screened for HIV in all reputable hospitals so the risk should be small. Catching the virus which causes AIDS does not necessarily produce an illness in itself; the only way to be sure if you feel you have been put at risk is to have a blood test for HIV antibodies on your return to a place where there are reliable laboratory facilities. However the test does not become positive for many weeks.

Malaria is prevalent in South East Asia and remains a serious disease and you are advised to protect yourself against mosquito bites as above and to take prophylactic (preventative) drugs. Start taking the tablets a few days before exposure and continue to take them six weeks after leaving the malarial zone. Remember to give the drugs to babies and children, pregnant women also.

Malaria

The subject of malaria prevention is becoming more complex as the malaria parasite becomes immune to some of the older drugs. Nowhere is this more apparent than in South East Asia especially parts of Laos and Cambodia. In particular, there has been an increase in the proportion of cases of falciparum malaria which are resistant to the normally used drugs. It would not be an exaggeration to say that we are near to the situation where some cases of malaria will be untreatable with presently available drugs.

Before you travel you must check with a reputable agency the likelihood and type of malaria in the countries which you intend to visit. Take note of advice on prophylaxis but be prepared to receive conflicting advice. Because of the rapidly changing situation in the South East Asian region the names and the dosage of the drugs have not been included but chloroquine and proganil may still be recommended for the areas where malaria is still fully sensitive, while Doxycycline, Mefloquine and Artemether are presently being used in resistant areas. Quinine, Halofantrine and Tetracycline drugs remain the mainstay of treatment. It is still possible to catch malaria even when taking prophylactic drugs, although it is unlikely. If you do develop symptoms (high fever, shivering, severe headache and sometimes diarrhoea) seek medical advice immediately. The risk of the disease is obviously greater the further you move from the cities into rural areas with primitive facilities and standing water.

The main symptoms are pains in the stomach, lack of appetite, lassitude and yellowness of the eyes and skin. Medically speaking there are two main types. The less serious, but more common is hepatitis A for which the best protection is the careful preparation of food, the avoidance of contaminated drinking water and scrupulous attention to toilet hygiene. The other, more serious, version is hepatitis B which is acquired usually as a sexually transmitted disease or by blood transfusion. It can less commonly be transmitted by injections with unclean needles and possibly by insect bites. The symptoms are the same as for hepatitis A. The incubation period is much longer (up to six months compared with six weeks) and there are more likely to be complications.

Infectious hepatitis (jaundice)

Hepatitis A can be protected against with gamma globulin. It should be obtained from a reputable source and is certainly useful for travellers who intend to live rough. You should have a shot before leaving and have it repeated every six months. The dose of gamma globulin depends on the concentration of the particular preparation used, so the manufacturers advice should be taken. The injection should be given as close as possible to your departure and as the dose depends on the likely time you are to spend in potentially affected areas. The manufacturer's instructions should be followed. Gamma globulin has really been superseded now by a proper vaccination against hepatitis A (Havrix), which gives immunity lasting up to 10 years. After that boosters are required. Havrix monodose is now widely available as is junior Havrix. The vaccination has negligible side effects and is extremely effective. Gamma globulin injection can be a bit painful, but it is cheaper than Havrix and may be more available in some places.

Hepatitis B can be effectively prevented by a specific vaccine (Engerix) – three shots over six months before travelling. If you have had jaundice in the past it would be worthwhile having a blood test to see if you are immune to either of these two types, because this might avoid the necessity and costs of vaccination or gamma globulin. There are other kinds of viral hepatitis (C, E etc) which are fairly similar to A and B, but vaccines are not available as yet.

Essentials

Typhus Can still occur carried by ticks. There is usually a reaction at the site of the bite and a fever. Seek medical advice.

Intestinal worms These are common and the more serious ones such as hookworm can be contracted from walking barefoot on infested earth or beaches. Some cause an itchy rash on the feet 'cutaneous larva migrans'.

Various other tropical diseases can be caught in jungle areas, usually transmitted by biting insects. Examples are leishmaniasis and filariasis.

Leptospirosis Various forms of leptospirosis occur throughout Latin America, transmitted by a bacterium which is excreted in rodent urine. Fresh water and moist soil harbour the organisms which enter the body through cuts and scratches. If you suffer from any form of prolonged fever consult a doctor.

Snake bite This is a very rare event indeed for travellers but if you are unlucky (or careless) enough to be bitten by a venomous snake, spider, scorpion or sea creature, try to identify the creature, without putting yourself in further danger. Snake bites in particular are very frightening, but in fact rarely poisonous – even venomous snakes bite without injecting venom. What you might expect if bitten are: fright, swelling, pain and bruising around the bite and soreness of the regional lymph glands, perhaps nausea, vomiting and a fever. Signs of serious poisoning would be the following symptoms: numbness and tingling of the face, muscular spasms, convulsions, shortness of breath or a failure of the blood to clot, causing generalized bleeding. Victims should be taken to a hospital or a doctor without delay. Commercial snake bite and scorpion kits are available, but are usually only useful for the specific types of snake or scorpion. Most serum has to be given intravenously so it is not much good equipping yourself with it unless you are used to making injections into veins. It is best to rely on local practice in these cases, because the particular creatures will be known about locally and appropriate treatment can be given.

Treatment of snake bite Reassure and comfort the victim frequently. Immobilize the limb by a bandage or a splint or by getting the person to lie still. Do not slash the bite area and try to suck out the poison because this sort of heroism does more harm than good. If you know how to use a tourniquet in these circumstances, you will not need this advice. If you are not experienced, do not apply a tourniquet.

Precautions Avoid walking in snake territory in bare feet or sandals – wear proper shoes or boots. If you encounter a snake stay put until it slithers away; do not investigate a wounded snake. Spiders and scorpions may be found in the more basic hotels. If stung, rest , take plenty of fluids and call a doctor. The best precaution is to keep beds away from the walls and look inside your shoes and under the toilet seat every morning.

Marine bites and stings Certain tropical sea fish when trodden upon inject venom into bathers' feet. This can be exceptionally painful. Wear plastic shoes when you go bathing if such creatures are reported. The pain can be relieved by immersing the foot in extremely hot water for as long as the pain persists.

Dengue fever This is increasing world-wide including in South East Asia. It can be completely prevented by avoiding mosquito bites in the same way as malaria. No vaccine is available. Dengue is an unpleasant and painful disease, presenting with a high temperature and body pains, but at least visitors are spared the more serious forms (haemorrhagic types) which are more of a problem for local people who have been exposed to the disease more than once. There is no specific treatment for dengue – just pain killers and rest.

Remember to take your anti-malarial tablets for six weeks after leaving the malarial area. If you have had attacks of diarrhoea it is worth having a stool specimen tested in case you have picked up amoebas. If you have been living rough, blood tests may be worthwhile to detect worms and other parasites. If you have been exposed to schistosomiasis by swimming in lakes etc check by means of a blood test when you get home, but leave it for six weeks because the test is slow to become positive. Report any untowards symptoms to your doctor and tell the doctor exactly where you have been and, if you know, what the likelihood of disease is to which you were exposed. **When you return home**

The above information has been compiled for us by Dr. David Snashall, who is presently Senior Lecturer in Occupational Health at the Guy's, King's & St. Thomas' Hospitals in London and until recently Chief Medical Advisor of the British Foreign and Commonwealth Office. He has travelled extensively in Central and South America and the Caribbean, worked in Peru and in East Africa and keeps in close touch with developments in preventative and tropical medicine.

For more information on health, take a look at the following websites: http://www.cdc.gov/travel/index.htm or http://www.tripprep.com/index.html.

Further reading

Books and magazines on the region

Asiaweek (weekly). A lightweight *Far Eastern Economic Review*; rather like a regional *Time* magazine in style. **Magazines**

Far Eastern Economic Review (weekly). Authoritative Hong Kong-based regional magazine; their correspondents based in each country provide knowledgeable, in-depth analysis particularly on economics and politics.

Dingwall, Alastair (1994) *Traveller's literary companion: South-east Asia*, In Print: Brighton. Experts on Southeast Asian language and literature select extracts from novels and other books by western and regional writers. The extracts are annoyingly brief, but it gives a good overview of what is available. **Books**

Dumarçay, Jacques (1991) *The palaces of South-East Asia: architecture and customs*, OUP: Singapore. A broad summary of palace art and architecture in both mainland and island Southeast Asia.

Fenton, James (1988) *All the wrong places: adrift in the politics of Asia*, Penguin: London. British journalist James Fenton skilfully and entertainingly recounts his experiences in Vietnam, Cambodia, the Philippines and Korea.

Fraser-Lu, Sylvia (1988) *Handwoven textiles of South-East Asia*, OUP: Singapore. Well illustrated, large-format book with informative text.

Higham, Charles (1989) *The archaeology of mainland Southeast Asia from 10,000 BC to the fall of Angkor*, Cambridge University Press: Cambridge. Best summary of changing views of the archaeology of the mainland.

Keyes, Charles F (1977) *The golden peninsula: culture and adaptation in mainland Southeast Asia*, Macmillan: New York. Academic, yet readable summary of the threads of continuity and change in Southeast Asia's culture. The volume has been recently republished by Hawaii University Press, but not updated or revised.

King, Ben F and **Dickinson, EC** (1975) *A field guide to the birds of South-East Asia*, Collins: London. Best regional guide to the birds of the region.

Miettinen, Jukko O (1992) *Classical dance and theatre in South-East Asia*, OUP, Singapore. Expensive, but accessible survey of dance and theatre, mostly focusing on Thailand, Myanmar and Indonesia.

Essentials

Osborne, Milton (1979) *Southeast Asia: an introductory history*, Allen & Unwin: Sydney. Good introductory history, clearly written, published in a portable paperback edition. A new revised edition is not on the shelves.

Rawson, Philip (1967) *The art of Southeast Asia*, Thames & Hudson: London. Portable general art history of Myanmar, Cambodia, Vietnam, Thailand, Laos, Java and Bali; by necessity, rather superficial, but a good place to start.

Reid, Anthony (1988) *Southeast Asia in the age of commerce 1450-1680: the lands below the winds*, Yale University Press: New Haven. Perhaps the best history of everyday life in Southeast Asia, looking at such themes as physical well-being, material culture and social organization.

Reid, Anthony (1993) *Southeast Asia in the age of commerce 1450-1680: expansion and crisis*, Yale University Press: New Haven. Volume 2 in this excellent history of the region.

Rigg, Jonathan (1991) *Southeast Asia: a region in transition*, Unwin Hyman: London. A thematic geography of the ASEAN region, providing an insight into some of the major issues affecting the region today.

Rigg, Jonathan (1997) *Southeast Asia: the human landscape of modernization and development*, London: Routledge. A book which covers both the market and former command economies (ie Myanmar, Vietnam, Laos and Cambodia) of the region. It focuses on how people in the region have responded to the challenges and tensions of modernization.

SarDesai, DR (1989) *Southeast Asia: past and present*, Macmillan: London. Skilful but at times frustratingly thin history of the region from the 1st century to the withdrawal of US forces from Vietnam.

Savage, Victor R (1984) *Western impressions of nature and landscape in Southeast Asia*, Singapore University Press: Singapore. Based on a geography PhD thesis, the book is a mine of quotations and observations from western travellers.

Steinberg, DJ *et al* (1987) *In search of Southeast Asia: a modern history*, University of Hawaii Press: Honolulu. The best standard history of the region; it skilfully examines and assesses general processes of change and their impacts from the arrival of the Europeans in the region.

Tarling, Nicholas (1992) (edit.) *Cambridge History of Southeast Asia*, Cambridge: Cambridge University Press. Two volume edited study, long and expensive with contributions from most of the leading historians of the region. A thematic and regional approach is taken, not a country one, although the history is fairly conventional.

Waterson, Roxana (1990) *The living house: an anthropology of architecture in South-East Asia*, OUP: Singapore. An academic but extensively-illustrated book on Southeast Asian architecture and how it links with lives and livelihoods. Fascinating material for those interested in such things.

Books on Vietnam

Novels **Duras, Marguerite** (1964) *The lover*, London: Flamingo. Now a film starring Jane March; this is the story of the illicit relationship between an expat French girl and a Chinese from Cholon set in the 1930s. The story is narrated by the French girl in her later years.

Greene, Graham (1954) *The quiet American*, Heinemann: London. What is remarkable about this novel is the way that it predicts America's experience in Vietnam. The two key figures are Alden Pyle, an idealistic young American, and Thomas Fowler, a hard-bitten and cynical British journalist. It is set in and around Saigon as the war between the French and the Viet Minh intensifies.

Grey, Anthony (1983) *Saigon*, Pan: London. Entertaining novel.

Nguyen Du (1983) *The tale of Kieu* (also known as *Truyen Kieu*), Yale University Press: New Haven, *tr.* Huynh Sanh Thong. Early 19th century Vietnamese classic and, for many, the masterpiece of Vietnamese poetry. It is also published locally in Vietnam (in English) by the Foreign Languages Publishing House. It tells the story of a beautiful girl and her doomed love affair with a soldier.

Vietnamese literature in English

Elliott, Mai (1999) *Sacred willow: four generations in the life of a Vietnamese family*, Oxford:Oxford University Press. Recounts the history of Vietnam through the life of the Duong family from the 19th century to the tragedy of Boat People. This is the story of Vietnam through Vietnamese eyes.

Taylor, Keith Weller (1983) *The birth of Vietnam*, University of California Press: Berkeley. Academic history of early Vietnam from the 3rd century BC to 10th century.

Wintle, Justin (1991) *The Vietnam Wars*, Weidenfeld and Nicholson: London. Not just about *the* War, but about all of Vietnam's interminable conflicts.

History

Essentials

There are more books on the Vietnam War than possibly any other conflict in global history. It has been examined in minute detail.

Books on the Vietnamese War

Bao Ninh (1993) *The sorrow of war*, Secker & Warburg, London. Wartime novel by a young North Vietnamese soldier, wonderful account of emotions during and after the war.

Cawthorne, Nigel (1992) *The bamboo cage*, Leo Cooper. The story of MIAs and POWs.

Fall, Bernard B (1967) *Hell in a very small place: the Siege of Dien Bien Phu*, Pall Mall Press.

Fitzgerald, Francis (1972) *Fire in the lake*, Vintage Books: New York. Pulitzer prize winner; a well-researched and readable account of the US involvement.

Harrison, James P (1982) *The endless war: fifty years of struggle in Vietnam*, Free Press: New York.

Herr, Michael (1977) *Dispatches*, Knopf: New York. An acclaimed 'account' of the war written by a correspondent who experienced the conflict first hand. It is the story of the war told through the eyes and words of the narrator – a journalist.

Karnow, Stanley (1983 and 1991) *Vietnam: a history*, Viking Press: New York. A comprehensive and readable history; second edition published in 1991; the best there is.

Lunn, Hugh (1985) *Vietnam: a reporter's war*, University of Queensland Press: St Lucia, Australia. Account of Australian reporter Hugh Lunn's year in Vietnam with Reuters between 1967 and 1968, including an account of his experiences during the Tet Offensive.

McNamara, Robert S and **Mark, Brian Van de** (1995) *In retrospect: the tragedy and lessons of Vietnam*, Times/Random House: New York. McNamara was Secretary for Defense from 1961 to 1968 and this is his cathartic account of the war. Informed from the inside, he concludes that the war was a big mistake.

Mangold, Tom and **Penycate, John** (1985), *The tunnels of Cu Chi*. Compelling account of the building of the tunnels and the VC who fought in them.

Mason, Robert (1984) *Chickenhawk*, Penguin: Harmondsworth. Autobiography of a helicopter pilot, excellent.

Sheehan, Neil (1989) *A bright shining lie*, Jonathan Cape: London. A meticulously researched 850-page account of the Vietnam War, based around the life of John Paul Vann; recommended.

Sheehan, Neil (1992) *Two cities: Hanoi and Saigon* (in US *After the war was over*), Jonathan Cape: London. A short but fascinating book which tries to link the past with the present in a part autobiography, part travelogue, part contemporary commentary.

SIPRI (1976) *Ecological consequences of the Second Indochina War*, Almqvist & Wiksell: Stockholm. Academic study of environmental side-effects of war.

Turley, William S (1986) *The Second Indochina War: a short political and military history 1954-1975*, Westview: Boulder. A clear, well-balanced academic account of the war.

Young, Gavin (1997) *A wavering grace: a Vietnamese family in war and peace*, London: Viking. This is Young's account of the war in Vietnam – he was a reporter in the country – told through the lives of a Vietnamese family. Moving and atmospheric.

Biography and autobiography
Fenn, Charles (1973) *Ho Chi Minh: a biographical introduction*, Studio Vista: London.
Greene, Graham (1980). *Ways of escape*. Autobiographical.
Ho Chi Minh (n.d.) *Prison diary*, Hanoi: Foreign Languages Publishing House. A collection of poems by Ho Chi Minh while he was incarcerated in China in 1942. They are autobiographical, recording his prison experiences and his yearning for home.
Page, Tim (1995) *Derailed in Uncle Ho's victory garden*, Touchstone Books, war photojournalist Tim Page makes a return visit to Vietnam, amusing in places.
Tin, Bui (1995) *Following Ho Chi Minh*, Hurst: London. Autobiographical account of a North Vietnamese Colonel's disillusionment with the Communist regime following Ho Chi Minh's death. Western readers may find it rather self-congratulatory in tone but nevertheless an interesting read.

Travel and Geography
Garstin, Crosbie (1928) *The Voyage from London to Indochina*: Heinemann. Hilarious, rather irreverent account of a journey through Vietnam.
Lewis, Norman (1951) *A dragon apparent: travels in Cambodia, Laos and Vietnam*. One of the finest of all travel books; now reprinted by Eland Books but also available second-hand from many bookshops.
Stewart, Lucretia (1998) *Tiger balm: travels in Laos, Cambodia and Vietnam*, London: Chatto & Windus.
Theroux, Paul (1977) *The great railway bazaar*, Penguin: London. Two chapters describe a graphic account of one American's attempt to travel by rail between Saigon and Hué.
Vu Tu Lap and **Taillard, Christian** (1994) *An Atlas of Vietnam*, Reclus – La Documentation Française. Marvellous summary of the population and economy of Vietnam in maps.

Economics, politics and development
Beresford, Melanie (1988) *Vietnam: politics, economics and society*, Pinter: London. Academic account of social, economic and political developments to mid-1980s; too early to include much discussion of economic reform programme.
Kemf, Elizabeth (1990) *Month of pure light: the regreening of Vietnam*, The Women's Press: London. Account of the attempts to overcome the after-effects of US defoliation and regreen the Vietnamese countryside; more a light travelogue than an objective book.
Kerkvliet, Benedict J Tria and **Porter, Doug J** (1995) (edits.) *Vietnam's rural transformation*, Boulder, Colorado: Westview and Singapore, Institute of Southeast Asian Studies. Up-to-date edited book on how the countryside in Vietnam has changed since *doi moi*.
Nrlund, Irene, Gates, Carolyn L and **Vu Cao Dam** (1995) (edits.) *Vietnam in a changing world*, Richmond, Surrey: Curzon Press. Up-to-date analysis of economic change in Vietnam incorporating many of the issues and tensions generated by the process of economic reform.
Nugent, Nicholas (1996) *Vietnam: the second revolution*, London: In Print. A good summary of the main changes in Vietnam's economy and society. Also covers the more recent changes dating from the early 1990s.
Popkin, Samuel L (1979) *The rational peasant: the political economy of rural society in Vietnam*, Berkeley: University of California Press. This book was written in response to James Scott's *The moral economy of the peasant*. Popkin contests the view that traditional Southeast Asia (here, Vietnam) was a moral economy where village solidarity and community spirit were dominant.

Scott, James C (1976) *The moral economy of the peasant: rebellion and subsistence in Southeast Asia*, New Haven: Yale University Press. The classic historical study of the 'moral' economy of the peasant. Available as a portable paperback.

Templer, Robert (1998) *Shadows and wind: a view of life in modern Vietnam*, London: Little Brown. Templer was a correspondent in Hanoi for Agence France – Presse and this is his account of modern Vietnam - and where it is headed. Overall it is a down-beat picture of the country, one where bureacratic inertia and political heavy handed-ness constrain progress.

Turner, Robert F (1975) *Vietnamese Communism: its origins and development*, Hoover Institution Press: Stanford. Academic study of rise of Communism in Vietnam.

Williams, Michael C (1992) *Vietnam at the crossroads*, Pinter: London. Most recent survey of political and economic reforms by a senior BBC World Service commentator; lucid and informed.

Young, Marilyn (1990) *The Vietnam Wars 1945-1990*, Harper Collins: New York. Good account of the origins, development and aftermath of the Vietnam wars.

Essentials

Books on doing business in Vietnam

Ashwood, Neil (1995) *Vietnam: a business handbook*, London: Graham and Trotman. One of the better of a whole spate of 'doing business in Vietnam' books. Well researched, with a good level of detail.

Quinlan, Joseph (1995) *Vietnam: business opportunities and risks*, Berkeley: Pacific View Press. Another book which can be recommended to businesspeople aiming to visit or invest in Vietnam.

Spencer, Cisca and **Heij, Gitte** (1995) *A guide to doing business in Vietnam*, Asia Research Centre, Murdoch University, Perth. This volume can also be recommended. Businesspeople say that it is generally accurate and usefully detailed.

Culture

Crawford, Ann Caddell (nd) *Customs and culture of Vietnam*, Charles Tuttle: Rutland, Vermont.

Hickey, Gerald (1964) *Village in Vietnam*, Yale University Press: New Haven; classic village study, only available second-hand.

Art and archaeology

Hejzlar, J (1973) *The art of Vietnam*, Hamlyn: London. The text is rather heavy going, but has numerous photographs.

Films

Along with the better-known films on the Vietnamese War including *Apocalypse Now*, *Hamburger Hill*, *Good Morning Vietnam* and Oliver Stone's trilogy *Platoon*, *Born on the Fourth of July* and *Heaven and Earth*, three French films have nicely captured the atmosphere of Vietnam at peace: *Indochine* starring Catherine Deneuve and *The Lover* with Jane March adapted from Margeurite Duras' book. The little known but delightful *Scent of green papaya*, an account of family relationships and love, was filmed entirely in a Paris studio. In all, Hollywood has made around 70 films on the Vietnam conflict. What they lack is any insight into the psyche and motivations of the Vietnamese. While US troops and journalists are portrayed as full human beings with emotions and desires, their foes are cut-out figures, devoid of character. In other words, don't expect to learn much about Vietnam and the Vietnamese by watching Vietnam War films made by Hollywood.

The internet

General tourism-related sites

http://www.vietvet.org. The Vietnam Veterans Webring offers not just the chance of a virtual visit but also provides details on specialist Veterans' tours to the country including visits to battle sites as well as reports and diaries from recent visitors.

http://www.bmi.net/vntours/. Vietnam Tours – Saigon-based and Vietnam Vet owned and operated – offers customised packages according to which US Army Corps a Vet belonged.

http://www.netspace.net.au/~mrfelix/bsa/. For potential bicycle tourists – Mr Pumpy offers a blow by blow account of one route through the Mekong Delta and another through Laos to Vietnam. The routes are well explained and the pitfalls are highlighted.

http://www.pata.org/. The Pacific Asia Travel Association, better known simply as PATA, with a useful news section arranged by country, links to airlines and cruise lines, and some information on educational, environmental and other initiatives.

http://webhead.com/asergio/asiaregion.html. Travel information on the Asian region.

http://www.yahoo.com/Regional Countries/[name of country]. Insert name of country to access practical information including material from other travel guides.

http://www.city.net/regions/asia/. Links to numerous country sites in Asia, including maps and some travel information, such as a travellers health advisory.

Maps   http://www.lib.utexas.edu/Libs/PLC/Map_collection/asia/htm. Up-to-date maps of Asia showing relief, political boundaries and major towns.

http://www.nationalgeographic.com/resources/ngo/maps/atlas/asia/asia.html. National Geographic's cartographic division, which takes maps from their current Atlas of the world.

http://emailhost.ait.ac.th/asia/asia. html. Clickable map of mainland Southeast Asia with pointer to sources of other information on the region.

http://www.expediamaps.com/. US biased but still pretty comprehensive. Key in a town and wait for it to magically appear.

Weather and geographical information   www.rainorshine.com/. A simple but effective weather site with five-day forecasts for 800 cities worldwide.

http://www.city.net/regions/asia. Pointer to information on Asian countries.

Travel advisories   http://travel.state.gov/travel_warnings.html. The US State Department's continually updated travel advisories on its Travel Warnings & Consular Information Sheets page.

http://www.fco.gov.uk/travel/. The UK Foreign and Commonwealth Office's travel warning section.

Travel and health   http://www.cdc.gov/travel/index.htm. Managed by the Center for Disease Control and Prevention (CDC) in Atlanta, this is one of the best health sites, providing detailed and authoritative information including special sections on such diseases, ailments and concerns as malaria, dengue fever, HIV/AIDS, rabies and Japanese encephalitis.

http://www.tripprep.com/index.html. Shoreland's Travel Health Online provides health advice by country.

Hotel sites   http://www3.sympatico.ca/donna.mcsherry/asia.htm. Stuck overnight at some international airport? Then check out the Budget Traveller's Guide to Sleeping in Airports.

Cyber cafés   www.netcafeguide.com/. Around 2,000 cyber cafés in 113 countries are listed here and it also provides discussion forums for travellers and a language section.

Newspapers, news and the media   http://www.vnagency.com.vn/. Vietnam's official news agency.

http://www.vietline.com. Vietnam Online site, with current affairs in Vietnam and links with other sites.

http://www.isop.ucla.edu/eas/web/radio-tv/htm. For information on Asian radio and television broadcasts access. Includes free downloadable software.
http://www.inesmedia.com. Site with links to 150-odd on-line newspapers in Asia and the Middle East.

http://www.oanda.com/converter/classic. Select your two currencies by clicking on a list, and wham – the exchange rate is provided. **Currencies**

http://none.coolware.com/infoasia/. Run by Infoasia which is a commercial firm that helps US and European firms get into Asia. **Business-related websites**
http://www.stern.nyu.edu/~nroubini/asia/AsiaHomepage.html. Homepage of a professor of economics – Roubini – who has collated all the information on the Asian financial and economic crisis, and there's a lot.

htttp://www.coombs.anu.edu.au/wwwVLPages/VietPages/wwwVL-Vietnam.html. This site has good links with other Vietnam sites – a good first stop. **General sites**
http://pears.lib.ohio-state.edu/asianstudies/asian studies.html. Huge range of links with information on topics from sports and travel to economics and engineering.
http://coombs.anu.edu.au/WWWVLPages/WhatsNewWWW/asian-www-news.html. Assortment of material from across Asian region.
http://coombs.anu.edu.au/asia-www-monitor.html. Produced by ANU's Research School of Pacific and Asian Studies, this site provides evaluations and summaries of Asian sites.
http://www.nbr.org. Centre for papers on Asia covering strategic, economic and political issues.
http://libweb.library.wisc.edu/guides/SEAsia/library.htm. `Gateway to Southeast Asia' from University of Wisconsin, numerous links.
http://www.pactoc.net.au/index/resindex.htm. Covers all Pacific, but good links into Southeast Asian material; emphasis on academic issues rather than travel.

http://www2.hawaii.edu/~tsomo. Resources on women and Buddhism. **History and culture**
http://www.asiasociety.org. Homepage of the Asia Society with papers, reports and speeches as well as nearly 1,000 links to what they consider to be the best educational, political and cultural sites on the Web.
http://www.hmongnet.org.usa. Information on Hmong culture, history and language.
http:vietconnection.com. Designed for travellers interested in Vietnam's culture.

http://nautilus.org. Homepage of the Nautilus Institute which focuses on issues connected with the environment and sustainability in the Asia-Pacific region. **Environment**

http://www.leidenuniv.nl/pun/ubhtm/mjkintro.htm. Library of slides from mainland Southeast Asian countries. **Picture libraries and books**

Useful addresses

For a list of embassies and consulates, see page 21

Tours and tour operators

Asian Journeys, 32-34 Semilong Rd, Northampton, NN2 6BT, T01604-234855. **UK**
Individual and group tours of the whole of Vietnam. *Encounter Overland*, 267 Old Brompton Rd, London, SW5 9JA, T0171-3706845. Long 6 to 8 week trips from Saigon or Hanoi ending up in Nepal on their "South China Sea to the Roof of the World" tour. Group expeditions with a maximum of 15 people. *Exodus Expeditions*, 9 Weir Rd,

London, SW12 0LT, T0181-6755550. Three tours of Vietnam each between 2-3 weeks, including cycling from Saigon to Hanoi, cultural tours of the whole country and a hill tribes and trekking tour. *Explore Worldwide*, 1 Frederick St, Aldershot, Hants, GU11 1LQ, T01252-344161, F01252-343170. *Guerba Expeditions Ltd*, Wessex House, 40 Station Rd, Westbury, Wiltshire, BA13 3JN, T01373-826611. Offer several land expeditions of the country. *The Imaginative Traveller*, 14 Barley Mow Passage, Chiswick, London, W4 4PH, 0181-742 8612, E info@imaginative-traveller.esm, W imaginative-traveller.com. Offer 15 tours of the country varying in length from 6-30 days and varying in content from trekking in the north to gourmet trips to travelling round the country on a 125cc Honda. *Indochina Travel*, Chiswick Gate, 598-608 Chiswick High Rd, London W4 5RT, T0181-9958280, F0181-9945346, recommended. *Regent Holidays*, 15 John St, Bristol, BS1 2HR, T0117-9211711, F0117-9254866, tailor made holidays, recommended. *Silk Steps*, 83 Quakers Rd, Downend, Bristol, BS16 6NH, T0117-9402800, E info@silksteps.co.uk, W www.silksteps.co.uk. Tailor-made tours and group travel arrangements. *Silverbird Travel*, 4 Northfields Prospect, Putney Bridge Rd, London, SW18 1PE, T0181-8759090. Tailor made tours covering the whole country. *Symbiosis Expedition Planning*, Bolingbroke Grove, London, SW11 1DA, T0171-9245906. Tailor made tours and they also offer 3 mountain biking tours, including a new one around the Mekong Delta. *Tour East*, King's Lodge, 28 Church St, Epsom, Surrey, KT17 42P, T01372-739799, F01372-739824. *Visit Vietnam*, T0171-2298612, E tennyson@visitvietnam, W www.visitvietnam.co.uk.

France *La Maison de L'Indochine*, 36 Rue des Bourdonnais, 75001 Paris, T1-40284360. *Nouvelles Frontières*, T1-42731064. *Vietnamtourism*, 4 Rue Cherubini 75002, Paris, T1-42868637. *Voyageurs Au Vietnam*, 55 Rue Sainte-Anne, 75002 Paris, T1-42861688.

Germany *Lernidee Reisen*, Dudenstr 78, D-10965 Berlin, T4930-7865056.

USA *Adventure Center*, T800-2278747. Tours from Hanoi to Saigon and from Hanoi to the northern Hilltribe areas. *Asia Pacific Adventures*, T800-8254680/213-9353156. Small group and tailor made tours. *Geographic Explorer* T800-7778183. Group and tailor made tours for the responsible tourist. *Global Spectrum*, 1901 Pennsylvania Avenue NW, Suite 204, Washington DC 20006, T202-2932065, F202-2960815, E gspectrum@gspectrum.com. This US-based company specialize in tours to Vietnam, many with a cultural twist and venturing off the usual routes. A professional and informed outfit. *Kim's Travel*, 8443 Westminster CA 92682. *Mekong Travel*, 151 First Ave, Suite 172, New York, T212-5292891, F212-5292891. *Nine Dragons Tours*, 6101 North Keystone Avenue, Indianapolis, T317-7261501, toll free within USA T800-9099050, E tours@nine-dragons.com, W www.nine-dragons.com. Offices in

Saigon, Da Nang and Hanoi offering guided and individually customized tours. *Quest Nature Tours*, T800-3871483. *Tour East*, 5120 West Goldleaf Circle, Suite 310, Los Angeles, California, 90056, T213-2906500, F213-2945531. *Viet Tours Holidays*, 8097 Westminster Av, Garden Grove, California, T714-8952588.

Australia *Intrepid*, PO Box 2781, Fitzroy DC, VIC 3065, T03-94732626, F03-94194426, E darrell@intrepidtravel.com.au, W www.intrepidtravel.com.au. Small group 'adventure' tours to Vietnam. *Tour East*, 99 Walker St, 12th floor, North Sydney, NSW 2060, T2-9569303, F2-9565340. *Intercontinental Travel*, 307 Victoria St, Abbotsford, Victoria 30567, T42877849. *Tara International Travel*, Level 3, 427 George St, Sydney 2645811. *World Expeditions*, T2643366, run mountain biking tours from Hanoi to Hué.

Vietnam **Hanoi** *Buffalo Tours*, 11 Hang Muoi St, T8280702, F8269370. Specialize in adventure and trekking tours. *Darling Café*, 33 Hang Quat St, T8269386, F8256562. Low cost tours around Hanoi and the north. *Especen*, 79E Hang Trong St, T8266856, F8269612. Organize mid-range tours of the north. *Exotissimo*, 26 Tran Nhat Duat, T8282150, F8282146. Specialize in weekend and more upmarket tours. *Green Bamboo*, 42 Nha Chung St, T8268752, F8264949. Quite a popular organizer of backpacker type tours and travel but for anything out of the ordinary not particularly cheap. *Hanoi Tourism*, 18 Ly Thuong Kiet St, T8268752, F8241101. Local state run tour provider, less dynamic than its southern counterpart. *Queen Café*, 65 Hang Bac St, T8260860, F8250000, queenaz@fpt.vn. One of the many tourist cafés but above average service. *Vietnam Tourism*, 30A Ly Thuong Kiet St, T8264154, F8257583. State tour operator better for group than individual travel.

Saigon *Ann Tourist*, Ton That Tung St, T8334356, F8323866. Generally excellent, knowledgeable guides. *Cam On Tour*, 32 Dong Du St, T8298443, F8298169. Efficient, knowledgeable and friendly staff. Can extend visas, book air tickets and hotels. *Diethelm*, 1A Me Linh Square, T8294932, F8294747. A good regional agent which can advise on visas, international rail connections and flights. *Exotissimo Travel*, 2B Dinh Tien Hoang St, T8251723, F8251684. Specialize in weekend and more upmarket tours. *Kim Café*, 270 De Tham St, T8369859, F8488369. *Saigontourist*, 49 Le Thanh Ton St, T8298129, F8224987. Local state tour operator that now operates on a national scale, chiefly used by group tours. *Sinh Café*, 246-248 De Tham St, T8367338, F8369322. The other half of the Kim – Sinh rivalry that invented budget travel in Vietnam. *Vidotour*, 41 Dinh Tien Hoang St, T8291438, F8291435. Probably the most highly regarded organizer of group travel in the country.

Thailand The greatest number of tour companies outside Vietnam are to be found in Bangkok, the 'gateway' to Vietnam. They are concentrated on Khaosan Rd and Soi Ngam Duphli and, for the more up-market operations, on Sukhumvit and Silom roads. There are also companies in the vicinity of the Vietnamese embassy.

BP Tour, 17 Khaosan Rd, T2815062, F2803642. *Diethelm Travel*, Kian Gwan Building II, 140/1 Witthayu Rd, T2559150, F2560248, E dto@dto.co.th. *East-West Group*, 135 Soi Sanam Khli, Witthayu Rd, T2530861, F2536178. *Educational Travel Centre*, *Royal Hotel*, 2 Rachdamnern Ave, T2240043, F2246930. *Exotissimo*, 21/17 Sukhumvit Soi 4, T2835240, F2547683 and 755 Silom Rd, T2359196, F2834885. *Marvel Holidays*, 279 Khaosan Rd, T2829339, F2813216. *MK Ways*, 57/11 Witthayu Rd, T2545583, F2545583/ 2802920. *Siam Wings Tours*, 173/1-3 Surawong Rd, T2534757, F2636808. *Vista Travel*, 244/4 Khaosan Rd, T2800348, F2800348.

Hong Kong *Skylion Ltd*, Suite D, 11 F Trust Tower, 68 Johnston Rd, Wanchai, T8650363, F8651306. *Vietnam Tours*, Friendship Travel, Houston Centre, 63 Moody Rd, Kowloon, T3666862.

Singapore *Tour East*, Head Office, 70 Anson Rd, No 12-00, Apex Tower, Singapore 0207, T2202200, F2258119.

Hanoi

3

Hanoi

Hanoi is the capital of the Socialist Republic of Vietnam. It lies nearly 100 kilometres from the sea on a bend in the Red River. From this geographical feature the city derives its name: Hanoi means 'within a river bend'. It is a city of broad, tree-lined boulevards, lakes, parks, weathered colonial buildings, elegant squares and some of the newest office blocks and hotels in Southeast Asia. The history of the city must be the most confusing of any oriental capital: established as a defensive citadel in the eighth century it has had at least seven names since then and has served a country of fluctuating borders; indeed, for much of the 19th century its capital status was taken away.

Hanoi

Phone code: 04
Colour map 1, grid B4

The original village on the site of the present city was located in a district with the local name of Long Do. The community seems to have existed as a small settlement as early as the third century AD, although the early history of the Red River Delta largely passed it by. At the beginning of the eighth century a general named Lu Yu became so enchanted with the scenery around the village of An Vien (close to Long Do), that he decided to move his headquarters there. Here he built a shrine to the Emperor Hsuan Tsung, erected an inscribed tablet, and dedicated a statue of the local earth spirit on which was inscribed a poem extolling the beauty of the spot.

Ins and outs

Getting there While Hanoi may be Vietnam's capital city, it is not as well connected as Saigon in the south. The airport is 50 kilometres from the city, about a 1 hour drive. There are flights to a handful of international and 7 local destinations. The train station is more central, about a 10-15 minute cyclo ride from the city centre. There are regular trains to Saigon, and all points on the route south, as to other destinations in the north like Haiphong and Lao Cai. There are also 4 trains each day to Kunming, the capital of China's Yunnan province. To confuse matters, there is not one bus terminal but several serving most destinations in the north and also major towns all the way south to Saigon. See the transport section at the end of this entry for details.

Getting around Hanoi is getting more frenetic by the minute as wealth is invested in the internal combustion engine, but it is still a quieter city than Saigon. With its elegant, tree-lined boulevards walking and bicycling can be delightful. If you like the idea of being bicycled, then a cyclo is the answer – but be prepared for some concentrated haggling. There are also motorbikes for hire for longer out-of-town journeys as well as a smattering of metered taxis.

History

The origins of Hanoi as a great city lie with a temple orphan: Ly Cong Uan. Ly rose through the ranks of the palace guards to become their commander and in 1010, four years after the death of the previous King Le Hoan, was enthroned, marking the beginning of the 200 year-long Ly Dynasty. On becoming king, Ly Cong Uan moved his capital from Hoa Lu to Dai La, which he renamed **Thang Long** or 'Soaring Dragon'. Thang Long is present day **Hanoi**. During the Ly Dynasty the heart of Thang Long was the king's sanctuary in the Forbidden City (Cam Thanh). Drawing both spiritual and physical protection, as well as economic well-being from their proximity to the king and his court, a city of commoners grew-up around the walls of Cam Thanh. The Ly kings established a Buddhist monarchical tradition which mirrored other courts in Southeast Asia. A number of pagodas were built at this time. Most have since disappeared, although the One Pillar Pagoda and the Tran Vu Temple both date from this period (see below).

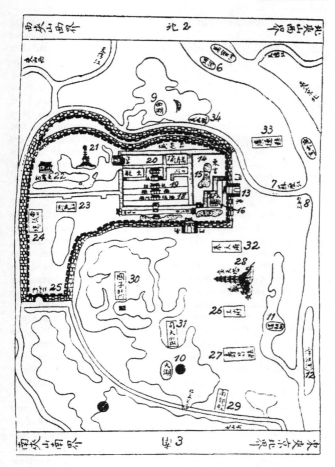

Map of Thang Long, former name of Hanoi, from Hong Duc Geography, dated 1490.

The map is orientated north (2), south (3), east (4) and west (5). The citadel is protected by walls, double in the north. It is situated between the Red River in the east (6) and the Tô Lich River (7) in the west which forms a protective moat to the north and west. Two great lakes lie to the north and south of the citadel. The first still exists as the Hà Nôi or Western Lake (Tây Hó) (9); a major part of the second, the Great Lake or Dai Ho (10) has been filled in and built over. Hoàn Kiém Lake (11) is shown to the south of the citadel, and draining into the Red River near Phu Sa Island (12). The Eastern Gate (Dông môn) (13), leads to the Heir Prince's Palace (Dông Cung) (14) with a large pond (tri) (15). To the south of the Palace is the Emperor's ancestors temple (Thái Miêu) (16), while to the west is the Imperial Palace with its Van Tho Palace (17) and its various buildings aligned south-north: Doan môn (18) Gate, the Audiences' Hall, Thân Triêu (19), Kinh Thiên Palace (20). In the western portion of the citadel are two temples, Khán Son (21) and Ling Lang (22); while to the south is the Military Instruction Palace (Giang võ diên) (23) and the Literary Examination Camp (Hôi thi duòng) (24). Outside the citadel's walls to the south (through the Bao Khanh Gate) (25) was the Lord Trinh's Palace (Vuong phú) (26), at Tho Xuong district (27). North of here and probably added to the map at a later date is the Bao Thiên Pagoda (28). Finally, to the northwest of the Trinh's Palace was the College of State Sons (Quôc Tu giám) (30), present-day Van Miéu, and the Observatory in the west (Tu Thiên Giám) (31).

Hanoi

Hanoi

☞ *Hanoi's names: (200 AD-present)*

Long Bien	*200 AD*
Dai La	*900-1010*
Thang Long	*1010-1400*
Dong Do	*1400-1428*
Dong Kinh	*1428-1789*
Bac Thanh	*1789-1831*
Hanoi	*1831-*

Thang Long, renamed **Tay Do** (Western Capital), was to remain the capital of Vietnam until 1400 when the Ho Dynasty (1400-1407) established a new capital at Thanh Hoa. But soon afterwards, the focus of power shifted back to Thang Long which, in turn, was renamed **Dong Kinh** (Eastern Capital) and **Bac Thanh** (Northern Citadel). It is from Dong Kinh that the French name for Northern Vietnam – Tonkin – is derived. The present name of the city dates from 1831 when the Nguyen Emperor Tu Duc (1847-1883) made it the capital of the province of Hanoi.

Colonial era During the period of French expansion into Indochina, the Red River was proposed as an alternative trade route to that of the Mekong. Francis Garnier was dispatched to the area in 1873 to ascertain the possibilities of establishing such a route. Despite having only a modest force of men under arms, when negotiations with Emperor Tu Duc failed in 1882, Garnier attacked and captured the citadel of Hanoi under the dubious pretext that the Vietnamese were about to attack him. Recognizing that if a small expeditionary force could be so successful, then there would be little chance against a full-strength army, Tu Duc acceded to French demands. At the time that the French took control of Annam, Hanoi could still be characterized more as a collection of villages than a city. As late as the 1870s, the French scholar André Masson, for example, argued that Hanoi "was not a city but a composite agglomeration where an administrative capital, a commercial town and numerous villages were juxtaposed ...". Indeed, the oldest name for Hanoi seems to have been *Ke Cho*, which means, 'a place where markets are'.

From 1882 onwards, Hanoi, along with the port city of Haiphong, became the focus of French activity in the north. Hanoi was made the capital of the new colony of Annam, and the French laid out a two square kilometres residential and business district, constructing mansions, villas and public buildings incorporating both French and Asian architectural styles. Many of these buildings still stand to the south and east of the Old City and Hoan Kiem Lake – almost as if they were grafted onto the older Annamese city. In the 1920s and 1930s, with conditions in the countryside deteriorating, there was an influx of landless and dispossessed labourers into the city. In their struggle to feed their families, many were willing to take jobs at subsistence wages in the textile, cigarette and other industries that grew up under French patronage. Before long, a poor underclass, living in squalid, pathetic conditions, had formed. At the end of the Second World War, with the French battling to keep Ho Chi Minh and his forces at bay, Hanoi became little more than a service centre. By 1954 there were about 40,000 stallholders, shopkeepers, peddlars and hawkers operating in the city – which at that time had a population of perhaps 400,000. It has been calculated that one family in two relied on the informal sector for their livelihoods.

War damage After the French withdrew in 1954, Ho Chi Minh concentrated on building up Vietnam and in particular Hanoi's industrial base. At that time the capital had only eight, small, privately-owned factories. By 1965, more than 1,000 enterprises had been added to this figure. However, as the US bombing of the north intensified with Operation Rolling Thunder in 1965, so the authorities began to evacuate non-essential civilians from Hanoi and to disperse industry into smaller, less vulnerable, units of operation. Between half and three-quarters of a million people were evacuated between 1965 and 1973: 75 percent of the inner city population. When hostilities ended in 1973, one Soviet reporter estimated that a quarter of all buildings had been destroyed. Nevertheless, the cessation of hostilities led to a spontaneous migration back into the capital. By 1984 the population of the city had reached 2.7 million, and today it is in excess of three million.

The physical damage wreaked upon the city during the war means that there is a grave shortage of housing and office space. Western companies opening up offices in the capital have found, to their surprise, that rents in one of the poorest countries in the world are approaching those in Tokyo and Hong Kong. Prime sites near Hoan Kiem Lake cost US$40-70 per square metre per month.

Hanoi

The French officer and hero Francis Garnier was killed in an assault on Hanoi's citadel on 21 December 1873. He was killed by a volley of bullets from Black Flag mercenaries, and not speared, as depicted here. Only 35 years old at his death, he became a symbol of courage and Gallic fortitude in France.
Source: Petit, M (nd) La France au Tonkin et en Chine

Hanoi

☞ *Beautiful Hanoi needs a miracle, says British MP*

When the French were unceremoniously bundled out of Vietnam in 1954 they did not leave much behind in the way of infrastructure, but they did leave Hanoi – one of the world's most beautiful cities. Built around more than twenty lakes, Hanoi consists of avenues lined with tamarind trees, elegant villas and magnificent public buildings. Decades of war and years of economic stagnation brought terrible decay, but not destruction. Hanoi has survived almost intact.

Alas the end is nigh. The arrival of the free market means that the planners now have the resources to succeed where the B-52 bombers failed. Unless a miracle occurs, Hanoi is about to be destroyed.

Already concrete monstrosities are rising in the most unlikely places. By Hoan Kiem lake in the city centre a ghastly confection of concrete and marble now dominates the skyline amid the yellow stucco and green wooden shutters of the public buildings left by the French. It is the new city hall. In this building dwell the very planners whose job is to regulate the development of the city. It is hard to think of a more ominous portent.

What is most lacking is not funds but political will. Government and local authority leaders pay lip service to the preservation of old Hanoi, but there has been little in the way of action. A ban on private cars in the old city would be a good start. Strict controls over new building would be another.

If the political will existed, it would not be hard to generate foreign support. "There is not one of my colleagues who has not raised this with the Vietnamese Government," an ambassador wrote to me. Another said, "I say to the Vietnamese, when you can demonstrate the will to preserve your city, I will find funds to pay for a consultant to advise how it might be done."

What irony. A country that has suffered so much at the hands of rapacious foreigners is now on the point of surrender to a culture at least as foreign and at least as destructive as that which it paid such a high price to defeat.

Source: *Extracted from an article written by Chris Mullin, MP, for the Vietnam Investment Review.*

Property development and the environment Although Saigon has attracted the lion's share of Vietnam's foreign inward investment, Hanoi, as the capital, also receives a large amount. But whereas Saigon's investment tends to be in industry, Hanoi has received a great deal of attention from property developers, notably in the hotel and office sectors. Unfortunately, much of the proposed development is in prestigious and historical central Hanoi.

British MP Chris Mullin has written an impassioned attack on the hideous and architecturally utterly incongruous schemes (see box) and drawn attention to the developers' blatant disregard for truth (such as a claim by Peter Purcell of Dragon Properties that a 20 storey office block will be "in total harmony with the character of the surrounding neighbourhood" of Hoan Kiem Lake) and Vietnamese politicians' disturbing haste to sell off prime, historical sites to overseas developers. In late 1994, the Chief Architect's Office proposed height limits on new development in the vicinity of Hoan Kiem Lake but failed to define the area this would apply to. By mid-1996 the crescendo of criticism from many quarters forced Hanoi's authorities to act. The first victim of their attention was the Golden Hanoi Hotel on the northwest bank of Hoan Kiem Lake. Work was halted while an embarrassed People's Committee tried to explain why they had authorized an illegal structure whilst at the same time trying to keep compensation to the foreign developer to a minimum.

Hanoi's streets

Street	Product	Date of Establishment	Origin of Inhabitants Village/District/Province
Hang Dong	Copper	18th century	Cau Nom/Khoai Chau/ Hai Hung
Hang Hom	Cupboards, Coffins	late 19th century	Ha Vi/Thuong Tin/Hay Tay
Hang Bac	Silver products, money Changing		Thanh Tri/Hanoi/Trau Khe/ Chau Giang/Hai Hung

A major development, the so-called Song Hong (Red River) City, is under construction between West Lake and the Red River. At a cost of US$260mn a Singaporean company is building luxury accommodation for 10,000, a 26-storey office, hotels and a hospital. Song Hong City will be built on the dyke that protects Hanoi from flooding. Interestingly 250 new houses built on the dyke illegally or with 'irresponsible licences' were torn down by the authorities because of the serious damage they have caused this ancient flood protection measure.

Pollution levels in Hanoi have soared as a result of the construction boom: dust from demolition, piling, bricks and tiles and sand blown from the back of trucks add an estimated 150 cubic metres of pollutants to the urban atmosphere every day. But while asthmatics may wheeze, Hanoi's army of builders grows daily ever stronger. Hundreds of farmers join the urban job market each week and one can see bands of men standing around at strategic points waiting to be recruited; on Duong Thanh Street, for example, carpenters with their tool boxes wait patiently for the call to a day's work. But can Hanoi's economy keep pace with the rate of migration in from the countryside. The situation in the past couple of years has looked ominous adding to the Party's woes. Nigel Thrift and Dean Forbes in their account of Vietnamese urbanization also identify the considerable social tension in what is still an austere and disciplined city between the wishes of the state for ideological rectitude and the desire of some of the population (especially the young) for a more colourful life, stimulated by the unification with the south and the growth of a market in consumer goods" (1986:151).

Sights

Hanoi is an ideal town to explore by bicycle or on foot with taxis and motorbikes available to the less energetic. The buses will probably remain a complete mystery, except to the long-term visitor. Much of the charm of Hanoi, and indeed of the rest of Vietnam, lies not so much in the official 'sights' (some of which can be decidedly uninspired) but in the unofficial and informal: the traffic, small shops, stalls, the bustle of pedestrians, clothing, parents treating their children to an ice cream, an evening visit to Hoan Kiem Lake ... Like China when it was 'opening-up' to Western tourists in the late 1970s, the primary interest lies in the novelty of exploring a city (and country) which, until recently, has opted for a firmly socialist road to development and has been insulated from the West. When Joleaud-Barral visited the city at the end of the 19th century he referred to it as a 'ville Française' and was of the opinion that whereas "at Saigon, one exists; at Hanoi, one *lives*". Humourist PJ O'Rourke describes the city along the same lines, if in a rather different style, in his book *Give war a chance*: "On first impression it seemed like Sixties

Hanoi

Hanoi

Related map
A Hoan Kiem,
page 89

N

| 0 metres | 200 |
| 0 yards | 218 |

■ **Sleeping**
1 Dan Chu
2 Dong Loi
3 Eden
4 Green Park
5 Gouman

6 Hilton Hanoi
7 Hoa Binh & Bank
   of America
8 Hoan Kiem
9 Mango
10 Sofitel Metropole

11 Thuy Nga
12 Trang Tien
13 Viet My
14 Villa Bleue

● **Eating**
1 202
2 252 Hang Bong
3 Al Fresco
4 Ban To Ho Tay
5 Bistrot

America – not pot, war and hirsute aggravation ... but the madras-clad, record hop, beach-bunny nation of my school days ... there was a doo-ron-ron in the air".

Hanoi's sights are centred in two main areas: around Hoan Kiem Lake, where many of the more expensive hotels are also located, and in the vicinity of Ho Chi Minh's Mausoleum. There are also some sights which fall outside these two areas.

Hoan Kiem Lake and Central Hanoi

Hoan Kiem Lake (the Lake of the Restored Sword) or Ho Guom, as it is more commonly referred to in Hanoi, is named after an incident that occurred during the 15th century. Emperor Le Thai To (1428-1433), following a momentous victory against an army of invading Ming Chinese, was sailing on the lake when a golden turtle appeared from the depths to take back the charmed sword which had secured the victory and restored it to the lake from whence it came. Like the sword in the stone of British Arthurian legend, Le Thai To's sword assures Vietnamese of divine intervention in time of national crisis and the story is graphically portrayed in water puppet theatres across the country. There is a modest and rather dilapidated tower (the *Tortoise Tower*) commemorating the event on an islet in the southern part of the lake. In fact, the lake does contain large turtles; one captured in 1968 was reputed to have weighed 250 kg. The park that surrounds the lake is used by the residents of the city every morning for jogging and tai chi (Chinese shadow boxing) and is regarded by locals as one of the city's beauty spots. When the French arrived in Hanoi at the end of the 19th century, the lake was an unhealthy lagoon surrounded by so many huts that it was impossible to see the shore.

The northeast corner is *the* place to have your photo taken, preferably with the **Ngoc Son (Jade Hill)**

6 Bodega
7 Club Opera
8 Coco Meeting Café
9 Green Bamboo Café
10 Gustave
11 Hanoi Gourmet
12 Hoa Sua
13 Indochine
14 Little Italian & Pear Tree
15 Mother's Pride
16 Seasons
17 Soho Deli

Tearaways terrorize townsfolk

A recent trend in contemporary society has manifested itself in the form of young male Hanoians racing each other on powerful motorbikes around the city streets. Up to 400 racers take part and, to add to the frisson, the more reckless cut their brake cables. The participants are drawn chiefly from the families of the nouveaux riches, some the sons of senior party members. A number of racers and spectators have died and police have so far proved unable to prevent the clandestinely organized events. Now a team of police riders equipped with fast bikes, guns and electric cattle prods has been assembled to maintain order. The Hanoi People's Committee has (a little naïvely) put forward the suggestion of building a special race track — presumably with the hope that legalizing and managing the `sport' will help to control it.

Pagoda (see diagram) in the background. The pagoda was built in the early 19th century on a small island and is linked to the shore by a red, arched wooden bridge (the **The Huc** – Sunbeam – **Bridge**) constructed in 1875. The temple is dedicated to Van Xuong, the God of Literature, although the 13th century hero Tran Hung Dao, the martial arts genius Quan Vu and the physician La To are also worshipped here. Shrouded by trees and surrounded by water, the pagoda's position is its strongest attribute. ■ *12,000d.*

Old City and 36 Streets
Stretching north from the lake is the **Old City**. Previously, it lay to the east of the citadel, where the emperor had his residence, and was squalid, dark, cramped and disease-ridden. This part of Hanoi has survived surprisingly intact, and today is the most beautiful area of the city. Narrow streets, each named after the produce that it sells or used to sell (Basket Street, Paper Street, Silk Street etc), create an intricate web of activity and colour. Another name for the area is '**36 Streets**' or **36 Pho Phuong**. By the 15th century there were 36 short lanes here, each specializing in a particular trade and representing one of the 36 guilds. Among them, for example, were the Phuong Hang Dao or Dyers' Guild, and the Phuong Hang Bac, the Silversmiths' Guild. The 36 streets have interested European visitors since they first started visiting Hanoi. Samuel Bacon, in 1685, for example, noted how "all the diverse objects sold in this town have a specially assigned street", remarking how different this was from "companies and corporations in European cities". The streets in question not only sold different products, but were usually also populated by people from different areas of the country – even from single villages. They would live, work and worship together because each of the occupational guilds had its own temple and its own community support networks.

Ngoc Son Pagoda

| Pavilion of the stele | Hall of cult | Sanctuary of Van Xuong | Sanctuary of Kouan Ti |

Longitudinal section of the Ngoc Son Pagoda
on Hoan Kiem Lake in Hanoi

Syndicated loans keep the sharks away

Throughout Vietnam, and indeed across the world wherever there are large numbers of Vietnamese, one will find hui in operation. Hui is a credit circle of 10 to 20 people who meet every month; the scheme lasts as many months as there are participants. In a blind auction the highest bidder takes home that month's capital. Credit is expensive in Vietnam, partly because there are few banks to make personal loans, so in time of crisis the needy have to borrow from money-lenders at crippling rates of interest. Alternatively they can join a hui and borrow at more modest rates.

It works like this: the hui is established with members agreeing to put in a fixed amount, say 100,000d, each month. Each month the members bid according to their financial needs, entering a zero bid if they need no cash. If, in month one, Mr Nam's daughter gets married he will require money for the wedding festivities and, moreover, he has to have the money so he must bid high, maybe 25,000d. Assuming this is the highest bid he will receive 75,000d from each member (ie 100,000 less 25,000). In future months Mr Nam cannot bid again but must pay 100,000d to whoever collects that month's

pot. Towards the end of the cycle several participants (those whose buffalo have not died and those whose daughters remain unmarried) will have taken nothing out but will have paid in 100,000 (minus x) dong each month; they can enter a zero bid and get the full 100,000d from all participants and with it a tidy profit.

There is, needless to say, strategy involved and this is where the Vietnamese love of gambling ("the besetting sin of the Vietnamese" according to Norman Lewis) colours the picture. One day, Mr Muoi wins 1 million dong on the Vinh Long lottery. He lets it be known that he intends to buy a Honda Dream, but to raise the necessary purchase price he must `win' that month's hui and will be bidding aggressively. In the same month Thuy, Mrs Phuoc's baby daughter, celebrates her first birthday so Mrs Phuoc needs money to throw a lavish thoi noi party (see box on page 372). She has heard of old Muoi's intentions but does not know if he is serious. In case he is, she will have to bid high. On the day, nice Mrs Phuoc enters a knock out bid of 30,000 but wily old Muoi was bluffing all along and he and the others make a lot of interest that month.

Some of this past is still in evidence: at the south end of Hang Dau Street, for example, is a mass of stalls selling nothing but shoes while Tin Street is still home to a community of tinkers. Generally however, the crafts and trades of the past have given way to new activities, karaoke bars, video rental and tourist shops – but it is remarkable the extent to which the streets still specialize in the production and sale of just one type of good. The dwellings in this area are known as 'tube houses' (*nha ong*); they are narrow, with shop fronts sometimes only three metres wide, but can be up to 50 metres long. The house at No 97 Hang Dao Street, for example, is a mere 1.6 metres wide. In the countryside the dimensions of houses were calculated on the basis of the owner's own physical dimensions; in urban areas no such regulations existed and tube houses evolved so that each house owner could have an, albeit very small, area of shop frontage facing onto the main street. The houses tend to be interspersed by courtyards or 'wells' to permit light into the house and allow some space for outside activities like washing and gardening. As geographers Brian Shaw and R Jones note in a paper on heritage conservation in Hanoi, the houses also had a natural air conditioning system: the difference in ambient temperature between the inner courtyards and the outside street created air flow, and the longer the house the greater the velocity of the flow. The older houses tend to be lower; commoners were not permitted to build higher than the Emperor's own residence. The structures were built of bricks 'cemented' together with sugar-cane juice.

A fear among conservationists is that this unique area will be destroyed as residents who have made small fortunes with the freeing-up of the economy, redevelop their houses insensitively. The desire is understandable: the tube houses are cramped and squalid, and often without any facilities. In an attempt to protect and renovate Hanoi's heritage an international foundation – the Friends of Hanoi Heritage – was established at the beginning of 1993 to raise funds to thwart the "bulldozers [that] wait in the wings to raze its heritage to the ground". Time, as they say, is very short. For information contact: Friends of Hanoi Heritage, Level 9, 287 Elizabeth Street, Sydney, NSW, Australia 2000.

Venturing further north, is the large and varied **Dong Xuan Market**, on Dong Xuan Street. This large covered market was destroyed in a disastrous fire in 1994. Stall holders lost an estimated US$4.5 million worth of stock and complained bitterly at the inadequacy of the fire services; one fire engine arrived with no water. The market is now rebuilt. **48 Hang Ngang Street** is the spot where Ho Chi Minh drew up the Vietnamese Declaration of Independence in 1945, unashamedly and ironically modelled on the US Declaration of Independence (Hang Ngang Street is at the north end of Hang Dao Street, before it becomes Hang Duong Street). Now a small museum with black and white photographs of Uncle Ho. The Old City is also a good area to eat, with a multitude of small and cheap eating houses (see page 92). Just to the east of the Dong Xuan market is the Red River, bridged at this point by the Cau Long Bien and Cau Chuong Duong. The former of these two bridges was built by the French in 1902 and named **Paul Doumer Bridge** after the Governor General of the time. Over 1.5 kilometres in length, it was the only river crossing in existence during the Vietnam War, and suffered repeated attacks from US planes only to be quickly repaired. The Chuong Duong Bridge was completed at the beginning of the 1980s.

To the south and east of Hoan Kiem Lake is the proud French-era **Municipal Theatre** or **Opera House**. It was built in 1911 and is one of the finest French colonial buildings in Hanoi. The exterior is a delightful mass of shutters, wrought iron work, little balconies and a tiled frieze. Inside, there are dozens of little boxes and fine decoration evocative of the French era. The Opera House has been lavishly restored, opening in time for the Francophone Summit held 1997. Just in front of the Opera House is the **Revolutionary Museum** (Bao Tang Cach Mang) at 25 Tong Dan Street. It is not a revolutionary museum as such, but a museum of the Vietnamese revolution, tracing the struggle of the Vietnamese people to establish their independence. The rooms are arranged chronologically beginning on the first floor, and as the first recounts the story of the destruction of the Mongol Chinese fleet at the mouth of the Bach Dang River in the autumn of 938 (see Ha Long Bay, page 157), it becomes clear that the American involvement in Vietnam has been just one episode in a centuries-long struggle against foreign aggressors. Also on display is a French guillotine (in the back passage on the first floor – one visitor was physically sick on seeing it), and an interesting room on the ground floor tracing the anti-war movement in the West. The final rooms show the peace and prosperity of reunification: bountiful harvests, the opening of large civil engineering projects, and smiling peasants. ■ *Open 0800-1230, 1400-1700 Tuesday-Sunday.*

A short distance south of the Revolutionary Museum, at 1 Pham Ngu Lao Street, is the **History Museum** (Bao Tang Lich Su). It is housed in a building which dates from the late 19th century, and which was originally an

Hanoi

The story of Quan Am

Quan Am was turned onto the streets by her husband for some unspecified wrong doing and, dressed as monk, took refuge in a monastery. There, a woman accused her of fathering, and then abandoning, her child. Accepting the blame (why, no one knows), she was again turned out onto the streets, only to return to the monastery much later when she was on the point of death – to confess her true identity. When the Emperor of China heard the tale, he made Quan Am the Guardian Spirit of Mother and Child, and couples without a son now pray to her. Quan Am's husband is sometimes depicted as a parakeet, with the Goddess usually holding her adopted son in one arm and standing on a lotus leaf (the symbol of purity).

archaeological research institute. The museum is now a centre of general cultural and historical research. The collection is large and rather confusing for the visitor without a working knowledge of the language or a guide to help as virtually all descriptions are in Vietnamese only. But fortunately, the rooms do proceed chronologically; from the prehistoric through to the Second World War. Exhibits include fine Dongson drums (see page 363), prehistoric artefacts, and Nguyen Dynasty pieces. Many of the pieces, though, are copies (for example the large 'tortoise' stelae). The curators will sometimes give visitors personal tours of the museum (for a small gratuity). ■ *Open 0800-1245, 1315-1700 Tuesday-Sunday.*

On Hai Ba Trung Street is the **Cho 19-12** – a market linking Hai Ba Trung with Ly Thuong Kiet Street – and selling primarily fresh fruit, vegetables and meat (including dog). A block to the west of the market is the site of the *Hoa Lo Prison* better known as the **Hanoi Hilton**, the prison where US POWs were incarcerated, some for six years, during the Vietnamese War. Up until 1969, prisoners were also tortured here. Two airforce officers Charles Tanner and Ross Terry, rather than face torture, concocted a story about two other members of their squadron who had been court-martialled for refusing to fly missions against the north. Thrilled with this piece of propaganda, visiting Japanese Communists were told the story and it filtered back to the US. Unfortunately for Tanner and Terry they had called their imaginary flyers Clark Kent and Ben Casey (both TV heroes). When the Vietnamese realized they had been made fools of, the two prisoners were again tortured. The final prisoners were not released until 1973, some having been held in the north since 1964. At the end of 1992 a US mission was shown around the prison where 2,000 inmates were housed in cramped and squalid conditions. Despite pleas from war veterans and party members, the site was sold to a Singapore-Vietnamese joint venture and is now a hotel and shopping complex, *Hanoi Towers*. As part of the deal the developers had to leave a portion of the prison for a museum, and quite a good one it is too. Maison Centrale, reads the legend over the prison's main gate which leads in to the museum. Unfortunately no captions were in English when we visited which is a pity as there are plenty of interesting-looking displays. There are recreations of conditions under colonial rule when the barbarous French incarcerated patriotic Vietnamese: by 1953 they were holding 2,000 prisoners in a space designed for 500. Less prominence is given to the role of the prison for holding American pilots, but of course, Douglas 'Pete' Peterson, the first post-war American Ambassador (1997-), who was one such occupant has his mug-shot on the wall. The revelry and fun the Vietnamese treated their captives to were, fortunately, recorded on film, strangely they contrast markedly with the version of events told by the prisoners. ■ *10,000d. Open 0800-1100 and 1330-1600.*

Nearby at 73 Quan Su Street is the **Quan Su** or **Ambassadors' Pagoda**. In the 15th century there was a guesthouse here for visiting Buddhist ambassadors. The current structure was built between 1936 and 1942. Chinese in appearance from the exterior, the temple contains some fine stone sculptures of the past, present and future Buddhas. It is very popular and crowded with scholars, pilgrims, beggars and incense sellers. The pagoda is one of the centres of Buddhist learning in Vietnam: at the back is a school room which is in regular use, students often spill-over to the surrounding corridors to listen.

A short distance south from the Ambassador's Pagoda, is **Thien Quang Lake** and **Lenin Park**. Not surprisingly, the park contains a statue of Lenin, together with the wreckage of a US B-52 bomber. You may be charged anything between 1,000 and 10,000d entrance depending on the entrance you use and how wealthy you look. Nearby, on Le Duan Street south of the railway station stalls sell a remarkable array of US, Soviet and Vietnamese army surplus kit.

Ho Chi Minh's Mausoleum and surrounding sights

Ho Chi Minh's Mausoleum (Lang Chu Tich Ho Chi Minh) is two kilometres to the west of Hoan Kiem Lake. Before entering the Mausoleum, visitors must leave cameras and possessions at the office (*Ban To Chuc*) on the corner of Doi Can (which becomes Le Hong Phong Street) and Ngoc Ha streets, a few minutes walk from the Mausoleum. Most cyclo drivers and locals will point it out. From the office, walk down Le Hong Phong Street and then north onto Hung Vuong Street – which leads onto **Ba Dinh Square** where Ho read out the Vietnamese Declaration of Independence on 2 September 1945 – and the Mausoleum. (Thereafter 2 September became Vietnam's National Day. Coincidentally 2 September also was the date on which Ho died in 1969, although his death was not officially announced until 3 September in order not to mar people's enjoyment of National Day in the beleaguered North.) Visitors march in file to see Ho's embalmed corpse. The Vietnamese have made his body a holy place of pilgrimage. This is contrary to Ho's own wishes: he wanted to be cremated and his ashes placed in three urns to be positioned atop three unmarked hills in the north, centre and south of the country. He once wrote that "cremation is not only good from the point of view of hygiene, but it also saves farmland". Visitors must be respectful: dress neatly, walk solemnly, and do not talk. The **Mausoleum**, built between 1973 and 1975, is a massive, square, forbidding structure and must be among the best constructed, maintained and air-conditioned (for obvious reasons) buildings in Vietnam. Opened in 1975, it is a fine example of the Mausoleum genre and modelled closely on Lenin's Mausoleum in Moscow. Ho lies, with a guard at each corner of his bier. The embalming of Ho's body was undertaken by the chief Soviet embalmer Dr. Sergei Debor who also pickled such Communist luminaries as Klenient Gottwald (President of Czechoslovakia), Georgi Dimitrov (Prime Minister of Bulgaria) and Forbes Burnham (President of Guyana). Debrov was flown to Hanoi from Moscow as Ho lay dying, bringing with him two transport planes packed with air conditioners (to keep the corpse cool) and other equipment. To escape US bombing, the team moved Ho to a cave, taking a full year to complete the embalming process. Russian scientists still check-up on their handiwork, servicing Ho's body regularly. Their embalming methods and the fluids they use are still a closely guarded secret, and in a recent interview, Debrov noted with pleasure the poor state of Mao's body, which was embalmed without Soviet help. "We had no part whatsoever in doing Mao", adding "I have heard reports that he is not in very good condition". ■ *Open 0730-1100 Tuesday-Thursday, Saturday and Sunday. The Mausoleum is closed in September and October.*

From the Mausoleum, visitors are directed to **Ho Chi Minh's house** built in the compound of the former **Presidential Palace**. The Palace, now a Party guesthouse, was the residence of the Governors-General of French Indochina and was built between 1900 and 1908. In 1954, when North Vietnam's struggle for independence was finally achieved, Ho Chi Minh declined to live in the palace, saying that it belonged to the people. Instead, he stayed in what is said to have been an electrician's house in the same compound. Here he lived from 1954-58, before moving to a new house built the other side of the small lake (Ho Chi Minh's 'Fish Farm', swarming with massive and well-fed carp). This modest house is airy and personal, and immaculately kept. Ho conducted meetings under the house which is raised up on wooden pillars (his books, slippers and telephones are still here), and slept and worked above. The typewriter on which it is said he typed the Declaration of Independence is on display. Built by the army, the house mirrors the one he lived in while fighting the French from his haven near the Chinese border. Behind the house is Ho's bomb shelter, and behind that the hut where he died in 1969. ■ *Open 0730-1130 Tuesday-Thursday, Saturday and Sunday.*

Behind Ho Chi Minh's house is the **One Pillar Pagoda** (**Chua Mot Cot**), one of the few structures remaining from the original foundation of the city. It was built in 1049 by Emperor Ly Thai Tong, although the shrine has since been rebuilt on several occasions, most recently in 1955 after the French destroyed it before withdrawing from the country. Emperor Ly built the pagoda in a fit of religious passion after he dreamt that he saw the goddess *Quan Am* (Chinese equivalent Kuan-yin) sitting on a lotus and holding a young boy, whom she handed to the Emperor. On the advice of counsellors who interpreted the dream, the Emperor built this little lotus-shaped temple in the centre of a water-lily pond and shortly afterwards his queen gave birth to a son. As the name suggests, it is supported on a single (concrete) pillar with a brick and stone staircase running up one side. The pagoda symbolizes the 'pure' lotus sprouting from the sea of sorrow. Original in design, with dragons running along the apex of the elegantly curved tiled roof, the temple is one of the most revered monuments in Vietnam. But the ungainly concrete pillar and the pond of green slime in which it is embedded detract considerably from the enchantment of the little pagoda. Adjacent is the inhabited Dien Huu Pagoda, a sign says they don't like people in shorts but actually they're quite friendly and it has a nice courtyard.

Ho Chi Minh Museum

Overshadowing the One Pillar Pagoda is the **Ho Chi Minh Museum** – opened in 1990 in celebration of the centenary of Ho's birth. Contained in a large and impressive modern building, it is the best arranged and most innovative museum in Vietnam. But, apart from newspaper clippings in French, everything is in Vietnamese. The display traces Ho's life and work from his early wanderings around the world to his death and final victory over the south. Traditional Vietnamese music performances. One of the guides may speak English. ■ *Open 0800-1100, 1330-1600 Tuesday-Thursday and Saturday; 0730-1100, 1330-1600 Sunday.*

Van Mieu Pagoda

South from Ho Chi Minh's Museum on Nguyen Thai Hoc are the walls of the Temple of Literature. The entrance to the pagoda is at the south end of this long and narrow block on Quoc Tu Giam Street. **The Temple of Literature** or **Van Mieu Pagoda** is the largest and probably the most important temple complex in Hanoi. It was founded in 1070 by Emperor Ly Thanh Tong, dedicated to Confucius who had a substantial following in Vietnam, and modelled, so it is said, on a temple in Shantung, China, the birthplace of the sage.

The examination of 1875

The examinations held at the Temple of Literature and which enabled, in theory, even the most lowly peasant to rise to the exalted position of a Mandarin were long and difficult, and conducted with great formality. André Masson quotes Monsieur de Kergaradec, the French Consul's, account of the examination of 1875:

"On the morning of the big day, from the third watch on, that is around one o'clock in the morning, the big drum which invites each one to present himself began to be beaten and soon students, intermingled with ordinary spectators, approached the Compound in front of the cordon formed around the outer wall by soldiers holding lances. In the middle of the fifth watch, towards four or five o'clock in the morning, the examiners in full dress came and installed themselves with their escorts at the different gates. Then began the roll call of the candidates, who were thoroughly searched at the entrance, and who carried with them a small tent of canvas and mats, cakes, rice, prepared tea, black ink, one or two brushes and a lamp. Everyone once inside, the gates were closed, and the examiners met in the central pavilion of the candidates' enclosure in order to post the subject of the composition. During the afternoon, the candidates who had finished withdrew a few at a time through the central gate...the last ones did not leave the Compound until midnight."

Doctor laureate on way home from an illustration by H Oger in 1905

Going to the examination camp with apparatus (bamboo bed, writing box, bamboo tube for examination papers) from an illustration by H Oger in 1905

Some researchers, while acknowledging the date of foundation, challenge the view that it was built as a Confucian institution pointing to the ascendancy of Buddhism during the Ly Dynasty. Confucian principles and teaching rapidly replaced Buddhism, however, and Van Mieu subsequently became the intellectual and spiritual centre of the kingdom as a cult of literature and education spread amongst the court, the mandarins and then among the common people. At one time there were said to be 20,000 schools teaching the Confucian classics in northern Vietnam alone.

The temple and its compound are arranged north-south, and visitors enter at the southern end from Quoc Tu Giam Street. On the pavement two pavilions house stelae bearing the inscription *ha ma*, (climb down from your horse) a nice reminder that even the most elevated dignitaries had to proceed on foot. The main Van Mieu Gate (Cong Van Mieu Mon) is adorned with 15th century dragons. Traditionally the large central gate was opened only on ceremonial occasions. The path leads through the Cong Dai Trung to a second courtyard and the Van Khue Gac Pavilion which was built in 1805 and dedicated to the Constellation of Literature. The roof is tiled according to the *yin-yang* principle.

Beyond lies the Courtyard of the Stelae at the centre of which is the rectangular pond or Cieng Thien Quang (Well of Heavenly Clarity). More important are the stelae themselves, 82 in all, on which are recorded the names of 1,306 successful examination scholars (*tien si*). Of the 82 that survive (30 are missing) the oldest dates back to 1442 and the most recent to 1779. Each stele is carried on the back of a tortoise, symbol of strength and longevity but they are arranged in no order; three chronological categories, however, can be identified. 14 date from the 15th and 16th centuries; they are the smallest and embellished with floral motifs and *yin-yang* symbols but not dragons (a royal emblem). 25 stelae are from the 17th century and ornamented with dragons (by now permitted), pairs of phoenix and other creatures mythical or real. The remaining 43 stelae are of 18th century origin; they are the largest and decorated with two stylized dragons, some merging with flame clouds. Passing was not easy: in 1733, out of some 3,000 entrants only eight passed the doctoral examination (*Thai Hoc Sinh*) and became Mandarins – a task that took 35 days. This tradition was begun in 1484 on the instruction of Emperor Le Thanh Tong, and continued through to 1878 – during which time 116 examinations were held. The Temple of Literature was not used only for examinations however: food was also distributed to the poor and infirm, 500 grammes of rice at a time. In 1880, the French Consul Monsieur de Kergaradec recorded that 22,000 impoverished people came to receive this meagre handout.

Continuing north, the *Dai Thanh Mon* or *Great Success Gate* leads on to a courtyard flanked by two buildings which date from 1954, the originals having been destroyed in 1947. These buildings were reserved for 72 disciples of Confucius. Facing is the *Dai Bai Duong (Great House of Ceremonies)* which was built in the 19th century but in the earlier style of the Le Dynasty. The carved wooden friezes with their dragons, phoenix, lotus flowers, fruits, clouds and *yin-yang* discs are all symbolically charged, depicting the order of the universe and by implication reflecting the god-given hierarchical nature of human society, each in his place. It is not surprising the Communist government has hitherto had reservations about preserving a temple extolling such heretical doctrine. Inside is an altar on which sit statues of Confucius and his closest disciples. Adjoining is the *Dai Thanh (Great Success) Sanctuary* which also contains a statue of Confucius.

The Trung sisters

Vietnamese history honours a number of heroines, of whom the Trung sisters are among the most revered. At the beginning of the Christian era, the Lac Lords of Vietnam began to agitate against Chinese control over their lands. Trung Trac, married to the Lac Lord Thi Sach, was apparently of a `brave and fearless disposition' and encouraged her husband and the other lords to rise up against the Chinese in 40 AD. The two sisters often fought while pregnant, apparently putting on gold plated armour over their enlarged bellies.

Although an independent kingdom was created for a short time, ultimately the uprising proved fruitless; a large Chinese army defeated the rebels in 43 AD, and eventually captured Trung Trac and her sister Trung Nhi, executing them and sending their heads to the Han court at Lo-yang. An alternative story of their death has it that the sisters threw themselves into the Hat Giang River to avoid being captured, and turned into stone statues. These were washed ashore and placed in Hanoi's Hai Ba Trung Temple for worship.

To the north once stood the first university in Vietnam, *Quoc Tu Giam*, which from the 11th to 18th centuries educated first the heir to the throne and later sons of mandarins. It was replaced with a temple dedicated to Confucius' parents and followers itself destroyed in 1947. ■ *12,000d. Open 0830-1600 Monday-Sunday.*

Fine Arts Museum Not far from the northern walls of the Van Mieu Pagoda at 66, Nguyen Thai Hoc Street is the **Fine Arts Museum** (Bao Tang My Thuat) contained in a large colonial building with an oriental-style roof. It has a large collection of contemporary Vietnamese art, along with some handicrafts. ■ *10,000d. Open 0800-1200, 1300-1600 Tuesday-Sunday.*

Army Museum A five-minute walk east from the Fine Arts Museum, situated at 30, Dien Bien Phu Street is the **Army Museum** (Bao Tang Quan Doi). Across the road from the front entrance is a statue of Lenin. The museum displays military memorabilia – mostly contemporary. Tanks, planes and artillery fill the courtyard. Symbolically, an untouched Mig-21 stands at the museum entrance while the wreckage of B52s, F1-11s and Q2Cs is piled up at the back. The museum illustrates battles and episodes in Vietnam's fight for independence (for instance, the battle at Dien Bien Phu), but unfortunately, all explanations are in Vietnamese. In the precincts of the museum is a flag tower, the **Cot Co**, raised up on three platforms. Built in 1812, it is the only substantial part of the original citadel still standing. ■ *10,000d. Open 0800-1130, 1330-1630 Tuesday-Sunday.*

Outer Hanoi North from the Old City is **Truc Bach (White Silk) Lake**. Truc Bach Lake was created in the 17th century by building a causeway across the southeast corner of Ho Tay. This was the site of the 11th century **Royal Palace** which had, so it is said, 'a hundred roofs'. All that is left is the terrace of *Kinh Thien* with its dragon staircase, and a number of stupas, bridges, gates and small pagodas. Judging by the ruins, the palace must have been an impressive sight. At the southwest corner of the lake, on the intersection of Hung Vuong, Quan Thanh and Thanh Nien streets is the **Quan Thanh Pagoda**, originally built in the early 11th century in honour of Huyen Thien Tran Vo (a genie) but since much remodelled. Despite renovation, it is still very beautiful. The large bronze bell was cast in 1677. ■ *5,000d.*

The much larger **West Lake** or **Ho Tay** was originally a meander in the Red River. It is fast losing its unique charm as the redevelopment disease spreads. Nguyen Ngoc Khoi, director of the Urban Planning Institute in Hanoi estimates that the area of the lake has shrunk by 20 percent, from 500 to 400 ha, as residents and hotel and office developers have reclaimed land. The lake is also suffering encroachment by water hyacinths which are fed by organic pollutants from factories (especially a tannery) and untreated sewage. The **Tran Quoc Pagoda** can be found on an islet on the east shores of the lake, linked to the causeway by a walkway. It was originally built on the banks of the Red River before being transferred to its present site by way of an intermediate location. The pagoda contains a stele dated 1639 recounting its unsettled history. A few kilometres north on the tip of a promontory stands **Tay Ho Pagoda**, notable chiefly for its setting. It is reached along a narrow lane lined with stalls selling fruit, roses and paper votives and a dozen restaurants serving giant snails with noodles (*bun oc*) and fried shrimp cakes.

South of the city centre, down Hue Street, is the hub of motorcycle sales, parts and repairs. Off this street, for example along Hoa Ma, Tran Nhan Tong and Thinh Yen are numerous **stalls and shops**, each specializing in a single type of product: TVs, electric fans, bicycle parts and so on. It is a fascinating area to explore. At the intersection of Thinh Yen and Pho 332 people congregate to sell second-hand and new bicycles, as well as bicycle parts. Not far away is the venerable **Hai Ba Trung Temple** – the temple of the Trung Sisters – overlooking a lake. Ask for **Den Hai Ba Trung**. The temple was built in 1142, but like others, has been restored on a number of occasions. It contains crude statues of the Trung sisters (see box), Trung Trac and Trung Nhi which are carried in procession once a year during February. The pagoda is not always open.

Further south still from the Hai Ba Trung, is another pagoda – **Chua Lien Phai**. This quiet pagoda which can be found just off Bach Mai Street, was built in 1732, although it has since been restored.

Excursions

Compared with Saigon and the south Hanoi and surrounds are rich in places of interest. Not only is the landscape more varied and attractive, the 1,000 year history of Hanoi has generated dozens of sights of architectural appeal many of which can be seen on a day trip.

Co Loa Citadel, the third century capital 16 kilometres north of Hanoi, built by King An Duong with walls in three concentric rings, the outer of which is eight kilometres in circumference. It is an important Bronze Age site and thousands of arrow heads and three bronze ploughshares have been excavated here. Today there is little to see as electricity sub-stations and farms have obliterated much of archaeological interest. ■ *Getting there: drive north up Highway 3, Co Loa is signposted to the east.* **To the north**

Hung Kings' Temples, **Phong Chau** South of Yen Bai and approximately 100 kilometres northwest of Hanoi near the industrial town of Viet Tri in Vinh Phu Province is popular with Vietnamese visitors especially during the Hung Kings' Festival. In purely topographical terms the site is striking, most obviously an almost perfectly circular hill rising unexpectedly out of the monotonous Red River floodplain with two lakes at the bottom. Given its peculiar physical setting it is easy to understand how the site acquired its mythical reputation as the birthplace of the Viet people and why the Hung Vuong kings chose it as the capital of their kingdom.

In this place, myth and historical fact have become intertwined. Legend has it that the Viet people are the product of the union of King Lac Long Quan, a dragon, and his fairy wife Au Co. Au Co gave birth to a pouch containing 100 eggs which hatched to produce 50 boys and 50 girls. Husband and wife decided to separate in order to populate the land and propagate the race, so half the children followed their mother to the highlands and half remained with their father on the plains giving rise to the Montagnards and lowland peoples of Vietnam. Historically easier to verify is the story of the Hung kings (Hung Vuong). They built a temple in order to commemorate the legendary progenitors of the Vietnamese people.

The **museum** is a hideous, Soviet inspired piece but there are on display interesting items excavated from the province. Exhibits include pottery, jewellery, fish hooks, arrow heads and axe heads (dated 1000-1300 BC) but of particular interest are the bronze drums dating from the Dongsonian period (see page 369). The Dongsonian was a transitional period between the neolithic and bronze ages and the drums are placed at around the fifth to the third centuries BC. Photographs show excavation in the 1960s when these items were uncovered. ■ *Open 0800-1130, 1300-1600, Monday-Sunday.*

Ascending the hill, a track leads to a **memorial to Ho Chi Minh**. Ho said he hoped that people would come from all over Vietnam to see this historic site. Nearby is the **Low Temple** dedicated to Au Co, mother of the country and

Day trips from Hanoi

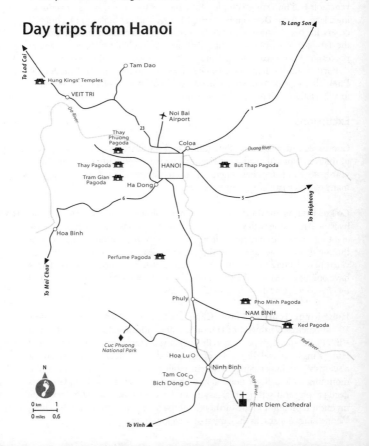

supposedly the site where the 100 eggs were produced. At the back of the temple is a statue of the Buddha of a thousand arms and a thousand eyes. Continuing up the hill is the **Middle Temple** where Prince Lang Lieu was crowned seventh Hung king and where the kings would play chess and discuss pressing affairs of state. Prince Lang Lieu was (like the English King Alfred) something of a dab hand in the kitchen and his most enduring creation is a pair of cakes, *banh trung* and *banh day*, which to this day (unlike Alfred's) remain popular delicacies, eaten at Tet. This temple has three altars and attractive murals.

Pressing on to the top of the hill is the **oath stone** on which the 18th Hung king, Thuc Phan, swore to defend the country from its enemies. Adjacent is the **Top Temple** dating from the 15th century. The roof is adorned with dragons and gaudily painted mural warriors stand guard outside. A not particularly ancient drum hangs from the ceiling but smoke rising from burning incense on the three altars helps add to the antiquity of the setting. Here it was that the kings would supplicate God for peace and prosperity.

Steps lead from the back right of this temple down the hill to the **mausoleum of the sixth Hung king**. These steps then continue down the far side of the hill to the **Well Temple** built in memory of the last princess of the Hung Dynasty. Inside is a well in the reflection of which this girl used to comb her hair. Today worshippers throw money in and, it is said, they even drink the water. Turn right to get back to the car park.

Festivals: *Hung Kings' festival* (10th day of the third lunar month). A two week celebration when the temple site comes alive as visitors from all over Vietnam descend on the area, as Ho Chi Minh encouraged them to. The place seethes with vendors of all descriptions and food stalls and fairground activities spring up. There are racing swan boats on one of the lakes.

■ *Getting there: turn off Highway 2 about 12 kilometres north of Viet Tri: a morning or afternoon's excursion by car from Hanoi.*

The Hung Kings' Temples

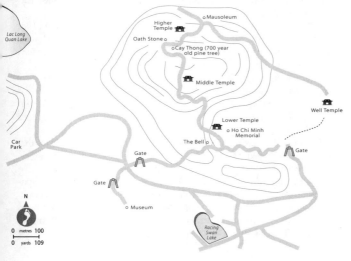

Lac Long Quan Lake

Mausoleum

Higher Temple

Oath Stone

Cay Thong (700 year old pine tree)

Middle Temple

Well Temple

Lower Temple

Ho Chi Minh Memorial

The Bell

Car Park

Gate

Gate

Gate

Museum

Racing Swan Lake

N

0 metres 100
0 yards 109

Tam Dao

Phone code: 021

Tam Dao lies in a mountain range of the same name, a chain of three mountains whose peaks constitute a natural border between Vinh Phu and Thai Nguyen provinces. Protruding from the clouds, the three peaks are said to resemble three islands, hence the name Tam Dao which means 'three islands'.

Construction of the town started in 1904; in 1915 the church, a post office, tennis courts and a swimming pool were added. As in Sapa, a mansion was built for the Governor General which, with its eight roofs, was the largest such villa in Indochina. And the 130-room *Metropole Hotel* was built to cater to the needs of the steady stream of affluent expatriates who came here to escape the summer heat of the Red River Delta.

Tam Dao was almost completely razed to the ground during the First Indochina War of 1945-1954; all that now remains of the original 200-plus French colonial buildings are the foundations of old villas and the shell of the old church building; the latter now functions as the club house of the Tam Dao Trades Union.

During the summer Tam Dao is a very busy resort – the month of July is the real high season for Vietnamese visitors – but from October through to March weather can become quite cold and the majority of its hotels and restaurants shut for the winter.

To describe Tam Dao's setting as stunning is an understatement. The town nestles in a giant rock bowl bitten out of the side of the mountain. All around steep cliffs soar high above, clad in a glorious jungle of trees entangled with lianas; early morning mist and cloud slowly burn off as the sun rises and the forest comes alive with the sound of bird call, animal cries and the humming of insects. It is said that the gods came down from heaven to play chess here. On a good day there are clear views over the plains below. Scrambling through the overgrowth one stumbles over colonial remains rather like discovering the remnants of some ancient classical civilization in the wilderness: crumbling walls, mysterious flights of steps, forlorn bridges, rocky balustrades and charming gateways.

And because of all this beauty Tam Dao is a tragedy. Modern day Tam Dao could justifiably claim to be the most odious, obnoxious and distasteful town in the country. It is utterly run-down. Most hotels are filthy and horribly managed. The people are unpleasant: rapacious, lazy and slovenly. Holiday makers are little better: their habits consist solely of being photographed, eating wild animals, getting drunk, karaoke and sex – if funds permit.

A 20-30 minute walk from the town centre is the **Silver Waterfall** (*Thac Bac*) which falls 45 metres. It is reached by way of a path and some old steps, lined with irritating vendors who stock everything except, unfortunately, 'Which part of 'NO' don't you understand' T-shirts.

■ *Getting there: all vehicles travelling along Highway 28 to Tam Dao are stopped at a checkpoint 11 kilometres before the town where a fee of 50,000d is levied from each foreign visitor. Thereafter the road climbs through some beautiful mountain scenery to the former colonial hill station, 930 metres above sea level. Best time to visit 80 years ago. Cold in winter, wet July-August.*

Sleeping There are numerous hotels and guesthouses but few, if any, that can be recommended. Many new ones have been erected with funny money, instantly recognizable by their spurious glitz, including a 5-storey monstrosity built by a recently retired driver. **A** *Cay Thong*, T824271, F824256. Japanese joint venture hotel 16 rooms all with adjoining bathroom, restaurant. **C-D** *Cong Doan* (*Trades Union*), T824210. Basic. **Eating** Expect boar, bear, porcupine, civet cat, bamboo rat, deer and jungle fowl to appear on the menu.

Directory Tourist offices *Tam Dao Tourism*, T824246, F824263.

The **Vietnam Museum of Ethnology**, some distance west of the city centre in   **To the west**
Cau Giay District (Nguyen Van Huyen Road), opened in November 1997 in a
modern purpose-built structure (which has been compared architecturally
with the Guggenheim Museum in New York). The collection here of some
25,000 artefacts and 15,000 photographs is excellent and, more to the point, is
attractively and informatively presented with labels in Vietnamese, English
and French. It displays the material culture (textiles, musical instruments,
jewellery, tools, baskets and the like) of the majority Kinh as well as Vietnam's
53 other designated minority peoples. While much is historical the museum
is also attempting to build up its contemporary collection. There is a shop
attached to the museum. ■ *10,000d. Open Tuesday-Sunday, 0830-1230,
1330-1630. Getting there: catch the No 14 minibus from Dinh Tien Hoang
Street, north of Hoan Kiem Lake, to the Nghia Tan stop. Turn right and walk
down Duong Hoang Quoc Viet for one block, before turning right at the
Petrolimex station down Nguyen Van Huyen. The Museum is down this street,
on the left.*

Perfume Pagoda (**Chua Huong** or Chua Huong Tich) is 60 kilometres   **To the south**
southwest of Hanoi. Dedicated to Quan Am (see page 77), it is one of a number of shrines and towers built amongst limestone caves and is regarded as
one of the most beautiful spots in Vietnam. The stone statue of Quan Am in
the principal pagoda was carved in 1793 after Tay Son rebels had stolen and
melted down its bronze predecessor to make cannon balls. Emperor Le
Thanh Tong (1460-1497) described it as 'Nam Thien de nhat dong' or 'foremost cave under the Vietnamese sky'. It is a popular pilgrimage spot, particularly during the festival months of March and April. A sampan takes visitors
along the Yen River, a diverting four kilometre ride through a flooded landscape to the Mountain of the Perfume Traces. From here it is a three kilometre
hike up the mountain to the cool, dark cave wherein lies the Perfume Pagoda.
The US$7 fare includes the return boat trip. ■ *Getting there: a half day excur-
sion, hire a car or take a tour.*

Keo Pagoda is seven kilometres outside the town of Thai Binh, which lies
to the southeast of Hanoi. This pagoda was built during the 11th century and
is a fine example of Vietnamese provincial architecture. ■ *Getting there: by
car or on a tour.* **Thien Truong** and **Pho Minh Pagodas** (see page 163), **Doi
Son** and **Doi Diap Pagodas** (see page 163).

Cuc Phuong National Park is about 160 kilometres south of Hanoi. This
can be done as day trip or over-nighter from Hanoi or as an excursion from
Ninh Binh (see page 167 for details).

Tay Phuong Pagoda is about six kilometres from the Thay Pagoda in the
village of Thac Xa. It may date back to the eighth century, although the present structure was rebuilt in 1794. Constructed of ironwood, it is sited at the
summit of a hill and is approached by way of a long stairway. The pagoda is
best known for its collection of 74 18th century *arhat* statues (statues of former monks). They are thought to be among the best examples of the wood-
carver's art from the period. ■ *Getting there: by tour or hire car.*

Thay Pagoda (Master's Pagoda), also known as Thien Phuc Tu Pagoda,
lies 40 kilometres southwest of Hanoi in the village of Sai Son, Ha Son Binh
Province. Built in the 11th century, the pagoda honours a herbalist, Dao
Hanh, who lived in Sai Son village. It is said that he was reborn as the son of
Emperor Le Thanh Tong after he and his wife had come to pray here. The
pagoda complex is divided into three sections. The outer section is used for
ceremonies, the middle is a Buddhist temple, while the inner part is dedicated
to the herbalist. The temple has some fine statues of the past, present and

future Buddhas with gold faces and lacquered red garments, as well as an impressive array of demons. Water puppet shows are performed during holidays and festivals on a stage built in the middle of the pond at the front of the pagoda (see page 387). Dao Hanh, who was a water puppet enthusiast, is said to have created the pond. It is spanned by two bridges built at the beginning of the 17th century. There are good views from the nearby Sai Son Hill – a path leads upwards from the pagoda. ■ *Getting there: by tour or hire car.*

Other possible day trips are excursions to **Haiphong** (see page 146), **Ninh Binh** (see page 164), **Hoa Lu** (see page 164), **Tam Coc** (see page 165), **Phat Diam Cathedral** (see page 166), **Hoa Binh** (see page 104) and **Mai Chau** (see page 106)

Essentials

Sleeping

■ *on maps*
Price codes:
see inside front cover

There has been a spate of hotel building and renovation in Hanoi in recent years and accommodation of all standards and at all prices is available. There are currently more rooms than visitors so discounts are available pretty much everywhere, particularly at the higher end although popular hotels can book up very quickly at certain times of year (December-March and summer holidays). The most expensive offer a range of business services and have IDD and satellite TV. Hotels north of Hoan Kiem Lake offer the best value.

City centre:
south of Hoan
Kiem Lake

L-A+ *Sofitel Metropole*, 15 Ngo Quyen St, T8266919, F8266920. Graham Greene stayed here in the 1950s. Until renovation in 1991-92 it oozed character. The only hotel in its class in central Hanoi and often full it boasts the essential Met Pub, restaurants, a business centre, useful bookshop and a small pool with attractive poolside bar. The hotel has retained most of its business despite competition from newer business hotels and remains a hub of activity. **L-A+** *Hilton Hanoi Opera*, 1 Le Thanh Tong St, T9330500, F9330530, E info_hanoi@hilton.com. Opened in February 1999, this is the genuine article. Built adjacent to and architecturally sympathetically with the Opera House it is a splendid building and aims to provide the highest levels of service and hospitality. **L-A+** *Chess Board*, 87 Nguyen Thai Hoc St, T8431548, F8236992. A/c, satellite TV etc but remarkably indifferent service for these prices. **L-A+** *De Syloia*, 17A Tran Hung Dao St, T8245346, F8241083. Business hotel with the popular *La Mousson* restaurant. **L-A+** *Guoman*, 83A Ly Thuong Kiet St, T8222800, F8222822. Proving to be one of the most popular of the new hotels: an attractive building, with pleasing decor, 152 comfortable rooms and a tip-top location. Friendly staff and highly efficient. **L-A+** *Green Park*, 48 Tran Nhan Tong St, T8227725, F8225977. 40 rooms, nice location, quite efficient with business facilities.

A+-B *Hoa Binh*, 27 Ly Thuong Kiet St, T8253315, F8269818. A/c, rambling old state-run hotel with quite large rooms. Renovated, but rather shoddy finish – poorly laid carpets, cracked doors, discounts negotiable. At US$150 per night guests would probably expect fresh rather than plastic flowers, *Le Splendide*, French restaurant attached. **A+-B** *Dan Chu*, 29 Trang Tien St, T8254937, F8266786. Good restaurant, very pleasant, friendly state-run hotel with clean and spacious rooms, some set well back from the street. **A+-A** *Thuy Nga*, 4 Ba Trieu St, T9341256, F9341262. New, privately owned hotel with 24 rooms in a prime position – front rooms overlook Hoan Kiem Lake. All mod cons, satellite TV, etc, scrupulously maintained and polished, attentive and engaging staff, breakfast included, recommended. **A** *Eden*, 78 To Nhuong St, T8245273, F8245619. Good location but small rooms whose price is hard

Hoan Kiem

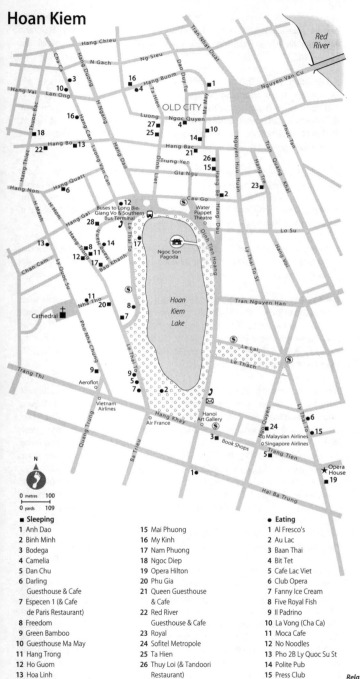

Red River

OLD CITY

Hoan Kiem Lake

Ngoc Son Pagoda

Water Puppet Theatre

Buses to Long Bien, Giang Vo & Southern Bus Terminal

Cathedral

Aeroflot

Vietnam Airlines

Air France

Hanoi Art Gallery

Book Shops

Malaysian Airlines
Singapore Airlines

Opera House

Hanoi

0 metres 100
0 yards 109

■ **Sleeping**
1 Anh Dao
2 Binh Minh
3 Bodega
4 Camelia
5 Dan Chu
6 Darling
   Guesthouse & Cafe
7 Especen 1 (& Cafe
   de Paris Restaurant)
8 Freedom
9 Green Bamboo
10 Guesthouse Ma May
11 Hang Trong
12 Ho Guom
13 Hoa Linh
14 Love Planet
   Guesthouse & Cafe

15 Mai Phuong
16 My Kinh
17 Nam Phuong
18 Ngoc Diep
19 Opera Hilton
20 Phu Gia
21 Queen Guesthouse
   & Cafe
22 Red River
   Guesthouse & Cafe
23 Royal
24 Sofitel Metropole
25 Ta Hien
26 Thuy Loi (& Tandoori
   Restaurant)
27 Thuy Nga
28 Win

● **Eating**
1 Al Fresco's
2 Au Lac
3 Baan Thai
4 Bit Tet
5 Cafe Lac Viet
6 Club Opera
7 Fanny Ice Cream
8 Five Royal Fish
9 Il Padrino
10 La Vong (Cha Ca)
11 Moca Cafe
12 No Noodles
13 Pho 2B Ly Quoc Su St
14 Polite Pub
15 Press Club
16 Restaurant 22
17 Thuy Ta

Related map
Hanoi, page 72

to justify: nevertheless popular, handy for *A Little Italian* and *The Pear Tree* restaurants. **A-B** *Bac Nam*, 20 Ngo Quyen St, T8257067, F8268998. Friendly, good restaurant. **A-B** *Hoan Kiem*, 25 Tran Hung Dao St, T8264204. A/c, big rooms, clean but overpriced.

B *Binh Minh*, 27 Ly Thai To St, T8266442, F8257725. Near the Metropole, a/c, pre-renovation but clean and perfectly good, a fair price for a central location. **B-D** *Hotel 35*, 35 Trang Tien St, T8256115. Some a/c, hot water, central, good value but often full, staff are not known for their friendliness. **C** *Bodega*, 57 Trang Tien St, T8252241. A/c, small hotel above restaurant and coffee shop and restaurant, well run, clean, recommended (2 sister hotels nearby are available for overspills).

Centre: north of Hoan Kiem Lake   In the Old Quarter buildings are tightly packed and rooms small, sometimes without windows – suffocating in a power cut, check first. Live cheek by jowl with your neighbours, enjoy their music and share with them the pleasures of tuning a motorbike engine at 0200 in the morning – remind them to test the horn while they're at it. Hotels in this area offer the best value for money.

L-A+ *Royal*, 20 Hang Tre St, T8244230, F8244234. Glacial, granite lobby, expensive but comfortable business hotel with restaurant and business centre, 65 rooms, ideal for extended stays.

A+-A *Galaxy*, 1 Phan Dinh Phung St, T8282888, F8282466. Recently renovated 3-star business hotel (built in 1918) with full accessories including the all-important bedside reading lights and switches which too many expensive hotels forget, 50 rooms. **A-B** *Freedom*, 57 Hang Trong St, T8267119, F8243918. Near Hoan Kiem lake and the cathedral. **A-B** *Ho Guom*, 76 Hang Trong St, T8252258, F8243564. Set back from the road, quiet, nice position.

B *Hoa Linh*, 35 Hang Bo St, T8243887, F8243886. Plumb in the centre of the bustling 36 Streets area, attractive lobby and willing staff but a bit pricey for what's on offer; **B** *Hong Ngoc*, 34 Hang Manh St, T8285053, F8285054. This is a real find. Small, family-run hotel, the rooms and bathrooms are huge and comfortable. Well positioned writing desk, bath tub, spotlessly clean throughout and a cheerful and helpful staff. **B-C** *Hang Trong*, 54-56 Hang Trong St, T8251346, F8285577. A/c, a few unusual and quite decent rooms set back from the road, good position. **B-C** *Nam Phuong*, 16 Bao Khanh St, T8258030, F8258964. Pleasant position near Hoan Kiem Lake but some rooms a little airless and cramped. **B-C** *Phu Gia*, 136 Hang Trong St, T8255493, F8259207. Some a/c, no frills, best rooms have views over Hoan Kiem Lake, others are arranged around an internal courtyard so quiet, cheapest rooms may have no window. **B** *Win*, 34 Hang Hanh St, T8267150, F8247448. Like an increasing number of hotels in Hanoi has satellite TV, cheaper rooms are on the top (4th) floor, fair size double rooms with bath.

C-D *Anh Dao*, 37 Ma May St, T8267151, F8282008. A/c, large clean rooms, hot water, bath tubs in all rooms, the more expensive rooms have breakfast included, excellent value, popular, recommended. **C-D** *Camelia*, 13 Luong Ngoc Quyen St, T8283583, F8244277. Sister hotel of Anh Dao and perfectly OK but slightly shabbier (when were the curtains last washed?), an excellent DIY breakfast is included. **C-D** *Guesthouse Ma May*, 73 Ma May St, T8244425. A/c, hot water, friendly and clean, large rooms. **C-D** *Red River*, 73 Hang Bo St, T8268427, F8287159. Part of the Red River travel empire, decent rooms, a/c, hot water, more expensive rooms include breakfast, accepts some credit cards (+4 percent). **C-D** *My Kinh*, 72-74 Hang Buom St, T8255726. Even cheapest rooms have a/c, private bathroom and hot water, restaurant; **C-D** *My Lan*, 70 Hang Bo St, T8245510, opposite Red River. Go through the dentist's surgery, elderly French-speaking doctor has a few rooms to rent, some a/c, spacious, light and breezy, nice roof-top terrace. **C-D** *Mai Phuong*, 32 Hang Be St, T/F8265341. Some a/c, cheaper rooms fan only and shared bathroom, friendly, also booking office for Green Bamboo Travel. **C-D** *Ngoc Diep*, 83 Thuoc Bac St, T8250020. Just around the corner from Red River, cheaper rooms have fan, hot water and TV, more expensive rooms a/c and breakfast included, popular.

D *Bao Khan*, 3 Bao Khanh St, T8250271, F8259228. Simple rooms, a/c, hot water, fair price, near Polite Pub. **D** *Hoa Long*, 94 Hang Trong St, T8269319, F8259228. Good value with a/c and hot water and good restaurant but some rooms lack windows, a common problem in some of Hanoi's cheaper hotels. **D** *Green Bamboo*, 42 Nha Chung St, T8268752, F8264949. Some a/c, cheaper rooms fan only, restaurant, bar and tour operator. **D** *Ta Hien*, 22 Ta Hien St, T8255888. Through a café, simple, no frills but quiet, clean, hot water, fan rooms only. **D** *Thuy Loi*, 24 Hang Be St, T8245359. Ac, hot water, good tandoori restaurant. **D** *Thuy Nga*, 24C Ta Hien St, T8266053, F8282892. A/c, hot water, clean and modern, friendly and good value, recommended. **D** *Tourist* Café, 6 To Tich St, T8243051. Good value with a/c and hot water**. D-E** *Darling Café*, 33 Hang Quat, T8269386, F8256562. Travellers' café but has a few rooms, some a/c and some dormitory rooms. **D-E** *Queen Café and Guesthouse*, 65 Hang Bac, T8260860, F8250000. Shared bathrooms, fan rooms, basic but OK, good tour operator. **D-E** *Binh Minh*, 50 Hang Be St, T8267356, F8247183. Some a/c. **D-E** *Love Planet*, 98 Ma May St, T8284864. Hotel, café and tour operator, a/c and fan dormitory rooms. The Especen Company runs 7 hotels northwest of Hoan Kiem Lake. They are known for their multilingual and very helpful staff, rooms sometimes a bit run down and some little small but generally good value. Rooms range **B-D, D** rooms have shared bathrooms. If one hotel is full they will find a room elsewhere. *Especen 1* (and head office), 79E Hang Trong St, T8266856, F8269612. *Especen 4*, 16 Trung Yen, T8261512. *Especen 7*, 23 Hang Quat St, T8251301. *Especen 8*, 30 Luong Van Can St, T8245923. *Especen 9*, 10B Dinh Liet St, T8253069. *Especen 10*, 2 Hang Vai St, T8281160. *Especen 11*, 28 Tho Xuong St, T8244401.

A+-A *Saigon*, 80 Ly Thuong Kiet St, T8268505, F8266631. Renovated, expensive, state-run business hotel. **A+-A** *Villa Bleue*, 82 Ly Thuong Kiet St, T8247733, F8245676. A/c, cable TV, nice villa, more expensive rooms are spacious and have bath tub but the place is not sufficiently well kept or managed to merit these prices. Features the unusual 'medieval' *Richard's Court Restaurant* with a European menu. **A** *Rose* (*Hoa Hong*) , 20 Phan Boi Chau St, T8254439, F8254437. A/c, one of the last state owned hotels to be built, expensive for what it offers. **A** *Dong Loi*, 94 Ly Thuong Kiet St, T8255721, F8267999. On the corner of Le Duan St. Spectacular pink building but does not represent particularly good value, in need of an overhaul. **A** *Thu Do*, 109 Tran Hung Dao St, T8252288, F8261266. Opposite European Commission, would be expensive at half the price.

Railway station area

B-C *Trai Xoai* (*Mango*, formerly *Railway*), 118 Le Duan St, T8243704, F8243966. Adjacent to station, *bia hoi* and *pho* stalls in the compound; **B-E** *Khach San 30-4*, 115 Tran Hung Dao St, T8260807, F8252611. Opposite railway station, newly renovated but still cheap and good value, cheaper fan rooms shared bathroom facilities.

C *Viet My III*, 84 Le Duan St, T8243035, F8249398. Private mini-hotel, clean, fair value, friendly, *Viet My II* is over the road.

D *Nhat Phuong*, 39 Le Duan St. A/c, hot water, fairly priced. **D-F** *Lotus*, 42V Ly Thuong Kiet St, T8268642. Rather small and cramped but cheap and welcoming, good café, food and meeting place, laundry service, Sinh Café Tours agent, popular. Recommended.

Hanoi

Out of town **L-A+** *Hanoi Daewoo*, Lieu Giai St, T8315000, F8315010. Several restaurants, pool, health club, business centre, indoor golf driving range – the works. Giant new hotel and apartment complex with pool, shops, bars and restaurants, could lay fair claim to be the country's only 5-star hotel. While it may be very well appointed the hotel is way out of the city centre to the west. **L-A+** *Meritus*, 1 Thanh Nien St, T8238888, F8293888. New Singaporean owned 322-room hotel overlooking the West Lake, opened just in time for the Asian Crisis. Italian and Chinese restaurants, excellent business facilities and an all-weather swimming pool. **L-A+** *Hanoi*, Giang Vo, Ba Dinh District, T8452270, F8459209. Refurbished 11 storey building, efficient but absurdly expensive and unfriendly state-run business hotel overlooking Giang Vo Lake. **L-A** *Asean*, 41 Chua Boc St, T8528262, F8529122. Claims to be Hanoi's friendliest hotel. *My Wife's Place* restaurant does excellent buffet lunch.

A+-A *Planet*, 120 Quan Thanh St, T8435888, F8435088. A/c, new business hotel in an odd location near West Lake. **A+-A** *Thang Loi*, Yen Phu, T8268211, F8252800. Occupies a wonderful position on West Lake but unsympathetic Cuban architecture, inconvenient location 4 kilometres north of town, and state-run, mosquitoes are a problem, pool. **A+-A** *Tay Ho*, Quang An, T8232380, F8232281. Even further out of town, its 3 concrete stumps ruin a gorgeous spot on West Lake, pool and reasonable facilities, state-run. **A+** *Hotel Nikko Hanoi*, 84 Tran Nhan Tong St, T8223535, F8223555, E sale-nikkohn@hn.vnn.vn. New hotel situated south of the city centre. Most facilities include business centre, good gym, pool. **A** *Heritage*, 80 Giang Vo St, T8344727, F8343882. 3-star, 65 room hotel currently offering fairly hefty discounts on published rates.

Eating

● *on maps* Hanoi is, after a 50 year aberration, returning to what it once was: a café society. It has Western-style coffee bars, restaurants and watering holes that stand up well to comparison with their equivalents in Europe. Hanoi's super-abundance of cafés, wine bars, pizzerias and grills not only serve food and drink of the highest standards they are also attractively styled (in a bamboo-meets-hi-tech stainless steel sort of way) and many create a lively or intimate ambience wholly unexpected in this Communist capital. This is a heartening renaissance; only 4 years ago we were lamenting the paucity of good places to eat in Hanoi.

A few words of caution: dog (*thit chó or thit cau*) is an esteemed delicacy in the north, 'who can resist a steaming bowl of broth with a pair of dogs paws?' demands one restauranter – but dog is usually served only in specialist outlets so unlikely to be ordered inadvertently. Second, old habits die hard: Communist ideals and recreational eating remain uncomfortable bed-fellows and, inevitably, at some stage you will suffer inedible food ungraciously served in dingy surroundings.

Vietnamese **Expensive** *Indochine*, 16 Nam Ngu St, T8246097. Excellent Vietnamese food served by elegantly attired staff, dinner for 2 for around US$25. *Seasons*, 95B Quan Thanh, T8435444. One would not wish this restaurant to become too well known but if readers of this guide promise to keep it to themselves – we rate this one of the most agreeable dining experiences in a long time. The building is a finely restored and authentically furnished colonial villa, food is fresh and delicious and service attentive. But this does not do it justice. At around US$5 per dish prices are very fair. *Banh Tom Ho Tay*, Thanh Nien St. Its speciality is banh tom, tasty deep-fried shrimp cakes, nice location between Truc Bach and West lakes from where we hope the shrimps have not been caught. *San Ho*, 58 Ly Thuong Kiet St, T8222184. This is Hanoi's seafood restaurant which does a set weekday lunch for US$7. Operates the popular 'first catch your lobster' system to ensure freshness.

Bites but no bark in a Vietnamese restaurant

Quang Vinh's restaurant was the ideal place for the ordeal to come. The palm-thatched house near the West Lake, on the outskirts of the Vietnamese capital Hanoi, was far from the accusing eyes of fellow-Englishmen.

It was dark outside. At one table, a Vietnamese couple were contentedly finishing their meal. At another, a man smoked a bamboo pipe. A television at the end of the room showed mildly pornographic Chinese videos.

But then came the moment of truth: could an Englishman eat a dog? Could he do so without his stomach rebelling, without his thoughts turning to labradors snoozing by Kentish fireplaces, Staffordshire bull terriers collecting sticks for children, and Pekinese perched on the laps of grandmothers?

One Englishman could: I ate roast dog, dog liver, barbecued dog with herbs and a deliciously spicy dog sausage, for it is the custom to dine on a selection of dog dishes when visiting a dog restaurant. The meat tastes faintly gamey. It is eaten with noodles, crispy rice-flour pancakes, fresh ginger, spring onions, apricot leaves and, for cowardly Englishmen, plenty of beer.

I had been inspired to undergo this traumatic experience – most un-British unless one is stranded with huskies on a polar ice cap – by a conversation earlier in the week with Do Duc Dinh, a Vietnamese economist, and Nguyen Thanh Tam, my official interpreter and guide.

They were much more anxious to tell me about the seven different ways of cooking a dog, and how unlucky it was to eat dog on the first 5 days of the month, than they were to explain Vietnam's economic reforms. "My favourite," began Tam, "is minced intestines roasted in the fire with green beans and onions." He remembered proudly how anti-Vietnamese protesters in Thailand in the 1980s had carried placards saying "Dog-eaters go home!"

During the Vietnam war, he said, a famous Vietnamese professor had discovered that wounded soldiers recovered much more quickly when their doctors prescribed half a kilogram of dog meat a day. Dinh insisted I should eat dog in Hanoi rather than Saigon. "I went to the S and ate dog, but they don't know how to cook it like we do in the N," he said. I asked where the dogs came from. "People breed it, then it becomes the family pet." And then they eat it? "Yes," he said with a laugh.

I told myself that the urban British, notorious animal lovers that they are, recoil particularly at the idea of eating dogs only because most of them never see the living versions of the pigs, cows, sheep and chickens that they eat in meat-form every day. And the French, after all, eat horses.

Resolutely unsentimental, we put aside our dog dinner and went to Vinh's kitchen. Two wire cages were on the floor; there was one large dog in the first and four small dogs in the second. 2 ft away, a cauldron of dog stew steamed and bubbled. Vinh told us about his flourishing business. The dogs are transported from villages in a nearby province. A 10 kg dog costs him about 120,000 Vietnamese dong, or just over US$10. At the end of the month – peak dog-eating time – his restaurant gets through about 30 dogs a day.

The restaurant, he said, was popular with Vietnamese, Koreans and Japanese. Squeamish westerners were sometimes tricked into eating dog by the Vietnamese friends, who would entertain them at the restaurant and tell them afterwards what it was they had so heartily consumed. ***Source***: Extracted from an article by Victor Mallet, Financial Times

---

Mid-range *La Vong* (aka *Cha Ca*), 14 Cha Ca St. Serves one dish only, the epony-mous cha ca Hanoi, fried fish fillets in mild spice and herbs served with noodles, (see page 671) popular with visitors and locals alike, new branch now open at 107 Nguyen Truong To St, T8239875. *Restaurant 202*, 202 Hue St, T9760487. Vietnam-ese and French menu, superb food, prices have edged up steadily but it still repre-sents excellent value. *Restaurant 22*, 22 Hang Can St. Good menu, popular and tasty

Vietnamese food, succulent duck. At just a couple of dollars per main course it represents brilliant value.

Cheap *Bodega*, 57 Trang Tien St. The ground floor is a popular coffee shop and ice-cream parlour, the first floor is a traditional restaurant with rather poor service and disappointing food. *Bit Tet (Beefsteak)*, 51 Hang Buom St. If asked to name the best diner in town it would be hard not to include this on one's list. The soups and steak frites are simply superb: it's rough and ready and you'll share your table, as at around US$3 per head is understandably crowded, evenings only, recommended. *Com Chay Nang Tam*, 79A Tran Hung Dao St. This popular little a/c restaurant is down an alley off Tran Hung Dao St, serves excellent and inexpensive vegetarian dishes. *Nos 9-25 Ta Hien St* represent a good selection of little local and inexpensive restaurants.

Other Asian *Baan Thai*, 3B Cha Ca St, T8281120. Authentic Thai fare, has received some good notices. *Edo*, Daewoo Hotel, 360 Kim Ma St, T8315000. Japanese restaurant, considered the finest. *Khazana*, 27 Quoc Tu Giam St, T8433477. Excellent Indian food, elegantly served, set lunch. *Mother's Pride*, 6C Phan Chu Trinh St, T8262168. Noodles and Malaysian dishes, slightly scruffy but OK and not too pricey. *Tandoor*, 24 Hang Be St, T8245359. In Thuy Loi Hotel, Indian food as good as any in Manchester or Bradford, highly popular with expat community.

International **Expensive** *Club Opera*, 59 Ly Thai To St, T8268802. Attractively restored colonial building, Vietnamese upstairs, western downstairs, decent dining options for US$10 per head. *Al Fresco's*, 23L Hai Ba Trung St, T8267782. A popular Australian grill bar serving steak, pasta, pizza and fantastic salads. Giant portions, lively atmosphere, a memorable experience. Recommended. *Gustave*, 17 Tran Tien St, T8250625. Named after the builder of Paris' most famous landmark, restaurant upstairs, piano bar and jazz downstairs. Food is regarded for quality and originality and homesick French visitors deem it well worth paying US$30 per person. *Il Grillo*, 116 Ba Trieu St, T8227720. Despite stiff competition from the Daewoo, the Press Club *et al* this still seems to hold the title as Hanoi's finest expat nosebag. Some find it over-rated and some over-priced at US$30+ per head. *Press Club*, 59A Ly Thai To St, T9340888. There are 3 outlets in this stylish complex directly behind the *Metropole Hotel*: bistro, top restaurant and cigar bar. Prices are not cheap but seldom will US$100 buy 2 people so much pleasure. Vietnamese dishes plus steaks, caesar salad, rack of lamb – and a fine wine list.

Mid-range *Bistrot*, 34 Tran Hung Dao St, T8266136, new polished granite entrance but the same erratic service, unpriced menu, paper table cloths and excellent French food: go! Dinner for 2 excluding wine costs around US$15. Steak rocquefort and duck are always good and so is the pâté and charcuterie. *Cafe de Paris*, 79 E Hang Trong St, T8266856. Relaxed French dining in an authentic setting, very decent food at around US$10 per person – leave room for the puds. *A Little Italian*, *The Pear Tree*, 78 Tho Nhuom St, (Eden Hotel), T8258167. 2 restaurants rolled into one, reasonable prices for European nosh and cocktails, generous servings, certainly we enjoyed our last visit. *Hanoi Gourmet*, 1B Ham Long, T9431009. Even in Europe this would be a place to rave about, it rates 'Top' in the Watkins ranking. For lovers of fine wine, cheese and cold cuts, Hanoi Gourmet is paradise. Find a free afternoon, go short on breakfast, then go for a long leisurely lunch. Freshly restocked from France every 2 weeks. US$3 and US$5 sandwiches delivered free. *Moca Cafe*, 14-16 Nha Tho, T8256334. From cinnamon flavoured cappuccino to smoked salmon, from dry martini to Bengali specials Moca is everything to all people. Its high open space, wafting fans and cool, marble-topped tables are hugely inviting. Open 0700-2400. *Il Padrino*, 42 Le Thai To St, T8288449. Italian excellence in Hanoi's culinary world is personified by this small restaurant overlooking Hoan Kiem Lake. Cafe downstairs, diner upstairs. Huge, mouth-watering pizzas (US$6) and frothy cappuccino (US$2). Grumpy service or was it a bad day? *Piano Bar and Restaurant*, 93 Phung Hung St, T8259425. Western and Vietnamese food, live music. *Soho*, 57 Ba Trieu St, T8266555. Places like this low-key but stylish deli/café make Saigon appear a cultural desert; Hanoians don't know how lucky they are. Main courses, sandwiches and salads to titillate the most jaded of palates. Around US$5 for main courses. Also delivers. *Sunset Pub*, 31 Cao Ba Quat St, T8230173. Pub and restaurant, pizza, burgers, cocktails and ice cream.

Cheap   *Hoa Sua*, 81 Tho Nhuom St, T8240448. French training restaurant (opposite Eden Hotel) where visitors can eat cheaply and well sitting around an attractive courtyard, popular. *Five Royal Fish (Ngu Ngu Ngu)*, 16 Le Thai To St. Terrace overlooks Hoan Kiem Lake, Vietnamese food and western, good reviews from some visitors.

Thuy Ta, 1 Le Thai To St. Nice setting on northwest corner of Hoan Kiem Lake, popular meeting place for Vietnamese and travellers, snacks, ice creams and drinks. *Bon Mua*, 38-40 Le Thai To St, popular ice-cream shop on the west bank of Hoan Kiem Lake. *Fanny Ice Cream*, 48 Le Thai To St. Nice refreshing ice cream and sorbet. 35 Trang Tien St remains a popular ice-cream outlet with the Vietnamese. *Baskin Robbins*, 20 Ngo Quyen St. Expensive and little better, if at all, than local ice cream, though fans will no doubt disagree. *Au Lac*, southwest corner of Hoan Kiem Lake, lovely spot under the trees overlooking the lake. Maddeningly, they have diversified into everything under the sun, fair, but no longer excellent at anything. *Cafe Lac Viet*, 46 Le Thai To St. Somewhat laid back sort of place with a library service. Their lemon juice is the perfect thirst quencher. *No Noodles*, 51 Luong Van Can St, T8257721. Delicious and inexpensive sandwiches so big you can't fit them in your mouth, free delivery in central Hanoi. Why can't Saigon have one? *252 Hang Bong*. Contrary to the cafe's own claim it is actually in what is now Cua Nam St although the owner pretends not to have noticed the new street sign. I sense a long-running feud with the People's Committee here. Excellent pastries, yoghurt and crême caramel, very popular for breakfast, 'frequented by Christine Deneuve' ... er, yes, during the filming of *Indochine* a number of years ago.

Bars & cafés

And then there are all the travel cafés   *Green Bamboo*, 42 Nha Chung St. Cafe, bar and guesthouse. *Meeting Café*, 59B Ba Trieu St, T8258813. Snacks and drinks and tour booking, usually pretty quiet. *Queen Cafe*, 65 Hang Bac St, T8260860. Pretty awful food but it is more a place to meet, book tours and -mail from than a place to lunch or dine. *Real Darling Cafe*, 33 Hang Quat St, popular rendezvous with back-packers, serves snacks. *Red River*, 73 Hang Bo St. Popular meeting place with reasonably good food, tours and accommodation. *Polite Pub*, 5 Bao Khanh St, good bar snacks and cocktails, popular expat haunt merging with *Gold Cock* next door. *Sunset Pub*, 31 Cao Ba Quat St, popular bar also serves lunch. *The Verandah*, 9 Nguyen Khac Can St. Popular with the expat crowd, film showings on Sunday. *Apocalypse Now*, 5C Hoa Ma St, T9712783. Like its Saigon counterpart, popular with all, music, pool and dancing; *Ship Inn*, 125A Lo Duc St, T8214138. Pool, darts and beer in a maritime setting. *Vortex*, 336 Ba Trieu St. Bar and club, busy Fri and Sat. Queen Bee, 42A Lang Ha St, T8352612. A little way out but especially good on Sat nights, dancing. *Library Bar*, Press Club, 59 Ly Thai To St, T9340888. Tranquil setting in which to tipple a few malts while chewing a fine Havana. *Met Pub*, Metropole Hotel, 56 Ly Thai To St. Excellent pub food and all the major sporting events screened.

36 Streets area is a good place to look around for cheap restaurants and foodstalls: To Tich St, between Hang Gai and Hang Quat, has pho and other noodles. Ta Hien St, north of Luong Ngoc Quyen St, offers an excellent selection of little restaurants. 2B Ly

Foodstalls

Quoc Su St does excellent pho: queue, pay, sit and eat. Junction of Hang Be and Cau Go streets scrumptious selection of delicious fillers: fried rice, fried noodles and chicken rice.

Entertainment

Evening entertainment in the traditional western sense is developing apace although still lacking the variety and sophistication of Saigon. See **Bars and cafés**, page 95.

Cinemas *Fansland*, 84 Ly Thuong Kiet St, T8257484. Sometimes without Vietnamese dubbing. *New Age*, 45 Hang Bai St, T8262954. Vietnamese and western films. *Alliance Française*, 42 Yel Kien St, T8266970. French films. See *Vietnam News* for current showings.

Dance & theatre The Municipal Theatre is housed in an impressive French-era building at the east end of Trang Tien St. Most performances are traditional or revolutionary.

Sports **Hanoi Hash House Harriers:** for details check flyers at Metropole, Club Opera etc. **Sports and Health Clubs**: *Sofitel Metropole* and the *Daewoo* boast the best facilities. *Asean Hotel*, 41 Chua Boc St. Small but well equipped. *Khuc Hao*, 1B Le Hong Phong St. Tennis courts. *Army Club*, 19 Hoang Dieu St. Pool and tennis courts open to the public. *Van Phuc and Trung Tu Diplomatic Compounds*, priority to diplomats but available to the public.

Water puppet theatre (See page 387): at the Water Puppetry House 32, Truong Chinh St. Set up in 1956 by Ho Chi Minh, weekly performances have been staged almost continually since. In 1984 the Australian government provided the theatre with wet suits and water resistant paints, and in recent years the troupe has performed in Japan, Australia and Europe. Entrance 20,000d. Performances every evening at 1830, 2000 and 2115 with live music (admission 20,000d-40,000d, camera 10,000d, video 50,000d). Fabulous performances, exciting music, the technical virtuosity of the puppeteers is astonishing. Also in the grounds of the Temple of Literature. A second water puppet theatre is at 57 Dinh Tien Hoang St at the northeast corner of Hoan Kiem Lake. ■ *Getting there: by taxi; the theatre is some 7 kilometres south of the centre.*

Festivals **January/February** *Dong Da Hill festival* (5th day of Tet) celebrates the battle of Dong Da in which Nguyen Hue routed 200,000 Chinese troops. Processions of dancers carry a flaming dragon of straw. **September** *National Day* (2nd) parades in Ba Dinh Square, boat races on Hoan Kiem Lake.

Shopping

Surprisingly – given the lack of consumer goods produced by Vietnam's moribund manufacturing sector – shopping is not a complete waste of time in Hanoi. One seasoned traveller was of the opinion that the city was a 'shopper's paradise' with cheap silk and good tailors, handicrafts and antiques. Hang Gai St is well geared to the foreign souvenir hunter and stocks an excellent range of clothes, ethnographia, fabrics and lacquerware. Hats of all descriptions abound.

Antiques Along Hang Khay and Trang Tien streets, south edge of Hoan Kiem Lake. Shops sell silver ornaments, porcelain, jewellery and carvings – much is not antique, not all is silver; bargain hard.

Art galleries Abound near Hoan Kiem Lake, especially Trang Tien St and on Dinh Tien Hoang St at northeast corner. *Hanoi Art Gallery*, 93 Dinh Tien Hoang St (although entrance is actually in Trang Tien St) sells interesting wood cuts and silk cards. Also look at the different qualities of hand-made papers.

Bicycles At the second-hand bike market at the intersection of Thinh Yen St and Pho 332, south of the city centre and on Ba Trieu St south of junction with Nguyen Du St.

Books On Trang Tien St. For example, at No 61 is the *Foreign Language Bookshop* and No 40 is the *State Bookshop*. The alley by the side of Foreign Languages Bookstore sells copies of books otherwise out of stock. Private booksellers operate on Trang Tien St and have pavement stalls in the evening (bargain). *Xunhasaba*, the state book distributor, has a shop at 32 Hai Ba Trung. *The Gioi*, Publisher's bookshop is at 46 Tran Hung Dao.

Handicrafts Hang Khay St, on southern shores of Hoan Kiem Lake, and Hai Gai St. A range of hand-woven fabrics and ethnographia from the hill tribes.

Maps From stalls and shops along Trang Tien St and outside GPO.

Photo shops Processing and film all around Hoan Kiem Lake. Slide film is available for sale in a few shops but it is recommended that you do not have it processed in Vietnam.

Shoes Walking boots, training shoes, flip flops and sandals, many of which are Western size are on sale in the shops around the northeast of Hoan Kiem Lake. Most are genuine brand name items and having 'fallen off the back of a lorry' are remarkably inexpensive – but do bargain.

Silk Countless shops on and around Hang Gai St; cheap tailoring services available. *Khai Silk* has several outlets including one in the Sofitel Metropole and one at 96 Hang Gai St, T8254237. Lovely fabrics and good designs.

Souvenirs Hang Gai St and around. For unusual souvenirs visit the shop making wooden percussion instruments at 76 Hang Bon St, great value at around US$3.

Transport

91 kilometres from Ninh Binh, 103 kilometres from Haiphong, 153 kilometres from Thanh Hoa, 165 kilometres from Ha Long Bay, 420 kilometres from Dien Bien Phu, 658 kilometres from Hué, 763 kilometres from Danang, 1,710 kilometres from Saigon.

Local The traffic in Hanoi is becoming more frantic – and lethal – as each month goes by. Bicycles, cyclos, mopeds, cars and Russian lorries fight for space with little sense of order, let alone a highway code. At night, with few street lamps and some vehicles without lights, it can seem positively murderous. Pedestrians should watch out.

Bicycle hire is the most popular form of local mass transport and is an excellent way to get around the city; they can be hired from *Tourist Meeting Café* at 59B Ba Trieu St, from 12 Trung Yen, just off Ta Hien St, from the little shops at 29-33 Ta Hien St, from the *Phu Gia Hotel* and from most tourist cafés, expect to pay about US$1 per day. As demand increases, the number of outlets should likewise increase. Start by asking at your hotel or guesthouse. For those staying longer, it might be worth buying a bicycle (see Shopping above). There are limited city bus services. Routes are marked on some tourist maps.

Hanoi's cyclo drivers must be among the most over-optimistic in Vietnam. They have obviously heard through the cyclo grapevine from Saigon that foreigners pay

Road to nowhere

Wholly symptomatic of the government's Gadarene rush to `modernize' the country is the new motorway between Hanoi and Noi Bai airport. It is both tragic and hilarious. Within days of its opening it was the scene of utter carnage as pedestrians, cyclists and buffalo exercised their right, laid down in black and white, to cross the road on zebra crossings in front of speeding traffic. Brazen hand-cart pushers obstinately cling to the fast lane swerving only to avoid the parked motorbikes of spectators squatting on the central reservation admiring the shambles, one

journalist on Vietnam News reported seeing 5 accidents on a single journey to the airport. So appalling is the planning of the motorway that it takes longer to reach town than using the old road. Although motorists might touch speeds of over 100 kilometres per hour they are deposited in such a remote part of Hanoi that it can take almost an hour to reach the city centre. Locals displayed their contempt for the scheme by hacking up the surface to excavate and sell the foundation sand and by cutting down and selling for scrap the metal handrails.

more than locals, but have taken this to extremes; prices quoted are usually 500 per-cent more than they should be. Drivers also have a disturbing tendency to forget the agreed fare and ask for more: be firm, some travellers even ask that the price be writ-ten down if communication is a problem. A trip from the railway station to Hoan Kiem Lake should not cost more than 5,000d.

Hiring a motorbike is a good way of getting to some of the more remote places, tourist cafés such as *Red River* and *Darling* rent a variety of machines for between US$5-8 per day.

There are now metered taxis in Hanoi: ***City Taxi***, T8222222. ***CP***, T8241999. ***Hanoi Taxi***, T8535252. ***PT Taxi***, T8533171. ***Red Taxi***, T8568686. Private cars can be chartered from the major hotels, from outside the Vietnam Airlines Office at 1 Quang Trung St and from many of the tour operators listed on page 100.

Air There are international air connections on Vietnam Airlines with Hong Kong, Guangzhou, Vientiane, Bangkok, Los Angeles, Paris and Moscow. A handful of other airlines also serve Hanoi. Domestic air connections with Saigon (1,900,000d), Danang (1,000,000d), Nha Trang (1,450,000d), Dien Bien Phu, Hué (1,000,000d), Na San, Ban Me Thuot and Pleiku. See timetable, page 407. ***Heli-Jet Vietnam*** offers charter heli-copter services from Hanoi's Gia Lam Airport to Vinh, US$3,200; Dien Bien Phu, US$4,000; Ha Long, US$1,800 and other destinations. For reservations, *Hotel Sofitel Metropole*, T8266919 x 8046, F8250168.

Transport to airport Hanoi's airport is 50 kilometres from the city (about 1 hour's drive). There is a minibus service from the front of the terminal building which costs foreigners US$4. If taking a taxi, ensure that the rate is for the whole car and not per person. If travelling in a group, taxis organized by the tourist cafés cost US$4. Minibuses leave for the airport from the Vietnam Airlines Office at 1 Quang Trung St, US$4 for foreigners, service at regular intervals from 0415 but check bus departure times at the Vietnam Airlines office. A taxi takes 1 hour from central Hanoi. Taxis can be chartered from the Vietnam Airlines Office for the airport. Expect to pay about US$16. An additional toll of 10,000d may be charged.

Train The central station (*Ga Hanoi*) is at 126 Le Duan St, at the end of Tran Hung Dao St (10-15 minutes cyclo ride from the centre of town). Regular daily connections with Saigon (see timetable, page 409). Advance booking is required. There are 4 trains daily to Haiphong, 1 from the platforms behind the central station, 3 from Long Bien (the station on the hill behind Chuong Duong Bridge) and also trains to the Chinese border at Lang Son and Lao Cai (walk down Nguyen Khuyen St and turn left into Tran Quy Cap St). Long Bien station is at the far end of Long Bien Bridge across the Red River, take a *xe ôm*. Giáp Bát station (bên xe Giáp Bát) is on Giai Phong St, the south continuation of Le Duan St 5 kilometres south of the railway station. Get there by *xe ôm*. Border opens 0700 Chinese time (1 hour ahead). Four trains a day to Kunming.

Bus: Hanoi has a number of bus stations. The **Southern bus terminal** is out of town, but linking buses run from the northern shore of Hoan Kiem Lake. The terminal serves destinations south of Hanoi: Saigon, Buon Ma Thuot, Vinh, Danang, Thanh Hoa, Nha Trang, Dalat, Qui Nhon, Ninh Binh and Nam Dinh. Express buses usually leave at 0500; advance booking is recommended. The **Kim Ma station** is on Nguyen Thai Hoc St (opposite No 168), just past Giang Vo St, and serves destinations to the northwest: Son Tay, Trung Ha, Phu To, Hat Lot, Moc Chau, Bat Bat, Tan Hong, Da Chong, Hoa Binh, Son La, Dien Bien Phu and Yen Bai. Buses and minibuses to Haiphong leave regularly from **Gia Lam station** (over Chuong Duong Bridge). 2½ hours (20,000d). Buses can be flagged down on Tran Quang Khai St before they cross the bridge. **Ha Dong station** in the southwest suburbs has buses to Hoa Binh. Take a local bus or *xe ôm* to the bus station. **Giap Bat station** on Giai Phong St serves destinations south.

Road

Hanoi

Directory

Airline offices *Vietnam Airlines*, 1 Quang Trung St, T8216666, F8248989. Vietnam Airlines is open 0700-1900 every day for both domestic and international bookings. *Air France*, 1 Ba Trieu St, T8253484, F8266694. *Aeroflot*, 4 Trang Thi St, T8256742. *Cathay Pacific*, 49 Hai Ba Trung St, T8267298 (Noi Bai, T8261113). *China Airlines*, 18 Tran Hung Dao St, T8242688. *China Southern Airlines*, 27 Ly Thai To St, T8269233. *Japan Airlines*, 1 Ba Trieu St, T8266693. *Malaysian Airlines*, 15 Ngo Quyen St, T8268820. *Pacific Airlines*, 100 Le Duan, T8515356. *Singapore Airlines*, 17 Ngo Quyen St, T8268888, F8268666. *Thai*, 44B Ly Thuong Kiet St, T8266893, F8267394. *Lao Aviation*, 41 Quang Trung St, T8229951.

Banks Foreign banks labour under a severe regime in Vietnam which is reflected in rates of commission which are higher than those charged by local banks. Commission on cashing TCs into US$ is higher than into dong. Major hotels will change US$ at poor rates. *ANZ Bank*, 14 Le Thai To St, T8258190. Open 0830-1530 Mon-Fri and 0830-1200 Sat, provides full banking services including cash advances on credit cards, 4% commission on TCs, 24-hr ATM. *Bank of Foreign Trade*, 47-49 Ly Thai To St. *Citibank*, 17 Ngo Quyen St, T8251950. *Commercial & Industrial Bank*, 37 Hang Bo St and 16 Phan Dinh Phung St. *Foreign Exchange Centre*, 2 Le Lai St. *National Bank*, 10 Le Lai. Open 0800-1100 and 1300-1600. *VID Public Bank*, 2 Ngo Quyen St. *Vietcombank*, 198 Tran Quang Khai St. No commission on TCs if converted to dong, 2% if converted to US$. **Black Market:** Do **not** change money with the women who hang around outside the GPO: they are fraudsters. Black market rates are seldom better than official rates: if they are, beware. **NB** It is also possible to change dong back into US$ in Hanoi; it is impossible to use dong for anything except wallpaper outside the country.

Communications Central GPO: 85 Dinh Tien Hoang St. **Express Mail Service:** (inland) at the GPO, T8255948. **International PO:** 87 Dinh Tien Hoang St. **International telephone, telex and fax services:** at the PO and from 66-68 Trang Tien St, 66 Luong Van Can St and in the PO on Le Duan next to the railway station. *TNT International Express*, 15 Ly Nam De St, T8434535. *UPS*, 4C Dinh Le St, T8246483. *DHL*, in GPO and 49 Nguyen Thai Hoc St, T8467020.

Embassies & consulates *Algeria*, 12 Phan Chu Trinh St, T8253865, F8260830. *Australia*, 8 Dao Tan St, T8317755, F8317711. *Belgium*, 48 Nguyen Thai Hoc St, T8452263, F8457165. *Burma*, A3 Van Phuc Diplomatic Compound, T8453396, F8452404. *Brazil*, 14 Thuy Khue St, T8430817, F8432542. *Cambodia*, 71 Tran Hung Dao St, T8253789, F8265225. *Canada*, 31 Hung Vuong St, T8235432, F8235333. *China*, 46 Hoang Dieu St, T8453736, F8232826. *Cuba*, 65 Ly Thuong Kiet St, T/F 8254775. *Czech Republic*, 13 Chu Van An St, T8454131. *Denmark*, 19 Dien Bien Phu St,

T8231888, F8231999. *Egypt*, Villa 6, Van Phuc Diplomatic Compound, T8460219, F8460218. European Union, 56 Ly Thai To St, T9341300, F9341361. *Finland*, Central Building, 31 Hai Ba Trung St, T8266788 , F8266766. *France*, 57 Tran Hung Dao St, T8252710, F8264236. *Germany*, 29 Tran Phu St, T8453836, F8453838. *Hungary*, 43-45 Dien Bien Phu St, T8452858, F8233049. *India*, 58-60 Tran Hung Dao St, T8244989, F8244998. *Indonesia*, 50 Ngo Quyen St, T8256316, F8259274. *Israel*, 68 Nguyen Thai Hoc St, T8430514, F8266920. *Italy*, 9 Le Phung Hieu St, T8256256, F8267602. *Japan*, 27 Lieu Gai St, T8692600, F8692595. *Laos*, 22 Tran Binh Trong St, T8463000, F8463043. *Malaysia*, A3 Van Phuc Diplomatic Compound, T8232056, F8232166. *Netherlands*, D1, Van Phuc Diplomatic Compound, T8430605, F8431013. *Philippines*, 27 Tran Hung Dao St, T8257873, F8265760. *Poland*, 3 Chua Mot Cot St, T8452027, F8236914. *Romania*, 5 Le Hong Phong St, T8254723, F8430922. *Russia*, 58 Tran Phu St, T8454631, F8456177. *Singapore*, 41-43 Tran Phu St, T8233966, F8233992. *South Korea*, 360 Kim Ma St, T8226677, F8226328. *Sweden*, Van Phuc Diplomatic Compound, T8315111, F8315117. *Switzerland*, 75 Kim Ma St, T8232019, F8235092. *Thailand*, 63-65 Hoang Dieu St, T8235092, F8235088. *UK*, Central Building, 31 Hai Ba Trung St, T8252510, F8265762. *USA*, 7 Lang Ha St, T8431500, F8431510.

Hospitals & medical services Hospitals: *AEA International*, Central Building, 31 Hai Ba Trung St, T9340555. 24-hr, US$65 for consultation with ex-pat doctor, US$45 for local doctor. *Hospital Bach Mai*, Giai Phong St, T8522004. English speaking doctors. *Eye Hospital*, 85 Ba Trieu St. *Friendship Hospital*, 1 Tran Khanh Du St, T8252231. *Hanoi Family Medical Practice*, 109-112 Van Phuc, T8430748. 24-hr 090401919. 24-hr medical and dental care, including intensive care. *International Hospital*, Phuong St, T5740740. *Hospital K*, 43 Quan Su St, T8252143. *Swedish Clinic*, opposite Swedish Embassy, Van Phuc, T8252464. *Vietnam-German Hospital*, 40 Trang Thi St, T8253531. **Dental treatment:** at *Vietnam-German Hospital*, T8269723, *Bach Mai Hospital* and B3 Van Phuc, T8430281.

Tour companies & travel agents The most popular option for travellers are the budget cafés that offer fairly priced tours, accommodation and a great opportunity to meet fellow travellers. While an excellent way to make friends these tours do tend to isolate the visitor from local people and while not as cocooned as the notorious Japanese coach tours they do not offer the real Vietnam that most independent travellers seek. Operators match their rival's prices and itineraries closely and indeed many operate a clearing system to consolidate passenger numbers to more profitable levels. Onward tickets to Hué and the south (US$22) and shared taxis to the airport (US$4) are also available. *NIC New Indochina Travel*, 1A Dang Thai Than, T9330599, F9330499, E helenp@netnam. org.vn.

Useful addresses *Business Centre*, Hanoi Business Centre, 51 Ly Thai To, T8268833, F8261222. *Hanoi People's Committee*, 12 Le Lai St, T8253536. *Hanoi Police*, 1 Hang Trong St, T8253131. *Immigration Dept*, 40A Hang Bai St, T8260919.

N.I.C
New Indochina Travel Co., Ltd

Your agent for Indochina

We have been selected in the Vietnam, Cambodia and Laos Handbook by Michael Buckley (Moon Travel Handbooks) as one of the most reliable agents in Vietnam.

Address: 1A Dang Thai Than, Hanoi, Vietnam
Tel: (84-4) 9330599
Fax: (84-4) 9330499
E-mail: helenp@netnam.org.vn

www.vietnamtourism.com/NIC Travel

- Specialist tour operator
- FIT package, tailor-made itineraries
- Worldwide hotel & ticket special rates
- Business meetings & conferences
- Transportation & limousine services

VIETNAM THE LAND OF ORIENTAL BEAUTY

The North

4

The North

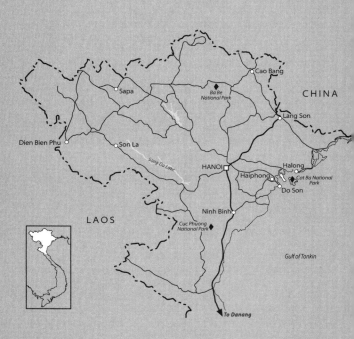

*To many the Northwest represents the finest Vietnam
has to offer. In terms of scenery, colour, human interest
and for the thrill of discovering the unknown, it is
unrivalled. Nor is the region without wider significance –
the course of world history was altered at Dien Bien Phu
in 1954. It is that myth of travellers' folklore: unspoilt
Vietnam.*

*There are good reasons why it is so. The distance,
rugged environment and primitive infrastructure have
all contributed to placing the Northwest at the edge of
Vietnamese space. But for those who wish to avoid the
backpacker's trail and are prepared to put up with a little
discomfort, the rewards are great. Pockets of the north
have been discovered. Sapa, for example, is no longer a
secret, but it is no less lovely for that.*

*The fertile river valleys dividing the mountain ranges
of North Vietnam have been settled by people of the
Austro-Asiatic language family, including forebears of
the modern Vietnamese and their upland cousins the
Muong. They are thought to have migrated into the area
from southern China during the latter half of the first
millennium BC; there they joined other groups including
the ancestors of the Mon-Khmer speaking peoples.*

Northwest

Hanoi to Hoa Binh, Son La, Dien Bien Phu, Lai Chau, Sapa and Lao Cai

The road from Hanoi to Dien Bien Phu winds its way for 420 kilometres into the Annamite mountains that mark the frontier with the Lao People's Democratic Republic. The round trip Hanoi to Hanoi via Dien Bien Phu and Sapa is about 1,200 kilometres and offers, perhaps, the most spectacular scenery anywhere in Vietnam. Opportunities to see something of the lives, customs and costumes of some of Vietnam's ethnic minorities (page 368) abound. The route can be taken in a clockwise or anti-clockwise direction; the advantage of following the clock is the opportunity to recover from the rigours of the journey in the tranquil setting of Sapa. While following the main roads and staying in registered guesthouses involves no special permission visitors wishing to stay in ethnic minority houses may require a permit from the provincial authorities to be presented to the local police; but regulations and the zeal with which they are enforced are constantly changing.

Highway 6 leads southwest out of Hanoi to Hoa Binh. Setting off in the early morning (this is a voyage of dawn starts and early nights) the important arterial function of this road to Hanoi can be clearly seen: ducks, chickens, pigs, bamboo and charcoal pour in; the energy and building materials of the capital – a remarkable volume transported by bicycle. Beyond the city limit the fields are highly productive, bounteous market gardens and intensive rice production.

The geology of much of Northwest Vietnam is limestone; the effect on this rock of the humid tropical climate and numerous streams and rivers is remarkable. Large cones and towers (hence tower karst) sometimes with vertical walls and overhangs rise dramatically from the flat alluvial plains. Dotted with bamboo thickets, this landscape is one of the most evocative in Vietnam; its hazy images seem to linger deep in the collective Vietnamese psyche and perhaps symbolize a sort of primaeval Garden of Eden, an irretrievable age when life was simpler and more innocent.

Hoa Binh

Phone code: 018
Colour map 1, grid B4

Hoa Binh, on the banks of the Da (Black) River, marks the southern limit of the interior highlands. Hoa Binh is 75 kilometres from Hanoi, a journey of about two and a half hours. A newly opened Hoa Binh Province museum (**Bao Tang Tinh Hoa Binh**) contains items of archaeological, historical and ethnographical importance. Relics of the First Indochina War, including a French amphibious landing craft remain from the bitterly fought campaign of 1951-2 which saw Viet Minh forces successfully dislodge the French. ■ *5,000d. Open 0800-1030, 1400-1700.* Major excavation sites of the Hoabinhian prehistoric civilization (10,000 BC) were found in the province, which is its main claim to international fame. In 1979, with Russian technical

People of the north

Ethnic groups belonging to the Sino-Tibetan language family such as the Hmong and Dao or the Ha Nhi and Phu La of the Tibeto-Burman language group are more recent arrivals. Migrating south from China only within the past 250-300 years, these people have lived almost exclusively on the upper mountain slopes, practising swidden agriculture and posing little threat to their more numerous lowland-dwelling neighbours, notably the Thai.

Thus was established the pattern of human and political settlement which would persist in North Vietnam for over 1,000 years right down to the colonial period – a centralized Viet state based in the Red River Delta area, with powerful Thai vassal lordships dominating the North West. Occupying lands located in some cases almost equidistant from Hanoi, Luang Prabang and Kunming, the Thai, Lao, Lu and Tay lords were obliged during the pre-colonial period to pay tribute to the royal courts of Nam Viet, Lang Xang (Laos) and China alike, though in times of upheaval they could and frequently did play one power off against the other for their own political gain.

Considerable effort was thus required by successive Viet kings in Thang Long

(Hanoi) and later in Hue to ensure that their writ and their writ alone ran in the far north. To this end there was ultimately no substitute for the occasional display of military force, but the enormous cost of mounting a campaign into the northern mountains obliged most Viet kings simply to endorse the prevailing balance of power there by investing the most powerful local lords as their local government mandarins, resorting to arms only when separatist tendencies became too strong.

Such was the political situation inherited by the French colonial government following its conquest of Indochina in the latter half of the 19th century. Its subsequent policy towards the ethnic minority chieftains of North Vietnam was to mirror that of the Vietnamese monarchy whose authority it assumed; throughout the colonial period responsibility for colonial administration at both local and provincial level was placed in the hands of seigneurial families of the dominant local ethnicity, a policy which culminated during the 1940s in the establishment of a series of ethnic minority 'autonomous zones` ruled over by the most powerful seigneurial families..

and financial assistance, work began on the Hoa Binh Dam and hydro-electric power station which 15 years later was complete. The reservoir has a volume of nine billion cubic meters: it provides two functions, to prevent flooding on the lower reaches of the Red River (ie Hanoi) and to generate power. Vietnam is so dependent on Hoa Binh for its electricity that when water levels fall below critical thresholds in the dry season large areas of the country are blacked out. More than 4,000 households had to be moved from the valley floor to rugged, infertile hillsides where ironically they are too poor to afford electricity.

Hoa Binh is a possible stopping off point en route for Son La but those who made an early start will press on to Mai Chau for lunch.

Muong and Dao Minority villages are accessible from Hoa Binh. **Xom Mo** is around eight kilometres from Hoa Binh, it is a village of the Muong minority. There are around 10 stilt houses, overnight stays are possible, nearby caves to visit. Duong and Phu are villages of the Dao Tien (Money Dao), located 25 kilometres up river. Boat hire (US$25) from Hoa Binh Tourism. Permit required for overnight stay. It is also possible to arrange a tour to the nearby **hydropower station**, most of which is built underground for strategic rather than environmental reasons but at vast expense.

Sleeping **B** *Hoa Binh 1*, 54 Phuong Lam, T852051, F854372. On Highway 6 out of Hoa Binh towards Mai Chau, clean and acceptable standards, some rooms built in minority style, also an ethnic minority dining experience complete with rice drunk through bamboo straws. The Hoa Binh Ethnic Minority Culture Troupe put on 1 hour shows featuring dance and music of the Muong, Thai, Hmông and Dao in the hotel. Gift shop stocks ethnic produce so for those venturing no further stock up now. **B** *Hoa Binh 2*, 160 An Duong Vuong, T852001. As above.

Eating *Thanh Toi*, 22a Cu Chinh Lan. Local specialities, wild boar and stir-fried eggplant.

Transport 75 kilometres from Hanoi. **Road Bus**: morning departures from Hanoi's Kim Ma terminal, 2 hours.

Directory **Tourist offices** *Hoa Binh Tourist Co*, Song Da, T854400. Can arrange boat hire and visits to minority villages.

Mai Chau

Colour map 1, grid B3

After leaving Hoa Binh, Highway 6 heads in a south-southwest direction as far as the Chu River. Thereafter it climbs through some spectacular mountain scenery before descending into the beautiful Mai Chau valley.

During the first half of this journey deep, the turtle shaped roofs of the Muong houses predominate, but after passing Man Duc the road enters the territory of the Thai, Northwest Vietnam's most prolific ethnic minority, heralding a subtle change in the style of stilted-house architecture. Whilst members of the Thai ethnic minority will be encountered in great abundance on this circuit, it is their Black Thai sub-ethnicity which will be seen most frequently. What makes the Mai Chau area interesting is that it is one of the few places en route where travellers can encounter their White Thai cousins.

An isolated farming community until 1993, Mai Chau has undergone significant change in just a few short years. That tourism has already reached Mai Chau becomes evident as each vehicle is flagged down on the approach to the town and a fee of 6,000d is levied from each foreign visitor. Its tranquil valley setting, engaging White Thai inhabitants and superb rice wine, however, continue to make Mai Chau a very worthwhile pit-stop, and an alternative overnight stop for those wishing to give Hoa Binh a miss.

The growing number of foreign tourists visiting the area in recent years has had a significant impact on the economy of Mai Chau and the lifestyles of its inhabitants. Some foreign visitors complain that the valley has already gone a long way down the same road as Chiang Mai in northern Thailand, offering a manicured hill tribe village experience to the less adventurous tourist who wants to sample the quaint lifestyle of the ethnic people without too much discomfort. There may be some truth in this allegation, yet there is another side to the coin.

Since the region first opened its doors to foreign tourists in 1993, the Mai Chau People's Committee has attempted to control the impact of tourism in the valley. Lac is the official tourist village to which tour groups are led and although it is possible to visit and even stay in the others, by 'sacrificing' one village to tourism it is hoped to limit the impact. Income generated from tourism by the villagers of Lac has brought about a significant enhancement of lifestyles, not just in Lac but also throughout the entire valley, enabling many villagers to tile their roofs and purchase consumer products such as television sets, refrigerators and motorbikes. Of course, for some foreign visitors the sight of a television aerial or a T-shirt is enough to prove that an ethnic village has already lost its traditional culture but in Lac they are wily enough to conceal their aerials in the roof space.

Lac is easily accessible from the main road – go a few hundred metres past the People's Committee Guesthouse then take a track to the right directly into the village of Lac, the village most popular with day-trippers and overnight visitors from Hanoi. Turning into the village one's heart may sink: minibuses are drawn up and stilt houses in the centre of the village all sport stickers of Hanoi tour operators. But before you turn and flee take a gentle stroll around the village, find a non-stickered house and by means of gestures, signs, broken English and the odd word of Vietnamese ask whether you can spend the night.

Lac White Thai village

Borrow or rent a bicycle from your hosts and wobble across narrow bunds to the neighbouring hamlets enjoying the ducks, buffaloes, children and lush rice fields. It is one of the most delightful of experiences. If you are lucky you will be offered a particularly refreshing tea made from the bark of a certain tree. Five kilometres south of Mai Chau on Route 15A is the Naon River on which, in the dry season, a boat can be taken to visit a number of large and **impressive grottoes**. Others can be reached on foot. Ask your hosts or at the People's Committee Guesthouse for details.

Excursions

D *People's Committee Guesthouse*, T851812. Fan rooms, basic, no restaurant. E *Ethnic Houses*, visitors can spend the night in a White Thai house on stilts. Mat, wicker pillow, mosquito net, basic washing facilities and sometimes fan provided. This is particularly recommended as the hospitality and easy manner of the people is a highlight of many visitors' stay in Vietnam. Food and local rice wine provided. Avoid the large houses in the centre if possible.

Sleeping

Ly Thuy, Route 15A, a kilometre or so from Lac. Good for dinner. *Nam Hai*, Route 15A. Good for breakfast.

Eating

Mai Chau Ethnic Minority Dance Troupe, Thai dancing culminating in the communal drinking of sweet sticky rice wine through straws from a large pot.

Entertainment

Villagers offer a range of woven goods and fabrics on which they are becoming dependent for a living. There are also local paintings and wicker baskets, pots, traps and pouches all well made. Mai Chau is probably the best place for buying handicrafts in the Northwest. The rice wine in Mai Chau is excellent, particularly when mixed with local honey.

Shopping

75 kilometres from Hoa Binh. **Road Bus**: connections with Hoa Binh (2 hours) and with Hanoi's Kim Ma station (4 hours). Onward buses northwest to Son La.

Transport

Son La

What the road to Son La lacks in comfort is more than compensated for by the scenery and superb **Black Thai** and **Muong villages**. The road passes close to several particularly attractive villages each with a suspension footbridge and fascinating hydraulic works. Mini hydro-electric generators on the river supply houses with enough power to run a light or television and water power is also used to husk and mill rice. The succession of picturesque little villages located just across the river to the left hand side of the road 85 to 78 kilometres before Son La affords an excellent opportunity to view Black Thai stilt house architecture. **Cuc Dua village** at the 84 kilometre mark is highly photogenic.

Phone code: 022
Colour map 1, grid B2

Typically there is a suspension bridge over the incised river in which are fish traps and swimming children. Clouds of butterflies flutter by on the breeze.

It was not until the 18th century under the patronage of the Black Thai seigneurial family of Ha that Son La began to develop as a town. During the late 1870s the region was invaded by renegade Chinese Yellow Flag bands taking refuge after the failed Taiping Uprising. Allying himself to Lin Yung-fu, commander of the pursuing Black Flag forces, Deo Van Tri, Black Thai chieftain, led a substantial army against the Yellow Flags in 1880, decisively defeating and expelling them from the country. Thus Tri established hegemony over all the Black and White Thai lords in the Son La area, enabling him to rely on their military support in his subsequent struggle against the French – indeed, the chieftains of Son La were to take an active role in the resistance effort between 1880 and 1888.

As the French moved their forces up the Da River valley during the campaign of 1888, the chieftains of the area were one by one obliged to surrender. A French garrison was quickly established at Son La. As elsewhere in the Northwest, the French chose to reward the chieftains of Son La district for their new found loyalty by reconfirming their authority as local government mandarins, albeit now on behalf of a colonial rather than a royal master.

While large-scale resistance to French rule in the Northwest effectively ceased after 1890, sporadic uprisings continued to create problems for the colonial administration. The French responded by establishing detention centres throughout the area which were known to the Thai as *huon mut* (dark houses). The culmination of this policy came in 1908 with the construction of a large penitentiary designed to incarcerate resistance leaders from the Northwest and other regions of Vietnam. Just one year after the opening of the new Son La Penitentiary, prisoners staged a mass-breakout, causing substantial damage to the prison itself before fleeing across the border into Laos.

During the final days of colonial rule Son La became an important French military outpost, and accordingly an air base was built at Na San, 20 kilometres from the town. Both Na San air base and the colonial government headquarters in Son La town were abandoned to the Viet Minh in November 1953, on the eve of the Battle of Dien Bien Phu.

Son La

Sights Contemporary Son La is undergoing a facelift, with gleaming new government buildings under construction in the centre of this provincial capital. There is little to see other than the **Son La Provincial Museum** on Youth Hill just off Highway 6 near the centre of town. Son La Provincial Museum is in fact the town's old **French Penitentiary**, constructed in 1908, damaged in 1909, bombed in 1952, and now partially rebuilt for tourists. The original three metre deep dungeon and tiny cells complete with food-serving hatches and leg-irons, can be seen together with an exhibition illustrating the history of the place and the key individuals who

■ **Sleeping**
1 Hoa Ban
2 People's Committee Guesthouse
3 Phong Lan I
4 Son La
5 Thanh Cong
6 Trade Union Guesthouse

were incarcerated here. ■ *5,000d. Open 0800-1030, 1400-1700 daily although a man with a key can normally be found at other times.*

To reach the **Coong caves** – or Tham Coong – walk or drive to the north end of town, after a few hundred metres are the tanks of the Son La water company; turn left and follow the stream or take the path and yomp across the bunds of the rice fields. There are two caves, the wet cave is now fenced off but a scramble up the limestone face brings you to a dry cave (entrance 5,000d if the man is there) from which are lovely views. As you have probably come to expect by now in Vietnam the caves are nothing, the walk a never-ending joy – in wet feet. The fields, ponds and streams below the caves are a miracle of inventiveness and beauty: stilt houses, gardens, hibiscus hedgerows, and a range of colours and smells that are particularly appealing in the late afternoon sunlight. Fish are bred in the ponds which are covered with water cress (*salad soong*) or what looks like a red algal bloom, actually a small floating weed (*beo hoa dau*) which is fed to ducks and pigs.

Excursions

Ban Co is a Black Thai village and a visit here can be combined with a trip to Tham Coong. Returning from the caves, rejoin the road then turn left and take a track across the fields to the village of Co. The village is a largeish and fairly ordinary Black Thai settlement but a diverting twilight hour can be spent watching its inhabitants returning from the fields with a fish or duck for the pot and a basket of greens, washing away the day's grime in the stream and settling down to a relaxing evening routine that has changed little in the last few hundred years.

There are **Hot Springs** in Mong village five kilometres south of Son La.

C *Hoa Ban*, 6 Chieng Le St, T852395, F852712. A/c or fan, clean and fairly comfortable, slightly pricy, restaurant. C *Nha Khach Uy Ban Nhan Dan (People's Committee Guesthouse)*, Highway 6, T852080. Signed *Nha Khach* just off Highway 6, a/c, fan, renovated and now the pick of the bunch, lovely setting overlooking hillsides and villages. C *Phong Lan 1*, T853515, opposite Central Market. A/c, clean and ordinary. C *Thanh Cong*, 278 Truong Chinh, T854691. On the road in from Mai Chau, new but stark. D *Son La*, Quang Thang St, opposite bus station, T852702. A/c and fan rooms, basic accommodation, restaurant. D *Nha Khach Cong Doan (Trade Union Guesthouse)*, Chieng Le St, T852864. A/c, fan rooms, basic, some English spoken. D *Nha Khach Song Da*, T852062. Fan rooms only.

Sleeping
■ *on map*
Price codes:
see inside front cover

Nha Hang Thit De, near the bridge. Goat specialities. *Nha Hang Thit Vit*, also near the bridge. Duck specialities.

Eating

310 kilometres northwest of Hanoi. **Road Bus**: connections with Hanoi's Kim Ma station and en route to Hanoi with Mai Chau and Hoa Binh. Continuing north from Son La, there are regular bus connections with Dien Bien Phu and Lai Chau.

Transport

Bank 186 Chieng Le St. **Communications Post Office:** 172 Chieng Le St.

Directory

Son La West to Dien Bien Phu or north to Lai Chau

The scenery leaving Son La is breath-taking. Reds and greens predominate. Red is the soil, the costumes and the newly tiled roofs. Green are the trees, the swaying fronds of bamboo, and the wet season rice. Early morning light brings out the colours in their finest and freshest hues. And as the sun rises colours transmute from orange to pink to ochre.

Around every bend in the road is a new visual treat. Most stunning are the valley floors, blessed with water throughout the year. Here generations of ceaseless human activity have engineered a land to man's design. Using nothing more than bamboo technology and human muscle terraces have been sculpted from the hills: little channels feed water from field to field illustrating a high level of social order and common purpose. Water powers devices of great ingenuity – water wheels for raising water from river level to field level, rice mills and huskers, mini electrical turbines. And quite inadvertently these people – who for centuries have been isolated from outside perceptions of beauty – have produced a fusion of natural and human landscape that cannot fail to please the eye. Shape, form, scale and colour blend and contrast in a pattern of sympathy and understanding wholly lost to the modern world. Then the road climbs away from the river to a rain-fed village: the grey and red dust and mean little houses indicate great poverty and one realizes the importance of a constant water supply.

There is a small and colourful market village 25 kilometres from Son La and 10 kilometres further on is **Thuan Chau** another little market town. In the early morning these two places are good for photographing people of different minorities in traditional dress bartering and trading. Thuan Chau is a good spot for breakfast and for buying headscarves. The settlements along this route nicely illustrate the law which describes the inverse relationship between the size of a place and the proportion of the population traditionally garbed. The road is remarkably good with crash barriers, mirrors positioned strategically on hair-pin bends and warning signs. Which considering the precipitous nature of the terrain from Thuan Chau to Tuan Giao and visibility obscured by cloud and fog is just as well.

Tuan Giao is 75 kilometres and approximately three hours from Son La. From Tuan Giao travellers have the choice of either proceeding north across the mountains direct to Lai Chau, or taking the longer route via Dien Bien Phu.

Highway 6 from Tuan Giao heads north across the Hoang Lien Son Range direct to Lai Chau. This journey of around 100 kilometres takes five hours. From Tuan Giao, the road climbs up through some spectacular scenery reaching altitudes of around 1800-1900 metres. Red and White Hmông villages are passed en route. It is the option taken by those who do not have time on their hands.

The journey from Tuan Giao to Dien Bien Phu on Highway 279 is 80 kilometres and takes around four hours and is chosen by those with a strong sense of Vietnamese history.

Dien Bien Phu

Situated in a region where even today ethnic Vietnamese still represent less than one third of the total population, Dien Bien Phu lies in the Muong Thanh valley, a heart-shaped basin 19 kilometres long and 13 kilometres wide, crossed by the Nam Yum River.

Phone code: 023
Colour map 1, grid B1

Ins and outs

Getting there Dien Bien Phu is deep in the highlands of northwest Vietnam, close to the border with Laos and 420 kilometres from Hanoi (although it feels much further). The airport is 2 kilometres north of town and there are 4 connections a week with Hanoi. Buses snake their way up from Hanoi via Hoa Binh and Son La, and there are also connections onward with Lai Chau, Sapa and Lao Cai. Expect overland journeys to be slow and sometimes arduous in this mountainous region – but the discomfort is more than compensated for by the sheer majesty of the landscapes. The road to Son La has been significantly upgraded over recent years but the route to Sapa is still poor.

Getting around The new town of Dien Bien, with its neat streets, is a small settlement, is easy to negotiate on foot. But while the streets may be built the local authorities haven't got around to giving them names – hence the absence of hotel addresses. Fortunately for a town of Dien Bien's size this oversight doesn't present any insurmountable problems. The battlefield of Dien Bien Phu is about 1.5 kilometres south of town and the bus station on highway 12 is also within easy walking distance of the town centre and its hotels.

The North

History

Modern Dien Bien Phu is a growing town. This reflects the decision to make it the provincial capital of Lai Chau Province and attempts to develop it as a tourist destination. But tucked away in one of Vietnam's remotest corners where only the most determined of travellers will find it, Dien Bien Phu's dreams of tapping the tourist dollar have been left largely unfulfilled.

Settled from an early date, Muong Thanh valley has been an important trading post on the caravan route between China and Burma for 2,000 years. Over the years numerous fortifications were constructed in and around Muong Thanh, the best-known being the fabled Citadel of the Thirty Thousand (*Thanh Tam Van*) built by the Lu during the 15th century. Remnants of this citadel can still be seen today, near Xam Mun.

The early years of the 18th century were a period of acute political instability throughout Vietnam. During this time the Northwest was overrun by armies of the Phe from southern Yunnan province who committed unspeakable acts of barbarism against the inhabitants of the area. In 1751, however, a Vietnamese peasant leader from the Red River Delta named Hoang Cong Chat, whose army had retreated into the region to escape from royal troops, rallied local Lu, Lao and Thai chieftains to his cause and expelled the Phe back across the border to China. Building a new fortress at Ban Phu, Chat set himself up as lord of a large area including most of modern Son La and Lai Chau provinces, winning the hearts of the local people by carrying out important land and taxation reforms.

The town of Dien Bien Phu itself only came into existence in 1841 when, in response to continued Lao, Siamese and Chinese banditry in the area, the Nguyen dynasty ordered the establishment of a royal district governed from a fortified settlement at Muong Thanh.

The Battle of Dien Bien Phu

On 20 November 1953, after a series of French successes, Colonel Christian de Castries and six battalions of French and French-colonial troops were parachuted into Dien Bien Phu. The location, in a narrow valley surrounded by steep wooded peaks, was chosen specifically because it was thought by the French strategists to be impregnable. From there, they believed, their forces could begin to harry the Viet Minh close to their bases as well as protect Laos from Viet Minh incursions. At the centre of the valley was the all-important airstrip – Colonel de Castries' only physical link with the outside world. In his history of Vietnam, Stanley Karnow writes of de Castries: "Irresistible to women and ridden with gambling debts, he had been a champion horseman, dare-devil pilot and courageous commando, his body scarred by three wounds earned during the Second World War and earlier in Indochina".

In response, the famous Vietnamese General Giap moved his forces, some 55,000 men, into the surrounding area, manhandling heavy guns (with the help, it is said of 200,000 porters) up the impossibly steep mountainsides until they had a view over the French forces. The French commander still believed however that his forces would have the upper hand in any set-piece confrontation, and set about strengthening his position. He created a series of heavily fortified strongholds, giving them women's names: Anne-Marie, Françoise, Huguette, Beatrice, Gabrielle, Dominique, Claudine, Isabelle and Eliane. It is said that they were named after de Castries' numerous mistresses.

As it turned out, de Castries was not luring the Viet Minh into a trap, but creating one for himself and his men. From the surrounding highlands, Giap had the French at his mercy. The shelling started in the middle of March, and the strongholds fell one-by-one; Beatrice first

and then Gabrielle and Anne-Marie by mid-March until de Castries' forces were concentrated around the airstrip. Poor weather, which prevented the French from using their air power, and human-wave attacks gradually wore the French troops down. By this time, de Castries had withdrawn to his bunker and command had effectively been taken over by his junior officers. A furious bombardment by the heavy guns of the Viet Minh from 1 May led to the final massed assault 5 days later. On the final night, the Viet Minh taunted the French defenders by playing the `Song of the Partisans', the theme of the French Resistance, over the garrison's radio frequencies. De Castries' HQ fell on 7 May at 1730 when 9,500 French and French colonial troops surrendered. A small force of paratroopers at the isolated southern position, Isabelle, continued to resist for a further 24 hours.

This humiliation at Dien Bien Phu led the French to sue for peace at a conference in Geneva. On 20 July 1954, it was agreed that Vietnam should be divided into two along the 17th parallel: a Communist north and a capitalist south. In total, 20,000 Viet Minh and over 3,000 French troops were killed at Dien Bien Phu. The Geneva agreement set terms so that the dead from both sides would be honoured in a massive ossuary. But when Ngo Dinh Diem, the President of the Republic of South Vietnam, symbolically urinated over Viet Minh dead in the South rather than bury them with honour, Giap and Ho decided to leave the French dead to lie where they had fallen. Over the 9 years of war between the Viet Minh and the French, the dead numbered between a quarter and 1 million civilians, 200,000-300,000 Viet Minh and 95,000 French colonial troops. Who was to guess another 20 years of warfare lay ahead.

Occupied by French forces during the course of their major Northwest campaign of 1888-1889, Dien Bien Phu was subsequently maintained as a garrison town. The town fell briefly to Thai insurgents during the latter stages of the 1908 Son La Penitentiary uprising (prompting the suicide of Dien Bien Phu's French commander) and again during the course of the 1914-1916 uprising of Son La chieftains but perhaps the most serious threat to French rule in the region came in 1918 when the Hmông rebelled against the harsh fiscal policies of the new Governor General Paul Doumer, by refusing to pay taxes in silver coins or to supply opium to the French and taking up arms against the garrison. The insurrection quickly spread east to Son La and south across the Lao border into Samneua, and although the French responded ruthlessly by devastating rebel areas, destroying food crops to provoke famine and setting a high price on the heads of prominent rebels, the revolt persisted until March 1921.

In Vietnam, as elsewhere in Asia, the defeat of the European Allies during the early years of the Second World War utterly shattered the image of western colonial supremacy, fuelling the forces of incipient nationalism. French attempts to resume their authority in the region in 1945 thus encountered stiff resistance from Viet Minh forces, and in the nine years of fighting which followed, the Northwest became a cradle of national resistance against French colonialism.

Following the French defeat at Hoa Binh in 1952 the Vietnamese army went on the offensive all over the Northwest, forcing the French to regroup at their two remaining strongholds of Na San (Son La) and Lai Chau. Early the following year, acting in conjunction with Pathet Lao forces, the Viet Minh overran Samneua in upper Laos and proceeded to sweep north, threatening the Lao capital of Luang Prabang. By November 1953 the French colonial government headquarters at Lai Chau, just 110 kilometres north of Dien Bien Phu, had also come under siege.

Dien Bien Phu was the site of the last calamitous battle between the forces of Ho Chi Minh's Viet Minh and the French, and was waged from March to May 1954. The French, who under Vichy rule had accepted the authority of the Japanese during the Second World War, attempted to regain control after the Japanese had surrendered. Ho, following his Declaration of Independence on 2 September 1945, thought otherwise, heralding nearly a decade of war before the French finally gave up the fight after their catastrophic defeat here. The lessons of the battle were numerous, but most of all it was a victory of determination over technology. In the aftermath, the French people, much like the Americans

en Bien Phu

e French Garrison, 13 March 1954
ortly before the siege began

GABRIELLE
Ford
Pavie Track
Nam Yum River
Rt 41
Ban Kéo
ANNE-MARIE
BEATRICE
HUGUETTE
DOMINIQUE
FRANCOISE
ELIANE
Phony Hill
Ban Ong Pet
CLAUDINE
Baldy Hill
Ban Hong
Lech Cang
Ban Na Loi
Ban Papé
MARCELLE
evacuated
Ban Ten
Ban Palech
Ban Bom La
Ban Nhong Nhai
Ban Kho Lai
Auxiliary
airstrip
Ban Hong Cum
N
ISABELLE
WIEME
CLAUDINE French strong points
|||||| Escarpment
······· Barbed-wire systems
km   1
miles 0.6

The North

two decades later, had no stomach left for a war in a distant, tropical and alien land.

Sights

On the battlefield General (as he was by the end of the battle) **de Castries' bunker** has been rebuilt and eight of the 10 French tanks (known as bisons) are scattered over the valley along with numerous US made artillery pieces. On **Hill A1** (known as **Eliane 2** to the French and scene of the fiercest fighting) is a bunker, the bison named Gazelle, a war memorial dedicated to the Vietnamese who died on the hill and around at the back is the entrance to a tunnel dug by coal miners from Hon Gai. Their tunnel ran several hundred metres to beneath French positions and was filled with 1,000 kilos of high explosives. It was detonated at 2300 on 6 May as a signal for the final assault. The huge crater is still there. The hill is a peaceful spot and a good place from which to watch the sun setting on the historic valley. After dark there are fireflies. Both places are fenced off so those wishing to get inside should check with the Historic Victory Museum first.

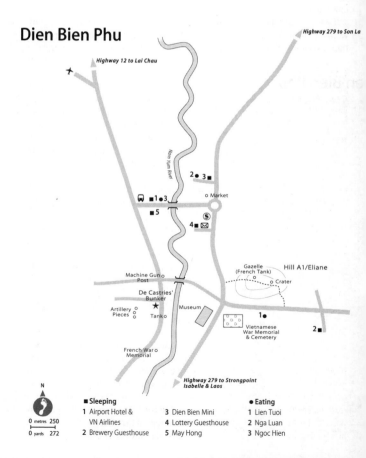

Dien Bien Phu

Highway 279 to Son La

Highway 12 to Lai Chau

Nom Yum River

2 ● 3 ■

■ 1 ● 3   ○ Market

■ 5

4 ■ ✉

Gazelle
(French Tank)   Hill A1/Eliane
○   ○ Crater

Machine Gun ○
Post

De Castries'
Bunker   ★

Artillery ○
Pieces ○   ★   Museum

Tank ○   1 ●

Vietnamese
War Memorial
& Cemetery   2 ■

French War ○
Memorial

*Highway 279 to Strongpoint
Isabelle & Laos*

N

0 metres 250
0 yards 272

■ **Sleeping**
1 Airport Hotel &
  VN Airlines
2 Brewery Guesthouse
3 Dien Bien Mini
4 Lottery Guesthouse
5 May Hong

● **Eating**
1 Lien Tuoi
2 Nga Luan
3 Ngoc Hien

The Historic Victory Exhibition Museum (Nha Trung Bay Thang Lich Su Dien Bien Phu) has a good collection of assorted weapons and artillery, Chinese, American and French in its grounds. There are photographs and other memorabilia together with a large illuminated model of the valley illustrating the course of the campaign. While every last piece of Vietnamese junk is carefully catalogued, displayed and described (in Vietnamese only, of course) French relics are heaped into tangled piles. It is interesting to note that while ordinary Vietnamese people forgive and forget so disarmingly readily the Communist propaganda machine gloats over its victory of almost half a century ago as though it were yesterday. ■ *5,000d. Open 0730-1130, 1330-1630 daily.*

Historic Victory Exhibition Museum

Revolutionary Heroes' Cemetery located directly opposite the Exhibition Centre adjacent to Hill A1, *(Nghia Trang Liet Si)* contains the graves of some 15,000 Vietnamese soldiers killed during the course of the Dien Bien Phu campaign. **French War Memorial** (Nghia Trang Phap) is located close to the command bunker of de Castries. It consists of a white obelisk surrounded by a grey concrete wall and black iron gates sitting on a bluff overlooking the Nam Yum River, unloved, unkempt and forgotten.

Revolutionary Heroes' Cemetery

The North

Essentials

Virtually all hotels are state run: customers mean extra work which hotel keepers on minimal salaries could do without. Expect a cool reception and to pay way over the odds for a very ordinary room.

Sleeping
■ *on map*
Price codes:
see inside front cover

C *Airport*, T824908, F826060. 6 rooms, a/c, hot water, fairly basic, near the bus station, Vietnam Airlines booking office is in the hotel and Ngoc Hien Restaurant next door. **C** *Dien Bien Mini Hotel*, T824319. Newish building with 23 rooms, a/c, fan rooms, restaurant, breakfast included. **C** *May Hong*, T826300. Opposite Vietnam Airlines booking office, a/c, hot water, new and possibly the smartest in town but soul-less. **D** *Brewery*, T824635. 10 rooms, out beyond Hill A1 at the east end of town. While not exactly welcoming we found them at lest amenable to bargaining, basic fan and a/c rooms, no restaurant but, as the name suggests, beer and plenty of it. A little *bia hoi* is next to the gate and fresh cool beer at 1,500d a glass slips down very easily – it gets our vote for the best in the Northwest. **D** *Lottery*, T825931. Centrally located and just 5 rooms, basic accommodation.

Lien Tuoi, next to the Vietnamese cemetery and Hill A1. Delicious local fare in a family restaurant. The family sits down to eat at 2000, don't expect much service (or food) after that. *Ngoc Hien*, next to *Airport Hotel*. Plain, ordinary but tasty food. *Nga Luan*, near maket. Unpretentious canteen-type eatery serving honest provender.

Eating
● *on map*

110 kilometres from Son La, 345 kilometres from Hoa Binh, 420 kilometres from Hanoi.

Transport

Air The airport (T824416) is 2 kilometres north of town, off Highway 12. 4 flights a week with Hanoi.

Road Bus: the bus station is close to the centre of town, on Highway 12. It is an easy walk to the hotels. There are now direct bus connections with Hanoi's Kim Ma station, depart 0430, 75,000d; Son La, 38,000d; Lai Chau, 5 buses per day, 25,000d. Note that road transport in the mountains is arduous. **Hire car**: roads via Son La are generally good (in the dry season) but via Sapa so bad in places that a four-wheel drive vehicle is highly recommended if not essential. Russian made army jeeps are ideal and can be hired, with driver, from hotels or tour operators in Hanoi (see page 86); expect to pay around US$300 for a 4 or 5 day round trip (1,200 kilometres via Sapa), quite reasonable if split four ways. For those willing to pay more Japanese land cruisers offer higher levels of comfort.

The road to Lai Chau

It is 104 kilometres on Highway 12 from Dien Bien Phu to Lai Chau. The road was originally built by an energetic French district governor, Auguste Pavie, and was used by soldiers fleeing from the French garrison at Lai Chau to the supposed safety of the garrison at Dien Bien Phu in 1953. Viet Minh ambushes along the Pavie Track meant that the French were forced to hack their way through the jungle and those few who made it to Dien Bien Phu found themselves almost immediately under siege again.

Within a few kilometres of Dien Bien Phu what has hitherto been a pleasant ride on decent metalled roads becomes a jarring, exhausting slog along particularly uncomfortable farm tracks. The five hour journey is scenically interesting and the few minority villages, Kho Mu and Thai on the valley floors and Hmông higher up, divert attention from the discomfort.

The scenery is different from any we have encountered so far. What drew gasps of amazement around Son La was the exquisite human landscape. From Dien Bien Phu to Lai Chau what impresses is the scenery in its natural state. It is unfriendly but spectacular. The agents at work here are rivers, rain, heat and gravity and the raw materials are rock and trees. There are no rice terraces but forested hills in which slash and burn farming takes place. This is the land of rockslide and flood. It is geologically young and dangerous: the steep slopes of thinly bedded shales collapse after heavy rain. The bands of limestone are more solid. The density of population is low and evidence abounds that the living here is harsh. We see a less romantic side to life in a minority village: tiny children of four stagger along with a baby strapped to their back, there is no colourful dress or elaborate costume just ragged kids in filthy t-shirts.

Pu Ka village, 46 kilometres from Lai Chau is a White Hmông settlement newly established by the authorities to transplant the Hmông away from their opium fields.

Lai Chau

Colour map 1, grid B1/2

If Son La is notable for the colour of its minorities and Dien Bien Phu for its history Lai Chau should be noted for the splendour of its trees. The town occupies a majestic setting in a valley deep and wide which is cloaked in dense stands of forest. For various reasons the trees have not been felled and the beauty they confer on Lai Chau presumably extended over a much wider reach of country in an age gone by.

Much of the present town of Lai Chau dates from 1969-72, when it was expanded to accommodate the large numbers of Chinese engineers posted here to upgrade the road from Dien Bien Phu to the Chinese border (the Friendship Road). In 1993 the status of capital of Lai Chau Province was transferred from Lai Chau town to Dien Bien Phu, partly in recognition of the latters' growing importance as hub of economic and tourist activity and partly in deference to plans to drown the entire Lai Chau valley. The floods of 1996 drove another nail into the coffin of this unhappy but lovely town: 29 people were killed and 4,000 lost their homes – flood damage can still be seen in the town centre.

The history of Lai Chau is inextricably entwined with that of the Black Thai **History** seigneurial family of Deo who had achieved ascendancy over the former White Thai lords of Muong Lay by the first half of the fifteenth century. In 1451 the Vietnamese King Le Thai To is recorded as having led a campaign against the Deo family of Muong Lay (today a village 13 kilometres south of the town) for its disloyalty to the crown.

The Deo family in fact comprised a number of separate Black Thai lineages dotted around what is now Northwest Vietnam and Yunnan province of China, but it was the marriage during the 1850s of Deo Van Xeng, a wealthy merchant from Yunnan, to the daughter of a Muong Lay Deo chieftain, which established the most notorious line of the Deo family. When his father-in-law died, Xeng seized control of the Muong Lay dominions and, with the support of the royal court in Luang Prabang and the mandarinate of Yunnan, quickly established himself as one of the most powerful lords in the Northwest.

Deo Van Xeng's eldest son, the energetic Deo Van Tri, continued his father's expansionist policies. Allying himself with Chinese Black Flag commander Lin Yung-fu, Tri succeeded in expelling a Chinese Yellow Flag occupation force from Son La, instantly winning the respect and allegiance of the Black and White Thai chieftains of that area. Apart from a small number who stayed and were subsequently integrated into the Thai community, the Black Flags also left the country shortly after this, enabling Tri to assume suzerainty over a large area of Northwest Vietnam.

When French forces launched their campaign to pacify the Northwest, Tri initially took an active part in the resistance, leading a joint Black and White Thai force against the colonial army at the battle of Cau Giay in 1883. Consequently king-in-exile Ham Nghi appointed Tri military governor of 16 districts. But the garrisoning of French troops at Lai Chau during the campaign of 1888-1889 marked a turning point in the war of resistance and Tri was ultimately obliged to surrender to the French at Lai Chau in 1890.

As elsewhere in the north, the French moved quickly to graft their colonial administrative systems onto those already established by the Nguyen court and they ensured Deo Van Tris future co-operation by awarding him the hereditary post of Supreme Thai Chieftain.

After his death in 1915, Tri was succeeded as Governor of Lai Chau by his son Deo Van Long who later took office as mandarin of the colonial government in 1940. However, as the Viet Minh war of resistance got under way in 1945, the colonial government sought to ensure the continued allegiance of ethnic minority leaders by offering them a measure of self-government. Accordingly, in 1947 Muong, Thai, Tày, Hmông and Nung Autonomous Regions were set up throughout the Northwest and in Lai Chau Deo Van Long was duly installed as king of the Thai.

King Deo Van Long is remembered with loathing by most older inhabitants of the Lai Chau area; by all accounts he was a tyrant who exercised absolute authority, striking fear into the hearts of the local people by occasionally having transgressors executed on the spot. The overgrown ruins of Long's mansion lie just across the river from Doi Cao (High Hill) and may be visited either by boat or by road (see below).

During the latter days of French rule, as the security situation began to deteriorate throughout the Northwest, Lai Chau became an important French military base; older citizens of the town remember clearly the large numbers of Moroccans, Algerians and Tunisians who were posted here between 1946 and 1953. The French were finally forced to abandon Lai Chau during the winter of 1953 on the eve of the momentous battle of Dien Bien Phu. Bereft of his colonial masters, a discredited Deo Van Long fled to Laos and then to Thailand, whence he is believed to have emigrated to France. A few remaining relatives still live in the area, but have wisely changed their family name to Dieu.

Sights The excellent little **Lai Chau Museum**, just a stone's throw from the People's Committee Guesthouse seems to have closed and exhibits transfered to Dien Bien Phu. **Former French Colonial Government Headquarters** are used as offices and the local hospital. To get there walk up High Hill past the hospital, fork left up a track leading to the crest of the hill 500 metres further along. Also, on a terrace above the river, a former airfield (*sang bay Phap*). A very pleasant couple of hours can be whiled away pottering around the largely overgrown and derelict French remains. In trying to identify French areas the budding Indiana Jones can put **Botanical Archaeology** to good use. The French were fond of ornamental trees and planted many exotic types: straight rows of huge century-old trees (*muong*) fringe what may have been a former parade ground or playing field; the vivid colours of the flame trees (*phuong*) flag the nascent archaeologist up flights of decaying steps and balustrades towards what looks to have been the sanitorium.

Black Thai Village and Deo Van Long's House the ruins of Deo Van Long's plush colonial mansion lie on Road 127 to Muong Te on the opposite bank of the Da River from High Hill (Doi Cao). The remains are wonderfully overgrown with creeper and strangling figs. Older inhabitants of the six or seven remaining houses recall that for many years Deo Van Long and his family lived in great luxury with a large retinue of servants. Some say that, before fleeing the country in 1953, Long had all his servants poisoned so they could not inform the advancing Viet Minh forces of his whereabouts. Beware of precarious piles of loose masonry and deep vaults (dungeons, wine cellars?) covered with only a matting of creeper. ■ *Getting there: by boat from below High Hill (not when river levels are too high or too low), or a circuitous eight kilometres road trip and crossing one especially rickety suspension bridge.*

Excursions **Phi Hay White Hmông village** makes an interesting morning's excursion for those who made the detour via Dien Bien Phu. It offers a snapshot of the stunning scenery along the more direct Lai Chau-Tuan Giao mountain route. Phi Hay village is very old and comprises some 50 houses. ■ *Getting there: take Highway 6 in the direction of Tuan Giao for 13 kilometres, stop next to a group of small shops as the road begins to level out, walk up the path to the left of the road, for a further two kilometres.*

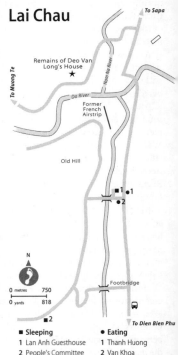

Lai Chau

To Sapa

To Muong Te

Nam Na River

Remains of Deo Van Long's House ★

Da River

Former French Airstrip

Old Hill

N

0 metres 750
0 yards 818

Footbridge

To Dien Bien Phu

■ **Sleeping**
1 Lan Anh Guesthouse
2 People's Committee Guesthouse

● **Eating**
1 Thanh Huong
2 Van Khoa

C *Lan Anh Guesthouse*, T852370. Fan and a/c rooms in the main part of town, not far from the treacherous Da River, a new block has wisely been built on stilts. Clean, comfortable, helpful, restaurant. **D-E** *People's Committee Guesthouse*, Nghe Toong, T852456. North of People's Committee Bridge (*Cau Uy Ban Nhan Dan*) and then up the zig-zag road, a/c and fan rooms, basic, clean and quiet accommodation with rock-hard beds, no restaurant. *Ethnic Houses*, overnight stays in ethnic houses are currently not possible.

Sleeping
■ *on map*
Price codes:
see inside front cover

Lan Anh Guesthouse (see above). *Thanh Huong*, on the main road nearly opposite bridge and *Van Khoa* restaurants, expect no menu or English, just point, mime and hope – or use the language section at the back of this book.

Eating
● *on map*

Road 103 kilometres and nearly 4 hours from Dien Bien Phu. **Bus**: connections south with Dien Bien Phu (and from there to Hanoi via Son La and Hoa Binh) and north and east with Sapa. Following the 1996 floods, the bus station was moved several kilometres west of the town; try to get dropped off by the bridge in the town centre. The People's Committee bridge is no longer open to traffic.

Transport

Sin Ho

Your driver will inform you of the latest outbreak of bubonic plague in the town, the absence of water and electricity and, when that does not dissuade you, he will remind you of the bus which plunged off the road in 1995 killing all 27 passengers. But your mind is made up and off you go. Your driver dodged American bombs, shells and napalm in the war and he applies the same degree of resolve and resignation to this modern day equivalent. Unfortunately the views from the back of a Russian army jeep are highly restricted so if the weather is clear you would be strongly advised to walk some of the way to appreciate the full majesty of the scenery. It will also give you a chance to absorb the delicious cool air, the forest sounds and smells and the wayside flowers. You also have the opportunity to witness the extraordinary perpendicular fields and to wonder how it is that man can actually harvest slopes on which we cannot even stand. And your driver can recover his shattered nerves.

Colour map 1, grid A2

After 20 kilometres the road levels off and meanders over the Sin Ho plateau passing hamlets of Red, White and Flower Hmông and Dao minorities. Sin Ho provides little that has not hitherto been seen although the **Sunday morning market** is worthy of note. As with other markets in the region, the Sunday market is an important social occasion – after their transactions are done, the men of various ethnic minorities gather around drinking wine and unattached boys and girls seek partners.

D *People's Committee Guesthouse*. In a competitive field this is one of the grottiest holes to spend a night in. Too late you realize your driver was not joking. The town is powered by a feeble generator that comes on at dusk providing just enough wattage (or should it be ampage?) to broadcast the Communist Party's latest propaganda over the public tannoy system and to excite light bulbs up to the equivalent of about two guttering candles. One or two drips of water may be coaxed from the tap but more likely the woman in charge will deliver two buckets of unclean water while muttering about the current drought and El Niño. Sheets have not been washed for months and while the mosquito nets *are* adequate for approximately half a bed the beds have to be cunningly manoeuvered so as to fall under the reach of the net while also keeping the door propped shut.

Sleeping

Eating Eat early. Little cafés around the market. May only have instant noodles at night. Eggs for breakfast. But washed down with the delicious local rice wine (purple or white and often sweetened with honey) it tastes like a feast. Wine costs less than US$0.50 a bottle. Bottled water and biscuits can be bought as too can the runny local honey but not much to eat with it.

Transport **Road** **Bus**: connections with Lai Chau and Phong Tho. A 40 kilometre detour off Highway 12. The first 20 kilometres is possibly the most spectacular and terrifying drive in Vietnam.

Directory **Communications** Post Office: near market.

Phong Tho

Colour map 1, grid A2

A small market town which will detain no one for long but a pleasant enough lunch stop or adequate overnighter for those with engine problems. The surrounding hamlets are home to the White Thai, Ha Nhi and Dao Tuyen ethnicities who can be encountered either at home or in Phong Tho's early morning market.

Sleeping **D** *Tam Duong*, on main drag, T875288. A surprisingly clean and comfortable little place, 8 fan rooms, hot water and a cheerful welcome. **D** *Phung Tam*. A little further along, one branch on either side of the road.

Eating A jolly good little road-sider opposite *Tam Duong Hotel* will knock up a delicious meal seemingly out of nothing.

Transport **Road** **Bus**: daily bus connections with Sapa and Lao Cai; foreigners get charged double the 35,000d local fare for the journey to Lao Cai. Also bus connections with Lai Chau.

Tam Duong

Sights
Colour map 1, grid A2

The chief attraction of Tam Duong is the colour and costume of the minority people, White and Flower Hmông, Dao Khau, Giay and White and Black Thai. There are some interesting walks to Na Bo (Pu Na minority village), Giang (Nhang minority) and (Hon minority) villages. Na Bo is seven kilometres from Tam Duong from which Giang is a further 1.5 kilometres and Hon a further five kilometres. Alternatively a motorbike and driver can be hired for around 80,000d. Pu Na and Nhang people are similar in culture and costume.

About 35 kilometres southeast of Tam Duong Highway 4D swings sharply to the northeast and the altitude climbs abruptly into the Hoang Lien Son range. Here is harsh mountain scenery on a scale previously unencountered on this circuit of Northwest Vietnam. The geology is hard and crystalline as is the skyline: sharp jagged peaks punch up into sky. Vertical cliffs drop below and soar above, friendly rolling scenery has been replaced by 3,000 metre high mountains.

Sleeping **D** *Phuong Thanh*, T875235. A/c and fan rooms, clean, comfortable, lovely views. **D-E** *People's Committee Guesthouse*. Some a/c, basic, clean. **E** guesthouse at the bus station.

Eating *Hong Nhung*, and others near the bus station.

From Lai Chau, Highway 12 heads almost due north following the picturesque Na river valley towards the Chinese border. At Pa So, 10 kilometres from China (border crossing closed), take Highway 4D, southeast. Tam Duong is in fact a collection of three small settlements, all new. **Road Bus**: connections with Sapa and Lao Cai and south with Lai Chau.

Transport

Sapa

Sapa remains a gem. Despite the countless thousands of tourists who have poured in every year for the past decade it has retained its charm and beauty. It may not feel so special at weekends when every tourist café in Hanoi buses in its independent travellers (and the minority people become just that) but during the week the few visitors who remain will have the town to themselves (bar the locals, of course): winsome Hmông girls, long quiet walks and the pick of the hotels.

Phone code: 020
Colour map 1, grid A2

Ins and outs

Most people arrive in Sapa on a tour from Hanoi, a 385 kilometre, 10 hour journey via Lao Cai. However, it is easy enough to travel by public transport, even if the level of comfort may be less. Those undertaking the full northern loop usually approach Sapa from the west, via Lai Chau, Dien Bien Phu and Son La. It is also possible to get to Sapa by train – or at least complete much of the journey by rail. There are daily trains from Hanoi to Lao Cai, 38 kilometres northeast of town.

Getting there

Sapa is a charming town, small enough to walk around and high enough to make walking a pleasurable activity.

Getting around

The town

Originally a Black Hmông settlement Sapa was first discovered by Europeans when a Jesuit missionary visited the area in 1918. By 1932 news of the quasi-European climate and beautiful scenery of the Tonkinese Alps had spread throughout French Indochina. Like Dalat in the south it served as a retreat for French administrators when the heat of the plains became unbearable. By the 1940s an estimated 300 French buildings – including a sizeable prison and the summer residence of the Governor of French Indochina – had sprung up. Until 1947 there were more French than Vietnamese, which became renowned for its many parks and flower gardens. However, as the security situation began to worsen during the latter days of French rule, the expatriate community steadily dwindled, and by 1953 virtually all had gone. Immediately following the French defeat at Dien Bien Phu in 1954, victorious Vietnamese forces razed a large number of Sapa's French buildings to the ground.

At 1,650 metres Sapa enjoys warm days and cool evenings in the summer but gets very cold in winter. Snow falls on average every couple of years and settles on the surrounding peaks of the Hoang Lien Son Mountains. Rain and cloud can occur at any time of year but the wettest months are May to September with nearly 1,000 millimetres of rain in July and August alone.

The huge scale of the Fan Si Pan range gives Sapa an Alpine feel and this impression is reinforced by Haut Savoie vernacular architecture with steep pitched roofs, window shutters and chimneys. But in an alluring blend of European and Vietnamese vegetation the gardeners of Sapa cultivate their foxgloves and apricot trees alongside thickets of bamboo and delicate orchids, just yards above the paddy fields.

The North

Ethnic minorities

Distinctly oriental but un-Vietnamese in manner and appearance are the Hmông, Dao and other minorities who come to Sapa to trade. Interestingly the Hmông (normally so reticent) have been the first to seize the commercial opportunities presented by tourism; they are engaging but persistent vendors of hand-loomed indigo clothing and handicrafts. Of the latter, particularly notable is a little brass and bamboo Jew's-harp. The Dao have also now started to latch on to the commercial opportunities presented by these tall, red-haired and red-faced strangers and have altered their weaving looms accordingly. Most other minorities hurry in and out of Sapa as quickly as business permits and appear anxious to have nothing to do with foreigners.

Saturday night is always a big occasion for Black Hmông and Red Dao teenagers in the Sapa area, as youngsters from miles around come to the so-called **Love Market** to find a partner. The girls sing or play taped music to attract the boys. A number of visitors have been dismayed by insensitive behaviour on the part of some tourists. The regular market is at its busiest and best on Sunday morning.

Sights

Church

Sapa is a pleasant place to relax and unwind, particularly after the arduous journey from Dien Bien Phu. Being comparatively new it has no important sights but several French buildings in and around are worth visiting. Most spectacular is the **church** in the centre of Sapa built in 1930. Recently rebuilt, the church was wrecked in 1952 by French artillerymen shelling the adjacent building in which Viet Minh troops were billeted. In the churchyard are the tombs of two former priests, including that of Father Thinh, who was brutally murdered. In the autumn of 1952 Father Thinh confronted a monk named Giao Linh who had been discovered having an affair with a nun at the Ta Phin seminary. Giao Linh obviously took great exception to the priest's interference, for shortly after this, when Father Thinh's congregation arrived at Sapa church for mass one foggy November morning, they discovered his decapitated body lying next to the altar.

Dragon's Jaw Hill

Ham Rong or **Dragon's Jaw Hill**, on which the district's TV transmitter is stuck, is located immediately above Sapa town centre and can be climbed by following the steps behind the *Ham Rong Hotel*. Apart from offering excellent views of the town, the path winds its way through a number of interesting limestone outcrops and miniature grottoes as it nears the summit.

Sapa was one of the places to be invaded by the Chinese in the 1979 border skirmish. Chinese soldiers found and destroyed the holiday retreat of the Vietnamese Communist Party Secretary-General Le Duan, no doubt infuriated by such uncomradely display of bourgeois tendencies.

Sapa Museum

This is located near the row of restaurants. The museum houses ethnic minority costumes and other ethnological exhibits relating to the Sapa region. ■ *5,000d. Open 0800-1130, 1330-1600 Saturday and Sunday only, at other times contact Service of Culture and Information opposite.*

Excursions

Abandoned French seminary

Near Ta Phin, the names of the Bishop who consecrated it and the presiding Governor of Indochina can be seen engraved on stones at the west end. Built in 1942 and under the ecclesiastical jurisdiction of the Parish of Sapa, the building was destroyed 10 years later by militant Vietnamese hostile to the intentions of the order.

Beyond the seminary the path descends into a valley of beautifully sculpted rice terraces past Black Hmông settlements to Ta Phin. Shy and reluctant people. ■ *Getting there: take the road eight kilometres east towards Lao Cai then a track left up towards Ta Phin, three kilometres to monastery four kilometres further to Ta Phin.*

Ta Phin Red Dao village

At 3,143 metres, Vietnam's highest mountain, is a three-day trek from Sapa. It lies on a bearing of 240° from Sapa; as the crow flies it is nine kilometres but by track it is 14 kilometres and involves dropping to 1,200 metres and crossing a rickety bamboo bridge before ascending. Enquire at Auberge or Cat Cat guesthouses for a local guide. A three-day expedition is recommended. There are few suitable spots for camping other than at the altitudes suggested below:

Mount Fan Si Pan

The North

Around Sapa With acknowledgment to Mr Dang Trung

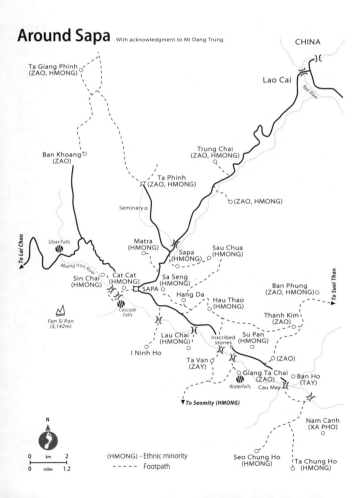

CHINA

Ta Giang Phinh (ZAO, HMONG)

Lao Cai

Red River

Ban Khoang (ZAO)

Trung Chai (ZAO, HMONG)

Ta Phinh (ZAO, HMONG)

Seminary

(ZAO, HMONG)

To Lai Chau

Silver Falls

Muong Hoa River

Matra (HMONG)

Sapa (HMONG)

Sau Chua (HMONG)

Sin Chai (HMONG)

Cat Cat (HMONG)

SAPA

Sa Seng (HMONG)

Hang Da

Ban Phung (ZAO, HMONG)

To Suoi Than

Cascade Falls

Hau Thao (HMONG)

Thanh Kim (ZAO)

Fan Si Pan (3,142m)

Lau Chai (HMONG)

Inscribed stones

Su Pan (HMONG)

I Ninh Ho

Ta Van (ZAY)

(ZAO)

Giang Ta Chai (ZAO)

Ban Ho (TAY)

Waterfalls

Cau May

To Seomity (HMONG)

Nam Canh (XA PHO)

N

0   km   2
0   miles   1.2

(HMONG) - Ethnic minority
- - - - - Footpath

Seo Chung Ho (HMONG)

Ta Chung Ho (HMONG)

Bridge of confusion

Cau may *means rattan bridge; it can also be translated as cloudy bridge. Originally all bridges were rattan, today only one. Villagers all refer to their own bridges as* cau may *and insist that theirs is the only true one.*

Day 1: Depart Sapa (1,650 metres) 0800. Lunch at 1,400 metres, 1200 noon. Camp at 2,285 metres.
Day 2: Reach summit late afternoon. Return to camp at 2,800 metres.
Day 3: Descend to Sapa.

Camping equipment is not available for hire but rucksacks, boots, fleeces and waterproofs can be bought in Hanoi. Porters are unwilling to carry more than about six kilos and are therefore of little use. The ascent involves some steep scrambles which are quite nasty in wet conditions. Only the very fit will make it to the summit.

Lau Chai village of the Black Hmông, Ta Van village of the Zay This is a round trip of 20 kilometres taking in minority villages and beautiful scenery. Head out of town in a southeast direction (past the *Auberge Guesthouse* – see Around Sapa map), Lao Chai is six kilometres on the far valley side. Follow the track leading from the right-hand side of the road down to the valley floor, cross the river by the footbridge (*cau may*) and then walk up through the rice fields into Lao Chai village. You will find Ta Van two kilometres further on.

A leisurely stroll through these villages could well be the highlight of a trip to Vietnam. It is chance to observe rural life led in reasonable prosperity. Wet rice forms the staple income, weaving for the tourist market puts a bit of meat on the table. Here nature is kind, there is rich soil and no shortage of water. Again we see how the landscape has been engineered to suit man's needs. The terracing is on an awesome scale (in places more than 100 steps): centuries of labour to convert steep slopes into level fields which can be flooded to grow rice. Technologically and in no sense pejoratively the villages might be described as belonging to a bamboo age. Bamboo trunks carry water huge distances from spring to village; water flows across barriers and tracks in bamboo aqueducts; mechanical rice huskers made of bamboo are driven by water requiring no human effort; houses are held up with bamboo; bottoms are parked on bamboo chairs and tobacco and other substances are inhaled through bamboo pipes. Any path chosen will lead to some hamlet or other; the Hmông in villages further from Sapa tend to be more reserved and suspicious: their fields and houses are often securely fenced off.

Cross back to the north side of the river by the suspension bridge. A dip in the deep pools of the Muong Hoa river is refreshingly invigorating. **Engraved stones** are a further two kilometres southeast (ie away from Sapa) by the side of road; they are believed to be inscribed in ancient Hmông. It is to be hoped they survive the current road repair and widening. The return walk to Sapa from the inscribed stones is a steady 10-kilometre uphill climb. Exhausting work but stimulated by the views and the air and fuelled by hard boiled eggs and warm Lao Cai beer from roadside shacks and the prospect of cold beer at home it is a pleasure, not an ordeal. In the late afternoon sun the rice glows with more shades of green than you would have thought possible and the lengthening shadows cast the entire landscape into vivid three dimensional relief – even through a camera lens.

Cat Cat and Sin Chai Villages The track heading west from Sapa through the market area offers either a short five kilometres round trip walk to Cat Cat Black Hmông village or a longer 10 kilometres round-trip walk to Sin Chai Black Hmông village; both options take in some beautiful scenery. The path to Cat Cat leads off to the left of the Sin Chai track after about one kilometre, following the line of pylons down through the rice paddies to Cat Cat village; beyond the village over the river bridge you can visit the **Cascade waterfall** (from which the village takes its name) and the ruins of a former French hydro-electric power station. Sin Chai village is four kilometres northwest of here.

The **Silver Falls** are 12 kilometres west of Sapa on the Lai Chau road, spectacular following rain. Hardly worth a special visit but if passing it's quite nice to stop for a paddle in the cold pools.

Essentials

A host of guesthouses has sprung up to cater for Sapa's rejuvenation. Prices tend to rise June-October to coincide with north hemisphere university vacs and at weekends. Hoteliers are accustomed to bargaining; healthy competition ensures rates in Sapa are fair market prices.

Sleeping
■ *on map*
Price codes:
see inside front cover

The North

A+-A *Victoria Sapa*, T871522, F871539. Opened in 1998 with 76 rooms, a nice position above the town and a pleasant aspect this hotel is easily the best in town. Comfortable well appointed rooms with that oh so important bath tub it is a lovely place in which to relax and enjoy the peace but it does not come cheap: the laundry bill after a drive from Dien Bien Phu would pay for a weekend at most other hotels in town. Because most people who can afford to stay at a hotel like the *Victoria Sapa* also dislike rough 10 hour journeys, the management have begun to offer soft sleeper berths on the Friday night sleeper from Hanoi. They even have plans to provide a purpose-built carriage along with restaurant car.

Sapa

Highway 4 to Lai Chau & Darling Hotel

To Cat Cat village

Highway 4 to Lao Cai

Photo shop

Football Pitch

Pharmacy

Weather station

Market

HAM RONG HILL

N

0   metres   50
0   yards   55

■ **Sleeping**		● **Eating**
1 Auberge	7 Post Office Guesthouse	1 Camelia
2 Bank Guesthouse	8 Rose	2 Chapa
3 Cat Cat Guesthouse	9 Student	3 Fan Si Pan
4 Ham Rong Guesthouse	10 Sunrise	
5 Forestry Guesthouse	11 Victoria	
6 Observatory Guesthouse	12 Waterfall	

B *Green Bamboo*, T871214. A lovely valley side location just beyond Auberge, breakfast included and nice enough rooms but a little on the pricey side.

C *Ham Rong Guesthouse*, T871251, F871303. French colonial villa, comfortable accommodation with good (but expensive) restaurant. **C** *Forestry Guesthouse*, T871230, F820080. All with private bathrooms and wonderful views, up a steep drive.

D *Auberge Guesthouse*, T871243, F871666. Dang Trung, the French-speaking owner shows guests his wonderful informal garden with pride: sweet peas, honeysuckle, snap dragons, foxgloves, roses and irises – all familiar to visitors from temperate climes – grow alongside sub-Alpine flora and a fantastic collection of orchids. The rooms are simply furnished but clean and boast hot water showers and log fires in winter. **D** *Cat Cat*, T871387. On the west (Cat Cat) side of town through the market, run by a half-Hmông lady, friendly, helpful, basic accommodation but clean, private bathroom, hot water, terrace, restaurant. **D** *Post Office Guesthouse*, T871244. Shower, toilet attached, clean and comfortable. **D** *Nha Khach Ke Hoach* (*Planning Committee Guest House*), T871289. 8 twin rooms with adjoining shower/toilet, newly-renovated French colonial villa, comfortable accommodation, no restaurant. **D-E** *Nha Khach Ngan Hang* (*Bank Guesthouse*), T871210. More expensive rooms en suite bathrooms, hot water, cheaper ones share, friendly. Recommended. **D** *Phuong Nam Guesthouse*, nice views and reasonable food.

E *Rose Guesthouse*, T871263. Rent jeeps and motorbikes. **E-F** *Darling*, T871349. A short walk from town to this secluded building but for those seeking peace worth every step of the way, simple, clean and a warm French welcome, stunning views and a colourful garden, top floor is dorm.

F *Observatory Guesthouse*. Very cheap dormitory accommodation, squeezes everyone in. *Nha San Dan Toc (Ethnic House)*. It is possible to spend the night in one of the ethnic houses in the Sapa district. Those of the Black Hmông are probably the best bet, though facilities are considerably more basic than in the Muong and Thai stilted houses of Hoa Binh, Mai Chau and Son La and travellers will need to bring their own bedding materials and mosquito net. A contribution of around 30,000d should be made.

Eating *Auberge*. Popular terrace, a lovely breakfast setting, full menu including vegetarian
● *on map* and several types of rice wine, also sells film and camera batteries. *Camelia*, just through market on the right. Long menu, delicious food and rice wine, very fair prices, sets a standard by which value for money should be judged: if there were more restaurants like this the French would never have left. *Chapa*, over-lit. Rather grubby but decent food. *Fansipan*. Good food and fruit wine. Rice and noodle stalls in the market.

Shopping Sapa is the place for buying ethnic clothes. Nowhere in Vietnam has the range of shirts, baggy trousers, caps, bags and other garments of Sapa. Sold by vendors or in shops, a lot is used but all the more authentic for that. A range of temperate fruit, plums and apricots, also delicious baby pineapples.

Transport 38 kilometres from Lao Cai, 385 kilometres from Hanoi (about 10 hours). **Road** Roads to Sapa have been improved but heavy rain and trucks can destroy a good road surface very quickly. **Bus**: connections with Lao Cai usually 0600 and 1330, US$3, 90 minutes. Honda ôm, jeep (US$3 per person) or local bus 20,000d from Lao Cai to Sapa. **Train** Connections from Hanoi to Lao Cai depart Hanoi 0530 arrive Lao Cai 1535; depart Hanoi 2020 arrive Lao Cai 0610. From Lao Cai to Hanoi depart 0940, arrive Hanoi 2015, depart Lao Cai 1830, arrive Hanoi 0445. Cost 155,000-180,000d depending on comfort level. Tickets from Lao Cai can be booked at the Post Office.

No man's land

Travellers with the correct exit visa for one country and the incorrect entry visa have often found themselves stranded on the bridge. This is particularly serious as most travellers have only single entry visas and can't get back into the country they've just left. Local traders are now accustomed to the almost daily battle of wills between *the two sets of immigration officials as forlorn visitors plead with these uniformed guards to release them from their Kafkaesque nightmare. Vietnamese officials usually prove the most intransigent. Keep a few dollar bills handy. Land travellers to Cambodia and Laos also take note.*

Banks The bank will change money US$ cash, most hotels too but at poor rates. Convert before you travel: as elsewhere in the Northwest beads and gold go further than plastic.

Directory

Lao Cai

Lao Cai is the most important border crossing with China. A two-way flow of people and trade cross through the town each day. But whereas the balance of human traffic is roughly equal the value of traded goods is highly one-sided: an endless flow of quality products from China's modern factories wreaks havoc on Vietnam's hapless state-owned enterprises struggling to fill quotas of shoddy goods that no one will buy.

Colour map 1, grid A2

This is open to railway passengers and pedestrians with the correct exit and entry visas for both countries (see box No Man's Land, above). From Ha Khau (Hekou) on the Chinese side rail connections with Kunming (20 hours). Visas into Vietnam must be obtained in Hong Kong or Peking and specify the Lao Cai crossing; they normally take a week to process and are not obtainable at the border. Visas for China must be obtained in Hanoi and must specify the Lao Cai crossing. Travellers crossing on foot must report to the Customs House south of the bridge and near level crossing for passport stamping and customs clearance, also to buy a 2,000d bridge ticket.

The border crossing

An important north-south transit stop for traders with caravans of pack oxen or horses since time immemorial, Lao Cai has changed hands many times over the past thousand years as rival Chinese, Vietnamese and ethnic minority chieftains fought for ascendancy in the region. The town itself dates back at least to 1463, when the Viet kings established it as the capital of their northernmost province of Hung Hoa.

Lao Cai fell to French in 1889 and thereafter served as an important administrative centre and garrison town. The direct rail link to Hanoi was built during the first decade of this century, a project remarkable for the 25,000 Vietnamese conscripted labourers who died during its seven-year construction period.

Following the Vietnamese invasion of Cambodia in late 1978 China, Cambodia's ally, responded in February 1979 by launching a massive invasion of northern Vietnam, 'to teach the Vietnamese a lesson'. Over 600,000 Chinese troops were deployed occupying territory from Phong Tho in the Northwest to Cao Bang and Lang Son in the Northeast. From the start of the campaign, however, the poorly trained Chinese forces encountered stiff resistance from local militia, and as the Vietnamese army got into gear the Chinese invasion force ground to a halt. After two weeks Chinese troops had penetrated no more than 30 kilometres into Vietnamese territory and with an estimated 20,000 casualties already incurred by the People's Army, the Chinese Government withdrew its troops, declaring the operation 'a great success'.

The North

Trade with China, much of it illegal, has turned this small town into a community of (dong if not dollar) millionaires and Lao Cai is experiencing something of a construction boom. Huge boulevards flanked by enormous local government buildings are sprouting up in the main part of town, west of the Red River. Other than for border-crossers Lao Cai holds little appeal.

Sleeping
■ *on map*
Price codes:
see inside front cover

Owing to the essentially ephemeral nature of Lao Cai's visitors hotels tend to be not much more than a bed for the night. The hotels are clustered in the border end of town, convenient for pedestrians but less so for rail travellers.

C-D *Binh Minh*, 39 Nguyen Hue, T830085. Perhaps the priciest of the hotels listed here but not necessarily any better, a/c, hot water, fridge and TV in top end rooms and fan only in cheaper. **D** *Hanoi*, 19 Nguyen Hue, T832487, F832486. 9 rooms all with a/c, hot water and fridge, perfectly OK. **D** *Hong Ha*, 26 Nguyen Hue, T830007. Sign outside just says 'Hotel', 10 a/c rooms, 4 fan rooms, next to bank and opposite Post Office. **D** *Ngoc Chung*, 27 Nguyen Hue, T832199. Just 6 rooms, quite busy, a/c, hot water and fridge, neat and clean. **D** *Petrolimex*, 67 Nguyen Hue, T831540. On a busy corner, 10 rooms, a/c, hot water, fridge. **D** *Song Hong*, facing border, near bridge, T830004. Simple but clean, 13 rooms overlooking China, a/c, hot water, quiet, probably the pick of the bunch. **D-E** *Post Office*, behind Post Office, T830006. The cheapest and a bit grubby, but quite friendly and a timely reminder to do something with all those unwritten postcards.

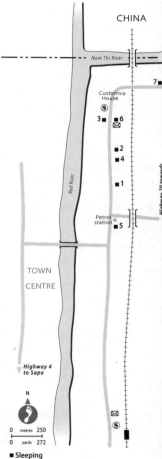

Lao Cai & Border Crossing to China

■ **Sleeping**
1 Binh Minh Guesthouse
2 Hanoi
3 Hong Ha
4 Ngoc Chung Guesthouse
5 Petrolimex Guesthouse
6 Post Office Guesthouse
7 Song Hong

Eating Nothing special to report.

Transport 38 kilometres from Sapa, 347 kilometres from Hanoi. **Road Bus**: connections with Sapa (2 hours) and Hanoi. **Train** Trains from Hanoi to Lao Cai depart Hanoi 0530 arrive Lao Cai 1535; depart Hanoi 2020 arrive Lao Cai 0610. From Lao Cai to Hanoi depart 0940, arrive Hanoi 2015, depart Lao Cai 1830, arrive Hanoi 0445. Cost 155,000-175,000d depending on comfort level. There is a twice weekly train service between Hanoi and Kunming (Con Minh) in each direction (one Vietnamese and one Chinese train) depart Monday and Saturday. Depart Hanoi 2130, arrive Lao Cai 0730, depart Lao Cai 0920 arrive Kunming 0500 next

The North

day. Hanoi-Kunming is 277,000d soft sleeper on the Vietnamese train but only 222,000d on the Chinese train, hard sleeper 199,000d Vietnamese and 159,000d Chinese. The station is 2-3 kilometres south of the hotel area so those arriving from China will need to take a *xe ôm* (around 10,000d).

Banks Next to railway station, cash only and just south of border opposite Post Office. **Communications** Post Office: opposite railway station and just south of border.

Directory

Bac Ha

Bac Ha is really only notable for one thing and that is its Sunday market. That 'one thing', however, is very special. Hundreds of local minority people flock in from the surrounding districts to shop and socialize while tourists from all corners of the earth pour in to watch them do it. Otherwise there is very little of interest and neither the appeal or comforts of Sapa.

The market
Phone code: 020
Colour map 1, grid A3

The Sunday market (0700-1300) draws in the Flower Hmông, Phu La, Dao Tuyen, La Chi and Tay – the latter being Vietnam's largest ethnic minority. It is a riot of colour and fun. While the women trade and gossip the men consume quantities of rice wine. By late morning they can no longer walk so are heaved onto donkeys by their wives and led home.

There are a number of walks to outlying villages. Pho village of the Flower Hmông is around four kilometres north; Thai Giang Pho village of Tay is four kilometres east and Na Hoi and Na Ang villages also of the Tay are two to four kilometres west.

C-D *Tran Sin*, T880240. Opposite market, clean and comfortable, restaurant. **D** *Anh Duong*, T880329. Opposite market, 12 rooms with toilet and shower. **D** *Buu Dien* (Post Office), T880360. 5 rooms with toilet/shower and hot water. **D** *Dang Khoa*, T880290. 14 rooms, basic but clean. **D** *Sao Mai*, T880288. Probably the best, a short hike from the centre, quiet, clean, 20 fan rooms with hot water.

Sleeping
■ *on map*
Price codes:
see inside front cover

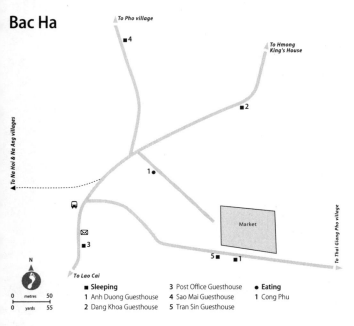

Bac Ha

■ **Sleeping**
1 Anh Duong Guesthouse
2 Dang Khoa Guesthouse
3 Post Office Guesthouse
4 Sao Mai Guesthouse
5 Tran Sin Guesthouse

● **Eating**
1 Cong Phu

Eating
● *on map*
A couple of the hotels have restaurants, otherwise there is *Cong Phu*, don't use the menu – most dishes are 'off', look in the pots in the kitchen, no fridge, no ice.

Transport **Train** From Lao Cai or Hanoi (10 hours) to Pho Lu, bus up to Bac Ha.

Road The drive from Sapa to Hanoi is very long – those intending just a quick detour to Bac Ha on the way home face a gruelling day – Sapa to Bac Ha is 3 hours, Bac Ha to Hanoi around 10 hours. Bus to Lao Cai departs 0900; 2 buses daily to Pho Lu 0900 and 1100, 15-20,000d. **Bus**: the simplest, as so often, is to buy a tour from a Hanoi travellers' café: Saturday night in Sapa (watching the Love Market), early departure for Bac Ha to see the market. Some hotels in Sapa run a Sunday morning minibus excursion to Bac Ha.

Routes **From Lao Cai to Hanoi** the road begins in a beautiful valley, colourful minorities, rice, cinnamon (in places the air is scented) and tea. By **Viet Tri** it has become a drab industrial landscape and remains so all the way back. Tam Dao (see page 86) is a detour that can be taken en route back to Hanoi.

Northeast

Rugged, but lacking the lofty grandeur of Northwest Vietnam, the scenery of the Northeast consists of limestone hills dissected by fast flowing streams – tributaries of the Gam and Red rivers – hurrying south with their burden of silt. Altitudes decline towards the coast and the river systems of the eastern quarter flow north into China and the You Jiang River. Once densely wooded, centuries of slash and burn cultivation and logging have taken their toll on the region and little tree cover remains. Localized landscapes draw admiration but extensive tracts are unremarkable. Hilltribe minorities, particularly the Dao, Nung and Tày are much in evidence.

Despite its sparse population Northeast Vietnam features prominently in the annals of nationalist and revolutionary history: decisive victories over invading Chinese, armed resistance against the French and momentous events in the founding of the Vietnamese Communist Party took place here.

Unlike Northwest Vietnam which has so conveniently aligned its attractions along one road circuit Northeast Vietnam is somewhat fragmented and until important roads are built or improved the traveller wishing to see everything must be prepared to double back over quite long distances. For those wishing to make forays from Hanoi into Northeast Vietnam the situation is better, broadly speaking there is a choice: Ha Giang and the far north or the Bac-Cao-Lang region.

The road to Ha Giang

Ha Giang can be reached comfortably in a day. Having acquired a special permit issued by the authorities there, it is possible to continue further north to the remote Dong Van-Meo Vac region. Beyond Meo Vac the road is impassable to motorized vehicles and travellers must therefore return to Tuyen Quang before proceeding to other destinations in Northeast Vietnam such as Cao Bang and Lang Son (although see Box Off-Road in the Northeast for an exception to this rule).

For much of its length the well-maintained Highway 2 follows the Lo River northwards through some delightful scenery. During the early stages of the journey as the road travels past the eastern shores of the Thac Ba Lake tea plantations may be seen everywhere, but northwards from Ham Yen, 41 kilometres beyond Tuyen Quang, it is orange plantations which carpet the hillsides.

Tuyen Quang Province has a large ethnic minority population, and not long after leaving the provincial capital travellers will begin to see people from the two main ethnic groups of this province, the Tày and the Dao (pronounced 'Zao'). The delightful little town of **Vinh Tuy**, near the banks of the Lo River, is a possible lunch stop. Boats may be seen on the river most days, dredging the bed for gold.

Bac Quang is a sizeable market town located some 60 kilometres before Ha Giang at the junction with Highway 279, the mountain road west to Bao Yen in Lao Cai Province. Unfortunately this road is currently impassable to motorized transport.

Ha Giang

Phone code: 019
Colour map 1, grid A3

The provincial capital of Ha Giang lies on the banks of the Lo River just south of its confluence with the River Mien, perched picturesquely between the beautiful Cam and Mo Neo mountains.

Archaeological evidence unearthed at Doi Thong (Pine Hill) in Ha Giang town indicates that there was human settlement in the region at least 30,000 years ago. It was during the Bronze Age, however, that the most important flowering of early culture took place under the Tay Vu, one of the most important tribes of the Hung kingdom of Van Lang whose centre of power was in the Ha Giang region. Some of the most beautiful Dong Son bronze drums were found in Ha Giang Province, most notably in the Meo Vac region where the tradition of making bronze drums for ceremonial purposes continues even to this day amongst the Lo Lo and Pu Peo ethnic minority communities.

The original settlement in Ha Giang lay on the east bank of the Lo River and it was here that the French established themelves following the conquest of the area in 1886. The town subsequently became an important military base, a development confirmed in 1905 when Ha Giang was formally established as one of four North Vietnamese military territories of French Indochina.

The Ha Giang area saw a number of important ethnic minority rebellions against the French during the early years of the colonial period, the most important being that of the Dao who rose up in 1901 under the leadership of Trieu Tien Kien and Trieu Tai Loc. The revolt was quickly put down and Trieu Tien Kien was killed during the fighting, but in 1913 Trieu Tai Loc rose up again, this time supported by another family member known as Trieu Tien Tien, marching under the slogans:

- 'No corvees, no taxes for the French,
- Drive out the French to recover our country,
- Liberty for the Dao'.

Carrying white flags embroidered with the four ideograms *To Quoc Bach Ky* (White Flag of the Fatherland) and wearing white conical hats (hence the French name 'The White Hat Revolt'), the rebels launched attacks against Tuyen Quang, Lao Cai and Yen Bai and managed to keep French troops at bay until 1915 when the revolt was savagely repressed. Hundreds of the insurgents were subsequently deported and 67 condemned to death by the colonial courts.

Like Cao Bang and Lang Son, Ha Giang was badly damaged during the border war with China in 1979 and has since undergone extensive reconstruction.

Sights in Ha Giang The **Ha Giang Museum** is next to Yen Bien Bridge in the centre of town. It contains important archaeological, historical and ethnological artefacts from in and around the region, including a very helpful display of ethnic minority costumes. Unfortunately the museum is normally locked and it is not always possible to visit.

Located close to the east bank of the River Lo in the old quarter of the town, **Ha Giang Market** is a daily market although it is busiest on Sunday. Tày, Nung and Red Dao people are always in evidence here, as are members of northern Ha Giang Province's prolific White Hmông ethnic minority.

Doi Thong or **Pine Hill** lies just behind the main Ha Giang Market. The pine trees are newly planted but the hill itself is an area of ancient human

....

Off-road in the North East

Ha Giang to Cho Ra via Bac Me, Bao Lac and Tinh Tuc *Those with sufficient faith in their Minsks and in their own ability to make running repairs to their bike can take an alternative route through some wild and unexplored country which will enable them to press forward without doubling back; but only in the dry season. The road from Ha Giang to Bao Lac (Highway 34) is passable by motorbike or jeep until Bac Me, although there are a couple of rivers to ford which will be impassable in the rainy season. From Bac Meon to Bao Lac is also very hard going and from Bac Me only motorcycles can continue over the rickety suspension bridges and through*

narrow jungle trails. Bao Lac from Ha Giang is about 12 hours and only worth it if you enjoy off-road biking. Bao Lac is a small town but visitors can put up for the night at the People's Committee Guesthouse. There is a busy morning market but this far from anywhere food is limited (no coffee or bread).

From Bao Lac to Tinh Tuc takes a whole day too; a very difficult road, again only for experienced bikers. Tinh Tuc is a tin mining town in a pretty valley. It has a simple but adequate hotel next to the Post Office; also a canteen type diner with very cold beer. Tinh Tuc to Cho Ra (for Ba Be Lake) is passable, scenic and rewarding.

....

settlement believed to date back some 30,000 years to the Son Vi period. Many ancient axe-heads and other primitive weapons were discovered on the hill during land clearance; these are now in the local museum and in the History Museum in Hanoi.

D *Electricity Company Guesthouse*, Tran Hung Dao St, T866317. 10 a/c rooms with adjoining shower/toilet. **D** *Huong Giang*, Tran Hung Dao St, T866015. 6 a/c and fan rooms, basic but comfortable accommodation. **D-E** *Ha Giang*, Tran Hung Dao St, T866640. 15 rooms, some a/c, some fan with outside shared facilities, basic with adjacent restaurant, steam bath/massage. **D-E** *River Mien*, Nguyen Trai St, T866746. Picturesque setting on a hill overlooking the river, 13 a/c and fan rooms, all with adjoining shower/toilet. **D-E** *Yen Bien*, Nguyen Trai St, T866333. The biggest hotel in town, 36 a/c and fan rooms, all have shower/toilet, restaurant. **Sleeping**

Tourist Company Quan Com Pho, Tran Hung Dao St. The most traveller-friendly place to eat in Ha Giang, located next to the *Ha Giang Hotel*. Another restaurant next door. There are also numerous other small places to eat located down side streets off Tran Hung Dao and on the other side of town near the main market. **Eating**

Tea is speciality product of the region, which grows many different varieties including green, yellow, black and flower-scented. Best known is *Shan Tuyet* tea, a flavoursome variety which is exported. **Shopping**

Ha Giang lies 333 kilometres and 6 hours north of Hanoi. **Road Bus**: early morning departures from Hanoi's Long Bien terminal. Four-wheel drive vehicle recommended in the far north, whatever the season. **Transport**

Communications Tour companies & travel agents *Ha Giang Tourist Company*, Tran Hung Dao St, T867054. Permits for Dong Van-Meo Vac region obtainable here, 150,000d, may take a day to issue. **Directory**

Dong Van-Meo Vac Region

Ins and outs All foreign visitors are required to obtain a special permit before proceeding beyond Ha Giang into the remote Dong Van/Meo Vac area on the Chinese border. This can be obtained either directly from the local police or alternatively through the Ha Giang Tourist Company – one possible advantage of booking a tour in Hanoi. Local bus services are infrequent and slow. The roads north of Ha Giang are in extremely poor condition and the going is very hard, four-wheel drive vehicle highly advisable. Ha Giang to Dong Van via Yen Minh is 148 kilometres, 7½ hours; Dong Van to Meo Vac 22 kilometres, 90 minutes. Returning from Meo Vac to Ha Giang head straight to Yen Minh via Highways 176 and 180 by-passing Dong Van and cutting off 22 kilometres. Since both Dong Van and Meo Vac are located very close to the Chinese border hill-walking by foreigners around both towns is forbidden, making the number of things to do in Dong Van and Meo Vac somewhat limited.

Local villages This is the northernmost tip of Vietnam, close to the Chinese border and just 30 kilometres south of the Tropic of Cancer. The primary tourist attraction of the area are the colourful costumes of the ethnic people and the fabulous mountainous scenery which compensate for the rather arduous journey along very bumpy roads. One particular highlight of the trip is the Ma Phi Leng Pass between Dong Van and Meo Vac, an area of breathtaking natural beauty.

Quan Ba is 45 kilometres from Ha Giang. the road climbs up the Quan Ba Pass to 'Heaven's Gate' – identifiable by the TV transmitter mast to the left of the summit – from where there are wonderful views of the Quan Ba valley with its extraordinary row of uniformly-shaped hills. Quan Ba has a Sunday market, one of the largest in the region which attracts not only White Hmông, Red Dao, Dao Ao Dai and Tày people but also members of the Bo Y ethnic minority who live in the mountains around the town.

Yen Minh is located 98 kilometres northwest of Ha Giang and is a convenient place to stop for lunch on the way to Dong Van and Meo Vac – a possible overnight stop for those planning to spend a little longer in the region. It too has a bustling Sunday market where in addition to the ethnic groups mentioned above can be seen Giay, Pu Peo, Co Lao, Lo Lo and the local branch of Red Dao.

The White Hmông village of **Lang Si** lies at the top of the Lang Si Pass (117 kilometres from Ha Giang); an ethnic minority market involving mainly White Hmông people is held here every six days. Just above the village, near the crest of the hill heading over towards Sa Phin, travellers can see sections of the substantial wall built by the French army at the end of the last century in order to delineate the westernmost frontier of the former White Hmông kingdom. Apiaries dot the hillside in this famed honey-producing area.

Sleeping **D** *People's Committee Guesthouse*, T852032. Basic rooms.

Sa Phin

Crossing the old border into the former demesne of the White Hmông kings the very distinctive architecture of the White Hmông houses of the area becomes apparent; it is quite unlike the small wooden huts characteristic of Hmông settlements elsewhere in North Vietnam. These are big, two-storey buildings, constructed using large bricks fashioned from the characteristic yellow earth of the region and invariably roofed in Chinese style. But it is not only the Hmông who construct their houses in this way – the dwellings of other ethnic minorities of the area such as the Co Lao and the Pu Peo are of similar design, no doubt a result of their having lived for generations within the borders of the former Hmông kingdom.

The remote Sa Phin valley is just two kilometres from the Chinese border. Below the road lies the village of Sa Phin, a small White Hmông settlement of no more than 20 buildings from which loom the twin white towers of the Hmông royal house, at one time the seat of government in the Dong Van-Meo Vac region:

Whilst it is clear that people of the Hmông ethnic minority have lived in the Dong Van-Meo Vac border region for many centuries, the ascendancy of White Hmông in the area is believed to date from the late 18th century, when the powerful Vuong family established its seat of government near Dong Van. In subsequent years the Vuong lords were endorsed as local government mandarins of Dong Van and Meo Vac by the Nguyen kings in Hue and later, following the French conquest of Indochina, by their colonial masters.

The Hmông Kings of Sa Phin

Keen to ensure the security of this key border region, the French authorities moved to further bolster the power of the Vuong family. Accordingly, in 1900 Vuong Chi Duc was recognized as king of the Hmông, and Chinese architects were brought in to design a residence befitting his newly-elevated status. A site was chosen at Sa Phin, 16 kilometres west of Dong Van; construction commenced in 1902 and was completed the following year.

During the early years of his reign, Vuong Chi Duc remained loyal to his French patrons, participating in numerous campaigns to quell uprisings against the colonial government. In 1927 he was made a general in the French army; a photograph of him in full military dress uniform may be seen on the family altar in the innermost room of the house. But as the struggle for Vietnamese independence got underway during the 1930s Duc adopted an increasingly neutral stance. Following his death in 1944 Duc was succeeded as king of the Hmông by his son, Vuong Chi Sinh, who the following year met and pledged his support for President Ho Chi Minh.

Built between 1902 and 1903, the **house of the former Hmông king** faces south in accordance with the geomantic principles which traditionally govern the construction of Northeast Asian royal residences, comprising four two-storey sections linked by three open courtyards. The building is surrounded by a moat and various ornately-carved tombs of members of the Vuong family lie outside the main gate. Both the outer and cross-sectional walls of the building are made of brick, but within that basic structure everything else is made of wood. The architecture, a development of late 19th-century Southern Chinese town house style, features *mui luyen* or *yin-yang* roof tiles.

No accommodation available here but there is a guesthouse in Dong Van, 16 kilometres away (see the next entry).

Sleeping

Dong Van

This remote market town is itself nothing special (situated 16 kilometres from Sa Phin) but is set in an attractive valley populated mainly by Tày people. Dong Van has a Sunday market but is very quiet at other times of the week. Since the town is only three kilometres from the Chinese border foreigners are not permitted to walk in the surrounding hills or visit villages in the vicinity. (Interestingly no two maps of this part of Vietnam tell the same story.) There is a simple government guesthouse in town.

Colour map 1, grid A4

The North

Sleeping **E** *People's Committee Guesthouse*, T856189. Very basic.

Meo Vac

Colour map 1, grid A4 Passing through the **Ma Phi Leng Pass** around 1,500 metres above the Nho Que River, the scenery is simply awesome. Like Dong Van, Meo Vac is a restricted border area and foreigners are not permitted to walk in the surrounding hills or visit villages outside the town. A small **market** is held every day in the town square, frequented mainly by White Hmông, Tày and Lo Lo people. Meo Vac is also the site of the famous Khau Vai 'Love Market' held once every year on the 27th day of the third month of the lunar calendar, which sees young people from all of the main ethnic groups of the region descending on the town to look for a partner. The highly colourful Lo Lo ethnic minority make up a large proportion of the town's population: a **Lo Lo village** is nearby, up the hill from the town centre.

Sleeping **E** *People's Committee Guesthouse*, T871176. Very basic.

Cao-Bac-Lang

The three provinces of Cao Bang, Bac Can and Lang Son – the famous Cao-Bac-Lang resistance zone of the 1947-1950 Frontier Campaign – form the heartland of the Viet Bac (literally North Vietnam), a mountainous region heavily populated by members of the Tày and Nung ethnic minorities which became the cradle of the revolution during the twilight of the French colonial period.

Ins and outs It is possible to tour this beautiful area by way of a circuit which leads north along Highway 3 from Thai Nguyen to Bac Can, making a small diversion to Ba Be National Park before continuing north to Cao Bang and the historic border district of Pac Bo. From here Highway 4, scene of some of the most bitter fighting during the First Indochina War, leads south to the important frontier town of Lang Son. The return journey from Lang Son to Hanoi may then be made either directly along Highway 1A or across the mountains along Highway 1B. Although it is possible to reach the larger centres by bus from Hanoi's Long Bien Terminal, the going is tough and detours are not possible, four-wheel drive vehicle (Russian jeep) is recommended. Tours available from Hanoi.

Bac Can

Phone code: 028
Colour map 1, grid A4 The market town and eponymous capital of Bac Can province lies on the River Cau. Bac Can acquired enormous strategic significance during the First Indochina War as the western-most stronghold of the Cao-Bac-Lang battle zone. The town was captured by the Viet Minh in 1944 and its recovery was considered crucial to the success of the 1947 French offensive against the Viet Bac resistance base. Although colonial troops did succeed in retaking Bac Can and building military outposts along Highway 3 in the autumn of 1947, guerilla attacks on the town's garrison subequently became so frequent that the French were forced to abandon the town two years later.

Bac Can's **daily market** is frequented by all of the main ethnic minority groups of the region, which include not only Tày but also local branches of the White Hmông and Red Dao plus Coin Dao (*Dao Tien*) and Tight-trousered Dao (*Dao Quan Chet*).

D-E *Bac Can*, T870440. Better rooms have a/c and adjoining shower/toilet, cheaper rooms have fan and shared outside facilities. *Thin Vien Restaurant*.

Sleeping & eating

Ba Be National Park *(Vuon Quoc Gia Ba Be)*

Ba Be National Park was established in 1992. It is Vietnam's eighth National Park and comprises 23,340 hectares of protected area plus an additional 8,079 hectares of buffer zone. The Park Centre is located on the eastern shore of Ba Be Lake.

Phone code: 026
Colour map 1, grid A4

Ba Be National Park lies 44 kilometres west of Na Phac on Highway 279, 1 hour. 15 kilometres before the Park is a checkpoint where a fee of 40,000d is levied.

Ins and outs

The park is centred on the beautiful Ba Be Lake (*Ba Be* means 'three basins'), 200 metres above sea level. The lake is surrounded by limestone hills carpeted in tropical evergreen forest. The park itself contains a very high diversity of flora and fauna, including an estimated 417 species of plant, 100 species of butterfly, 23 species of amphibian and reptile, 110 species of bird and 50 species of mammal. Amongst the latter are 10 seriously endangered species, including the Tonkinese snub-nosed monkey (*Rhinopitecus avunculus*) and the black gibbon (*Hylobates concolor*). Within the Park there are a number of villages inhabited by people of the Tày, Red Dao, Coin Dao and White Hmông ethnic minorities.

The area

The National Park Centre runs many different tours led by English-speaking guides with an expert knowledge of the area and its wildlfe These tours range from two-hour boat trips to two-day mountain treks staying overnight in Tày or Dao ethnic minority villages and visiting caves, waterfalls and other local beauty spots.

C *Ba Be National Park Guesthouse*, T876127 and 876131. 5 guesthouses each of 3 twin rooms with adjoining bathroom, prices rise in the summer, basic but comfortable accommodation. Meals available in Park office.

Sleeping & eating

About 15 kilometres east of Ba Be National Park Cho Ra has accommodation in the form of **C** *Ba Be Hotel*, T876115. 9 twin fan rooms with hot water, shower/toilet, in the event that the National Park Guesthouse is full. The hotel manager can arrange a whole-day boat trip for US$20; the trip includes 2 hours on the river to the lake passing a small ethnic community homestead where you will be fed and filled with rice wine for 20,000d. Opposite the hotel is a 5-day market for Dao and Tày people, some of whom have walked through the night to get there.

Cho Ra
Colour map 1, grid A4

Cao Bang

Cao Bang stands in a valley on a narrow peninsula between the Bang Giang and Hien Rivers, which join just to the northwest of the town. Cao Bang was badly damaged during the 1979 border war with China and has since been extensively rebuilt. At the time of writing many new government buildings, hotels and commercial developments are taking shape in and around the town; the gleaming new market is one of the largest in the country.

Phone code: 026
Colour map 1, grid A5

The North

Ins and outs

Getting there Na Phac to Cao Bang is 83 kilometres, 1¾ hours along a well metalled road. The Cao Bac Pass runs between 39 and 29 kilometres before Cao Bang, with stunning scenery all the way and breathtaking views at its summit. Arriving in Cao Bang fork left over a bridge and keep going until the *Bang Giang Hotel* appears straight in front of you.

History

Tay-Thai settlement in the area began at a very early date, leading to the emergence of the powerful Tay Au kingdom here during the Bronze Age. The Tay Au kings moved their capital south to Co Loa in the Red River Delta where, over the ensuing centuries, they gradually succumbed to the dominant Viet culture.

In the mid-10th century the Viet kings set about establishing fortifications in and around Cao Bang owing to its strategic position near the Chinese border, but the region continued to pose a significant security problem throughout the feudal era, as indicated by the revolts of Tay lords Be Khac Thieu and Nung Dac Thai against the Le Dynasty during the 1430s.

During the late 16th and early 17th centuries Cao Bang became a hotbed of revolt against royal authority. The essential background to the events of that period was the usurpation of the Le throne in 1527 by the Mac; although the Le kings were reinstated in 1592, members of the Mac family subsequently seized Cao Bang and proceeded to rule the region as an independent kingdom for a further 75 years. The ruins of a temple which once functioned as the palace of the Mac kings may still be seen today near the small market town of Cao Binh, 12 kilometres northwest of Cao Bang town.

Before the arrival of the French, the market town of Cao Binh served as the administrative headquarters of Cao Bang Province. However, the Cao Bang peninsula had also been settled from an early date, and following the French conquest of the area in 1884 the colonial authorities decided to transfer the provincial capital to the current site. A substantial fortress was subsequently constructed on the hill overlooking the town centre – the outer walls of this fortress still stand today, although what's left of the fortress itself currently serves as a base for the People's Army and is therefore off-limits to visitors.

From the late 1920s onwards Cao Bang became a cradle of the revolutionary movement in the north. The following years saw the establishment of many party cells through which a substantial programme of subversive activity against the colonial regime was organized. It was thus no accident that in 1940, when he returned to Vietnam after his long sojourn overseas, Ho Chi Minh chose to make remote Cao Bang Province his revolutionary headquarters during the crucial period from 1940 to 1945.

Sights

There is not a lot to see in the town. A few late 19th century French buildings have survived the ravages of war and redevelopment in the old quarter of town which stretches down the hill from the fortress to the Hien River Bridge making that area worth exploring on foot. **Cao Bang Exhibition Centre**, Kim Dong St. Located just behind the new market, this museum records the history of the revolutionary struggle in Cao Bang Province, with particular reference to the years leading up to the establishment of the Democratic Republic of Vietnam when Ho Chi Minh's headquarters were based at Pac

Bo, 56 kilometres north of Cao Bang. Pride of place in the exhibition hall is given to Ho's old staff car, registration number 'BAC 808'. Unfortunately all information is in Vietnamese only.

Excursions

The temple honours the memory of Nung Tri Cao, Nung lord of Quang Nguyen, who led one of the most important revolts of the ethnic minority people against the Vietnamese monarchy during the 11th century.

Ky Sam Temple

The story of Nung Tri Cao began in 1039 when Nung Tri Cao's father Nung Ton Phuc and his elder brother Nung Tri Thong rose in rebellion against Le Thai Tong. An expeditionary force was swiftly assembled by the Viets and the rebels were caught and summarily executed. However, two years later Nung Tri Cao himself gathered an army, seizing neighbouring territories and declaring himself ruler of a Nung kingdom which he called Dai Lich. He too was quickly captured by Viet troops, but having put his father and elder brother to death two years earlier, King Le Thai Tong took pity on Nung Tri Cao and let him return to Quang Nguyen. For the next seven years peace returned to the area, but in 1048 Nung Tri Cao rose up in revolt yet again, this time declaring himself 'Emperor of Dai Nam' and seizing territories in southern China. For the next five years he managed to play the Viet and Chinese kings off against each other until Le Thai Tong finally captured and executed him in 1053.

There has been a temple in the village of Ngan for many centuries, but the one standing today dates from the 19th century. It comprises two buildings, the outer building housing an altar dedicated to one of Nung Tri Cao's generals, the inner sanctum originally containing statues of the king, his wife and his mother; unfortunately these statues were stolen many years ago. The poem etched onto the walls in the outer building talks of Nung Tri Cao's campaigns and declares that his spirit is ever ready to come to the aid of his country in times of need. ■ *Getting there: Ky Sam Temple 18 kilometres north of Cao Bang town on Highway 203 to Pac Bo. It is located in the Nung village of Ngan, 200 metres east of Highway 203.*

Constructed in 1906, Cao Binh Church was one of three churches administered from Cao Bang during the French period, the others being those of Cao Bang and That Khe. There used to be many French houses in the vicinity of the church, but the majority of those that survived the French war were destroyed in 1979. However, the former vicar's house still stands relatively intact, adjacent to the ruins of the church. The family which currently occupies it runs one of the Cao Bang region's most famous apiaries. ■ *Getting there: five kilometres north of Ky Sam Temple along Highway 203 to Pac Bo, fork left at a junction; the ruins are half a kilometre from the junction.*

Ruins of Cao Binh Church

Cao Binh is situated on the east bank of the Dau Genh River, a tributary of the River Bang Giang. On the opposite bank of that river lies Lang Den (Temple village), which takes its name from the ruined 16th-century palace of the Mac Dynasty located on a hill just above the village.

Mac Kings' Temple

This structure is believed to have been built during the early 1520s by Mac Dang Dung, a general of the Le army who in 1521-1522 seized control of the kingdom, forcing the 11 year-old King Le Chieu Tong into exile and setting up his younger brother Le Thung as king. Two years later Mac Dang Dung forced Le Thung to abdicate, declaring himself king of Dai Viet.

The North

The Mac Dynasty retained control of Dai Viet for 65 years, during which period representatives of the deposed Le Dynasty mounted numerous military campaigns against the usurpers. The Le kings were finally restored to power in 1592 by the powerful Trinh family, but in that year a nephew of Mac Mau Hop, the last Mac king, seized Cao Bang and set up a small kingdom there. Over the next 75 years three successive generations of the Mac family managed to keep the royal armies at bay, even managing to launch two successful attacks on Thang Long (Hanoi) before Cao Bang was finally recaptured by Trinh armies in 1667.

It is clear that this building was originally constructed as a small royal residence; the original cannon placements may still be seen on the hill in front of the main entrance. ■ *Getting there: one and a half kilometres beyond Lang Den (Temple village), located on the west bank of the Dau Genh River, opposite Cao Binh. Accessible either on foot or by four-wheel drive capable of fording the river.*

Pac Bo
Colour map 1, grid A5

On 28 January 1941 Ho Chi Minh crossed the Sino-Vietnamese border, returning home to take charge of the resistance movement after 30 years overseas. In the days which followed he and his colleagues set up their revolutionary headquarters in a cave in the Pac Bo valley. Of interest primarily to scholars of the fledgling Vietnamese Socialist Party Pac Bo is the sort of pilgrimage spot that model carpet weavers or revolutionary railwaymen might be brought to as a reward.

The road to Ba Dinh Square

Taking advantage of the surrender of the French administration to the Japanese Ho Chi Minh returned to Vietnam setting up his HQ at Pac Bo, an area populated mainly by the Nung ethnic minority. It was from here that Ho Chi Minh – dressed in the traditional costume of the Nung people – guided the growing revolutionary movement, organizing training programmes for cadres, translating 'The History of the Communist Party in the USSR' into Vietnamese and editing the revolutionary newspaper 'Independent Vietnam'.

The eighth Congress of the Communist Party Central Committee, convened by Ho Chi Minh at Pac Bo between 10 and 19 March 1941, was an event of great historic importance which saw the establishment of the Vietnam Independence League (*Vietnam Doc Lap Dong Minh Hoi*), better known as the Viet Minh. This Congress also speeded up preparations for the future armed uprising, establishing guerilla bases throughout the Viet Bac.

The years from 1941 to 1945 were a period of severe hardship for the Vietnamese people, as the colonial government colluded with Japanese demands to exploit the country's natural resources to the full in order to support the Japanese war effort. But by 1945 the Vichy government in France had fallen and the French colonial administration belatedly drew up plans to resist the Japanese, but on 9 March 1945 their plans were foiled by the Japanese who set up a new government with King Bao Dai as head of state.

At this juncture Viet Minh guerilla activity was intensified all over the country, with the result that by June 1945 almost all of the six provinces north of the Red River Delta were under Communist control. On 13 August Japan surrendered to the Allied forces; three days later Ho Chi Minh headed south from Pac Bo to Tan Trao near Tuyen Quang to preside over a People's Congress which declared a general insurrection and established the Democratic Republic of Vietnam. The August Revolution which followed swept all in its wake; within a matter of weeks the three major cities of Hanoi, Hue and Saigon had fallen to the Viet Minh and King Bao Dai had abdicated. On 2 September 1945 President Ho Chi Minh made a historic address to the people in Hanoi's Ba Dinh Square, proclaiming the nation's independence.

The museum houses artefacts concerning the revolution and Ho Chi Minh's part in it. ■ *5,000d. Open 0800-1700.* **Coc Bo Cave** is where Ho lived and worked after his return from overseas. The area is not unattractive with its streams and trees but the charm is rendered somewhat comic by the commemorative plaques which festoon the place complete with names dubbed by Ho: Karl Marx mountain, Lenin stream and so on. ■ *Getting there: Cao Bang to Pac Bo is 56 kilometres of stunning scenery, one and a half hours. Despite its proximity to China no special permit is needed but walking outside the area is not permitted.*

Pac Bo Exhibition Centre

Ban Doc (Ban Zop), Vietnam's most recently discovered **waterfall** and apparently the highest is about 80 kilometres due north of Cao Bang. Cao Bang Guesthouse can provide details. They also reckon to be able to arrange permits for three-day trips into China but quite what there is to see and whether you can get back in to Vietnam you will have to find out for yourself.

Essentials

B-C *Bang Giang Hotel*, Be Van Dan St, T853431. New 80-room building 1st floor a/c, 2nd Floor fan, all with adjoining bathroom. **C** *Cao Bang Guesthouse*, Kim Dong St, T851023. 28 rooms a/c and fan. **D** *Phong Lan*, 83 Be Van Dan St, T852260. 40 rooms, better ones a/c cheaper fan and shared facility; **C** *Duc Trung Mini*, Be Van Dan St, T853424. 6 a/c rooms. **D** *Phuong Dong*, T853178. On Bang Giang River opposite town centre, 8 rooms fan and a/c, restaurant.

Sleeping

Bac Lam, Kim Dong St. *Thanh Truc*, 278 Vuon Cam. *Ngoc Diep*, B53 Be Van Dan St.

Eating

Northeast Frontier

From Cao Bang to Lang Son along Highway 4 is a journey of 135 kilometres; the road is in relatively poor condition and the going can be quite hard, taking three and a half hours but it is not without its rewards.

10 kilometres south of Dong Khe Highway 4 climbs up to the infamous Lung Phay Pass. From here to the village of Bong Lau the wonderful mountain scenery makes it difficult to imagine the carnage which took place 1947-1950, when convoy after convoy of French supply trucks ran into carefully-planned Viet Minh ambushes. The War Heroes' Cemetery at Bong Lau is sited on a hill where a French military outpost once stood and marks the border between Cao Bang and Lang Son provinces.

Lung Phay Pass

30 kilometres south of That Khe the road passes through more towering limestone outcrops before commencing its climb up through another of the Frontier Campaign's infamous battle zones, the beautiful Bo Cung Pass.

Bo Cung Pass

The government established by Ho Chi Minh in September 1945 soon found itself in a cleft stick. The terms of the Potsdam Conference had provided for the surrender of Japanese forces to be accepted south of the 16th parallel by British-Indian forces and north of that line by the Chinese Kuomintang (Nationalist Party) troops of Chiang Kai-shek. In the south, General Gracey promptly freed thousands of French troops detained in the wake of the Japanese coup.

The Frontier Campaign of 1947-1950

Unable to confront both the French and the Chinese, Ho Chi Minh decided to negotiate with the French concluding, as we have already seen, that they were the lesser of the two evils. In February 1946 the French signed a treaty with the Chinese Nationalists which secured their withdrawal from Vietnamese territory; the following month a Franco-Vietnamese agreement confirmed the status of Vietnam as a free state within the French Union and the Indochinese Federation.

After consolidating their positions in the Red River Delta, the French resolved to launch a major offensive against the Viet Bac in October 1947 with the objective of destroying the resistance leadership. Their plan involved a pincer movement of two armed columns – one under Colonel Communal moving by water up the Red and Lo Rivers to attack and occupy Tuyen Quang and Chiem Hoa, the other under Colonel Beaufre travelling to Lang Son and then north along Highway 4 to That Khe, Dong Khe and Cao Bang before heading southwards to Bac Can. The offensive was intended to take the Viet Minh by surprise but, just six days after the attack had begun, an aircraft carrying the French chief of staff was shot down near Cao Bang, allowing the plans to fall into the hands of the Viet Minh High Command.

Sailing up the Lo River, Communal's column fell into a Viet Minh ambush suffering a humiliating defeat and losing some 38 gunboats before being forced to retreat to Tuyen Quang. Meanwhile Beaufre's forces suffered repeated ambushes at the hands of Viet Minh before finally managing to recapture the fortresses of Cao Bang and Bac Can in late October 1947. Having failed to achieve the objective of their offensive, the French were now obliged to dig in for a long and costly war.

The position of the French became steadily more and more precarious. Supply convoys travelling from Lang Son to Cao Bang and Bac Can were ambushed repeatedly, particularly along Highway 4. Thousands of colonial troops lost their lives whilst travelling along what French press dubbed the 'Road of Death', the most dangerous stretches of which were the Lung Phay Pass 10 kilometres south of Dong Khe and the Bo Cung Pass 30 kilometres south of That Khe.

Despite massive subsidy from the United States under the emerging Truman doctrine of containing communism, the cost of air-dropping supplies into the region was becoming an intolerable burden. The French High Command finally concluded that their position in the Viet Bac was no longer tenable and began to draw up plans for the abandonment of Cao Bang.

Before these plans could be implemented, however, the Viet Minh launched a surprise attack on Dong Khe, capturing the post. Taken aback by this bold move and desperate to secure the speedy and safe retreat of its Cao Bang garrison, the French High Command ordered the post's commander, Colonel Charton, to withdraw to Lang Son.

Leaving Cao Bang on 3 October 1950, Charton's column made it no further than Nam Nang, 17 kilometres south of the town, before running into a Viet Minh ambush. Travelling northwards from That Khe to rendezvous with Charton, Lepage's forces were also intercepted in the vicinity of Dong Khe. The subsequent battle in the hills to the west of Highway 4 resulted in a resounding Viet Minh victory, in the aftermath of which on 8 October some 8,000 French troops had been either killed or taken prisoner. Within days the French had abandoned all their remaining posts on Highway 4.

The Viet Minh victory on Highway 4 was a major turning point in the war which threw the colonial forces throughout the north into complete disarray. During the following two weeks the French were obliged to withdraw all their forces from Lang Son, Thai Nguyen and Tuyen Quang, whilst in the northwest the French garrisons at Hoa Binh and Lao Cai were also driven out. Thus was the scene set for the final stage of the First Indochina War, which would culminate four years later in the momentous battle at Dien Bien Phu.

Lang Son

The town of Lang Son lies on the Ky Lung River in a small alluvial plain sur-   *Phone code: 025*
rounded by 1,000 metres high mountains. Like Cao Bang, Lang Son was badly   *Colour map 1, grid B5*
damaged during the border war of 1979 and has since been substantially rebuilt.
But the old quarter of the town south of the Ky Cung River still contains a num-
ber of interesting historic buildings and the town's markets see a regular
throughput of ethnic minority people.

Ins and outs

The direct route from Hanoi is along Highway 1A via Chi Lang and Bac Giang, 154 kilometres, $3\frac{1}{2}$ hours. Chi Lang Pass is the site of Le Loi's historic victory over 100,000
Ming invaders in 1427, effectively bringing to an end 1,000 years of Chinese hegemony. The longer, more scenic route is along Highway 1B via Bac Son and Thai
Nguyen, 237 kilometres, 7 hours. The road passes through some delightful highland
countryside settled by Tày, Nung and Dao ethnic people. There are early morning bus
departures from Hanoi's Long Bien terminal. Two trains run daily from Hanoi and back
– one during the day, one overnight – from Dong Dang (Border Gate) and Dong Kinh
(ie Lang Son Central) to Hanoi.

History

Lang Son arose to prominence as early as the Bronze Age, when emergent
trade routes between India and China turned it into an important transit stop
on the main road from the Red River Delta through Nanning to Guangzhou.

    Between 1527 and 1592 the Mac devoted considerable attention to the task
of fortifying the strategically important Lang Son border region. Vestiges of a
number of Mac Dynasty fortifications may still be seen today in Lang Son
Province, the best preserved of which is the citadel which lies on a limestone
outcrop to the west of the present town.

    By the time of its seizure by French troops in 1885 Lang Son had developed
into a sizeable and prosperous market town. In subsequent years it became a
French military base second in importance only to Cao Bang.

Sights

Dong Kinh Market has been recently rebuilt and is chock-full of Chinese   **Markets**
consumer goods brought through Dong Dang. Although rebuilt many times
and finally sidelined by the gleaming new structure at Dong Kinh, **Ky Lua
Market** is the oldest in Lang Son and still sees a trickle of trading activity every
day. Members of the Tày and Nung ethnicity are regular visitors here. **Lang
Son Citadel** A large section of the ancient city walls, dating back to the 18th
century, may still be seen. The former Lang Son monastery once stood on the
other side of the city walls. ■ *Getting there: south down Nguyen Thai Hoc St
from the old quarter to My Son junction.*

Excursions

The east and west facing walls of the imposing 16th century Mac Dynasty cita-   **Mac Dynasty**
del are located on a limestone outcrop west of Lang Son. ■ *Getting there: head*   **Citadel**
out of town past the six-way junction on the Tam Thanh road.

The border crossing

12 kilometres north of Lang Son, Highway 4 meets Highway 1. From this junction it is just 8 kilometres to the Dong Dang Friendship Gate (Cua Khau Huu Nghi Dong Dang), the border with China. The border is open in both directions to those with the correct entry and exit visas specifying the Friendship crossing. Visas cannot be obtained at the border and must be picked up in Saigon/Hanoi or Hong Kong/Peking. Vietnamese visas normally specify air routes only; a special stamp for land crossings must be obtained from the immigration police or travel agents.

Crossing from China *From the border town of Ping Xiang in China catch a minibus near the main bus station (¥3 per person) to the border. Tell the driver you want to go to YuteLarm GorGwarn (Cantonese for Vietnam border). At the drop-off point you will be greeted by a crowd of willing motorbike drivers who can take you to the border, a 5-10 minute drive, for around ¥5 per person. He will take you to the policed border-gate*

leaving you to walk the 500 or so odd metres down an almost deserted road before reaching the Chinese Immigration Building. After paying ¥10 for the privilege of leaving China at this border point (the cheek!) and other obligatory stages of red tape, you have to continue, unescorted, down the same road for another 5 minutes with the occasional truck going past but little else. The silence is quite eerie and out-of-the-place for a border point. On average only about 20 or 30 people cross at this point per day. The Vietnamese border control looks more like a restaurant and the Vietnamese guards are relaxed and cheeky (a contrast to the stern Chinese!). From Dong Dang, the trip to Lang Son itself is easily managed, as hordes of hopefuls wait outside the Immigration Building with vans, cars and bikes. They will also change money at terrible rates. The journey to Lang Son takes about 30 minutes and will cost around US$5 for a van which can hold 5 or 6 people.

Tam Thanh Cave A poem by Ngo Thi Sy (1726-1780), military commander of the Lang Son garrison, who first discovered these and other caves in the area, is carved on the wall near the entrance. There are three chambers; the outer one functions as a pagoda with two shrines and the second one contains a fresh water pool. ■ *10,000d. Getting there: on the road to the Mac citadel.*

Nhi Thanh Cave Nhi Thanh, perhaps the best known of Lang Son's caves, is located south of Tam Thanh cave. There are in fact two separate caves here – the one on the right contains the Tam Giao Pagoda, established in 1777 by Ngo Thi Sy, in which are six shrines, whilst the one on the left follows the Ngoc Tuyen stream deep into the mountain: this one is particularly dramatic. More of Ngo Thi Sy's poetry adorns the walls. The ladies who sit in front of the pagoda are lovely and very friendly, they will offer visitors tea and bananas. ■ *10,000d. Getting there: from the six-way junction take the Nhi Thanh road.*

Essentials

Sleeping **B-C** *Dong Kinh*, 25 Nguyen Du St, T870166. Near market, better rooms with own bathroom, a/c, fridge etc, cheapest rooms shared facilities, basic but comfortable accommodation, restaurant. **B-C** *Kim Son*, 3 Minh Khai St, T870378, F872118. Comfortable Chinese joint-venture hotel, 29 rooms all a/c, adjoining bathroom, Quang Chau Chinese restaurant. **C** *A1 Guesthouse*, 32 Dinh Tien Hoang St, T870221. The only hotel in the old quarter of town, 30 twin rooms all with adjoining bathroom, basic. **C** *Anh Dao*, 1 Nhi Thanh St, T870543. 16 twin a/c rooms all with bathroom, restaurant.

C *Bac Son*, 41 Le Loi St, T871849, F871507. 22 rooms, all with adjoining bathroom, pricier rooms have a/c. **C** *Hoa Binh*, 127 Tran Dang Ninh St, T870807, F871507. 12 rooms all a/c, adjoining bathroom, comfortable accommodation. **C** *KDN*, 233 Tran Dang Ninh St, T871272. 18 a/c rooms, own bathroom, comfortable enough with Gia Canh Restaurant next door. **C-D** *Tam Thanh*, 117 Tran Dang Ninh St, T870979. 18 a/c and fan rooms all with adjoining bathroom, basic but comfortable accommodation next to *Tam Thanh Restaurant*.

A number of hotels have restaurants attached, see above. Also *Cua Hang An Uong*, corner of Le Loi and the market street looks like a 70s built English club house but serves fantastic lau (steamboat) at good prices. **Eating**

Train 1 day time and 1 night time train connections each day with Hanoi. **Transport**

Road A main highway links Lang Son with Hanoi and public buses travel along this route. More interesting is the road via Bac Son and Thai Nguyen. It is possible to return (on a Minsk) via Halong Bay and the coast; the road to Tien Yen is a shocker, and carry lunch and spare fuel with you as there are no supplies en route. From Tien Yen the road improves but as it passes through the dusty coal-mining areas of Quang Ninh you will end up as black as a miner.

The North

Bac Son

Settled mainly by members of the Tày and Nung ethnicity, this small market town has two important reasons to claim significance in the history of the Vietnamese nation. *Colour map 1, grid B5*

The first derives from the very large number of prehistoric artefacts unearthed here by archaeologists. The so-called Bac Son period (5000-3000 BC) was characterized by the development of pottery and the widespread use of refined stone implements, including distinctive axes with polished edges known as Bacsonian axes.

The second is the Bac Son Uprising. In September 1940 revolutionaries detained in Lang Son prison seized the opportunity afforded by the Japanese attack on the town to escape, heading northwest across the mountains to Bac Son. With the support of the local Party organization they organized a general insurrection in the town, disarming the fleeing French troops and taking over the district centre to set up the first revolutionary power base in the Viet Bac.

The following year French forces responded by launching a campaign of terror in the Viet Bac, forcing the leaders of the uprising to retreat into the mountains. The Bac Son uprising did, however, prove to be an important milestone in the revolutionary struggle and in the years which followed the tide turned steadily against the French throughout the region.

On the way into the town the road passes an unmarked white building on stilts with a Vietnamese flag fluttering on its roof – this is the Museum of the Bac Son Rebellion which contains a small collection of prehistoric axe-heads and other tools dating from the Bac Son period plus a large display of artefacts relating to the Bac Son Uprising. These include the weapons and personal effects of those involved in the uprising, plus letters and other documents written by Ho Chi Minh and leading revolutionaries such as Hoang Van Thu. No English translation, unfortunately. **Bac Son Museum**

Road **Bus**: connections with Hanoi and Lang Son. **Transport**

Hanoi to Haiphong, Do Son, Cat Ba Island and Halong Bay

The 100 kilometre road from Hanoi to Haiphong, the north's principal port, passes through the flood-prone riceland of the Red River Delta. In places the land lies below sea-level and an elaborate system of dykes and bunds has been built up over the centuries to keep the river in place. Haiphong was heavily bombed during the American War, but still retains a surprising amount of French-era architecture. From Haiphong it is just a 40 minute drive to the resort town of Do Son or a four hour ferry ride to Cat Ba Island, Vietnam's most accessible national park. Cat Ba's rugged scenery and forests make it an attractive place in which to spend a few days. It is also an ideal spot from which to explore the wonderful scenery of Halong Bay.

Haiphong

Phone code: 031
Colour map 1, grid B5

The port of Haiphong was established in 1888 on the Cua Cam River, a major distributory of the Red River. It is the largest port and the second largest city in the north (with a population of over 1.6 million and rising fast). Over and above its natural attributes Haiphong is blessed with a go-ahead and entrepreneurial People's Committee (no surprises that the district sports Vietnam's only casino) and this attitude vitality is reflected in the bustle of the town and the industry and vitality of the population. Haiphong's prosperity looks set to redouble with heavy investment in port and communications infrastructure and major investment from overseas in manufacturing plant. Despite this (from the tourists' viewpoint) seemingly inauspicious framework central Haiphong remains remarkably attractive and its people open and warm. Although its role in the tourist trade is unlikely to exceed by far the provision of a bed for those who have missed the last Cat Ba ferry there is sufficient in and around Haiphong to justify a closer look.

Ins and outs

Getting there As the north's second city after Hanoi, and the region's premier port, Haiphong is well connected. Cat Bi, Haiphong's airport, is 7 kilometres from the city and there are 5 departures a week for Saigon (but none with Hanoi). The road from Hanoi is now excellent (for Vietnam) and there are numerous bus and minibus connections. There are 5 trains each day between the two cities. Haiphong is the departure point for Cat Ba Island and from there with Ha Long Bay.

Getting around Central Haiphong is sufficiently compact for most sights to be visited on foot. But the distance from, for example, the railway station to port merits a cyclo or xe ôm as do the outer temples.

History

Haiphong witnessed the initial arrival of the French in 1872 (they occupied Hanoi a year later) and, appropriately, their final departure from the north at 1500 in the afternoon of 15 May 1955. As the major port of the north, it was subjected to sustained bombing during the War. To prevent petrol and diesel fuel reaching the Viet Cong nearly 80 percent of all above-ground tanks were obliterated by American bombing in 1966. The US did not realize that the

The Battles of Bach Dang River (938 AD and 1288 AD)

The battles of Bach Dang River were both won in a style reminiscent of many battles fought against the US. In 938 AD, unable to confront the powerful Chinese fleet on equal terms, the Vietnamese General Ngo Quyen sunk sharpened poles tipped with iron into the bed of the river that the Chinese were about to sail up. When the Chinese fleet appeared off the mouth of the river, Quyen sent a small flotilla of shallow draught boats to taunt the Chinese. Rising to the bait they attacked and, as the tide fell, their heavy ships were impaled on the stakes that lay just below the surface. Over half the Chinese, including the Admiral Hung-ts'ao were drowned. In 1288, apparently not having learnt the lessons of history, another Mongol Chinese fleet of 400 ships appeared off the coast. This time the famous Vietnamese general Tran Hung Dao laid the trap, again luring the enemy onto sunken stakes. In both instances, the victories were so emphatic as to terminate the Chinese invasion plans.

North Vietnamese, anticipating such an action, had dispersed much of their supplies to underground and concealed tanks. This did not prevent the city from receiving a battering, although Haiphong's air defence units are said to have retaliated by shooting down 317 US planes.

Sights

Much of outer Haiphong is an ugly industrial sprawl that will win no environmental beauty contests. But, considering the bombing the city sustained, there is still a surprising amount of attractive **colonial-style architecture** in the city centre. Central Haiphong is pleasantly green with tree-lined streets. Right in the heart of town, where Tran Hung Dao and Quang Trung streets meet, is the **Great Theatre**, built in 1904 of imported French materials, with a colonnaded front, facing a wide tree-lined boulevard. In November 1946 40 Viet Minh fighters died here in a pitched battle with the French, triggered by the French government's decision to open a customs house in Haiphong. A plaque outside commemorates the battle. The **museum** (*Bao Tang Hai Phong*), 66 Dien Bien Phu Street, is an impressive colonial edifice in a wash of desert sand red, contains records of the city's turbulent past. ■ *Open 0800-1100 and 1400-1630, Tuesday, Wednesday, Sunday.* The streets around the theatre support the greatest concentration of foodstalls and shops. There are a number of **street markets** and **flower stalls** off Cao Dat Street, which runs south from the theatre, along Tran Nhat Duat and Luong Khanh Thien streets. Sat Market is to be found in the west quarter of town, at the end of Phan Boi Chau Street. A market has stood on this site since 1876. The present building is a huge concrete edifice six storeys high that has never quite taken off. Near the centre of town on Me Linh Street is the **Nghe Pagoda** built at the beginning of the 20th century. The pagoda is dedicated to the memory of heroine General Le Chan who fought with the Trung sisters against the Chinese. A festival is held on the eighth day of the second lunar month to commemorate her birthday and offerings of crab and noodles, her favourite foods, are made.

Two kilometres south of the city centre on Chua, Hang Street, is the **Du Hang Pagoda**. Originally built in 1672 by wealthy mandarin turned monk Nguyen Dinh Sach, it has been renovated and remodelled several times since. Arranged around a courtyard, this small temple has some fine traditional woodcarving. Get there by *xe ôm*, along a pot-holed road, past workers' cottages. Also two kilometres south of the centre, on Nyuyen Cong Tru Street, is

Dinh Hang Kenh (Hang Kenh communal house or *dinh*) which dates back to 1856. The main building is supported by 32 columns of iron wood and the wood carvings in the window grilles are a notable feature. There are a number of dinh around Haiphong reflecting the importance of Chinese in the local ethnic mix.

The **Foreign Language Teaching Institute** (which has no foreign teachers!) in Nguyen Duc Canh Street, has a crowd of eager young Vietnamese students more than willing to chat to you for an afternoon and show you around Haiphong in exchange for practising their English.

Essentials

Sleeping Haiphong offers plenty of accommodation to meet the demands of industrialists and expats rather than travellers, therefore standards tend to be fairly good but prices a little high. There is value to be found, however.

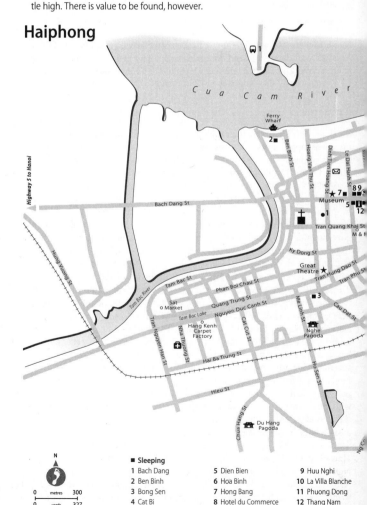

Haiphong

■ Sleeping		
1 Bach Dang	5 Dien Bien	9 Huu Nghi
2 Ben Binh	6 Hoa Binh	10 La Villa Blanche
3 Bong Sen	7 Hong Bang	11 Phuong Dong
4 Cat Bi	8 Hotel du Commerce	12 Thang Nam

A+-A *Huu Nghi*, 60 Dien Bien Phu St, T823310, F823245. Central, and at 11 storeys and 126 rooms one of Haiphong's largest, efficient enough but prices, like the building itself, nudge the stratosphere, perhaps the opening of the Royal Garden will bring them down. **A+-A** *Royal Garden*, 4 Tran Phu St, T827827, 827828, E royalgarden@ hn.vnn.vn. Haiphong's newest, largest and most luxurious hotel. Near the river, this 127-room hotel has restaurant and bar, it is well managed and comfortable. **A** *La Villa Blanche*, 5 Tran Hung Dao St, T841113, F842278. Belongs to the navy, glittering foyer, mirrors and expensive looking ladies, all mod cons. **A-B** *Royal*, 275 Lach Tray St, T847857, F843368. On the airport/Do Son road 3 kilometres south of centre, new, comfortable, well appointed and good value (breakfast included), particularly recommended for longer stays.

B *Dien Bien*, 67 Dien Bien Phu St, T842264, F842977. Similar to most in this area, fairly large rooms but somewhat plasticky decor. **B** *Hotel du Commerce*, 62 Dien Bien Phu St, T842706, F842560. Attractive colonial style, renovated but still atmospheric, large rooms, restaurant. **B-C** *Cat Bi*, 30 Tran Phu St, T836284, F845181. Short distance south of centre, a/c, newly renovated, a range of rooms. **B-C** *Thang Nam*, 55 Dien Bien Phu St, T823460, F841019. 18 rooms all a/c, central, well run, fair value. **B-D** *Bach Dang*, 42 Dien Bien Phu St, T842444. Somewhat run-down but a range of rooms available some with shared facilities, central, restaurant.

C *Hong Bang*, 64 Dien Bien Phu St, T842229, F841044. Colonial façade, 70s renovation, largeish rooms. **C** *Ben Binh*, 6 Ben Binh St, T842260, F842524. Set in a lovely garden opposite ferry dock, a/c, hot water, fridge in more expensive rooms, could be cleaner, a nice spot to have breakfast while waiting for the fast boat to Cat Ba. **C-D** *Bong Sen*, 15-16 Nguyen Duc Canh St, T846019, F855184. South of theatre, short trek from the station, run by quite a cheerful bunch. Hotel is behind the restaurant which provides useful sound insulation, a/c, hot water, quite clean but beds a little lumpy.

D *Phuong Dong*, 19 Luong Khanh Thien St, T855391. Immediately in front of railway station, clean, good value for money. **D-E** *Hoa Binh*, 104 Luong Khanh Thien St, T846909, F846907. Opposite station, some very basic but clean fan rooms and others a little smarter with a/c.

Foreign business influence is reflected in the form of at least two Japanese restaurants.

Eating
● *on map*

● **Eating**
1 Atlantic
2 Lucky
3 Saigon Thien Bao
4 Sake

🚌 **Buses**
1 Binh Bus Station
  (Buses to Halong)
2 Lach Tray Bus Station
  (Buses to Do Son)

■ *on map*
Price codes:
see inside front cover

The North

Atlantic, 30 Dinh Tien Hoang St. Vietnamese with some Western, central, inexpensive and good. *Bong Sen*, 15-16 Nguyen Duc Canh St. Vietnamese and Asian dishes at modest prices, quite popular with locals. *Lucky*, 22 Minh Khai St. Next to Quang Minh Hotel. A local legend. *Saigon Thien Bao*, 6 Tran Binh Trong St, T859152. South of town centre, reckons to be the town's top venue, cavernous and somewhat intimidating to the lone diner, Vietnamese and Western dishes, rather bland food and erratic service, staff are more absorbed in the latest twist in the current TV soap than in their customers' vain wishes for more rice. Hence bills for one can be kept below US$7. *Sake*, 55 Dien Bien Phu St. Next to Thang Nam Hotel, Japanese food at fair prices. *Thien Nhat*, 97 Dien Bien Phu St, T823327. Another well regarded Japanese restaurant. Numerous popular, cheap local eateries and *bia hois* west of Theatre on Quang Trung and Nguyen Duc Canh streets and around especially *Trong Khach*, 93 Nguyen Duc Canh St, seafood and *Thien Nhien*, 43 Quang Trung St, Vietnamese.

Bars Really only one to report, *M & N Club*, 17 Tran Quang Khai St, T822603. Vast and normally vacant but at least it's there serving up beer, Baskin Robbins ice cream and music from pirated Cds.

Transport **Local** Metered taxis T841999, cyclos or xe ôm.

Air Connections with Saigon each day except Mondays and Fridays.

Train There are 5 train departures daily from Hanoi; 0600 from central station (Tran Qui Cap St entrance), 0820, 1000, 1500 and 1705 depart from Long Bien station on Gam Cau St, 52,000d, 2½ hours.

Road **Bus**: regular connections with Hanoi. Cat Bi, Haiphong's airport, lies 7 kilometres southeast of town, the only air connections are with Saigon. Highway 5 has been newly relaid (with a little help from our Japanese friends) and is now a fast motorway connecting capital with coast. There are regular bus departures from Hanoi. Frequent train connections with Hanoi too. Long Bien and Gia Lam terminals to Haiphong's central Tam Bac station; minibuses from Hanoi's Tran Quang Khai St. From Bai Chay to Binh bus station north of Cua Cam River, 3 hours (ferry into town).

Ferry Connections with Cat Ba and Hon Gai from wharf on Ben Binh St, ticket office open 1 hour before departures. Dept for Cat Hai and Cat Ba at 0630 and 1330, 60,000d, 4 hours. Depart for Cat Hai and Hon Gai 0900, 50,000d. **Express boat**, a/c, to Cat Ba depart 0900 and 1400, 90,000d, 1 hour. From Cat Ba express boat to Haiphong dept 1130 and 1600

Directory **Airline offices** *Vietnam Airlines*, 30 Tran Phu St, T849242, F859497. **Banks** *ACB*, 69 Dien Bien Phu St. Changes US$ cash only. *Indovina Bank*, 30 Tran Phu St. *VID Bank*, 56 Dien Bien Phu St. Changes US$, Sing $ and Malay $ TCs and cash. *Vietcombank*, 11 Hoang Dieu St. Cashes TCs. **Communications** GPO: 3 Nguyen Tri Phuong St. Full international telephone and fax services. TNT International Express: T 847180. **Hospital and medical services** *Vietnam-Czech Friendship Hospital*, 1 Nha Thuong St, T 846236. **Tourist offices** *Haiphong Toserco*, 40 Tran Quang Khai St, T842288, F843977. *Haiphong Tourist*, 87 Dien Bien Phu St, T842709. *Vietnam Tourism*, 15 Le Dai Hanh St, T842989, F842674. All have cars for rent and will arrange tours to Halong Bay, Cat Ba etc but nothing that cannot be done by most individuals for considerably cheaper.

Do Son

Do Son is a tourist resort 21 kilometres southeast of Haiphong sitting on the southern end of the Do Son peninsula. Not really a 'Pattaya' it would, nevertheless, desperately love to become one. It is primarily a Vietnamese holiday and weekend destination that has not caught on with foreigners. Indeed, it is likely to be a while before it does but anyone caught in Haiphong with a day to spare would find Do Son a refreshing break. Do Son boasts Vietnam's only casino.

Phone code: 031
Colour map 1, grid B5

Sights

The Do Son Peninsula was originally developed as a resort by the French and it is currently experiencing a renaissance as joint ventures are signed, old hotels renovated and Haiphong Tourist cranks the marketing machine into action. The small *Ba De Temple* on Doc Mountain, at the north end of the peninsula, honours a young girl who threw herself to her death after spending a night with a courtier (this theme is a popular one in Vietnam – the idea of honourable maidens choosing death in preference to despoilation being seen as highly romantic; although in this case the poor girl got both). Buffalo fights are held on the ninth day of the eighth lunar month at Do Son village. Preparation for the fights takes months – the normally docile bulls are fed special diets and kept in isolation. The fighting takes place at the end of the fishing season and attracts thousands of drinking and gambling visitors. The buffaloes charge each other, smashing skulls and gouging each other with horns. The victor is electrocuted and sliced up for everyone to enjoy. The festival celebrates delivery from a huge storm in the 15th century and honours the great bird king (*Diem Tuoc Dai Vuong*) who saved them.

Do Son does have potential as a resort and it does have charm but these attributes need working on. Considering what it is (a Vietnamese holiday resort four hours drive from Hanoi, see tinted box 'Cultural expectations and tolerance levels on holiday') it could be a lot worse. Beaches are quite white and clean but rather than being fringed by gently swaying palms are lined by austere sea pines which shed sharp needles; the sea itself is an unappealing rust colour from silt discharged into the sea by the Red River. The peninsula is too narrow to permit space to roam and escape but there are secluded spots to breath deeply the fresh air blowing in from the South China Sea, or the Eastern Sea as the Vietnamese would prefer we call it. It has a friendly and relaxed feel as sea-side retreats invariably do.

Do Son is regimented into three zones or *khu*. Khu 1 is nearest Do Son town. It has a prom and a front with waves and several huge hotels; it is the least attractive of the three zones so if it does not appeal press on. Khu 2 is better geared to tourists: there are a couple of quite attractive small hotels, the beach is nothing special but there are plenty of restaurants, it is breezy and fresh. Khu 3 at the distal end of the peninsula is the least developed and most wooded zone. Hotels here tend to be small and there is a fairly secluded beach. Right at the southern tip is the casino, formerly *Hotel de la Pointe*.

Essentials

There are one or two hotels which Westerners would feel relaxed in. Most hotels are concrete monoliths owned by trade unions, state enterprises or utilities and geared to providing holidays for 100 factory workers and their families at a time.

Sleeping

The North

■ *on map*
Price codes:
see inside front cover

Khu 1: **C** *Cong Doan* (*Trade Union*), T861300. 100 rooms, cheaper on higher floors, fan only and no lift, simply furnished but clean, Party conference venue rather than riotous holiday getaway. **C** *Forestry*, T861104, F861105. Grim concrete block, 76 rooms all with a/c and hot water. There are new hotels going up in Khu 1 that might, when finished, look OK.

Khu 2: **B-C** *Garden Resort*, T861226, F861186. A series of villas set in well kept and wooded grounds, each with two large and two small rooms, a/c, hot water, fridge, IDD, TV etc, larger rooms have bath tub, smaller ones shower only, clean, friendly, rec. Note that prices here, as at many other hotels in Do Son, rise by 50 percent Friday-Sunday. **B-C** *Van Thong*, T861331, F861131. Clean but relatively small a/c rooms around a nice courtyard setting at back, like a number of other Do Son hotels this one offers 'Thai massage'. **C** *Hai Au*, T861272, F861176. Nothing special about the hotel, large and slightly forbidding aspect but set among trees and has tennis court at rear.

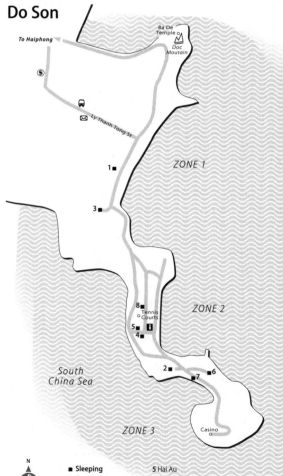

Do Son

To Haiphong

Ba De Temple

Doc Moutain

Ly Thanh Tong St

ZONE 1

1

3

8
Tennis Courts

5
4

ZONE 2

2
7 6

South China Sea

ZONE 3

Casino

Dau Island

N

0 metres 250
0 yards 274

■ **Sleeping**
1 Cong Doan
2 Doi Tien
3 Forestry
4 Garden Resort

5 Hai Au
6 Hoa Sua
7 Huong Dua
8 Van Thong

The North

Khu 3: D *Doi Tien*, T861182. 14 fan rooms on a slight rise, no hot water, views but pretty grotty buildings, poorly maintained and managed. **D** *Hoa Sua*, T861202. 12 a/c rooms with hot water, in a concrete block that could be Le Corbusier in a dark mood. Although some rooms have a view not all do and one side is dangerously near a karaoke strip, a common enough hazard in Do Son. **D** *Huong Dua*, T861181. Last hotel before the casino and possibly the best. Small, colonial style buildings in yellow wash overlooking a secluded beach, nice and airy, well maintained and clean, simple, some a/c some fan, restaurant. Recommended.

Many of the hotels have restaurants but the best option is to dive into one of the countless restaurants offering seafood specialities (*dac san bien*) which line the roads. All fairly indistinguishable but not undistinguished. Khu 2 offers the more attractive options for eating. **Eating**

Casino Located at the very southern tip in Khu 3 occupying the former *Hotel de la Pointe*, T861888. Open 1100-0500, no Vietnamese allowed, passport needed for entrance, restaurant. **Entertainment**

Communications Tourist offices *Do Son Tourism Company*, Khu 2, T861330, F861186. Next to *Hai Au Hotel*. Rare among state tourism offices for a high level of enthusiasm and eagerness to help, but a limited range of services, chiefly a very expensive boat to Cat Ba or a cheaper one to the small island of Dau, just off the southern tip of the peninsula. **Useful services** Post Office and Bank in Do Son town but for sophisticated financial transactions Haiphong is not far away. **Directory**

Road Bus: there are frequent bus services between Haiphong's Lach Tray station and Do Son 45 minutes, 7,000d. Do Son bus station is 4-5 kilometres from the nicest hotels (see the map for location). **Xe ôm**: US$2 one way. **Transport**

Cat Ba Island

Whilst not quite the tropical island paradise of our dreams (too rocky) Cat Ba nevertheless matches our highest expectations in terms of its remoteness (quite but not too); its mellifluousness; its perfect harmony between too little to do but just enough to keep boredom at bay; and its stunning physical setting – lying, as it does, just south of the famous Halong Bay where it enjoys all the advantages of the beauty but suffers none of the arrogance or squalor of poor Halong City. In short Cat Ba is a gem and proves the highlight of many visits to Vietnam.

Phone code: 031
Colour map 1, grid B5

Ins and outs

The **express boat**, a/c, from Haiphong departs at 0900 and 1400, costs 90,000d and takes an hour. If it is not running late the 0600 train from Hanoi will get you to Haiphong just in time to *xe ôm* across town to catch the 0900. **Ferry**: from Haiphong (usually crowded) depart 0630 and 1330, 60,000d, 4 hours. Alternatively take the Hon Gai ferry at 0900 stopping off at Cat Hai; from there small boat to Phu Long on the west of Cat Ba Island and *xe ôm* or bus (erratic service) to Cat Ba town. **Getting there**

Either by organized tour or *xe ôm* (US$3 should get you anywhere on the island) or hired motorbike (Minsk), US$5 per day. There is a bus service between Cat Ba town and Phu Long. Boats usually use the new Cat Ba pier in the middle of town but when strong westerly winds are blowing they use the old harbour. From the old harbour it is a 10 minute bus ride or *xe ôm* around to the hotels. **Getting around**

The North

The Island

Cat Ba is the largest island in a coastal archipelago which includes over 350 limestone outcrops. It is adjacent to and geologically similar to the islands and peaks of Halong Bay but separated by a broad channel as the map on page 156 illustrates. The islands around Cat Ba are larger than the outcrops of Halong Bay and generally more dramatic. Cat Ba is the ideal place from which to explore the whole coastal area: besides the quality of its scenery it is a more agreeable town in which to stay, although the countless new hotels springing up are slowly eroding the difference. The island is rugged and sparsely inhabited. Outside Cat Ba town there are only a few small villages. Perhaps the greatest pleasure is to hire a motorbike and explore, a simple enough process given the island's limited road network.

For an island of its size Cat Ba has remarkably few **beaches** – only two within easy access, creatively named **Cat Ga One** and **Cat Ga Two**. These lie just to the east of town behind a steep hill in the southern fringes of the National Park. They are popular with locals and visitors alike, especially in the late afternoon and at weekends but are also tending to attract tourist paraphernalia and litter, National Park status notwithstanding. A two kilometre walk to the first and a further one kilometre to the second which is quieter and cleaner. 5,000d. There are cold drinks and peanutty snacks for sale, tyres for hire, showers and toilets.

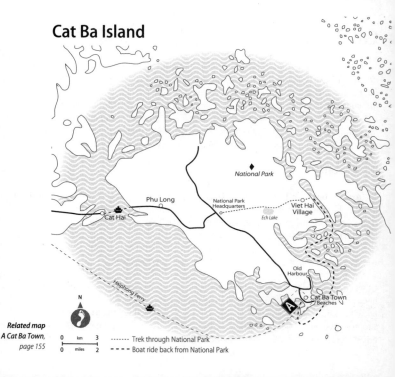

Cat Ba Island

National Park

Phu Long

National Park
Headquarters

Viet Hai
Village

Cat Hai

Ech Lake

Old
Harbour

Cat Ba Town
Beaches

Haiphong Ferry

N

Related map
A Cat Ba Town,
page 155

| 0 | km | 3 |
| 0 | miles | 2 |

------ Trek through National Park
- - - - Boat ride back from National Park

Cat Ba National Park (*Vuon Quoc Gia Cat Ba*)

Colour map 1, grid B5

The National Park, established in 1986 covers roughly half the island. Of this area a third consists of coast and inland waters. Home to 109 bird and animal species, of particular importance is the world's last remaining troupe of white-headed langur (around 200 animals). These elusive creatures are rarely spotted and then only from the sea as they inhabit wild and remote cliff habitats. There are also several types of rare macaque (rhesus, pig-tailed and red-faced) and moose deer. Vegetation ranges from mangrove swamps in sheltered bays to densely wooded hollows to high, rugged limestone crags sprouting caps of hardy willows.

The marine section of the park is no less bounteous: perhaps less fortunate is the high economic value of its fish and crustacea populations which keeps the local fishing fleet hard at work and prosperous. In common with other coastal areas in the region the potential for snorkelling here is zero – it is not called the Red River for nothing.

Visitors are free to roam through the forest but advised not to wander too far from the path. Many hotels arrange treks from the park gate through the forest to Ao Ech (frog lake) on to the village of Viet Hai for a light lunch then down to the coast for a boat ride home. This takes the best part of a day and costs around US$10. It is a good way to see the park but those preferring solitude can go their own way or go with a park guide, US$5 for half a day US$10 for the full day. July to October is the wet season when leeches are a problem and mosquitoes are at their worst. Bring leech socks if you have them and plenty of insect repellent. Collar, long sleeves and long trousers advisable. Fauna and flora enthusiasts who fancy staying longer and chatting to the friendly park wardens can put up at one of the several species of *park guesthouse* (**D-E**) T848336. Park office 0700-1130, 1140-1730. ∎ *US$1. Town to park gate 30 minutes on a motorbike.*

Best time to visit
Cat Ba is at its wettest July-August, driest and coolest (15°C) November-January, busiest (and most expensive) May-September.

*Related map
Cat Ba Island, page 154*

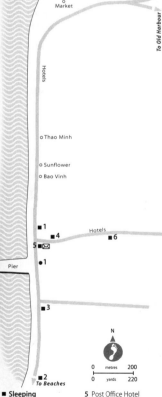

Cat Ba Town

To National Park & Phu Long

To Old Harbour

Market

Hotels

Thao Minh

Sunflower

Bao Vinh

Hotels

Pier

N

0 metres 200
0 yards 220

To Beaches

■ **Sleeping**
1 Family
2 Gieng Ngoc
3 Hoang Huong
4 Pacific
5 Post Office Hotel
6 Sun & Sea

● **Eating**
1 Milo's Cafe

The North

The North

Sleeping
■ *on map*
Price codes:
see inside front cover

Currently a boom town there are already dozens of hotels and guesthouses and more are completed every month. During quieter periods substantial discounts can and should be negotiated. There are no addresses and to confuse matters further many hotels claim the same name (*Gia Dinh* or *Family* is the current favourite). A small selection of the better accommodation is listed although frankly the newer places are virtually indisinguishable:

C *Sun and Sea*, past the PO on the right, T888315, F888475. Currently the plushest in town, 20 rooms, all mod cons including satellite TV, tall but no seaview, slightly tacky finish but enthusiastic owners. **C** *Sunflower*, west of pier in the busiest part of town (karaoke is a real menace here), T888215, F888451. 15 rooms, 10 with seaview, a/c and comfortable, good restaurant. **C** *PO Guesthouse*. Central, new and clean. **D** *Gieng Ngoc 1 and 2*, east of the new pier, T888286. Among the best of the budget hotels, quiet (a rare commodity in Cat Ba town), front rooms overlook sea, fair sized rooms, basic but clean, fan only, hot water in winter, Gieng Ngoc 1 is the smaller, older and cheaper of the two. **D** *Family* (*Quang Duc*), just west of pier, T888231. The original 'Family' Hotel, fan, hot water, spotlessly clean, views from most rooms, a very well run little hotel, owners are knowledgeable on local matters and helpful, restaurant. Recommended. **D** *Hoang Huong*, near pier, T888274. Clean and central. **D** *Pacific*, opposite PO, T888331, F888325. Popular with tour groups, friendly and efficient. **D** *Thao Minh*, west of pier, T888408. 20 fan rooms with hot water, new, clean, tour group type hotel, popular restaurant. **E** *Hoa Phong*, east of pier, T888412. Cheap but sparsely furnished, a grubby, karaoke-type establishment.

Eating
● *on map*

After dark there is a charged atmosphere along the front as tanned Westerners crowd into small restaurants to quaff large bottles of chilled beer, consume fresh seafood and strike up lively conversations and friendships. Some hotels listed above have

Cat Ba Island & Halong Bay

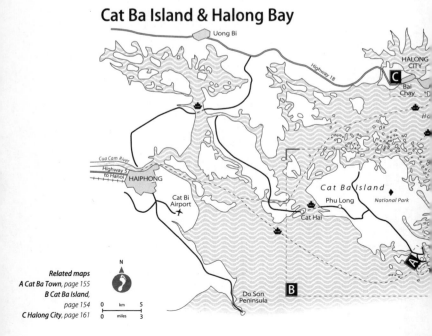

Related maps
A Cat Ba Town, page 155
B Cat Ba Island,
page 154
C Halong City, page 161

restaurants. Of particular note are Family (*Quang Duc*), *Thao Minh* and *Sunflower*. Also many restaurants serving seafood, Vietnamese/Chinese and vegetarian. Smack opp the pier is a little joint of indeterminate name (currently *Milos*) run by a lovely young lady: serves food and drink and is an agent for boat and trekking tours, helpful.

Express boat From Cat Ba express boats to Haiphong depart 1130 and 1600. **Transport**
Ferry From Cat Ba to Haiphong: depart 0600 and 1300. From Cat Ba to Hon Gai: most hotels on the island offer tours of Halong Bay that will drop off passengers in Hon Gai. **Tours** All Hanoi tourist cafés offer tours to Cat Ba: you are well advised not to take one but to make your own way via the Haiphong train and ferry; this is a far cheaper option, very easy and more flexible.

Banks None, hotels will exchange US$ cash at poor rates. **Communications** Post Office: in **Directory** town centre, opposite pier. International calls and faxes, may also change money. No Email cafés yet reported but it will not be long.

Halong Bay

Halong means descending dragon, and an enormous beast is said to have   *Colour map 1, grid B6*
careered into the sea at this point, cutting the fantastic bay from the rocks as it thrashed its way into the depths. Vietnamese poets (including the 'Poet King' Le Thanh Tong) have traditionally extolled the beauty of this romantic area with its rugged islands that protrude from a sea dotted with sailing junks; and artists have been just as quick to draw inspiration from the crooked islands seeing the forms of monks and gods in the rock faces and dragon's lairs and fairy lakes in the depths of the caves. Another myth has it that the islands are dragons sent by the gods to impede the progress of an invasion flotilla. Historically more believable, if substantially embellished, the area was the location of two famous sea battles, in the 10th and 13th centuries (see box Battles of Bach Dang River).

Ins and outs

There are two bases from which to **Getting there** explore Halong Bay – Halong City or Cat Ba. Traditionally, visitors went direct to Halong City (see the Halong City entry for details) and took a boat from there. This is still a valid option, especially for those who are short of time. But Cat Ba is becoming increasingly popular as a springboard to Halong Bay, largely because Cat Ba itself is interesting.

Boat tours of the Bay can be booked in **Getting around** Halong City and Cat Ba Town. To see the Bay properly, allocate 4-5 hours. See the end of this section for details and the separate entries on Cat Ba Town and Halong City for local transport.

The area

Geologically the tower karst scenery of Halong Bay is the product of millions of years of chemical action and river erosion working on the limestone to produce a pitted landscape. At the end of the last ice age when glaciers melted the sea level rose and inundated the area turning hills into islands. The islands of the bay are divided by a broad channel: to the east are the smaller outcrops of Bai Tu Long while to the east are the larger islands with caves and secluded beaches.

Among the more spectacular caves are **Hang Hanh** which extends for two kilometres. Tour guides will point out fantastic stalagmites and stalactites which, with imagination, become heroes, demons and animals. **Hang Luon** is another flooded cave which leads to the hollow core in a doughnut or Polo-shaped island. It can be swum or navigated by coracle. **Hang Dau Go** is the cave wherein Tran Hung Dao stored his wooden stakes prior to studding them in the bed of the Bach Dang River in 1288 to destroy the boats of invading Mongol hordes. **Hang Thien Cung** is a hanging cave, a short 50 metres haul above sea level, with dripping stalactites, stumpy stalagmites and solid rock pillars. All these and more, Grotto of Wonders, Customs House Cave and Surprise Grotto charge US$1. Many are a disappointment with harrying vendors, mounds of litter and disfiguring graffito. Many are lit but some are not so bring a torch. Rocks can be treacherously slippery so sensible footwear is advised. A good boatman (and some speak English) will take you to more secluded islands where you can swim and rest free of charge and free of hassles while he knocks up a delicious seafood lunch (not free of charge).

Getting there from Halong
Boat tours can be booked from hotels although it may be cheaper to organize the trip independently; try the tourist wharf opposite *Van Hai Hotel*. You will be approached by numerous touts along the seafront in Bai Chay, most are prepared to bargain. Because it takes about one hour to get into the bay proper, one long trip represents better value than two short ones. A tour of the bay including a cave or two and a swim needs four to five hours. Charter rates are around 50,000-80,000d per hour for a boat that will accommodate eight to 10, food extra. Boats can be hired overnight for upwards of 400,000d, which considering the saving on hotel bills is fairly economical (take warm clothes). **Tourist cafés** in Hanoi offer tours of the bay with one night in Bai Chay, at prices ranging from US$16-35 plus the US$3 tax which Quang Ninh province in its wisdom has started to levy on all foreign visitors (how Haiphong and Cat Ba must be rubbing their hands). OK for those short of time but more economical and fun to do it yourself.

Getting there from Cat Ba
Cat Ba is an increasingly popular alternative springboard to Halong Bay. The chief advantage is that there is a lot to see on the island: unlike Bai Chay it is an attractive destination in its own right. From Cat Ba there are two further options: either return to Hanoi via Halong City (most tours of Halong Bay will drop passengers off in Hon Gai) or double back via Haiphong. But the journey from Halong to Hanoi is wretched and the minibus operators some of the least pleasant in the country (and note the last bus to Hanoi from Bai Chay leaves at 1600). The preferred alternative, therefore, is to arrive and depart Cat Ba via Haiphong and take a one day or half day tour of the bay, thus cutting out Halong City altogether. The final nail in the coffin for Halong City is that all foreign visitors to this wretched town are taxed US$3 through the compulsory purchase of a 'sightseeing ticket'. A one day tour of Halong Bay costs US$10 per person plus US$2 for lunch but groups can bargain.

Halong City

The route from Hanoi passes newly industrializing satellite towns whose facto-
ries, petrol stations and houses spill onto what were recently paddy fields. After
Uong Bi the scenery improves with the limestone hills which rise out of the allu-
vial plain giving a foretaste of the better things to come. Following the admission
of Halong Bay to UNESCO's hallowed roll of World Heritage Sites the two small
towns of Bai Chay and Hon Gai were in 1994 collectively elevated in status by
the government and dubbed Halong City, a moniker largely ignored by locals.

Phone code: 033
Colour map 1, grid B6

Ins and outs

There are regular bus connections from Hanoi's Gia Lam terminal to Bai Chay, across **Getting there**
the water from Hon Gai, 4-5 hours, 35,000d. The Bai Chay station is on the waterfront,
near the Post Office. Or you can take the train to Haiphong and get a bus or ferry from
there.

Given the paucity of sites in the town, pretty much anywhere of relevance can be **Getting around**
reached on foot. For venturing further afield the town has the usual gangs of xe ôm
drivers.

The town

It was at Halong that, arguably, Vietnam's fate under the French was sealed.
In late 1882 Captain Henri Rivière led two companies of troops to Hon Gai to
seize the coal mines for France. Shortly afterwards he was ambushed and
killed and his head paraded on a stake from village to village. His death persuaded the French parliament to fund a full scale expedition to make all of
Vietnam a protectorate of France. As the politician Jules Delafosse remarked
at the time: "Let us, gentlemen, call things by their name. It is not a protectorate you want, but a possession."

The twin towns, Bai Chay to the west and Hon Gai to the east, separated by
a river estuary and linked by a ferry, could not be more different. Few visitors
make the short crossing to Hon Gai which, with its port and adjacent coal-
mines, could fairly be described as the industrial end of town.

Bai Chay has made great efforts and not a little progress towards turning
itself into an attractive destination rather than merely a dormitory for those
visiting Ha Long Bay. At huge expense a narrow beach has been constructed
in front of the hotels; casuarina, palm and flame trees have been planted along
the prom, old hotels renovated and new ones built. There is no denying the
effect, an attractive feel, a seaside town. But the charm is not likely to work its
magic with travellers from abroad in the same way that it does with Vietnamese who are drawn in huge numbers rapidly swamping the little beach every
weekend. Several large and attractive modern hotels have been built, including the Halong Plaza, one of the most luxurious in the country. But quite who
is going to occupy all these junior and executive suites is a problem the marketing men appear to have overlooked.

A five minute, 500d ferry ride brings us to the bustling port of **Hon Gai**.
The Vietnamese government would dearly like to bridge the estuary which
divides the town but owing to the disted stataus of Halong must first obtain
UNESCO's approval. As mining areas go this is quite a nice one but it does not
live up to the 'natural wonderland' image Quang Ninh Tourism is trying to
promote. The port of Hon Gai is busy with plenty of little bamboo and resin

coracles (*thung chai*) which are used by the fishermen as tenders to get out to their boats and to bring ashore the catch. There is a thriving market and near the ferry dock is the 106 metre high **Poem Mountain** (*Nui Bao Tho*) so named following a visit in 1486 by King Le Thanh Tong who was so taken by the beauty of Ha Long Bay that he composed a poem celebrating the scenery and carved his verse into the rock. It is quite a scramble up the hill and finding the right path may require some help. At the foot of the mountain nestles the little **Long Thien Pagoda** which dates from earlier this century. 20 minutes walk north up from Hon Gai is a **ruined colonial church** damaged by a bomb in 1972 but the site affords lovely views. About one kilometre east of central Hon Gai is a small **museum** on Coc 3 Street.

Excursions

The **limestone outcrops** and spectacular **caves and grottoes** of Ha Long Bay constitute the chief attraction, see Halong Bay on page 157 for details of how to visit.

Cat Ba Island   Two ferry rides or charter a boat, see page 157.

Yen Tu Mountains   The Yen Tu Mountains are 14 kilometres northwest of Uong Bi and climb to a maximum elevation of 1,068 metres. Peppered with pagodas from the 13th-16th centuries, much has been lost to the ravages of war and climate but stupas and temples of more recent foundation survive. The site has attracted pilgrims since the 13th century when King Tran Nhan Tong abandoned the throne in favour of a spiritual life. He washed the secular dust from his body in the Tam stream and entered the Cam Thuc (Abstinence) Pagoda. His 100 concubines traced him here and tried to persuade him of the folly of his ways but despite their undoubted allure he resisted all appeals and clung to his ascetic existence. Distraught by their failure, the poor women drowned themselves. Tran Nhan Tong later built a temple to their memory. Climbing the hills, visiting the temples and admiring the views can take a full day.

Halong City

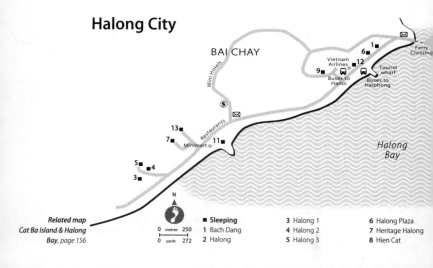

BAI CHAY

Mini Hotels

Vietnam Airlines

Buses to Hanoi

Tourist wharf

Buses to Haiphong

Ferry Crossing

Restaurants

Minimart

Halong Bay

13

7

11

5   4

3

N

Related map
Cat Ba Island & Halong
Bay, page 156

0 metres 250	■ **Sleeping**	3 Halong 1	6 Halong Plaza
0 yards 272	1 Bach Dang	4 Halong 2	7 Heritage Halong
	2 Halong	5 Halong 3	8 Hien Cat

The North

Essentials

The past couple of years has seen an explosion in the number of hotels and guest-houses in Bai Chay and Hon Gai; this reflects the popularity of Halong Bay as a destination for both Vietnamese and foreign visitors. The enthusiasm of the hotel builders has, for the time being at least, outstripped demand so owners are having to accept hard bargaining as an uncomfortable fact of life. Many of the newer hotels are badly built and, apart from the fact that some of the taller ones look structurally unsound, are hideously damp and musty; check the room first.

Sleeping
■ *on map*
Price codes:
see inside front cover

Hon Gai There are few hotels here but they tend to be more competitively priced than those in Bai Chay. **B-C** *Queen*, 70 Le Thanh Tong St, T826193, F827268. A/c, hot water, bathrooms attached, smallish rooms but clean and well run, disco on Saturday evenings – finishes early. **C** *Halong Guesthouse*, 80 Le Thanh Tong, T826509. Just 8 rooms, but a/c, hot water, private bathroom, clean and good value. Several other guesthouses on Le Thanh Tong St. **D** *Hien Cat*, 252 Ben Tau St, T827417. Nearest to the ferry wharf, cheapest and possibly the best, only 5 rooms, the best is at the top, airy, breezy, clean, fan only, outside bathroom, hot water, the family will invite guests to join them for meals. Recommended.

Bai Chay There are two main groups of hotels, 2 kilometres apart. Most are to be found at the west end on the way in to town, set back a little from the sea front and include Vuon Dao St composed entirely of 5-8 rooms mini hotels. 2 kilometres further on, near the ferry to Hon Gai is a smaller group some of which have good views.

Ferry end **L-A+** *Halong Plaza*, 8 Halong Rd, T845810, F846867. A Thai joint venture with 200 rooms and suites and fantastic views over the sea, especially from upper floors, luxuriously finished, huge bathrooms, every comfort and extravagance as the Thais do so well, swimming pool, restaurants and engaging staff, a lovely hotel by any standards. **B** *Bach Dang*, Halong Rd, T846330, F846026. Old but a clean and well run establishment, a/c, sea views. **B** *Van Hai*, Halong Rd, T846403, F846115. Opposite tourist wharf, beginning to show its age, furnishings of flimsy construction and public areas rather shabby but staff are friendly. **D** *Minh Tuan*, Ho Xuan Huong St, T846200. Up a quiet lane 50 metres before the bus station, 14 a/c rooms with bathroom, clean, well managed.

The North

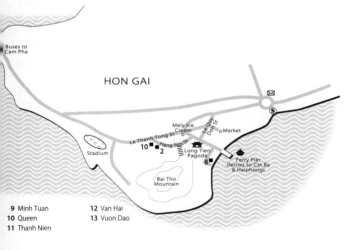

HON GAI

Buses to
Cam Pha

Mely Ice
Cream

Le Thanh Tong St

Hang Noi St

Le Quy Don St

○ Market

Stadium

10 ■ ■
2

Long Tien
Pagoda

8 ■

Ferry Pier
(ferries to Cat Ba
& Haiphong)

Bai Tho
Mountain

West end A+ *Heritage Halong*, 88 Halong Rd, T846888, F846999. A Singapore joint venture lacking the oppulence of the Plaza but nevertheless extremely comfortable and cheaper, all rooms have sea views. 24 hour coffee shop, disco and pool. **A** *Ha Long 1*, Halong Rd, T846014, F846318. A converted French villa with stacks of charm set amongst frangipani, some of the 23 rooms have sea outlook, huge bathrooms, bathtubs, bidets etc. **A** *Saigon Halong*, Halong Rd, T845845, F845849. Newly built and run by Saigon Tourist, 23 rooms in 5 'villas', comfortable, all mod cons, set back from the road on the way into town, relaxed and attractive surroundings, ring in advance to negotiate discount or package. **B** *Vuon Dao*, Halong Rd, T846370, F846287. Set at the top of a drive, large concrete edifice but fairly breezy and airy. **C** *Ha Long 2 & 3*, Halong Rd, T846014, F846318. Set behind Ha Long 1, some large and some smaller blocks that chiefly cater for the Vietnamese market, not particularly clean or comfortable. **C** *Thanh Nien*, Halong Rd, T846715, F846226. Occupies a nice spot on a little promontory jutting into the sea but can be a bit noisy from surrounding cafés etc, attractive bungalow accommodation, a/c, hot water. **D** *Huong Tram*, Halong Rd, T846365. Up a track off Halong Rd, 500 metres east of Post Office, nice views from the top floor of this a/c mini hotel, helpful with advice for local walks and boat trips.

Vuon Dao St A plethora of mini hotels all offering similar accommodation at similar prices (**C-D**) and all willing to bargain during quiet periods.

Eating Seafood is fresh and abundant and fairly priced. **Hon Gai**, Le Qui Don St has good seafood restaurants. *Kem Mely* on Le Thanh Tong St has ice cream and cakes.

Bai Chay: other than the hotels, Halong Rd, near the junction with Vuon Dao St is lined for several hundred metres with restaurants all much of a muchness and all pretty good. *Café Indochine* is useful for local information as well as the usual *ca phe sua da*. At the ferry end there is a decent restaurant opposite the tourist wharf.

Entertainment Discos in *Halong Heritage*, Bai Chay and *Queen Hotel*, Hon Gai.

Shopping Quang Ninh traditional coal sculpture available in Hon Gai.

Transport **Road Bus**: regular connections from Bai Chay to Hanoi from 0700, last bus departs 1600. Buses are slow, crowded, uncomfortable and full of pickpockets. Bai Chay bus station demands foreigners pay double the published fare (35,000d), bus operators will demand triple. Regular connections with Haiphong's Binh bus station 0900-1500, 20,000d (published fare).

Sea Charter boat: to and from Cat Ba try the tourist wharf opposite *Van Hai Hotel*. **Ferries** depart for Haiphong from Hon Gai 0600, 0830, 1100 and 1600, 45,000d, 3 hours. The trip itself is worthwhile; the ferry is packed with people and their produce and threads its way through the limestone islands and outcrops that are so characteristic of the area, before winding up the Cua Cam River to the port of Haiphong. For Cat Ba take the Haiphong ferry to Cat Hai and either transfer to the Haiphong-Cat Ba ferry or hop over to Phu Long and take a *xe ôm* from there.

Directory **Banks** Hon Gai has three banks, *Vietcombank* on Le Thanh Tong offers same rates as Hanoi. *GPO* also changes money. **Communications** GPO in Hon Gai, Le Thanh Tong St. Open 0700-2000, international telephone and fax. In Bai Chay at junction of Halong Rd and Vuon Dao St and opposite Hon Gai ferry. **Hospitals & medical services** *Bai Chay Hospital*, T846566. *Hon Gai Hospital*, T825499. **Tourist offices** *Quang Ninh Tourism*, near *Ha Long Hotel*, Bai Chay, T846274. *Vietnam Tourism*, 2 Le Thanh Tong St T827250, near Hon Gai bus station.

Hanoi to Ninh Binh

From Hanoi, the route south runs through the rather grey, industrial towns of Ha Nam, Nam Dinh and Ninh Binh. The last few years have brought rapid expansion to these industrial centres which are being convulsed with change: road widenings and realignments, wholesale demolition of old buildings to make way for new, huge industrial zones and factories gobbling up prime 'ricefield' sites. The traffic is dominated by trucks and buses which sweep bicycles, pedestrians and hand cart pushers into the ditch. Communities which for centuries were divided by nothing more than a dirt track now find themselves rent asunder by four-lane highways, but ancient ties of kith and kin and tradition have yet to adjust. Thus we see gaggles of little children dodging the wheels of juggernauts, racing to get to school on time and a little old lady trying to avoid spilling the three delicately balanced, steaming bowls of noodle soup in her hands destined for the officers of the Planning and Investment Committee of Ward No 8 while simultaneously trying to dodge the oncoming Hanoi to Vinh express bus which is overtaking the Ha Nam to Ninh Binh stopping bus, which in turn has swerved to avoid the heavy truck of Construction Company No 17 of Ha Tay Province whose driver has pulled up to enable his mate to jump down and buy two 555 cigarettes – and while he's at it to have a pee; and all the time, coming up from the south, a similar contingent of fast and slow moving vehicles duel to overtake all in their path while desperately trying to prevent anything else from getting in front.

Nam Dinh

Nam Dinh is a large and diverse industrial centre, with a reputation for its textiles. The Nam Dinh Textile Mill was built by the French in 1899, and is still operating (which says a lot for the state of Vietnamese industry and Vietnamese resourcefulness). The city is the third largest urban centre in the north with a population exceeding 300,000.

Phone code: 035
Colour map 1, grid C5

Thien Truong and Pho Minh Pagodas – both highly regarded – are to be found in the village of Tuc Mac (My Loc district), three kilometres north of Nam Dinh. Also here are the few remains of the Tran Dynasty. Thien Truong was built in 1238 and dedicated to the kings of the Tran family; Pho Minh was built rather later, in 1305, and contains an impressive 13-storey tower.

Excursions

    Doi Son and **Doi Diep Pagodas** are situated on two neighbouring mountains (*Nui Doi Son* and *Nui Doi Diep*). The former was originally built at some point during the early Ly Dynasty (544-602 AD). When the Emperor Le Dai Hanh (980-1005) planted rice at the foot of the mountain, legend has it that he uncovered two vessels, one filled with gold and the other with silver. From that season on, the harvests were always bountiful.

    Keo Pagoda North of the main channel of the Red River, 10 kilometres southwest of Thai Binh is the site of the 11th century Keo Pagoda, which was destroyed in a flood. The present building dates back to the seventeenth century but has been remodelled several times. Its chief architectural attraction is a wooden three-storey campanile containing two bronze bells.

    ■ *Getting to the pagodas: either by xe ôm from Nam Dinh or as part of a day trip by car (including Hoa Lu) from Hanoi.*

Sleeping **B-C** *Son Nam*, 26 Le Hong Phong St, T848920, F848915. A range of accommodation in three buildings. **C** *Vi Hoang*, 115 Nguyen Du St. Somewhat uncared for, restaurant.

Transport 80 kilometres south of Hanoi. At the eastern apex of the Ha Nam, Nam Dinh, Ninh Binh growth triangle; cut off by Highway 1 but the railway detours two sides of the triangle to get there. **Train** 5 daily connections with Hanoi, 2-3 hours, also with Ninh Binh. **Road Bus**: regular connections with Hanoi's Southern terminal, 3 hours, and with Haiphong on Highway 10, 4 hours.

Directory **Communications** Post Office: Ha Huy Tap St. **Tourist offices** *Nam Dinh Tourist*, 115 Nguyen Du St.

Ninh Binh

Phone code: 030
Colour map 1, grid C4

Ninh Binh is capital of the densely populated and newly formed province of Ninh Binh. It marks the most southerly point of the northern region. The town itself has little to commend to the tourist but it is a useful and accessible hub from which to visit some of the most interesting and attractive sights in the north. Within a short drive lie the ancient capital of Hoa Lu with its temples dedicated to two of Vietnam's great kings; the exquisite watery landscape of Tam Coc, an 'inland Halong Bay', where sampans carry visitors up a meandering river, through inundated grottoes and past verdant fields of rice; the Catholic landscape around Phat Diem Cathedral, spires and towers, bells and smells; and the lovely Cuc Phuong National Park with its glorious butterflies, flowers and trees.

Excursions

Hoa Lu
Colour map 1, grid C4

Hoa Lu lies about 13 kilometres from Ninh Binh near the village of Truong Yen. It was the capital of Vietnam from 968 to 1010 AD, during the Dinh and Early Le dynasties. Prior to the establishment of Hoa Lu as the centre of the new kingdom, there was nothing here. But the location was a good one in the narrow valley of the Hong River – on the 'dragon's belly', as the Vietnamese say. The passes leading to the citadel could be easily defended with a small force, and defenders could keep watch over the plains to the north and guard against the Chinese. The kings of Hoa Lu were, in essence, rustics. This is reflected in the art and architecture of the temples of the ancient city: primitive in form, massive in conception. Animals – elephants, rhinoceros, horses – were the dominant motifs, monumentally carved in stone. The inhabitants were not, by all accounts, sophisticated aesthetes.

Much of this former capital, which covered over 200 hectares, has been destroyed, although archaeological excavations have revealed a great deal of historical and artistic interest. The two principal temples of Hoa Lu are those of Dinh Bo Linh who assumed the title King Dinh Tien Hoang on ascending the throne (reigned 968-980) and Le Hoan who assumed the title King Le Dai Hanh on ascending the throne (ruled 980-1009). The **Temple of Dinh Tien Hoang** was originally constructed in the 11th century but was reconstructed in 1696. It is arranged as a series of courtyards, gates and buildings. The inscription on one of the pillars in the temple, in ancient Vietnamese, reads 'Dai Co Viet', from which the name 'Vietnam' is derived. The temple also contains statues of various animals, often crude, which came to represent higher beings. The back room of the temple is dedicated to Dinh Tien Hoang, whose statue occupies the central position, surrounded by those of his sons. In the 960s, Dinh Tien Hoang managed to pacify much of the Red River plain, undermining the position of a competing ruling family, the Ngos, who eventually accepted Dinh Tien Hoang's supremacy. However, this was not done willingly, and banditry and insubordination continued to afflict Hoang's Kingdom. He responded by placing a large kettle and a tiger in a cage in the courtyard of his palace and decreed: 'those who violate the law will be boiled and gnawed'. An uneasy calm descended on Dinh Tien Hoang's kingdom, and he could concern himself with promoting Buddhism and geomancy, arranging strategic marriages, and implementing administrative reforms. But, by making his infant son Hang Lang heir apparent, rather than Dinh Lien (his only adult son), he sealed his fate. History records that the announcement was followed by earthquakes and hailstorms, a sign of dissension in the court, and in 979 Lien sent an assassin to kill his younger brother Hang Lang. A few months later in the same year, an official named Do Thich killed both Dinh Tien Hoang and Dinh Lien as they lay drunk and asleep in the palace courtyard. When Do Thich was apprehended, it is said that he was executed and his flesh fed to the people of the city.

The **Temple of King Le Dai Hanh** is dedicated to the founder of the Le Dynasty who seized power after the regicide of Dinh Tien Hoang. In fact Le Dai Hanh took not only Hoang's throne but also his wife, Duong Van Nga, and representations of her, Le Dai Hanh and Le Ngoa Trieu (Hanh's eldest son) each sit on their own altar in the rear temple.

A short walk beyond Le Dai Hanh's temple is Nhat Tru Pagoda, a 'working' temple. In front of it stands a stone pillar engraved with excerpts from the Buddhist bible (*kinh phat*). Adjacent to Dinh Tien Hoang's temple is a small hill, Nui Ma Yen, at the top of which is Dinh Tien Hoang's tomb. Local children will tell you it is 265 steps to the top. There are also boat trips on the river to Xuyen Thay cave (15,000d), less spectacular than Tam Coc. ■ *US$1. Getting there: by bicycle or xe ôm, six kilometres north of Ninh Binh and six kilometres west of Highway 1, follow signs to Truong Yen. From Hanoi, by chartered car, two hours, or on an organized tour. Cheaper, especially for three or four persons, and more flexible to hire a car with driver, no need for a guide.* **Sleeping B-C** *Van Xuan*, just off Highway 1 (T030-860648, F030-860647). New hotel, a/c, hot water, clean, restaurant.

Hoa Lu and the Temple of Dinh Tien Hoang

To Highway 1

Nhat Tru Pagoda

Le Dai Hanh Temple

Dinh Tien Hoang's Temple

Car Park

Boats for hire

N

Dinh Tien Hoang's Grave

Ma Yen Mountain

To Xuyen Thuy Cave

| 0 | metres | 50 |
| 0 | yards | 55 |

······· Footpath

Tam Coc

Some 10 kilometres south of Ninh Binh a few kilometres west of Highway 1. Tam Coc means three caves; and the highlight of this excursion is an enchanting boat ride up the little Ngo Dong River through the eponymous three caves. Those who have seen the film *Indochine*, some of which was shot here, will be familiar with the nature of the bee-hive type scenery created by limestone towers, similar to those of Halong Bay. The exact form varies from wet to dry season; when flooded the channel disappears and one or two of the caves may be drowned. In the dry season the shallow river meanders between fields of golden rice. Women row and punt pitch and resin tubs that look like elongated coracles through the tunnels. It is a most leisurely experience and a chance to observe at close quarters the extraordinary method of rowing with the feet. Take plenty of sun cream and a hat. The villagers have a rota to decide whose turn it is to row and to supplement their fee will try and sell visitors embroidered table cloths and napkins. Enterprising photographers snap you setting off from the bank and will surprise you one kilometre up stream with copies of your cheesy grin already printed. On a busy day the scene from above is like a two way, nose to tail procession of waterboatmen, so to enjoy Tam Coc at its best make it your first port of call in the morning.

Bich Dong A short drive to the south is **Bich Dong**. This is much harder work, so not surprisingly it is a lot quieter than Tam Coc. Bich Dong consists of a series of temples and caves built into and carved out of a limestone mountain. The temples date from the reign of Le Thai To in the early 15th century. It is typical of many Vietnamese cave temples but with more than the average number of legends attached, while the number of interpretations of its rock formations defies belief. The cliff face into which the lower temple is built is beautifully covered with the roots and trunks of banyan trees. Next to the temple is a pivoted and carved rock that resonates beautifully when tapped with a stone. Next see Buddha's footprints embedded in the rock (size 12, for the curious) and the tombs of the two founding monks. Leading upwards is the middle temple, an 18th-century bell, a memorial stone into which are carved the names of benefactors and a cave festooned with rock forms. Here, clear as can be, are likeness of Uncle Ho, a turtle and an elephant. More resonant rock pillars follow and a rock which enables pregnant women to choose the sex of their baby: touch the top for a boy and the middle for a girl. But best of all scramble right to the pinnacle of the peak for a glorious view over the whole area. ■ *US$2 plus US$1.5 per person for the boat ride (tip or purchase will be requested). Getting there: the turning to Tam Coc and Bich Dong is four kilometres south of Ninh Binh on Highway 1. A small road leads two to three kilometres west to Tam Coc and a further two kilometres to Bich Dong. Can easily be reached by bicycle or xe ôm from Ninh Binh or by car from Hanoi (on a day trip including Hoa Lu); again the same reservations about taking an organized tour apply.*

Phat Diem Cathedral The Red River Delta was the first part of the country to be influenced by Western missionaries: Portuguese priests were proselytizing here as early as 1627. Christian influence is still strong despite the mass exodus of Catholics to the south in 1954 and decades of communist rule. Villages in these coastal provinces (which are built of red brick, often walled and densely populated) may have more than half a dozen churches, all with packed congregations, not only on Sundays. It is hard to escape the feeling visiting some of these Catholic villages that it is the trappings of the religion that are the objects of worship rather than the founder of the religion. The churches, the shrines, the holy grottoes, the photographs of the parish priest on bedroom walls and the holy relics clearly assume huge significance in people's lives.

Phat Diem Cathedral is the most spectacular of the church buildings in the area, partly for its scale but also for its remarkable oriental style. Completed in 1891, it boasts a bell tower in the form of a pagoda behind which stretches for 74 metres the nave of the cathedral held up by 52 ironwood pillars. Several services daily. ■ *Getting there: 24 kilometres southwest of Ninh Binh in the village of Kim Son. The journey takes in a number of more conventional churches, waterways and paddy fields. Motorbike from Ninh Binh or hire car from Hanoi. Hoa Lu, Tam Coc and Phat Diem can all be comfortably covered in one day.*

This is probably the second most accessible of Vietnam's national parks and for nature lovers not intending to visit Cat Ba island it is worthy of consideration. Located in an area of deeply-cut limestone and reaching elevations of up to 800 metres, the park is covered by 22,000 hectares of humid tropical montagne forest. It is home to an estimated 1,880 species of flora including the giant *parashorea*, *cinamomum* and *sandoricum* trees. Wildlife has been much depleted by hunting, only 64 mammal and 137 bird species are thought to remain. The government has resettled a number of the park's 30,000 Muong minority people although Muong villages do remain and can be visited. April and May sees fat grubs and pupae metamorphosing into swarms of beautiful butterflies that mantle the forest in fantastic shades of greens and yellows. ■ *US$5. Getting there: around 120 kilometres south of Hanoi and 45 kilometres west of Ninh Binh. Can be done as a day trip from Ninh Binh, or from Hanoi (early start). Access by car only. Organized tour from Hanoi may be a sensible option for lone travellers or pairs, otherwise charter a car.* Accommodation at the Park Gate (fan or a/c, hot water, US$25-40) or in the interior (hot water, no a/c US$20-40). One or two day treks can be arranged with a guide (US$10 per day). Park office T030-866085.

**Cuc Phuong
National Park**
*Colour map 2,
grid A1/2*

B-D *Hoa Lu*, Tran Hung Dao St, T871217, F874126. On Highway 1 towards Hanoi, 120 rooms at a range of prices for a range of standards, cars and motorbikes for rent, tours arranged, including hunting, friendly. **C-D** *Thuy Anh*, 55A Truong Han Sieu St, T/F871602. 8 a/c rooms, with fridge etc in this spotless hotel, 30 additional rooms in their sister hotel, car for hire 300,000d per day, motorbike 60,000d per day and bicycle, will arrange tours, useful source of information. **D** *Queen*, Hoanh Hoa Tham St, T871874. Near station, simple but clean.

Sleeping

94 kilometres south of Hanoi on Highway 1 and the main north-south railway line. **Train** There are regular local train connections with Hanoi, 3 hours, soft seats 48,000d, hard seats 38,000d. 13 hrs from Hué, soft seats 213,000d. It may be difficult getting connections on from Ninh Binh because of Ninh Binh's limited allocation of tickets. In case of difficulty board the train and negotiate once under way. **Road Bus**: there are regular bus connections with Hanoi's Southern terminal, 3 hours.

Transport

Bank *Vietincombank*, Tran Hung Dao St. Cashes Tcs.

Directory

Communications GPO: Tran Hung Dao St.

The North

The Central Region

5

The Central Region

The Central Region extends over 1,000 kilometres north to south. It includes the mountains of the Annamite chain which form a natural frontier with Laos to the west and in places extend almost all the way to the sea, in the east. Many of Vietnam's hill peoples are concentrated in these mountains. The narrow coastal strip, sometimes only a few kilometres wide, supported the former artistically accomplished kingdom of Champa.

The narrow central region is traversed by a single road – Highway 1 – which runs all the way from Hanoi to Saigon. Along much of its route, the road runs close to the coast, passing through a succession of interesting, though rather unattractive, towns. These northern provinces – such as Nghe Tinh – are among the poorest in the country but their inhabitants are among the friendliest. Villagers here grow barely enough to feed themselves. 654 kilometres south of Hanoi and 1,071 kilometres north of Saigon, is the former imperial capital of Hué. Though devastated during the Vietnam War, the Imperial Palace and tombs represent the most impressive collection of historical sights in Vietnam.

Thanh Hoa to Hué

Thanh Hoa

Phone code: 037
Colour map 2, grid A2
The **citadel of Ho** was built in 1397 when Thanh Hoa was the capital of Vietnam. Much of this great city has been destroyed, although the massive city gates are preserved. Art historians believe that they rival the finest Chinese buildings, and the site is in the process of being excavated. This town and province mark the most northerly point of the central region.

The 160 metres long **Ham Rong Bridge** or 'Dragon's Jaw' which crosses the Ma River south of Thanh Hoa was a highly significant spot during the Vietnam War. The bridge, a crucial transport link with the south, was heavily fortified and the US lost 70 planes in successive abortive raids from 1965. Eventually, in 1972, they succeeded using laser-guided 'smart' bombs – at which point the Vietnamese promptly built a replacement pontoon bridge. Significantly, however, during the attack in 1972, as well as one at the same time using the same technology against the Paul Doumer Bridge in Hanoi, no US aircraft were lost. 15 kilometres east of Thanh Hoa lies the coastal resort of **Sam Son**. This is truly a bizarre place catering mainly for the holidaying Vietnamese. The place is teeming with karaoke cafés and commercial sex workers. The beach is long and crowded with deckchairs. It is impossible to stroll around without the hirers of these chairs following you. If you walk south along the beach and over the hill you can find a deserted cove (walk past the temple). This beach is full of tiny crabs.

Sleeping   **B-E** *Thanh Hoa*, 25 Quang Trung St, T852517, F853963. 93 rooms at a wide range of prices offering everything from a/c and satellite TV to shared bathrooms with cold water only. **C** *Binh Minh*, 102 Trien Quoc Dat St, near Post Office and railway station, T852088. Satellite TV, a/c and restaurant.

Transport   153 kilometres from Hanoi. **Train** Express trains to and from Hanoi and Saigon stop here, 4¼ hours. **Road Bus**: regular connections with Hanoi's Ha Dong bus station, 4 hours, Ninh Binh, Vinh and other towns on Highway 1.

Directory   **Tourist offices** *Thanh Hoa Province Tourism* in *Thanh Hoa Hotel*.

Vinh

Phone code: 038
Colour map 2, grid B2
Vinh is a diversified industrial centre and capital of Nghe Tinh Province. It was damaged by the French before 1954, and then suffered sustained bombing by US and ARVN (Army of the Republic of Vietnam) aircraft from 1964 through to 1972. In the process it was virtually razed. Vinh lies at the important point where the coastal plain narrows, forcing roads and railways to squeeze down a slender coastal strip of land. The town has since been rebuilt with assistance from former East Germany, in startlingly unimaginative style. The dirty-brown apartment blocks make Vinh one of the most inhuman and uninspired cities in Vietnam. The province of Nghe Tinh also happens to be one of the poorest, and the mini-famine of 1989 struck hard.

There is nothing of historical interest here, unless socialist architecture can be thought of as such. The **Central Market**, at the south end of Gao Thang Street (the continuation of Quang Trung Street), is a bustle of colour and activity.

Kim Lien village, 14 kilometres west of Vinh, is the birthplace of Ho Chi **Excursions** Minh who was born here in 1890. There is a reconstruction of the house Ho was born in together with a memorial altar. **Sen** is another village close to Kim Lien, where Ho lived with his father from the age of six. Although the community and surrounding area were hardly wealthy, Ho was fortunate to be born into a family of modest means and his father was highly educated. The house where he lived (in fact a replica built in 1955) may be thatched and rude, but it was a great deal better than the squalor that most of his countrymen had to endure (see page 336 for a short account of Ho's life). The province of Nghe Tinh has a reputation for producing charismatic revolutionary leaders; not only Ho Chi Minh but also Phan Boi Chau – another fervant anti-colonialist – was born here (see page 347).

Cua Lo is a beach 20 kilometres from Vinh. It boasts eight kilometres of white sandy beach and is a very popular (if slightly downmarket) holiday spot with the locals. There are a number of hotels but finding a room during holiday time (June-August) can be tricky. **C-D** *Thai Binh Duong*, 92 Binh Minh St, T824164.

Because so few visitors stay in Vinh, hotel rates can be bargained down considerably. **Sleeping** **B-D** *Giao Te*, 9 Ho Tung Mau St, T843175. A/c, large and unattractive. **C** *Hong Ngoi*, 86B Le Loi St, T841314. Mini hotel offering comfortable accommodation. Prices can be bargained to very reasonable levels. **C** *Kim Lien*, 12 Quang Trung St, T844751, F843699. Perhaps the best in town. **C** *Nghe An Guesthouse*, 4 Phan Dang Lum St, T846112. A/c. **C-E** *Song Lan*, 13 Quang Trung St, T840603. 20 rooms, some a/c. **D-E** *Railway Station Hotel*, Le Nin St (adjacent to the station), T853754. Some a/c.

197 kilometres from Dong Hoi, 291 kilometres from Hanoi, 368 kilometres from Hué. **Transport** **Train** The station is in the west quarter of town, 3 kilometres from the central market. Connections with Hanoi and all points south to Saigon; express trains stop here. **Road** **Bus**: the bus station is on Le Loi St. Express buses leave for Hanoi, Saigon and Danang at 0500. **Local** Honda ôm. Cars available from Vinh Tourist or most hotels.

Banks *Vietcombank*, Nguyen Si Sach St. **Communications** Post Office: Nguyen Thi Minh Khai **Directory** St. **Tourist offices** *Vinh Tourist Office*, 13 Quang Trung St, T844692.

Ngang Pass or Porte d'Annam

Running between the Central Highlands and the coast is a small range of mountains, the Hoanh Son, which neatly divide the north from Central Vietnam. In French times the range marked the southern limit of Tonkin and northern limit of Annam. The mountains which reach up to 1,000 metres have a marked effect on climate blocking cold northerly winds in winter and receiving up to 3,000 millimetres of rain. During the reign of Minh Mang a gate was built, the Hoanh Son Quan. Subsequently, Emperor Thieu Tri on a visit north composed a poem which is inscribed on a nearby rock.

Dong Hoi

Travelling either south from Vinh towards Hué, or north to Vinh, there is lit- *Phone code: 052* tle to entice the traveller to stop. Along this stretch of coastal plain, which *Colour map 2, grid B2* crosses from the province of Nghe An to Ha Tinh to Quang Binh to Quang Tri to Thua Thien Hué, the inhabitants have been struggling against floods and encroaching sand dunes for years. During the Vietnam War, the area was pounded by bombs and shells, and sprayed with defoliants. Unexploded bombs still regularly maim farmers (one million bombs have been unearthed since the end of hostilities), and it is claimed that the enduring effects of Agent Orange can be seen in the high rates of physical deformity in both animals and humans.

The town of Dong Hoi can be used as a stopping-off point on the way north or south. It was virtually annihilated during the war as it lies just north of the 17th parallel, marking the border between North and South Vietnam. Just south of the town is the **Hien Luong Bridge** which spans the Ben Hai River – the river forming the border between the two halves of former North and South Vietnam.

Excursions **Phong Nha Cave** is about 50 kilometres from Dong Hoil. It is a true speleological wonder – if not of the world then certainly of Vietnam. Visitors are taken only 600 metres into the cave by boat and are dropped off to explore. The brick foundations of a Cham temple remain in one of the chambers. There are stalagmites and stalactites and those with a powerful torch can pick out the form of every manner of ghoul and god in the rocks. A team of British divers explored nine kilometres of the main cave system in 1990 but less than one kilometre is accessible to visitors. ■ *US$6 including boat ride. Getting there: north on Highway 1 for 20 kilometres, 30 kilometres west to the Son River landing stage.*

Sleeping **C** *Phuong Nam*, T052-823194. A/c, restaurant.

Transport 522 kilometres from Hanoi, 166 kilometres from Hué, 197 kilometres from Vinh. **Train** Regular connections with Hanoi and Saigon. **Road** Buses travelling up Highway 1 linking Saigon with Hanoi pass through Dong Hoi.

Dong Ha

Phone code: 053
Colour map 3, grid A4

Dong Ha sits on the junction of Highways 1 and 9 and is prospering with the growth of trade with Laos. Dong Ha is a convenient overnight stop for those crossing into or coming from Laos. Travellers have reported successfully hitching lifts with trucks bound for Laos.

Excursions **The DMZ, Khe Sanh and the Ho Chi Minh Trail** lie to the south of Dong Hoi. These war-time sights are normally visited on a tour from Hué and are described in detail on page 190. 94 kilometres south at Dong Ha, Highway 9 branches off the main coastal Highway 1 and proceeds to the border with Laos. Along this route is Khe Sanh (now called Huong Hoa) – one of the most evocative names associated with American involvement in Vietnam (see page 189). Close to Khe Sanh are parts of the famous Ho Chi Minh Trail along which supplies were ferried from the north to the south (see page 190). Highway 9 has been extensively improved in recent years to provide land-locked Laos with an alternative access route to the sea.

International Crossing This border crossing to Savannakhet is open to foreigners with the appropriate visa for the **Lao Bao crossing**. The crossing is two kilometres beyond Lao Bao village. Bus connections from Hué to Khe Sanh, also from Khe Sanh to Lao Bao village (**E** *Mountain*, simple, clean, friendly). Honda ôm from Khe Sanh to the border, US$3, or from Lao Bao village to the border US$1. Those crossing into Vietnam may be able to get a ride with the DMZ tour bus from Khe Sanh back to Hué in the late afternoon.

C *Ngan Ha Guesthouse*, Le Quay Don St, T852806. Some a/c. **E** *Thai Son Guesthouse*. **Sleeping**
Good restaurant nearby.

74 kilometres from Hué, 80 kilometres from Lao Bao, border crossing. Bus to Vinh, 12 **Transport**
hours.

Hué

A trip to Vietnam should, if possible, include a trip to Hué , 100 kilometres south   *Population: 350,000*
of the 17th parallel and built on the banks of the Huong Giang or Perfume River.   *Phone code: 054*
The river is named after a scented shrub which is supposed to grow at its source.   *Colour map 3, grid A4*

Ins and outs

Hué's Phu Bai airport is a 40-minute drive from the city. There are daily connections **Getting there**
with Hanoi and Saigon. The two bus stations and one train station are more central
and there are connections north to Hanoi and south to Saigon – and all points between. The trains tend to fill up, so advance booking is recommended, especially for
sleepers. Many foreign visitors arriving by road do so on tourist minibuses.

For the city itself, walking is an option – interspersed, perhaps, with the odd cyclo **Getting around**
journey. However, most guesthouses hire out bicycles and this is a very pleasant and
slightly more flexible way of exploring Hué and some of the surrounding countryside.
A motorbike provides even more flexibility. Boats are available for hire on the river
(and up stream to the tombs) and there is also the usual array of xe ôm.

History

Hué was the capital of Vietnam during the Nguyen Dynasty and is one of the **Ancient capital**
cultural cores of the country. The Nguyen Dynasty ruled Vietnam between
1802 and 1945, and for the first time in Vietnamese history a single court controlled the land from Yunnan (southern China) southwards to the Gulf of
Siam. To link the north and south – over 1,500 kilometres – the Nguyen
emperors built and maintained the Mandarin Road (*Quan Lo*), interspersed
with relay stations. Even in 1802 when it was not yet complete, it took couriers
13 days to travel between Hué and Saigon, and five days between Hué and
Hanoi. If they arrived more than two days late, the punishment was a flogging. There cannot have been a better road in Southeast Asia, or a more effective incentive system.

The city of Hué was equally impressive. George Finlayson, a British visitor
in 1821-22 wrote that its "style of neatness, magnitude, and perfection" made
other Asian cities look "like the works of children". Although the Confucian
bureaucracy and some of the dynasty's technical achievements may have
been remarkable, there was continual discontent and uprisings against the
Nguyen emperors. The court was packed with scheming mandarins, princesses, eunuchs and scholars writing wicked poetry. The female writer Ho
Xuan Huong, wrote of the court and its eunuchs:

*"Why do the twelve midwives who cared for you hate each other? Where have they
thrown away your youthful sexual passions? Damned be you if you should care
about the twitterings of mice-like lovers, or about a bee-like male gallant caressing
his adored one ... At least, a thousand years from now you will be more able to avoid
the posthumous slander that you indulged in mulberry-grove intrigues."*

The Central Region

**Nguyen Dynasty Emperors
(1802-1945)**

Gia Long	1802-1819
Minh Mang	1820-1840
Thieu Tri	1841-1847
Tu Duc	1847-1883
Duc Duc	1883
Hiep Hoa	1883
Kien Phuc	1883-1884
Ham Nghi	1884-1885
Dong Khanh	1885-1889
Thanh Thai	1889-1907
Duy Tan	1907-1916
Khai Dinh	1916-1925
Bao Dai	1925-1945

In 1883 a French fleet assembled at the mouth of the Perfume River, not far from Hué, and opened fire. After taking heavy casualties, Emperor Hiep Hoa sued for peace, and signed a treaty making Vietnam a protectorate of France. As French influence over Vietnam increased, the power and influence of the Nguyen waned. The undermining effect of the French presence was compounded by significant schisms in Vietnamese society. In particular, the spread of Christianity was undermining traditional hierarchies. Despite the impressive imperial tombs and palace (see below), many scholars maintain that the Nguyen Dynasty was simply too short-lived to have ever had a 'golden age'. Emperor Tu Duc may have reigned for 36 years (1847-1883), but by then the imperial family had grown so large that he had to contend with a series of damaging attempted coups d'état as family members vied for the throne. Although the French, and then the Japanese during the Second World War, found it to their advantage to maintain the framework of Vietnamese imperial rule, the system became hollow and, eventually, irrelevant. The last Nguyen Emperor, Bao Dai, abdicated on 30 August 1945.

Unfortunately for art lovers, the relative peace which descended upon Hué at the end of the Second World War was not to last. During the 1968 Tet offensive, Viet Cong soldiers holed up in the Citadel for 25 days. The bombardment which ensued, as US troops attempted to root them out, caused extensive damage to the Thai Hoa Palace and other monuments, much of which has still to be repaired. During their occupation of Hué, the NVA forces settled old scores, shooting, beheading and even burning alive 3,000 people, including civil servants, police officers and anyone connected with, or suspected of being sympathetic to, the government in Saigon. This action lent support to the notion that should the north ever achieve victory over the south it would result in mass killings. The irony was that this series of atrocities went unremarked in the US: at the time the Western media were pre-occupied with the infamous My Lai massacre by American troops (see page 210).

**Best time
to visit** Hué has a reputation for its bad weather. The rainy season extends from September to January, and rainfall is particularly heavy between September and November; the best time to visit is therefore between February and August. However, even in the 'dry' season an umbrella is handy, especially when venturing out of town to the pagodas and tombs. Rainfall of 2,770 millimetres has been recorded in a single month.

Sights

**The Imperial
City** The **Imperial City** at Hué is built on the same principles as the Forbidden Palace in Peking. It is enclosed by seven to 10 metre thick **outer walls** (Kinh Thanh), along with moats, canals and towers. Emperor Gia Long commenced construction in 1804 after geomancers had decreed a suitable

location and orientation for the palace. The site enclosed the land of eight villages (for which the inhabitants received compensation), and covers six square kilometres; sufficient area to house the Emperor and all his family, courtiers, bodyguards and servants. It took 20,000 men to construct the walls alone. Ten gates pierce the four walls of the citadel, although many are in poor condition. Not only has the city been damaged by war and incessant conflict, but also by natural disasters such as floods which, in the mid-19th century, inundated the city to a depth of several metres.

Chinese custom decreed that the 'front' of the palace should face south (like the Emperor) and this is the direction from which visitors approach the site. Over the outer moat, a pair of gates pierce the outer walls: the **Hien Nhon** and **Chuong Duc gates**. Just inside are two groups of massive cannon; four through the Hien Nhon Gate and five through the Chuong Duc Gate. These are the Nine Holy Cannon (Cuu Vi Than Cong), cast in 1803 on the orders of Gia Long from bronzeware seized from the Tay Son revolutionaries. The cannon are named after the four seasons and the five elements, and on each is carved its name, rank, firing instructions and how the bronze of which they are made was acquired. They are five metres in length, but have never been fired. Like the giant urns outside the Hien Lam Cac (see below), they are

The Central Region

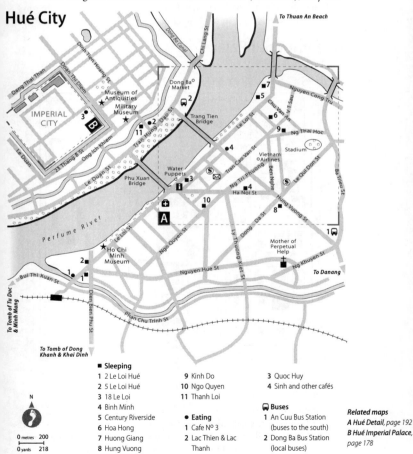

Hué City

To Thuan An Beach

Dong Ba Market

IMPERIAL CITY

Museum of Antiquities
Military Museum

Trang Tien Bridge

Water Puppets

Phu Xuan Bridge

Perfume River

Ho Chi Minh Museum

Stadium

Vietnam Airlines

Mother of Perpetual Help

To Danang

To Tomb of Tu Duc & Minh Mang

To Tomb of Dong Khanh & Khai Dinh

N

| 0 metres | 200 |
| 0 yards | 218 |

■ Sleeping
1 2 Le Loi Hué
2 5 Le Loi Hué
3 18 Le Loi
4 Binh Minh
5 Century Riverside
6 Hoa Hong
7 Huong Giang
8 Hung Vuong
9 Kinh Do
10 Ngo Quyen
11 Thanh Loi

● Eating
1 Cafe Nº 3
2 Lac Thien & Lac Thanh
3 Quoc Huy
4 Sinh and other cafés

🚌 Buses
1 An Cuu Bus Station (buses to the south)
2 Dong Ba Bus Station (local buses)

Related maps
A Hué Detail, page 192
B Hué Imperial Palace, page 178

meant to symbolize the permanence of the empire. Between the two gates is a massive **flag tower**. The flag of the National Liberation Front flew here for 24 days during the Tet Offensive in 1968 – a picture of the event is displayed in Hué's Ho Chi Minh Museum.

Northwards from the cannon, and over one of three bridges which span a second moat, is the **Ngo Mon** (or Noon Gate), built in 1833 during the reign of Emperor Minh Mang. The ticket office is just to the right. The gate, remodelled on a number of occasions since its original construction, is surmounted by a pavilion from where the emperor would view palace ceremonies. Of the five entrances, the central one – the Ngo Mon – was only opened for the emperor to pass through. UNESCO has thrown itself into the restoration of Ngo Mon with vigour and the newly finished pavilion atop the gate now gleams and glints in the sun; those who consider it garish can console themselves with the thought that this is how it might have appeared in Minh Mang's time. On an upper floor are photographs showing Ngo Mon before and after restoration.

North from the Ngo Mon, is the **Golden Water Bridge** (again reserved solely for the emperor's use) between two tanks, lined with laterite blocks. This leads to the **Dai Trieu Nghi** (the Great Rites Courtyard) on the north side of which is the **Dien Thai Hoa Palace** (the Palace of Supreme Harmony) constructed by Gia Long in 1805 and used for his coronation in 1806. From

Hué Imperial Palace

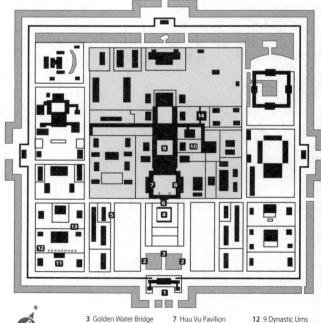

0 metres 100
0 yards 109

1 Ngo Mon (Royal Gate)
2 Tanks
3 Golden Water Bridge
4 Throne Hall & Great Rites Courtyard, Thai Hoa Palace
5 Waiting Pavilion, (Huu Ta Dai Lam Vien)
6 Red Gate
7 Huu Vu Pavilion
8 Ta Pavilion
9 Central Pavilion, Private Apartments of the Emperor
10 Quang Minh Palace
11 Hien Lam Cac
12 9 Dynastic Urns
13 Thé Temple
14 Royal Reading Pavilion

Forbidden Purple City

here, sitting on his golden throne raised up on a dais, the emperor would receive ministers, foreign emissaries, mandarins and military officers during formal ceremonial occasions. In front of the palace are 18 stone stelae, which stipulate the arrangement of the nine mandarinate ranks on the Great Rites Courtyard: the upper level was for ministers, mandarins and officers of the upper grade; the lower for those of lower grades. Civil servants would stand on the left, and the military on the right. Only royal princes were allowed to stand in the palace itself, which is perhaps the best preserved building in the Imperial City complex. Its red and gold columns, tiled floor, and fine ceiling have been restored and the rear of the palace is now a tourist shop.

North of the Palace of Supreme Harmony is the **Tu Cam Thanh** (the Purple Forbidden City). This would have been reserved for the use of the emperor and his family, and was surrounded by one metre thick walls: a city within a city. Tragically, the Forbidden City was virtually destroyed during the 1968 Tet offensive. The two **Mandarin Palaces** and the **Royal Reading Pavilion** are all that survive.

At the far side of the Thai Hoa Palace, are two enormous **bronze urns** (Vac Dong) decorated with birds, plants and wild animals, and weighing about 1,500 kilos each. To either side of the urns are the **Ta** and **Huu Vu Pavilions** – one converted into a souvenir art shop, the other a mock throne room in which tourists can pay US$5 to dress up and play the part of king for five minutes. The Royal Reading Pavilion has been rebuilt but, needless to say, has no books. At least they still stand: much of the rest of the Forbidden City is a depressing pile of rubble with a few bullet marked walls, scrub and vegetable plots. It is an artistic tragedy. On the far side of the palace are the outer northern walls of the citadel and the north gate.

Most of the surviving buildings of interest are to be found on the west side of the palace, running between the outer walls and the walls of the Forbidden City. At the southwest corner is the well-preserved and beautiful **Hien Lam Cac**, a pavilion built in 1821, in front of which stand nine massive bronze urns cast between 1835 and 1837 on the orders of Emperor Minh Mang. It is estimated that they weigh between 1,500 kilos and 2,600 kilos, and each has 17 decorative figures, animals, rivers, flowers and landscapes representing between them the wealth, beauty and unity of the country. The central, largest and most ornate urn is dedicated to the founder of the empire, Emperor Gia Long. Next to the urns walking northwards is the **The Temple** (the Temple of Generations). Built in 1821, it contains altars honouring 10 of the kings of the Nguyen Dynasty (Duc Duc and Hiep Hoa are missing) behind which are meant to be kept a selection of their personal belongings. It was only in 1954, however, that the stelae of the three Revolutionary emperors Ham Nghi, Thanh Thai, and Duy Tan were brought into the temple. The French, perhaps fearing that they would become a focus of discontent, prevented the Vietnamese from erecting altars in their memory. North of the The Temple is **Hung Temple** built in 1804 for the worship of Gia Long's father, Nguyen Phuc Luan, the father of the founder of the Nguyen Dynasty. The temple was renovated in 1951.

UNESCO began the arduous process of renovating the complex in 1983, but they have a very long way still to go: Vietnam at that time was a pariah state due to its invasion of Cambodia in 1978-9 and the appeal for funds and assistance fell on deaf ears. It was therefore fitting testimony to Vietnam's rehabilitation in the eyes of the world that in 1993 UNESCO declared Hué a World Heritage site. Although it is the battle of 1968 which is normally blamed for the destruction, the city has in fact been gradually destroyed over a period of 50 years. The French shelled it, fervent revolutionaries burnt down its buildings, typhoons and rains have battered it, thieves have ransacked its contents, and termites have eaten away at its foundations. In some respects it is surprising that as many as a third of the monuments have survived relatively intact. ■ *Entrance to Imperial City US$5.*

Other sights On the north bank of the river next to the Dong Ba bus station on Tran Hung Dao Street is the covered **Dong Ba Market**. The **Bao Quoc Pagoda** (just off Dien Bien Phu Street to the right, over the railway line), is said to have been built in the early 18th century by a Buddhist monk named Giac Phong. Note the 'stupa' that is behind and to the left of the central pagoda and the fine doors inscribed with Chinese and Sanskrit characters. Further along Dien Bien Phu Street, at the intersection with Tu Dam Street is the **Tu Dam Pagoda**. According to the Hué Buddhist Association this was originally founded in 1690-1695 but has been rebuilt many times. The present day Pagoda was built shortly before the Second World War. In August 1963 the Diem government sent its forces to suppress the monks here who were alleged to be fermenting discontent among the people. The specially selected forces – they were Catholic – clubbed and shot to death about 30 monks and their student followers, and smashed the great Buddha image here.

The Perfume River is spanned by two bridges; downstream is the unfortunate **Trang Tien Bridge**, named after the royal mint that once stood at its northern end. It was built in 1896 and destroyed soon after by a typhoon; after having been rebuilt it was then razed once more in 1968 during the Tet Offensive. Upstream is Phu Xuan bridge, built by the US Army in 1970.

The skyline of modern Hué is adorned by the striking pagoda-like tower of the **Church of Mother of Perpetual Help**. This three-storeyed, octagonal steel tower is 53 metres high and an attractive blend of Asian and European styles. The church was completed in 1962 and marble from the Marble Mountain in Danang was used for the altar. The church lies at the junction of Nguyen Hue and Nguyen Khuyen streets.

Museums

Hué also has a number of museums. The best is the **Hué Museum of Antiquities** at 3 Le Truc Street. Housed in the Long An Palace, the museum contains a reasonable (although unlabelled) collection of ceramics, furniture, screens and bronzeware. In the front courtyard are stone mandarins, gongs and giant bells. The building itself is worthy of note for its elegant construction, built by Emperor Thieu Tri in 1845 it was dismantled and erected on the present site in 1909. Directly opposite the museum is the **Royal College** established in 1803 and moved to this site in 1908. It is usually closed to visitors. Close by at 23 Thang 8 Street (between Dinh Tien Hoang and Doan Thi Diem streets) is the **Military Museum**. Missiles, tanks and armoured personnel carriers fill the courtyard. Across the river at 7 Le Loi Street is the requisite **Ho Chi Minh Museum** which displays pictures of Ho's life plus a few models and personal possessions. The 'tour' begins at the end of the corridor on the second floor. Some interesting photographs (eg of Ho as a cook's assistant at the Carlton Hotel, London), but does not compare with the Ho Chi Minh Museum in Hanoi. ■ *Open 0730-1130, 1330-1630 Monday-Sunday.*

Excursions

As the geographical and spiritual centre of the Nguyen Dynasty, Hué and the surrounding area is the site of numerous pagodas and seven imperial tombs, along with the tombs of numerous other royal personages. Few visitors will wish to see them all – some are extensively damaged – time and war have taken their toll.

Around Hué

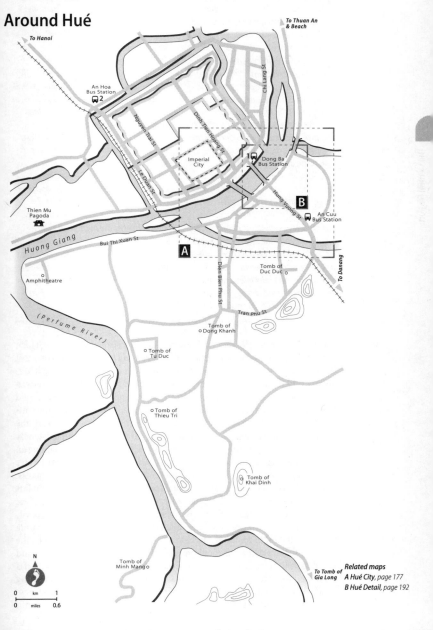

Related maps
A *Hué City*, page 177
B *Hué Detail*, page 192

The death and burial of Emperor Gia Long (1820)

When the Emperor Gia Long died on 3 February 1820, the thread on the ancestors' altar (representing his soul) was tied. The following day the corpse was bathed and clothed in rich garments, and precious stones and pearls were placed in his mouth. Then a ritual offering of food, drink and incense was made before the body was placed in a coffin made of catalpa wood (Bignonia catalpa) – a wood impervious to insect attack. At this time, the crown prince announced the period of mourning that was to be observed – a minimum of 3 years. Relatives of the dead emperor, mandarins and their wives each had different forms and periods of mourning to observe, depending upon their position.

3 days after Gia Long's death, a messenger was sent to the Hoang Nhon Pagoda to inform the Empress, who was already dead, of the demise of her husband. Meanwhile, the new Emperor Minh Mang had the former ruler's deeds recorded and engraved on golden sheets which were bound together as a book. Then astrologers selected an auspicious date for the funeral, picking 27 May after some argument (11 May also had its supporters). On 17 May court officials told the heaven, the earth, and the dynastic ancestors, of the details for the funeral and at the same time opened the imperial tomb. On 20 May the corpse was informed of the ceremony. 4 days later the coffin left the palace for the 3 day journey to its final resting place. Then, at the appointed time, the coffin was lowered into the sepulchre – its orientation correct – shrouded in silk cloth, protected by a second outer coffin, covered in resin, and finally bricked in. Next to Gia Long, a second grave was dug into which were placed an assortment of objects useful in his next life. The following morning, Emperor Minh Mang, in full mourning robes, stood outside the tomb facing east, while a mandarin facing in the opposite direction inscribed ritual titles on the tomb. The silk thread on the ancestors' altar – the symbol of the soul – was untied, animals slaughtered, and the thread then buried in the vicinity of the tomb.
(This account is adapted from James Dumarçay's The palaces of South-East Asia, 1991.)

Thien Mu Pagoda   Thien Mu Pagoda (the Elderly Goddess Pagoda), also known as the Thien Mau Tu Pagoda, and locally as the **Linh Mu Pagoda** (the name used on most local maps), is the finest in Hué. It is beautifully sited on the Perfume River, about four kilometres upstream from the city. It was built in 1601 by Nguyen Hoang, the governor of Hué, after an old woman appeared to him and said that the site had supernatural significance and should be marked by the construction of a pagoda. The monastery is the oldest in Hué, and the seven-storey *Phuoc Duyen* (Happiness and Grace Tower), built later by Emperor Thieu Tri in 1844, is 21 metres high, with each storey containing an altar to a different Buddha. The summit of the tower is crowned with a water pitcher to catch the rain, water representing the source of happiness. Arranged around the tower are four smaller buildings one of which contains the *Great Bell* cast in 1710 under the orders of the Nguyen Lord, Nguyen Phuc Chu, and weighing 2,200 kilos. Beneath another of these surrounding pavilions is a monstrous *marble turtle* on which is a 2.6 metre high stele recounting the development of Buddhism in Hué carved in 1715. Beyond the tower, the entrance to the pagoda is through a triple gateway patrolled by six carved and vividly painted guardians – two on each gate. The roof of the sanctuary itself is decorated with jataka stories. At the front of the sanctuary is a brass laughing Buddha. Behind that are an assortment of gilded Buddhas and a crescent-shaped gong cast in 1677 by Jean de la Croix. The first monk to commit suicide through self immolation, Thich Quang Duc, came from this pagoda (see page 262) and the grey Austin in which he made the journey to his death in Saigon is still kept here in a garage in the temple garden. In May 1993 a Vietnamese – this time not a monk – immolated himself at Thieu Mu. Why is not clear: some maintain it was linked to the persecution of Buddhists: others because of the man's frustrated love life. ■ *Getting there: it is an easy three kilometre bicycle (or cyclo) ride from the city, following the north bank of river upstream (west).*

After the Imperial Palace, the tombs of the former emperors which dot the countryside to the south of the city are Hué's most spectacular tourist attraction (see map). Each of the tombs follows the same stylistic formula, although at the same time they reflect the tastes and predilections of the emperor in question. The tombs were built during the lifetime of each emperor, who took a great interest in their design and construction; after all they were meant to ensure his comfort in the next life. Each mausoleum, variously arranged, has five design elements: a courtyard with statues of elephants, horses and military and civil mandarins (originally, usually approached through a park of rare trees), a stele pavilion (with an engraved eulogy composed by the king's son and heir), a Temple of the Soul's Tablets, a pleasure pavilion, and a grave. Geomancers decreed that they should also have a stream and a mountainous screen in front. The tombs faithfully copy Chinese prototypes, although most art historians claim that they fall short in terms of execution. ■ *Entrance to each of the tombs US$5. An extra US$5 is charged for video cameras. Getting to and around the Imperial Tombs: is easiest by car/minibus as they are spread over a large area. Most hotels organize tours. A cyclo for the day should cost about 40,000-50,000d (with some walking up the hills), bicycle hire about US$1 (see Local transport). Set out early if bicycling; all the tombs are easily accessible by bicycle, with the exception of Gia Long's. It is also possible to go on the back of a motorcycle taxi (Honda ôm). Finally, boats can be chartered to sail up the Perfume River – the most peaceful way to travel, but only a few of the tombs can be reached in this way (see Tours).*

Imperial Tombs

Plan of Gia Long's Tomb

The Tomb of Emperor Gia Long is rarely visited – it is accessible by bicycle or motorbike (which can be taken by boat across the Perfume River) or by boat, with a long walk – but is well worth the effort. The tomb is overgrown with cassava bushes and several huge mango trees, and the pavilions are shoddily roofed with corrugated iron but the setting is quiet and peaceful. It was built between 1814 and 1820 (see box on preceeding page for an account of his burial). Gia Long's mausoleum follows the same formula as the other tombs: there is a surrounding lotus

Tomb of Emperor Gia Long

The Central Region

pond; a courtyard with five now headless mandarins, horses and elephants; steps leading up to a further courtyard with an ancestral temple at the rear; and to the right of this a double walled and locked burial chamber where Gia Long and his wife are interred (the Emperor's tomb is fractionally taller); the stele eulogizing the Emperor's reign is beyond the burial chamber. Ask the custodian for admittance to the burial chamber for which you should make a small contribution.

Nguyen Anh, or Gia Long as he was crowned in 1802, came to power with French support. Back in 1787 Gia Long's son, the young Prince Canh, had caused a sensation in French salon life when, with soldier/missionary Georges Pigneau de Béhaine, the two had sought military support against the Tay Son from Louis XVI. In return for Tourane (Danang) and Poulo Condore the French offered men and weapons – an offer that was subsequently withdrawn. Pigneau then raised military support from French merchants in India and in 1799 Prince Canh's French-trained army defeated the Tay Son at Qui Nhon.

Gia Long's reign was despotic – to his European advisers who pointed out that encouragement of industry would lead to the betterment of the poor, he replied that he preferred them poor. The poor were virtual slaves – the price for one healthy young buffalo was one healthy young girl – and *vice versa*. Flogging was the norm; it has been described as the 'bamboo's golden age'. One study by a Vietnamese scholar estimated that there were 105 peasant uprisings between 1802 and 1820 alone. For this and the fact that he gave the French a foothold in Vietnam the Vietnamese have never forgiven Gia Long. Of him they still say *"cong ran can ga nha"* (he carried home the snake that killed the chicken). ■ *Getting there: from Minh Mang's tomb (see below for travel information) take the road southeast for several kilometres through Minh Mang Village to a tributary of the Perfume River; a boat ferries travellers to the opposite bank where a single track path, which almost peters out in places, leads to the tomb after several more kilometres. The familiar twin pillars appear, miraculously, amidst the undergrowth. Ask directions along the way.*

Tomb of Emperor Minh Mang

The Tomb of Emperor Minh Mang is possibly the finest of all the imperial tombs. Built between 1841 and 1843, it is sited among peaceful ponds, about 12 kilometres from the city of Hué. In terms of architectural poise and balance, and richness of decoration, it has no peer in the area. The layout is unusual in its symmetry along a single central and sacred axis (*Shendao*); no other tomb, with the possible exception of Khai Dinh, achieves the same unity of constituent parts, nor draws the eye onwards so easily and pleasantly from one visual element to the next. The tomb was traditionally approached through the **Dai Hong Mon** – today visitors pass through a side gate – a gate which leads into the ceremonial courtyard containing an array of statuary. Next is the stele pavilion in which there is a carved eulogy to the dead Emperor composed by his son, Thieu Tri. Continuing downwards through a series

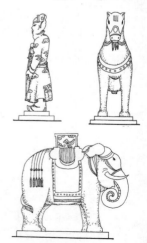

Statues in the front courtyard of Minh Mang's mausoleum

of courtyards there is, in turn, the **Sung An Temple** dedicated to Minh Mang and his Empress, a small garden with flower beds that once formed the Chinese character for 'longevity', and two sets of stone bridges. The first consists of three spans, the central one of which (**Trung Dao Bridge**) was for the sole use of the Emperor. The second, single, bridge leads to a short flight of stairs with naga balustrades at the end of which is a locked bronze door. The door leads to the tomb itself which is surrounded by a circular wall. ■ *Getting there: by bicycle, visitors must cross the Perfume River by boat. There are also boat tours to the tomb from Hué (see Tours, page 191).*

Tomb of Thieu Tri

The Tomb of Thieu Tri (seven kilometres southwest of Hué in the village of Thuy Bang) was built in 1848 by his son Tu Duc, who took into account his father's wishes that it be 'economical and convenient'. Thieu Tri reigned for just seven years and unlike his forebears did not start planning his mausoleum the moment he ascended the throne. Upon his death his body was temporarily interred in Long An Temple (now the Hué Museum of Antiquities). The tomb is in two adjacent parts, with separate tomb and temple areas; the layout of each follows the symmetrical axis arrangement of Minh Mang's tomb which has also inspired the architectural style.

Tomb of Tu Duc

The Tomb of Tu Duc is seven kilometres from the city and was built between 1864 and 1867 in a pine wood. It is enclosed by a wall within which is a lake. The lake, with lotus and water hyacinth, contains a small island where the king built a number of replicas of famous temples – which are now rather difficult to discern. He often came here to relax, and from the pavilions that reach out over the lake, composed poetry and listened to music. The **Xung Khiem Pavilion** built in 1865 has recently been restored with UNESCO's help and is the most attractive building here (although it is usually overrun with Vietnamese picnickers). The tomb complex follows the formula described above: ceremonial square, mourning yard with pavilion, and then the tomb itself. To the left of Tu Duc's tomb are the tombs of his Empress, Le Thien Anh and adopted son, Kien Phuc. Many of the pavilions are crumbling

(margin, vertical) The Central Region

Plan of Minh Mang's Tomb

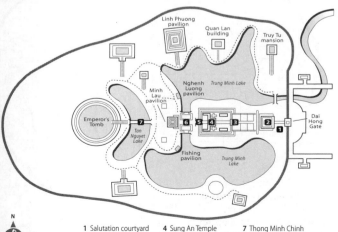

N
Not to scale

1 Salutation courtyard	4 Sung An Temple
2 Stela House	5 Hoang Trach Gate
3 Hien Duc Gate	6 Trung Dao bridge
	7 Thong Minh Chinh Truc bridge

and ramshackle – lending the tomb a rather tragic air. This is appropriate: though he had 104 wives, Tu Duc fathered no sons. He was therefore forced to write his own eulogy, a fact which he took as a bad omen. The eulogy itself recounts the sadness in Tu Duc's life. A flavour of its sentiment can be gleaned from a confession he wrote in 1867 following French seizure of territory (see box). It was during Tu Duc's reign, and shortly after his death, that France gained full control of Vietnam.

Tomb of Duc Duc The Tomb of Duc Duc is the closest to Hué, two kilometres south of the city centre on Tan Lang Street. Despite ruling for just three days and then dying in prison, Emperor Duc Duc (1852-1883) has a tomb, built posthumously by his son, Thanh Thai, in 1889 on the spot where, it is said, the body was dumped by gaolers. Emperors **Thanh Thai** and **Duy Tan** are buried in the same complex. Unlike Duc Duc, though, both were strongly anti-French and were exiled for a period in Africa. Although Thanh Thai later returned to Vietnam and died in Vung Tau in 1953, his son Duy Tan was killed in an air crash in central Africa in 1945. It was not until 1987 that Duy Tan's body was repatriated and interred alongside Thanh Thai, his father. The tomb is in three parts: the Long An Temple; Duc Duc's tomb to the south; and Thanh Thai and Duy Tan's tombs adjacent to each other.

Tomb of Dong Khanh The Tomb of Dong Khanh is 500 metres from Tu Duc's tomb: walk up the path on the other side of the road from the main entrance to Tu Duc's tomb – the path is partly hidden in amongst the stalls. Built in 1889, it is the smallest of the imperial mausoleums, but nonetheless one of the most individual. Unusually, it has two separate sections. One is a walled area containing the usual series of pavilions and courtyards and with an historically interesting collection of personal objects that belonged to the Emperor. The second, 100

Plan of Tu Duc's Tomb

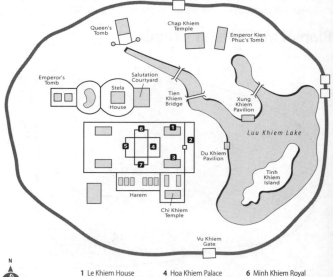

N
Not to scale

1 Le Khiem House
2 Khiem Cung Gate
3 Phap Khiem House
4 Hoa Khiem Palace
5 Luong Khiem Palace
6 Minh Khiem Royal Theatre
7 On Khiem Mansion

The Central Region

Tu Duc's lament

Never has an era seen such sadness, never a year more anguish. Above me, I fear the edicts of heaven. Below, the tribulations of the people trouble my days and nights. Deep in my heart I tremble and blush, finding neither words or actions to help my subjects.

Alone, I am speechless. My pulse is feeble, my body pale and thin, my beard and hair white. Though not yet 40, I have already reached old age, so that I lack the strength to pay homage to my ancestors every morning and evening. Evil must be suppressed and goodness sought. The wise must offer their counsel, the strong their force, the rich their wealth, and all those with skills should devote them to the needs of the army and the kingdom. Let us together mend our errors and rebuild.

Alas! The centuries are fraught with pain, and man is burdened by fear and woe. Thus we express our feelings that they may be known to the world.
(Taken from Vietnam, Karnow, S.)

metres away, consists of an open series of platforms. The lower platform has the honour guard of mandarins, horses and elephants along with a stele pavilion; the third platform is a tiled area which would have had an awning; and the highest platform, the tomb itself. The tomb is enclosed within three open walls, the entrance protected by a dragon screen (to prevent spirits entering).

Tomb of Khai Dinh

The Tomb of Khai Dinh is 10 kilometres from Hué and was built between 1920 and 1932. It is the last of the mausoleums of the Nguyen Dynasty, and by the time Khai Dinh was contemplating the afterlife, brick had given way to concrete (which is beginning to deteriorate). Nevertheless, it occupies a fine position on the Chau Mountain facing southwest towards a large white statue of Quan Am, also built by Khai Dinh. The valley, cultivated to cassava and sugar cane, and the pine-covered mountains, make this one of the most beautifully sited and peaceful of the tombs. Indeed, before construction could begin, Khai Dinh had to remove the tombs of Chinese nobles who had already

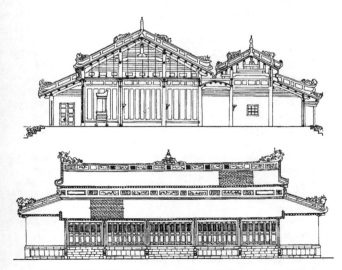

Two views of Sung An Temple, Minh Mang's Tomb: a cross section through the temple (top) and the southern elevation (bottom)

The Central Region

The funeral of a King

On 6 November 1925, Dai-Hanh-Hoang-Khai-Dinh, King of Annam, `mounted the dragon's back,' or, to put it briefly, died. Seven diamonds were put in the mouth of the corpse, which was washed, embalmed, dressed in state robes, placed in a huge red and gold lacquer coffin and covered over with young tea-leaves. 10 days later official mourning was inaugurated with the sacrifice of a bullock, a goat and a pig. A portrait of the late monarch, painted on silk, was placed on the throne. Paper invocations were burnt, massed lamentations rent the air 4 times daily for 60 days.

All Annam was in Hué, dressed in its best and brightest. Sampans swarmed about the bridge, packed with expectant people. Gay shrines lined the way, hung with flowers and paper streamers. Bunting, citron and scarlet, fluttered in the breeze. Route-keepers in green and red held the crowds in check, chasing small boys out of the way, swacking them over their mushroom hats – chastisement that produced a maximum of noise with a minimum of pain.

At the head of the column were two elephants, hung with tassels and embroidered cloths and topped with crimson howdahs and yellow umbrellas. Never have I seen animals so unutterably bored. They lolled against each other, eyes closed – and slumbered. But for an occasional twitch of an ear or tail they might have been dead. Their boredom was understandable when you came to think of it. An elephant is a long-lived beast. No elephant gets his photograph in the papers on reaching the century: it is far too common an occurrence. These two were full-grown; elderly, even. It is possible that they featured at the obsequies of Thieu-Tri, and there have been innumerable royal funerals since. At one period kings weren't stopping on the throne of Annam long enough to get the cushions warm. What was a very novel and splendid exhibition to me was stale stuff to these beasts.

"All very fine for you, mister," they might have said. "First time and all that. Can drop out and buy yourself a drink any time you like. All very well for you, Henry, in a feather-weight gent's suiting; but what about us, tight-laced front and back with about a ton of passengers, brollies, flags and furniture up top?"

An old bearded mandarin in a gorgeous coat of royal blue struck with a wooden hammer on a silver gong. The procession began to shuffle slowly forward – somebody in front had found means to rouse the elephants, apparently. 160 trained porters, clad in black and white, crouched under the red lacquer poles of the giant bier – slips of bamboo had been placed between their teeth to stop them from chattering.

Slowly, steadily, keeping the prescribed horizontal, the huge thing rose. 6 tons it weighed and special bridges had to be built to accommodate it. Slowly, steadily it moved towards us, preceded by solemn-stepping heralds in white; flagbearers in sea-green carrying dragon banners of crimson and emerald, blue and gold.

The second day was spent in getting the coffin from Nam-Gio to the mausoleum and was a mere repetition of the first. The actual interment took place on the morning of the 3rd day. In a few minutes the mourners were out in the daylight again and the vault doors were being sealed. The spirit of Khai-Dinh was on its way to the Ten Judgement Halls of the Infernal Regions, to pass before the Mirror of the Past wherein he would see all his deeds reflected, together with their consequences; to drink the Water of Forgetfulness, and pass on through transmigration to transmigration till he attained the Pure Land and a state of blessed nothingness. And Bao-Dai—weeping bitterly, poor little chap – reigned in his stead.
(Adapted from The Voyage from London to Indochina, Crosbie Garstin.)

The battle at Khe Sanh (1968)

Khe Sanh (already the site of a bloody confrontation in April and May 1967) is the place where the North Vietnamese Army (NVA) tried to achieve another Dien Bien Phu; in other words, an American humiliation. One of the NVA divisions, the 304th, even had Dien Bien Phu emblazoned on its battle streamers. Westmoreland would have nothing of it, and prepared for massive confrontation. He hoped to bury Ho Chi Minh's troops under tonnes of high explosive and achieve a Dien Bien Phu in reverse. But, the American high command had some warning of the attack: a North Vietnamese regimental commander was killed while he was surveying the base on 2 January and that was interpreted as meaning the NVA were planning a major assault. Special forces long-range patrols were dropped into the area around the base and photo reconnaissance increased. It became clear that 20,000-40,000 NVA troops were converging on Khe Sanh.

With the US Marines effectively surrounded in a place which the assistant commander of the 3rd Marine Division referred to as 'not really anywhere', there was a heavy exchange of fire in January 1968. The Marine artillery fired 159,000 shells, B-52s carpet-bombed the surrounding area, obliterating each 'box' with 162 tonnes of bombs. But, despite the haggard faces of the Marines, the attack on Khe Sanh was merely a cover for the Tet offensive – the commanders of the NVA realized that there was no chance of repeating their success at Dien Bien Phu against the US military. The Tet offensive proved to be a remarkable psychological victory for the NVA – even if their 77-day seige of Khe Sanh cost many 1,000s (one estimate is 10,000-15,000) of NVA lives, while only 248 Americans were killed (43 of those in a C-123 transporter crash). Again, a problem for the US military was one of presentation. Even Walter Cronkite, the doyen of TV reporters, informed his audience that the parallels between Khe Sanh and Dien Bien Phu were "there for all to see".

The Central Region

selected the site for its beauty and auspicious orientation. 127 steep steps lead up to the Honour Courtyard with statuary of mandarins, elephants and horses. An octagonal Stele Pavilion in the centre of the mourning yard contains a stone stele with an eulogy to the Emperor. At the top of some more stairs, are the tomb and shrine of Khai Dinh, containing a bronze statue of the Emperor sitting on his throne and holding a jade sceptre. The body is interred nine metres below ground level (see box describing Khai Dinh's interment). The interior is richly decorated with ornate and colourful murals (the artist incurred the wrath of the emperor and only just escaped execution), floor tiles, and decorations built up with fragments of porcelain. It is the most elaborate of all the tombs and took 11 years to build. Such was the cost of construction that Khai Dinh had to levy additional taxes to fund the project. The tomb shows distinct European stylistic influences.

Ho Quyen Ho Quyen (Amphitheatre) lies about four kilometres upstream of Hué on the south bank of the Perfume River. It was built in 1830 by Emperor Minh Mang as a venue for the popular duels between elephants and tigers. This royal sport was in earlier centuries staged on an island in the Perfume River or on the river banks but by 1830 it was considered desirable for the royal party to be able to observe the duels without placing themselves at risk from escaping tigers. The amphitheatre is said to have been last used in 1904 when, as usual, the elephant emerged victorious: 'The elephant rushed ahead and pressed the tiger to the wall with all the force he could gain. Then he raised his head, threw the enemy to the ground and smashed him to death.' The walls of the amphitheatre are five metres high and the arena is 44 metres in diameter. At the south side, beneath the royal box, is one large gateway (for the elephant) and to the north, five smaller entrances for the tigers. The walls are in good condition and the centre filled with immaculately tended rows of vegetables. ■ *Getting there: by cyclo or bicycle about three kilometres west of Hué station on Bui Thi Xuan Street.*

Thanh Toan bridge

Thanh Toan covered bridge is eight kilometres west of Hué. Built in the reign of King Le Hien Tong (1740-1786) by Tran Thi Dao, a childless woman as an act of charity hoping that God would bless her with a baby. The bridge with its shelter for the tired and homeless attracted the interest of several kings who granted the village immunity from several taxes. The original yin-yang tiles have been replaced with ugly green enamelled tube tiles, unfortunately, but the structure is still healthy.

Thuan An Beach

Thuan An Beach is 13 kilometres to the northeast of Hué, about four kilometres off the road to Danang. Six kilometres in length, it offers swimming in both a protected lagoon (into which flows the Perfume River) and in the South China Sea. ■ *Getting there: local buses leave for Thuan An from the Dong Ba bus station; boats can be chartered from the dock behind the Dong Ba Market, one hour (30,000-40,000d). NB Intermittent buses return from Thuan An village to Hué (16 kilometres); an alternative would be to take bicycles on the boat and cycle back. At the main gate to the beach there is a bicycle park which charges 5,000d for a bicycle.* **Sleeping** Thuan An Hotel is 100 metres from the beach, dirty and unhelpful. **C** *Dong Hai Hotel*, T866115. About one kilometre from the beach, new and clean.

DMZ

The incongruously named Demilitarized Zone (DMZ), scene of some of the fiercest fighting of the Vietnam War, lies along the Ben Hai River and the better known 17th Parallel. The DMZ was the creation of the 1954 Geneva Peace Accord which divided the country into two spheres of influence prior to elections that were never held. Like its counterpart in Germany the boundary evolved into a national border separating Communist from capitalist but unlike its European equivalent it was the triumph of Communism that saw its demise. A number of wartime sights can be seen on a single, rather gruelling, day's tour from Hué. ■ *Getting to the sights of DMZ: most visitors visit the sights of the DMZ, including Khe Sanh and the Ho Chi Minh Trail, on a tour. But buses do leave for the town of Khe Sanh from the An Hoa bus station; the site of the US base is three kilometres from Khe Sanh Bus Station. From here it is possible to arrange transport to the Ho Chi Minh Trail and to other sights, but it is probably more trouble than it is worth. A one-day tour of all the DMZ sights can be booked from a number of Hué hotels. Cost about US$15, depart early, return late.*

Khe Sanh is the site of one of the most famous battles of the War. The battleground lies along Highway 9 which runs west towards Laos, to the north of Hué, and south of Dong Hoi and is three kilometres from the village of the same name. There is not much to see here; it is of most interest to war veterans.

Ho Chi Minh Trail is another popular, but necessarily disappointing, sight given that its whole purpose was to be as inconspicuous as possible. Anything you see was designed to be invisible – from the air at least; rather an artificial 'sight' but a worthy pilgrimage considering the sacrifice of millions of Vietnamese porters and the role it played in the American defeat (see box, page 189). A section runs close to Khe Sanh.

The tunnels of Vinh Moc served a similar function to the better known Cu Chi tunnels. They evolved as families in the heavily bombed village dug themselves shelters beneath their houses and then joined up with their neighbours. Later the tunnels developed a more offensive role when Viet Cong soldiers fought from them. Some visitors regard these tunnels as more 'authentic' than the 'touristy' tunnels of Cu Chi. Offshore is **Con Co Island**, an important supply depot and anti-aircraft stronghold in the war. Life for ordinary peasants in the battle zone just north of the DMZ was terrifying: some idea of conditions (for revolutionary peasants at least) can be gained from the 1970 North Vietnamese film *Vinh Linh Steel Ramparts*. ■ *Getting to the tunnels: six kilometres north of Ben Hai River turn right in Ho Xa village. Vinh Moc, 13 kilometres off Highway 1.*

The Rock Pile is a 230 metres high limestone outcrop just south of the DMZ. It served as a US observation post. An apparently unassailable position, troops, ammunition, Budweiser and prostitutes all had to be helicoptered in. The sheer walls of the Rock Pile were eventually scaled by the Viet Cong. The **Hien Luong Bridge** on the 17th parallel which marked the boundary between north and south (see page 174) is included in most tours. As all war paraphernalia has been stripped from the DMZ the visit is more of a 'pilgrimage' than a visual experience. Those who are short of time should visit one or two tombs instead.

Tours

The more expensive hotels organize bus and boat tours to the **Imperial Tombs**. It is also possible to charter boats to the tombs (the most romantic way to see them) and to **Thuan An Beach** (see page 190). *DMZ Tours*, 26 Le Loi Street, charges US$3 per person to visit Linh Mu Pagoda, Tu Duc and Minh Mang's Tombs extra for Gia Long's Tomb, depart 0800, return 1500. Boats are available on the stretch of river bank between the *Huong Giang Hotel* and the Trang Tien Bridge, and also from the dock behind the Dong Ba Market. For Thuan An Beach, a one hour journey, expect to pay 40,000-50,000d. From Hué, there are also tours organized to some of the sights of the Vietnam War. DMZ Tours (see above) charge US$15 for a day's programme, taking in nine sights including Vinh Moc tunnels and museum, the Ho Chi Minh Trail and Khe Sanh, depart 0600, return 2000. Those wishing to travel overland to Laos can arrange to be dropped off in Khe Sanh, pay just US$10-12.

New provincial hostilities are reportedly hotting up in the DMZ as Quang Tri Province, in which the DMZ lies, and which technically has jurisdiction over the DMZ sights is losing out from the tourist trade. Tours begin in Hué, Thua Thien-Hué Province, so it is the tour operators from here that gain all the benefit. Quang Tri Tourism claims to be owed a fortune in back fees by *DMZ Tours* which it described as 'the most legal among the under-the-table tour companies'.

The Central Region

Essentials

Sleeping
■ *on maps*
Price codes:
see inside front cover

Most hotels lie to the south of the Perfume River although there are a couple to the north in the old Vietnamese part of town. Conditions in many hotels have improved but bargaining is still very much the order of the day if you are to pay a fair price.

L-A *Saigon Morin*, 30 Le Loi St, T823526, F825155. At long last re-opened and recognizable as the fine hotel originally built by the Morin brothers in the 1880s. Arranged around a courtyard with a small pool the rooms are large and comfortable. All a/c, satellite TV and hot water. The courtyard is a delightful place to sit in the evening and enjoy a quiet drink. Despite minor drawbacks (nylon towels, hot water tank too small to fill a bath etc) the service is friendly and the overall effect most agreeable, particularly if you like the colour pink. Recommended.

A+-A *Century Riverside*, 49 Le Loi St, T823390, F823394. Fabulous river views but several reports suggest service is poor. Bargaining should elicit major discounts. **A+-A** *Huong Giang* (*Perfume River Hotel*), 51 Le Loi St, T822122, F823424. Gorgeous position on the river, comfortable rooms, despite the heavy, wooden, lacquered 'royal' furniture many Hué hotels do insist on using, and efficient service. Only some rooms look on to the river, there's a good pool but the top-floor restaurant is for emergencies only. **A-B** *Hoa Hong 2*, 1 Pham Ngu Lao St, T824377, F826949. Large and a

The Central Region

Hué Detail

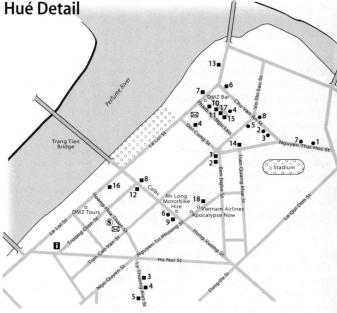

little impersonal but popular with tour groups, breakfast included. **A-B** *Le Loi Hué*, 5 Le Loi St, T824668. Large yellow wash and green-shuttered villa on the river, expansive rooms, attractive ambience although in the rainy season rooms can be dank and chilly, overpriced. **A-C** *Hung Vuong*, 2 Hung Vuong St, T823866, F825910. Priciest rooms in the old villa in front, building behind is modern and sterile, cheapest rooms around the back.

B *Kinh Do*, 1 Nguyen Thai Hoc St, T823566, F821190. Architecturally unattractive and smallish rooms but comfortable, quiet, friendly staff. **B** *Dong Duong*, 3 Hung Vuong St, T826070. 12 rooms in a villa whose renovation has removed most of the charm but an excellent and cheap restaurant. **B** *Thuan Hoa*, 7 Nguyen Tri Phuong St, T822553, F822470. Large and not particularly appealing place, restaurant, dancing and handy for *Apocalypse Now*.

C *18 Le Loi*, 18 Le Loi St, T823720. Nice position not far from the river, 10 rooms, avoid downstairs and try the larger airy first floor rooms, all a/c, hot water. Bicycles for rent. **C** *A Dong 1*, 1 bis Chu Van An St, T824148, F828074. 7 rooms in this friendly hotel, a/c, fridge and bathtub but nothing out of the ordinary apart from an attractive upstairs terrace. **C-D** *Ngo Quyen*, 9 Ngo Quyen St, T823278, F828372. Cheaper rooms have fan and shared bathroom, better rooms have a/c, bathtub and hot water, quite good value. **C-D** Thanh Loi, 7 Dinh Tien Hoang St, T824803, F825344. North of the river, opposite Lac Thien Restaurant, newish building, rather flimsy fittings but clean, bicycles for rent. **C-E** *Le Loi Hué*, 2 Le Loi St, T822153, F824527. Not far from the station, consists of 6 blocks of differing comfort, some a/c, clean, hot water showers, good value.

D *Nha Khach*, 2 Ben Nghe St. Externally an attractive building but sadly the insides have been allowed to run down, better value elsewhere. **D** *Nha Khach Ben Nghe*, 4 Ben Nghe St, T823687. Some quite comfortable rooms, fan and a/c, offering reasonable value. **D** *Duy Tan*, 12 Hung Vuong St, T826479, F826477. Has slashed its prices to realistic levels, spartan rooms. **C** *Tourist villas* on Ly Thuong Kiet St run by Hué Tourist. All a little shabby, but have atmosphere, a/c, hot water and include breakfast in the price. *No 5*, T822167. Nice colonial façade, one room has a lovely balcony. *No 9*, T825163. Large and small rooms (all same price), curtains consist of nylon sheets pocked with cigarette burns. *16*, several large rooms. Friendly. **D** *Tourist Villa*, 14 Ly Thuong Kiet St, T825461. Unsigned. Privately run, 4 spacious rooms, lovely garden, good breakfast (not included). Recommended. The little hem (alley) opposite the *Century Riverside* has some really nice little rooms in comfortable and cheerful guesthouses in what is easily the best value accommodation in Hué. Particularly recommended are: **D** *Mimosa*, 46/6 Le Loi St, T828068, F823858. 6 rooms, a/c, hot water, bathtub. quiet, simple and clean, French spoken. **D** *Thanh Thuy*, 46/? Le Loi St, T824585. Another small, peaceful, clean, family-run guesthouse with a/c and hot water. **D-F** *Hoang Huong*, 46/2 Le Loi St, T828509. Some a/c, cheaper room with fan and only US$3 for a dorm bed, friendly and helpful.

Hué specialities are excellent and although a few years ago they were quite hard to obtain in Hué the situation has improved greatly. The influence of the royal court on Hué cuisine is evident in a number of ways: there are a large number of dishes served – it tends to be nibble food – each dish is relatively light, delicately flavoured (although some are quite spicy) and most require painstaking preparation in the kitchen: in short, a veritable culinary harem in which even the most pampered and surfeited king could find something to tickle his palate. Other Hué dishes are more robust, notably the famed *bun bo Hue*, round white noodles in soup with slices of beef and laced with chilli oil of extravagant piquancy.

Eating
● *on maps*

The Central Region

Of the hotels the Saigon Morin does excellent barbecues at around 5 bucks a plate. *Huong Giang* sometimes offers special Hué banquets but these are normally for large groups and tours only. *Club Garden*, 12 Vo Thi Sau St, T826327. A relaxed and attractive setting, Vietnamese and fairly ambitious Western menu, the food is OK. *An Dinh Palace*, 97 Phan Dinh Phung St (Front Gate) or 78A Nguyen Hue St Back Gate), T833019. Set in the home of a minor royal, it is, nevertheless, grand enough to boast two addresses and the only restaurant in this book to do so. Rather shabby as you might expect, it is an unusual dining experience with a decent Vietnamese menu and slightly better than expected food. *Ong Tao*, 96 Chu Van An St. A not particularly atmospheric restaurant located in the eating quarter. Serves excellent Vietnamese dishes at very fair prices. *Quoc Huy*, 43 Dinh Cung Trang. This is a wonderful open-air restaurant by the Northeast Gate of the Imperial Palace under the shade of a large tree, an ideal place for lunch after a morning's royal sight-seeing, well prepared food at very fair prices. *Am Phu* (*Hell*), 35 Nguyen Thai Hoc St. Do not confuse with An Phu – suggest you spell it for your cyclo driver rather than rely on your Vietnamese pronunciation. Excellent Vietnamese dishes in this spit and sawdust type eatery. Popular with locals which is always a good sign, two will dine and drink for less than US$5. *Ngoc An*, 29 Nguyen Thai Hoc St. Yet another fine diner in this end of town. Some Western, but Vietnamese dishes are what it's best at. Cheap and cheerful. *An Phu 1* and *2*, 18 Chu Van An St. Slightly more polished and therefore favoured by cautious tour leaders. Decent enough food, Western and local, but lots of pestering kids selling postcards. *Lac Thien* and *Lac Than*, 6 Dinh Tien Hoang St. Arguably Hué's most famous restaurants. Run by schismatic branches of the same deaf-mute family in adjacent buildings. You go to one or the other: under no circumstances should clients patronise both establishments. 10 years ago providence took us to *Lac Thien* which serves excellent dishes from a diverse and inexpensive menu, its Huda beers are long and cold, the family is riotous and entertaining and we have never looked back. We hear similar reports of next door but cannot believe it is as good. *Dong Tam*, 48/17 Le Loi St. Tucked away in the little hem opposite Century Riverside this is Hué's veggie restaurant. Sit in a pleasant and quiet little yard surrounded by plants and topiary while choosing from the very reasonably priced menu. Its credentials are reflected in its popularity with the city's monkish population. *Café no.3*, 3 Le Loi St. Near station and opposite *Le Loi Hué Hotel*, a cheap and popular café serving standard Vietnamese, Western and vegetarian food, useful source of information, bikes for rent. *Mandarin*, 12 Hung Vuong St. Backpacker food at its worst. Everything comes swimming in its own little pond of liquid or grease. Fly-blown, grunge, but nevertheless popular: let's be charitable and ascribe that to its bike rental service.

Cafés On Hung Vuong St opposite *Hung Vuong Hotel*, all pretty much alike in serving excellent snacks, fried noodles and breakfasts etc at low prices.

Bars *DMZ Bar*, 44 Le Loi St, T822585. Hué's first bar, cold beer and spirits at low prices, pool table and a friendly crowd including Hué's tiny core of ex-pats. *Apocalypse Now*, Nguyen Tri Phuong St, near corner of Hung Vuong St. Attracts a slightly younger crowd, pool table, music and beer to the usual A.N. formula.

Entertainment The water puppet troupe at 11 Le Loi St appear to have packed up which is a great pity because they were excellent, worth checking though. Otherwise rent a dragon boat and sail up the Perfume River with your own private singers and musicians. Tour offices and major hotels will arrange groups.

Shopping *Non bai tho* or poem hats. These are a form of the standard conical hat, *non la*, which are peculiar to Hué. Made from bamboo and palm leaves, love poetry, songs, proverbs or simply a design are stencilled on to them, which are only visible if the hat is held up to the light and viewed from the inside. No Vietnamese visitor would shake the dust of Hué off his feet without having previously stocked up on *me xung*, a sugary, peanut, toffee confection coated in sesame seeds: quite a pleasant energy booster to carry while cycling around the tombs, and with the significant advantage over Mars Bars, that while it may pull out your teeth out it won't melt in your pocket.

Local Bicycles and motorbikes can be hired from most hotels and guesthouses or from the men who hang around outside the *Huong Giang Hotel*; bicycles are less than a dollar a day, motorbikes around US$6 per day. Both represent an ideal way of touring the outlying sights. Boat hire: through tour agents, from outside the Huong Giang Hotel and from any berth on the south bank of the river, east of Trang Tien Bridge. Either for a gentle cruise, with singers in the evening or an attractive way of getting to some of the temples and mausoleums. Cyclo and xe ôm: everywhere. The latter is the speedier way to see the temples as the terrain south of town is quite hilly but the cyclo, of course, is the more civilized despite the occasional walk up hill. Taxi: *Hué Taxi* (metered) T833333.

Transport

Air Phu Bai Airport is a 40 minute drive south of Hué, Vietnam Airlines run a bus service in to town or you can take a taxi (around 80,000d on the meter, don't pay more for an unmetered vehicle). 2 connections daily with Hanoi (70-105 minutes, depending on aircraft type) and the same with Saigon (90-120 minutes).

Train The station is at the west end of Le Loi St, and serves all stations south to Saigon and north to Hanoi. Advance booking, especially for sleepers, is essential. The four hour journey to Danang is especially recommended for its scenic views.

Road Bus: the An Cuu station at 43 Hung Vuong St serves destinations south of Hué. The An Hoa station up at the northwest corner of the citadel serves destinations to the north of Hué. **Minibus**: to major destinations can be booked from hotels or from most of the agencies listed above.

Airline offices *Vietnam Airlines*, 7 Nguyen Tri Phuong St, T/F8824709. **Banks** *Industrial & Commercial Bank*, 2A Le Quy Don St. 0700-1130 and 1330-1700, closed Thur afternoon. *Vietcom Bank*, 6 Hoang Nhoa Tham St, next to GPO. GPO also changes money. **Communications** GPO: 8 Hoang Hoa Tham St. Open 0630-2100. International telephone and fax, poste restante and money change. **Hospitals & medical services** *Hué General Hospital*, 16 Le Loi St, T822325. **Tour companies & travel agents** *DMZ Tours*, 26 Le Loi St, T825242, F824806. They know the area well and run tours of the DMZ (all day tour, around US$18), boat trips on the river to see the tombs and temples, and sell tickets to onward destinations, Danang, Hoi An, Saigon etc. *Sinh Café*, 2 Hung Vuong St, T822121. Offer a very similar package at matching prices. *Café no 3*, 3 Le Loi St. Provide a small range of tours at competitive prices. *Le Van Tam*, 126 Phan Chu Trinh St, T826848. Rent cars at reasonable prices (US$26 to Hoi An). *Mr Long*, 9 Hung Vuong St. Rents motorbikes as does *Mr Franky*, 11 Tran Hung Dao St. An entertaining veteran. **Tourist offices** *Hué City Tourism*, 1 Truong Dinh St, T823577. *Thua-Thien Hue Tourism*, 9 Ngo Quyen St, T823288. Neither is very helpful from the information and map perspective but can arrange tours, the latter to other parts of the province too.

Directory

Hué to Danang

Between Hué and Danang a finger of the Truong Son Mountains juts eastwards, extending all the way to the sea: almost as though God were somewhat roguishly trying to divide the country into two equal halves. This barrier to north-south communication has resulted in some spectacular engineering solutions: the railway line closely follows the coastline (fortunately it's single

👉 **By train from Hué to Danang**

The train journey from Hué to Danang is regarded as not just one of the most scenic in Vietnam, but in the world. Paul Theroux in his book The Great Railway Bazaar (Penguin) recounts his impressions as the train reached the narrow coastal strip, south of Hué and approaching Danang. "The drizzle, so interminable in the former Royal Capital, gave way to bright sunshine and warmth; 'I had no idea,' I said. Of all the places the railway had taken me since London, this was the loveliest. We were at the fringes of a bay that was green and sparkling in bright sunlight. Beyond the leaping jade plates of the sea was an overhang of cliffs and the sight of a valley so large it contained sun, smoke, rain, and cloud – all at once – independent quantities of colour. I had been unprepared for this beauty; it surprised and humbled me ... Who has mentioned the simple fact that the heights of Vietnam are places of unimaginable grandeur? Though we can hardly blame a frightened draftee for not noticing this magnificence, we should have known all along that the French would not have colonized it, nor would the Americans have fought so long, if such ripeness did not invite the eye to take it."

track and narrow gauge) sometimes almost hanging over the sea – while Highway 1 winds its way equally precariously over the Hai Van Pass. It is to be hoped that the government's plans to build a tunnel through the mountains do materialize as it will remove the trucks and buses from the pass. The route is spectacular and should not be missed, see box above.

Lang Co
Colour map 3, grid A5

The road passes through many pretty, red-tiled villages, compact and surrounded by clumps of bamboo and fruit trees which provide shade, shelter and sustenance. And for colour the bougainvillea – which through grafting produce pink and white leaves on the same branch. Windowless jalopies from the French era trundle along picking up passengers and their bundles while station wagons from the American era provide an inter-village shared taxi service. Just north of Hai Van pass lies the idyllic fishing village of **Lang Co** (about 65 kilometres south of Hué) which has a number of cheap and good seafood restaurants along the road as well as the *Lang Co Hotel*, T054-874426, which has a few simple but slightly overpriced rooms (US$12-14) at the top of the dunes looking down to the sea, fan and cold water (and that sporadically) only. The beach here is wide, clean and usually deserted, but somewhat spoilt by the high voltage power lines which run its length. Shortly after crossing the Lang Co lagoon, dotted with coracles and fish traps, the road begins the long haul up to Hai Van Pass.

Hai Van Pass
Colour map 3, grid A5

Hai Van Pass (Deo Hai Van) 'Pass of the Ocean Clouds' or, to the French, Col des Nuages lies 497 metres above the dancing white waves that can be seen at its foot. In historic times the pass marked the border between the kingdoms of Vietnam and Champa. The mountains also act as an important climatic barrier trapping the cooler, damper air masses to the north and bottling it up over Hué, which accounts for Hué's shocking weather. They also mark an abrupt linguistic divide, with the Hué dialect (the language of the royal court) to the north the source of bemusement to many southerners.

The pass is peppered with abandoned pillboxes and crowned with an old fort, originally built by the dynasty from Hué and used as a relay station for the pony express on the old Mandarin Road. Subsequently used by the French, today it is a pretty shabby affair collecting wind-blown litter and sometimes used by the People's Army for a quiet brew-up and a smoke.

Looking back to the north, stretching into the haze is the littoral and lagoon of Lang Co. To the south, Danang Bay and Monkey Mountain; and at your feet a patch of green paddies which belong to the Leper Colony, accessible only by boat. Hai Van Pass will not detain anyone long, unless their engine has blown up, the litter and vendors will see to that.

Highway 1 passes through the village of **Nam O**, once famous for firework manufacture. Pages of old school books were once dyed pink, laid out in the sun to dry, rolled up and filled with gunpowder. But alas, no more. Like other pyrotechnical villages, Nam O has suffered from the government's ban on firecrackers. Just south of Nam O is **Xuan Thieu Beach**, dubbed *Red Beach II* by US Marines who landed here in March 1965, marking the beginning of direct intervention by the US in the Second Indochina War. The tarmac and concrete foundations of the military base remain.

Danang

Danang is yet another name to conjure with. It is a city with a history: originally Danang was known as Cua Han ('Mouth of the Han River'); when the French took control they renamed it Tourane, a rough transliteration of Cua Han. Then it acquired the title Thai Phien, and finally Danang. The city is sited on a peninsula of land at the point where the Han River flows into the South China Sea. An important port from French times, Danang gained world-wide fame when two US Marine battalions landed here in March 1965 to secure the airfield. They were the first of a great many more who would land on the beaches and airfields of South Vietnam.

*Phone code: 051
Colour map 3,
grid A5*

Ins and outs

The airport is on the edge of the city. There are daily connections with Hanoi and Saigon and less regularly with Buon Ma Thuot, Dalat, Pleiku and Nha Trang. Danang is on the north-south railway line linking Hanoi and Saigon and there are also regular bus and minibus connections with all major cities in the south as far as Saigon, and in the north as far as Hanoi. A few years ago the border with Laos at Lao Bao opened to foreign travellers and daily buses leave Danang for the Lao town of Savannakhet, on the Mekong. Visas are available from the Lao consulate in town.

Getting there

Danang is a sizeable town and there is abundant public transport including cyclos, taxis and Honda om. Bicycles and motorbikes are available for hire from some guesthouses.

Getting around

History

Danang lies in a region of great historical significance. Fairly close to – but not often within particularly easy reach of – the city lie ruins of the powerful kingdom of Champa, one of the most glorious in ancient Southeast Asia (see page 328). The Cham were probably of Indonesian descent, and Chinese texts give the date 192 AD as the year when a group of tribes formed a union known as Lin-Yi, later to become Champa. The polytheistic religion of Champa was a fusion of Buddhism, Sivaism and local elements – and later Islam – producing an abundance of religious (and secular) sculptures and monuments. The goddess Uroja is of central importance; the 'mother' of the nation, she is normally represented as a breast and nipple. Siva is represented as a linga. The kingdom reached its apogee in the 10th and 11th centuries, but unlike the

Khmers, Champa never had the opportunity to create a capital city matching the magnificence of Angkor. For long periods the Cham were compelled to pay tribute to the Chinese, and after that they were dominated in turn by the Javanese, Annamese (the Vietnamese) and then the Khmers. The Cham 'nation' was finally eradicated in 1471, although there are still an estimated 90,000 Cham living in central Vietnam (mostly Brahmanists and Muslims). Given this turbulent history, it is perhaps surprising that the Cham found any opportunity for artistic endeavours. It should perhaps be added that since the demise of the kingdom, the number of Cham sculptures has grown enormously as forgers have carved more of the beautiful images.

Danang today has a population of 600,000 making it the fourth largest city in Vietnam and is once more extending its influence as a commercial and trading city. Its position, roughly equidistant between Hanoi and Saigon, gives Danang strategic significance and its port facilities are being upgraded. An Export Processing Zone has been created which has yet to excite foreign interest but will no doubt do so when Saigon overheats.

Sights

Cham
Museum

The **Cham Museum** is at the intersection of Tran Phu and Le Dinh Duong streets. It was established by academics of the École Française d'Extrême Orient, and contains the largest display of Cham art anywhere in the world (see page 363 and Excursions, below, to My Son and Dong Duong). The museum buildings alone are worth the visit: constructed in 1916 in a beautiful setting, the complex is open-plan in design, providing an environment in which the pieces can be exhibited to their best advantage. There are a number of rooms, each dedicated to a different period or style of Cham art, dating from the fourth to the 14th centuries. The Cham Period, spanning more than 1,000 years, produced abundant sculpture. Facial features on earlier works tend to be accentuated, and the bodies rather heavily sculpted. From the 10th century, under the influence of the Khmers, faces become less stylistic, more human, and the bodies of the figures more graceful and flowing. One problem with the display is the lack of any background information – not even dates are provided. The museum booklet (10,000d) has been written as an art history, not as a guide to the collection, and is of little help. The pieces are wonderful, but the visitor may leave the museum rather befuddled by the display. ■ *20,000d. Open 0700-1800 Monday-Sunday.*

Danang's **Cao Dai Temple** is at 35 Haiphong Street and is the second largest in Vietnam. The priest here is particularly friendly and informative – especially regarding Cao Dai-ism and its links with other religions. Services are held at 0600, 1200, 1800 and 2400 (see page 382). **Danang Cathedral**, single-spired with a pink sandstone coloured wash and built in 1923, can be found at 156 Tran Phu Street. The stained glass windows were made in Grenoble, in 1927, by Louis Balmet who was also responsible for the windows of Dalat Cathedral. The city has a fair array of markets. There is a covered **general market** (**Cho Han**) in a new building at the intersection of Tran Phu and Hung Vuong streets. Another market, **Cho Con**, is at the intersection of Hung Vuong and Ong Ich Khiem streets. The stalls close by sell basketwork and other handicrafts. On Haiphong Street, running east from the railway station, there is a **street market** selling fresh produce. Danang still retains some fine **French colonial architecture**, for instance, the house at 46 Tran Quoc Toan Street.

Excursions

Once a fabled resort celebrated in rock songs, China Beach is now a quiet sea-shore, with souvenir and food stalls. Of course, it retains the white sand and surf that brought it such popularity with American soldiers. At times too, a strong and dangerous cross-current and undertow. China Beach was the GI name for this US military R & R retreat during the Vietnam War. Since 1975 it has been called T20 Beach; T20 was the military code by which the North Vietnamese Army referred to the beach. The local Vietnamese name is My Khe. **C-D** *My Khe Hotel*, T821180. Plenty of stalls selling fresh seafood: cuttlefish, crab and shrimp steamed or grilled to taste, delicious and reasonable

China Beach

The Central Region

Danang

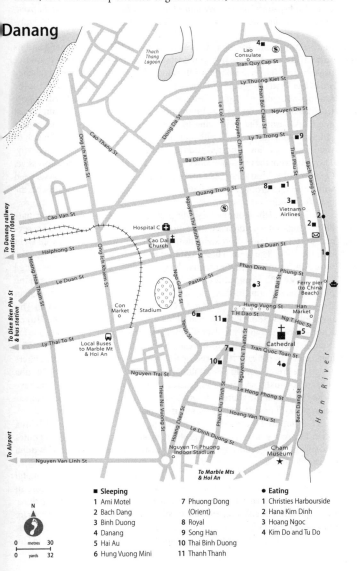

■ Sleeping		● Eating
1 Ami Motel	7 Phuong Dong	1 Christies Harbourside
2 Bach Dang	(Orient)	2 Hana Kim Dinh
3 Binh Duong	8 Royal	3 Hoang Ngoc
4 Danang	9 Song Han	4 Kim Do and Tu Do
5 Hai Au	10 Thai Binh Duong	
6 Hung Vuong Mini	11 Thanh Thanh	

prices. ■ *Getting there: take the red and white bus to Hoi An, ask the driver to put you down after crossing Nguyen Van Troi Bridge, a three kilometres hike from here. Or take the ferry crossing from Bach Dang Street with a bicycle. Alternatively, to go the whole way by xe ôm shouldn't cost more than the price of a cold beer.*

Two kilometres south of China Beach is **Bac My An Beach**, next to the *Furama Resort*. This is a clean and attractive beach with some seafood stalls.

Hoi An is a beautiful, historic town (see page 204), situated 32 kilometres south of Danang. Although a few years ago most visitors saw the town as an excursion from Danang, roles are now reversed, most people prefer to stay here and make an excursion to Danang. ■ *Getting there: by bus from 350 Hung Vuong Street look for a red and white bus with the Hoi An sign at the front, one hour; the last bus returns at about 1700.*

Marble Mountains

Marble Mountains (or Ngu Hanh Son) overlook the city of Danang and its airfield, about 12 kilometres to the west. The name was given to these five peaks by the Nguyen Emperor Minh Mang on his visit in 1825 – although they are in fact limestone crags with marble outcrops. They are also known as the mountains of the five elements (fire, water, soil, wood and metal). An important religious spot for the Cham, the peaks became havens for Communist guerrillas during the war owing to their commanding view over Danang airbase. From here, a force with sufficient firepower could control much of what went on below, and the guerrillas harried the Americans mercilessly. The views from the mountain sides, overlooking Danang Bay, are impressive. On the Marble Mountains are a number of important sights, often associated with caves and grottoes which have formed through chemical action on the limestone rock.

At the foot of the mountains is a village with a number of shops selling marble carvings. Of the mountains, the most visited is **Thuy Son**. There are several grottoes and cave pagodas in the mountain which are marked by steps cut into the rock. The **Tam Thai Pagoda**, reached by a staircase cut into the mountain, is on the site of a much older Cham place of worship. Constructed in 1825 by Minh Mang, and subsequently rebuilt, the central statue is of the Buddha Sakyamuni (the historic Buddha) flanked by the Bodhisattva Quan Am (a future Buddha and the Goddess of Mercy), and a statue of Van Thu (symbolizing wisdom). At the rear of the grotto is another cave, the **Huyen Khong Cave**. Originally a place of animist worship, it later became a site for Buddhist pilgrimage. The entrance is protected by four door guardians. The high ceiling of the cave is pierced by five holes through which the sun filters and in the hour before midday it illuminates the central statue of the Buddha Sakyamuni. In the cave are various natural rock formations which, if you have picked up one of the young cave guides along the way, will be pointed out as being stork-like birds, elephants, an arm, a fish and a face.

A few hundred metres to the south on the right is a track leading to Chua Quan The Am which has its own grotto complete with stalactites, stalagmites and pillars. Local children will point out formations resembling the Buddha and an elephant.

■ *Entrance to Marble Mountain, US$2. Guides, usually young girls, useful for pointing out the various caves dotted over the mountain but complaints of harassment from tourists seem to have ended this useful service. Getting there: 12 kilometres from Danang 20 kilometres from Hoi An, red and white bus to Hoi An from Danang's local bus station opposite 350 Hung Vuong Street, 25 minutes or take a xe ôm. Many visitors stop off at Marble Mountain en route to Hoi An.*

Non Nuoc Beach is a one kilometre walk from Marble Mountain. A huge, white sandy beach it was developed as a beach resort for Russians after 1975 which perhaps explains the ugliness of the concrete Non Nuoc Beach Resort. Visitors are charged for using the beach and the usual for bike parking.

Sleeping C *Non Nuoc Beach Resort*, T821470. Three blocks, some a/c, restaurants. **E** *Hoa's Place*, T836188. Fan, no hot water, has received enthusiastic reviews from backpackers for its simplicity, value and cheery reception.

My Son and **Dong Duong** are two centres of the former Cham Kingdom (see page 211). **My Son** is located about 60 kilometres south of Danang (28 kilometres west of Tra Kieu) and consists of over 70 monuments spread over a large area. The characteristic Cham architectural structure is the tower, built to reflect the divinity of the king: tall and rectangular, with four porticoes, each of which is 'blind' except for that on the west face. Because Cham kings were far less powerful than, say, the deva-rajas of Angkor, the monuments are correspondingly smaller and more personal. Orginally built of wood (not surprisingly, none remains), they were later made of brick, of which the earliest (seventh century) are located at My Son. These are so-called Mi-Son E1 – the unromantic identifying sequence of letters and numbers being given, uncharacteristically, by the French archaeologists who rediscovered and initially investigated the monuments in 1898. Although little of these early examples remains, the temples seem to show similarities with post-Gupta Indian forms, while also embodying Chen-La stylistic influences. Bricks are exactly laid and held together with a form of vegetable cement probably the resin of the cay day tree. It is thought that on completion, each tower was surrounded by wood and fired over several days in what amounted to a vast outdoor kiln. Unfortunately, My Son was a Vietcong field headquarters and therefore located within one of the US 'free fire' zones and was extensively damaged – in particular, the finest sanctuary in the complex was demolished by US sappers.

My Son
Colour map 3, grid A5

The Central Region

60 kilometres south of Danang and 20 kilometres from My Son, **Dong Duong** supplanted My Son as the centre of Cham art and culture when King Indravarman II built a large Buddhist monastery there at the end of the ninth century. Artistically, little changed – the decoration of the towers simply became more ornate, flamboyant and involved, and the reliefs more deeply cut. Then, in the early 10th century, the focus of Cham art returned to My Son once again under the patronage of Indravarman III (so-called Mi-Son A1 style). Here, a new and far more elegant architecture, evolved. The towers became taller and more balanced, and the decoration purer and less crude.

Of the temple groupings, Groups A, E and H were badly damaged in the war. Groups B and C have largely retained their temples but many statues, altars and linga have been removed to the **Cham Museum** in Danang or by French collectors.

■ *50,000d. Getting to My Son: from Danang, drive south on Highway 1 and turn right towards Tra Kieu after 34 kilometres (some two kilometres after crossing the Thu Bon River). Drive through Tra Kieu to the village of Kim Lam. Turn left; the path to My Son is about six kilometres further along this road. At this point is the ticket office, a short bamboo bridge crossing and a two kilometre jeep ride (included in the ticket price) with a short walk at the end to My Son. It is not clear how thoroughly the area has been de-mined so it is advisable not to stray too far from the road and path. Take a hat, sun cream and water – it is hot and dry. My Son can be reached just as easily from Hoi An, two hours each way by Honda om (US$7) or by boat (US$15), which takes all day. The boat will carry bicycles; negotiate with riverside restaurants in Hoi An.*

Bana Hill Station **Bana** is the most recently rehabilitated **Hill Station** in Vietnam. It is 38 kilometres west of Danang on Chua Mountain (Nui Chua). The mountain rises to a height of 1,467 metres, while Bana itself is tucked in at 1,200 metres. The view in all directions is spectacular, the air is fresh and cool and encompassed into each day are four seasons: morning is spring, noon the summer, afternoon is autumn and night the winter. Bana was founded in 1902 by the French who brought their febrile and palsied here to convalesce in a most benevolent clime. Flora and fauna are diverse and interesting, and villas have been fashioned from the foundations of former French fabrications, some of which accept guests. ■ *10,000d per person, 5,000d per motorbike. Accommodation available. Getting there: a short hitch north up Highway 1, before the village of Nam turn left. Easily accessible by motorbike from Danang.*

Essentials

Sleeping
■ *on map*
Price codes:
see inside front cover

A number of new hotels have opened and, together with renovated hotels, Danang now offers reasonable accommodation at a range of prices.

L-A+ *Furama Resort*, 68 Xuan Huong St, T847888, F847666, E furamadn@hn.vnn.vn. 200 rooms and suites beautifully designed and furnished. Cool and comfortable and with its own beach, a welcome addition to Vietnam's small but growing number of such resorts. Excellent watersports facilities, mountain biking, free form pool, golf driving range and tennis.

A *Phuong Dong (Orient)*, 93 Phan Chu Trinh St, T821266, F822854. A/c, still rather grand, good size rooms. **A-B** *Bach Dang Hotel*, 50 Bach Dang St, T823649, F821659. Rather cramped for the price, some with river views and quite a good restaurant, cheaper rooms in and old building at the back, all with satellite TV and bath tub, central location. **A-B** *Royal* (formerly *Marco Polo*), 17 Quang Trung St, T823295. 28 rooms, with its discounted rates (breakfast included) this smart hotel offers excellent value. Restaurant and nightclub. **A-C** *Song Han*, 36 Bach Dang St, T822540. 60 rooms, a/c and some river views.

B *Hai Au*, 177 Tran Phu St, T822722, F824165. Central, large rooms, friendly reception, indifferent restaurant. **B-C** *Ami Motel*, 7 Quang Trung, T824494. Clean, friendly. **B-C** *Binh Duong*, 30, 32 Tran Phu St, T821930, F827666. Clean and friendly. **B-C** *Thai Binh Duong (Pacific)*, 92 Phan Chu Trinh St, T822137. A/c, large and central but rather characterless. **B-C** *White Snow*, 177 Phan Chu Trinh St, T834333, F834332. Considered to be one of the best hotels in Danang, good breakfasts. **B-D** *Danang*, 3-5 Dong Da St, T821986. Some a/c, restaurant and tour services, now merged with the old Marble Mountain hotel next door.

C *Canary*, 30 Ngo Gia Tu St, T829800, F828900. A/c, all have bath tub and hot water, good value. **C** *Phuong Lan*, 142 Hoang Dieu St, T820373, F820382. A/c, satellite TV, hot water, good value (after some bargaining), free airport pick-up, motorbikes for rent.

D *Hung Vuong Mini*, 95 Hung Vuong St, T823967. 10 rooms, some a/c, hot water, bicycle, motorbike and cars for hire at competitive prices. **D** *Thanh Thanh*, 54 Phan Chu Trinh St, T830684, F829886. Some a/c, a bit run down but good location.

Seafood is good here, and Danang has its own beer, Da Nang 'Export'. There are a number of cafés and restaurants along Bach Dang St, overlooking the river.

Eating
● *on map*

Mid-range *Bach Dang Hotel*, 50 Bach Dang St. Informal, glimpses of river and decent food. *Christies Harbourside Grill*, 9 Bach Dang St, T826645. Some American, some Vietnamese, fish and chips are excellent value, paperback book exchange. Recommended. *Hoang Ngoc*, 106 Nguyen Chi Thanh St, T821214. Extensive menu, good food and welcoming atmosphere, popular. *Hana Kim Dinh*, 7 Bach Dang St. Riverside restaurant, opposite *Bach Dang Hotel*, Western and Vietnamese menus, sit in or overlooking the river. *Kim Do*, 174 Tran Phu St, T821846. Now a huge Chinese restaurant on the site of the popular old restaurant. Typical Chinese menu, reasonable food at fair prices. Popular with tour groups. *Tu Do*, 172 Tran Phu St. Extensive menu and excellent food, deservedly popular and good value. Recommended.

There is a nightclub at the *Royal Hotel*.

Nightclubs

Marble carvings From shops in town, but particularly from the stalls around the foot of Marble Mountain (see Excursions).

Shopping

108 kilometres from Hué, 130 from Quang Ngai. Local buses to Hoi An run from the station at the west end of Hung Vuong St, opposite Con Market. **International connections**: it is possible to get a visa for Laos in Danang from the Laotian consulate here (US$25 for a 7-day transit visa), takes 1 day. There are daily departures for the Lao town of Savannakhet, on the Mekong River. The road runs west from Dong Ha into the Annamite mountains and crosses the border at Lao Bao, not far from the battlefield of Khe Sanh.

Transport

Local Bicycles available from many hotels from around US$1 per day. Some cafés and hotels also rent motorbikes for US$5-7 per day. Otherwise the usual cyclo or Honda om. Taxis, *Airport Taxi* T825555, *Dana Taxi*, T815815.

Air The airport is 2½ kilometres southwest of the city. There are 2-3 connections daily from Saigon and Hanoi, 70-85 minutes. Connections with Buon Ma Thuot (65 minutes) and Dalat (85 minutes) 3 times a week and with Nha Trang (80 minutes) 5 days a week. Vietnam Airlines, 35 Tran Phu St, T821130, F832759.

Train The train station is on Haiphong St, 2 kilometres west of town and there are express trains to and from Hanoi, Saigon and Hue.

Road Bus: the inter-province bus station is on Dien Bien Phu St, about 3 kilometres from town from which there are connections with all major cities.

Airline offices *Vietnam Airlines Booking Office*, 35 Tran Phu St, T821130, F832759. **Banks** *VID Public Bank*, 2 Tran Phu St. *Vietcombank*, 104 Le Loi St. Will change most major currencies, cash and TCs. **Communications** GPO: 60 Bach Dang St, corner of Bach Dang and Le Duan streets. Telex, fax and telephone facilities here. Poste restante at 62 Bach Dang St. **TNT International:** T821685/822582. **Embassies & consulates** *Lao Consulate*, 12 Tran Qui Cap St, T821208, F822628. **Hospitals & medical services** Hospital: *C Hospital*, 74 Haiphong St, T821480. **Tourist offices** *Danang Tourist Office*, 92 Phan Chu Trinh St, T821423, F822854. Arranges cars and guides. *Vietnamtourism*, 158 Phan Chu Trinh St, T822990. **Useful addresses** Immigration Police: Nguyen Thi Minh Khai St, opposite *Hai Van Hotel*.

Directory

The Central Region

Hoi An

Phone code: 051
Colour map 3, grid A5

The ancient town of Hoi An (formerly Faifo) lies 32 kilometres south of Danang on the banks of the Thu Bon River. Originally a Champa port, the town has a distinct Chinese atmosphere with low, tiled-roof houses and narrow streets.

Ins and outs

Getting there   Hoi An is a small town and most people who come here base themselves in the much bigger city of Danang, just 32 kilometres away (see the Danang entry for details on getting there). However, there are direct minibus connections with Saigon, Hanoi, Hué and Nha Trang. The quickest way of getting from Hanoi or Saigon is by flying to Danang and then catching a taxi from the airport direct to Hoian.

Getting around   Hoi An is compact best explored on foot. Guesthouses hire out bicycles and vehicles are also available for out-of-town excursions.

The town

Hoi An is divided into five quarters or 'bangs', each of which would traditionally have had its own pagoda and supported one Chinese clan group. The Chinese, along with some Japanese, settled here in the 16th century and controlled trade between island Southeast Asia, East Asia (China and Japan) and India. Portuguese and Dutch vessels also docked at the port. During the Tay Son rebellion (1771-1788) the town was almost totally destroyed, although this is not apparent to the visitor. By the end of the 19th century the Thu Bon River had started to silt up and Hoi An was gradually eclipsed by Danang as the most important port of the area.

Hoi An has emerged as one of the most popular tourist destinations in Vietnam and there has been no diminution in its status. Quite the reverse. Walking along Tran Phu Street one often sees more Western than Vietnamese faces.

Hoi An's historic character is being slowly submerged by the rising tide of tourism. Although remaining physically intact virtually every one of its fine historic buildings either markets some aspect of its own heritage or touts in some other way for the tourist dollar; increasingly it is coming to resemble the 'Vietnam' pavilion in a Disney theme park. Nevertheless, visitors to Hoi An are charmed by the gentleness of the people and the sedate pace of life. Hoi An is friendly and quiet. Everything is small and slow. Hoi An also has a number of highly praised restaurants and the nearby Cua Dai Beach.

Sights

Most of Hoi An's more attractive buildings and assembly halls (known as hoi quan) are found either on (or just off) Tran Phu Street. Tran Phu stretches west-east from the Japanese Covered Bridge to the market, running parallel to, and one street in from, the river. The best way to explore this small, intimate town is on foot. People are friendly and will generally not mind inquisitive, but polite, foreigners. A day is needed to see the town properly. Entrance to most buildings is by **sightseeing ticket**, 50,000d for four separate sights on sale at Hoi An Tourist Office at the junction of Phan Chu Trinh and Nguyen Hue streets, and Hoi An Museum. Tickets for additional sights cost 10,000d.

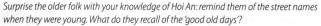

At the west end of Tran Phu Street is Hoi An's most famous landmark: the covered bridge – variously known as the Pagoda Bridge, the Faraway People's Bridge and, popularly, as the **Japanese Covered Bridge** (*Cau Nhat Ban*). The bridge was built in the 16th century, perhaps even earlier. On its north side there is a pagoda, Japanese in style, which protects sailors. At the west end of the bridge are statues of two dogs, and at the east end, of two monkeys – it is said that the bridge was begun in the year of the monkey and finished in the year of the dog. Some scholars have pointed out that this would mean a two-year period of construction, an inordinately long time for such a small bridge; they maintain that the two animals represent points of the compass, WSW (monkey) and NW (dog). Father Benigne Vachet, a missionary who lived in Hoi An between 1673 and 1683 notes in his memoirs that the bridge was the haunt of beggars and fortune tellers hoping to benefit from the stream of people crossing over it. Its popular name – Japanese Covered Bridge – reflects a long-standing belief that it was built by the Japanese, although no documentary evidence exists to support this. One of its other names, the Faraway People's Bridge, is said to have been coined because vessels from faraway would moor close to the bridge. ■ *1 token – keep your ticket to get back.* **Japanese Covered Bridge**

Just south of the Covered Bridge is **Bach Dang Street** which runs along the banks of the Thu Bon River. Here there are boats, activity and often a cooling breeze. The road loops round to the Hoi An Market (see below). The small but interesting French quarter around Phan Boi Chau St is worth taking time over; it's not on the regular 'tourist circuit' and requires no entry fee although a small gratuity is always welcomed.

Chinese traders in Hoi An (like elsewhere in Southeast Asia) established self-governing dialect associations or clan houses which owned their own schools, cemeteries, hospitals and temples. The clan houses (*hoi quan*) may be dedicated to a god or an illustrious individual and may contain a temple but are not themselves temples. There are five clan houses in Hoi An, four for use by people of specific ethnicities: Fukien, Cantonese, Hainan, Chaozhou and the fifth for use by any visiting Chinese sailors or merchants. **Assembly Halls**

Strolling east from the Covered Bridge down Tran Phu St all the assembly halls can be seen. Merchants from Guangdong would meet at the **Cantonese Assembly Hall** or **Quang Dong Hoi Quan**, 176 Tran Phu St. This assembly hall is dedicated to Quan Cong, a Han Chinese general and dates from 1786. The hall with fine embroidered hangings is in a cool, tree filled compound, a good place to rest. Admission, one token.

Next is the **All Chinese Assembly Hall**, **Ngu Bang Hoi Quan**, and sometimes referred to as **Chua Ba** (Goddess Temple) 64 Tran Phu St. Unusually for an assembly hall, it was a mutual aid society open to any Chinese trader or seaman, regardless of dialect or region of origin. Chinese vessels tended to visit Hoi An during the spring, returning to China in the summer. The assembly hall would help ship-wrecked and ill sailors and perform the burial rites of merchants with no relatives in Hoi An. Built in 1773 as a meeting place for all five groups (the four listed above plus Hakka) and also for those with no clan house of their own it today accommodates a Chinese School, *Truong Le Nghia*, where children of the diaspora learn the language of their forebears. Admission, one token.

The **Fukien Assembly Hall** or **Phuc Kien Hoi Quan**, 46 Tran Phu St, founded around 1690, served Hoi An's largest Chinese ethnic group, those from Fukien. It is an intimate building within a large compound and is dedicated to Thien Hau, goddess of the sea and protector of sailors. She is the central figure on the main altar, clothed in gilded robes who, together with her assistants, can hear the cries of distress of drowning sailors. Immediately on the right on entering the temple is a mural depicting Thien Hau rescuing a sinking vessel. Behind the main altar is a second sanctuary which houses the image of Van Thien whose blessings pregnant women invoke on the lives of their unborn children. Admission, one token.

With a rather more colourful history comes the **Hainan Assembly Hall** or **Hai Nam Hoi Quan**, 100 metres further east at 10 Tran Phu St. Founded in 1883 in memory of the more than 100 sailors and passengers who were killed when three ships were plundered by an admiral in Emperor Tu Duc's navy. In his defence the admiral claimed the victims were pirates and some sources maintain he even had the ships painted black to strengthen his case.

Exquisite wood carving is the highlight of the **Chaozhou** or **Trieu Chau Assembly Hall**, 157 Nguyen Duy Hieu St. The altar and its panels depict images from the sea and women from the Peking court, presumably intended to console homesick traders. Admission, one token.

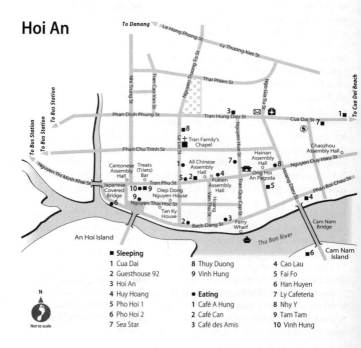

Hoi An

■ Sleeping

1 Cua Dai	8 Thuy Duong
2 Guesthouse 92	9 Vinh Hung
3 Hoi An	
4 Huy Hoang	● Eating
5 Pho Hoi 1	1 Café A Hung
6 Pho Hoi 2	2 Café Can
7 Sea Star	3 Café des Amis

4 Cao Lau	
5 Fai Fo	
6 Han Huyen	
7 Ly Cafeteria	
8 Nhy Y	
9 Tam Tam	
10 Vinh Hung	

N

Not to scale

Tan Ky House, 101 Nguyen Thai Hoc St, dates from the late eighteenth century. Built by later generations of the Tan Ky family (they originally arrived in
Hoi An from China two hundred years earlier) it reflects not only the prosperity the family had acquired but also the architecture of their Japanese and
Vietnamese neighbours, whose styles had presumably worked their influence
on the aesthetic taste and appreciation of the younger family members.

At the east end of Tran Phu Street at No 24, close to the intersection with
Nguyen Hue Street, is the **Ong Hoi An Pagoda**. This temple is in fact two
interlinked pagodas built back-to-back: *Chua Quan Cong*, and behind that
Chua Quan Am. Their date of construction is not known, although both certainly existed in 1653. In 1824 Emperor Minh Mang made a donation of 300
luong (1 luong = 1.5 oz) of silver for the support of the pagodas. They are dedicated to Quan Cong and Quan Am respectively.

Virtually opposite the Ong Hoi An Pagoda, is the **Hoi An Market** (*Cho Hoi
An*). The market extends down to the river and then along the river road
(Bach Dang Street). At the Tran Phu Street end it is a covered market selling
mostly dry goods, numerous cloth merchants and seamstresses will produce
made-to-measure shirts in a few hours for US$5 but not all to the same high
standards. Mr Thuc, Tran Quy Cap and Yaly, 27 Tran Qui Cap have been recommended by visitors, also 60 Le Loi Street. The riverside of the market is the
local **fish market** which comes alive at 0500-0600 as boats arrive with the
night's catch.

On the junction of Le Loi and Phan Chu Trinh streets stands the **Tran
Family Temple** which has survived for 15 generations; the current generation has no son which means the lineage has been broken. The building exem-
plifies well Hoi An's construction methods and the harmonious fusion of
Chinese and Japanese styles. It is roofed with heavy *yin* and *yang* tiling which
requires strong roof beams; these are held up by a triple beamed support in
the Japanese style (seen in the roof of the covered bridge). Some beams have
ornately carved dragons of Chinese inspiration. The outer doors are Japanese, the inner are Chinese. On a central altar rest small wooden boxes which
contain the photograph or likeness of the deceased together with biographical
details; beyond, at the back of the house is a small raised Chinese herb, spice
and flower garden with a row of bonzai trees. As with all Hoi An's family
houses guests are received warmly and courteously and served lotus tea and
dried coconut. ■ *1 coupon.*

Diep Dong Nguyen House, 80 Nguyen Thai Hoc Street, with two Chinese
lanterns hanging outside, was once a Chinese dispensary. The owner is
friendly, hospitable and not commercially-minded. He takes visitors into his
house and shows everything with pride and smiles.

Just east of the Japanese Bridge is **Phung Hung House**, 4 Nguyen Thi
Minh Khai Street. Built over 200 years ago it has been in the same family for
eight generations. The house is constructed of 80 columns of ironwood on
marble pedestals. During the floods of 1964 Phung Hung House became
home to 160 locals who camped upstairs for three days as water rose 2.5
metres.

Museums

Adjacent to Ong Hoi An Pagoda is **Hoi An Museum of History and Culture**,
7 Nguyen Hue St, is housed in a former pagoda. The museum sets the history
of the town in its trading context with sections on all the main cultural influences. Admission, one token. The **Museum of Trade Ceramics**, 80 Tran Phu
St, was opened with financial and technical support from Japan; it contains an

interesting range of ancient wares, some of them from shipwrecks in surrounding waters. There are also detailed architectural drawings of various houses in Hoi An. Upstairs, from the front balcony there is a fascinating roofscape. Admission, one token.

Excursions

Cua Dai Beach, five kilometres from Hoi An, east down Tran Hung Dao Street, a pleasant 20 minute cycle ride. White sand and clear water. Refreshments available. **Boat rides** on the Thu Bon River. Local boatwomen charge a dollar or so an hour, a very tranquil and relaxed way of spending the early evening.

Essentials

Sleeping
■ *on map*
Price codes:
see inside front cover

There has been a dramatic increase in the number of hotel rooms available in Hoi An and so the chances of being left bedless for the night have fallen dramatically. It is still as well to book in advance, however. During slack periods substantial discounts can be reckoned on.

B-C *Pho Hoi 2*, Cam Nam Island, T/F862628. South of Cam Nam Bridge, new 45 room hotel, all a/c, bathtubs and satellite TV, some rooms have river view, motorbikes and sampans for rent. **B-C** *Vinh Hung*, 143 Tran Phu St, T861621, F861893. An attractive old building with a splendid and ornate reception room decorated with dark wood in Chinese style. Rooms at a range of prices, some large and traditionally furnished, others rather small. Popular and recommended. **B-D** *Hoi An*, 6 Tran Hung Dao St, T861445, F861636. Attractive colonial building set well back from the road in spacious grounds, cheaper rooms have fan and shared bathroom, staff not particularly welcoming. **B-D** *Thuy Duong 1*, 11 Le Loi St, T861574, F861330. 10 rooms, some a/c, friendly.

C-D *Cua Dai*, 18A Cua Dai St, T862231, F862232. On the beach road, a little way from town but comfortable, clean, well-run and a friendly reception, perhaps can be charmed into including breakfast. **C-D** *Guesthouse 92*, 92 Tran Phu St, T861331. Very obliging and helpful, reluctant to turn anyone away hence often looks like a refugee camp, rents bicycles. **C-D** *Huy Hoang*, 73 Phan Boi Chau St, T861453. 19 a/c rooms, bath, hot water, terrace on the river, clean and very friendly. A decent hotel spoilt by the excessive noise from the neighbours which affect the cheaper downstairs rooms in particular. **C-D** *Pho Hoi 1*, 7/2 Tran Phu St, T861633, near market. Some a/c, cheaper rooms share facilities. **C-D** *Sea Star*, 15 Cua Dai St, on the road to the beach, T861589. New, travel services, car hire on offer.

D-E *Thuy Duong 2*, 68 Huynh Thuc Khang St, T861394, F861330. All a/c with bath tub and hot water, friendly and a short walk out of the centre, near bus station but friendly and good value.

Eating
● *on map*

A Hoi An speciality is *Cao Lau* – a special wanton soup made with water from one particular well. Fresh seafood is also readily available. There are new restaurants and cafés springing up all over town but especially on Tran Phu St.

Café A Hung, 29 Le Loi St. Seafood, vegetarian dishes. *Café Can*, 74 Bach Dang St. Good Vietnamese and Western menu, seafood specialities by the river. *Café des Amis*, 52 Bach Dang St, near the river. Fish and seafood, set menu changes daily, widely acclaimed food, excellent value. Highly recommended. *Fukien*, 31 Tran Phu St. Family run Chinese. *Han Huyen (Floating Restaurant)*, Bach Dang St, just east of footbridge. Excellent seafood. *Nhu y (aka Miss Vy's)*, 2 Tran Phu St. Miss Vy turns out all the local specialities as well as some of her own. The set 5-course dinner is particularly recommended. *Restaurant 79*, 79 Huynh Thuc Khang St, opposite *Thuy Duong 2 Hotel*. Good and cheap. *Tam Tam Café*, 110 Nguyen Thai Hoc. This is a great little café in a renovated tea house. Cocktails, draft beer, music, book exchange, plus attached restaurant serving French and Italian cuisine. A relaxing place for a drink, expresso or meal. *Thanh*, 76 Bach Dang St. A charming old house overlooking the river which is recognizable by its Chinese temple style, the shrimp is excellent. *Vinh Hung*, 147 Tran Phu St, T862203. Belongs to the hotel of the same name. Another fine building finely decked with Chinese lanterns and traditional furniture, An excellent range of seafood and Vietnamese specials at fair prices. *Yellow River*, 38 Tran Phu St. Good Hoi An family restaurant, fried wanton is recommended, especially for francophones. *Fai Fo*, 104 Tran Phu St. Especially good for breakfast and ice cream. *Ly Cafeteria 22*, 22 Nguyen Hue St. Cheap, cheerful and very popular. *Cao Lau*, 42 Tran Phu St. For the best Cao Lau and cheap. Recommended.

Bars *Treats (Triets)*, 158 Tran Phu St, T861125. One of Hoi An's few bars and a very well run one. Two pool tables, airy, attractive and popular happy hour.

Shopping Hoi An is a shopper's paradise – Tran Phu and Le Loi streets being the main shopping areas. Look out for galleries selling original works of art, fabric shops which will knock up silk or cotton clothing in 24 hours (insist on double stitching or it will fall apart in 24 hours), embroidered table cloths and antiques. Note, however, that it is illegal to take items more than 200 years old out of the country and the customs officials are likely to confiscate anything that takes their fancy.

Transport 32 kilometres from Danang.

Local Hoi An itself is best explored on foot but for venturing further abroad hotels have 2- and 4-wheel vehicles for hire, bicycle still only 5,000d per day, motorbike US$4 per day.

Air Flights to Danang from Saigon and Hanoi, taxi from Danang airport to Hoi An will cost about US$15 or less (bargain hard), 40 minutes.

Road The road from Danang runs just inland from the coast and passes the skeleton of a former US Airforce base. This is an area of war scrap recycling. Further on towards Hoi An, the road becomes narrow, almost a rural lane, skirting past paddy fields, vegetable farms and cassava plots. **Bus**: the bus station is about 1 kilometre west of the centre of town. There are regular connections from Danang's local bus station, 1 hour. If on a day's excursion from Danang, the last bus returns at about 1700. **Minibus**: to Hué, Nha Trang (US$10), Saigon (US$25), Hanoi (US$25).

Directory **Banks** *Hoi An Bank*, 4 Hoang Dieu. Exchanges cash and TCs. **Communications** Post Office: 5 Tran Hung Dao St, next to *Hoi An Hotel*. Has poste restante international telephone and fax service. **Email:** widely available, often in tailors' shops, 1,000d per minute. **Hospitals & medical services** Hospital: 4 Tran Hung Dao St. **Tour companies & travel agents** *My Son Tours*, 17/2 Tran Hung Dao St, T861121. Cheap minibus tickets to Hué (US$3). Nha Trang (US$5) and Saigon (US$15) plus car and motorbike hire and useful advice. **Tourist offices** *Tourist Office*, 12 Phan Chu Trinh St, T861276. English-speaking, car and minibus hire and guides to Hoi An.

The Son My (My Lai) Massacre

The massacre at Son My was a turning point in the American public's view of the war, and the role that the US was playing. Were American forces defending Vietnam and the world from the evils of communism? Or were they merely shoring up a despotic government which had lost all legitimacy among the population it ostensibly served?

The massacre occurred on the morning of 16 March 1968. Units from the 23rd Infantry Division were dropped into the village of Son My. The area was regarded as an area of intense Communist presence – so much so that soldiers referred to the villages as Pinkville. Only 2 weeks beforehand, 6 soldiers had been killed after stumbling into a mine field. The leader of the platoon that was charged with the job of investigating the hamlet of My Lai was 2nd Lt. William Calley. Under his orders, 347 people, all unarmed and many women and children, were massacred. Some of Calley's men refused to participate, but nonetheless most did. Neil Sheehan, in his book A Bright Shining Lie, writes:

"One soldier missed a baby lying on the ground twice with a .45 pistol as his comrades laughed at his marksmanship. He stood over the child and fired a third time. The soldiers beat women with rifle butts and raped some and sodomized others before shooting them. They shot the water buffalos, the pigs, and the chickens. They threw the dead animals into the wells to poison the water. They tossed satchel charges into the bomb shelters under the houses. A lot of the inhabitants had fled into the shelters. Those who leaped out to escape the explosives were gunned down. All of the houses were put to the torch" (1989:689). In total, over 500 people were killed at Son My; most in the hamlet of My Lai, but another 90 at another hamlet (by another platoon) in the same village. The story of the massacre was filed by Seymour Hersh, but not until 13 November – 8 months later. The subsequent court-martial only convicted Calley, who was by all accounts a sadist. He was sentenced to life imprisonment, but had served only 3 years before President Nixon intervened on his behalf (he was personally convicted of the murder of 109 of the victims). As Sheehan argues, the massacre was, in some regards, not surprising. The nature of the war had led to the killing and maiming of countless unarmed and innocent peasants; it was often done from a distance. In the minds of most GIs, every Vietnamese was a potential Communist; from this position it was only a small step to believing that all Vietnamese were legitimate targets.

Quang Ngai to Phan Rang via Nha Trang

This 500 kilometre stretch of Highway 1 runs along the coast, sometimes within sight of the sea. Areas of lowland suitable for rice cultivation are few, and the soils generally poor. The beach resort of Nha Trang is situated in the heartland of the former Cham Kingdom and along this stretch of Vietnam's central region are innumerable Cham towers, most unrestored and only rudimentarily studied. The former US Navy base at Cam Ranh Bay lies 50 kilometres south of Nha Trang, and another 55 kilometres south from here is the town of Phan Rang. Phan Rang is notable for the group of Cham Towers that lie just outside the town. From here the road divides: Highway 1 and the railway continue southwards to Phan Thiet and from there to Saigon, a total of 318 kilometres; another road runs northwest to Dalat, 110 kilometres.

The Tay Son Rebellion (1771-1788)

At the time of the Tay Son rebellion in 1771, Vietnam was in turmoil and conditions in the countryside were deteriorating to the point of famine. The three Tay Son brothers found a rich lode of dissatisfaction among the peasantry, which they successfully mined. Exploiting the latent discontent, they redistributed property from hostile mandarins to the peasants and raised a motley army of clerks, cattle-dealers, farmers, hill people, even scholars, to fight the Trinh and Nguyen lords. Brilliant strategists and demonstrating considerable skills of leadership, the brothers and their supporters swept through the country extending the area under their control south as far as Saigon and north to Trinh.

The Chinese, sensing that the disorder and dissent caused by the conflict gave them an opportunity to bring the entire nation under their control, sent a 200,000-strong army southwards in 1788. In the same year, the most intelligent (by all accounts) of the brothers, Nguyen Hue, proclaimed himself emperor under the name of Quang Trung and began to prepare for battle against the cursed Chinese. On the 5th day of Tet in 1789, the brothers attacked the Chinese near Thang Long catching them unawares as they celebrated the New Year. (The Viet Cong were to do the same during the Tet Offensive nearly 200 years later.) With great military skill, they routed the enemy, who fled in panic back towards China. Rather than face capture, one of the Chinese generals committed suicide. This victory at the Battle of Dong Da is regarded as one of the greatest in the annals of Vietnamese history. Quang Trung, having saved the nation from the Chinese, had visions of recreating the great Nam Viet Empire of the 2nd century BC, and of invading China. Among the reforms that he introduced were a degree of land reform, a wider programme of education, and a fairer system of taxation. He even tried to get all peasants to carry identity cards with the slogan `the great trust of the empire' emblazoned on them. These greater visions were not to be however: Quang Trung died suddenly in 1792, failing to provide the dynastic continuity that was necessary if Vietnam was to survive the impending French arrival. As a postscript to the Tay Son rebellion, in 1802 the new Emperor Gia Long ordered his soldiers to exhume the body of the last of the brothers and urinate upon it in front of the deceased's wife and son. They were then torn apart by 4 elephants. Quang Trung and the other Tay Son brothers – like many former nationalist and peasant leaders – are revered by the Vietnamese and honoured by the Communists.

Quang Ngai

Quang Ngai is a modest provincial capital on Highway 1, situated on the south bank of the Tra Khuc River. Few people stay here as facilities are still pretty basic. Its greatest claim to fame is its proximity to **Son My** – the site of the **My Lai massacre** (see below, Excursions). There is an extensive **market** running north from the bus station, along Ngo Quyen Street (just east of Quang Trung Street – Highway 1). Also in the city is a **citadel** built during the reign of Gia Long (1802-1819).

Phone code: 055
Colour map 3, grid B6

Son My (My Lai) lies 13 kilometres from Quang Ngai. Just over one kilometre north of town on Highway 1, soon after crossing the bridge over the Tra Khuc River, is a plaque indicating the way to Son My (My Lai). Turn right, and continue for 12 kilometres to the subdistrict of Son My where one of the worst, and certainly the most publicized, atrocities committed by US troops during the Vietnam War occurred (see box). The massacre of innocent

Excursions

The Central Region

My Lai – 30 years on

It was thought that pretty much everything that happened that awful day in My Lai was known. Thirty years ago Hugh C Thompson Jr and Lawrence Colburn received medals for heroism under enemy fire, but in 1998 the US Army corrected an oversight: there was no enemy in My Lai; or rather, the enemy was the US. Thompson, a 24-year-old helicopter pilot, Colburn, his gunner and a third man, Glenn U. Andreotta (who was later killed in action) stopped the My Lai massacre before more people were killed. Thompson spotted women and children hiding in a bunker and put his helicopter down between them and advancing American soldiers. He called up another chopper and between them they evacuated the 10 civilians. At the same time Thompson reported the massacre to his CO who called off all action in the sector, thus ending the killing. On 7 March 1998 at the Vietnam Veterans Memorial in Washington the 2 survivors, Thompson and Colburn, were awarded the highest medal for bravery not involving conflict with an enemy.

Vietnamese villagers is better known as the My Lai Massacre – after one of the four hamlets of Son My. In the centre of the village of Son My is a memorial and a military cemetery 400 metres beyond. There is an exhibition of contemporaneous US military photos of the massacre and a reconstruction of an underground bomb shelter; the creek where many villagers were dumped after being shot has been preserved. A sign prohibits photos, but permission may be given by the informative English-speaking guide. There is no charge but visitors are invited to contribute to the upkeep of the memorial. The track to Son My from the main road is in poor condition (difficult except in a four-wheel drive vehicle) but is under reconstruction.

Sleeping **B** *Nha Khach Uy Ban*, Phan Boi Chau St (west of the Post Office), a/c. **E** *Khach San So 2*, 41 Phan Boi Chau St.

Transport 130 kilometres from Danang, 174 kilometres from Quy Nhon, 238 kilometres from Hué, 411 kilometres from Nha Trang, 888 kilometres from Hanoi, 840 kilometres from Saigon. **Train** The station is about 3 kilometres west of town. Regular connections with Hanoi and Saigon and all stops between the two. **Road Bus**: the bus station is a short distance east of Quang Trung St (Highway 1), on Nguyen Nghiem St.

Directory **Communications** Post Office: intersection of Phan Dinh Phung and Phan Boi Chau streets (west of Quang Trung St – Highway 1).

Quy Nhon

Phone code: 056
Colour map 3, grid C6

Quy Nhon, the capital of Binh Dinh Province, has a population of nearly 250,000 and is situated on a spur just 10 kilometres off Highway 1. The town was established by royal decree in 1898 so has thus just celebrated its first century. The town is taking a breather after a flurry of economic growth based on the export of logs and smuggling so don't expect much of the hotels or restaurants. It can be used as a stopping-off point on the long journey north or south between Danang and Nha Trang. A seaside town, it has reasonable swimming off sandy **Quy Nhon Beach** and a number of sights in the vicinity. A leper colony was founded in 1929 by a French priest, Paul Maheu, and patients and their families were cared for by nuns. The colony survives (at the western end of Nguyen Hue St) but is now run by the health department.

Thap Doi Cham towers are situated on the edge of town. The area around **Excursions**
Quy Nhon was a focus of the Cham Empire, and a number of monuments
(13, it is said) have survived the intervening years. These two impressive
Cham towers are about three kilometres from the centre of town. ■ *Getting*
there: walk or bicycle northwest on Tran Hung Dao Street, past the bus station,
and after two kilometres turn right onto Thap Doi Street. The towers are a short
distance along this street.

Tay Son District is about 50 kilometres from Quy Nhon off Highway 19
running west towards Play Ku. It is famous as the place where three brothers
led a peasant revolt in 1771 (see box). The Vietnamese have a penchant for
celebrating the exploits of the poor and the weak, and those of the Tay Son
brothers are displayed in the **Quang Trung Museum**. ■ *Getting there: take a*
bus from the station on Tran Hung Dao Street.

Hoang De Citadel (also known as Cha Ban) is situated about 27 kilometres north of Quy Nhon. Originally a Cham capital which was repeatedly
attacked by the Vietnamese, it was taken over by the Tay Son brothers in the
18th century and made the capital of their short-lived kingdom. Not much
remains except some **Cham ruins**, within the citadel walls, in the vicinity of
the old capital. 50 kilometres south of Quy Nhon is the small town of Song
Cau, two kilometres north of which is the *Sao Bien Restaurant*, recommended
for crab.

174 kilometres from Quang Ngai, 223 kilometres from Buon Ma Thuot, 238 kilometres **Transport**
from Nha Trang, 304 kilometres from Danang, 412 kilometres from Hué. **Air** Airport
is 35 kilometres north, 3 connections weekly with Saigon, 1 hour. *Vietnam Airlines*, 4
Ly Thuong Kiot St, T823125, F821280. **Train** The station is just over 1 kilometre
northwest of the town centre, on Hoang Hoa Tham St which runs off Tran Hung Dao
St. Express trains do not stop here. To catch the express, take the shuttle train to Dieu
Tri, 10 kilometres away. **Road Bus**: the bus station is 1 kilometre northwest of the
town centre, on Tran Hung Dao St (near the intersection with Le Hong Phong St).
Express buses leave at 0500 for Hanoi, Saigon, Nha Trang, Danang, Dalat, Hué.

Banks *Vietcombank*, 152 Le Loi St. Changes US$, cash and TCs. **Communications** Post Office: **Directory**
127 Hai Ba Trung. **TNT International Express:** T82193/82600. **Hospitals & medical**
services *General Hospital*, 102 Nguyen Hue St. **Tourist offices** *Binh Dinh Tourism Company*, 4
Nguyen Hue St, T822524.

Central Highlands

Despite its many splendours the Central Highlands does not quite match, in
terms of botanical greenery and ethnic colour, the huge attractions of the
mountainous north. Nevertheless, it has vibrant markets, exotic traditions
and extraordinary vernacular architecture. A National Park, beautiful
montagne and high plateau scenery, wild animals – all can be seen in the 250
kilometre span that separates Kontum in the north from Buon Ma Thuot in
the south. At elevations high enough to produce cool evenings the Central
Highlands offers the advantage to the visitor that the warm coastal plain and
beaches of Nha Trang are just a few hours away.

Play Ku

Phone code: 059
Colour map 3, grid C5

186 kilometres from Quy Nhon, 197 kilometres from Buon Ma Thuot, Play Ku (or still commonly Pleiku), with a population of 35,000, is located high on the Play Ku Plateau, one of many such structural features in the Central Highlands. It is the capital of Gia Lai Province which, with a population density of just 34 per square kilometre, is one of the most sparsely inhabited areas of Vietnam. Historically, this was a densely forested part of the country and it remains home to a large number of hill tribes. Play Ku was HQ to II Corps, one of the four military tactical zones into which South Vietnam was divided during the American war. John Vann (see Neil Sheehan's *Bright Shining Lie* – recommended reading) controlled massive B52 bombing raids against the encroaching NVA from here and, in June 1972, he was killed in a helicopter crash just outside Play Ku.

Play Ku the town has little to offer the tourist; during the monsoon the streets turn into muddy torrents and chill damp pervades hotel rooms and bedding. There is a small **museum** at 28 Quang Trung St which houses little of interest. The attractions of the area lie outside the town on the road north to Kontum.

Excursions There are a number of places to visit on the Kontum road. **Bien Ho** is a large **volcanic lake** and the main source of water for Play Ku, so no fishing or swimming. A raised platform on a promontory jutting out into the lake is a good place from which to appreciate the beauty and peace of the setting. ■ *1,000d. Getting there: by car or xe ôm, five kilometres north of Play Ku turn right on to the Quy Nhon road (Highway 19) and after a further two kilometres turn left past a derelict ARVN barracks.*

Bien Ho tea factory which occupies an unlovely concrete building 14 kilometres north of Play Ku sometimes allows visits. Two kilometres further is the turn left to the once spectacular **Yaly Falls**. Now there is a hydro-electric plant to which the water is diverted there is not much to see, but along the road are several **Jarai villages** which are worth a visit. It would appear that foreigners no longer need a license to do so. For the sake of preserving the traditional way of life it would seem sensible to stick to those villages. The first such village is **Plei Mrong**, about two kilometres on the left. This is the least interesting of the three as it has no *rong* or communal house or graveyard statues, but it still affords a glimpse of Jarai life to those in a hurry. **Plei Fun** is about 20 kilometres along the Yaly road and is the village Gia Lai Tourist will take you to if you book a tour through them. The local villagers have wised up to tourism and may try and charge you 30,000d to see their graveyard. The graves are covered by tiled or wooden roofs which shelter the worldly possessions of the deceased – bottles, bowls, even the odd bicycle. Carved hardwood statues guard the graves, a peculiarly Jarai tradition. Push on to **Plei Mun**, another five kilometres down the road and left two kilometres down a dirt road for some even finer examples. There is also a traditional wooden rong house with a corrugated iron roof.

Sleeping Play Ku has something of a shortage of hotel accommodation and some hotels still do not accept foreigners. Don't expect any bargains either.

B-C *Pleiku*, 124 Le Loi St, T824296. Recently revamped, some nice rooms with satellite TV and cheaper ones that represent good value. **B-C** *Yaly*, 89 Hung Vuong St, T824843. The cheapest rooms are on the top floor and quite good value for Pleiku, restaurant. **C** *Hung Vuong*, 215 Hung Vuong St, T824270. A/c, fridge and TV in every room, friendly staff. **C-D** *Movie Star*, 6 Vo Thi Sau St, T823855. Very friendly and comfortable.

Apart from noodle stalls and *com binh dan* there is only *Than Lich*, part of *Pleiku Hotel*. **Eating**
Spotless restaurant with a good choice of dishes, meals for under US$3. *Yaly Hotel*, 89
Hung Vuong St. Decent Vietnamese and Western fare.

Air Daily connections with Saigon, 3 per week with Vinh and Danang. **Road Bus**: **Transport**
regular connections with Quy Nhon, Buon Ma Thuot and Kontum. **Minibuses**: depart
from the market.

Banks *Vietcombank*, 12 Tran Hung Dao St. The only place in town that changes TCs (as there's **Directory**
nowhere in Kontum this is probably the most compelling reason to stop in Play Ku at all).
Communications Post Office: 87 Hung Vuong St. **Tourist offices** *Gia Lai Tourist*, 215 Hung
Vuong St, T824891. Expensive and unhelpful. Organizes some specialist veterans and trekking
tours. The independent tourist should try ringing Nhung of *Nhung's Tours*, 48 Hung Vuong St,
T822666. Very friendly one-man outfit which can organize all sorts of programmes at reasonable
prices. *Vietnam Airlines*, 89 Hung Vuong St, T824680, F825097.

Kontum

Kontum is a charming, sleepy little town 49 kilometres north of Play Ku and is *Phone code*: 060
an attractive stopping off point from which to visit the surrounding Bahnar *Colour map 3,*
villages. It has a population of 35,000 many of whom are from minority *grid B5*
ethnicities.

About 12 kilometres south of Kontum the road crosses the **Chu Pao Pass**,
the former site of a US and ARVN base. There is nothing to see in particular,
but one can imagine its strategic importance with its commanding views over
the Kontum Plateau. The road descends past sugar cane plantations before
crossing the Dakbla River, the lighter soil of Kontum is much more suitable
for sugar than the red loam of Play Ku, which is best for coffee and rubber.

In town there is the **Tan Huong Church** on Nguyen Hue Street, whose
whitewashed façade bears an interesting depiction of St George and the
dragon. Further east on the same street is the superb **Wooden Church**, well
worth a visit. Built by the French with Bahnar labour in 1913, it has now been
restored to its spectacular former glory. Inside, the blue walls and
stained-glass windows combine with the dark brown polished wood to produce a very serene effect. In the grounds to the right stands a rong house and a
statue of Stephano Theodore Cuenot, the first Catholic bishop of Kontum
diocese. He died on 14 November 1861 and every year a fête is held to commemorate him.

Kontum Prison, the former residence of several prominent revolutionaries is now being added to visitors' itineraries by Kontum Tourist. In fact it was
completely demolished and has been rebuilt from scratch, so if it's authentic-
ity you're after, don't bother.

There are scores of Bahnar villages around Kontum that can be reached by **Excursions**
motorbike. **Kon D'Re** is a fine example of a community almost untouched by
modern life. A perfect rong communal house dominates the hamlet, and all
other dwellings in the village are made from bamboo or mud and reeds. The
stilt house nearest the well is in fact a small Catholic church (most Bahnar are
Christian). Nearby **Kon Kotu** is similar. ■ *Getting there: take Nguyen Hue
Street and turn right into Tran Hung Dao Street, cross the suspension bridge
over the Dakbla River (built in 1997 after a flood washed the old one away).
After a few hundred meters turn left (just before the centre for traditional medicine) and continue for three kilometres bearing left for Kon Kotu and right for
Kon D'Re.* A more lively Bahnar community can be found at **Kontum**

K'Nam. Turn right off Nguyen Hue past the Wooden Church. Here the stilt houses are crowded close together and the village bustles with activity.

Sleeping **B-D** *Dakbla*, 2 Phan Dinh Phung St, T863333, F863336. Some a/c, all hot water, satellite TV, friendly welcome and quite good value. **C-D** *Quang Trung*, 168 Ba Trieu St, T862249. Some a/c, all rooms have hot water, nice rooms but a touch overpriced. **D-E** *Ngoc Linh*, 12 A Phan Dinh Phung St, T864560. All a/c, even the dormitory rooms, clean, good value.

Eating *Dakbla Restaurant*, under the *Dakbla Hotel*. Some good Vietnamese and Western dishes. *Dakbla's Café*, 168 Nguyen Hue St, T862584. Café and souvenir shop (fancy a crossbow?) with English menu and friendly staff. Recommended. *Thien Long*, 40 Nguyen Hue St, T864198. Decent Vietnamese menu but check the prices before ordering. *Thuc Don*, 90 Nguyen Hue St, T862594. Enormous menu broken down into sections: 'à la carte', 'lunch', 'special' and 'celebration', good food.

Transport **Road** Kontum is reached via Pleiku on Highway 14 by bus, car or motorbike. Coming from Danang it is possible to cut across via the road 10 kilometres south of Quang Ngai, but only by four-wheel drive. Surrounding villages are best toured by motorbike.

Directory **Banks** *Agriculture Bank* is on the corner of Tran Phu and Phan Chu Trinh but doesn't cash TCs. **Communications** Post Office: *GPO*, 205 Le Hong Phong St. **Tour companies & travel agents** The offices of *Dakbla Tourist* can be found in *Dakbla Hotel*, T863333. **Motorbike rental:** bicycles and motorbikes can be hired at *Dakbla's Café*.

Buon Ma Thuot

Phone code: 050
Colour map 4, grid A5

Buon Ma Thuot, the capital of Dac Lac Province with a population of 100,000, is inland from Nha Trang, not far from the Cambodian border. It is rarely visited by tourists as it is difficult to get to and lies off the main tourist route. The town is sited on the Daclac Plateau at an altitude of about 1,000 metres. Unofficial capital of the Central Highlands Buon Ma Thuot is surrounded by forests, waterfalls and large numbers of montagnards, the ethnic minorities of the hills or hill tribes. Within a short drive is a National Park and several accessible minority villages where visitors can spend the night.

History Since reunification in 1975, areas of this part of Vietnam have been designated New Economic Zones. 'Excess' population from Saigon and from the overpopulated lands of the Red River Delta have been resettled in new villages, and the forest cleared. Many of the resettlement communities have been unsuccessful: the poor quality of the land was not fully appreciated and yields of crops have been disappointingly low. There has also been some friction between the settlers and the minority ethnic groups (mostly E-de) who live in the area, who have been discriminated against for many years.

Sights There is a **Museum of Cultural Heritage**, 4 Nguyen Du St, in Bao Dai's old palace; it contains a smallish collection of clothes, tools and other artefacts of the various minority groups 'montagnards' that live in the area, and admission is free. Buon Ma Thuot prison is at 18 Tan Thuat Street and is worth a visit. Here you can see guardrooms, watch towers and the tiny cells where revolutionaries from the 1930s to the 1970s were imprisoned. A small museum in the former governor's residence contains paintings of prison life and photographs of distinguished former inmates. The buildings are grim but the compound is actually a rather peaceful place with well-tended and attractive gardens. ■ *Entrance is free but if the caretaker has to open it up especially for you a small donation is appreciated.*

The serene **Lak Lake** is about 50 kilometres southeast of Buon Ma Thuot. It is an attraction in its own right but all the more compelling a visit on account of the surrounding **M'nong villages**. Early morning mists hang above the calm waters and mingle with the columns of woodsmoke rising from the longhouses. The lake can be explored by dugout (about US$3 per hour). The canoes are painstakingly hollowed out from tree trunks by axe and the steady chopping echoes around the lake from dawn to dusk. The M'nong have been famed as elephant catchers for hundreds of years and although the elephant populations in the forests are declining the M'nong still use them in their traditional role for dragging logs from the forest. It is possible to stay overnight at a M'nong village, *Buon Juin* (Buon means village), indeed it is the only way to watch the elephants taking their evening wallow in the cool waters and to appreciate the tranquility of sunrise over the lake. The M'nong number about 50,000 and are matriarchal. An evening supping with your hosts, sharing rice

The Central Region

Buon Ma Thuot

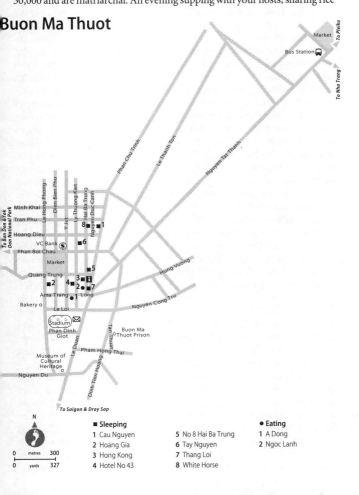

■ **Sleeping**		● **Eating**
1 Cau Nguyen	5 No 8 Hai Ba Trung	1 A Dong
2 Hoang Gia	6 Tay Nguyen	2 Ngoc Lanh
3 Hong Kong	7 Thang Loi	
4 Hotel No 43	8 White Horse	

N

0   metres   300
0   yards   327

wine and sleeping in the simplicity of a M'nong longhouse is an ideal introduction to these genial people. ■ *Getting there: take Highway 27 (the Dalat road) turn right down a track just before a sign advising 'Dalat 156 kilometres'. Expect to pay about US$6 to spend a night in a longhouse and a little extra for food and rice wine.*

Yet another of Bao Dai's hunting lodges overlooks the lake about three kilometres from Buon Juin: whatever his other faults the last emperor was blessed with a good eye for location. The building looks nothing like a palace now, having long ago been stripped of the precious woods with which it was panelled. In fact the rather ugly concrete shell is now a television broadcasting station, hence the large aerial. A quick climb to the top of the stairs inside, however, brings its reward of superb views of the lake and surrounding plateau.

The lake can be explored by dugout (US$10 per hour through Daklak Tourist or for less than one third if done independently). Yet another of Bao Dai's villas overlooks the lake about three kilometres from Buon Juin. The building looks nothing like a palace now, having long ago been stripped of the precious woods with which it was panelled. In fact the rather ugly concrete shell is now a television broadcasting station, hence the large aerial. If one climbs the stairs inside, however, one is rewarded with superb views of the lake and surrounding plateau.

The best **Ede village** to visit is *Buon Tur*. Apart from the odd TV aerial, life is unchanged in this community of 20 stilt houses and despite the efforts of the government to stop it Ede is still taught in school. The village headman was born in 1916, he speaks no English or Vietnamese so if he invites you for tea under his house the conversation will have to be conducted in French. Visitors used to be able to stay overnight in the village but the local police have put a stop to this pleasant and harmless practice. This is for our own safety, they explain in their customary thoughtful way, because the doors on Ede houses have no locks. ■ *Getting there: 15 kilometres southwest of Buon Ma Thuot on Highway 14.* A further six kilometres on is **Dray Sap waterfall**, a low but 100 metres wide cascade, particularly spectacular in the wet season when it fully justifies its name 'waterfall of smoke'. A beautiful spot with huge trees and lush greenery. A new red barrier replaces the painted line beyond which you venture at your peril. ■ *5,000d.*

Yok Don National Park is a 58,000 ha wildlife reserve about 40 kilometres northwest of Buon Ma Thuot. The park contains at least 63 species of animal and 196 species of birds and is thought to be the home of several rare white elephants. There are treks and tours some of which can be undertaken on the back of an elephant: a two day elephant safari costs US$180 for two people, trekking deep into the park staying in tents near Yok Don mountain; this is probably the only chance of seeing wildlife of any great rarity but, alas, the rare become rarer with each passing year. The less adventurous (or those with smaller elephant-trekking budgets) will have to make do with one hour rides at US$15 or simply watching one of the village's elephants at work. ■ *Admission to the park US$5.* **D** *Park Guesthouse*, T853110. Four rooms near the park gate, they hope to get electricity in 1999.

Ban Don village is a harmonious, multi-racial village near the park. It is home to Ede, M'nong, Lao, Thai, Khmer and a few Giarai people. The village has a long tradition of taming the forest's elephants and beyond the third sub-hamlet is the tomb of Khun Ju-Nop, known as the king elephant catcher, who died in 1924. His tomb is the square one next to the taller white stupa commemorating his brother, also a famous elephant catcher, who died in 1950. Both of these men were of Lao origin. Behind these is a more modern tomb of a Mnong elephant catcher, Y Pum B'Ya, a son of Khun Ju-Nop.

Daklak Tourist operates seven hotels in town, all demanding US$ cash in hand and plenty of it, from foreigners and not much room for bargain.

A-B *Thang Loi*, 1 Phan Chu Trinh St, T857615, F857622. All mod cons, recently refurbished, very comfortable and best in town, restaurant. **B** *Cau Nguyen*, 57 Phan Chu Trinh St, T851913, F851942. All rooms have satellite TV, bath. There are 6 truly enormous suites for which it would seem worth paying the extra US$5. **B-C** *Hai Ba Trung*, 8 Hai Ba Trung St, T852407. Comfortable and cheerful but overpriced. **C** *Tay Nguyen*, 110 Ly Thuong Kiet St, T851010, F852250. All rooms have a/c, hot water etc. The Vietnamese price would be good value but at 3 times that for foreigners it is horribly overpriced. **D** *Hong Kong*, 30 Hai Ba Trung St, T852630. Some a/c, all hot water, clean. **D** *Hoang Gia*, 62 Le Hong Phong St, T852161. Fan only, some decent sized but shabby rooms. **D-E** *43 Ly Thuong Kiet*, 43 Ly Thuong Kiet, T853921. Fan only, some hot water, grotty and cheap.

Independent hotels are just arriving: B-C *White Horse*, 50-54 Hai Ba Trung St, T850379, F852121. All rooms a/c, hot water, IDD, satellite TV. Friendly and good value. Recommended. **C-D** *Buon Ma Thuot Airport*, 23-25 Nguyen Chi Thanh St, T856266. All a/c, a little way out of town but nice rooms with bath, Vietnam Airlines office is in the hotel. **E** *Hai Duong*, 33 Ly Thuong Kiet St, T857790. Nice rooms, shared bathroom with hot water, a/c rooms are very good value.

Thang Loi Hotel has the best restaurant in town, closely followed by the *White Horse*, whose seafood is particularly good. **A** *Dong*, 29 Ama Trang Long St. Has a range of Vietnamese, Chinese, Thai and western foods. *Hua Thai*, 40 Hoang Dieu St. Serves good Vietnamese and Chinese food. *Ngoc Lanh*, 24 Hai Ba Trung St. Simple and tasty Vietnamese food. *Thanh Tuan*, 18 Hai Ba Trung St. Cheap rice dishes. *Nguyen*, 55 Hai Ba Trung St. Very cheap and reputedly does the best *pho* in town. *Banh Mi Hanoi*, 17-19 Le Hong Phong St. Bakery, sells sandwiches, drinks and a range of goodies such as cheese and Mars Bars, ideal picnic provisions.

190 kilometres from Nha Trang, 396 kilometres from Dalat (via Nha Trang), 217 kilometres direct, 350 kilometres from Saigon. **Air** Daily connections with Saigon, 55 minutes; 3 flights weekly from Danang, 65 minutes. **Road** Possible to take four-wheel drive from Dalat over the mountain road only in the dry season. **Bus**: regular connections with Saigon (4 hours by minibus via the upgraded Highway 14), Nha Trang and Quy Nhon. The bus terminal is about 2½ kilometres northeast of the town centre (see map).

Banks *Vietcombank*, 92-94 Y Jut, changes TCs. **Communications** Post Office: *GPO*, 6 Le Duan St. Cyber cafés have yet to make an appearance. **Tour companies & travel agents** Motorbike **rental:** there are no official motorbike rental shops in Buon Ma Thuot but many Honda ôm drivers will happily rent you their bike for US$5-8 per day. Note, however, that this is about the same as hiring the driver too: that would cost you an additional 40 cigarettes. **Tourist offices** *Daklak Tourist*, 3 Phan Chu Trinh St, T852108, F852865. Quite expensive tours but helpful. **Useful addresses** *Vietnam Airlines*, 25 Nguyen Chi Thanh St, T855055, F862086.

Sleeping
■ *on map*
Price codes:
see inside front cover

Eating
● *on map*

Transport

Directory

The Central Region

Nha Trang

Phone code: 058
Colour map, 4 grid A6

Nha Trang is a centuries old fishing town established in the sheltered mouth of the Cai Estuary. An important Cham settlement, it retains distinguished and well preserved Cham towers. A port was built in 1924 which can handle small coastal traders. Its clear waters and offshore islands won wide acclaim in the 1960s and while its new found prosperity is based on tourism the coral reefs and teaming shoals are, sadly, things of the past.

Ins and outs

Getting there Nha Trang's airport on the southern edge of town – a cyclo journey away from the centre. There are daily flights to Hanoi and Saigon and five departures a week for Danang. The town is on the main north-south railway line and there are trains to Saigon and Hanoi – and stops between. The main bus terminal is west of the town centre – note that some inter-provincial buses do not make a detour into Nha Trang but drop off at the junction with Highway 1. Xe ôms take passengers into town.

Getting around Nha Trang is negotiable on foot – just. But there are bicycles for hire, and the usual cyclos. Some guesthouses also hire out motorbikes and a few tour companies stretch to cars for out-of-town excursions.

The town

Word has spread, and Nha Trang's days as an undiscovered treasure are over. Nha Trang is a firmly established favourite of Vietnamese as well as foreign visitors and Nha Trangites of all backgrounds and persuasions endeavour to ease the dollar from the traveller's sweaty paw: clamouring beggars at Po Nagar; schoolgirls and toothless crones offering a massage on the beach (US$3-5 – nice work, in a country where a teacher might earn only US$30 a month); hawkers of all kinds pestering sunbathers with sickly confections and postcards. But the beach is long and you do not have to walk far to escape the madding crowds. The people of Nha Trang are also gloriously friendly.

The name Nha Trang is thought to be derived from the Cham word *yakram*, meaning bamboo river, and the surrounding area was a focal point of the Cham Kingdom – some of the country's best preserved Cham towers lie close by (see below). Nha Trang was besieged for nine months during the Tay Son rebellion of the late 18th century (see page 211), before eventually falling to the rebel troops. There are, in reality, two Nha Trangs: popular Nha Trang is a sleepy, sedate and genteel seaside town consisting of a long palm and casuarina-fringed beach, one or two streets running parallel to it, and a smattering of elegant colonial era buildings; commercial Nha Trang to the north of Yersin Street is a bustling city with an attractive array of Chinese shop houses interspersed among the socialist – municipal architecture. Most Western tourists confine their activities to the former part of town, venturing north only to visit the Cham Ponagar Temple and south to see Bao Dai's Villa at Cau Da.

Sights

Cham Ponagar Temple complex On a hill just outside the city is the **Cham Ponagar Temple complex**, known locally as Thap Ba. Originally the complex consisted of eight towers, four of which remain. Their stylistic differences indicate that they were built at different times between the seventh and 12th centuries. The largest (at 23 metres

Alexandre Yersin

Alexandre John Emille Yersin was born in 1863 in Canton Vaud, Switzerland. He enrolled at the University of Lausanne and completed his medical education in Paris where he became an assistant to Louis Pasteur. In 1888, Yersin adopted French citizenship. To the astonishment of all he became a ship's doctor; he visited the Far East and in 1891 landed in Nha Trang. 2 years later, as part of his exploration of Vietnam he `discovered' the Dalat Plateau which he recommended for development as a hill resort owing to its beauty and temperate climate. The following year, in 1894, he was urged to visit Hong Kong to assist in an outbreak of the plague. He identified the baccilus which was named Yersinia pestis. In 1895 he set up a laboratory in Nha Trang which, in 1902, became a Pasteur Institute, the first to be established outside France. Here he developed an anti-serum for the treatment of plague. He established a cattle farm for the production of serum and vaccines and for the improvement of breeding stock at Suoi Dau, 25 kilometres south of Nha Trang. Yersin was responsible for the introduction to Vietnam of commercial crops such as coffee, rubber and the cinchona (quinine) tree. In his retirement he indulged his passions, astrology, photography and observation of the hydrographic conditions of Nha Trang Bay. Yersin died in 1943 and was buried at Suoi Dau. His tombstone, simply engraved `Alexandre Yersin 1863–1943', can be seen today at Suoi Dau. Take Highway 1, 25 kilometres south of Nha Trang, look for the sign `Tombeau de Alexandre Yersin'. The key to the gate is kept with a local family. The tomb is 1.5 kilometres from the gate.

The Central Region

high) was built in 817 AD and contains a statue of Lady Thien Y-ana, also known as Ponagar (who was the beautiful wife of Prince Bac Hai) as well as a fine and very large lingam. She taught the people of the area weaving and new agricultural techniques, and they built the tower in her honour. The other towers are dedicated to gods: the central tower to Cri Cambhu (which has become a fertility temple for childless couples), the northwest tower to Sandhaka (wood cutter and foster father to Lady Thien Y-ana), and the south tower to Ganeca (Lady Thien Y-ana's daughter). The best time to visit the towers is in the late afternoon, 1600-1700. ■ *5,000d. Getting there: either walk or catch a cyclo. Take 2 Thang 4 Street north out of town; Cham Ponagar is just over the second of two bridges (Xom Bong bridge), a couple of kilometres from the city centre.* En route to the towers, the road crosses the **Cai River estuary** where there is a diversity of fishing craft – including coracles (*cái thúng*) and mechanical fish traps. The traps take the form of nets which are supported by long arms; the arms are hinged to a platform on stilts and are raised and lowered by wires connected to a capstan which is turned, sometimes by hand but commonly by foot. In places the water is shallow enough for fishermen to wade out to their machine. Otherwise they paddle a coracle.

The best known pagoda in Nha Trang is the Long Son Pagoda, built in 1963, which can be found on 23 Thang 10 Street (the west extension of Yersin Street). Inside the sanctuary is an unusual image of the Buddha, backlit with natural light (ask a monk for access if the building is closed). Murals depicting the jataka stories decorate the upper walls. To the right of the sanctuary, stairs lead up to a nine metre high white Buddha, perched on a hill top, from where there are fine views. The pagoda commemorates those monks and nuns who died demonstrating against the Diem government. In particular those who, through their self-immolation, brought the despotic nature of the Diem regime and its human rights abuses to the attention of the American public.

Long Son Pagoda

Nha Trang Cathedral, granite-coloured (though built of concrete) and imposing, was built in 1933 on a small rock outcrop. The cathedral has a single, crennelated tower, with stained glass in the upper sections of its windows and pierced metal in the lower. The path to the cathedral runs off Nguyen Trai Street. Daily mass is said here.

Museums

The Yersin Museum, 8 Tran Phu Street south of the Post Office, is contained within the colonnaded Pasteur Institute founded by the great scientist's protégé, Dr Alexandre Yersin. Swiss-born Yersin first arrived in Vietnam in 1891 and spent much of the rest of his life in Nha Trang (see box). The museum contains the lab equipment used by Yersin, his library and stereoscope through which visitors can see in 3-d the black and white slides including shots taken by Yersin on his visits to the highlands. The curator is helpful and friendly and fluent in French and English. ■ *26,000d. Open Monday-Saturday 0730-1100.* The Khanh Hoa Museum is at 16 Tran Phu Street. It contains a Dongson bronze drum and a palaeolithic stone xylophone. There is a room of ethnographics and, of course, a Ho Chi Minh room which contains several items of interest. English speaking curators will be pleased to show you around and should be tipped. The Central Market (*Cho Dam*) close to Nguyen Hong Son Street is a good place to wander, although it is surrounded by rather unattractive mansion blocks. In the vicinity of the market, along Phan Boi Chau Street for example, are some bustling streets with old colonial-style shuttered houses.

Excursions

South of Nha Trang Cau Da is a small fishing port five kilometres south of Nha Trang, taking the beach road (Tran Phu). Attractively sited on a small promontory outside Cau Da with magnificent views on all sides is yet another villa of the last emperor of Vietnam, Bao Dai – now a hotel. Born into an era of air travel he took advantage of this mode of travel to enjoy the most enchanting places in Vietnam. With his penchant for fresh air this must have been one of his favourites.

Cau Da is home to the Institute of Oceanography. Built in 1922, it claims to be the only institute of its kind in Vietnam: it contains a selection of poorly displayed marine fauna in pickling jars and glass cases and in the front courtyard are tanks of live fish, turtles and seahorses. The Institute conducts research and tries to promote marine conservation (see box) but wages an uphill struggle against the powerful fishing industry which dynamites and trawls its way through the bay with little heed for tomorrow. ■ *Open 0730-1130, 1330-1630.*

Islands From Cau Da pier boats can be taken to the islands in Nha Trang Bay. Mieu Island boasts the Tri Nguyen aquarium, a series of tanks in which fish and crustacea are reared, ostensibly for scientific purposes, but as the adjacent retaurant makes plain it is the science of the tummy that is being served. Not a particularly noteworthy trip.

Other nearby islands are Hon Mun, Hon Tam and Hon Mot. The islands are usually a bit of an anticlimax for, as so often in Vietnam, to travel is better than to arrive: lovely boat trip, disappointing beach. The best part is anchoring offshore and jumping into the exquisitely cool water while your skipper prepares a sumptuous seafood feast and the beers chill in the ice bucket. These islands are sometimes known as the Salangane islands after the sea swallows that nest here in such profusion. The sea swallow (*yen* in Vietnamese) produces the highly prized bird's nest from which the famous soup is made (see box on page 40). **Hon Yen** (Swallow Island) is out of bounds and strictly government controlled presumably to deter any would-be private nest collectors. ■ *Getting there: best known are the tours run by Mama Hanh (Hanh's Green Hat) and Mama Linh. These admirable ladies run daily tours (see tour operators) departing 0900; best to book the night before. They have established US$7 as the benchmark price for a day trip out which should include a seafood lunch and snorkelling equipment, cold beers (not unreasonably) cost extra.* A number of other captains and their wives are keen to cash in on the

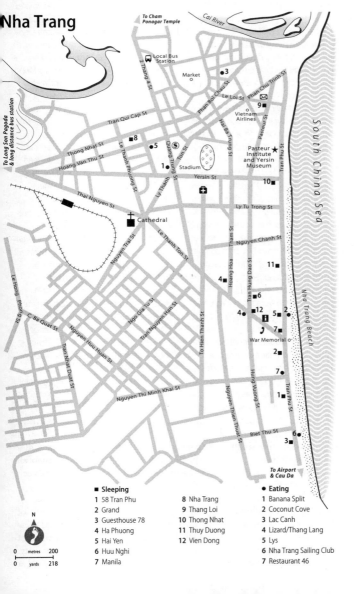

The Central Region

■ Sleeping
1 58 Tran Phu
2 Grand
3 Guesthouse 78
4 Ha Phuong
5 Hai Yen
6 Huu Nghi
7 Manila
8 Nha Trang
9 Thang Loi
10 Thong Nhat
11 Thuy Duong
12 Vien Dong

● Eating
1 Banana Split
2 Coconut Cove
3 Lac Canh
4 Lizard/Thang Lang
5 Lys
6 Nha Trang Sailing Club
7 Restaurant 46

'Marine conservation in Vietnam': a personal view

In the summer of 1992, I came to this fascinating country as a marine scientist. My first research vessel was a small 10 metres wooden boat hired from a local fisherman. For three days, we snorkelled around the scenic limestone islands of Halong Bay, investigating the life under the turbid water. Since then, I have travelled up and down the coast with Vietnamese scientists, searching for sites worthy of conservation.

Not surprisingly, all the sites we surveyed harbour a diversity of fish, coral and other invertebrates; some are frequented by turtles and dugongs. Sadly, all sites suffer a cocktail of human-induced threats. While much of Halong Bay remains spectacular above water, the corals beneath are smothered by silt washed down from deforested hillsides.

South on the Son Tra Peninsula, near Danang, are beautiful beaches where women, young and old, in their non la wade in the water harvesting seaweed and shells. Beneath the water the coral is dead, infested with tall seaweed. Back on shore are huge mounds of dead corals the height of a man, waiting for transport to nearby kilns and cement factories. Further south still is the famous seaside town of Nha Trang. Away from major rivers, Nha Trang is blessed with crystal blue sea where coral reefs with arrays of colourful fish, seastars and shells flourish. Here the country's first marine park was proposed in 1994. But as most of the nearby reefs have been dynamited by poverty-driven fishermen, more and more tourists crowd this tiny island and its surrounding waters

throwing their devastating anchors and beer cans onto the previously undisturbed reefs. More subtle interference is taking place as the ornamental fish trade and aquarium business become lucrative.

But the tale is not entirely one of devastation. I did witness schools of jacks, barracuda and parrot fish on pristine reefs in some more remote areas. Two examples are the island groups of Con Dao some 200 kilometres south of Ho Chi Minh City, and Phu Quoc, the 'wealthy kingdom' in the Gulf of Thailand. The two island groups remain blanketed in healthy forest and both areas support rich coral reefs. Con Dao, in particular, has escaped human pressure, thanks to its historical significance and low population. Until the ambitious development plans of the government materialize, Con Dao should remain relatively unspoilt. The coral reefs off the An Thoi Islands at the southern tip of Phu Quoc, are also in good condition, although certain species such as the highly priced groupers and sea cucumbers have been heavily exploited to satiate gourmands in Hong Kong and other Asian cities. There are more undisturbed areas, but for the sake of their safety, these locations will not be disclosed here.

The real encouragement lies not in discovering a new, pristine site, but in the growing awareness of my Vietnamese counterparts. The reward is the change from their cheers over trophies of dead squid and triton, to the vigorous criticism they now voice: "when we visited the island, the ranger offered us turtle eggs for tea, it's ridiculous!"
by Catherine Cheung

trade and for those seeking a little more solitude in Nha Trang Bay or something a little less routine it may be preferable to negotiate terms – but establish exactly what those terms are before setting sail as some poor souls have been charged extortionate sums for their lunch.

North of town **Hon Chong Headland** or Husband Rocks lie a short distance north of Ponagar Towers and from there can be reached easily on foot. Proceed a few hundred yards north then turn off to the right down to the sea. The water of the crescent-shaped bay is clear and calm although the beach is rather dirty. At the south end of the bay is Non Chong Promontory. The rock perched at the end of the promontory has a large, rather pudgy indentation in it – said to have been made by the hand of a male giant. It looks more like a paw print and is disfigured with grafitti. There are numerous cafés here but the appeal of the whole area, saga and all, is distinctly Vietnamese. Westerners would probably have a better day advancing no further north than Ponagar then taking a leisurely seafood lunch on the way back into town followed by a lie on the beach, cocktails, a slap-up Italian dinner and an early night with a good book.

Ba Ho is the name given to a sequence of three pools and rapids to be found in a remote and attractive woodland setting. Huge granite boulders have been sculpted and smoothed by the dashing torrent, but it is easy enough to find a lazy pool to soak in. ■ *Getting there: 20 kilometres north up Highway 1 followed by a two kilometre hike.*

Essentials

There has been a considerable increase in the number of hotel rooms available in Nha Trang but even so rooms in the more popular hotels get snapped up quickly, often long in advance by tour groups. Best to book before arriving.

L-A+ *Ana Mandara*, Tran Phu St, T829829, F829629. Nha Trang's beach resort where those that can afford it relax in unashamed and exquisitive luxury. Simple but elegant designs are set against cool woods, wafting fans and icy a/c – all pitched in battle against the scorching sun that blazes down on the beach outside. Pool, restaurants and every facility in this enchanting retreat.

A+-A *Nha Trang Lodge*, 42 Tran Phu St, T810500, F828800. A 14-storey monster overlooking the beach. Looks better from inside than out. Comfortable with all mod-cons, pool, tennis court and restaurant. **A-B** *Cau Da*, Tran Phu St (just before Cau Da village), T881049, F881471. A/c, a villa of former Emperor Bao Dai, with magnificent views over the harbour and outlying islands, sited on a small promontory, with large elegant rooms. An additional 40 rooms in assorted buildings that lack the scale and elegance, not surprisingly, of the emperor's own quarters. **A-C** *Hai Yen*, 40 Tran Phu St, T822974, F821902. Large, some a/c, characterless but comfortable and friendly with large rooms some with bathtub, sea view, access to *Vien Dong Hotel's* pool. **A-C** *Vien Dong*, 1 Tran Hung Dao St, T821606, F821912. A/c, hot water, suites, pool (open to outsiders for 15,000d), tennis, cheapest rooms are good value, most popular in Nha Trang, sometimes booked up weeks ahead. Recommended.

B-D *Grand*, 44 Tran Phu St, T822445, F825395. Large colonial mansion with spacious elegant rooms overlooking the sea, cheaper fan rooms at the back. Recommended. **B-C** *Nha Trang*, 129 Thong Nhat St, T822347, F823594. A/c, bicycles and motorbikes for rent. **B-D** *Que Huong*, 60 Tran Phu St, T825047, F825344. Restaurant, clean, friendly but a bit pricey. **B-D** *Thang Loi*, 4 Pasteur St, T822241, F821905. Some a/c, newly renovated, clean, friendly, arranged around courtyard, bicycles and Hondas for rent. Recommended.

C-D *Guesthouse 78*, 78 Tran Phu St, T826342. 47 rooms, some a/c. **C-D** *Huu Nghi*, 3 Tran Hung Dao St, T822246, F827416. Formerly Hung Dao. A range of rooms, some a/c, some satellite TV, friendly. **C-D** *Phuong Anh (Mini Hotel)*, 16 Hoang Hoa Tham St, T821813, F829020. A/c, fan, hot water, very clean hotel, with helpful French and English speaking proprietor, only 4 rooms. **C-D** *Tulip*, 30 Hoang Van Thu St, T821302. 15 rooms, a/c, hot water, good new middle range hotel with English, French and Dutch speaking staff, very clean.

Sleeping
■ *on map*
Price codes:
see inside front cover

The Central Region

D *Ha Phuong 1*, 30 Hoang Hoa Tham St, T/F829015. 10-minute walk from the beach but good value, rooms with hot water and fan. **D** *Hai Quan* (Navy Guesthouse), 58 Tran Phu St, T822997. Nicely restored bungalow overlooks the beach, rather barrack-like block at the back. **D** *Thong Nhat*, 5 Yersin, St, T822966, F825221. Some a/c, friendly staff, good large clean rooms, hot showers, dorm beds available (**F**), restaurant. Recommended. **D-E** `Railway' Hotel*, 40 Thai Nguyen St, T822298. Some a/c, a little decrepit, but cheap. **D-E** *Thuy Duong*, 36A Tran Phu St, T822534. Some a/c, 4 and 6-bedrooms, good value. Recommended.

Eating
● *on map*

There are a number of seafood restaurants and cafés along the beach front road. US$2 for a freshly cooked seafood platter. Sandwich stalls make good peanut butter sandwiches. The French bread in Nha Trang is excellent.

Nha Hang Hai Son, 304 2 Thang 4 St. North of town on the way to Ponagar Towers and a great place to stop off for lunch on the way back in from sight-seeing. Located on an island from where great views over the rivers, the Cham towers. Food is nice, all seafood recommended, but service is erratic.

Vien Dong Hotel. Poolside restaurant, candle-lit at night, entertainment, a bit touristy but good food. *Café des Amis*, 16 Tran Phu St. Off-shoot of the Hoi An parent, good for breakfast, vegetarian and seafood dinners. *Lac Canh*, 11 Hang Ca St. Serves excellent Chinese and Vietnamese food, with seafood specialities, best are the meats, squid and prawns barbecued at your table, smoky atmosphere and can be hard to get a table. Recommended. *Nha Trang Sailing Club*, 76 Tran Phu St. Bar and restaurant are in two separate sections, slump back in a vast rattan chair enjoying sun-downers then walk over to the Italian/Vietnamese restaurant or stay put with a plate of comfort food. The bar attracts a lively crowd. *Restaurant Lys*, 117A Hoang Van Thu St. Vietnamese and other Asian, long-standing favourite of ours. Recommended. *Coconut Cove*, on the beach opposite *Hai Yen Hotel*. Italian specials: pizzas, pasta but for ambience the Sailing Club wins. *Restaurant 46*, 46 Tran Phu. Open-air diner with seafood specials but try and get a table well away from the go-carts next door. *Thang Lang (Lizard)*, Le Thanh Ton St, opposite *Vien Dong Hotel*. This place has transformed itself beyond all recognition. It is now a bar with real atmosphere and a restaurant offering a range of Western dishes. Worth at least an aperitif. *Thong Nhat Hotel Restaurant*, 18 Tran Phu St. Vietnamese, seafood, excellent spring rolls and 'rocket shrimps'. *Thuy Duong*, 36A Tran Phu St. Seafood specialities in 60s-style diner building, service leaves a little to be desired. *Banana Split*, 58 Quang Trung St. Excellent breakfasts, delicious banana, chocolate and nut pancakes, popular meeting place. Recommended.

Bars

Sailing Club, 76 Tran Phu St. Lively bar, especially on Saturday nights when a wide spectrum of ex-pats, locals and tourists congregate to enjoy pool, cold beer and music. *Lizard*, opposite *Vien Dong Hotel*, make sure they don't substitute local gin for Gordons. *Rainbow Bar*, 52 Tran Phu St. Friendly staff and the atmosphere is great if a bit hazy at times. They serve reasonably priced beer and the food isn't bad. Pool table and Happy Hour 2100-2200.

Entertainment

Sports Diving: dry season only: January-May. Nha Trang has two Western-run diving schools. *Rainbow Dive* (Rainbow Club) is run by a British couple from Reading (Ian and Angie Thompson). Their open water diving course (PADI) that takes 4 days costs US$340. The boat is a newly renovated Russian spy boat, with polished wooden floors. The Vietnamese crew are excellent. There is also a good French-run outfit. Around US$85 per day. **Fishing**: boats and equipment can be hired from Cau Da Pier (see Excursions); contact Khanh Hoa Tourism, 1 Tran Hung Dao St for more information.

Book exchanges At beach cafés opposite *Hai Au Hotel* and near War Memorial. Second-hand paperbacks, not cheap, however.

Local speciality *Banh trang duong* – local sugar rock.

Seashells, coral and shell jewellery Mounted marine life (lobsters, horseshoe crabs, turtles etc) – environmentalism and conservation are not words on the lips of many Vietnamese.

Nha Trang lies 105 kilometres from Phan Rang, 215 kilometres from Dalat, 445 kilometres from Saigon.

Local Bicycles and motorbikes can be hired from some hotels for around 10,000d per day for a bicycle and 70,000d per day for a motorbike, and from the cafés and tour agents along the beach front. Car hire from *Vieng Dong Hotel*, 1 Tran Hung Dao St, or one of the private tour operators listed on page 227.

Air 3 connections daily with Saigon, 65 minutes, daily with Hanoi, 2 hours 40 minutes and 5 per week with Danang, 80 minutes. The airport is just south of town and taxis and cyclos run from here. There was a scam in operation when we last visited trying to get taxi passengers to pay a `tax' to leave the airport; we declined and nothing more was said.

Train There are regular train connections with Hanoi and Saigon and all stops between the two. The station is a yellow wash colonial building with blue shutters on Thai Nguyen St, T822113.

Road Bus: The long distance bus station (*ben xe lien tinh*) is west out of town on 23 Thang 10 St (ie 23rd October St) and has connections with Saigon, Phan Rang, Danang, Quy Nhon, Dalat, Hué and Vinh. Note that inter-province buses do not go into Nha Trang, they drop off at junctions on Highway 1 from where a *xe ôm* will deliver you to your destination (pay no more than US$1).

Airline offices *Vietnam Airlines*, 91 Nguyen Thien Thuan St, T826768, F825956. *Vietnam Airlines sales agent*, 12B Hoang Hoa Tham St, T823797. Open 0700-1100, 1330-1615, and 91 Nguyen Thien Thuat St, T826768, F825956. **Banks** *Vietcombank*, 17 Quang Trung. Will change most major currencies, cash, TCs (2% commission), and cash advances on some credit cards. Gold shops near Dam market will also change money. **Communications** Post Office: 2 Tran Phu St, also 50 Le Thanh Tan St, opposite *Vien Dong Hotel* (international calls and faxes). **TNT International Express:** T821043. **Hospital & medical services** *General Hospital*, 19 Yersin St, T822168. **Tour companies & travel agents** *Hanh's Green Hat*, on the beach opposite 52 Tran Phu St (*Rainbow Bar*), T824494, F825117. Boat trips (US$7 including lunch and pick-up from hotel). Also other local tours, car, motorbike and bicycle hire. *Mama Linh*, 1 Phan Chu Trinh, T826693. Organizes good boat trips and minibuses to Hoi An and Dalat. *Chau's Tour* is run by the engaging Chau (Captain Cook), 22 Le Thanh Phuong St, T827877, F822000. He is highly entertaining and runs a good ship. **Tourist offices** *Khanh Hoa Tourism*, 1 Tran Hung Dao St, T822226, F821092.

Cam Ranh Bay

Cam Ranh Bay lies 50 kilometres south of Nha Trang. Highway 1 skirts around this bay – one of the world's largest natural harbours – once an important US naval base and then taken over by the Soviets. In fact the Soviets, or at least the Russians, were here before the Americans: they used it for re-provisioning during the Russo-Japanese war of 1904, which they emphatically lost. After re-unification in 1975, the Vietnamese allowed the Soviets to

Colour map 4, grid A6

use this fine natural harbour once again as part-payment for the support (political and financial) that they were receiving. However, from the late 1980s, the former Soviet fleet began to wind down its presence here as Cold War tensions in the area eased and economic pressures forced the former USSR to reduce military expenditure. Now the port is almost deserted. Cam Ranh is also a centre for Vietnam's salt industry; for miles around the scenery is white with salt pans (looking like wintry paddy fields) produce pure, crystalline sea salt. There is a modest **Cao Dai Church** near the intersection of Highway 1 and the road leading towards the Bay (Da Bac Street). Contining east along Da Bac Street, the road leads to a thriving fish market (down a pair of narrow alleys) and then to a busy boatyard producing small fishing vessels. At 120 Da Bac Street is Chua Phuoc Hai, an attractive little Buddhist temple. There is nowhere to stay in Cam Ranh, but following Highway 1, two kilometres south is *Hotel Restaurant Nguyen Quang*, which has two rooms on stilts over a lake. ■ *Getting there: by bus from the local station opposite 115 2 Thang 4 Street.*

Phan Rang

Phone code: 068
Colour map 4,
grid B6

Few tourists stop at Phan Rang, a small seaside town of about 50,000 people and the capital of Ninh Thuan Province. Phan Rang was once the capital of Champa when it was known as Panduranga and there are a number of **Cham towers** (*thap Cham*) nearby. The town and surrounding area are still home to a small population of **Cham**. In the centre of town at 305 Thong Nhat Street (Highway 1) is a large salmon-pink **pagoda** with fine roof decoration. South from the pagoda, opposite 326 Thong Nhat Street is the entrance to **Phan Rang Market** (*Cho Phan Rang*). The beach here is beautiful and, no doubt, prospective developers have their eye on creating another Nha Trang, but for now it remains unspoilt.

Excursions **Po Klong Garai** is a group of three Cham towers on the road towards Dalat, six kilometres from Phan Rang. Built during the 13th century, they are located on a cactus and boulder-strewn hill with commanding views over the surrounding countryside. Raised up on a brick base, the towers have been extensively renovated. The central tower has a figure of dancing Siva over the main entrance and, tucked inside the dimly lit main chamber full of incense smoke, Siva's vehicle, the bull Nandi and other statues. Other than My Son, perhaps the best Cham relics in the country. ■ *5,000d. Getting there: bicycle or take a xe ôm (US$1-2) or local bus towards Dalat; two kilometres beyond the village of Thap Cham turn right when a concrete water tank comes into view. The towers are visible a short distance along this track. The temple complex has been looked after by a Cham caretaker since 1968.*

Phan Rang

To Hanoi & Nha Trang

To Thap, Cham & Railway Station

Tran Phu

Thong Nhat Hotel

Tower o   ■ Huu Nghi II Hote

■ Ninh Thuan Hotel

Konica Film Processing

Pho 129 Restaurant

Hiep Thanh Restaurant

O Market

Thuong Kuong

Thong Nhat

N

Not to scale

Huu Nghi Hotel

To Saigon

Po Ro Me is another group of more recently constructed Cham buildings, which can be seen in the distance from Po Klong Garai, rising up from the valley floor. Po Ro Me was the last king of independent Champa (1627-1651), and he died a prisoner of the Vietnamese. ■ *Getting there: it is not easy: drive south on Highway 1 from Phan Rang towards Saigon; the towers are a five kilometres walk from the road. Ask for Thap Cham Po Ro Me.*

Finally, there is a **third group of Cham towers**, in poor condition, 16 kilometres north of town right at the side of Highway 1.

Tuan Tu is a small Cham village, about five kilometres south of Phan Rang. Like most Cham these villagers have renounced Hinduism in favour of Islam and their names reflect this, boys are called Mo Ham Mat, Su Le Man and so on.

Ninh Chu Beach About six to seven kilometres northeast of Phan Rang is Ninh Chu beach. Overall, not a bad beach. At least it's fairly quiet. There are several cafés along the beach which rent chairs and umbrellas in addition to selling drinks. **B-C** *Ninh Chu Hotel*, T873000, F822600. A nice beach hotel with some concrete bungalows scattered about. Prices start at a reasonable level but can rise pretty high for rooms with a/c, satellite TV, hot water tub and so on. The usual karaoke and massage services available, a decent, reasonably priced restaurant and a small Post Office nearby. Some of the staff now speak English and credit cards are accepted.

Sleeping Most hotels in Phan Rang are either old dumpy things that look like prisons or newly finished, 'modern' mini-hotels. Expensive and poor. Eventually someone will figure out that a renovated, old style, French building with modern conveniences would be a real hit, but until then it might be a good idea to stay somewhere near the beach.

B *Thong Nhat*, 99 Thong Nhat St, T827201, F822943. One of the mini-hotels with all the modern conveniences but absolutely no charm or character. Clean but over-priced, restaurant and all the usual karaoke, sauna and massage paraphernalia. **B-C** *Ninh Thuan*, 1 Le Hong Phong, T827100, F822142. Fan and a/c rooms, restaurant. **D** *Huu Nghi 1, 2* and *3*, 13, 194 and 354 Thong Nhat St, T822606, F822943. Maybe the Russians felt at home with the neo-gulag styling, 'looks like a prison', depressing and filthy.

Eating As is usually the case in towns of this size, there are no cafés or restaurants catering to backpackers. There are, however, quite a few pho stands and *bia hoi* joints on the west end of Quang Trung St, as well as some rice stalls near the bus station and the usual local cafés scattered around town. If you're feeling lucky just point to something randomly on the menu and enjoy the surprise of seeing what you get.

Transport 105 kilometres from Nha Trang, 110 kilometres from Dalat, 318 kilometres from Saigon. Train the closest stop is Thap Cham, about 5 kilometres west of town. **Road Bus**: the bus station is on the east side of Thong Nhat, near the Post Office. Local buses, however, leave from the south side of town. Regular connections with Saigon, Dalat Nha Trang.

Directory **Banks** The foreign exchange service is at 334 Thong Nhat St, *Agribank* also on Thong Nhat. Most hotels and jewellery shops will change US$, but cashing TCs may be a bit difficult. **Communications** Post Office: is at the north end of Thong Nhat St, near the turn-off to Ninh Chu. **Tourist office** *Ninh Thuan Tourist*, 404 Thong Nhat St.

The Central Region

Ca Na

Phone code: 068
Colour map 4, grid B6

This is just a wide place in the road between Phan Thiet and Phan Rang. It's about 36 kilometres south of Phan Rang, nestled between boulder-strewn hills to the west and wild rocky surf to the east. There are a couple of small restaurants selling decent road-food and drinks and a couple of guesthouses that are as close to the highway as they are to the beach. It's worth a stop for fried noodles with seafood and a quick walk up the hill to see the small pagoda that is visible from the road and maybe a stroll on the beach.

Sleeping **D** *Ca Na*, T861320. A few rooms between road and beach, simple but clean. **D** *Hai Son*, T861322. Similar.

Phan Thiet

Phone code: 062
Colour map 4,
grid B5

Phan Thiet is a little fishing town at the mouth of the Cai River. For the traveller, however, the real attractions lie east of town on the 20 kilometre coastal road to Mui Ne. The beaches along this stretch have been well developed, with quality hotels and resorts and one of Vietnam's finest golf courses.

Phan Thiet is capital of Binh Thuan province. There are still significant numbers of Cham (50,000) and Raglai (30,000) minorities, who until a few hundred years ago dominated the ethnic scene. There are relics of the Cham era, the best and easiest to find being two **Cham towers** on the Mui Ne road, they are now somewhat broken down and considering the long walk uphill to see them they are probably best viewed from the road. Like Cham towers elsewhere in this part of the country they are constructed of brick bound together with resin of the Cay Day tree. Once the tower was completed timber was

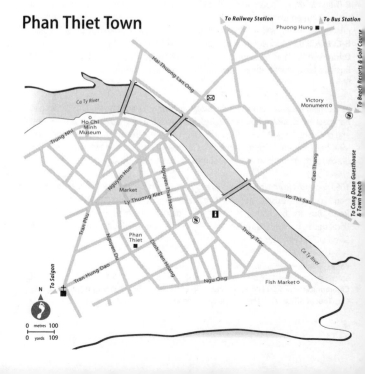

Phan Thiet Town

piled around it and ignited; the heat from the flames melted the resin which solidified on cooling. There are a few **Ho Chi Minh relics**, including a museum on Nguyen Truong To Street and the Duc Thanh school next door where he taught in 1911, but nothing of any special interest.

Mui Ne (or Cape Ne) is a small fishing village. Mui Ne's two claims to fame are its nuoc mam (fish sauce) and its beaches. On the cape itself are some impressive sand dunes. Around the village the air is fragranced with a heady mix of fresh sea air and fermenting fish sauce.

But overwhelmingly Phan Thiet is a place to hole up in for a few days, relax with a book, jog along the beach, lie around the pool, indulge in a seafood dinner or two, and for those with an inclination play a round or two of golf on the course designed by Nick Faldo.

Those interested in learning more about the Cham might care to visit the house of Nguyen Thi Them, a Cham princess who died in 1998. The house where she lived is 60 kilometres north of Phan Thiet in Phan Thanh village, Bac Binh commune where a few vestigial treasures from the past are kept. **Excursions**

Phan Thiet town A-B *Phuong Hung*, 112 Tran Hung Dao, T825619, F825300. One of the newer hotels in town, Phuong Hung is a fairly comfortable place to pass an evening but at fairly stiff prices. Some of the staff speak quite good English, restaurant, karaoke and massage. **C** *Phan Thiet*, 276 Tran Hung Dao St, T821694, F817139. 21 rooms with phone and TV in a fairly nice and fairly non-descript state-run hotel. All with a/c and hot water. Mastercard and Visa are accepted. **C-D** *Khach San 19/4*, 1 Tu Van Tu St, T821794, F825184. Conveniently located near the bus station and little else. Some fan, some a/c, all hot water. **D** *Cong Doan*, Vo Thi Sau St. A strange and slightly depressing concrete compound on the beach just outside town. Some a/c. **D-E** *Thanh Cong*, Tran Hung Dao St, T823905. Prices start at US$6 for fan rooms rising to US$12 for a/c. **Sleeping**

Mui Ne Beach All fairly expensive but well run and attractive resort type hotels. In the high season and at weekends it can be hard to find a room but at other times easy to find a bargain. Some good value family deals can be found.

A+-A *Coco Beach (Hai Duong)*, T847111, F847115, E paradise@cocobeach.net. The European owners live here and ensure the place is well run. Not luxurious (no bathtub for example) but friendly and impeccably kept bungalows facing the beach. Beautiful setting, lovely pool, relaxing. Good restaurant. **A+-A** *Novotel Ocean Dunes Resort*, T823393, F825682, E novotel@netnam2.org.vn. The largest of the three, not a bungalow resort, but comfortable and with good facilities, pool, restaurant, bar, two pools, tennis courts and gym, guests enjoy a 20 percent discount on green fees at the adjacent Ocean Dunes golf club. **A+-A** *Victoria Phan Thiet*, T847170, F848440, E victoriapt@ bdvn.net. Part of the French-run Victoria chain, 50 bungalows, doubles and family in an attractive landscaped setting. Restaurants, bars, pool and health club. **A-B** *Bamboo Village*, T847007, F847095, E dephan@netnam2.org.vn. 15 attractive and simple bamboo huts at the top of the beach. More expensive rooms have a/c and hot water showers, cheaper ones make do with cold water only (unreasonable at these prices). A lovely shady spot with an excellent restaurant.

There are also some cheaper places along the beach road, **C-D** *Khu Bai Tam Mui Ne*. They offer some decent concrete and thatch bungalows with two beds. There is a restaurant serving local food and a nice stretch of beach outside your front door. Not a bad way to relax for a few days. Tents are also rented out for 50,000d per night. Cheaper eating places can be found along the road east to Mui Ne.

Eating   As you would expect, fish is the speciality in Phan Thiet. Some of the hotels listed above have restaurants. There are many restaurants in town, look for signs that say 'nha hang' or 'quan an'. If the place looks busy, the food is probably pretty good. There are no backpacker cafés in town.

Entertainment   **Sport   Golf**: *Ocean Dunes Golf Club*, T823366, F821511. This IMG managed, 18 hole, 6746 yard course is highly regarded. It has a fully equipped club house with bar and restaurant. Green fee US$80, caddy US$15. **Tennis**: at *Novotel*. **Beach sports**: wind surfing etc offered by the resorts.

Transport   198 kilometres from Saigon, 250 kilometres from Nha Trang, 146 kilometres from Phan Rang and 247 kilometres from Dalat. **Road   Bus**: the bus station is a few kilometres north of town past the Victory monument on Tran Hung Dao St. Connections with all neighbouring towns. A local bus plies the Phan Thiet bus station to Mui Ne route, 8,000d each way, taxis too. **Train** Although Phan Thiet has a station it connects only with Muong Man, 12 kilometres to the west. From Muong Man 1 train daily south to Saigon and north to Hanoi.

Local   Cyclos and *xe ôms* are abundant in Phan Thiet town. A *xe ôm* from town to Mui Ne should cost under US$2. Binh Thuan Tourist, 82 Trung Trac St can arrange car hire as can the larger hotels. Bicycle and motorbikes can also be rented from some hotels and represent a great way to explore the vicinity.

Directory   **Banks**   *The Foreign Currency Exchange*, on Tran Hung Dao, is open from 0730 to 1630, but they do not cash TCs. Industrial and Commercial Bank, near the Victory Monument, cashes TCs. The larger hotels will exchange money. **Communications**   Post Office: 2 Le Hong Phong St. **Tourist office**   *Binh Thuan Tourist*, 82 Trung Trac St, T816821, F817139. Can arrange tours and car rentals.

Phan Rang to Dalat

The 100 kilometres trip between Dalat and Phan Rang is spectacular but sometimes excruciatingly uncomfortable by bus. The narrow strip of land between the highlands and the coast is an area of intensive rice, tobacco and grape cultivation. Winding upwards, the road passes under a massive pipe carrying water from the mountains down to the turbines of a hydropower plant in the valley. It then works its way through the dramatic Ngoan Muc Pass to the Dalat Plateau.

Dalat

Phone code: 063
Colour map 4, grid A5

Dalat is situated on a plateau in the Central Highlands, at an altitude of almost 1,500 metres, and has a population of 130,000. To the north are the five volcanic peaks of the Lang Biang mountains, rising to 2,400 metres. The town itself is centred on a lake – Xuan Huong – amidst rolling countryside. In the vicinity are forests, waterfalls, and an abundance of orchids and other temperate flora.

Ins and outs

Getting there   Dalat airport is 30 kilometres from town and there are multiple daily connections with Saigon. However, most people arrive here by road from Saigon, a 6-hour journey. There are also bus connections with Nha Trang via Phan Rang (4 hours) and direct buses to Buon Ma Thuot, another hill station to the north.

Dalat is a former French hill station, established to give hassled expats the chance to **Getting around** escape from the heat of the lowlands. It is cool in the evening throughout the year – and can be cold during the winter months between October and March. Walking is the best way to see the town. Mountain bikes and motorbikes are available for hire, and there are also motorcycle taxis and ordinary taxis.

The town

As in other colonial possessions in Southeast Asia, the French developed this highland area as a hill resort to which hot and flustered colonial servants and businessmen and their families, could retire during the summer heat. The city was founded in 1897 after the site had been discovered by Dr Alexandre Yersin who recommended that it be developed as a hill resort. By 1935 a railway line had been laid linking it with Saigon, via Phan Rang. The French built timber frame houses to remind them of Europe, and complained about the locals and the stinking heat of Saigon.

Dalat is a city in the European sense: it has a cathedral, a university, a research institute (nuclear physics) and a royal history (albeit neither a long nor particularly proud one). But in reality it appears to be nothing so much as a large market town (albeit rather a grand one). The modern economy of Dalat owes much to the prosperity generated by sales of the vegetables and flowers grown intensively in the plateau to lowland Vietnam. Several international agribusinesses have set up in Dalat to develop the huge potential the region offers, cut flowers from Dalat are to be found ornamenting all the leading hotels in Saigon.

Dalat's economy is also heavily dependent on tourism (nine tenths or more Vietnamese) and there are countless guesthouses, restaurants and shops dependent on this trade. Despite huge investment in the sector Dalat

The Central Region

Dalat

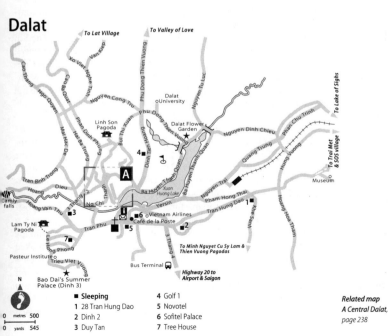

Sleeping
1 28 Tran Hung Dao
2 Dinh 2
3 Duy Tan

4 Golf 1
5 Novotel
6 Sofitel Palace
7 Tree House

0 metres 500
0 yards 545

Related map
A Central Dalat,
page 238

has not really taken off as a destination with foreigners in the way it should have. Business at the top end of the market will undoubtedly grow now the reputation of the excellent golf course and the two newly renovated hotels is more widely known. At the other end of the spectrum opportunities for trekking, visiting minority villages and so on have been curtailed by the state run Dalat Tourism whose monopoly suffocates initiative and stifles enterprise. Fortunately Dalat's appeal is more enduring and the independent traveller can find plenty of diversion as well as peace and quiet to fill a couple of pleasant days.

Climate Nights are cool throughout the year in Dalat, especially so from October to March. Temperatures range from 4°C in December and January, to 26°C in March and April. The rainy season stretches from May to November, with heaviest rains in August and September. Even during the warmest months it can be chilly in the evening.

Sights

Xuan Huong Lake The Central Xuan Huong Lake (originally the Grand Lake – renamed in 1954) was created in 1919 after a small dam was constructed on the Cam Ly River. A road runs round the perimeter of the lake, a pleasant and easy bicycle ride. In general, however, the hills and the dispersed nature of Dalat's sights make hiring a motorbike a more popular option.

Dalat Flower Garden At the northeast end of the lake is the **Dalat Flower Garden**. Established in 1966, it supports a modest range of temperate and tropical plants including orchids (in the orchid house), roses, camelias, lilies and hydrangeas. ■ *10,000d. Open 0730-1600 Monday-Sunday.*

Dalat Cathedral Visible from the lake, and next to the *Novotel Hotel*, is the single-spired Dalat Cathedral. Construction began in 1931, although the building was not completed until the Japanese 'occupation' in the 1940s. The stained-glass windows, with their vivid colours and use of pure, clean lines, were crafted in France by Louis Balmet between 1934 and 1940. Sadly most have not survived the ravages of time or revolution. Lining the nave are blocks of woodcarvings of Jesus and the crucifixion. Mass is held twice a day at 0515 and 1715 Monday-Saturday and 0515, 0700, 0830, 1430 and 1600 on Sunday. The cathedral has a choir and attracts a large and enthusiastic congregation.

Colonial villas Many of the large colonial villas – universally washed in pastel yellow – are 1930s and 40s vintage. Some have curved walls, railings and are almost nautical in inspiration; others are reminiscent of houses in Provence. Many of the larger villas can be found along Tran Hung Dao Street. Perhaps the largest and most impressive house is the **former residence of the Governor General** at 12 Tran Hung Dao Street – now the *Hotel Dinh II*. 1930s in style, with large airy rooms and uncomfortable furniture, it occupies a magnificent position set among mountain pines and overlooking the town. The house is a popular place for domestic tourists to have their photographs taken with the requisite stuffed animals. It is possible to stay here although it is often booked up by state enterprises and it is popular with members of Lam Dong People's Committee, modest and unassuming. North of here, in the valley and off Quang Trung Street, is the **Dalat Railway Station**. It was opened in 1938, five years after the completion of the rack and pinion track from Saigon and was closed in 1964. Dalat station is the last in Vietnam to retain its original French art-deco architecture, the coloured glass windows remain intact. Its steep pitched roofs could handle the heaviest of Alpine snowfalls for which, presumably they were designed. Despite the fact it is virtually unused the building is surprisingly well maintained and beds of geraniums flourish under the sun and the careful hand of an unseen gardner. In 1991 a seven kilometre stretch to the village of Trai Mat was reopened and twice a day a small Russian-built diesel car makes the journey (see Excursions page 237). There is also an old steam engine which is occasionally fired up and a Renault diesel car.

Lam Ty Ni Pagoda is down a track off Le Hong Phong Street. Unremarkable, save for a charming monk, Vien Thuc, who lives here. The main sanctuary was built in 1961 and contains an image of the Buddha with an electric halo. Vien Thuc arrived in 1968 and in 1987 he finished the gateway that leads up through a garden to the figure of Quan Am. Vien Thuc originally named his garden – which is almost Japanese in inspiration – An Lac Vien or Peace Garden but has now decided that Divine Calmness Bamboo Garden has a better ring to it. Vien Thuc is a scholar, poet, artist, philosopher, mystic, divine and entrepreneur but is best known for his paintings, of which, by his own reckoning, there are more than 100,000. And wandering through the maze of rustic huts and shacks tacked on to the back of the temple one can easily believe this: the walls are lined deep with hanging sheets which bear his simple but distinctive calligraphy and philosophy: "Living in the present how beautiful this very moment is", "Zen painting destroys millennium sorrows", "The mystique, silence and melody universal of love" and so on. Vien Thuc shows visitors around with a mixture of pride "I work very hard" and self deprecating modesty, chuckling to himself as if to say "I must be mad". His work is widely known. He has exhibited in Paris, New York and Holland and on the web where he can be found at http//:www.well.com/user/ gdisf/cyclo.htm. His paintings and books of poetry are for sale at prices that are creeping up to levels high enough for you to wish you could buy shares in him.

Lam Ty Ni Pagoda

The slightly wacky theme is maintained at the nearby Tree House, 3 Huynh Thuc Khang, leading many to wonder what they put in the water for this corner of Dalat to nurture so many creative eccentrics. Dr Dang Viet Nga, has over a period of many years built up her hotel in organic fashion. The rooms and gardens are scenes taken from the pages of a fairy story book. Guests sleep inside mushrooms, trees and giraffes and sip tea under giant cobwebs. There is a honeymoon room, an ant room and plenty more. It is not a particularly comfortable place to stay and privacy is limited by the number of visitors but it is a sight well worth the 4,000d entrance ticket.

Tree House

The **Linh Son Pagoda** is at 120 Nguyen Van Troi Street, just up from the intersection with Phan Dinh Phung Street. Built in 1942 and still in good condition, the pagoda is reserved for men. Perched on a small hillock, the sanctuary is fronted by two dragon balustrades, themselves flanked by two ponds with miniature mountain scenes. To the right is a military-looking turret.

Linh Son Pagoda

Four kilometres from the centre of town, at the end of Khe Sanh Street, is the **Thien Vuong Pagoda**. Begun in the 1950s, this stark pagoda has recently been expanded and renovated. In the main sanctuary are three massive bronze-coloured sandalwood standing figures with Sakyamuni, the historic Buddha, in the centre. Just before Thien Vuong Street is another pagoda: **Minh Nguyet Cu Sy Lam**. The sanctuary is to the right of the main gates. These two pagodas, though in no way artistically significant, are popular with local visitors and stalls nearby sell local jams, artichoke tea, cordials and dried mushrooms.

Thien Vuong Pagoda

Summer Palace Vietnam's last emperor, Bao Dai, had a **Summer Palace** on Le Hong Phong Street, about two kilometres from the town centre and now known as **Dinh 3**. Built on a hill with views on every side, it is Art Deco in style both inside and out, and rather modest for a palace. The stark interior contains little to indicate that this was the home of an emperor – perhaps many of Bao Dai's personal belongings have been removed. The impressive dining-room contains an etched glass map of Vietnam, while the study has Bao Dai's desk, a few personal ornaments and photographs, and a small collection of his books: Shakespeare's comedies, Voltaire, Brontë and the Bible. According to US reports, by 1952 Bao Dai was receiving an official stipend of US$4 million per year. Much of this was ferreted away in US and Swiss bank accounts – insurance against the day when his reign would end. The rest was spent on his four private planes – leaving little to lavish on his home. The palace is very popular with Vietnamese tourists who run riot lying on the beds, sitting in the chairs and having their photographs taken wherever they can. Bao Dai also had a **hunting lodge** which was recently restored as a museum and opened to the public by the *Sofitel hotel*. Now known as **Dinh 1** the lodge sports 1930s furniture, antique telephone switchboards and although it is not sumptious nevertheless has a feel of authenticity. The gardens are green but lacking in intimacy but as very few tourists visit one can have the place to oneself and scribble a diary entry while sitting unobserved on the foot of the late emperor's bed. ■ *10,000d. Open 0700-1130, 1300-1630 Monday-Sunday.*

Dalat University Out near the golf course on Phu Dong Thien Vung Street **Dalat University** was founded as a Roman Catholic University in 1957 and taken over by the government in 1975. It currently provides for 8,000 students from central and southern Vietnam. It is strong on English teaching and science and has links with the Nuclear Research Institute. Symbolic of the change in political fortunes. A huge red communist star atop the obelisk in the University's grounds actually conceals a crucifix.

Dalat Market Dalat Market (*Cho Dalat*) is at the end of Nguyen Thi Minh Khai Street and sells, to the eyes of an average lowland Vietnamese, a dazzling array of exotic fruits and vegetables grown in the temperate climate of the area: plums, strawberries, carrots, potatoes, loganberries, cherries, apples, onions and avocados It is also well stocked with cut flowers: gladioli, irises, roses, chrysanthemums and marigolds.

Excursions

The area surrounding Dalat was a beautiful wilderness until fairly recently. It is still beautiful, but no longer a wilderness. It is said that during the War, US soldiers would come to hunt tiger, leopard, stag, bear and other game, only to find that they themselves were being hunted – not by the animals, but by the Viet Cong who lived and fought in the forests and mountains. Despite the admonitory posters the authorities have not controlled deforestation in the Dalat area: the land on either side of the road up from Saigon is almost entirely cleared, except for a narrow band of pine forest around Dalat itself and on the steeper slopes.

Cam Ly Waterfall The landscape around Dalat is characterized by fast-flowing rivers and waterfalls. **Cam Ly Waterfall** is the closest waterfall to Dalat, two kilometres west of the town centre on Hoang Van Thu Street. Not exactly spectacular but relatively uncluttered and not overrun. ■ *Open 0700-1800 Monday-Sunday.*

Dantania Falls are along a track, five kilometres out of town on the road towards Saigon. The path leads steeply downwards into a forested ravine; it is an easy hike there, but tiring on the return journey. The falls – really a cascade – are hardly spectacular, but few people come here except at weekends so it is usually peaceful. ■ *5,000d*. **Prenn Falls** are also on the route to Saigon, next to the road, 15 kilometres from Dalat. The falls were dedicated to Queen Sirikit of Thailand when she visited them in 1959. Burdened with tourist tat, swan boats, stuffed animals and vendors of everything you could ever conceivably not want, Prenn tends to appeal more to the dramatic than the international market. There is a restaurant here. ■ *10,000d. Getting there: by bus en route towards Saigon.*

Lake of Sighs

Lake of Sighs lies five kilometres northeast of Dalat. The lake is said by some to be named after the sighs of the girls being courted by handsome young men from the military academy in Dalat. Another unlikely theory is that the name was coined after a young Vietnamese maiden, Mai Nuong, drowned herself in the lake in the 18th century. The story is that her lover, Hoang Tung, had joined the army to fight the Chinese who were mounting one of their periodic invasions of the country, and had thoughtlessly failed to tell her. Devastated, and thinking that Hoang Tung no longer loved her, she committed suicide in the lake. Not long ago the lake was surrounded by thick forest; today it is a thin wood. Souvenir shops, incredibly, sell stuffed tigers (no environmental movement here), while Montagnard 'cowboys' with plastic guns and holsters lead horses along the forest trails. The area is busy at weekends. The **Valley of Love** or Thung Lung Tinh Yeu is five kilometres due north of Dalat. Boats can be hired on the lake here, there is horse 'riding' and a few refreshment stands. ■ *8,000d or free if you take a path to the side. Getting to the waterfalls and lakes: because of the cool climate, it is very pleasant to reach the lakes, forests and waterfalls around Dalat by bicycle. In fact a day spent travelling is probably more enjoyable than the sites themselves.*

Trai Mat Village and others

Trai Mat Village can be reached by train from Dalat. In 1991 a seven kilometre stretch of track from Dalat Railway Station to the village of Trai Mat was reopened after 15 years of inoperation and every day at 0800 and 1330 a small Russian-built diesel car makes the return journey. The train can be hired at other times for a cost of around US$12. The journey to Trai Mat village takes you near the Lake of Sighs and past immaculately tended vegetable gardens; no space on the valley floors or sides is wasted and the high intensity agriculture is a marvellous sight. Trai Mat is a prosperous market village with piles of produce from the surrounding area. Walk 300 metres up the road and to the left a narrow lane leads down to Chua Linh Phuoc, an attractive Buddhist temple more than 50 years old. It is notable for its huge Buddha and mosaic adorned pillars. The mosaics are made of broken rice bowls and fragments of beer bottle. ■ *Getting there: by train or motorbike, follow Tran Hung Dao Street which becomes Hung Vuong, past SOS Village as left, keep going.*

In the vicinity of Dalat are a number of **villages**, both of **tribal minorities**, and of **migrants** who have been relocated here by the authorities – in some cases former inmates of re-education camps. The best known group of such villages are the **Lat** communities, 10 kilometres northwest of town. At present, local officials are not keen to have foreigners visiting the villages. There have been numerous reports of fines being imposed – anything up to US$100 per person (one group managed to bargain their fine down from US$100 to US$15 per person). In theory, it should be possible to obtain a permit from the police in Dalat, although these are not always granted.

The Central Region

Essentials

Sleeping

■ *on maps*
Price codes:
see inside front cover

Dalat has a large number of hotels and guesthouses most of which cater for Vietnamese visitors only. Most cheaper hotels for foreigners are controlled by Dalat Tourist and therefore tend not to represent particularly good value for money. Dalat's chilly evenings make cold showers an uninviting prospect, the hotels listed below all have

Central Dalat

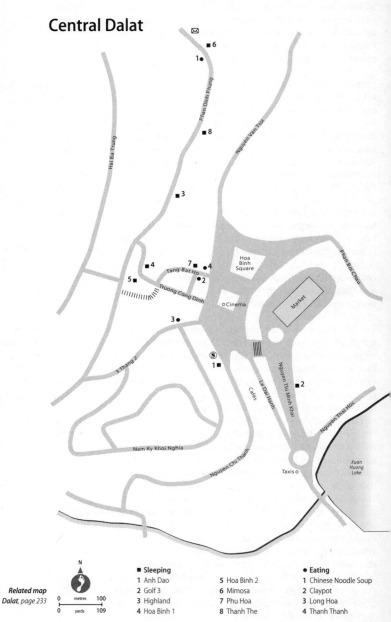

Related map
Dalat, page 233

N

0 metres 100
0 yards 109

■ Sleeping		● Eating
1 Anh Dao	5 Hoa Binh 2	1 Chinese Noodle Soup
2 Golf 3	6 Mimosa	2 Claypot
3 Highland	7 Phu Hoa	3 Long Hoa
4 Hoa Binh 1	8 Thanh The	4 Thanh Thanh

hot water and by the same token no a/c. Prices tend to rise in the high season, October-May.

L-A+ *Sofitel Dalat Palace*, 12 Tran Phu St, T825444, F825666, E sofitel@netnam2. org.vn. This rambling old building was built in 1922 and in 1995 was restored to its former glory. Those that knew it before restoration will be amazed: the renovation is superb, curtains, furniture, statues, gilt mirrors, chandeliers adorn the rooms which are tastefully arranged as the French do best. The view over Xuan Huong lake to the hills beyond is lovely and the extensive grounds of the hotel are beautifully laid out. One of the finest hotels in Vietnam. The hotel offers guests special green fees on the golf course.

A *Novotel*, 7 Tran Phu St, T825777, F825888, E novotel@netnam2.org.vn. Formerly the *Dalat Hotel*, opposite PO and near Sofitel with whom it shares management and many facilities. Rooms nicely restored and comfortably furnished. No restaurant but breakfast served here and *Café de la Poste* just over the road. **A-B** *Golf 3*, 4 Nguyen Thi Minh Khai St, T826042, F830396. Smart new centrally located hotel, comfortable rooms, cheaper rooms showers only. Nightclub and restaurant. **A-B** *Tree House (Hang Nga)*, 3 Huynh Thuc Khang St, T822070, F831480. If you fancy a fantasy night in a mushroom or tree or your name is Alice then this is the place for you. Most unusual but rather over run by visitors, restaurant.

B *Anh Dao*, 50-52 Hoa Binh Square, T823577, F823570. 27 rooms, central location, plasticky furnishings, cheaper rooms have no window. **B** *Golf 1*, 11 Dinh Tien Hoang St, T821281, F824945. Little way from centre, opposite the golf course, popular with golfers, clean, comfortable quiet, busy at weekend, book in advance. **B** *Dinh 2*, 12 Tran Hung Dao St, T822092, F825885. Formerly the residence of the French Governor General. 3 buildings, 22 rooms in all. Lovely setting but not a particularly welcoming place. **B** *Duy Tan*, 83 3 Thang 2 St, T822216, F822677. Low rise buildings arranged around a courtyard, all the usual amenities at this price, satellite TV, fridge, bath tub etc but not particularly good value.

C-D *Thanh The*, 118 Phan Dinh Phung St, T822180. Prices vary seasonally and you should bargain if it's not full. A bit of a rabbit warren clean but nothing special, restaurant. **C-D** *28 Tran Hung Dao*, 28 Tran Hung Dao St, T822764. Further up the road from Dinh 2, about 2 kilometres from the centre. A lovely old villa that has seen better days, comfort levels not great but nice views and a friendly welcome. Irregular rambling rooms, airy and clean, small garden at the back, ideal for those looking for peace and relaxation. Some dorm rooms, breakfast included.

D *Hoa Binh 1*, 64 Truong Cong Dinh St, T822787. Good location, one of the better low cost places, 15 rooms including 5 at the back around a small yard, quiet but not much view, rooms at the front have a view but can be a bit noisy, furniture a bit battered but friendly and an all day café. *Dalat by Night* bar next door. **D** *Hoa Binh 2*, 67 Truong Cong Dinh St, T822982. Newer and near its sister hotel, clean, some rooms have small balconies, not much in the way of curtains (a common complaint). **D** *Mimosa*, 170 Phan Dinh Phung St, T822656. A bit like all the other unremarkable *Dalat Tourist* hotels in this area, fairly central, not terribly quiet at the front, 30 rooms, showers, fridge, TV. **D** *Phu Hoa*, 16 Tang Bat Ho St, T822194, F822661. Central, simple but clean, 32 rooms, rear facing ones are quieter, the rooms for 3 are best equipped, including bath tub, approaching fair value.

The Central Region

Eating
● *on maps*

A number of popular eateries have closed but few have sprung up to replace them: lean times in the tourist trade. Cafés and street stalls line Nguyen Thi Minh Khai St, leading to Dalat market, which is itself the ideal place to buy picnic provisions. There are lakeside cafés and restaurants which may look attractive places to eat but they are badly staffed and serve indifferent food.

Le Rabelais, *Sofitel Dalat Palace*, 12 Tran Phu St, T825444. French specialities, superb dining room with views down to the lake, starters around US$12, main courses US$25, excellent. *Le Café de la Poste*, 12 Tran Phu St. Adjacent to *Sofitel Hotel* and under the same management, international food and a not very well stocked deli but spot on if you are craving cheese. Bar and nightclub upstairs. *Long Hoa*, 6 3 Thang 2, T822934. In the best traditions of French family restaurants, delicious food, super breakfasts, popular with Dalat's few ex-pats and visitors alike, fairly priced. Do sample Madam's home made strawberry wine which can be bought by the bottle for around US$6. *Thanh Thanh*, 4 Tang Bat Ho St, T821836. Delicious French and Vietnamese dishes served up in this smart unpretentious little restaurant, clean, white table cloths and a fresh rose on every table; attentive service. Crab soup, baked crab, lotus salad, French onion soup, beef Napoleon and venison are some of the mouth watering delights on offer at around US$3 each. *Hoa Binh 1*, 67 Truong Cong Dinh St. An all day eatery serving standard back packer fare – fried noodles, veggie dishes and pancakes at low prices. *Chinese Rice Noodle Soup*, 217 Phan Dinh Phung St, opposite *Mimosa Hotel*. Pretty self explanatory really, steaming soups with or without wan tun. *Clay Pot*, Tang Bat Ho St, opposite *Phu Hoa Hotel*. Decent Vietnamese fare at low prices. Pho and banh mi stalls, Tang Bat Ho St in front of Phu Hoa Hotel. Noodle soup and filled baguettes (paté, cold cuts or Vache Qui Rit) available from early morning 'til late in this little side street.

Bakery *Le Café de la Poste*, part of *Sofitel/Novotel*, pastries, coffee etc, European style.

Entertainment

Dancing *PK's Nightclub* upstairs at *Le Café de la Poste* more for Vietnamese cha cha cha couples than Western clubbers. Entrance ticket 30,000d, free to guests. *Golf 3 Hotel* is slightly more racy.

Bars *Larry's Bar* in the Sofitel is not exactly a theme pub but resembles a European dungeon. *Dalat by Night*, adjacent to *Hoa Binh 1 Hotel*. A bit grungy, has pool table.

Sports Golf: *Dalat Palace Golf Club*, T823507. IMG managed 18-hole golf course originally developed by Emperor Bao Dai and rebuilt in 1994. Rated by some, including Gordon Simmonds, as the finest in Vietnam and one of the best in the region. Beautiful setting overlooking Xuan Huong Lake. Green fee US$85 reduced to US$50 after 1500, US$60 at weekends, US$10 caddy fee. **Tennis**: 2 courts at *Sofitel Dalat Palace*.

Shopping

Wood carvings, minority handicrafts, fabrics etc from shops on Hoa Binh Square. **Local delicacies**: jams, artichoke teas, cordials and dried mushrooms; also local fruit wines, smooth and fiery.

Transport

110 kilometres from Phan Rang, 210 from Nha Trang, 299 kilometres from Saigon, 1,505 kilometres from Hanoi.

Local For short hops and longer excursions the motorbike taxi (*xe ôm*) is probably the simplest option. Negotiate the fare in advance but expect to pay around 5,000d for a short distance, 80,000d for a day. For those desiring a little more independence, mountain bikes and motorbikes can be rented from many hotels and from the kiosks along Nguyen Thi Minh Khai St in front of *Golf 3 Hotel* and the market, 20,000d per day for the former, 80,000d per day for the latter. Shared taxis to outlying villages from Hoa Binh Square or the roundabout by the dam. Metered taxis *TT Taxi*, T820082.

Air Lien Khang airport is 30 kilometres south of Dalat, a 40 minute drive. There are daily connections from Saigon. The Vietnam Airlines airport bus costs 40,000d.

Road Bus: long distance buses and minibuses arrive at Dalat bus station (Ben Xe Dalat) on 3 Thang 4, the main road in from the south. From here take a *xe ôm* the 2 or so kilometres into town. Inter-province buses (*xe lien tinh*) for major destinations depart 0500 onwards, check times the evening before. Minibuses ply the Saigon (US$10, 6 hours) and Nha Trang (US$8, 4 hours) routes, also bookable from most hotels. Direct connection with Buon Ma Thuot.

Banks *Incombank*, 42 Hoa Bin Square. 0700-1100, 1300-1600 Mon-Fri and 0700-1100 Sat. **Directory**
Changes cash also £, US$, FF, AU$, CA$ TCs at 1% commission. **Communications** Post Office: 14 Tran Phu St, opposite *Novotel*. **Hospitals & medical services** 4 Pham Ngoc Thach St, T822154. **Tour companies & travel agents** *Action Dalat*, 114 3 Thang 2 St, T829422, F820532. Trekking, boat rides, camping, climbing and abseiling on Lang Bian mountain and excursions to minority villages. A number of set pieces from around US$20 per day including lunch, English speaking guide. *Dalat Tourist*, 9 Le Dai Hanh St, T/F822479 and 4 Tran Quoc Toan St, T822125. Provide no information just offer 2 standard tours of Dalat and surrounds taking in waterfalls, lakes, ethnic villages from US$7-13. Many hotels, particularly budget sell these tours, start from your hotel at 0800. *Vietnam Airlines*, 3 Thang 4 St, in front of *Sofitel*, T822895.

Dalat to Saigon

For the first 20 kilometres out of Dalat on Highway 20 to Saigon the land is forested. But as the road descends on to the Bao Loc Plateau the forest is replaced by tea plantations and fruit orchards. Many of the farmers on the plateau settled here after fleeing from the north following partition in 1954. At the centre of the plateau is the town of Bao Loc (180 kilometres from Saigon, 120 kilometres from Dalat). 20 kilometres north of Bao Loc are the **Dambri Falls** considered the most impressive in southern Vietnam and worth an excursion for those who have time (July-November only). ■ *US$1. Getting there: by xe ôm from Bao Loc.*

Nam Cat Tien National Park

This newly created national park is about 150 kilometres north of Saigon, off Highway 20 en route for Dalat. The park is one of the last surviving areas of natural bamboo and dipterocarp forest in southern Vietnam. It is also one of the few places where populations of large mammals can be found in Vietnam: tiger, elephant, bear and the last remaining Javan rhino (see page 359). There are also 300 species of bird, smaller mammals, reptiles and butterflies. The park is managed by 20 rangers who besides helping protect the flora and fauna also conduct research and show visitors around. They do not speak English. A two-hour trek with guide costs around US$3, full day and two-day treks (sleeping out in hammocks) also possible. Take tough long-sleeved and long-legged clothing, jungle boots and leech socks if possible and plenty of insect repellent.

Sleeping (**E**) Very primitive lodgings for about 20, four beds per rooms, mosquito nets provided, outside toilet block with sink and cold shower, limited food available (instant noodles) and beer.

Transport Get there by car about 50 kilometres south of Bao Loc on Highway 20 (at the small town of Tan Phu) turn off to Nam Cat Tien, which is about 25 kilometres down a rough road, not well sign-posted. Some of the larger tour operators in Saigon offer two-day trips to Nam Cat Tien.

Routes The road then works its way down from the plateau through scrub bamboo forest towards the rolling landscape around Saigon, heavily cultivated with rubber and fruit trees. About 30 kilometres before Highway 20 joins Highway 1 the road crosses **La Nga Lake**. Fishermen live in floating houses on the lake; besides fishing in conventional ways they also keep fish in cages under their houses. The road between Dalat and Saigon is good. At the important industrial centre of Bien Hoa, 26 kilometres northeast of Saigon, a road runs south to the beach resort of Vung Tau.

Vung Tau

Phone code: 064
Colour map 4,
grid B4

Vung Tau is the hub of the country's oil industry, it is a significant port and home to a major fishing fleet. Despite the town's best endeavours tourism has never really taken off and with gas now being piped ashore to fuel power stations and fertilizer factories a little way inland it seems unlikely that it ever will. Vung Tau does have a certain appeal, however, it also boasts good hotels and some excellent restaurants.

Ins and outs

Getting there Vung Tau is a painless 2-3 hour road journey from Saigon. The bus and minibus stations are both relatively central and there are regular connections with Saigon. There is an even quicker hydrofoil service from central Saigon and for those who find even that too demanding to contemplate, helicopters ferry people here three days a week in just 30 minutes.

Getting around Vung Tau has the normal fleets of cyclos, honda ôms and taxis: take your pick.

History

Before the 17th century, Vung Tau was under the control of the Khmer kings of Cambodia. A large dam and reservoir to the north was built by one of the Cambodian kings to water his horses and elephants. In the 17th century, the Vietnamese annexed the surrounding territory, and later still the French gained control. The town began to develop as a seaside resort at the beginning of the 20th century when roads linking it to Saigon were constructed. At this time it was known as Cap Saint-Jacques and considered a fairly fine resort by the French adequate, at least, for the Governor General of Indochina to build himself a retreat here.

Vung Tau is situated on a rocky and hilly promontory that juts into the sea. This is the last piece of solid coastal geology until Hon Chong on the very far side of the Mekong Delta, some indication of the hundreds of square miles of mud that lie to the south. It is now a popular resort town for Vietnamese day-trippers and enjoys a relatively high level of prosperity, its wealth based on oil, trade and its role as provincial capital of Ba Ria-Vung Tau Province.

Oil was found off the coast of Vung Tau in the 1970s and the Russians

Superior God of the Southern Sea

The whale has long been worshipped in Vietnam. Ever since the days of early Champa the whale has been credited with saving the lives of drowning fishermen. The Cham believed that Cha-Aih-Va, a powerful god could assume the form of a whale in order to rescue those in need. Gia Long is said to have been rescued by a whale when his boat sank. After he ascended the throne, Emperor Gia Long awarded the whale the title Nam Hai Cu Toc Ngoc Lam Thuong Dang Than, Superior God of the Southern Sea. Coastal inhabitants always try to help whales in difficulty and cut them free of their nets. If a whale should die a full funeral is arranged. The person who discovered its dead body is considered to be the whale's 'eldest son' and will head the funeral procession dressed in white as if it were his own father's funeral.

moved in to help develop the fields. And in what now seem the heady days of the early 1990s British, Japanese and Canadian firms headed a long list of foreign oil companies pouring vast sums of money into the search for more of the black stuff. But with the exception of a few minor gas deposits nothing was found and most oilmen have stuffed their kitbags and gone in search of new seas to despoil. Some cling on but more from inertia than any real sense of optimism. Those few exploration companies remaining in Vietnam find obtaining a license-to-drill harder than finding the hydro-carbons they are looking for, so have relocated in Hanoi to grease a few palms. As a result the construction boom and easy riches which poured into the town have come to an end. In addition the Russians, while not exactly the biggest of spenders, are also coming to an end: from 5,000 in 1996 the contingent was down to 1,000 in 1998 and likely to be no more than 100 by the year 2000.

Sadly, the ending of the boom coincided with a gradual dawning on the part of foreign visitors that Vung Tau was not such a nice place after all, and that the best seaside holidays were to be had in Phan Thiet and Nha Trang. Tourism, though much vaunted in the nineties, never amounted to much and is even less now (although Long Hai attracts quite a few escapees from Saigon).

So all of this has left Vung Tau with a lot of hotels, some quite decent ones, and not many people to sleep in them; consequently there are some bargains to be had.

Sights

Being a beach resort one would expect good beaches but with the exception of Back Beach or Bai Sau, they are poor: narrow, with little or no sand, no coral and second-rate swimming. In the town itself is **Bai Truoc** or Front Beach, lined with kiosks and restaurants and really not a beach at all. Freighters moor offshore and fishing boats unload their catch at the south end of the bay, opposite the *Hai Au Hotel*. South from town, taking the coast road (Halong Street), is **Bai Dua** (formerly Roches Noires Beach) and a small collection of guesthouses. Again, the beach is poor. At Bai Dua there are two temples, one with a **large Buddha** looking out to sea, the other with an equally **large figure of Quan Am**. Also at Bai Dua is **Niet Ban Tinh Xa**, a pagoda built on a hill in 1971. It is said to be one of the largest temples in Vietnam, and contains a 5,000 kilos bronze bell and a 12 metres-long reclining Buddha.

Around the headland is a small and peaceful cove with good surf – **Mui Nghinh Phong** (formerly Au Vents Beach); swimming can be dangerous here. Northeast from the headland, on Thuy Van Street, and just past the

island pagoda of Hon Ba, is the longest stretch of sand – **Bai Sau** (Back Beach). Bai Sau is about two kilometres southeast from town, taking Hoang Hoa Tham Street. This is a beach in the usual sense of the word: five kilometres of sand. It is exposed to the wind and the South China Sea and the surf is usually good, sometimes ferocious. A system of flags indicates whether swimming is safe: white (safe), red (unsafe). Regulations state: "People suffering from mental, blood pressure disorders and epilepsy must not bathe". Overlooking the South China Sea at the south end of Bai Sau is a **giant Jesus** with arms outstretched. Behind the figure, on another hill, is a **lighthouse** built in 1910 which can be reached by path either from Halong Street (near the *Hai Au Hotel*) or from the southern end of Bai Sau. Good views of the town, bays and sea.

North of town, at 12 Tran Phu Street (the coast road) is **Bach Dinh** (Villa Blanche) built in the early part of this century as a summer residence for Governor General Paul Doumer. In 1909 King Thanh Thai was kept here prior to being sent into exile on the island of Reunion and it was later used by President Thieu. The house and later gardens are open to visitors. The house serves

Vung Tau

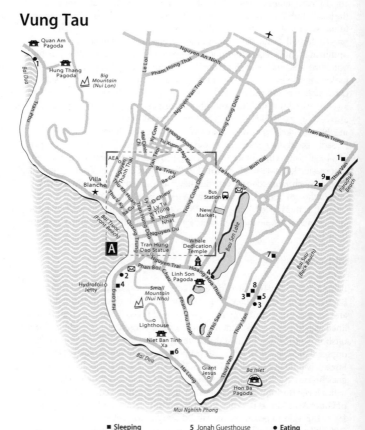

Related map
A Vung Tau Centre,
page 246

N
Not to scale

■ Sleeping	5 Jonah Guesthouse	● Eating
1 Bimexco	6 Neptune	1 69 Cay Bang
2 Cap Saint Jaques	7 Sammy	2 Bi Ti
3 Dang Gia Trang	8 Thang Muoi	3 Cuu Long Cafe
4 Hai Au	9 Thuy Duong	4 Ngoc Thuy

as a sort of repository storing *bric a brac* that no one wants, yet can't quite bring themselves to throwing it away. ■ *20,000d. Open 0700-1130, 1330-1700.* **Bai Dau Beach** is three kilometres northwest of town at the fishing village of Ben Dinh (now geared primarily to the demands of domestic tourists). Again, the beach is nothing special, but it is the quietest spot on the peninsula. The pagoda on the hill here is called **Hung Thang Tu**.

Although there are numerous pagodas and churches in Vung Tau none is particularly noteworthy. At the south end of Tran Hung Dao Boulevard is a massive and rather crude **statue of General Tran Hung Dao** who defeated a Chinese invasion force in the mid-13th century (see page 147). At 61 Hoang Hoa Tham Street, on the way to Bai Sau, is the 100-year old **Linh Son Co Tu Pagoda**. Across the road from the Linh Son Pagoda is the **Lang Ca Ong** or Whale Dedication Temple, which – not surprisingly – is dedicated to the whale, the patron god of Vung Tau fishermen (worship of the whale was inherited from the Cham). It was built in 1911 and contains a number of whale skeletons displayed in cabinets. Whale and dolphin bones are brought to the temple and worshipped before being cremated: they are credited with saving drowning sailors and fishermen. Rather quietly the Vietnamese regard large sea mammals as big fish: the whale is **ca voi** (jumbo fish) and the dolphin **ca heo** (pig fish).

Vung Tau market is near Le Quy Don Street.

Essentials

Competition for customers is intense and quality accommodation is available at sensible prices.

Sleeping

■ *on maps*
Price codes:
see inside front cover

In town   A+-A *Royal* (formerly *Canadian*), 48 Quang Trung St, T859852, F859851. Friendly, smart and comfortable, occupies a prime seafront site, some rooms have spectacular views. **A** *Rang Dong*, 5 Duy Tan St, T854933, F858306. Utilitarian rather than comfortable. **A-B** *Rex*, 1 Duy Tan St, T856335, F859862. Set a short way back from the beach but good views from the upper floors, good restaurant. **A-C** *Palace*, 11 Nguyen Trai St, T856411, F856878. Offers a wide range of business and recreational services, swimming pool on the 1st floor. **B** *Petro House*, 89 Tran Hung Dao St, T852014, F852015. New, central, satellite TV, business centre, French restaurant. **B** *Sea Breeze*, 11 Nguyen Trai St, T856392, F856856. Popular with oilmen and other expats. **B-C** *Grand*, 26 Quang Trung St, T852469. Occupies a nice position overlooking the sea, offers the usual entertainments. **B-C** *Hai Au*, 100 Halong St, T852178. Restaurant and small pool. **B-C** *Pacific*, 4 Le Loi Blvd, T852391. Large and sprawling with little character. **B-C** *Song Hong*, 12 Hoang Dieu St, T852452. Decent rooms, large downstairs restaurant.

Bai Dau   C-D Quiet, guesthouse-type accommodation along Tran Phu St, eg nos 28, 29, 47, 142 (about 6-7 of them), catering mostly to Vietnamese.

Bai Sau (Back Beach)   A *Sammy*, 18 Thuy Van St, T854755, F854762. Large and very comfortable new hotel, good views, business facilities and good Chinese restaurant. Recommended. **B-C** *Thang Muoi*, 4-6 Thuy Van St, T859876. A/c, large restaurant, small pool (not always filled with water). **C-D** *Bimexco*, Thuy Van St (north end of Bai Sau), T853470. Bungalows in casuarina-filled compound. Recommended. **C-D** *Cong Doan*, 4 Tran Hung Dao St, T856500. Large, some a/c and private bathrooms, friendly, but characterless. **C-D** *Dang Gia Trang*, 38/22 Thuy Van St, T859249. 100 metres up a small track, opposite *Jonah's*, some large a/c rooms, clean and good value. **D** *Jonah Guesthouse*, 29 Thuy Van St, T853481. Friendly, English, Japanese and French spoken.

Bai Dua Number of smaller hotels and guesthouses in this quiet, almost Mediterranean, enclave. **A-B** *Neptune Hotel*, 60A Halong St, T856192, F856439. Large and friendly new hotel with some superb suites overlooking the sea. Restaurant and roof terrace also with good views, private (rather rocky) beach across the road.

Eating

● *on maps*

In town/Front Beach Restaurants in town are often associated with hotels but there are plenty of independents. *Hung Ky*, 26 Quang Trung St, T850260 (*Grand Hotel*). Chinese restaurant with traditional Chinese dishes and seafood. *Hue Anh*, 446 Truong Cong Dinh St, T856663. Hue Anh has a bigger sister inside the *Sammy Hotel*. Chinese with healthy portions at middle of the road prices. *Huu Nghi*, 14 Tran Hung Dao St, T852017. Chinese/Vietnamese menu. Recommended. *Oasis*, 1 Le Loi St, T858088. Fairly large Western and Vietnamese menu, decent pizzas. *Thanh Tam*, 13 Quang Trung St, T856144. Excellent Vietnamese fare at a reasonable price. Seafood especially good: try the stir-fried squid. *Whispers*, 12 Nguyen Trai St, T856028. Very good, if slightly over-priced Western food, including beef imported from the US and Australia. Sunday lunch recommended. *Bi Ti*, 124/4 Halong St, T856652. Attractive restaurant swathed in greenery, extensive Vietnamese menu and good views over the bay. *Viet An Halal*, 40 Quang Trung St, T853735. A range of Halal foods prepared

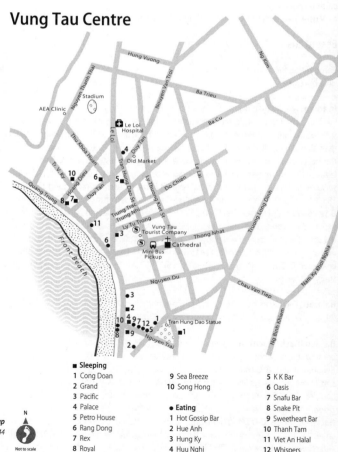

Vung Tau Centre

■ **Sleeping**
1 Cong Doan
2 Grand
3 Pacific
4 Palace
5 Petro House
6 Rang Dong
7 Rex
8 Royal
9 Sea Breeze
10 Song Hong

● **Eating**
1 Hot Gossip Bar
2 Hue Anh
3 Hung Ky
4 Huu Nghi
5 K K Bar
6 Oasis
7 Snafu Bar
8 Snake Pit
9 Sweetheart Bar
10 Thanh Tam
11 Viet An Halal
12 Whispers

Related map
Vung Tau, page 244

N

Not to scale

by an Indian/Vietnamese chef. Best curries in town. There are a number of cafés along the seafront, eg Thanh Nien, 55 Quang Trung St.

Bai Sau There are numerous seafood restaurants on the beach, all of which are much of a muchness. Two places in this area deserve mention, however: *Ngoc Thuy*, 63/3 Hoang Hoa Tham St, T859188. Interesting setting, backing onto and over the lake, gigantic Vietnamese menu. *Cuu Long Café*, 57 Thuy Van St. Cheap and friendly backpacker-oriented café with bicycles and motorbikes for hire.

On Bai Dau *69 Cay Bang*, 69 Tran Phu St. Overlooking sea, straightforward, no frills, good seafood.

Bars Bars open, close and change hands regularly. There are 3 or 4 bars on Nguyen Trai St which are popular with expats: *KK* at no 4, *Snafu*, 14 and *Sweetheart* at 18, all are a/c with cold beer, pool and Western snacks. *Hot Gossip*, 436 Trong Cong Dinh St, is just around the corner. On the front is *Snake Pit*, 15 Quang Trung St. A friendly new bar, also favoured by expats.

Nightclubs **Dancing** *Rex Hotel*, 1 Duy Tan St. *Hollywood Club*, south end of Quang Trung St.

Sports **Fishing**: rods can be hired on Halong St, opposite hydrofoil jetty for 25,000d per hour and fishing trips organized at 23 Quang Trung St.

Local festivals *Whale festival* (16th day of the 8th lunar month), fishermen make offerings at the Lang Ca Ong (Whale) Temple on Hoang Hoa Tham St.

Shopping Shells, shell ornaments and shell jewellery and stuffed lobsters are all to be found on the seafront along Quang Trung St.

Transport 113 kilometres from Saigon, 85 kilometres from Bien Hoa, 20 kilometres from Long Hai. **Air** There is a helicopter service from Saigon, Monday, Thursday and Saturday, 30 minutes, US$20, T08-8443289. **Road** **Bus**: Vung Tau bus station is sandwiched between Nam Ky Khoi Nghia and Xo Viet Nghe Tinh streets. Regular connections with Saigon (2½ hours) and other major destinations. Minibuses arrive and depart from Tran Hung Dao St in front of the church. Taxi or car chartered from a hotel should cost no more than US$20 to Saigon, 2 hours. **Boat** **Hydrofoil**: from wharf at end of Ham Nghi St in Saigon to Halong St jetty in Vung Tau, 4 services daily in each direction, 1 hour 20 minutes, US$10 each way, *Vinaexpress* T08-8253888 and 064-856530.

Directory **Banks** *Vietcombank*, 27 Tran Hung Dao Blvd (closed Thursday afternoon). Changes TCs and cash in major currencies. *VCSB*, 59 Tran Hung Dao St. Foreign exchange but not TCs. Most major hotels will change US$ cash. **Communications** GPO: 45 Le Hong Phong St. International telephone and faxes. Poste Restante service. **Hospitals & medical services** Hospital: *AEA International*, 1 Thanh Thai St, T858776. **Tour companies & travel agents** *OTAS*, 4 Le Loi St (*Pacific Hotel*), T852279. Tours to surrounding sights. **Tourist offices** *Ba Ria-Vung Tau Tourist Co*, 33-35 Tran Hung Dao St, T856445.

The Central Region

Long Hai to Ho Coc

Long Hai

Phone code: 064
Colour map 4, grid B4

Long Hai is a small town a few kilometres up the coast from Vung Tau, although in order to get here from Vung Tau you have to retreat inland as far as Ba Ria. It is such a non-descript little place that you could easily pass through without realising you had ever got there. Glimpses of the sea can be had from the road through the trees, but only just. Long expanses of clean sand and beaches far superior to Vung Tau's are the main attraction, although the town itself is rather shabby and in recent years has become very popular with Vietnamese tourists. Along the stretch of road that runs north of Long Hai several resorts have opened and more will surely follow to take advantage of the natural and unspoilt coast.

Sleeping **L-A+** *Anoasis Beach Resort*, T868227, F868229, E Anoasis@hcm.vnn.vn. 2-3 kilometres east of Long Hai. The latest addition to Vietnam's luxury resorts, it consists of 15 standard and 3 giant bungalows in a park setting with fantastic views over the sea. It is owned and run by Anoa, the spunky French lady of Vietnamese origin who in 1992 flew her helicopter from Paris to Hanoi. Scenically, it is probably the most appealing of all Vietnams resorts, it is attractively finished and everything is on a generous scale: each bungalow has a bath big enough for 2, comfortable and beautifully designed furnishings, there is a gigantic pool, a private beach and a jetty. **B** *Long Hai*, T868976. 30 rooms, all a/c and hot water, comfortable. **C** *Palace*, T868364. Some a/c, 18 large, wood-panelled rooms in this imposing domed mansion set amidst trees on a small hill, smacks of faded grandeur and a touch overpriced. **C** *Rang Dong*, T868356. Some a/c, grubby and unfriendly. **C-D** *Cong Doan*, T868312. Some a/c, many rooms have a balcony, comfortable and clean, gardens back onto the beach. **D-E** *Green*, T868337. Some a/c, friendly and fairly clean. **E** *Ngoc Minh*, T868429. Fan only, shared bathrooms but cleanish.

Eating Apart from the restaurant at *Anoasis* with its lovely outlook and European and Vietnamese menus, there are no noteworthy eateries, the restaurants inside the Palace, *Cong Doan* and *Ngoc Minh* hotels being the pick of the bunch. Seafood, naturally, is the speciality.

Transport **Road Bus**: some direct services from Saigon but probably quicker to take the Vung Tau bus, alight at Ba Ria and *xe ôm* from there. **Hydrofoil**: catch the Vung Tau hydrofoil and take a taxi or motorbike from there.

Directory **Tourist offices** *Long Hai Tourist Co*, is inside the *Rang Dong Hotel*, T868401.

Thuy Duong

The coastal road from Long Hai first ducks inland past large sand dunes then rejoins the sea, winding its merry way around rocky headlands and passing within a few feet of small, sandy beaches. The **caves** at **Minh Danh**, five kilometres from Long Hai, are soon reached. Signposted, it is a scramble up the hill to reach them. The caves and crevices were used by Communist soldiers as a hide-out from 1948 to 1975. ■ *20,000d, if you are unlucky.*

Thuy Duong is soon reached. This amounts to nothing except a quite comfortable hotel, a few beach cafés and shelters. But at weekends the place comes alive with families from Saigon, Bien Hoa and, one suspects, Vung

Vo Thi Sau

Born Ba Ria 1933, executed Con Dao 1952. At the precociously early age of 14 this Vietnamese revolutionary heroine developed an interest in politics and a passionate hatred for the French. In 1949 she obtained three hand-grenades and with just one of them she killed one French soldier and injured 20 others. She became a messenger and supplied food and ammunition to the Viet Minh. In 1950 she tried to assassinate a village headman working for the French but the hand-grenade failed to go off. She was caught, tortured and sentenced to death. She was executed on 23 January 1952 at the age of 18.

Tau. The beaches here are superb, gently shelving and golden: lovely swimming, safe for kids and peaceful mid-week. Even at weekends a short walk will take you well away from the crowds to coves, which romantically minded couples thought they had to themselves.

A-B *Thuy Duong Hotel*, T886215, F886180. A/c, comfortable hotel with pool, tennis court (US$5-7 per hour), restaurant. Also some cheaper bungalows which are run by the same establishment.   **Sleeping**

The beach cafés don't look much but the food is plentiful, cheap and good.   **Eating**

Ho Coc

The road then turns inland again to the quaint Dat Do, rejoining the main road from Ba Ria. Head east until reaching Bong Trang from where a straight and narrow road cuts a swathe through some lovely trees almost due south to the sea at tiny **Ho Coc**. The beach here is long and wide, another idyllic place for swimming and relaxing. This is a true escape, very few visitors and almost wholly undeveloped. There is simple accommodation in 6 A-frame huts on the beach, which have fans and showers. There is now reported to be electricity all night. (**D**), T874255. Only recently the local policeman would stroll along at 2100 and suggest to visitors that it was late and perhaps time for bed – maybe he still does. There is a decent restaurant and a friendly reception is assured. ■ *Getting there: buses from Ba Ria stop at Bong Trang, Minsk om from there to Ho Coc, 5,000d. Some Saigon cafés organize day trips. Three to three and a half hours from Saigon by car.*   *Phone code: 064*

Rejoining the main road, continue a further 10 kilometres or so east to the **hot springs** at **Binh Chau**. Here one can immerse oneself in a communal pool or a private one, although be careful where you bathe: in places the sulphorous water bubbles out of springs at 82°C. See for yourself by buying an egg and boiling it. For those wishing to take the waters accommodation is available at: **C-D** *Cu Mi Hotel*, T871131. A/c, hot water, clean. ■ *5,000d, private pool an additional 30,000d-50,000d per hour.*

Con Dao

The prison island of Con Dao was originally used by the French to incarcerate their more obstinate political prisoners. Built in 1861 the prison could hold up to 12,000 people and was later used by the government of South Vietnam to hold political prisoners. The infamous 'tiger cages' where prisoners were chained and tortured still stand. One kilometre beyond the prison is a cemetery where many of the victims of the prison are buried. The grave of Vo Thi   *Phone code: 064*

Sau (1933-1952) can be seen among them. There is a **museum** (*Bao Tang Tong Ho Tinh*) in the town of Con Dao in the house of the former prison governor which contains artefacts relating to the island's past. ■ *5,000d.*

The chief reason for visiting the island is that it is a beautiful, remote and unspoilt place. Its high mountains, many swathed in forest, plunge straight into the sea. There are countless isolated coves and beaches. Being at the earliest stage in the cycle of tourism, facilities for the foreign visitor are very primitive – some way behind those of that other and more accessible island retreat, Phu Quoc.

Sleeping **C** *Phi Yen*, Con Dao town, T830168. 10 clean rooms, overspills accommodated in guesthouses.

Transport **Air** Helicopter service Monday, Thursday and Saturday, 1 hour 15 minutes US$80 one way. T08-8443289. **Sea Boat**: 12-hour sailing from Vung Tau.

Saigon

6

Saigon

Saigon, Pearl of the Orient, is the largest city in Vietnam. It is also the nation's foremost commercial and industrial centre. Founded as a Khmer trading and fishing port on the west bank of the Dong Nai River it fell into Vietnamese hands in the late 17th century. Early in the 18th century the Nguyen emperors established Gia Dinh Citadel, destroyed by French naval forces in 1859. Rebuilt as a French colonial city it was named Saigon (Soai-gon – wood of the kapok tree). Officially Ho Chi Minh City since 1975, it remains to most the bi-syllabic, familiar, old 'Saigon'.

Saigon

Phone code: 08
Colour map 4, grid B3

The population of Saigon today is officially six million and rising fast as the rural poor are lured by the tales of streets paved with gold. Actual numbers are thought to be considerably higher when all the recent migrants without residence cards are added. But it has been a roller-coaster ride over the last 35 years. During the course of the Vietnam War, as refugees spilled in from a devastated countryside, the population of Saigon almost doubled from 2.4 million in 1965 to around 4.5 million by 1975. With reunification in 1976, the new Communist authorities pursued a policy of depopulation, believing that the city had become too large – that it was parasitic and was preying on the surrounding countryside. Certainly, most of the jobs were in the service sector, and were linked to the United States presence. For example, Saigon had 56,000 registered prostitutes alone (and many, many, more unregistered 'amateurs') – most of them country girls.

Ins and outs

Getting there Saigon may not be Vietnam's capital, but it is the economic powerhouse of the country and the largest city. Reflecting its premier economic position, it is well connected with the wider world – indeed, more airlines fly here from more places than they do from Hanoi. Tan Son Nhat airport is 30 minutes from town. There are direct domestic connections with Hanoi and Haiphong in the north, Hué, Danang, Play Ku, Buon Ma Thuot, Qui Nhon and Nha Trang in the central region, and Phu Quoc and Rach Gia in the Mekong region. The train station is northwest of the city centre and there are regular daily connections with Hanoi and all stops on the line north. As well as international air connections, there is a bus service from Saigon to Phnom Penh (Cambodia). Buses for destinations within the country leave from two main city bus terminals and connect Saigon with many larger towns in the central and northern regions, and for most places in the Mekong Delta.

Getting around Saigon has abundant public transport – which is fortunate, because it is a hot, large and frenetic city. Metered taxis, motorcycle taxis and cyclos vie for business in a healthy spirit of capitalism. Many tourists who prefer some level of independence opt to hire (or even buy) a bicycle or motorbike.

History

Prior to the 15th century, Saigon was a small Khmer village surrounded by a wilderness of forest and swamp. Through the years it had ostensibly been incorporated into the Funan and then the Khmer empires, although it is hard to believe that these kingdoms had any direct, long-term influence on the inhabitants of the community. The Khmers, who called the region *Prei Nokor*, used the area for hunting.

By 1623 Saigon had become an important commercial centre, and in the mid 17th century it became the residence of the so-called Vice-King of Cambodia. In 1698, the Viets managed to extend their control this far south and finally Saigon was brought under Vietnamese control – and hence celebrated the city's tercentenary in 1998. By 1790, the city had a population of 50,000 and before Hué was selected as the capital of the Nguyen Dynasty, Emperor Gia Long made Saigon his place of residence.

In the middle of the 19th century, the French began to challenge Vietnamese authority in the south of Vietnam and Saigon. Between 1859 and 1862, in response to the Nguyen persecution of Catholics in Vietnam, the French attacked and captured Saigon, along with the southern provinces of Vinh Long, An Giang and Ha Tien. The Treaty of Saigon in 1862 ratified the conquest and created the new French colony of Cochin China. Saigon was developed in French style: wide, tree-lined boulevards, street-side cafés, elegant French architecture, boutiques and the smell of baking baguettes. The map of French Saigon in the 1930s shows a city that owes more to Haussmann than Vietnamese geomancers. And French insensitivity can be judged from the street names which include, astonishingly, a Cambodian King and minor French dignitaries but not a single Vietnamese person, place or event.

The city

Saigon or Ho Chi Minh City is divided, administratively, into 12 urban districts or *quan*, and six suburban districts *huyen*. These are further sub-divided into wards and the wards into neighbourhoods; each district and ward has its own People's Committee or local government who guard and protect their responsibilities and rights jealously and maintain a high degree of administrative autonomy. A city-wide People's Committee, elected every four years, oversees the functioning of the entire metropolis.

Saigon

Saigon in the 1930s

Crossing the road

Saigon's streets may look anarchic but they are not. A strict code of conduct applies: the main difference between Vietnam's roads and those of the West is that in Vietnam the individual abdicates responsibility for his personal safety and assumes an obligation to everyone else; it is the closest Vietnam has ever come to true communism! Watch Vietnamese cross a busy street: unlike Westerners they do not wait for a lull in the traffic but launch themselves straight into the flow, chatting and laughing with their friends, eyes ahead so as to avoid walking into a passing bicycle (their sole duty), no looking left and right, no ducking and weaving: responsibility for their safety rests entirely with the oncoming cyclists. In order to make it easier for cyclists not to hit them they walk at a steady, even pace with no deviation from a clearly signalled route, for any slight change in trajectory or velocity would spell certain disaster.

With the 'freeing-up' of the Vietnamese economy and the influx of Westerners, conmen and touts have come out of the woodwork to plague visitors, as they did during the War. It is necessary to be careful, especially if lulled into a false sense of security by the people of Hanoi. See the warning on Safety, page 26.

Vietnam's economic reforms are most in evidence in Saigon (see page 395) and average incomes here at US$480 are over double the national average. It is here that the highest concentration of *Hoa* (ethnic Chinese) is to be found – 380,000 – and, although once persecuted for their economic success (see page 265), they still have the greatest economic influence, and acumen. Most of Saigon's ethnic Chinese live in the district of Cholon, and from there control two-thirds of small-scale commercial enterprises. The reforms have encouraged the *Hoa* to begin investing in business again. Drawing on their links with fellow Chinese in Taiwan, Hong Kong, Bangkok, and among the overseas Vietnamese, they are viewed by the government as crucial in improving prospects for the economy. The reforms have also brought economic inefficiencies into the open. Although the changes have brought wealth to a few, and increased the range of goods on sale, they have also created a much clearer division between the haves and the have-nots.

In its short history Saigon has had a number of keepers. Each has rebuilt the city in their own style. First the Khmer, then the early Vietnamese, followed by the French who tore it all down and started from scratch were succeeded by the Americans and the 'Puppet' Régime, and finally the Communist North who engineered society rather than the buildings, locking the urban fabric in a timewarp. Under the current régime, best described as crony capitalist, the city is once more being rebuilt. Ever larger holes are being torn in the heart of central Saigon. Whereas two years ago it was common to see buildings disappear, now whole blocks fall to the wrecker's ball. From the holes left behind, concrete, steel and glass monuments emerge. There is, of course, a difference from earlier periods of remodelling of the city. Then, it was conducted on a human scale and the largest buildings, though grand, were on a scale that was in keeping with the dimensions of the streets and ordinary shophouses. French buildings in Dong Khoi Street, for example, were consistent with the Vietnamese way of life: street level trading with a few residential floors above. By late 1998, however, the Asian malaise had caught up. Certainly office and apartment blocks and hotels were being topped out and some were opening their doors for business but the great swathes of clearance that characterized the early nineties had dwindled away to nothing more

Street wise

Cyclists and motorbike drivers in Saigon might like to be aware of the laws they could unwittingly breach and the level of fine they might thereby incur.

Bicycle infringements	*Fine (Dong)*
● *not moving in the right hand lane*	10,000
● *three riders cycling shoulder by shoulder*	20,000
● *clinging to automobiles or motorbikes, carrying cumbersome things or 'worming' in the street*	50,000
● *illegal racing and fleeing after causing accidents*	500,000
● *protesting the police officer's decision*	confiscation of bike plus 1,000,000
● *organizing illegal races*	2,000,000

Motorbike infringements	
● *not moving in the right hand lane*	50,000
● *speeding*	100,000
● *riding an unlicensed vehicle*	200,000
● *riding when drunk*	500,000
● *running away after accidents*	up to 2,000,000
● *illegal racing*	5,000,000
● *illegal racing and protesting the decisions of police officials*	50,000,000

than minor vandalism. And as for new construction, there was virtually nothing at all; so, as with the post-war bombsites nature quickly moved in to colonize the wasteland. In celebration of Saigon's 300th anniversary the municipal authorities decided the city could do with a face lift: a lot of shacks and extensions that extended on to pavements were swept away, sometimes revealing lost and attractive colonial façades behind. The pavements themselves were relaid and widened (superior motorbike parks, the cynics muttered); and several municipal buildings were renovated, in particular the Opera House to which replicas of the original statuary were added – the effect being somewhat spoilt by the tin roof.

Sights

Central Saigon

All the sights of Central Saigon can be reached on foot or cyclo in no more than 30 minutes from the major hotel areas of Nguyen Hue, Dong Khoi and Ton Duc Thang streets. Visiting all the sights described will take several days, not that we would particularly recommend visiting them all. Quite a good first port of call, however, is the **Panorama Café** on the 33rd floor of **Saigon Trade Centre**, the tallest building in Vietnam at 37 Ton Duc Thang Street. From this vantage point you can see, stretching before you, the whole city and its position and layout in relation to the river and surrounding swampland becomes strikingly clear.

Rex Hotel The Rex Hotel, a pre-Liberation favourite with US officers, stands at the intersection of Le Loi and Nguyen Hue Boulevards. This was the scene of the daily 'Five O'Clock Follies' where the military briefed an increasingly sceptical press corps during the Vietnam War. Fully renovated, the crown on the fifth floor terrace of the *Rex* (a good place to have a beer) is rotating once again after a number of years of immobility. Some maintain that it symbolizes Saigon's newly discovered (or rediscovered) vitality. A short distance northeast from the *Rex*, at the end of Le Loi Boulevard, is the once impressive French-era **Opera House**. The opera house was once home to the National Assembly and when it is functioning provides a varied programme of events: for example, traditional theatre, contemporary dance and gymnastics. At the northwest end of Nguyen Hue Boulevard, again close to the *Rex*, is the yellow and white **City Hall**, now home to Ho Chi Minh City People's Committee, which overlooks a **statue of Bac Ho** (Uncle Ho) offering comfort, or perhaps advice, to a child. This is a favourite spot for Vietnamese to have their photograph taken, especially newly-weds who believe old Ho confers some sort of blessing. On weekend evenings literally thousands of young Saigon men and women cruise up and down Nguyen Hue and Le Loi Boulevards and Dong

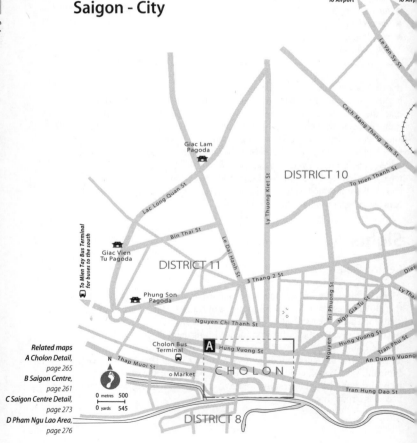

Saigon - City

Khoi Street (formerly the bar-lined Tu Do Street, the old Rue Catinat) on bicycles and motorbikes; this whirl of people and machines is known as *chay long rong* or *song voi* – meaning 'living fast'. There are now so many bicycles and motorbikes on the streets of Saigon that intersections seem lethally confused. Miraculously, the riders miss each other (most of the time) while pedestrians safely make their way through waves of machines (see box, page 256).

North up Dong Khoi Street in the middle of Paris Square (Cong xa Pari) is the imposing but austere red-brick, twin-spired Notre Dame Cathedral, overlooking a grassed square in which is a statue of the Virgin Mary holding an orb. The cathedral was built between 1877 and 1880, and is said to be on the site of an ancient pagoda. A number of homeless sleep under its walls at night, as the Lord would no doubt wish; unfortunately the signs asking Vietnamese men not to treat the walls as a public urinal do not deter this unpleasant but widespread practice. Communion is celebrated here six times on Sundays and three times on weekdays. The late Sunday afternoon and evening services draw particularly large congregations.

Notre Dame Cathedral

Saigon

General Post Office Facing onto the square is the General Post Office, built in the 1880s, a particularly distinguished building despite the veneer of junk that has been slapped onto it. The front façade has attractive cornices with French and Khmer motifs and the names of distinguished French men of letters and science. Inside, the high vaulted ceiling and fans create a deliciously cool atmosphere in which to scribble a post card. Note the old wall map of Cochin-China which has miraculously survived.

Archibishop's Palace Around this area are a number of very fine French-era buildings; some have been allowed to fall into decay but others have been nicely maintained. In particular the Archbishop's Palace on the corner of Nguyen Dinh Chieu and Tran Quoc Thao streets and the high schools, Le Qui Don at 2 Le Qui Don Street and Marie Curie on Nam Ky Khoi Nghia Street.

North of the Cathedral is Le Duan Street, the former corridor of power with Ngo Dinh Diem's Palace at one end, the zoo at the other and the former embassies of the three major powers France, the US and the UK in between. Quite who was aping who and who the puppet and who the master was a tangled question. Nearest the Palace is the compound of the **French Consulate**. A block away is the **former US Embassy**. After diplomatic ties were resumed the Americans lost little time in demolishing the 1960s building which held so many bad memories. The new Consulate General is being built on this site. A plaque outside records the attack by Viet Cong special forces during the Tet offensive of 1968 and the final victory in 1975. On the other side of the road, a little further northeast at 25 Le Duan, is the former **British Embassy**, now the British Consulate General and British Council. At 2 Le Duan Street is the **War Museum** (Bao Tang Quan Doi) with a tank and warplane in the front compound. It contains an indifferent display of photographs and articles of war. ■ *Open 0800-1130, 1330-1600 Tuesday-Sunday.*

Botanical Gardens At the end of Le Duan Street are the Botanical Gardens which run alongside Nguyen Binh Khiem Street at the point where the Thi Nghe channel flows into the Saigon River. The gardens were established in 1864 by French botanist Jean-Batiste Louis Pierre; by the 1970s they had a collection of nearly 2,000 species, and a particularly fine display of orchids. With the dislocations of the immediate postwar years, the gardens went into decline, a situation from which they are still trying to recover. In the south quarter of the grounds of the gardens is a mediocre **zoo** with a rather moth-eaten collection of animals which form a backdrop to smartly dressed Vietnamese families posing for photographs. The latest addition to the zoo is a life size family of Vietnamese-speaking model dinosaurs. To popular dismay the local authorities are now driving a road through the southern side site. ■ *Entrance to gardens and zoo 10,000d.*

Historical Museum More stimulating and impressive, at 2 Nguyen Binh Khiem Street, just to the left of the main gates to the Botanical Gardens, is the Historical Museum, formerly the National Museum, and before that the Musée Blanchard de la Bosse (from 1929-1956). This elegant building was constructed in 1928 and is pagodaesque in style. It displays a wide range of artefacts from the prehistoric (300,000 years ago) and the Dongson periods (3,500 BC – 100 AD) through to the birth of the Vietnamese Communist Party in 1930. Particularly impressive are the Cham sculptures, of which the standing bronze Buddha from the fourth to sixth century is probably the finest. There are also representative pieces from the Chen-la, Funan, Khmer, Oc-eo and Han Chinese periods, and from the various Vietnamese dynasties together with some hill tribe artefacts. Little of the labelling is in English and even the English booklet available from the ticket office is of little help. Water puppet shows (see page 387) are held here daily, 10,000d. ■ *10,000d. Open 0830-1130, 1330-1630 Tuesday-Sunday.* Opposite the Historical Museum is the **Memorial Temple**, constructed in 1928 and dedicated to famous Vietnamese. ■ *Open 0800-1130, 1300-1600 Tuesday-Sunday.*

Saigon Centre

Saigon

■ **Sleeping**
1 Embassy
2 International
3 Liberty
4 Mercury
5 New World
6 Sofitel Plaza

● **Eating**
1 ABC
2 Blue Ginger
3 Hoa Vien
4 La Bibliotheque
5 Mandarin
6 Thanh Nien
7 Thien Nam
8 Tib
9 VY

Related maps
A Saigon Centre Detail,
page 273
B Pham Ngu Lao Area,
page 276
Saigon Centre,
page 261

☞ **The Buddhist martyrs: self-immolation as protest**

In August 1963 there was a demonstration of 15,000 people at the Xa Loi Pagoda, with speakers denouncing the Diem régime and telling jokes about Diem's sister-in-law, Madame Nhu (she was later on a speaking tour in the US to call monks "hooligans in robes"). Two nights later, ARVN special forces (from Catholic families) raided the pagoda, battering down the gate, wounding 30 and killing 7 people. Soon afterwards Diem declared martial law. The pagoda became a focus of discontent, with several monks committing suicide through self-immolation to protest against the Diem régime. The first monk to immolate himself was 66-year-old Thich Quang Du, from Hué. On 11 June 1963, his companions poured petrol over him and set him alight as he sat in the lotus position. Pedestrians prostrated

themselves at the sight; even a policeman threw himself to the ground in reverence. The next day, the picture of the monk in flames filled the front pages of newspapers across the world. Some 30 monks and nuns followed Thich's example in protesting against the Diem government and US involvement in South Vietnam. Two young US protesters also followed suit, one committing suicide by self-immolation outside the Pentagon and the other next to the UN, both in November 1968. Madame Nhu, a Catholic, is reported as having said after the monks' death: "Let them burn, and we shall clap our hands". Within 5 months Diem had been killed in a military coup. In May 1993 a Vietnamese man immolated himself at the Thien Mu Pagoda in Hué – the pagoda where the first monk-martyr was based (see page 182).

War Crimes Museum The popular War Crimes Museum is on Vo Van Tan Street, close to the intersection with Le Qui Don Street. In the courtyard are tanks, bombs and helicopters, while in the museum itself are countless photographs, and a few exhibits, illustrating man's inhumanity. The display covers the Son My (My Lai) massacre on 16 March 1968 (see box, page 210), the effects of napalm and phosphorous, and the after-effects of Agent Orange defoliation (this is particularly disturbing, with bottled malformed human foetuses). Understandably, there is no record of North Vietnamese atrocities to US and South Vietnamese troops. There is also a rather laughable exhibit of such latter-day Western atrocities as heavy metal music. This museum has gone through some interesting name changes in recent years. It began life as the Exhibition House of American and Chinese War Crimes. In 1990, 'Chinese' was dropped from the name, and in 1994 'American' was too. From 1996 it was simply called the 'War Remnants Museum'. ■ *10,000d. Open 0730-1145, 1330-1645 Tuesday-Sunday.*

Xa Loi Pagoda In total, Saigon has close to 200 pagodas – far too many to see. Many of the finest are in Cholon (see below), although there is a selection closer to the main hotel area in central Saigon. The Xa Loi Pagoda is not far from the War Crimes Museum at 89 Ba Huyen Thanh Quan Street (see Saigon General map), surrounded by foodstalls. If the main gate is shut, try the side entrance on Su Thien Chieu Street. Built in 1956, the pagoda contains a multi-storeyed tower which is particularly revered, as it houses a relic of the Buddha. The main sanctuary contains a large, bronze-gilded Buddha in an attitude of meditation. Around the walls is a series of silk paintings depicting the previous lives of the Buddha (with an explanation of each life to the right of the entrance into the sanctuary). The pagoda is historically, rather than artistically, important as it became a focus of dissent against the Diem regime (see box). ■ *Open 0630-1100, 1430-1700 Monday-Sunday.*

The **Presidential Palace**, now renamed **Reunification Hall**, or the **Thong Nhat Conference Hall**, is in a large park to the southeast of Nguyen Thi Minh Khai Street, and southwest of Nam Ky Khoi Nghia Street. The residence of the French governor was built on this site in 1868, which was later renamed the Presidential Palace. In February 1962, a pair of planes took off to attack Viet Cong emplacements – piloted by two of the south's finest airmen – but they turned back to bomb the Presidential Palace in a futile attempt to assassinate Diem. The president escaped with his family to the cellar, but the Palace had to be demolished and replaced with a new building. One of the most memorable photographs taken during the War was of a NVA tank crashing through the gates to the Palace on 30 April 1975 – symbolizing the end of South Vietnam and its government. The President of South Vietnam, General Duong Van Minh, and his entire cabinet, were arrested in the Palace shortly afterwards. The hall has been preserved as it was found in 1975 and visitors can take a guided tour. In the *Vice President's Guest Room*, there is a lacquered painting of the Temple of Literature in Hanoi, while the *Presenting of Credentials Room* contains a fine 40-piece lacquer work showing diplomats presenting their credentials during the Le Dynasty (15th century). In the basement there are operations rooms, military maps, radios and other paraphernalia. In essence, it is a 60s-style building filled with 60s-style official furnishings. Visitors are shown a poorly made, but nonetheless interesting, film of the Revolution. ■ *40,000d. Open 0730-1030, 1300-1530 Monday-Sunday.* The guides are friendly, but their English is not always very good. **NB** The hall is sometimes closed for state occasions. The visitors' entrance is at 106 Nguyen Du Street.

Reunification Hall

Close by, the Revolutionary Museum is at 65 Ly Tu Trong Street. Like the equivalent in Hanoi, this is not a revolutionary museum but a museum of the revolution, with a display of photographs, a few pieces of hardware (helicopter, anti-aircraft guns) in the back compound, and some memorabilia. All the labelling is in Vietnamese, and the museum is usually filled with red-scarved school children. ■ *Open 0800-1130, 1330-1630 Tuesday-Sunday.* Opposite the museum is a small park with open-air café. Southeast from the Revolutionary Museum along Ly Tu Trong Street is the centre of Saigon's 'fashion' industry selling some genuine brand names but mostly quite good fakes.

Revolutionary Museum

Not far away at 45 Truong Dinh Street is the Mariamman Hindu Temple. Although clearly Hindu, with a statue of Mariamman flanked by Maduraiveeran and Pechiamman, it is largely frequented by Chinese worshippers, providing the strange sight of Chinese Vietnamese clasping incense sticks and prostrating themselves in front of a Hindu deity, as they would to a Buddha image. The Chinese have always been pragmatic when it comes to religions.

Mariamman Hindu Temple

A large covered central market, Ben Thanh Market faces a statue of Tran Nguyen Han at a large and chaotic roundabout, the Ben Thanh gyratory system, which marks the intersection of Le Loi, Ham Nghi and Tran Hung Dao boulevards. Ben Thanh is well stocked with clothes (cheap souvenir t-shirts), household goods, a wide range of soap, shampoo and sun cream, a good choice of souvenirs, lacquerware, embroidery and so on, as well as some terrific lines in food: cold meats, fresh and dried fruits. It is not cheap (most local people 'window-shop' here and purchase elsewhere) but the quality is high and the selection probably without equal. It is a terrific experience just to wander through and marvel at the range of produce on offer, all the more so

Ben Thanh Market (Cho Ben Thanh)

Saigon

now most beggars have been eased out. Outside the north gate (cua bac) on Le Thanh Ton Street are particularly tempting displays of fresh fruit (the oranges and apples are imported) and beautiful cut flowers. Saigon has a number of markets; this one and the Binh Tay Market in Cholon (see below) are the largest. Many of the markets are surprisingly well stocked for a country which a few years ago was close to economic collapse. The people of the south, and particularly the Chinese of Saigon, have not forgotten what it is like to conduct business, and with the economic reforms, private traders have reappeared on the streets to make a quick dong or buck.

Fine Art Museum The Fine Art Museum (*Bao Tang My Thuat*), in an impressive cream-coloured mansion at 97A Pho Duc Chinh Street, displays work from the classical period through to socialist realist. On the third floor is a museum of ancient art which contains artefacts from the ancient civilizations of Oc Eo. ■ *Open 0800-1130, 1400-1700 Tuesday-Sunday*. At 338 Nguyen Cong Tru Street is the **Phung Son Tu Pagoda**. This is a small temple built just after the Second World War by Fukien Chinese; its most notable feature is the wonderful painted entrance doors with their fearsome armed warriors. Incense spirals hang in the open well of the pagoda, which is dedicated to Ong Bon, the Guardian of Happiness and Virtue. The **War Surplus** or **Dan Sinh Market** is close to the Phung Son Tu Pagoda at 104 Nguyen Cong Tru Street. Merchandise on sale includes dog tags and military clothing and equipment (not all of it authentic). The market is popular with Western visitors looking for mementoes of their visit, so bargain particularly hard.

Old Market The Old Market is on Ton That Dam Street, running between Ham Nghi Boulevard and Ton That Thiep Street. It is the centre for the sale of black market goods (particularly consumer electronics) – now openly displayed. There is also a good range of foodstalls and fruit sellers. Close by on Ben Chuong Duong Street is the old **Hong Kong and Shanghai Bank building** which overlooks Saigon's **pet market** where sad mangy looking animals – birds, monkeys, dogs – await a new home in a different cage or a cooking pot. Nguyen Tat Thanh Street runs south from here over the Ben Nghe Channel to **Dragon House Wharf**, at the confluence of the Ben Nghe Channel and the Saigon River. The building has been converted into a **museum** (predominantly on the first floor) celebrating the life and exploits of Ho Chi Minh, mostly through pictures and the odd piece of memorabilia. School children are brought here to be told of their country's recent history, and people of all ages have their photographs taken with a portrait of Bac Ho in the background. ■ *Open 0800-1130, 1400-1800 Tuesday-Thursday and Saturday, 0800-1130, 1400-2000 Sunday*.

Ton Duc Thang Museum A short distance north up Ton Duc Thang Street from the broad Me Linh Square (in the centre of which an imposing statue of Vietnamese hero Tran Hung Dao glares down at the site vacated by the *Floating Hotel*) is the rarely visited Ton Duc Thang Museum. Opened in 1989, it is dedicated to the life of Ton Duc Thang or Bac (Uncle) Ton. A comrade of Ho Chi Minh with whom he fought, Bac Ton became President of Vietnam and died in 1980. The museum contains an array of photographs and other memorabilia. ■ *Open 0800-1100, 1400-1800 Tuesday-Sunday*.

Cholon

Cholon (*Cho lon* = big market) or Chinatown is an area inhabited predominantly by Vietnamese of Chinese origin. Since 1975, the authorities have alienated many Chinese, causing hundreds of thousands to leave the country. In making their escape many have died – either through drowning, as their perilously small and overladen craft foundered, or at the hands of pirates in the South China Sea (see page 348). In total, between 1977 and 1982, 709,570 refugees were recorded by the UNHCR as having fled Vietnam. By the late 1980s, the flow of boat people was being driven more by economic, than by political, forces; there was little chance of making good in a country as poor, and in an economy as moribund, as that of Vietnam. Today, although economic conditions have barely changed, the stream has dried to a trickle as the opportunities for claiming refugee status and gaining asylum have disappeared. Even with this flow of Chinese out of the country, there is still a large population of Chinese Vietnamese living in Cholon, an area which encompasses the fifth and the sixth precincts or *quan*, to the southwest of the city centre. Cholon appears to the casual visitor to be the most populated, noisiest, and in general the most vigorous part of Saigon, if not of Vietnam. It is here that entrepreneurial talent and private funds are concentrated; both resources that the government are keen to mobilize in their attempts to reinvigorate the economy.

Cholon is worth visiting not only for the bustle and activity, but also because the temples and assembly halls found here are the finest in Saigon. As with any town in Southeast Asia boasting a sizeable Chinese population the early settlers established meeting rooms which offered social, cultural and spiritual support to members of a dialect group. These assembly halls or *hoi quan* are most common in Hoi An and Cholon. There are temples in the buildings which attract Vietnamese as well as Chinese worshippers and indeed today serve little of their former purpose. The elderly meet here occasionally for a natter and a cup of tea. The sights outlined below can be walked in half a day, although hiring a cyclo for a few hours is a more relaxing way to get around.

The Nghia An Assembly Hall can be found at 678 Nguyen Trai Street, not far from the *Arc en Ciel Hotel*, the best hotel in Cholon. A magnificent carved gold-painted wooden boat hangs over the entrance. To the left, on entering the temple, is a larger than life representation of Quan Cong's horse and

Chinatown

**Nghia An
Assembly Hall**

Saigon

Cholon Detail

*Related map
Saigon - City,
page 258*

groom. At the main altar are three figures in glass cases: the central red-faced figure with a green cloak is Quan Cong himself; to the left and right are his trusty companions, the General Chau Xuong (very fierce) and the mandarin Quan Binh respectively. On leaving note the fine gold figures of guardians on the inside of the door panels.

Tam Son Assembly Hall The Tam Son Assembly Hall is nearby at 118 Trieu Quang Phuc Street, just off Nguyen Trai Street. The temple is frequented by childless mothers as it is dedicated to Chua Thai Sanh, the Goddess of Fertility, and was built in the 19th century by Fukien immigrants. It is an uncluttered, 'pure' example of a Chinese/Vietnamese pagoda; peaceful and quiet. Like Nghia An Hoi Quan, the temple contains figures of Quan Cong, his horse and two companions (see above).

Thien Hau Pagoda The Thien Hau Pagoda, on 710 Nguyen Trai Street, is one of the largest in the city. Constructed in the early 19th century, it is Chinese in inspiration and is dedicated to the worship of both the Buddha and to the Goddess Thien Hau. She is the goddess of the sea and the protector of sailors. Two enormous incense urns can be seen through the main doors. Inside, the principal altar supports the gilded form of Thien Hau, with a boat to one side. Silk paintings depicting religious scenes decorate the walls. By far the most interesting part of the pagoda is the roof, which can be best seen looking up from the small open courtyard. It must be one of the finest and most richly ornamented in Vietnam, with the high-relief frieze depicting episodes from the Legends of the Three Kingdoms. In the post 1975 era, many would-be refugees prayed here for safe deliverance before casting themselves adrift on the South China Sea. A number of those who survived the perilous voyage sent offerings to the merciful goddess and the pagoda has been well maintained since.

Quan Am Pagoda Close to Thien Hau, at 12 Lao Tu Street (just off Luong Nhu Hoc Street), is the Quan Am Pagoda, thought to be one of the oldest in the city. The roof supports four sets of impressive mosaic-encrusted figures, while inside, the main building is fronted with old gold and lacquer panels of guardian spirits. The main altar supports a seated statue of A-Pho, the Holy Mother. In front of the main altar is a white ceramic statue of *Quan Am, the Goddess of Purity and Motherhood* (Goddess of Mercy) (see page 77). The pagoda complex also contains a series of courtyards and altars dedicated to a range of deities and spirits. Outside, hawkers sell caged birds and vast quantities of incense sticks to pilgrims.

Binh Tay Market The Binh Tay Market, sandwiched between Thap Muoi and Ben Phan Van Khoe streets, is one of the most colourful and exciting markets in Saigon, with a wonderful array of noises, smells and colours. It sprawls over a large area and is contained in what looks like a rather decayed Forbidden Palace. Beware of pickpockets here. A new high-rise market – the five-storey **An Dong Market** – opened at the end of 1991 in Cholon. It was built with an investment of US$5 million from local ethnic Chinese businessmen.

Phung Son Pagoda A 25 minute walk from the Binh Tay Market and set back from the road at 1408 3 Thang 2 Boulevard is the Phung Son Pagoda, also known as **Go Pagoda**. It was built at the beginning of the 19th century on the site of an earlier Cambodian structure and has been rebuilt several times. At one time, it was decided to move the pagoda, and all the temple valuables were loaded on to the back of a white elephant. The beast stumbled and the valuables tumbled out into the pond that surrounds the temple. This was taken as a sign from the gods that the pagoda was to stay where it was. In the sanctuary, there is a large seated gilded Buddha, surrounded by a variety of other figures from several Asian and Southeast Asian countries.

Outer Saigon

The Phuoc Hai Tu (Emperor of Jade Pagoda) can be found off Dien Bien Phu Street at 73 Mai Thi Luu Street, nestling behind low pink walls, just before the Thi Nghe Channel. Women sell birds that are set free to gain merit, and a pond to the right contains large turtles. The Emperor of Jade is the supreme god of the Taoists, although this temple, built in 1900, contains a wide range of other deities. These include the archangel Michael of the Buddhists, a Sakyamuni (historic) Buddha, statues of the two generals who tamed the Green Dragon (representing the east) and the White Dragon (representing the west) (to the left and right of the first altar) and Quan Am (see page 77). The Hall of Ten Hells in the left-hand sanctuary has reliefs depicting the 1,000 tortures of hell. **Phuoc Hai Tu (Emperor of Jade Pagoda)**

Not far from the Emperor of Jade Pagoda is the small Tran Hung Dao Temple at 34 Vo Thi Sau Street. Built in 1932, it was dedicated to the worship of the victorious 13th century General Hung Dao, and contains a series of bas-reliefs depicting the general's successes, along with weapons and carved dragons (see page 147). In the front courtyard is a larger than life bronze statue of this hero of Vietnamese nationalism. ■ *Open 0700-1100, 1430-1700 Monday-Sunday.* **Tran Hung Dao Temple**

To the west, on Nguyen Van Troi Street, and just to the south of the Thi Nghe Channel is another modern pagoda, the Vinh Nghiem Pagoda. It was completed in 1967 and is one of the largest in Vietnam. Built in Japanese style, it displays a seven-storey pagoda in the classic style (only open on holidays) and a large, airy, sanctuary. On either side of the entrance are two fearsome warriors; inside is a large Japanese-style Buddha in an attitude of meditation, flanked by two goddesses. Along the walls are a series of scrolls depicting the jataka tales, with rather quaint (and difficult to interpret) explanations in English. ■ *Open 0730-1130, 1400-1800 Monday-Sunday.* **Vinh Nghiem Pagoda**

A 10-15 minutes cyclo ride across the Thi Nghe Channel and almost into the suburbs leads to the Tomb and Temple of Marshal Le Van Duyet at 126 Dinh Tien Hoang Street. Le Van Duyet was a highly respected Vietnamese soldier who put down the Tay Son rebellion (see page 211) and died in 1831. The pagoda was renovated in 1937 – a plaque on the left lists those who made donations to the renovation fund. The main sanctuary contains a weird assortment of objects: a stuffed tiger, a miniature mountain, whale baleen, carved elephants, crystal goblets, spears and other weapons of war. Much of the collection is made up of the Marshal's personal possessions. In front of the temple is the tomb itself, surrounded by a low wall and flanked, at the front, by two guardian lions and two lotus buds. The pagoda's attractive roof is best seen from the tomb. **Tomb and Temple of Marshal Le Van Duyet**

Giac Vien Pagoda (Buddha's Complete Enlightenment) can be found at the end of a narrow 200 metre-long dirt road running off Lac Long Quan Street (just after No 247), set among vegetable plots. It is similar in layout, content and inspiration to Giac Lam Pagoda (see below). Visiting just one of the two **Giac Vien Pagoda**

Saigon

pagodas would be enough for most visitors. The Giac Vien Pagoda was built in 1771 and dedicated to the worship of the Emperor Gia Long. Although restored, Giac Vien remains one of the best preserved temples in Vietnam. It is lavishly decorated, with over 100 carvings of various divinities and spirits, dominated by a large gilded image of the Buddha of the Past (Amitabha or *A Di Da* in Vietnamese). It is everything a pagoda should be: demons and gods jump out around every corner, a confusion of fantastic characters. With the smoke and smells, the richness of colour, and the darkness, it assaults the senses. Among the decorations, note the 'Buddha lamp', funerary tablets, and urns with photographs of the deceased.

Giac Lam Pagoda The Giac Lam Pagoda (Forest of Enlightenment) is at 118 Lac Long Quan Street, about two kilometres northeast from Giac Vien Pagoda, through an arch and down a short track about 200 metres from the intersection with Le Dai Hanh Street. Built in 1744, it is the oldest pagoda in Saigon. There is a sacred Bodhi tree in the temple courtyard and the pagoda is set among fruit trees and vegetable plots. Inside Giac Lam it feels, initially, like a rather cluttered private house. In one section, there are rows of funerary tablets with pictures of the deceased; a rather moving display of man's mortality. The main altar is particularly impressive, with layers of Buddhas, dominated by the gilded form of the Buddha of the Past. Note the 49-Buddha oil lamp. The monks are very friendly and will probably offer tea. Some have good English and French as well as detailed knowledge of the history of the pagoda. It is a small haven of peace. An unusual unique feature is the use of blue and white porcelain plates to decorate the roof and some of the small towers in the garden facing the pagoda.

Excursions

Unlike Hanoi which is so rich in sights to visit on a day out the Saigon region is woefully under-endowed (thank goodness the city itself has so much to offer). The Cu Chi Tunnels are the most popular day trip followed closely by an excursion to the Mekong Delta. It is possible to get to the coast and back in a day, Vung Tau, Long Hai and Ho Coc being the obvious candidates. Saigon does, on the other hand, have several out of town sports facilities with three golf courses and the exhilarating Saigon Water Park within an hour's drive.

Cu Chi Tunnels Cu Chi Tunnels are about 40 kilometres northwest of Saigon (see map, page 340). Cu Chi town is on the main road to Tay Ninh and the Cao Dai Cathedral, and both the tunnels and the cathedral can be visited in a single day trip. Dug by the Viet Minh who began work in 1948, they were later expanded by the VC and used for storage, and refuge, and contained sleeping quarters, hospitals and schools. The tunnels are too narrow for most Westerners, but a short section of the 200 kilometres of tunnels has been especially widened to allow tourists to share the experience. Tall or large people might still find it a claustrophobic squeeze. Cu Chi was one of the most fervently Communist of the districts around Saigon and the tunnels were used as the base from which the VC mounted the operations of the Tet Offensive in 1968. Communist cadres were active in this area of rubber plantations, even before the Second World War. Vann and Ramsey, two American soldiers, were to notice the difference between this area and other parts of the south in the early 60s: "No children laughed and shouted for gum and candy in these hamlets. Everyone, adult and child, had a cold look" (Sheehan 1989:539-40). When the

Americans first discovered this underground base on their doorstep they would simply pump CS gas down the tunnel openings and then set explosives. Later, realizing that the tunnels might also yield valuable intelligence, they sent volunteer 'tunnel rats' into the earth to capture prisoners. Cu Chi district was a free fire zone and assaulted with the full battery of ecological warfare. Defoliants were sprayed and 20 tonne Rome Ploughs carved up the area in the search for tunnels. It was said that even a crow flying over Cu Chi district had to carry its own lunch. There are in fact two sets of Cu Chi Tunnels open to visitors. Cu Chi 1 is more 'touristy' and consists largely of reconstructions. Visitors are shown a somewhat antique but nevertheless interesting video and invited to a firing range to try their hand with equally ancient AK47s at a buck a bang. ■ *US$5.* Cu Chi 2 has fewer tourists and more original tunnels. It also has a 'minefield' where visitors have to avoid tripwires. ■ *US$3. Getting there: most visitors reach Cu Chi on a tour or charter a car (about US$20-30 per day, including a visit to Tay Ninh – see below). Regular buses leave for Cu Chi town from the Mien Tay station (Cholon) and the Ham Nghi station; from Cu Chi it is necessary to take a Honda ôm to the tunnels or the infrequent Ben Suc bus. It is also possible to take a motorbike the whole way from Saigon. Go up Cach Mang Thang Tam Street which turns into Highway 22 to Cu Chi.*

Saigon

Day Trips from Saigon

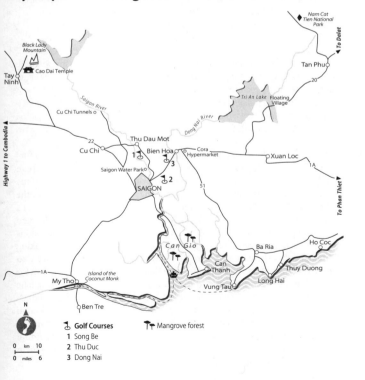

Nam Cat Tien National Park

To Dalat

Black Lady Mountain

Cao Dai Temple

Tay Ninh

Tan Phu

20

Saigon River

Tri An Lake Floating Village

Cu Chi Tunnels

Dong Nai River

Highway 1 to Cambodia

22

Thu Dau Mot

Cu Chi

Bien Hoa Cora Hypermarket

Xuan Loc

1A

Saigon Water Park

SAIGON

51

To Phan Thiet

Can Gio

Ba Ria

Ho Coc

1A

Island of the Coconut Monk

My Tho

Can Thanh

Thuy Duong

Long Hai

Vung Tau

Ben Tre

N

🏌 **Golf Courses**   🌴 Mangrove forest

1 Song Be
2 Thu Duc
3 Dong Nai

0 km 10
0 miles 6

👉 *Rebirth of a forest*

25 kilometres southeast of Saigon, stretching down to the coast, lies the district of Can Gio. A low lying area, it is watered by the silty Saigon River and twice daily washed by the salty tides of the South China Sea. Conditions are ideal for mangrove forest, one of the most diverse and prolific of all woodland types, and the 30,000 hectare forest in Can Gio is no exception. The forest visitors see today is, however, less than 16 years old, having been replanted by Vietnamese forestry workers to replace the dead stumps that remained after the US Air Force defoliated the old mangroves with herbicides, chiefly Agent Orange.

Ho Chi Minh's famous dictum "Rùng là vàng, nêu ta biét bao vê, thi rung rât qúy" (forests are gold, if we know how to protect them we can be rich) was prescient; the great man understood environmental issues long before the 'greens' made them trendy. Happily the Can Gio mangrove swamps reflect the truth of Ho's words proving fertile spawning and nursery grounds for commercially valuable fish and crustacea stocks as well as providing habitat for numerous semi-aquatic and rare species such as otters. The Rhizophora tree species (distinguished by their stilt roots like 'flying buttresses') deliver a sustainable harvest of charcoal, building materials, fruit, edible leaves and tannin when carefully managed.

Vietnamese and international scientists have been impressed by the extent of re-colonization of the forest by wildlife because while new flora species are slow to colonize the fauna has developed apace: otters, crocodiles, kingfishers, storks and many other species have returned and in growing numbers. No scientific enumeration has been completed but preliminary observations look promising.

Given the fantastic achievement this represents it is dismaying that government planners have, to their eternal shame, now decided to turn the mangrove forest into a Special Economic Zone. The proposals for the area sound like the rantings of a mad World Bank economist: 'infrastructure', EZ, EPZ, multi-sectoral lps, sea-port, eco-tourism ...' ie long on jargon and short on coherance. But in a totalitarian society like Vietnam where no opposition is permitted, the media is tightly controlled and there are no genuine people's or environmental movements these government officials wield absolute power. The damage has begun: the central road through the forest is being widened and metalled and bridges are being built to connect the coast with Saigon.

Tay Ninh
Colour map 4, grid B3

Tay Ninh is a town 96 kilometres northwest of Saigon and 64 kilometres further on from Cu Chi town. It can be visited on a day trip from the city and can easily be combined with a visit to the tunnels of Cu Chi. The province of the same name borders Cambodia and, before the 17th century, was part of the Khmer Kingdom. Between 1975 and December 1978, soldiers of Pol Pot's Khmer Rouge periodically attacked villages in this province, killing the men and raping the women. Ostensibly, it was in order to stop these incursions that the Vietnamese army invaded Cambodia on Christmas Day 1978, taking Phnom Penh by January 1979. Tay Ninh town contains the idiosyncratic **Cao Dai Great Temple**, the 'cathedral' of the Cao Dai religion (see page 382 for background on Cao Daism) and is the main reason to visit the town. The cathedral is set within a large complex of schools and administrative buildings, all washed in pastel yellow. The twin-towered cathedral is European in inspiration but with distinct Oriental features. On the façade are figures of Cao Dai saints in high relief, and at the entrance to the Cathedral is a mural depicting Victor Hugo flanked by the Vietnamese poet Nguyen Binh Khiem and the Chinese nationalist Sun Yat Sen. The latter holds an inkstone, symbolizing, strangely, the link between Confucianism and Christianity. Graham Greene in *The Quiet American* called it "The Walt Disney Fantasia of the East". Monsieur Ferry, an acquaintance of Norman Lewis, described the cathedral in even more outlandish terms, saying it "looked like a fantasy from the brain of Disney, and all the faiths of the Orient had been ransacked to create the pompous ritual ...". Lewis himself was clearly unimpressed with the structure and the religion, writing in *A Dragon Apparent* that "This cathedral must be the most outrageously vulgar building ever to have been erected with serious intent".

After removing shoes and hats, women enter the cathedral through a door to the left, men to the right, and they then proceed down their respective aisles towards the altar, usually accompanied by a Cao Dai priest dressed in white with a black turban. During services they don red, blue and yellow robes signifying Confucianism, Taoism and Buddhism respectively. Two rows of pink pillars entwined with green dragons line the nave, leading up to the main altar which supports a large globe on which is painted a single staring eye – the divine, all seeing, eye. The roof is blue and cloud dotted, representing the heavens, and the walls are pierced by open, lattice-work, windows. Ceremonies are held each day at 0600, 1200, 1800 and 2400 and visitors can watch from the cathedral's balcony. **NB** Visitors should not enter the central portion of the nave – keep to the side aisles – and also should not wander in and out during services. If you go in at the beginning of the service you should stay until the end (one hour). Photography is allowed. About 500 metres from the cathedral (turn right when facing the main façade) is the *Doan Ket*, a formal garden.

Tay Ninh also has a good **market** and some **Cham temples** one kilometre to the southwest of the town. ■ *Getting there: a tour, or charter a car in Saigon. Regular buses leave for Tay Ninh, via Cu Chi, from Mien Tay station (two and a half hours) or motorbike.*

Nui Ba Den
Colour map 4, grid B4

Also known as Nui Ba Den Black Lady Mountain is 10 kilometres to the northeast of Tay Ninh and 106 kilometres from Saigon. The peak rises dramatically from the plain to a height of almost 1,000 metres and can be seen in the distance, to the right, on entering Tay Ninh. The Black Lady was a certain Ly-thi Huong who, while her lover was bravely fighting the occupying forces, was ordered to marry the son of a local mandarin. Rather than complying, she threw herself from the mountain. Another version of this story is that she was kidnapped by local scoundrels. A number of shrines to the Black Woman are located on the mountain, and pilgrims still visit the site. Fierce battles were also fought here between the French and Americans, and the Viet Minh. There are excellent views of the surrounding plain from the summit.

Can Gia

This mangrove forest is the green lung of Saigon. Within an hour or two of setting off visitors can be motoring through mile after mile of unspoilt woodland, albeit woods with a difference. For these trees grow in salty water and are inundated by rising tides twice a day (see box *Rebirth of a forest*, above). Within the forest is a monkey sanctuary and a rather poor crocodile farm (both are very hard to find). While not a day out for the kids those of a botanical disposition will find it interesting. There are no beaches, just mud banks and food is likely to be no more than a packet of instant noodles. ■ *Getting there: easiest by motorbike. Go through District 4, past Ho Chi Minh Museum and the port and just go straight. Take a ferry from Nha Be to Binh Khanh and keep driving. After three kilometres it starts getting green. Another ferry crossing awaits at Dan Xay those wishing to go down to the coast. Very muddy in the wet season.*

Bien Hoa A town 26 kilometres north of Saigon, Bien Hoa is on Highway 1. It is the capital of the province of Dong Nai and was established by Chinese migrants on the banks of the Dong Nai River in the late 17th century when the town was known by the name Dong Nai Dai Pho. During the war it was a massive US air base and although there is little to see today there are suggestions that it could replace Tan Son Nhat as Saigon's airport, owing to the latter's cramped site. Paul Theroux in *The Great Railway Bazaar* (Penguin) wrote of Bien Hoa:

> "... out here in the suburbs of Bien Hoa, created by the pressure of American occupation, the roads were falling to pieces and cholera streamed into the backyards. Planning and maintenance characterize even the briefest and most brutish empire; apart from the institution of a legal system there aren't many more imperial virtues. But Americans weren't pledged to maintain. There is Bien Hoa Station, built fifty years ago. It is falling down, but that is not the point. There is no sign that it was ever mended by the Americans; even sagging under its corona of barbed wire it looks a good deal sturdier than the hangars at Bien Hoa airbase."

My Tho My Tho is another town it is quite possible to visit in a day. My Tho is in the Mekong Delta about 70 kilometres from Saigon (see page 296). While My Tho does not represent the rest of the Mekong Delta those for whom time is pressing should consider a day trip to My Tho, for while the journey there is an unexciting trip on the river giving a taste of the huge delta region.

Essentials

Sleeping

All in District 1, Quan 1 – Q1, unless stated otherwise.

■ *on maps*
Price codes: see inside front cover

There is a good choice of reasonable places to stay and many have been renovated in the past couple of years. Saigon's hotel-building spree has run well ahead of even the most optimistic visitor arrival forecasts and has, for the customer, resulted in a very satisfying correction in the balance of market forces; the downward pressure on prices has provided a sharp lesson in applied economics. Hotels which just two years ago were charging US$200 per night are now offering the same room for as little as US$40 to regular business customers.

Central Saigon **L-A+** *Oscar* (formerly *Saigon Century*), 68A Nguyen Hue Blvd, T8231818, F8292732. A/c, satellite TV, friendly staff, excellent buffet lunch, coffee shop, business centre, small health club, hairdresser, disco, central location but somewhat cramped and quite expensive rooms. **L-A+** *Saigon Prince*, 63 Nguyen Hue Blvd, T8222999, F8228748. A/c, satellite TV, health club (but no pool), several restaurants including Japanese. The building itself is a rather ungainly pink giant, quite popular but low occupancy rates, discounts should be negotiable, Chatterbox Restaurant serves popular Sunday brunch 1100-1500, (US$13). **L-A+** *Sofitel Plaza Saigon*, 17 Le Duan St, T8241555, F8241666, E sofitelsgn@hcmc.netnam.vn. One of Saigon's newest hotels, smart, fashionable and comfortable, 300 rooms, roof-top pool and gym, Asian restaurant and coffee shop. **L-A** *Continental*, 132-134, Dong Khoi St, T8299201, F8290936. A/c, built in 1880 and an integral part of the city's history, Graham Greene stayed here and the hotel features in *The Quiet American*. Old journalists' haunt – *Continental Shelf* was "a famous verandah where correspondents, spies, speculators, traffickers, intellectuals and soldiers used to meet during the war to glean information and pick up secret reports, half false, half true or half disclosed. All of this is more than enough for it to be known as Radio Catinat". A delightful enclosed garden, ("I sometimes went there for a late evening drink among the frangipani and hibiscus blossom ...It was the reverse of the frenzy of the war, and a good place to think." wrote war journalist Jon Swain), faded colonial splendour and large rooms – just ripe for the Raffles Group to renovate and run. **L-A** *Norfolk Hotel*, 117 Le Thanh Ton St, T8295368, F8293415. A/c, satellite TV, in a bustling area near Ben Thanh market, business facilities, restaurant

Saigon Centre Detail

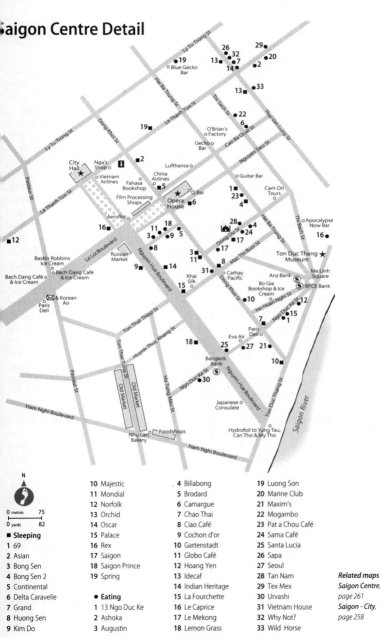

Saigon

and excellent staff, popular with visiting and expat businessmen, especially Australians. **L-A** *Rex*, 141 Nguyen Hue Blvd, T8292185, F8296536. A/c, satellite TV, restaurants, pool, good rooms with famous roof top terrace bar, popular with journalists and upmarket tour groups. **L-A** *Kim Do*, 133 Nguyen Hue Blvd, T8225914, F8225913. Renovated back-packers hotel masquerading as a business hotel, absurd prices, centrality is its only redeeming feature (Saigontourist).

A+-A *Asian*, 146-150 Dong Khoi St, T8296979, F8297433. A/c, satellite TV, restaurant, breakfast included, central, rooms a little small, eclipsed by newer business hotels. **A+-A** *Delta Caravelle*, 19-23 Lam Son Square, T8234999, F8243999. A/c, satellite TV, central, recently reopened with a huge 20 storey tower it has already established itself as one of Saigon's top hotels, it does a fantastic buffet lunch and dinner and *Saigon Saigon*, a roof top bar, draws the crowds until the early hours of the morning. Recommended. **A+-A** *Bong Sen*, 117-123 Dong Khoi St, T8291516, F8298076, E bongsen@hcm.vnn.vn. Newly enlarged (136 rooms) and upgraded hotel with decent business facilities. A Saigon-tourist property, but considered to be well run, a/c, restaurant, price includes breakfast, central, expect massive discounts. **A+-A** *Majestic*, 1 Dong Khoi St, T8295517, 8228750 (reservations), F8295510. Built in 1925 the hotel has character and charm and has been tastefully restored. A/c, satellite TV, price includes breakfast; restaurant, small kidney shaped pool, more expensive and large rooms have superb views over the river (pool view and quieter at the back), from the bar on the top floor there are magnificent views of the river-front, especially at night. **A+-B** *Grand*, 8 Dong Khoi St, T8230163, F8235781. A/c, satellite TV. Newly emerged from extensive renovation, happily the stained glass and marble staircase have largely survived the process. Lovely pool and a very reasonably priced restaurant. **A** *Orchid*, 29A Thai Van Lung St, T8231809, F8292245. A/c, satellite TV, central, surrounded by restaurants and bars, a former tour group hotel now badly in need of renovation. **A-B** *Embassy*, 35 Nguyen Trung Truc St, T8231981, F8231978. Rather unappealing lobby area but quite comfortable rooms, newly found favour with tour groups, moderately efficient. **A-B** *Huong Sen*, 66-70 Dong Khoi St, T8291415, F8290916. A/c, popular with tour groups. **A-B** *Palace*, 56-64 Nguyen Hue Blvd, T8292860, F8244230. Newly expanded government-run hotel with some decent sized rooms in the old part. A/c, central, restaurant, small roof top pool, dancing, price includes breakfast. **A-B** *Spring*, 44-46 Le Thanh Ton St, T8297362, F8221383. Central, comfortable, charming and helpful staff, book well in advance if you want to stay in this well-run family hotel, excellent value, breakfast includes. Recommended.

B *Bong Sen 2*, 61-63 Hai Ba Trung St, T8235818, F8235816. A/c, restaurant, well managed, price includes breakfast. **B** *Mogambo*, 20 Thi Sach St, T8251311, F8226031. A/c, satellite TV, a few good rooms above this popular bar-diner. **B** *Mondial*, 109 Dong Khoi St, T8296291, F8296273. A/c, roof restaurant, well managed, price includes breakfast, good value for downtown. **B-C** *Saigon*, 45-47 Dong Du St, T8299734, F8291466. Some a/c, central, some rooms a bit dark and small, popular, clean and good value. **C-D** *Khach San 69*, 69 Hai Ba Trung St, T8291513, F8258903. Some a/c, backs on to Saigon's Indian mosque, clean rooms, fairly priced.

Borders of central Saigon These hotels are a little out of the centre – a 10-30 minute walk or short taxi ride. **L-A+** *Omni Saigon*, 251 Nguyen Van Troi St, Q Phu Nhuan, T8449222, F8449200. A/c, satellite TV, pool, health club, presidential suite, restaurants, the popular R & R Bar, full business facilities, a highly rated hair-dresser, dry-cleaning service, but inconvenient for town: a courtesy shuttle connects with town centre. **L-A** *Equatorial*, 242 Tran Binh Trong St, Q5, T8390000, F8390011, E eghcmc@hcm.vnn.vn. A/c, satellite TV, a marble-cool oasis of calm with charming staff; large and lovely pool, well equipped gym, Japanese, Chinese and Western restaurants, a bakery and the largest ball-room in

Vietnam, offers the keenest deals both for weekend packages, short stay, long stay and office accommodation, try here first. Highly recommended but not much on the doorstep. **L-A** *New World*, 76 Le Lai St, T8228888, F8230710. A/c, satellite TV, large attractive pool and gym, business facilities, Chinese and Western restaurants, popular among visiting Asian businessmen; patisserie and bakery, dry cleaning service, night club and all the features one would expect of a good international, 4 star hotel. Currently offering large discounts.

A+ *Sol Chancery Saigon*, 196 Nguyen Thi Minh Khai St, Q3, T8299152, F8251464. A/c, satellite TV, overlooks Lao Dong Sports Club, all the rooms are suites, comfortable, good service, popular. **A+** *Windsor Saigon*, 193 Tran Hung Dao Blvd, T8367848, F8367889. High quality finish, a/c, satellite TV, suites and studios, gym, restaurant, business facilities and the Gourmet Royale, a first class delicatessen selling bread, pies, cheese, ham, sausages, sandwiches and other goodies. **A+-A** *Mercury*, 79 Tran Hung Dao Blvd, T8242525, F8242602. A/c, satellite TV, originally built as a cinema and now a hotel with welcoming, friendly staff, plus a rooftop barbecue restaurant and the famed Gossip nightclub. **A+-A** *Saigon Star*, 204 Nguyen Thi Minh Khai St, Q3, T8230260, F8230255. A/c, satellite TV, business centre and secretarial facilities, a friendly, well run hotel. **A-B** *International*, 19 Vo Van Tan St, Q3, T8290009, F8290066. A/c, satellite TV, comfortable and elegant, Chinese seafood restaurant and noodle shop, business centre, breakfast included.

B *Liberty* (*Que Huong*), 167 Hai Ba Trung St, Q3, T8294227, F8290919. A/c, popular restaurant, decent enough rooms but a little pricy for what it offers. **B** *Nha Khach Bo Giao Duc*, 3 Cong Truong Quoc Te, T8258628, F8242066, university guesthouse located behind university building (Vien Dai Hoc).

C-D *Architecture Guesthouse*, 134 Nguyen Dinh Chieu St, T8225583. Some huge rooms, a/c, quiet.

D *Khach San Ga Saigon* (*Station Hotel*), 1 Nguyen Thong St, T8436189. Overlooks the railway station, noisy area, rather run down. **D** *Huong*, 46 Le Thi Rieng St, T8322452, F8298540. Friendly, helpful French educated owner, comfortable. **D-F** *Miss Loi's Guesthouse*, 178/20 Co Giang St, T8367973. Cheap and cheerful, well kept, some a/c, breakfast included, popular. Recommended.

Most backpackers head straight for this bustling district, a 10-15 minute walk from downtown. There are countless hotels, guesthouses and rooms to rent which open and close and change name or owner with remarkable speed. Shared rooms can be had for as little as US$4-5 per night and dormitory rooms for less but facilities and comfort levels at the bottom end are very basic. The area is littered with restaurants, cafés, email services, tour agencies and money changers, all fiercely competitive; there are mini-supermarkets and shops selling rucksacks, footwear, CDs and ethnic knick-knacks. The concentration of services means the area is popular with younger expats as well as with tourists.

Pham Ngu Lao Area

A+-A *Que Huong (Liberty 4)*, 265 Pham Ngu Lao St, T8365822, F8365435. Formerly Hoang Vu, well renovated but priced way too high for this area. **A-B** *Vien Dong*, 275A Pham Ngu Lao St, T8368941, F8368812. Refurbished, marble clad lobby which in no way justifies these room rates, popular Cheers disco and the little visited but decent (if pricey) Omar Khyyam Indian restaurant.

Saigon

B *Dai Hoang Long* (*Giant Dragon*), 173 Pham Ngu Lao St, T8369268, F8367279. With a small ground floor area but soaring many stories into the air this type of building is sometimes known as a rocket building, we shall no doubt know in a few years whether they skimped on the cement. **B-D** *Le Le 1*, 171 Pham Ngu Lao St, T8368686, F8368787. Small rooms and rather pricey.

C-D *Hong Hoa*, 185/28 Pham Ngu Lao St, T836 1915, E honhoarr@hcm.vnn.vn. A well run family hotel of 7 rooms, all a/c, hot water and private bathroom, 3 rooms have bathtubs. Conveniently the downstairs has banks of email terminals and a supermarket. **C-D** *Huong*, 40/19 Bui Vien St, T8369158. A/c and hot water, private bathrooms. **C-D** *Le Le 2*, 269 De Tham St, T8368585, F8368787. Fan, some a/c. **C-D** *Mimi Guesthouse*, 40/5 Bui Vien St, T8369645. 6 rooms with private bathroom, a/c and hot water. **C-D** *Yen Nhi*, 283/24 Pham Ngu Lao St, T/F8367232. Hot water, bath tubs, a/c, friendly, clean, English speaking hotel.

D *Linh*, 40/10 Bui Vien St, T/F8369641, E linh.hb@hcm.vnn.vn. A well priced, clean, friendly, family-run hotel with a/c and hot water. Attracts some longer-staying guests. **D** *Ngoc Dang*, 254 De Tham St. Clean friendly and pleasant, some a/c. **D** *Linh Thu Guesthouse*, 72 Bui Vien St, T8368421. Fan and bathroom, some a/c. **D** *Phuong Lan Guesthouse*, 70 Bui Vien St, T/F8369569. Fan, 2 shared bathrooms for 7 guest rooms, some a/c. **D-E** *211*, 211 Pham Ngu Lao St, T8367353, F8361883. Some a/c, clean, roof top terrace. **D-E** *Minh Chau*, 75 Bui Vien St, T8367588. Some a/c, hot water and private bathrooms, spotlessly clean, run by two sisters it has been recommended by lone women travellers. **D-E** *Tan Thanh Thanh*, 205 Pham Ngu Lao St, T8367027, F8371238. A/c, fan, some dorm accommodation, roof top bar and 'grill', best stick to the beer and enjoy the breeze. **D-E** *Thanh Huyen*, 175/1 Pham Ngu Lao St, T8368435, 3 rooms (1 a/c, 2 fan) above a small eatery, clean and, being off the main drag, quiet. **D-E** *Que Huong (Liberty 3)*, 187 Pham Ngu Lao St, T8369522, F8364557. Now less popular with travellers as there is more choice, cheapest on the upper floors, rather noisy.

Pham Ngu Lao Area

N	7 Liberty 4	17 Vien Dong
Not to scale	8 Linh Thu	18 Yen Nhi
	9 Lucy	19 211
■ **Sleeping**	10 Mimi	
Related maps	11 Minh Chau	● **Eating**
Saigon Centre, 1 Giant Dragon	12 Ngoc Dang	1 Bodhi Tree
page 261 2 Huong	13 Phuong Lan	(Vegetarian)
3 Hong Hoa	14 Tan Thanh Thanh	2 Back packer bar
Saigon - City, 4 Le Le 1	15 Thai Binh	3 Café Van
page 258 5 Le Le 2	16 Thanh Huyen &	4 Cappuccino
6 Liberty 3	Margherita restaurant	

5 Kim Café & Booking Office
6 Long Phi Bar & Chez Papa
7 Lucky Café
8 Saigon Café
9 Shanti
10 Sinh Café & Booking Office
11 Zen (Vegetarian)
12 333

Saigon

E *Thai Binh*, 325 Pham Ngu Lao St, T8369544, basic old building, fans only, cold water. Those intending to stay a month more might consider the funished apartments of *Lucy Hotel*, 61 Do Quang Dau St, T8368285, F8367281, US$450 per month – negotiable.

Few people stay in Cholon, but it does have the best pagodas in Saigon and is only a short cyclo ride from the centre of town. **A** *Arc en Ciel* (*Thien Hong*), 52-56 Tan Da St, Q5, T8552869, F8550332. A/c, restaurant, best in Cholon with roof top bar, price includes breakfast.

Cholon

D *Phuong Hoang* (*Phénix*), 411 Tran Hung Dao St (entrance is down a side street), T8556599. Cheap but rather dingy, a/c.

These hotels are located several kilometres northwest of the city centre. Prices tend to be marginally more competitive as a result.

Near airport

A+-A *Garden Plaza*, 309 Nguyen Van Troi St, Q Tan Binh, T8421111, F8424370. Comfortable, well-run, business oriented hotel just a stone's throw from the airport. Popular bar and excellent buffet lunch. **A+-A** *Saigon Lodge*, 215 Nam Ky Khoi Nghia St, Q3, T8230112, F8251070. Geared to the needs of Malay businessmen, halal food, Karaoke etc. **A-B** *De Nhat (formerly Chains First Hotel)*, 18 Hoang Viet St, Q Tan Binh, T8441199, F8444282. A/c, Wing A old and cheaper Wing B new and pricier, free airport pickup and downtown shuttle, tennis court, business services. **B** *Cosevina*, 311 Nguyen Van Troi St, Q Phu Nhuan, T8442088, F8445898. A/c, comfortable with good restaurant. **B** *Orient*, 261 Hoang Van Thu St, Q Phu Nhuan, T8441322, F8444809. Functional and fairly priced, perfectly good for a night, breakfast included. **B-C** *Airport*, 108 Hong Ha St, Q Tan Binh, T8445761, F8440166. Closest to the airport and reasonable value. Just 100 metres east a café sits beneath the wings of a grounded Boeing 707.

Eating

Saigon has a rich culinary tradition. You could quite easily eat a different national cuisine every night for several weeks. There is everything from the starchy expense account restaurant to wayside cafés. Pham Ngu Lao, the backpackers' area, is chock-a-block with low cost restaurants many of which are just as good as the more expensive places elsewhere. Do not overlook street-side stalls whose staples consist of *pho* (noodle soup), *bánh xeo* (savoury pancakes), *cha giò* (spring rolls) and baguettes stuffed with pâté and salad (*banh mi pate*) – usually fresh and very cheap; *binh dân* (popular) street restaurants where food is set out on a counter – simply point to what you want – are frequented by shop and office workers at lunch time and provide excellent value and normally good food.

● *on maps*

Expensive *Mandarin*, 11A Ngo Van Nam St, T8229783. One of the finest Vietnamese restaurants in Saigon. Elegant decor, exquisite service and delicious food. Two can have a truly enjoyable evening out for the US$25 mark.

Vietnamese

Mid-range *Blue Ginger (Saigon Times Club)*, 37 Nam Ky Khoi Nghia St, T8298676. Delicious food, courteous and discrete service, dine indoors or in a small courtyard, menu includes *cha ca Hanoi*. Recommended. *Com Nieu Saigon*, 6C Tu Xuong St, Q3, T8203188. Well known for the theatricals which accompany the serving of the speciality baked rice. One waiter smashes the earthenware pot before tossing the contents across the room to his nimble fingered colleague standing by your table. Deserves attention for its excellent food and a good selection of soups. Four can eat well for

US$12. *Lemon Grass*, 4 Nguyen Thiep St, T8220496. Good food attractively served, set lunch menu is good value, popular with tourists wishing to sample typical Vietnamese food, convenient location in the heart of town. *Tan Nam*, 60-62 Dong Du St, T8298634. Another popular and central restaurant serving national dishes from an extensive menu. *Tib*, 187 Hai Ba Trung St, Q3, T8297242. Quiet, good service, extensive menu which includes a good selection of Hué specialities, nice for Sunday lunch, which for two costs around US$10. *Vietnam House*, 93-95 Dong Khoi St, T8291623. Attractively restored building, waiters and waitresses wear traditional Vietnamese costume and traditional music is played on an array of exotic instruments, excellent food. Recommended. *VY*, 164 Pasteur St, T8296210. Indoor and open-air sections, attractive ambience and first class Vietnamese food. *Cha Ca Hanoi*, 5A Tran Nhat Duat, T8444240. A little way out of town beyond Tan Dinh Market, now in a new modern and characterless building but still serving same excellent dish *cha ca Hanoi*. Small cubes of boneless, white fish fried in a mildly spicy sauce at the table on a charcoal burner; flavoured with dill and spring onions and eaten with rice noodles, green leaves and peanuts, a glorious fusion of flavours, circa US$6 for two but unpriced menu and an unattractive tendency to rook foreigners on the drinks. *Givral*, 169 Dong Khoi. Café, patisserie and convenient snacks and drinks in the city centre. *13 Ngo Duc Ke*. Fresh, well cooked, honest Vietnamese fare, chicken in lemon grass (no skin no bone) is a great fave and the beef (*bo luc lac*) melts in the mouth. Open 0600-2300, popular with locals, expats and travellers alike, eat out on the pavement or indoors (a/c and one of the few places in Saigon without music). *Quan An Hue*, 7/1 Ky Dong, Q3, T8445934. Hué specialities. Work your way down the list sampling the many delicate dishes. Each dish is cheap but multiplied by the number of diners the cost rises more quickly than you might expect. *Thanh Nien*, 11 Nguyen Van Chiem St. Popular with young Vietnamese, indoor and outdoor seating, excellent Vietnamese cooking, live music, attached is *Kem Y* (Italian ice cream café). *Restaurant 95*, 95 Dinh Tien Hoang St, crab specialities: fried noodles, crab soup and spring rolls, small, scruffy room, delicious food but over-priced; (numbers 94 and 96 also specialize in noodles and seafood).

Cheap *Giac Duc*, 492 Nguyen Dinh Chieu St, Q3. Vietnamese vegetarian restaurant. *Luong Son*, aka *Bo Tuong Xeo*, 31 Ly Tu Trong St. Noisy, smoky and chaotic, usually packed, specializes in bo tung xeo (sliced beef barbecued at the table served with mustard sauce – the name also refers to a gruesome torture, ask Vietnamese friends for details). The beef, barbecued squid and other delicacies are truly superb, two people will eat and drink well for US$8. Recommended. *Hoang Yen*, 5-9 Ngo Duc Ke St. Utterly plain setting and decor but absolutely fabulous Vietnamese dishes, as the throngs of local lunchtime customers testify, soups and chicken dishes are ravishing, you cannot go wrong at US$3-4 per head. *Ngu Binh*, 82 Cu Xa Nguyen Van Troi St, Q Phu Nhuan. Specializes in Hué dishes and closes early, simple and stylish setting, just north of Nguyen Van Troi bridge on the airport road. *May Bon Phuong*, 335/5 Dien Bien Phu St, Q3. Tucked away between Dien Bien Phu and Nguyen Dinh Chieu sts, closed Tues, outstanding fish salad, popular with Vietnamese, a little rough and ready but good value. *Tinh Tam Trai*, 170A Vo Thi Sau St, Q3. Another inexpensive and good little vegetarian restaurant. *Pho Hoa Pasteur*, 260C Pasteur St. Probably the best known of all *pho* restaurants, costs more than average but it serves good *pho* and is usually packed. *Pho Hung*, 46 Mac Dinh Chi St. Another highly recommended pho outlet. *Kem Bach Dang*, 26-28 Le Loi St, on opposite corners with Pasteur St. A very popular café serving fruit juice, shakes and ice cream. Try the coconut ice cream (kem dua) served in a coconut.

Seafood In *Thi Sach St* numerous restaurants specializing in seafood spill out on to the pavement, expect spirited neighbours ploughing their way through a case of Heineken. One restaurant owner enthused 'customers are impressed because they see these fresh animals which minutes ago were swimming in water'. For some reason most of the restaurants are named after trees, look out for Mango or *Cay Xoai*. **Minh Thanh**, 2 Ham Tu St, just west of the junction with Nguyen Van Cu St, Q5. Half way to Cholon this is not an easy restaurant to find. Very rough and ready, plastic chairs and stools but reckoned by some to have the most succulent crab and prawn.

Saigon, it is said, has the cheapest Japanese food in the world. Unable to verify the truth of that claim we would certainly testify to the excellence of Saigon's Japanese restaurants. Long may the Japanese salaryman live away from home. The city's Chinese population is concentrated in Cholon and a cruise of District 5 will reveal a number of good Chinese eating houses. **Other Asian**

Expensive *Nanbantei*, 37 Nguyen Trung Truc St, T8298071. Yakitori-style food. *Ritz Taiwanese*, 333 Tran Hung Dao St, T8324325. Superb Chinese food with specialities from this off-shore republic, but jolly expensive, not hard for four to notch up a bill for US$100. *Chao Thai*, 16 Thai Van Lung St, T8241457. Probably the best Thai fare in town. Attractive setting. Rates as the priciest Thai in town, a decent spread for two could easily cost US$30. *Dynasty* (New World Hotel), 76 Le Lai St, T8228888. A long Chinese menu, excellent lunchtime dim sun. *Ohan*, 71-73 Pasteur St, T8244896. Japanese, decent sized portions, welcoming atmosphere, popular with Japanese. A huge lunch will set you back US$40 for two. *Sawaddee*, 29B Thai Van Lung St, T8221402. Good Thai food at a fair price. For those in need of a fix of tom yam and green curry. Form reports suggest irregular quality, however. *Seoul*, 35 Ngo Duc Ke St, T8294297. Good Korean food, extensive menu, popular with Saigon's dwindling Korean business fraternity. *Tandoor*, 103 Vo Van Tan St, T8244839. Another popular Northern Indian restaurant. Delivery service.

Mid-range *ABC*, 172 Nguyen Dinh Chieu St, Q3, T8230388. Nightime refuge for those in need of solid Chinese fare (excellent fried noodles for around US$4 a plate). Stays open until 0300 and serves as a clearing house for girls not yet fixed up with a partner for the night. *Ashoka*, 17A/10 Le Thanh Ton St, T8231372. Has collapsed in the face of stiff competition. Expensive and poor quality. *Indian Heritage* over the road is far better. *Indian Heritage*, 12 Thai Van Lung St, T8234687. Our favourite Indian. Long menu includes Tandoori dishes. Excellent quality, charming service and fair prices. Lunchtime buffet at US$5 is good value. Recommended.

Cheap *Mosque*, 66 Dong Du St, opposite Saigon Hotel. Walk around to the back of the mosque (infidels, women and shoes permitted) superb vegetarian and meat curries and stuffed bread, lunch only, especially popular on Fridays, get there by 1200.

Expensive *Le Bordeaux*, F7-F8 D2 St, Cu Xa Van Thanh Bac, Q Binh Thanh, T8999831. If you can find it you are in for a treat. Lovely décor and warm atmosphere, receives the highest accolades for its French cuisine, expect to pay at least US$60 for two if drinking wine. *Le Caprice*, 15th Floor, Landmark Building, 5B Ton Duc Thang St, T8228337. Lovely views over the river, very expensive and thought to be a little starchy, generates more complaints than compliments, at these prices you would not expect the cheese to be served in horrid plastic packages. The rooftop bar is well worth a visit, however. *Camargue*, 16 Cao Ba Quat St, T8243148, corner of Thi Sach St. Unsigned, large French villa, lovely open-air terrace, *chic*, consistently excellent food, several bars and pool tables, dinner for two with wine won't come for much less than US$60. *Maxim's*, 13-17 Dong Khoi St, T8225554. Massive menu; the food receives mixed reviews but the floorshows are widely acclaimed. *Sandro*, 142 Vo Thi Sau St, T8203552. Authentic Italian. Its fans rave about it but we cannot see what the fuss is about, especially at these prices. **International**

Saigon

Mid-range *Le Mekong*, 57 Dong Du St, T8295047. Now in its third location, this time in the centre of town, excellent French cuisine. *A*, 361/8 Nguyen Dinh Chieu St, Q3, T8359190. Russian restaurant run by a Russo-Vietnamese family, 2 private rooms and a lower price lunchtime menu. *Annie's Pizzas*, 21 Bui Thi Xuan St, T8392577. Great pizzas, eat in, take away or home delivery, much improved delivery service. *Augustin*, 10 Nguyen Thiep St (between Dong Khoi St & Nguyen Hue Blvd), T8292941. Fairly priced and some of the best, unstuffy French cooking in Saigon; tables pretty closely packed, congenial atmosphere. Recommended. *Bavaria*, 20 Le Anh Xuan St, T8222673. Near New World Hotel, large German portions. *Billabong and Café Latin*, 25 Dong Du St, T8226363. Spanish tapas bar with French restaurant above, attracts the young expat trendies. *Brodard*, 131 Dong Khoi St, T8223966. Decades old international restaurant run in the old style. Good meals at a decent price. Bang in the centre. *Gartenstadt*, 34 Dong Khoi St, T8223623. Inviting menu, plates of wurst, rosti, spatzli, sauerkraut and draught German beer. Two can add pounds of lard for US$15 (beer extra). *Globo Café*, 6 Nguyen Thiep St, T8228855. Emphasis on design: the cocktails and glittering clientele are more impressive than the food. *La Bibliothèque* (aka *Madame Dai's*), 84A Nguyen Du St, T8231438. French. Madame Dai was a member of the National Assembly of the former régime and a lawyer: customers eat in her study surrounded by law tomes, rather pretentious. It is either packed with tour groups or deserted but nevertheless serves a valuable function by reminding us how much better Saigon's restaurants have become. As recently as the late 80s and early 90s dinner at Madam Dai's was a real treat; now, however, the humblest café in Pham Ngu Lao serves steak and chips that's just as good and a fraction the price. *La Fourchette*, 9 Ngo Duc Ke St, T8298143. A truly excellent and authentic little French bistrot. Warm welcome, well prepared dishes, generous portions, local steak as tender as any import, fairly priced (an extravagent dinner for two need cost no more than US$20 excluding wine), booking advised. Recommended. *Marine Club*, 17A4 Le Thanh Ton St, T8292249. Louche nightspot, *Cabaret*-like atmosphere, sizzling cocktails and good food (especially the pizzas), popular with racy young ex-pats. *Mogambo*, 20 bis Thi Sach St, T8251311. Bar and restaurant, serves up excellent burgers, steaks, pies and fries but not the tarts that are such a popular feature of Mogambo's in Manila. *Port Orient*, Delta Caravelle Hotel, Lam Son Square, T8234999. Buffet lunch and dinner. Japanese sushi, Chinese dim sun, seafood, a range of hot dishes, cheeses and puddings galore. Weekends are especially extravagant. Wildly popular particularly as wine is currently included in the modest price of US$15, cannot do better. *Restaurant 180*, 180 Nguyen Van Thu St, T8251673. Ambitious European and Asian menu, large portions and excellent food, perennial favourite. *Rex Hotel*, 141 Nguyen Hue Blvd, T8292185. 5th floor restaurant and terrace bar, Western and Vietnamese food is quite good, service notoriously slow, drink prices absurdly high. *Santa Lucia*, 14 Nguyen Hue Blvd, T8226562. One of the best Italian restaurants in Saigon, pleasing Italian décor and style, excellent food and service. *Tex-Mex*, 24 Le Thanh Ton St, T8295950. American and Mexican specialities, a friendly and well run bar with pool tables, a great place to watch rugby, football or other international sporting highlights (especially if the French are losing). Independent research proves its waitresses do have the shortest skirts in town. *Thien Nam*, 53 Nam Ky Khoi Nghia St, T8223634. Was popular with US servicemen in the 60's, its décor remains largely unaltered, a Chinese, a Vietnamese and a Western menu. Fantastic cauliflower cheese – just when you least expected it. *Why Not?*, 24 Thai Van Lung St, T8226138. French bistro-type restaurant with character, fine French cooking and a charming welcome in the appealing shape of Miss Thu Anh. The daily menu offers unparalleled value, 3 courses for around US$6. A la carte one is spoilt for choice. Evenings tend to be quieter but the bar downstairs is intimate and an increasingly popular venue. *Wild Horse Saloon*, 8A1/2D1 Thai Van Lung St, T8251901. With its rustic exterior this bar-cum-diner would look more at home in Wyoming than in a Saigon street. Friendly and attentive service from Vietnamese cowgirls and squaws, a long menu, often with special promotions. Excellent roasts for Sunday lunch. Recommended. *Ciao Café*, 72 Nguyen Hue Blvd, T8251203. Corner with Nguyen Thiep St, ice creams, pasta, fruit juice, coffee, popular rendezvous.

Cheap *Chez Guido*, T8983747. An excellent delivery service specializing in Italian (fab pizzas, excellent pasta) and with much more besides, quick, efficient and very good value for money, perfect for a monsoon night with a few beers and a video. *Hoa Vien*, 30 Mac Dinh Chi St, T8258605. An amazing and vast Czech restaurant, usually packed. No doubt chiefly on account of the draught Pilsner Urquell but the unusual menu makes a change. *Sapa*, 26 Thai Van Lung St, T8295754. New owner seems to have lost the plot, but still features Swiss dishes, including rösti, on its menu. *Idecaf*, 31 Thai Van Lung St, T8258465. Excellent little French café, part of the French Cutural Institute, eat in or out, good food, fairly priced, check out the French films being screened.

Cheap *Cay Bo De* (*Bodhi Tree*), 175/6 Pham Ngu Lao St. Saigon's most popular vegetarian eatery in the heart of backpacker land, excellent food and amazing prices. Mexican pancake, vegetable curry, rice in coconut and braised mushrooms are classics. It is struggle to spend US$2 per head. Recommended. *Zen*, 175/18 Pham Ngu Lao St, another popular vegetarian restaurant nearby. *Margherita*, 175/1, Pham Ngu Lao St, is opposite Bodhi Tree and serves good Italian fare at tremendous price. *Cappuccino*, 258 De Tham St, T8371467. Excellent range of well prepared Italian food at sensible prices, US$2 for a good pizza, same for pasta dishes. *Chez Papa*, 163 Pham Ngu Lao St, T8369319. Small and quiet French restaurant above the busy Long Phi Bar, limited menu but good food at fair prices, US$15 for two excluding wine. *Café Van*, 169B De Tham St, T8360636. A good little sandwich bar which also does free deliveries, try BLT or chicken curry baguette, also baked potatoes with chilli-con-carné and other tempting fillings. Well worth popping in for a drink and a bite and a chat with the English owner whose experience and knowledge of travel in Vietnam is unrivalled (assuming he's not in Sapa). *Lucky*, 224 De Tham St. Italian food (Japanese upstairs), bar and good breakfasts. *Kim Café*, 268 De Tham St. Wide range of food, open from early till late, popular with travellers and expats. At US$2, Peter's breakfast is the best, cheapest and lardiest breakfast in the country, it would fuel a trooper for a day. *Sinh Café*, 246-248 De Tham St. Good value food and drink all day.

Pham Ngu Lao Area

Anh Thu, 49 Dinh Cong Trang St, and numerous other stalls nearby on the south side of Tan Dinh market serve excellent *cha gio*, *banh xeo*, *bi cuon* and other Vietnamese street food. *Nguyen Trai St* (extreme east end of, by the *New World Hotel* roundabout) late night pho can be had from the stalls in this area. *Tran Cao Van St*, east of Cong Truong Quoc Te, Q3, the restaurants and stalls here serve delicious noodles of all kinds, especially noodle soup with duck (*my vit*). *362-376*, Hai Ba Trung St, just north of Tan Dinh market. Everyone has their favourite but these restaurants serve excellent chicken rice (*com ga*), 381, *Hong Phat* is particularly good. All charge just over US$2.00 for steamed chicken and rice (*com gà hap*) with soup. *Thinh Phat*, 177 Vo Van Tan St, Q3, also does good chicken rice.

Foodstalls

The major hotels all have gourmet shops selling bread and pastries: Equatorial, Omni, New World and Windsor are all good.

Bakeries

Nhu Lan, 66-68 Ham Nghi St. If there are more delicious baguettes than these we should like to know where. Churns out freshly baked bread until 2200. *Paris Deli*, 31 Dong Khoi St, T8297533 and Saigon Centre, 65 Le Loi St, T8216127. Bread, sandwiches and patisserie, eat in café or have delivered. *Saigon Bakery*, 281c Hai Ba Trung St, Q3 (just north of Vo Thi Sau St). Delicious selection of doughnuts, tarts, bread rolls, mini

Saigon

quiches and other tempting savouries. *Sama*, 35 Dong Khoi St is well known for its sandwiches. *Brodard*, 11 Nguyen Thiep St its cakes are a little too sweet and gooey for European tastes, as are those at *Givral*, 169 Dong Khoi St, although they look superb.

Bars Along with the influx of foreigners and the freeing up of Vietnamese society has come a rapid increase in the number of bars in Saigon and they cater to just about all tastes – drink, music and company-wise. At one time hotel bars were just about the only safe and legal place for foreigners to drink but now they are beginning to look much the same as hotel bars the world over. The roof-top bar at the *Rex Hotel* is an exception, it has strange fish tanks, song birds, topiary, good views, cooling breeze, snacks and meals – and a link with history; sadly it suffers chronic *Saigon Touristiensis*, massive overcharging syndrome. *R & R*, at the *Omni Hotel*, Nguyen Van Troi St, with its 60s theme and girls around the pool table generates a happy mood.

Countless bars have opened and countless bars have closed since the first edition of this book, but of those remaining two stand out: ***Apocalypse Now*** and ***Q Bar***. But painful as it is for us to admit it *Apocalypse Now*, 2C Thi Sach St, is not what it was. No longer cheap and the music is repetitive. Expats tend to go elsewhere most nights leaving crowds of tourists in search of a legend. But on a good night there are few places that generate quite so much steam.

The most sophisticated of Saigon's bars was ***Q Bar***, 7 Lam Son Square, T8291299, under the Opera House. The sophisticated, intelligent, witty, rich, handsome, cute, curvaceous, camp, glittering and famous are welcome; unwashed *tay ba lo* trying to eke out a bottle of BGI for the evening are not. Striking decor and Caravaggio murals, haunt of a wide cross-section of Saigon society, open till the small hours. Closed for 'renovation' the Vietnamese government is currently preventing the owners from re-entering the country. Directly opposite is the towering form of the Delta Caravelle Hotel which is home to the popular *Saigon Saigon* (10th floor). Saigon Saigon is breezy and cool, it has large comfortable chairs in which to loll and has superb views. Strongly recommended for a glimpse into a more civilized and better past. Not far away, at 74 Hai Ba Trung St is ***Gecko Bar*** which purveys, among other things, chocolate vodka. Like all of Saigon's bars its popularity waxes and wanes but it has a hard core of loyal fans. Gecko is home to Saigon's rugby football teams. Towards the river is ***Guitar Bar***, 62 Hai Ba Trung St, T8222166. Quite a scenic spot in which to waste a few hours, an excellent Vietnamese band plays 60's classics occasionally. A couple of hundred yards north up Hai Ba Trung St is the admirably run ***O'Brien's Factory*** (formerly Bernie's), T8293198, which also does excellent food, especially pizzas. Around the corner is ***Blue Gecko*** at 31 Ly Tu Trong St, T8243483. It has a pool table and usually a friendly crowd, a decent band plays at weekends. ***Bar No 5***, 5 Ly Tu Trong St, T8256300, is a nicely converted building, attracts an interesting selection of expats and with its engaging bar girls and excellent comfort food is well worth looking in.

The Pham Ngu Lao area has a large number of reasonably priced bars, most have pool tables: ***Long Phi***, 163 Pham Ngu Lao St, pool, is one of the best, popular with expats who prefer Pham Ngu Lao prices. ***Rolling Stone***, 177 Pham Ngu Lao and ***Saigon Café*** on the corner of De Tham St attract a good number.

A characteristic feature of Vietnamese nightlife is *bia om*, dimly-lit bars with young female hostesses to entertain clients: this they do by rehearsing their English, or at least certain well-worn phrases, and general flirtatiousness. The girls expect to be bought drinks and should be tipped. Bia om bars spring up like mushrooms and survive until the police close them down and arrest the girls; a number are to be found in Hai Ba Trung St, notably ***Monkey Bar***, at 97 (formerly Linda's Pub), and a clutch of others around 74 Hai Ba Trung St.

AIDS in Vietnam

Like the other countries of Southeast Asia, Vietnam is thought to have the potential for 'rapid increase' in the HIV/AIDS epidemic. As of the end of June 1994 there were 106 reported AIDS cases in Vietnam, and 9 percent of intravenous drug users were HIV-infected in 1993. This comparatively low level of infection probably reflects the absence of research, rather than the absence of a problem. It is thought that the epidemic will soon (if it has not done so already) cross over from the drug-using population into the heterosexual population, and has the potential of becoming almost as serious a problem as it currently is in Thailand.

The government has launched a visible but somewhat ineffective campaign against AIDS. AIDS is always referred to in Vietnam by its French name SIDA which Vietnamese pronounce with a rather sinister hissing sound. But bowing to pressure from the similarly acronymed Swedish International Development Agency, which has been very generous to Vietnam, the government adopted the more international sounding AIDS, a word which few Vietnamese can pronounce.

Star of the SIDA campaign, appearing on countless posters, is the durian fruit. With its putrid smell and perilous spikes the analogy between durian and the HIV virus was presumably considered obvious to all and sufficient warning to Vietnamese youth – while still within the strict limits of decency set by the Cultural Checking and Information Department. Inevitably, the hapless durian is now dubbed trai SIDA, the AIDS fruit.

The ineffectiveness of the campaign can be gauged from the still commonly held belief that SIDA is spread by white foreign males only. Fortunately the protection offered by condoms (rain coats, ao mua) is generally understood although unfortunately ao mua are usually used in pre- and extra-marital romantic relationships only – in which they are prized for their contraceptive effect. A disadvantage the maligned white male labours under is that locally sold rain coats (including those exported from Japan) don't quite measure up to the task.

Further complicating the matter, large quantities of good quality second-hand garments are sent from abroad to clothe the poor of Vietnam. Often these find their way into the hands of vendors and are sold on the street. Popular belief was that these were the clothes of Westerners who had died of SIDA, hence the common street sign 'Ao SIDA' advertising a second-hand clothing stall.

Vietnamese tend to prefer non-alcoholic drinks and huge numbers of cafés exist to cater to this market. Young romantic couples sit in virtual darkness listening to Vietnamese love songs while sipping coffee. The furniture tends to be rather small for the Western frame but these cafés are an agreeable way of relaxing after dinner in a more typically Vietnamese setting. *Thien Ha Café* at 25A Tu Xuong, Q3 which features piano and violin duets is a prime and popular example.

Entertainment

Cinemas There were 44 'picture houses' in Saigon at last count; Western films are beginning to be shown. French films are screened at the **French Cultural Institute (Idecaf)**, 31 Thai Van Lung, T8295451. *Tan Son Nhat Cinema*, 186 Nguyen Van Troi St, Tan Binh District. Shows carefully chosen English language films from time to time. *Film Archive Club*, 212 Ly Chinh Thang St, District 3, T8468883. Shows a good selection of modern and classic Western movies.

Dancing At the *Rex*, *Caravelle*, *Majestic* and *Palace Hotels*. Also at some restaurants eg *Liberty*, 80 Dong Khoi St. *Maxim's* (from 2000, 15,000d).

Horse races

The commencement was a race of 12 horses, or rather ponies; for, however great were the prizes for competition, the rivalship had not caused them to improve the breed of their cattle; a more meagre, dwarfish, crippled, puny lot of horses, I never before beheld. Chinese horses are bad enough, but these were ten times worse; and I think the best mode the Quong or the King could adopt to improve them would be, to have races twice or thrice a year, and give prizes to be run for, that would pay the natives to buy foreign horses, and mix the breed.

Well, these twelve animals started; but with all their whips, rattans, spurs, and shouting, they could not get more than a very slow canter out of the best of them. I pitied the poor beasts; they looked far more in want of a feed of corn, than fit to run a race. They made two or three more trials, but it was "no go"; I could have run faster myself, weak as I was. The poor brutes broke down before they got half-way round the course; and, out of the twelve that started, only three managed to come in anything at all like "racers". Taken from Cochin-China and My Experience of It by Edward Brown, London 1861.

Discos *Cheers*, *Vien Dong Hotel*, crowded, is as popular as ever. *Hoan Kiem*, 27 Ngo Duc Ke St (1730-2400). *Gossip*, at *Mercury Hotel*. US$8 for men, free for women Monday-Friday, US$4, Saturday and Sunday, currently the most popular in town. *Catwalk*, *New World Hotel*. *Planet Europa*, Truong Son St, near the airport. Part of the superbowl complex, is thought to attract more girls than any other.

Sports **Bowling** There are 2 venues, *International Club*, 285 Cach Mang Thang Tam St, T8651709. 12 lanes, 40,000d per person per game; and the enormous *Superbowl*, Truong Son St. 32 lanes, just outside the airport, 40,000d per person per game plus shoe hire, video arcades and fast food outlets – a great hit with the Vietnamese – book, T8458119. **Golf** *Song Be Golf Resort*, 20 kilometres from Saigon, T065-855802. An attractive course an hour's drive from town with basic amenities. *Golf Vietnam and Country Club*, Thu Duc, T8252951. Green fees Monday-Friday US$73, Saturday-Sunday, US$92. **Hash House Harriers** Hash House Harriers meet 1500, Sunday, *Delta Caravelle Hotel*. **Racing** The *Phu Tho Racecourse*, 2 Le Dai Hanh St, District II. Stages races on Thursday, Saturday and Sunday afternoons. Both the winner and the second horse have to be selected to collect. The course has been reopened with financing from an interested Chinese entrepreneur but not a lot has changed since 1858 when Edward Brown recorded his impressions of Vietnamese racing, see box, above. He would be delighted to know of plans by fellow Britons to introduce new breeding stock to Vietnam. Entrance to Turf Club 20,000d. Beware pickpockets. **Swimming** Some hotels (like the *New World* and *Equatorial*) allow non-residents to use their pool for a charge that can be pretty steep. Apart from these two, other hotels with decent pools are the Sofitel Plaza, Omni, Grand and Delta Carvelle. The Lao Dong Club (old Cercle Sportif) on the corner of Nguyen Thi Minh Khai and Huyen Tran Cong Chua St has a good size pool; the old US Embassy pool on Nguyen Thi Minh Khai St opposite Phung Khac Khoan St, tends to be crowded but one can imagine the conversations that must have taken place there. Also the *International Club*, 285 Cach Mang Thang Tam St. 20,000d Monday-Friday, 30,000d on Saturday and Sunday. *Saigon Water Park*, T8970456. A little way out but is enormous fun. Just hop in a taxi and ask for Saigon Water Park, 40,000d. **Tennis** Courts at the *Rex Hotel*. Also at the Lao Dong Club in Van Hoa Park, behind Reunification Hall.

Shopping

Most shops are on Dong Khoi, Mac Thi Buoi and Ngo Duc Ke streets (the latter two both run off Dong Khoi). For the knowledgeable, there are bargains to be found, especially Chinese and Vietnamese ceramics – the difficulty is getting them out of the country (see page 22, Export restrictions). Also available are old watches, colonial bric-à-brac, lacquerware and carvings etc. For the less touristy stuff visitors would be advised to spend an hour or so browsing the shops in Le Cong Trieu St. Le Cong Trieu is not marked on any maps but runs between Nam Ky Khoi Nghia and Pho Duc Chinh streets just south of Ben Thanh Market. Among the bric-à-brac and tat are some interesting items of furniture, statuary and ceramics. Bargaining is the order of the day and some pretty good deals can be struck. Mr *Lac Long*, 143 Le Thanh Ton St, sometimes has some unusual items for sale even if there is nothing of interest on display.

From the stalls along Le Thanh Ton St close to the Ben Thanh market and Vo Thi Sau west of junction with Pham Ngoc Thach St. US$40 for a Vietnamese bike, at least US$70 for a better built Chinese one.

Bookazine, 28 Dong Khoi St. New, a decent range of English language books. *Lan Anh Bookshop*, 201 Dong Khoi St. For second-hand books in French and English. Bookshop, at 20 Ho Huan Nghiep sells French, English and Vietnamese books including bound photocopies of volumes. Some old books have 'US Embassy Library' stamped in the front. It doubles as a café selling some of the tastiest ice cream in Saigon. *Hong Ha*, 40 Ngo Duc Ke St, and shops at 60-62 and 56 Le Loi Blvd and 40 Nguyen Hue Blvd sell English-Vietnamese dictionaries and phrase books and some books on Vietnam. *Fahasa*, foreign language bookstore on Dong Khoi St, opposite *Continental Hotel*, sells books imported from England and France as well as pirated versions of Western books. The Vietnamese authorities quite happily sanction pirating by state publishers. *The Cat*, 243 De Tham St. Sells, buys and exchanges books, CDs, tapes, also buys cameras, Walkmans and watches from hard up travellers.

Shops specializing in western staples (which, in Vietnam, seem suddenly luxurious) such as milk, cornflakes, peanut butter etc abound on Ham Nghi Blvd around number 62 and 64 (*Kim Thanh*). Also sell baby products, nappies etc at a price. 66 Ham Nghi, excellent bakery. *Le Cochon d'or*, 7 Nguyen Thiep St, T8293856. Purveys an excellent range of charcuterie, cheese and delicatessen, imported and local. Those wishing to sample pure yoghurt will enjoy tracking down *Hoa Sinh*, 20/10 Ho Hao Hon St, T8367181. An unsigned 'dairy', not easy to find but only 5 minutes on a bicycle from Pham Ngu Lao St, it sells locally produced goat and other cheeses and dairy products as well at very reasonable prices.

There are a number of shops along Dong Khoi St and Nguyen Hue Blvd. Handicrafts include embroidered and woven fabrics, lacquerware, mother-of-pearl inlaid screens and ceramics. Nice decorative items from *Arts and Crafts Gallery*, 26 Le Thanh Ton St. *Mai Handicrafts*, 298 Nguyen Trong Tuyen St, Q Tan Binh, T8440988. A little way out of town but sells an interesting selection of goods, fabrics and handmade paper all made by disadvantaged people in little income generating schemes. A number of shops in De Tham St sell woven and embroidered goods including scarves, bags and clothes. *East Meets West*, 24 Le Loi Blvd. Nicely made Vietnamese and ethnic handicrafts, reasonably priced.

Vietnamese lacquerware has a long history, and a reputation of sorts (see page 388). Visitors to the workshop can witness the production process and, of course, buy the products if they wish. Lacquerware is available from many of the handicraft shops on

Raid

Overwhelmed by the pent-up forces of capitalism, freer since *dòi mòi*, Saigon's authorities have lost the control they once exercised over the city's business activities. Frightened by their diminishing power the authorities want to be seen to be in charge. Coupled with a crusading zeal as part of the 'social evils' campaign police activity is highly visible.

The victims of a police raid usually consist of those least able to protect themselves. Thus in Hai Ba Trung St or Pham Ngu Lao rarely an evening passes without a sudden rush in the street. Word flashes down the street: 'can sat' – police. Street vendors rapidly gather their stock in trade, stack their little plastic chairs, gather empty soup bowls and wheel their cigarette or noodle stall down a side street or into an accommodating neighbour's yard and hold their breath.

A typical raid is heralded by uniformed policemen on motorbikes backed up by colleagues, often not in uniform, lounging in the back of an open yellow police jeep. They proceed at a leisurely pace enjoying the fear they create. Justice is blind. A random strike. Into the back of a police truck goes a cigarette trolley together with its wailing elderly female owner, somebody's grandmother. A dozen plastic stools are thrown in followed by six collapsible wooden tables, a small drinks cart and another protesting granny. They are driven off and normality descends. Out pop the concealed bottles, cigarettes and the usual street furniture – business as usual.

Poor and unlicensed street vendors whose stock may represent their entirely worldly wealth bear the brunt of these raids while the owners of cafés and restaurants whose furniture and customers spill onto the street, breaking every ordinance in the book, stand calmly by. They have greased the right palms. The poor have no protection and lack the wherewithall to buy it.

The other group of people to suffer are those lacking official residence papers along with other undesirables. Midnight raids strike terror. Police wielding sledge hammers smash down unlicensed wooden shacks while terrified children and screaming mothers are thrown into the back of police trucks. On one night in August 1996 1,900 were rounded up including "homeless children, old people and migrants from other parts of the country, many of whom were beggars and pickpockets". The official report continued, "homes would be found for the homeless, drug addicts would be sent to rehabilitation centres and prostitutes would go to education centres".

And thank goodness: "Social evils have decreased by 50-70 percent since the government issued the anti-social vices decision".

Nguyen Hue Blvd and Dong Khoi St. Also from the ***Lamson Laquerware Factory***, 106 Nguyen Van Troi St (opposite *Omni Hotel*, Visa and Mastercard). ***Miss Nga*** sells lacquer and other top quality handicrafts suitable for souvenirs from her shop, 61 Le Thanh Ton St.

Linen Good quality linen table cloths, sheets, avaliable from shops on Dong Khoi St.

Maps Saigon has the best selection in Vietnam; from the stalls on Le Loi Blvd between Dong Khoi St and Nguyen Hue Blvd. Bargain hard – the bookshops listed above are probably cheaper.

Outdoor Gear Vietnam produces a list of equipment for climbing and camping, such as walking boots, fleeces and rucksacks. Top quality brand name goods can be bought cheaply, especially around Pham Ngu Lao and De Tham streets.

(See page 388)   Vietnamese silk and traditional dresses (*ao dai*) are to be found in the **Silk/Ao Dai** shops on Dong Khoi St and in Ben Thanh market.

From 336 Nguyen Cong Tru St.   **War surplus**

Sold in the main hotels. Same day *Bangkok Post* and *The Nation* newspapers (English **Western** language Thai papers), and up-to-date *Financial Times*, *Straits Times*, *South China* **newspapers** *Morning Post*, *Newsweek* and *The Economist*, available from Fahasa on Dong Khoi St. **and magazines** Numerous vendors around the Continental Hotel.

Transport

72 kilometres from My Tho, 147 kilometres from Vinh Long, 113 kilometres from Vung Tau, 165 kilometres from Can Tho, 299 kilometres from Dalat, 338 kilometres from Hatien, 445 kilometres from Nha Trang, 965 kilometres from Danang, 1,071 kilometres from Hué, 1,710 kilometres from Hanoi.

If staying in Saigon for any length of time (or intending to travel by bus with the bike) **Local** it might be a good idea to buy a bicycle (see Shopping, above and page 285). Bicycles and motorbikes can be hired from some of the cheaper hotels and cafés, especially in Pham Ngu Lao St. Bikes should always be parked in the roped-off compounds (*Gui xe*) that are all over town; they will be looked after for a small charge (500d by day, 1,000d after dark, 2,000d for motorbikes – always get a ticket).

Cyclos are a peaceful way to get around the city. They can be hired by the hour (approximately US$2 per hour) or to reach a specific destination. Some drivers speak English. Each tends to have his own patch which is jealously guarded. Expect to pay more outside the major hotels – it is worth walking around the corner. Cyclos found waiting in tourist spots will often offer additional services such as money changing and 'girls'. Some visitors complain of cyclo drivers in Saigon having an annoying habit of forgetting the agreed price (though Hanoi is worse). Cyclos are being banned from more and more streets in the centre of Saigon which may involve a longer journey.

Motorcycle taxis (*Honda* or *xe ôm*) are quickest way to get around town and cheaper than cyclo; agree a price and hop on the back. *Xe ôm* drivers can be recognized by their baseball caps, clapped out Honda Cubs and tendency to chain smoke, they hang around on most street corners. Saigon has quite a large fleet of meter taxis. There are more than 14 taxi companies fighting bitterly for trade on the streets of Saigon. Competition has brought down prices so they are now reasonably inexpensive and for two or more are cheaper than cyclo or *xe ôm*. All taxis are metered, ensure the meter is set after you get in. The standard of vehicle and service vary widely and some companies are more expensive than others. All taxis are numbered, in the event of forgotten luggage or other problems ring the company and quote the number of your taxi.

Tan Son Nhat Airport is 30 minutes northwest of the city. Taxis to the city centre cost **Air** US$5-7. Airport facilities include a branch of the **Vietcombank** and **First Vinabank**, for changing money and Post Office.

The station (*Nha ga*) is 2 kilometres from the centre of the city at the end of Nguyen **Train** Thong St. Much improved facilities for the traveller include a/c waiting room, Post Office and bank (no travellers' cheques). Regular daily connections with Hanoi and all points north. Express trains take between 36 and 40 hours to reach Hanoi; hard and soft berths are available. Sleepers should be booked in advance. (See page 409 for more information on rail travel and a condensed timetable with selected fares.)

Taxis

Name	Colour	Telephone
Airport	white	844 6666
Saigon	green and white	842 4242
Ben Thanh	red	842 2422
Mai Linh	green and white	822 6666
Davi	grey or white	829 0290
Festival	grey	845 4545
Saigon Tourist	red	822 2206
Tanaco	red	822 6226
V Taxi	red	820 2020
Vinataxi	yellow	8110888
S Taxi	white	821 2121

Road **Bus** There are 2 main bus stations (see map for location). Buses north to Dalat, Hué, Danang and all significant points on the road to Hanoi leave from the Mien Dong terminal, north of the city centre on Xo Viet Nghe Tinh St, before the road crosses the Saigon River. Buses south to Ca Mau, Rach Gia, Ha Tien, Long Xuyen, My Tho, An Long, Can Tho, Long Xuyen and elsewhere leave from the Mien Tay terminal, some distance southwest of town on Hung Vuong Blvd. There is also a bus station in Cholon which serves destinations such as Long An, My Thuan, Ben Luc and My Tho. A new fleet of a/c buses connects central Saigon with the bus terminals, 3,000d. Buses depart from the bus station opposite Ben Thanh Market. Minibuses for Vung Tau depart from Ham Nghi Blvd – hop in quickly as they are not allowed to pick up passengers in town. Ask at your hotel for updated information.

Hydrofoil *Vinaexpress*, T8253888, 8215609, operates hydrofoils to Vung Tau, My Tho and Can Tho. 4 per day to Vung Tau (US$10) and 1 per day to My Tho (US$12) and Can Tho (US$24).

International connections **Air** (See list page 23). **Road** To Phnom Penh *Sinh Café* run a minibus to Moc Bai, on the border, US$5, depart 0800, bus or *xe ôm* from there to Phnom Penh.

Directory

Airline offices *Asiana Airlines*, 141-143 Ham Nghi St, T8222663, F8222710. *Air France*, 130 Dong Khoi St, T8290981, F8220537. *Aeroflot*, 4H Le Loi St, T8293489, F8290076. *British Airways*, c/o Jardine Pacific, 58 Dong Khoi St, T8291288, F8230030. *Cathay Pacific*, 58 Dong Khoi St, T8223203 (airport, T8441895), F8258276. *China Airlines*, 132-134 Dong Khoi St, T8251388, F8251390. *China Southern Airlines*, 52B Pham Hong Thai St, T8291172, F8296800. *Emirates Airlines*, 17 Han Thuyen St, T8256575, F8256578. *Eva Air*, 32-34 Ngo Duc Ke St, T8224488, F8223567. *Garuda*, 132-134 Dong Khoi St, T8293644, F8293688. *JAL*, 115 Nguyen Hue St, T8219098, F8219097. *KLM*, 2A-4A Ton Duc Thang St, T8231990, F8231989. *Korean Air*, 65 Le Loi St, T8242879, F8242877. *Lufthansa*, Continental Hotel,132 Dong Khoi St, T8298549, F8298537. *Lauda Air*, 9 Dong Khoi St, T8297117, F8295832. *Malaysian*, 132-134 Dong Khoi St, T8292529, F8242884. *Pacific Airlines*, 177 Vo Thi Sau St, Q3, T8200979, F8200980 (airport, T8442705). *Qantas*, 65 Le Loi St, T8214660, F8214669. *Royal Air Cambodge*, 343 Le Van Sy St, T8440126, F8421578. *Singapore Airlines*, 29 Le Duan St, T823 1588, F8231554. *Thai Airways*, 65 Nguyen Du St, T8223365, F8223465. *United Airlines*, 58 Dong Khoi St, T8234755, F8230030. *Vietnam Airlines*, 116 Nguyen Hue Blvd, T8292118, F8230273.

Banks It is easy to change money in Saigon. Money changers on Le Loi St, corner of Dong Khoi St, central, quick and easy. *ANZ Bank*, Me Linh Square. 4% commission charged on cashing TCs into US$ ATM cashpoint. *Foreign Exchange Bank*, 101 Nam Ky Khoi Nghia St. *Hong Kong Bank*, New World Hotel,

Ly Tu Trong St. 24-hr ATM. *Vietcombank*: Nguyen Hue Blvd (opposite the *Rex Hotel*); 123 Dong Khoi St. *Vietnam Export-Import Bank*, Le Thi Hong Gam St. *Thai Military Bank*, 11 Ben Chuong Duong St. *VID Public Bank*, 15A Ben Chuong Duong. *BFCE*, 11 Me Linh Square. *Sacom Bank*, Pham Ngu Lao St. 1% commission on TCs cashed in dong. 2% on TCs cashed in US$.

GPO: 2 Cong Xa Paris (facing the Cathedral). Open 0630-1930 Mon-Sun. Telex, telegram and international telephone services available. Long-distance calls between US$12 (Hong Kong, Thailand, Malaysia) and US$20 for the first 5 mins (UK call = US$20 for 5 mins). **Communications**

Australia, Landmark Building, 5B Ton Duc Thang St, T8296035, F8296031. *Belgium*, 230G Pasteur, Q3, T/F8243571. *Cambodia*, 41 Phung Khac Khoan St, T8292751, F8292744. *Canada*, Mondial Business Centre, 203 Dong Khoi St, T8242000 x 1209, F8294528. *China*, 39 Nguyen Thi Minh Khai St, T8292457, F8295009. *Cuba*, 45 Phung Khac Khoan St, T8297350, F8295293. *Denmark*, 20 Phung Khac Khoan St, T8228289, F8224888. *France*, 27 Nguyen Thi Minh Khai St, T8297235, F8291675. *Germany*, 126 Nguyen Dinh Chieu St, Q3, T8291967, F8231919. *Hungary*, 22 Phung Khac Khoan St, T8290130, F8292410. *India*, 49 Tran Quoc Thao St, Q3, T8294498, F8294495. *Indonesia*, 18 Phung Khac Khoan St, T8223799, F8299493. *Italy*, 4 Dong Khoi St, T8298721, F8298723. *Japan*, 13-17 Nguyen Hue Blvd, T8225314, F8225316. *Laos*, 93 Pasteur St, T8297667, F8299272. *Malaysia*, 53 Nguyen Dinh Chieu St, Q3, T8299023, F8299027. *New Zealand*, 41 Nguyen Thi Minh Khai St, Q3, T8226907, F8226905. *Netherlands*, 29 Le Duan St, T8235932, F8235934. *Panama*, 7A Le Thanh Ton St, T8250334, F8236447. *Philippines*, 12 Nam Ky Khoi Nghia St, T8214593, F8210026. *Poland*, 2-2A Tran Cao Van St, T/F8290114. *Russia*, 40 Ba Huyen Thanh Quan St, T8292936, F8292937. *Singapore*, 65 Le Loi St, T8225174, F8251600. *South Korea*, 107 Nguyen Du St, T8225757, F8225750. *Sweden*, 8A/11D1 Thai Van Lung St, T8236865, F823 6817. *Switzerland*, 270A Bach Dang St, Q Binh Thanh, T8412211, F8412028. *Thailand*, 77 Tran Quoc Thao St, Q3, T8222637, F8291002. *Ukranian*, 213 Nguyen Van Thu St, T8222490, F8250559. *United Kingdom*, 25 Le Duan St, T8298433, F8225740. *USA*, 51 Nguyen Dinh Chieu St, (will move to Le Duan St in mid 1999) T8234642, F8229434. **Embassies & consulates**

AEA International Clinic, 65 Nguyen Du St, T8298520, F8298551. Comprehensive 24 hr medical and dental service and medical evacuation, US$45 for consultation with local doctor, US$65 with overseas doctor, check insurance policy before going. *Cho Ray Hospital*, 201 Nguyen Chi Thanh Blvd, Q5, T8554137. *Emergency Centre*, 125 Le Loi Blvd, T8292071. 24 hr, some English and French-speaking doctors; *Institut du Coeur*, 520 Nguyen Tri Phuong St, Q10, T8654025 – also has French doctors (expensive). *St Paul's Eye Hospital*, 280 Dien Bien Phu St, T8357644. **Dental treatment:** available at *St Paul's Hospital*, 280 Dien Bien Phu St, Q3, T8225052 or *AEA*. *Colombia-Gia Dinh International Clinic*, 1 No Trang Long St, Q Binh Thanh, T8030678, F8030677. American run emergency clinic with medivac and GP services. **Hospitals & medical services**

Places of worship Church services: Communion held 6 times on Sun and 3 times on weekdays and Sat at the Cathedral at the north end of Dong Khoi St.

Ann Tourist, 58 Ton That Tung St, T8334356, F8323866 (generally excellent, knowledgeable guides). *Cam On Tour*, 32 Dong Du St, T8298443, F8298169. Efficient, knowledgeable and friendly staff and helpful, English-speaking drivers). Highly recommended. *Davi Tour*, 119 Lu Tu Trong St, T8295499, F8228990. Very helpful tour company, good value tours. Recommended. *Diethelm Travel*, 1A Me Linn Square, District 1, T8294932, F8294747. *Exotissimo*, Saigon Trade Centre, 37 Ton Duc Thang, T8251723, F8295800. An efficient agency that can handle all travel needs of visitors to Vietnam. Also popular with overseas tour operators for whom it handles group travel. *Far East Tourist*, 61 Le Thanh Ton St, T8225187, F8295361. *Fiditourist*, 195 Pham Ngu Lao St, T/F8361922. A rival of Sinh and Kim Cafés, vying for the budget traveller's dollar, has a money exchange which remains open long after the banks have closed. *Kim Café*, 270 De Tham St. Organize minibuses to Nha Trang, Dalat etc and tours of the Mekong, good source of information. *Oriental Pearls*, 2812 Cach Mang Thang Tam, Q Tan Binh, T8640500. *Peace Tour Co*, 60 Vo Van Tan, Q3, T8294416, F8294416. *Sinh Café*, 179 Pham Ngu Lao St. Organize tours of the south and arrange travel to the north via their open tour: US$35 to Hué, US$57 to Hanoi. *Vacation Planners*, 39/3 Tran Nhat Duat St, T8242807, F8299744. Recommended. *Vidotour*, Le Thanh Ton St, T8291438. *Youth Tourist Centre*, 51 Nguyen Dinh Chieu St, T8296743, F8290919. **Tour companies & travel agents**

Saigon

Tourist offices *Cuu Long Tourist*, 45 Dinh Tien Hoang St, T8293990. For tours to Mekong Delta. *Saigontourist*, 49 Le Thanh Ton St, T8295834, F8224987. Organize expensive tours, maybe useful for advice and a few useful handouts. *Vietnamtourism*, 69-71 Nguyen Hue Blvd, T8290772, F8290775. Again, only helpful if booking one of their tours.

Useful addresses Chamber of Commerce and Industry: 171 Vo Thi Sau St, Q3, T8230301. **Foreign Affairs Service:** 6 Alexandre de Rhodes St, T8224128. **Immigration Office:** 254 Nguyen Trai St, change visa to specify overland exit via Moc Bai if travelling to Cambodia or for overland travel to Laos or China. Also for visa extensions.

The Mekong Delta and the South

7

The Mekong Delta and the South

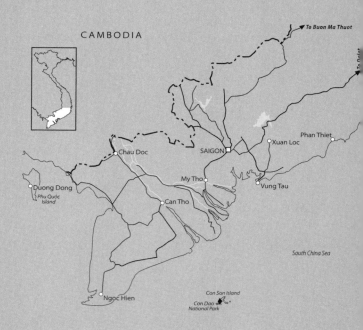

Formal sights are thin on the ground in the Mekong Delta region and travel can be slow, involving ferry crossings and boat rides. But perhaps herein lies the first contradiction of the Delta, for to travel is often better than to arrive. Boat trips along canals, down rivers and around islands hold more appeal than many of the towns. Biking past paddy fields or cycling through orchards is often more enchanting than the official tourist stops. The region has had a restless history: struggle between Cambodians and Vietnamese for ownership of the wide plains resulted in Viet supremacy although important Khmer relics remain. And during the French and American wars the Mekong Delta produced many of the most fervent fighters for independence.

The Mekong Delta

History

The Mekong Delta or *Cuu Long* (nine dragons), is Vietnam's rice bowl, and before the partition of the country in 1954, rice was traded from the south where there was a rice surplus, to the north where there was a rice deficit, as well as internationally. Even prior to the creation of French Cochin China in the 19th century, rice was being transported from here to Hué, the imperial capital. Since reunification in 1975 this pattern of trade has reasserted itself. The delta covers 67,000 square kilometres, of which about half is cultivated. Rice yields are in fact generally lower than in the north, but the huge area under cultivation and the larger size of farms means that both the region and individual households tend to produce a surplus for sale. In the Mekong Delta, there is nearly three times as much riceland per person as there is in the north. It is this which accounts for the relative wealth of the region.

The Mekong Delta was not opened up to agriculture on an extensive scale until the late 19th and early 20th centuries. Initially it seems that this was a spontaneous process: peasants, responding to the market incentives introduced by the French, slowly began to push the frontier of cultivation southwards into this wilderness area. The process gathered pace when the French colonial government began to construct canals and drainage projects to open more land to wet rice agriculture. By the

1930s the population of the Delta had reached 4.5 million with 2.2 million hectares of land under rice cultivation. The Mekong Delta, along with the Irrawaddy (Burma/Myanmar) and Chao Phraya (Thailand) became one of the great rice exporting areas of Southeast Asia, shipping over 1.2 million tonnes annually.

Given their close proximity to prosperous Saigon the inhabitants of the Mekong Delta might have expected some of the benefits of development to trickle their way: in this they have been disappointed. Many of the Delta

provinces have hardline Communist People's Committees which have staunchly resisted social and economic change, so foreign investment has gone to the more welcoming provinces of Dong Nai and Ho Chi Minh City. The iron grip of the state companies on the tourist industry has resulted in dismal and dingy hotels that look upon customers as an irritant rather than a source of business. The contrast with private hotels that eagerly scour the bus stations looking for custom could not be more marked. Province tourist companies offer tedious and unimaginative tours at high prices in contrast to the more interesting tours at low prices run by private operators in Saigon, although there are now one or two exceptions. Despite its potential, tourism in the Mekong Delta remains woefully underdeveloped.

Travel in the Mekong Delta The road is relatively good from Saigon to Long Xuyen, Chau Doc, and Can Tho, but beyond these towns roads are narrow and pot-holed and travel is generally slow but improving. Ferry crossings slow travel down still further and if travelling by bus expect long delays waiting in queues (private cars push straight to the front). Remember that banks are few and far between – take dong with you and a few small US$ bills for unforeseen expenses along the way.

Best time to visit December-May. During the monsoon from June-November the weather is poor, constant background drizzle interrupted by short bursts of torrential rain. In October flooding may interrupt movement particularly in the remoter areas and around Chau Doc and Dong Thap Province.

My Tho

History

Phone code: 075
Colour map 4, grid B3

My Tho, the capital of Tien Giang Province, is 71 kilometres southwest of Saigon on the banks of the My Tho River, a 'distributary' of the mighty Mekong and about 40 kilometres from the South China Sea. The town has had a turbulent history: it was Khmer until the 17th century, when the advancing Vietnamese took control of the surrounding area. In the 18th century Thai forces annexed the territory, before being driven out in 1784. Finally, the French gained control in 1862.

Not far from My Tho is the hamlet of **Ap Bac**, the site of the Communists' first major military victory against the ARVN. The battle demonstrated that without direct US involvement the Communists could never be defeated. John Paul Vann was harsh in his criticism of the tactics and motivation of the South Vietnamese Army who failed to dislodge a weak VC position. As he observed from the air, almost speechless with rage, he realized how feeble his Vietnamese ally was; an opinion that few senior US officers heeded – to their cost (see *Bright Shining Lie* by Neil Sheehan).

Sights

Today, My Tho is an important riverside market town, five kilometres off the main 'highway' to Vinh Long and points south. On the corner of Nguyen Trai Street and Hung Vuong Boulevard, and a five minutes walk from the central market, is **My Tho church**: yellow wash with a newer, white campanile. The **central market** covers a large area from Le Loi Boulevard, down to the river. The river is the most enjoyable spot to watch My Tho life go by. **Vinh Trang**

Pagoda is at 60 Nguyen Trung Truc Street. The temple is on the right, through a painted bamboo archway. The entrance to the temple is through an ornate porcelain- encrusted gate. The pagoda was built in 1849, and displays a mixture of architectural styles – Chinese, Vietnamese and colonial. The façade is almost fairytale in inspiration. The temple also has a small collection of animals that would be far happier elsewhere. ■ *Open 0900-1200, 1400-1700, Monday-Sunday. Getting there: it is a long walk; best by bicycle or cyclo.*

Excursions

Also known as Con Phung, this is about three kilometres from My Tho. The 'Coconut Monk', established a retreat on this island shortly after the end of the Second World War where he developed a new 'religion', a fusion of Buddhism and Christianity. He is said to have meditated for three years on a stone slab, eating nothing but coconuts (why, is not clear) – hence the name. Persecuted by both the South Vietnamese government and by the Communists, the monastery has fallen into disuse.

Island of the Coconut Monk

About 10 kilometres from town at Dong Tam, this farm raises snakes for their medicinal qualities – not to remove their venom for use in serum. The belief is that their flesh and gall have strong healing powers. In addition to the snakes, a bear, crocodiles and others are tormented by their Vietnamese visitors. A restaurant serves snake specialities. ■ *US$1. Getting there: take Highway 1 towards Vinh Long, at Dong Tam follow signs to Trai Ran or take the road past the Ben Tre ferry, turn right up a mud lane where you see the sign.*

Snake farm

The Mekong Delta & the South

My Tho

■ **Sleeping**
1 Khach San 43
2 Hung Vuong
3 Huong Duong
4 Lao Dong
5 Rang Dong
6 Song Tien

Tan Long Island Opposite My Tho, this is a pleasant to wander along narrow paths. Tan Long is noted for its longan production but many other fruits and honey to sample as well as rice whisky. ■ *Getting there: either by tourist boat from the corner of 30 Thang 4 and Trung Trac streets (50,000d) or by ferry from the terminal in Le Thi Hong Gam Street (1,000d).*

Essentials

Sleeping
■ *on map*
Price codes:
see inside front cover
C *Hung Vuong*, 40 Hung Vuong St, T876868. Away from the river, private hotel. **C** *Khach San 43*, 43 Ngo Quyen St. Astonishingly expensive for the broken down and filthy rooms, avoid at all costs. **C** *Rang Dong*, 25 30 Thang 4 St, T874400. Private mini hotel, near river, a/c and hot water. **C-E** *Song Tien* (used to be the *Grand*), 101 Trung Trac St, T872009. A/c and fan rooms, dingy conditions and lack of customers have forced the authorities to cut prices. Cannot be recommended, bargain hard. **D** *Huong Duong*, 33 Trung Trac St, T872011. Good river views from upper floors. **E** *Lao Dong*, corner of Le Loi and 30 Thang 4 streets. Clean hotel with fan rooms, good views. Recommended.

Eating A speciality of the area is *hu tieu my tho* – a spicy soup of vermicilli, sliced pork, dried shrimps and fresh herbs. *Cay Bo De*, 32 Nam Ky Khoi Nghia St. Good, cheap vegetarian dishes including a delicious veggie *hu tieu* for 6,000d. *Chi Thanh*, Trung Trac St. Good fried noodles and shrimps. Recommended. *Nha Hang 52*, 52 Trung Trac St. Excellent food at good prices. *Nha Hang 54*, 54 Trung Trac St. Delicious ice cream. *Nha Hang 46*. Savoury pancakes *bánh xèo* filled with beansprouts, mushrooms and prawns, delicious. *Truc Café*, 36 Trung Trac St. Good for an evening beer and excellent breakfast.

Transport 72 kilometres from Saigon, 70 kilometres from Vinh Long, 103 kilometres from Can Tho, 179 kilometres from Chau Doc, 182 kilometres from Rach Gia. The bus station (*Ben Xe My Tho*) is 3-4 kilometres from town on Ap Bac St towards Saigon with regular connections from Saigon's Mien Tay station (2 hours). **Local** As in all Mekong Delta towns local travel is often by boat – to visit the orchards, islands and remoter places. On land there are the usual *xe ôms* and the local version of a cyclo – a trailer towed by a bicycle. **Road Bus**: to Vinh Long, Chau Doc, Ca Mau, Tay Ninh, Cai Be, Can Tho. Buses to Can Tho and Vinh Long 0430, 0630 and 0830, to Chau Doc at 0430; and to other destinations in the Mekong Delta. **Boat** The Hydrofoil from end of Ham Nghi St in Saigon departs 0730 daily, 2 hours, US$12, return 1520. T08-8215609. Ferry to Chau Doc leaves from the Ben Tre ferry terminal at 1300, 30,000d plus 10,000d for hammock, 24 hours.

Directory **Banks** 5 Le Van Duyet St. **Communications** Post Office and international calls: at 59 30 Thang 4 St. **Tourist offices** *Tien Giang Tourism*, 8 30 Thang 4, T873184, F873578. *Tien Giang Youth Tourist*, 25 Nam Ky Khoi Nghia St, T875189. Probably the best of a poor bunch. 2, 3 and 4-hr trips surrounding islands, orchards and farms. *Chuong Duong Tourist*, 12 30 Thang 4 St, T873379. Visitors might therefore look favourably on Mr Truc who will approach them in Trung Trac St: his prices are cheaper, he speaks English and is an interesting and helpful guide.

Ben Tre

Phone code: 075
Colour map 4, grid B3
Ben Tre has its fans but as it is a cul-de-sac you can't just pass through. Consequently it does not attract a lot of foreign, or for that matter, Vietnamese visitors. The province is essentially a huge island of mud at one of the nine mouths of the Mekong. It depends heavily on farming, fishing and coconuts although there are some light industries engaged in processing the local farm output and refining sugar. During the wars of resistance against the French

and Americans Ben Tre earned itself a reputation as a staunch Viet Minh/Viet Cong stronghold. Ben Tre is not geared to tourism so do not expect tours or facilities, but for the truly independent traveller there is plenty of interest to be seen in the day to day way of life. There are, however, plans to recreate a guerrilla base in one village but quite how compelling an attraction that will prove remains to be seen.

C-D *Dong Khoi*, 16 Hai Ba Trung St, T822632, F822440. Some a/c with fridge, bathroom and hot water, restaurant. **C-D** *People's Committee Guesthouse*, 143 Hung Vuong St, T826134. All a/c, some hot water. **C-D** *Trade Union Guesthouse*, 36 Hai Ba Trung St, T825082. Some a/c, all have bathroom but only some have hot water. **C-E** *Party Committee Guesthouse*, 5 Cach Mang Thang Tam St, T822339, F826205. Some a/c, hot water, most have bathroom attached, and some very simple rooms.
    Sleeping

Most of the hotels have restaurants, there is a floating restaurant on the river, but best to stick to local noodle and rice stands.
    Eating

Vinh Long

Vinh Long is a rather ramshackle, but nonetheless clean, riverside town on the banks of the Co Chien River and is the capital of Vinh Long Province. It was one of the focal points in the spread of Christianity in the Mekong Delta, and there is a **cathedral** and Catholic **seminary** in town. The richly stocked and well-ordered **Cho Vinh Long**, the central market, is on Hung Dao Vuong Street, near the local bus station. Vinh Long makes a reasonable stopping-off point on the road to Long Xuyen, Rach Gia and Ha Tien. There is a **Cao Dai church** not far from the second bridge leading into town from Saigon and My Tho, visible on the right-hand side. The lack of sights and stifling effect of the province's state-run tourist monopoly encourage most travellers to press on to Can Tho.
    Phone code: 070
    Colour map 4, grid B3

River trips There are islands and orchards around Vinh Long as charming as any in the Delta. But getting there can be expensive. Officially, Cuu Long Tourist has a monopoly on excursions by foreigners and charges US$20-30 per hour, although there have been reports of bargaining them down. Local boatmen are prepared to risk a fine and take tourists for one-tenth of that amount. Binh Hoa Phuoc Island makes a pleasant side trip and visitors can
    Excursions

The Mekong Delta & the South

Vinh Long at the end of the 19th century
Source: The French in Indochina, first published in 1884

stay at (**C**) *Mr Giao's House*, with an attractive orchard and bonsai garden, but as it is part of Cuu Long's package deal it is expensive for the individual traveller.

An Binh Island This is just a 10 minute ferry ride from Phan Boi Chau Street; and it represents a great example of delta landscape. The island can be explored either by boat, paddling down narrow canals, or by following the dirt tracks and crossing monkey bridges on foot. Monkey bridges are those single bamboo poles with, if you are lucky, a flimsy handrail – which is there for psychological reassurance rather than for stopping you from falling off. But don't worry, the water is warm and usually shallow and the mud soft. On the island is also the ancient Tien Chau Pagoda and a nuoc mam (fish sauce factory). Try and find a local boatman to bring you here.

The Khmer Temples at Tra Vinh (see page 301) These can be visited on a day trip from Vinh Long. ■ *Getting there: by bus or by motorbike or, for the fabulously wealthy, a trip with Cuu Long Tourist.*

Sleeping **B** *Cuu Long (A)*, 1 1 Thang 5 St (ie No 1 1st May St), T822494, F823357. A/c (not far from the market, on the river), a/c, best in town, some rooms with river views, price including breakfast. **B-C** *Cuu Long (B)*, has the same address and telephone number, but is further up 1 Thang 5 St, set back from the river. Poor value for money, cheaper rooms, no hot water. **B-D** *An Binh*, 3 Hoang Thai Hien St, opposite Post Office, T823190. A/c, fan rooms, dark, unwelcoming, only more expensive rooms (US$20) have hot water, restaurant. **D** *Long Chau*, adjacent to Cuu Long (A), also lays claim to the Thang 5 St address, T823611. Cheapest rooms have shared WC, gloomy accommodation in which to wile away the midnight hours, at 0200 the river boats start, at which point abandon further thoughts of slumber. **D-E** *Nam Phuong*, 11 Le Lai St, T822226. Some a/c, clean and cheap.

Eating There are a number of restaurants and riverside cafés along 1 Thang 5 St, just beyond *Cuu Long (A) Hotel* including *Phuong Thuy Restaurant*, and *Tong Dai*, 16 1 Thang 5. Friendly café, good for breakfast. All close early. **2** *Lan Que*, 2 2 Thang 9 St, T823262. Away from the hotels but worth finding, friendly, good food, open till 2200.

Transport 70 kilometres from My Tho, 32 kilometres from Can Tho, 147 kilometres from Saigon. **Road Bus**: the inter-province bus station is 4-5 kilometres from the centre of town, from here to town take a bicycle cyclo, pay no more than 4-5,000d and insist on being taken to the centre. Regular connections, along a reasonable road, with Saigon's Mien Tay station (3½ hours). Links with Can Tho, My Tho, Long Xuyen, Rach Gia and other Mekong Delta destinations, Sa Dec.

Directory **Banks** *Agricultural Bank (Ngan Hang Nong Nghiep)*, 22 3 Thang 2 St. **Communications Post Office:** 10 Doan Thi Diem St (behind local bus station). **Tourist offices** *Cuu Long Tourist*, 1 Thang 5 St, T823616, F823357.

Tra Vinh

Phone code: 074
Colour map 4, grid C3

Tra Vinh is the capital of the province of the same name and has a large Khmer population – 30 percent of the province's population is Khmer, and at the last count there were 1,431 Khmer temples.

The town itself is an attractive one, with almost every street lined with huge **Sights** trees, some well over 100 feet tall. The market is on the central square between Dien Bien Phu Street – the town's main thoroughfare – and the Tra Vinh River – a relatively small branch of the Mekong, compared with most Delta towns. A walk through the market and along the river bank makes a pleasant late afternoon or early evening stroll. Otherwise there's not a lot to do in Tra Vinh, although it's a nice enough place to spend time. The Ong Met Pagoda on Dien Bien Phu Street north of the town centre is a gilded Chinese-style temple where the monks will be only too happy to ply you with tea and practice their English, although the building itself is fairly unremarkable.

The two best reasons to come to Tra Vinh are to see the storks and the Khmer **Excursions** temples. Fortunately, these can be combined at two nearby pagodas. **Hang Pagoda** is about five kilometres south of town, while **Giong Long** is 43 kilometres southeast. Neither is particularly special architecturally, but the sight of hundreds of storks that rest in their grounds and wheel around their pointed roofs at dawn and dusk is truly spectacular.

B-D *Thanh Tra*, 1 Pham Thai Buong St, T863622. Most room have a/c, satellite TV, **Sleeping** spotless and very comfortable. Recommended. **D-E** *Cuu Long*, 999 Nguyen Thi Minh Khai St, T862615. About 2 kilometres out of town, some a/c, stained walls, but they try to please. **D-E** *Huong Tra*, 67 Ly Thuong Kiet, T862433. Some a/c, hot water, somewhat grubby bathrooms but cheap. **D-E** *Thanh Binh*, 1 Bis Le Thanh Ton St, T866170. Some a/c, hot water, karaoke. **D-E** *Phuong Hoang*, 1 Le Thanh Ton St, T862270. Some a/c, hot water, not particularly clean but cheap.

Thanh Tra Hotel, 1 Pham Thai Buong St. Better than your average hotel diner. *Tuy* **Eating** *Huong*, 8 Dien Bien Phu St. Opposite the market, good, simple Vietnamese dishes.

Road Bus: the bus station is on Chua Phung St, about 500 metres south of town. **Transport** Regular connections with Vinh Long.

Banks *Agribank*, corner of Le Loi and Nam Ky Khoi Nghia streets. Does not change TCs. **Directory** **Communications Post Office:** corner of Phan Dinh Phung and Le Thanh Ton streets. **Tourist office** *Tra Vinh Tourist Co*, in *Cuu Long Hotel*.

Can Tho

The town

Can Tho is a large thriving and rapidly growing commercial town of 200,000 *Phone code: 07* situated in the heart of the Mekong Delta on the banks of the Can Tho River, *Colour map 4, grid B2* surrounded by canals and ricelands. It is the capital of Can Tho Province, the largest city in the Delta, and the region's principal transport hub, with roads and canals running to most other important towns. It is also the most welcoming and agreeable of the Delta towns. A small settlement was established at Can Tho at the end of the 18th century, although the town did not prosper until the French took control of the Delta a century later and rice production for export began to take off. Can Tho was also an important US base. Paul Theroux in *The Great Railway Bazaar* writes:

"Can Tho was once the home of thousands of GIs. With the brothels and bars closed, it had the abandoned look of an unused fairground after a busy summer. In a matter of time, very few years, there will be little evidence that the Americans were ever there. There are poisoned rice fields between the straggling fingers of the Mekong Delta and there are hundreds of blond and fuzzy-haired children, but in a generation even these unusual features will change."

Sights

There is a university, founded in 1966, part of which is a famous **rice research institute**, located 25 kilometres away on Highway 91A. Like International Rice Research Institute (IRRI), its more famous counterpart in the Philippines (and to which it is attached), one of its key functions is developing rice hybrids that will flourish in the varied conditions of the delta. Near the coast, rice has to be tolerant of salt and tidal flooding. In Dong Thap Province near Cambodia floating rice has to grow stalks of four to five metres in order to keep its head above the annual flood. Here also is a teacher training college.

There is a bustling **market** on Hai Ba Trung Street which runs along the banks of the river. The **Munirangsyaram Pagoda** at 36 Hoa Binh Boulevard (southwest from the post office) was built just after the war and is a Khmer Hinayana Buddhist sanctuary. The **Vang Pagoda** is on Hoa Binh Street.

Can Tho

To Bus Station & Long Xuyen

Ngo Gia Tu

Vo Thi Sau

Ngo Quyen

Tran Quoc Toan

Hoa Binh

Ngo Quyen

Ly Thuong Kiet

Hai Ba Trung

Munirangsyaram Pagoda

Ngo Van So

Can Tho River

Tan   Trao

Le Thanh Ton

Nguyen Thai Hoc

Vo Van Tan

Nam Ky Khoi Nghia

Dong Khoi

Nguyen An Ninh

Chau Van Liem

Phan Dinh Phung

Nguyen Thi Minh Khai

Related map
A Can Tho Centre,
page 303

N

0 metres 100
0 yards 109

■ **Sleeping**
1 Hau Giang 'A'
2 Hau Giang 'B'
3 Saigon Can Tho

● **Eating**
1 Cay Sung
2 Rainbow

Excursions

Boat trips to the **floating markets** at **Phung Hiep**, 33 kilometres (nine hour round trip by sampan or take a bus to Phung Hiep and rent a boat there) and **Phong Dien**, 15 kilometres down the Can Tho River. Bustling affairs, the vendors attach a sample of their wares to a bamboo pole to attract customers. Housewives paddle their sampan from boat to boat and barter, haggle and gossip in the usual way. Phung Hiep also boasts a snake market (on land) and yards making traditional fishing boats and rice barges. Markets are busiest 0600-0900. **Orchards** and **gardens** abound, small sampans are best as they can negotiate the narrowest canals to take the visitor into the heart of the area, a veritable Garden of Eden. Take at least a five-hour trip in order to see the landscape at a leisurely pace. Highly recommended. Women with sampans to rent will approach travellers in Hai Ba Trung Street near the market waving a book of testimonials from previous satisfied customers. Expect to pay about 20,000d per hour for two people or 30,000d per hour for four people. **Binh Thuy Temple** which is six kilometres along the road to Long Xuyen dates from the mid-19th century; festivals are held here in the middle of the fourth and twelfth lunar months.

Can Tho Centre

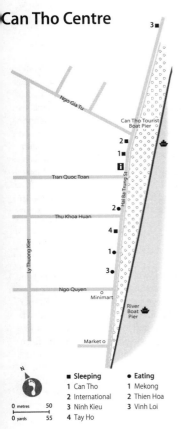

Sleeping
1 Can Tho
2 International
3 Ninh Kieu
4 Tay Ho

Eating
1 Mekong
2 Thien Hoa
3 Vinh Loi

0 metres 50
0 yards 55

Essentials

A lot of hotel-building has taken place in Can Tho recently, a reflection on the growing economy of this dynamically run province.

A *Saigon Can Tho*, 55 Phan Dinh Phung St, T825831, F823288. A/c, comfortable, new, business hotel. **A** *Victoria Can Tho*, T810111, F829259, E victoria@bdvn. vnd.net. Brand new 92-room riverside hotel, office and conference facilities. With places like this and the hydrofoil link from Saigon a genuinely comfortable break in the Mekong Delta is a real possibility. Located a short way across the river, a car or minibus meets the hydrofoil.

B *Hau Giang A*, 34 Nam Ky Khoi Nghia St, T821851, F821806. A/c, restaurant, dancing. **B** *International (Quoc Te)*, 10-12 Hai Ba Trung St, T822079, F821039. A/c, overlooks river, good, if rather soulless restaurant. **B** *Ninh Kieu*, 2 Hai Ba Trung St, T821171, F821104. A/c, lovely position on the river and good restaurant.

C *Phuong Tran*, 118/44A Tran Phu St, T824723, F820437. Near stadium located out of town north of Rach Kai Khe in the

The Mekong Delta & the South

Sleeping
■ *on maps*
Price codes:
see inside front cover

heart of *bia ôm* territory but new, large rooms, good value, no restaurant. **C-D** *Can Tho*, 14-16 Hai Ba Trung St, T822218. A/c, fan rooms, on the river.

D *Tay Ho*, 36 Hai Ba Trung St, T823392. Central, no hot water, fair value. **D-E** *Hau Giang B*, 27 Chau Van Liem St, T821950, F821806. A/c, fan rooms all with hot water, used by backpacker tour groups from Saigon, good value.

Eating
● *on maps*

Hai Ba Trung St by the river offers a good range of excellent and very well priced little restaurants, the riverside setting is an attractive one.

Ninh Kieu, 2 Hai Ba Trung St. On the river, good seafood and some western dishes. *Cay Sung*, 14 6 Nam Ky Khoi Nghia St. Excellent local fare served in an everyday setting. *Mekong*, 38 Hai Ba Trung St. Serves good Vietnamese fare. *Nam Bo*, 50 Hai Ba Trung St, T823908. Excellent little place serving tasty Vietnamese and French dishes in smart surroundings. Recommended. *Rainbow*, 54 Nam Ky Khoi Nghia St. Mixed Western and Vietnamese menu, good fare at the pricier end of the Can Tho spectrum, still represents value for money. *Tan Thanh*, 182 A 3 Thang 2 St. 'Serving merry-making, wedding, birthday, longlive toasting party', a little way out. *Thien Hoa*, 26 Hai Ba Trung St. Used by tour groups but remains good, friendly owner speaks no English. *Vinh Loi*, 42 Hai Ba Trung St. Claims to be 24 hour, popular with tourists.

Entertainment

Dancing *International Hotel*, 12 Hai Ba Trung St and *Hau Giang A Hotel*, 34 Nam Ky Khoi Nghia St.

Shopping

Minimart No 1, 1 Ngo Quyen St. By the market for alcohol and other useful items.

Transport

32 kilometres from Vinh Long, 64 kilometres from Long Xuyen, 103 kilometres from My Tho, 115 kilometres from Rach Gia, 120 kilometres from Chau Doc, 165 kilometres from Saigon, 206 kilometres from Ha Tien. **Local** *Xe ôm*, cyclo and sampan. Cars can be hired from the larger hotels. **Road Bus**: the bus station is about 2 kilometres northwest of town along Nguyen Trai St, near the intersection with Hung Vuong St and route 4. Regular connections from Saigon's Mien Tay terminal, 4-5 hours and other centres in the Mekong Delta. Rach Gia, 5 hours, 10,000d; Chau Doc, 4 hours, 9,600d. **Sea Hydrofoil**: the daily hydrofoil to Can Tho from Saigon is a popular alternative to the gruelling bus ride. 4 hours (via My Tho), US$24 one way, T08-8215609.

Directory

Communications Post Office: intersection of Hoa Binh Blvd and Ngo Quyen St. **Tourist offices** *Can Tho Tourist*, 20 Hai Ba Trung St, T821852, F822719. Quite expensive, tours in powerful boats – not the best way to see the delta.

Soc Trang

Phone code: 079
Colour map 4, grid C3

Soc Trang is a large, sprawling and scruffy town which sits astride a narrow branch of the Mekong distributory system and is dominated by a huge telecommunications mast. Historically the town was home to a large Khmer community, as is witnessed by the darker skins of many inhabitants. Indeed, most of its attraction lies in this connection, and for those running to a leisurely timetable it might warrant a visit which can be done as a day trip from Can Tho. On the tenth day of the tenth lunar month (around late November/early December) the town dusts itself down and generates a carnival atmosphere for the lively *Ghe Nho Festival*. People come from miles around to watch Khmer boats racing on the river, with hundreds of young men paddling furiously.

At the top end of town on Nguyen Thi Minh Khai Street is the **Kleang**
Pagoda, a temple built in traditional Cambodian style, perched on a two-level
terrace. Vivid colours adorn the windows and doors while inside sits a fine
golden sakyamuni statue which would look better without its tacky electric
halo. Opposite the pagoda is the **Khmer Museum** in which musical instruments, traditional clothing and agricultural tools form the rather uninspired
display.

About three kilometres out of town is the **Matoc Pagoda** or (Maha Tup as it is
properly called in Khmer). Follow Le Hong Phong Street and fork right after
the fire station. The main pagoda is on the right and is decorated with superb
brightly coloured murals; recently restored with donations from the Vietnamese and Khmer diaspora. Buddhists have worshipped on this holy site for
over 400 years, but the pagoda's current incarnation is relatively modern. The
chief attraction of the place, Megachiropteraphobes excepted, is the fruit bat.
Thousands of these enormous mammals roost in the trees behind the pagoda
and at dusk are an impressive sight as they fly off en masse to find food, literally blackening the sky. Also behind the pagoda are the monks' living quarters
and the tombs of two five-toed pigs, which are special to this community.
Look carefully at the picture on the grave! Some living examples can be seen in
the pens, lovingly cared for by the monks.

B-D *Khanh Hung*, 15 Tran Hung Dao St, T821026. All a/c, hot water, satellite TV, some
very nice rooms, friendly. Recommended. **C** *Phong Lan*, 124 Dong khoi St, T812619.
A/c, hot water, some rooms have a balcony overlooking the river. **C-D** *Cong Doan*, 4
Tran Van Sac, T825614. Some a/c, no hot water, walls stained with damp but nevertheless clean if spartan. **D-E** *Dong Tien*. Has girls.

Soc Trang has no outstanding eateries, but several restaurants on Hai Ba Trung St do
simple and cheap rice dishes. *Khanh Hung Hotel* offers a range of good food. *Phong
Lan Hotel* has some Western dishes on a largely Vietnamese menu.

Road Bus: the bus station is N of the river on Nguyen Chi Thanh St.

Communications Post Office: 2 Tran Hung Dao St.

Long Xuyen

This is an airy, albeit rather shabby, town and the capital of An Giang Prov- *Phone code: 076*
ince. It is situated on the west bank of the Bassac River and has a population of *Colour map 4, grid B2*
100,000. It falls slightly short, however, of the claims made by An Giang Tour-
ism: "Travellers are invited to take a glimpse of Angiang's good decor. Elegant, comfortable hotels: particularly, perfect services with special dishes that
are so delicious and fetching that hardly may another place be found out."

The large **Catholic Cathedral** on Hung Vuong Street is visible from out of
town – two clasped hands form the spire. It was completed shortly before
reunification in 1975. A short walk away at 8 Le Minh Nguyen Street is the
Quan Thanh Pagoda. It contains lively murals on the entrance wall and the
figure of General Quan Cong and his two mandarin companions General
Chau Xuong and Mandarin Quan Binh at the altar. Also on Le Minh Nguyen
Street, close to the intersection with Huynh Thi Huong Street, is the **Dinh
Than My Phuoc Pagoda**. Note the roof and the murals on the wooden walls
near the altar.

An Giang Museum is at 77 Thoai Ngoc Hau Street. It fails to rise far above the 'dull' rating so keep it for a rainy day. On display are war relics and Ton Duc Thang's personal affects (such as the leg irons he wore in prison) and some Oc Eo artefacts. Ton Duc Thang was born on nearby Ong Ho island. He later worked in the Bason Shipyard where he incited agitation against the French for which he served a term on Con Dao Island. In 1946 he went to Hanoi and became friends with Ho Chi Minh. Upon the latter's death in 1969 Ton Duc Thang became president of North Vietnam, and in 1975 president of the United Vietnam. On the outskirts of town on Tran Hung Dao Street travelling towards Chau Doc (just after the second bridge, about 500 metres), the **Cao Dai church** is worth visiting if unable to see the Cao Dai Cathedral at Tay Ninh (see page 270).

Excursions   **Ong Ho Island** is a pleasant trip up the Hau River for fans of Bac Ton (Uncle Ton). Take a boat from the river front.

Sleeping   **B** *Cuu Long (Mekong)*, 21 Nguyen Van Cung, T852365. A/c, hot water, large rooms, clean. **B** *Long Xuyen*, 17 Nguyen Van Cung St, T852927. A/c, hot water. **C-D** *An Giang*, 40 Hai Ba Trung St, T852297. A/c, hot water, clean and good value. **C-D** *Thai Binh 2*, 4 Nguyen Hue St, T841859. Some a/c, hot water, average. **D** *Song Hau*, 243 Nguyen Luong Duyet St, T852308. A/c. **D** *Thai Binh*, 12 Nguyen Hue, T852184. Restaurant. **D** *Tien Thanh*, 240 Tran Hung Dao St. Out of town on way in from Can Tho. **D** *Xuan Phuong*, 68 Nguyen Trai St, T852041. A/c, clean. **D-E** *Hun Dung*, 283 Tran Hung Dao St, T853882. Some a/c, very clean and friendly. **E** *Phat Thanh*, 2 Ly Tu Trong St, T841708. Pretty grubby.

Transport   64 kilometres from Can Tho, 126 kilometres from My Tho. **Road Bus**: the station is 1 ½ kilometres east of town on Tran Hung Dao St. Minibuses stop on Hung Vuong St, not far from the cathedral. Regular connections with Saigon's Mien Tay station 6-7 hours, Chau Doc 1½ hours, Can Tho, Vinh Long and other destinations in the delta. There are a number of private minibus companies in town offering a faster and more comfortable service than the regular buses.

Directory   **Banks** *Vietcombank*, 1 Hung Vuong (at the junction of Hung Vuong and Nguyen Thi Minh Khai streets). Those going to Chau Doc should cash their TCs here. **Communications** **Post Office:** 101 Tran Hung Dao St (quite a way over the Hoang Dieu Bridge and more centrally on Ngo Gia Tu St). **Tourist offices** *An Giang Tourist Office*, 17 Nguyen Van Cung St, T841036.

Sa Dec

Phone code: 067
Colour map 4, grid B2

Sa Dec was formerly the capital of Dong Thap province, a privilege that was removed in 1984. It is a friendly town about 20 kilometres west of Vinh Long. Its biggest claim to fame is that it was the birthplace of French novelist Margueritte Duras, and the town's three main avenues – Nguyen Hue, Tran Hung Dao and Hung Vuong – together with the odd colonial villa betray the French influence on this relatively young town.

Sights   Sa Dec's bustling riverside **market** on Nguyen Hue Street is worth a visit. Many of the scenes from the film adaption of Duras' novel *The Lover* were filmed in front of the shop terraces and merchants' houses here. Sit in one of the many riverside cafés to watch the world float by – which presumably, as a young woman, is what Duras did.

Duras' childhood home is across the river and can be reached by ferry from the covered fish market. Hers is the first of two villas near the wharf, now rather tired looking and in use as a school, which would perhaps be of consolation to Duras mère who was herself the local teacher.

Phuoc Hung Pagoda at 75/5 Hung Vuong Street is a splendid Chinese-style pagoda constructed in 1838 when Sa Dec was a humble one-road village. Surrounded by ornamental gardens, lotus ponds and cypress trees, the main temple to the right is decorated with fabulous animals assembled from pieces of porcelain rice bowls. Inside are some marvellous wooden statues of Buddhist holies made in 1838 by the venerable sculptor Cam. There are also some superbly preserved gilded wooden beams and two antique prayer tocsins. The smaller one was made in 1888 and its resounding mellow tone changes with the weather. The West Hall contains a valuable copy of the 101 volume Great Buddhist Canon. There are also some very interesting and ancient old photos of dead devotees and of pagoda life in the past. In the courtyard take care not to squash the old turtles that plod about amid the greenery.

Tu Ton Rose Garden is a few kilometres west of Sa Dec and can be reached either on foot or by Honda om to Tan Qui Don village. This 6,000 hectare nursery borders the river and is home to more than 40 varieties of rose and 540 other types of plant, from medicinal herbs to exotic orchids. For once the local tourist company's breathless prose turns out to be correct.

Excursions

D *Sa Dec*, 108/5A Hung Vuong St, T861430. Some a/c, comfortable but a touch overpriced. **D-E** *Bong Hong*, 5/74 Quoc Lo (National Highway), T861301. Some good value a/c rooms if you don't mind the peeling paintwork.

Sleeping

Cay Sung, 2/4 Hung Vuong St and the next door *Thuy*, 2/3 Hung Vuong St. Both serve good Vietnamese rice dishes for a dollar or less.

Eating

143 kilometres from Saigon, 102 kilometres from Chau Doc and 20 kilometres from Vinh Long. **Road Bus**: the bus station is about 500 metres southeast of town down Nguyen Hue St and across the bridge.

Transport

Tourist offices The local branch of *Dong Thap Tourist Co* is in *Sa Dec Hotel*.

Directory

Cao Lanh

Cao Lanh is another typically sleepy delta town and provincial capital; this one is the administrative centre of Dong Thap province and hard either to like or dislike.

Phone code: 067
Colour map 4, grid B2

To the northeast along Nguyen Hue Street is the **war memorial**, while the road southwest leads to the birthplace of Ho Chi Minh's father, Nguyen Sinh Sac. The vast **Plain of Reeds** (Dong Thap Muoi) is a swamp that extends for miles on all sides, particularly in the late season monsoon (September-November). It is an important wildlife habitat but in the wet season, when the water levels rise, getting about on dry land can be a real problem. Extraordinarily, the Vietnamese have not adapted the stilt house solution used by the Khmer and every year get flooded out. In the rural districts houses are built on the highest land available and in a good year the floor will be just inches above the lapping water. At these times all transport is by boat. When the sky is grey the scene is unutterably desolate and in the isolation of the plain one can truly feel the end of the Earth has been reached.

Sights

Excursions Excursions are the only real reason to visit Cao Lanh, particularly if you are a bird lover or a Ho Chi Minh biographer. **Tam Nong Bird Sanctuary** (Chim Tram) is an 8,000 hectares reserve 45 kilometres northwest of Cao Lanh. It contains 182 species of bird at different times of year, but most spectacular is the red-headed crane, rarest of the world's 15 crane species. Between August and November these spectacular creatures migrate across the nearby Cambodian border to avoid the floods (cranes feed on land), but at any other time, and particularly at dawn and dusk, they are a magnificent sight. Floating rice is grown in the area around the Bird Sanctuary and although the acreage planted diminishes each year this is another of nature's truly prodigious feats. The leaves float on the surface while the roots are anchored in mud as much as four to five metres below; but as so much energy goes into growing the stalk little is left over for the ears of rice, so yields are low.

My An Bird Garden lies 44 kilometres northeast of Cao Lanh near Thap Muoi town. Here humans and birds live in close proximity to each other, the main species being the storks and ibises. Again, dawn and dusk are the best times to visit as the sky is darkened by tens of thousands of birds flying off to feed or coming home to roost. This can be combined with a boat trip to **Xeo Quyt Base**, about 20 kilometres northwest of Cao Lanh. There was so little vegetation cover that fast-growing eucalyptus trees were planted; but even these took three years to provide sufficient cover to conceal humans. As the waterlogged ground prevented tunnelling waterproof chambers sealed with plastic and resin were sunk into the mud. Stocked with rice, water and candles Communist cadres co-ordinated their resistance strategy from here for almost 15 years. Despite frequent land and air raids the US forces never succeeded in finding or damaging the base.

Tower Mound (Go Thap), is the best place from which to get a view of the immensity and beauty of the surrounding Plain of Reeds. Here also visitors can see a 10-storey pagoda originally erected by President Ngo Dinh Diem, as a visual pun (Dong Thap Muoi can be translated as '10-storey tower') which was quite rightly destroyed by the Viet Minh but rebuilt in 1992; also the tomb of emperor Gia Long's sister and the earthworks from which General Duong and Admiral Kieu conducted their resistance against the French invaders between 1861 and 1866.

Sleeping **B-C** *Song Tra*, 175 Nguyen Hue St, T852504. Currently Cao Lanh's best hotel, very comfortable. **C** *Xuan Mai*, 2 Cong Ly St, T852852. Clean and spacious new hotel, all a/c, fridge and bath. **C-D** *My Tra*, T851218. East of town on Highway 30 towards the war memorial, all a/c, some nice rooms. **D-E** *Cao Lanh*, 72 Nguyen Hue St, T851061. Some a/c rooms, the cheapest of which are good value. Don't expect too many smiles, however. **D-E** *Thien Loi*, 32 Doc Binh Kieu St, T851370. Some a/c, quiet and cheap. **E** *Du Lich*, 30 Thang 4 St. Fan only, a truly grubby little place.

Eating *Song Tra*, *Xuan Mai* and *My Tra* hotels all have restaurants. *Tiem Com 44*, 44 Nguyen Hue St. Simple Vietnamese food, fried rice for 10,000d for example. *A Dong*, 64 Nguyen Hue St. Tasty and clean.

Transport **Road** **Bus**: the bus station is located at the southeast end of Ly Thuong Kiet St. Connections with all delta towns and with Saigon.

Directory **Banks** *Incombank* is on the opposite corner to the Post Office but does not cash TCs. **Communications** Post Office: on the corner of Nguyen Hue and Ly Thuong Kiet streets. **Tourist offices** *Dong Thap Tourist Co*, 2 Doc Binh Kieu St, T851343, F852136. Unusually friendly and helpful and good value for a province tourist company, organizes boat trips to all local sites (US$20-30).

Chau Doc

The town

Chau Doc is an attractive bustling riverside town (formerly called Chau Phu) in An Giang Province on the west bank of the Hau or Bassac River (sometimes also called the Hau River) and bordering Cambodia. With a population of 96,000, it is an important trading and marketing centre for the surrounding agricultural communities. Until the mid-18th century this was part of Cambodia: it was given to the Nguyen lord, Nguyen Phuc Khoat, after he had helped to put down an insurrection in the area. The area still supports a large Khmer population, as well as the largest Cham settlement in the Delta. Cambodia's influence can be seen in the tendency for women to wear scarves instead of the non la conical hat, and in the people's darker skin, indicating Khmer blood. The Chau Doc district (it was a separate province for a while) is the seat of the Hoa Hao religion which claims about one to one and a half million adherents and was founded in the village of Hoa Hao in 1939 (see page 382).

Phone code: 076
Colour map 4, grid B2

Sights

A large **market** sprawls from the river-front down and along Le Cong Thanh Doc, Phu Thu, Bach Dang and Chi Lang streets. It sells fresh produce and black market goods smuggled in from Thailand. Near the market and the river, at the intersection of Gia Long and Nguyen Van Thoai streets is the **Chau Phu Pagoda**. Built in 1926, it is dedicated to Thai Ngoc Hau, a former local mandarin: rather dilapidated, but with some fine carved pillars.

Excursions

Nui Sam or Sam Mountain lies about 5 kilometres southwest of town and is one reason to visit Chau Doc. This mountain was designated a 'Famed Beauty Spot' in 1980 by the Ministry of Culture. Rising from the flood plain, Nui Sam is a favourite spot for Vietnamese tourists who throng here, especially at festival time. The mountain, really a barren rock-strewn hill, can be seen at the

Nui Sam

The Mekong Delta & the South

Chau Doc

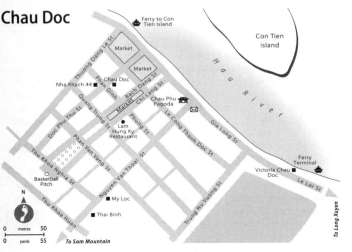

end of the continuation of Nguyen Van Thoai Street. It is literally honeycombed with tombs, sanctuaries and temples. Most visitors come only to see Tay An Pagoda, Lady Xu Temple, and the tomb of Thoai Ngoc Hau. But it is possible to walk or drive right up the hill for good views of the surrounding countryside: from the summit it is easy to appreciate that this is some of the most productive land in Vietnam. At the top is a military base formerly occupied by American soldiers and now by Vietnamese protecting their Cambodia flank.

Tay An Pagoda The Tay An Pagoda is at the foot of the hill, facing the road. Built originally in 1847, it has been extended twice and now represents an eclectic mixture of styles – Chinese, Islamic, perhaps even Italian. The pagoda contains a bewildering display of over 200 statues. A short distance on from the pagoda, past shops and stalls, is the **Chua Xu**. This temple was originally constructed in the late 19th century, and then rebuilt in 1972. It is rather a featureless building, though highly revered by the Vietnamese and honours the holy Lady Xu whose statue is enshrined in the new multi-roofed pagoda. The 23rd to the 25th of the fourth lunar month is the date of the holy Lady during which time, if the blurb of An Giang Tourist is to be believed (it is not), two million Vietnamese flock to see her being washed and reclothed. Hyperbole aside Lady Xu is a major pilgrimage for traders and business from Saigon and the south all hoping that sales will thereby soar and profits leap. On the other side of the road is the tomb of **Thoai Ngoc Hau** (1761-1829); an enormous head of the man graces the entranceway. The real reason to come here is to watch the pilgrims, rather than study the temples and tombs – which are rather poor – and to climb the hill. ■ *Getting there: either by bus (there is a stop at the foot of the mountain) or, more peacefully, by the local equivalent of the cyclo.*

Temples on the mountain Hang Pagoda is a 200-year-old temple situated half way up and is worth visiting for several reasons. In the first level of the temple are some vivid cartoon drawings of the tortures of hell. The second level is built at the mouth of a cave which last century was home to a woman named Thich Gieu Thien. Her likeness and tomb can be seen in the first pagoda. Fed up with her lazy and abusive husband she left her home in Cholon and came to live in this cave, as an ascetic supposedly waited on by two snakes.

Essentials

Sleeping *Victoria Chau Doc*, Le Loi St. An entire renovation by this excellent French hotel group should produce top quality accommodation. **C-D** *My Loc*, 51 Nguyen Van Thoai, T866455. Some a/c, friendly, including breakfast, quiet area. **C-E** *Thanh Tra*, 77 Thu Khoa Nghia St, T866788. Some a/c, nice and quiet. **D-E** *Thuan Loi*, 18 Tran Hung Dao St, T866134. Some a/c and good river views, clean and friendly. Recommended. **E** *Chau Doc*, 17 Doc Phu Thu St, T866484. Friendly but grubby, popular and central. **E** *Hotel 777*, 47 Doc Phu Thu, T866409. Small but friendly. **E** *Nha Khach 44*, 44 Doc Phu Thu St, T866540. Friendly and clean. **E** *Tai Ngan*, Nguyen Huu Canh, T866435. A very new place and still neat and clean. Extra charges for a/c and hot water. **E** *Thai Binh*, 37 Nguyen Van Thoai, T866221.

Nui Sam Almost every café near Sam Mountain has a room for rent and good value can be found by shopping around and bargaining hard. Two at the foot are: **D-E** *Guesthouse 27*, T861006. Some a/c, big rooms. On the mountain itself is **D-E** *Tango*, T861775. Some a/c, restaurant. **E** *Guesthouse 333*, T861048. Some a/c, friendly and clean.

Try the **Bong Mai** restaurant at the corner of Phan Dinh Phung and Doc Phu Thu **Eating**
streets (next to the *Chau Doc Hotel*), 17 Doc Phu Thu St. Vietnamese and Western
dishes in an old colonial mansion, cheap and cheerful. **Lam Hung Ky**, 71 Chi Lang St.
Excellent freshly prepared and cooked food. There is a wide range of good foodstalls
in the market area.

96 kilometres from Ha Tien, 117 kilometres from Can Tho, 179 kilometres from My **Transport**
Tho. **Road Bus**: the station is southeast of town on the south side of Le Loi St. 1-2
kilometres from town centre, past the church; minibuses stop in town on Quang
Trung St. Regular connections with Saigon's Mien Tay station (6-7 hours), including
two ferry crossings. Buses to Long Xuyen (1½ hours), Can Tho, and other destinations
in the delta. **Boat Ferries**: there are daily ferries along the canal to Ha Tien, journey
time 10 hours, a fascinating way to see village life, take plenty of water and food.

Communications Post Office: corner of Gia Long and Nguyen Van Thoai streets (on riverfront, **Directory**
opposite the Chau Phu Pagoda).

Ha Tien can be reached either by boat or by road. The road is in a pitiful state **From Chau Doc**
but can be traversed by four-wheel drive, Minsk or bicycle. Nevertheless it is **to Ha Tien**
well worth attempting as it means the south coast can be reached without trail-
ing back the 38 kilometres to Long Xuyen. Also the scenery as the road skirts the
Cambodian border is beautiful and the local way of life little changed in hundreds of years. It passes Ba Chuc where the bones of 1,000 Vietnamese killed in
1978 by the Khmer Rouge are displayed in a glass-sided memorial. The nearby
Tan Buu Memorial contains grisly photographs of the carnage.

Rach Gia

Rach Gia is the capital of Kien Giang Province. The wealth of the province is *Phone code: 077*
based on rice and seafood. *Nuoc mam*, a renowned fish sauce is produced *Colour map 4,*
here. The city is an important deep water port on the Gulf of Thailand with a *grid B2*
population of 125,000. Already an entry point for goods, both smuggled and
legal, from Thailand, it should grow in significance if Vietnam continues to
follow the path of economic reform and rapprochement with the market
economies of the region. The centre of the town is in fact an island at the
mouth of the **Cai Lon River**.

Unfortunately, Rach Gia is a rather unpleasant little town, best known for its **Sights**
bia ôm bars and prostitution. There are a number of pagodas in town including the **Phat Lon Pagoda**, which is on the mainland north of town just off
Quang Trung Street, and the **Nguyen Trung Truc Temple** which is not far
away at 18 Nguyen Cong Tru Street. The latter is dedicated to the 19th century
Vietnamese resistance leader of the same name. Nguyen Trung Truc was
active in Cochin China during the 1860s, and led the raid that resulted in the
firing of the French warship *Esperance*. As the French closed in, he retreated
to the island of Phu Quoc. From here, the French only managed to dislodge
him after threatening to kill his mother. He gave himself up and was executed
at the market place in Rach Gia on 27 October 1868. **Tam Bao Temple** dates
from the 18th century but was rebuilt in 1917. During the First Indochina
War it was used to conceal Viet Minh nationalists who published a newspaper
from here. There is a small **museum** at 21 Nguyen Van Troi Street in the heart
of town and a **market** in the northeast quarter of the island. The wharf area is
interesting and the bustling fish market displays the wealth of the seas. Some
attractive colonial architecture survives.

The Mekong Delta & the South

Excursions **Oc-eo** is an ancient city about 10 kilometres inland from Rach Gia. It is of great interest and significance to archaeologists, but there is not a great deal for the tourist to see bar a pile of stones on which sits a small bamboo shrine. The site is overseen by an elderly custodian who lives adjacent. This port city of the ancient kingdom of Funan (see page 327) was at its height from the first to sixth centuries AD. Excavations have shown that buildings were constructed on piles and the city was inter-linked by a complex network of irrigation and transport canals. Like many of the ancient empires of the region, Oc-eo built its wealth on controlling trade between the east (China) and the west (India, Mediterranean). Vessels from Malaya, Indonesia and Persia docked here. No sculpture has yet been found, but a gold medallion with the profile of the Roman emperor Antonius Pius (152 AD) has been unearthed.

■ *Getting there: the site is near the village of Tan Hoi, and is only accessible by boat. Hire a small boat (the approach canal is very shallow and narrow) from the river front beyond the Vinh Tan Van Market, northeast along Bach Dang Street. The trip takes several hours; expect to pay about US$12.*

Rach Gia

N

| 0 | metres | 100 |
| 0 | yards | 109 |

■ **Sleeping**
1 1 Thang 5
2 Binh Minh
3 Palace
4 Thanh Binh
5 To Chau

(All listed below are on the island.) **B** *To Chau*, 41 Ho Chi Minh St (aka 41 Le Loi St), T863718. A/c. **C-D** *Palace*, 41 Tran Phu St, T863049. A/c, fan rooms, breakfast included. **C-D** *1 Thang 5 (1 May Hotel)*, 38 Nguyen Hung Son St, T862103. Reasonable. **E** *Binh Minh*, 48 Pham Hong Thai St, T862154. Not a very welcoming place. **E-F** *Thanh Binh*, 11 Ly Tu Trong St, T863053. Shared WC but clean, motorbikes for rent.

Sleeping
■ *on map*
Price codes:
see inside front cover

Hoa Bien, end of Nguyen Hung Son St, by sea. Cool breeze, good service. Thien Nga, 4A Le Loi St. Kindly helpful owner, good freshly prepared food. **Rach Soi**: *Khanh Ngoc*, near Sua Dua Bridge. Specializes in game including venison and hedgehog.

Eating

92 kilometres from Ha Tien, 115 kilometres from Can Tho, 182 kilometres from My Tho, 250 kilometres from Saigon. **Air** Connections with Phu Quoc Island, 30 minutes and Saigon (via Phu Quoc), 2 hours, twice a week. The airport is at Rach Soi about 10 kilometres east of Rach Gia.

Transport

Road **Bus**: the station is south of town on Nguyen Trung Truc St. Regular connections with Saigon's Mien Tay terminal (8 hours). Also connections with Can Tho and Long Xuyen. Local buses to Ha Tien leave from an office at 33 30 Thang 4 St. **Boat** Daily connections to Phu Quoc, depart ferry terminal on Nguyen Cong Tru St, west of the island, 0800, journey time approximately 9 hours.

Banks *Vietcombank*, 1 Huynh Man Dat St, adjacent to Post Office. *Vietnam Airlines*, 180 Nguyen Trung Truc St, T861848. **Communications** Post Office: Tu Duc St (on the mainland, north bank). **Tourist offices** *Kien Giang Tourism*, 12 Ly Tu Trong St (on the island), T862081.

Directory

Rach Gia to Ha Tien

Highway 80 from Rach Gia to Ha Tien follows the Rach Gia-Ha Tien canal virtually the entire way. The road begins well enough with a decent surface and coconut palms and emerald paddies to charm the eye. But it soon degenerates into a pot-holed, dusty track. Add clouds of dust from the Kien Luong cement works and the need for a hotel with running water becomes urgent. Ba Hon village, near the cement works, is the turning for Hon Chong. Towards Ha Tien the road nears the sea where rooted in the inter-tidal zone are miles of mangrove forest, most newly replanted. The palms of *Nypa fruticans*, and the distinctively stilt-rooted *Rhizophora apiculata* predominate. The former is extensively used for thatch while the latter produces excellent charcoal.

Ha Tien

The town is located west of a lagoon called Dong Ho (East Lake) which is bridged by a floating pontoon (toll charged for vehicles and pedestrians). The bridge was built by US Army engineers who would, no doubt, be pleased by the longevity of their construction.

Phone code: 077
Colour map 4, grid B1

Ha Tien's history is strongly coloured by its proximity to Cambodia to which the area belonged until the 18th century. The numerical and agricultural superiority of the Vietnamese allowed them to gradually displace the Khmer occupants and eventually military might, under Mac Cuu prevailed. But it is not an argument the Khmer are prepared to walk away from, as their incursions in the late 1970s showed, and bitter resentments remain on both sides of the border.

The Mekong Delta & the South

Sights   Despite its colourful history, modern Ha Tien does not contain a great deal of interest to the visitor and apart from a handful of buildings there is little of architectural merit. The most interesting historical sights and landscapes can be viewed in about a day.

There are a number of pagodas in town. The **Tam Bao Temple** at 328 Phuong Thanh Street was founded in the 18th century as too was **Chua Phu Dung** (Phu Dung Pagoda) which can be found not far away, a short distance along a path to the northwest just off Phuong Thanh Street. A lengthy story is attached to this temple, the Cotton Rose Hibiscus Pagoda. In 1730 newly widowed Nguyen Nghi fled invaders from Laos and landed in Ha Tien with his son and 10-year-old daughter, Phu Cu (the ancient form of Phu Dung with the same floral meaning). Nguyen Nghi was soon appointed Professor of Literature and Poetry to Duke Mac Cuu's son, Mac Tu, and privately tutored his own little daughter, who had taken to dressing as a boy in order to be able to attend school. After Duke Mac Cuu's untimely death in 1735 his son was granted the name Mac Thien Tich and the title Great Admiral Commander- in-Chief, Plenipotentiary Minister of Ha Tien Province. Later he inaugurated a poetry club at which young Phu Cu, still in the guise of a boy, declaimed exquisitely, setting passions ablaze. Surreptitious investigations put the Great Admiral's mind at rest: 'he' was in fact a girl. A long poetic romance and royal wedding followed. After years of happy marriage the angelic Phu Cu one day begged her husband to let her break with their poetic love of the past and become a nun. The Great Admiral realized he could not but comply. He built the Phu Cu, Cotton Rose Hibiscus Pagoda, wherein his beloved wife spent the rest of her life in prayer and contemplation. The towering pagoda was built so high that it served as a constant reminder and could, in due course, be seen from his own tomb.

Den Mac Cuu, the temple dedicated to the worship of the Mac Cuu and his clan was built 1898-1902. Mac Cuu was provincial governor under the waning Khmer and in 1708 established a Vietnamese protectorate. The temple lies a short way from the town and sits at the foot of **nui lang**, tomb mountain. To the left of the altar house is a map showing the location of the tombs of members of the clan. Mac Cuu's own tomb lies a short distance up the hill along a path leading from the right of the temple – nice views of the sea. Around the back of nui lang (a short drive, or longish trek) is **Lang Mo Ba Co Nam** (tomb of Great Aunt number five), an honorary title given to the three-year-old daughter of Mac Cuu who was buried alive. It has become an important shrine to Vietnamese seeking her divine intercession in time of family crisis and more visited than Mac Cuu's tomb.

Excursions   **Mui Nai** lies in a 'tourist park' about five kilometres west of town. There are some nicely wooded hills and a muddy beach from where Phu Quoc Island and Cambodia can be seen. The beach gets very crowded and litter-strewn during public holidays. Rock scrambling for the nimble footed but disappointing compared with the sandy beach at Hon Chong. ■ *500d, cars 3,000d.*
Thach Dong Pagoda, three kilometres from Ha Tien, and a short hike up from the road, is dedicated to the goddess Quan Am; at the bottom of the mountain is *Bia Cam Thu* (Monument of Hate – the Vietnamese don't mince their words) a memorial to the 130 slain by the Khmer Rouge in March 1978. The temple is inside a limestone hill which consists of a series of caves and clefts in the rock. Good views of the surrounding, remarkably flat, country. ■ *5,000d, cameras 5,000d.* About two kilometres beyond Thach Dong Pagoda is the **Cambodian border**: do not let the fact that it is permeable to locals and contraband of all sorts encourage you to follow; this is not an authorized crossing for foreigners.

Hon Chong is a popular and well known beach area about 30 kilometres east of Ha Tien. Unlike Ha Tien, Hon Chong has clean white sand and miles of unspoilt beach – much nicer than Ha Tien but not a patch on Phu Quoc. Apart from the beach its main claim to fame is the holy grotto and the interesting limestone formations, **Hon Phu Tu**, Father and Son rocks which lie 100 metres or so offshore (5,000d for a boat ride). Follow the path through **Chua Hang (Hang Pagoda)** to the beach. The temple with its Buddha of 100 hands loses much of its religious significance and atmosphere at holiday times

Ha Tien

The Mekong Delta & the South

■ Sleeping
1 Dong Ho
2 Du Lich
3 Duc Tai Guesthouse
4 Ha Tien
5 Khai Hoan
6 Phuong Thanh
7 To Chau

● Eating
1 Huong Bien
2 Khai Hoan

(notably Tet) when noisy throngs of trippers file through on their way to the beach. Boats accommodating more than 10 people can be hired from some of the cafés for about US$70 per day, smaller boats should be much less. A number of elementary guesthouses including **E** *Hon Trem*, T854331, and **E** *Huong Bien*, T853466. No fan, hot, cramped, very basic, but an excellent restaurant with good food. ■ *Getting there: by car, turn south off Highway 80 at Ba Hon village, 11 kilometres down an appallingly uncomfortable and slow track. Or by bus to Ba Hon, 45 minutes, xe ôm to Hon Chong, 10,000d, one and a half hours, very dusty.*

Phu Quoc Island lies 45 kilometres west of Ha Tien, it is not possible to get there by boat from Ha Tien as the route is so near Cambodian waters; travellers have managed to get from Phu Quoc back to Ha Tien by boat, however (two to three hours).

Sleeping
■ *on map*
Price codes:
see inside front cover

D-E *Dong Ho*, Tran Hau St, T852141. Basic, noisy and lack of clean water reported. **D-E** *Du Lich*, Mac Thien Tich St. Large fan rooms. **D-E** *Khai Hoan*, 239 Phuong Thanh St, T852254. Recommended. **E** *Duc Tai Guesthouse*, Phuong Thanh St. **E** *Ha Tien*, corner of Ben Tran Hau and Phuong Thanh streets. A real treat for nature lovers: *Listen* to the dogs singing in the courtyard, *Feel* the pain that the bedbugs inflict, *Witness* plagues of mosquitoes unseen since biblical times, *Hear* the cockroaches scuttle home from the party under your bed and *Enjoy* the sound of rats copulating in the corner. **E** *Phuong Thanh*, Phuong Thanh St. Old, fan only, may not accept westerners. **E** *To Chau*, To Chau St, T852148. Fan only, run down.

Eating
● *on map*

Numerous food stalls along the river and Ben Tran Hau. *Khai Hoan*, Ben Tran Hau. Looks scruffy from the outside but food is good. *Huong Bien*, Ben Tran Hau. Not bad, but may run out of food.

Shopping

Ha Tien is known for its tortoiseshell products: carved fans, boxes, combs and other items made from the shells of specially bred tortoises, 999 Tham Tuong Xanh St.

Transport

92 kilometres from Rach Gia, 96 kilometres from Chau Doc (by canal), 206 kilometres from Can Tho, 272 kilometres from My Tho, 338 kilometres from Saigon. **Road Bus**: the bus station is on the southeast edge of town, south of the pontoon bridge that crosses the Chau To River. Buses from Saigon's Mien Tay station, 10 hours, regular connections with Rach Gia, 4 hours, and Can Tho. **Boat** It appears to be possible to get to Ha Tien from Phu Quoc – don't bank on it – although not vice versa. **Ferry** The ferry wharf is just to the northeast of the pontoon bridge. Ferries to Chau Doc (70,000d, 7-10 hours) depart 0600, take food and water.

Directory   **Communications** Post Office: to Chau St.

Phu Quoc Island

Phu Quoc's northernmost tip lies just outside Cambodian territorial waters and, like other parts of present day Vietnam in this area, it has been fought over, claimed and reclaimed by Thai, Khmer and Viet. The island is today renowned for its *nuoc mam* (fish sauce), which is exported globally. Fishing and pepper are mainstays of the local economy although smuggling provides a living for some of the island's 46,000 population. The waters around the island are clear and unpolluted, sufficiently so for pearls to be cultivated in oyster beds. Snorkelling is good. None of the ambitious plans for transforming Phu Quoc into a tropical playground for wealthy tourists has come to fruition: given the current economic outlook it will be some time before they do.

Phone code: 077
Colour map 4, grid B1

Historically, the island is renowned for its small part in the triumph of the Nguyen Dynasty. In 1765 Pigneau de Behaine was sent here as a young seminarist to train Roman Catholic missionaries; by chance he was on the island when Nguyen Anh (son of emperor-to-be Gia Long) arrived, fleeing the Tay Son. Pigneau's role in the rise of the Nguyen Dynasty is described more fully on page 184. Another link between the island and wider Vietnamese history is that it was here, in 1919, that the civil servant Ngo Van Chieu communed with the spirit world and made contact with the Supreme Being, leading to the establishment of the Cao Dai religion (see page 382).

Duong Dong is the largest town on the island, the airport is a short drive outside.

D *Huong Bien*, Duong Dong. Clean rooms with bathroom, on the beach. **D** *Kim Linh*, Duong To Village, T846611. On the beach, excellent restaurant, helpful staff, motorbikes to rent, boat trips cost around US$50 per day including lunch (for up to 8 people).

Sleeping

Air 4 connections weekly with Saigon, 50 minutes and 2 with Rach Gia, 30 minutes. *Vietnam Airlines*, in the airport, T846086, F846693.

Transport

Boat It is not possible to get to Phu Quoc by boat from Ha Tien although reports suggest the return journey, which follows a slightly more southerly route, is possible, 2-3 hours. About 9 hours from Rach Gia. Ferry reaches An Thui at the south tip of Phu Quoc around 1700, *xe ôm* to Duong Dong, 30 minutes, or bus, 1 hour. Boats will not sail in rough conditions or if there are too few passengers.

Communications Tourist offices *Phu Quoc Tourist Company*, Duong Dong, T846050/ 846113.

Directory

hu Quoc Island

Bai Thom Beach
Cape Da Chong
Cape Ganh Dau
Mong Tay
Cua Can Beach
Ben Tranh Waterfall
Duong Dong
Duong To Hotel
Ham Ninh
Gulf of Thailand
Phu Quoc Prison
An Thoi
Bai Khem Beach
Cape Hanh
Gia Long's Stone Chair
An Thoi Ferry Quay
Roi
Thom
Vong
Vang
Kim Quy
Xuong
May Rut
Mong Tay
N
Not to scale

Background

8

Background

Vietnam - Provinces

CHINA

Lai Châu

Lào Cai

Hà Giang

Cao Bang

Tuyên Quang

Bac Thai

Lang Son

Yên Bái

Vinh Phú

Hà Bac

1

Quang Ninh

Son La

2

Hòa Bình

Hai Hung

3

4

6 5

Thanh Hóa

Gulf of Tonkin

LAOS

Nghê An

Hà Tinh

Quang Bình

Quang Tri

Thùa Thiên Huê

THAILAND

Quang Nam Dà Nang

Quang Ngai

Kon Tum

Bình Dinh

Gia Lai

Phú Yên

CAMBODIA

Dac Lac

Khánh Hòa

Sông Bé

Lâm Dong

Ninh Thuan

Tây Ninh

Dong Nai

Bình Thuan

An Giang

9

Long An

7

8

11

10

Can Tho

Ben Tre

South China Sea

Kiên Giang

Trà Vinh

Sóc Trang

Gulf of Thailand

Minh Hai

N

Provinces	4 Thái Bình	8 Ba Ria-Vung Tau
1 Hanoi	5 Nam Ha	9 Dong Tháp
2 Hà Tay	6 Ninh Bình	10 Vinh Long
3 Hai Phong	7 Ho Chi Minh City	11 Tien Giang

Background

After the war

The Socialist Republic of Vietnam (SRV) was born from the ashes of the Vietnam War on 2 July 1976 when former North and South Vietnam were reunified. Hanoi was proclaimed as the capital of the new country. But few Vietnamese would have guessed that their emergent country would be cast by the US in the mould of a pariah state for almost 18 years. First President George Bush, and then his successor Bill Clinton, eased the US trade embargo bit by bit in a dance of appeasement and procrastination, as they tried to comfort American business clamouring for a slice of the Vietnamese pie, while also trying to stay on the right side of the vociferous lobby in the US demanding more action on the MIA issue. Appropriately, the embargo, which was first imposed on the former North in May 1964, and then nationwide in 1975, was finally lifted a few days before the celebrations of Tet, Vietnamese New Year, on 4 February 1994.

On the morning of the 30 April 1975, just before 1100, a T-54 tank crashed through the gates of the Presidential Palace in Saigon, symbolically marking the end of the Vietnam War. 20 years later, the same tank – number 843 – became a symbol of the past as parades and celebrations, and a good deal of soul searching, marked the anniversary of the end of the War. To many Vietnamese, in retrospect, 1975 was more a beginning than an end: it was the beginning of a collective struggle to come to terms with the War, to build a nation, to reinvigorate the economy, and to excise the ghosts of the past. Two decades after the armies of the South laid down their arms and the last US servicemen and officials frantically fled by helicopter to carriers waiting in the South China Sea, the Vietnamese government is still trying, as they put it, to get people to recognize that 'Vietnam is a country, not a war'. A further 20 years from now, it may seem that only in 1995 did the War truly end. It was not until 1986 that the economic reforms enshrined in *doi moi* were formally adopted; not until September 1989 that Vietnamese forces withdrew from the tragedy of Cambodia; not until February 1994 that the US finally lifted its trade embargo of Vietnam; and not until July 1995 that Vietnam joined the Association of Southeast Asian Nations (ASEAN). In one of those twists of fate, which the concerns of the present tend to obscure, in joining ASEAN Vietnam became part of an organization that was initially established to counteract the Communist threat of Vietnam itself.

Vietnam is almost schizophrenic in complexion: it has adroitly reformed its economy and has some of the most liberal foreign investment laws in Asia; yet the Communist Party maintains an almost Stalinist grip on political dissent. It consists of two halves which, for 20 years developed along diverging paths and appear to be diverging once more as the reforms bite. Northerners and Southerners often have little time for one another and have been characterized, respectively, as temperamentally 'temperate' and 'tropical' – reflecting the environments of the north and south. In short, Vietnam is almost two countries in one.

Isolated from the Western world both economically and diplomatically since 1975, and so far as the north is concerned since 1954, Vietnam has an ambience and character not matched by any of the more Westernized nations of Southeast Asia. Many visitors find it difficult to disassociate the country from the Vietnam War – a conflict which managed to wreak such destruction in this corner of Asia, while traumatizing not one but two nations. But Vietnam has far more to offer than this sequence of recent historical events: there are the impressive temples of the ancient

Kingdom of Champa, verdant rice paddys (during the wet season), palm fringed tropical beaches, and the former imperial palace at Hué. For those with revolutionary predilections, there are agricultural cooperatives and communes, innovative drug rehabilitation centres, and ideologically sound carpet factories – although such is the pace of economic reform that these may not last much longer. Vietnam is changing almost before one's eyes. Although the war may be ever-so-slowly fading from the memory (and from the landscape) there are, as journalist Lincoln Kaye writes "places where the fixed enormity of past horrors inexorably glares through the banal ephemera of the present."

But to talk of Vietnam as a single, unified country disguises the deep differences which divide the north from the south, and the cities from the countryside. The brash, bright, vital and economically energetic city of Saigon could not be further removed from the grave, elegant and romantically decrepit city of Hanoi over 1,500 kilometres to the north. Between the two stretches a succession of cities remembered largely for their role in a war which in Vietnamese history occupies only a small slice of a centuries-long battle against outsiders: Nha Trang, Danang, Hué, Khe Sanh, Vinh and Dong Hoi.

The common view of Vietnam as one of the last bastions of Communism is already obsolete. The country is undergoing a fundamental reform of its economic system – known locally as *doi moi* or 'renovation'. In the south, the effects of these changes are already very much in evidence. New private businesses spring up almost overnight, foreign investors are moving in, and local enterprise is waking from its 15-year slumber. But although economic reform and market economics may be at the top of the government's agenda, political reform – in other words, *glasnost* to go with the *perestroika* – is actively discouraged. Journalists, novelists and academics who dare to question the supremacy of the Party are quickly silenced. It is uncertain how long the government will be able to maintain this balancing act.

Despite the visible signs of wealth in Saigon, or Ho Chi Minh City as it is officially known (see page 251), Vietnam is still among the poorest countries in the world. The government may be able to mobilize one of the world's largest armies, but producing consumer goods for its long-suffering population seems to be beyond its capabilities. *Doi moi* is reaping results, but it is still not clear whether this will create more than just small pockets of wealth among an otherwise destitute and increasingly dissatisfied population. Average incomes are still only US$230 per year, nearly half of children aged less than five are malnourished, and there are a mere four television sets per 100 people.

In economic terms, there are two Vietnams emerging. There are the major cities and towns where most things are available – for a price: fax facilities, photocopying, hamburgers, imported beers and soft drinks and whose citizens enjoy not only the fruits of international capitalism but profit by it. And then there is the rest of the country, where it is difficult to buy anything beyond life's basic necessities and where life has changed little in decades. Trying to narrow this yawning – and some would say widening – chasm will be the chief task of the Communist Party if it is to retain its legitimacy into the next century.

Background

History

Vietnam before history

The earliest record of humans in Vietnam is from an archaeological site on Do Mountain, in the northern Thanh Hoa Province. The remains discovered here have been dated to the Lower Palaeolithic (early Stone Age). So far, all early human remains have been unearthed in North Vietnam, invariably in association with limestone cliff dwellings. Unusually, tools are made of basalt rather than flint, the more common material found at similar sites in other parts of the world.

Archaeological excavations have shown that between 5,000 and 3,000 BC, two important Mesolithic cultures occupied North Vietnam: these are referred to as the **Hoa Binh** and **Bac Son** cultures after the principal excavation sites in Tonkin. Refined stone implements and distinctive hand axes with polished edges (known as Bacsonian axes) are characteristic of the two cultures. These early inhabitants of Vietnam were probably small and dark-skinned, probably of Melanesian or Austronesian stock.

There are 2,000 years of recorded Vietnamese history and another 2,000 years of legend. The Vietnamese people trace their origins back to 15 tribal groups known as the **Lac Viet** who settled in what is now North Vietnam at the beginning of the Bronze Age. Here they established an agrarian kingdom known as Van-lang which seems to have vanished during the third century BC.

A problem with early **French archaeological studies** in Vietnam was that most of the scholars were either Sinologists or Indologists. In consequence, they looked to Vietnam as a receptacle of Chinese or Indian cultural influences, and spent little time uncovering those aspects of culture, art and life that were indigenous in origin and inspiration. The French archaeologist Bezacier for example, expressed the generally held view that 'Vietnamese' history only began in the seventh century AD. Such sites as Hoa Binh, Dong Son and Oc-eo, which predate the seventh century, were regarded as essentially Chinese or 'Indonesian', their only 'Vietnameseness' being their geographical location. This perspective was more often than not based on faulty and slapdash scholarship, and reflected the prevailing view that Southeast Asian art was basically derivative.

Pre-colonial history

The beginning of Vietnamese recorded history coincides with the start of **Chinese cultural hegenomy** over the north, in the second century BC. The Chinese dominated Vietnam for over 1,000 years until the 10th century AD, and the cultural legacy is still very much in evidence, making Vietnam distinctive in Southeast Asia. Even after the 10th century, and despite breaking away from Chinese political domination, Vietnam was still overshadowed and greatly influenced by its illustrious neighbour to the north. Nonetheless, the fact that Vietnam could shrug off 1,000 years of Chinese subjugation and emerge with a distinct cultural heritage and language says a lot for Vietnam's strength of national identity. Indeed, it might be argued, as William Duiker does, that the Vietnamese nation "has been formed in the crucible of its historic resistance to Chinese conquest and assimilation".

The Ly Dynasty (1009-1225) was the first independent Vietnamese dynasty. Its capital, Thang Long, was at the site of present day Hanoi and the dynasty based its system of government and social relations closely upon the Chinese Confucianist model (see page 380). The Vietnamese owe a considerable debt to the Chinese (government, philosophy and arts) but they have always been determined to maintain their independence. Vietnamese Confucianist scholars were unsparing in their criticism of Chinese imperialism. Continuous Chinese

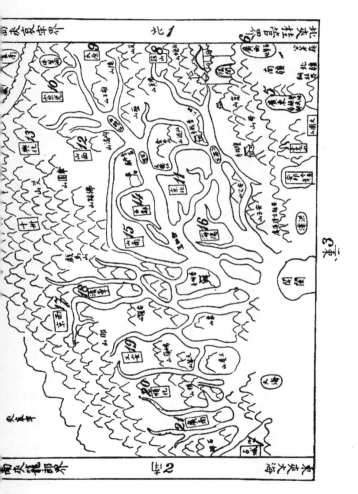

Map of Vietnam under the Lê Dynasty, taken from a manuscript dated 1490 and entitled *Geography of Hong Duc.* The orientation given is North (1), South (2), East (3), West (4); one can distinguish in the N, Kouang-tong (5), Kouang-si (6) and in the S, Champa (7). Between these two limits Vietnamese provinces are shown: from N to S and E to W: Lang Son (8), Thái Nguyên (9), Tuyên Quang (10), Kinh Bác (11), Son Tây (12), Hung Hoá (13), Trung Dô (14), Son Nam (15), Hai Durong (16), Tây Kinh (17), Thanh Hoá (18), Nghè An (19), Thuân Hoá (20), Quáng Nam (21).

invasions, all ultimately futile, served to cement an enmity between the two countries, which is still in evidence today – despite their having normalized diplomatic relations in October 1991.

The first Ly emperor, and one of Vietnam's great kings was Ly Cong Uan who was born in 974. He is usually known by his posthumous title, **Ly Thai To** and reigned for 19 years from 1009-1028. Ly Cong Uan was raised and educated by monks and acceded to the throne when, as the commander of the palace guard in Hoa Lu (the capital of Vietnam before Thang Long or Hanoi) and with the support of his great patron, the monk Van Hanh, he managed to gain the support of the Buddhist establishment and many local lords. During his reign, he enjoyed a reputation not just as a great soldier, but also as a devout man who paid attention to the interests and well-being of his people. He also seemed, if the contemporary records are to be believed, to have been remarkably sensitive to those he ruled. He tried to re-establish the harmony between ruler and ruled which had suffered during the previous years, and he even sent his son to live outside the walls of the palace so that he could gain a taste of ordinary life and an understanding of ordinary people. As he approached death he is said to have increasingly retired from everyday life, preparing himself for the everlasting.

Ly Cong Uan was succeeded by his son, Ly Phat Ma who is better known as **Ly Thai Tong** (reigned 1028-1054). Ly Phat Ma had been prepared for kingship since birth and he proved to be an excellent ruler during his long 26-year reign. It is hard to generalize about this period in Vietnamese history because Ly Phat Ma adapted his pattern of rule no less than six times during his reign. Early on he challenged the establishment, contending for example that good governance was not merely a consequence of following best practice (which the logic of bureaucratic Confucianism would maintain) but depended upon good kingship – in other words, depended upon the qualities of the man at the helm. Later he was more of an establishment figure, holding much greater store by the institutions of kingship. Perhaps his greatest military success was the mounting of a campaign to defeat the Cham in 1044 from which he returned with shiploads of plunder. His greatest artistic legacy was the construction of the One Pillar Pagoda or Chua Mot Cot in Hanoi (see page 79).

Ly Phat Ma was succeeded by his son, Ly Nhat Ton, posthumously known as **Ly Thanh Tong** (reigned 1054-1072). History is not as kind about Ly Thanh Tong as it is about his two forebears. Nonetheless he did challenge the might of the Chinese along Vietnam's northern borders – largely successfully – and like his father also mounted a campaign against Champa in 1069. Indeed his expedition against the Cham mirrored his father's in most respects and, like his father, he won. (But unlike his father, he did not execute the Cham king.) Records indicate that he spent a great deal of time trying to father a son and worked his way through numerous concubines and a great deal of incense in the process. At last, after much labour (on his part, and probably on the mother's too, although the texts do not say as much), a son was born to a concubine of common blood in 1066 and named Ly Can Duc.

Ly Can Duc was proclaimed emperor in 1072 when he was only six years old and, surprisingly, remained king until he died in 1127. During the early years of his reign the kingdom faced a succession of crises, largely due to the fact that his young age meant that there was no paramount leader. His death marks the end of the Ly Dynasty for he left no heir, and the crown passed to the maternal clan of his nephew. There followed a period of instability and it was not until 1225 that a new dynasty – the Tran Dynasty – managed to subdue the various competing cliques and bring a semblance of order to the country.

Tran Dynasty Scholars do not know a great deal about the four generations of kings of the Tran Dynasty. It seems that they established the habit of marrying within the clan, and each king took queens who were either their cousins or, in one case, a half-sister. Such a long period of intermarriage, one imagines, would have had some far-reaching mental consequences although ironically the collapse of the dynasty seems to have been brought about after one foolish king decided to marry outside the Tran clan. The great achievement of the Tran Dynasty was to resist the expansionist tendencies of the Mongol forces who conquered China in the 1250s and then set their sights on Vietnam. In 1284 a huge Mongol-Yuan force, consisting of no fewer than four armies, massed on the border to crush the Vietnamese. Fortunately the Tran were blessed with a group of brave and resourceful princes, the most notable of whom was Tran Quoc Tuan better known – and now immortalized in street names in just about every Vietnamese town – as **Tran Hung Dao**. Although the invading forces captured Thang Long (Hanoi) they never managed to defeat the Vietnamese in a decisive battle and in the end the forces of the Tran Dynasty were victorious.

Funan (1st-6th century AD)

According to Chinese sources, Funan was a Hindu kingdom founded in the first century AD with its capital, Vyadhapura, close to the Mekong River near the border with Cambodia. A local legend records that Kaundinya, a great Indian Brahmin, acting on a dream, sailed to the coast of Vietnam carrying with him a bow and arrow. When he arrived, Kaundinya shot the arrow and where it landed he established the capital of Funan. Following this act, Kaundinya married the princess Soma, daughter of the local King of the Nagas (giant water serpents). The legend symbolizes the union between Indian and local cultural traditions – the naga representing indigenous fertility rites and customs, and the arrow, the potency of the Hindu religion.

Funan built its wealth and power on its **strategic location** on the sea route **Oc-eo** between China and the islands to the south. Maritime technology at the time forced seafarers travelling between China and island Southeast Asia and India to stop and wait for the winds to change before they could continue on their way. This sometimes meant a stay of up to five months. The large port city of Oc-eo (see page 312) offered a safe harbour for merchant vessels and the revenues generated enabled the kings of the empire to expand rice cultivation, dominate a host of surrounding vassal states as far away as the Malay coast and South Burma, and build a series of impressive temples, cities and irrigation works. Although the Chinese chronicler K'ang T'ai records that the Funanese were barbarians – "ugly, black, and frizzy-haired" – it is clear from Chinese court annals that they were artistically and technologically accomplished. It is recorded for example that one Chinese emperor was so impressed by the skill of some visiting musicians in 263 AD that he ordered the establishment of an institute of Funanese music.

Funan reached the peak of its powers in the fourth century and went into decline during the fifth century AD when improving maritime technology made Oc-eo redundant as a haven for sailing vessels. No longer did merchants hug the coastline; ships were now large enough, and navigation skills sophisticated enough, to make the journey from South China to the Malacca Strait without landfall. By the mid-sixth century, Funan, having suffered from a drawn-out leadership crisis, was severely weakened. Neighbouring competing powers took advantage of this crisis, absorbing previously Funan-controlled lands. Irrigation works fell into disrepair as state control weakened, and peasants left the fields to seek more productive lands elsewhere. Funan, having lost both the economic wealth and the religious legitimacy on which its power had been based, was ultimately conquered by the Cham.

Background

A Spanish account of Champa circa 1595

This account of Champa is taken from an anonymous manuscript compiled in Manila about 1590-95, possibly as part of the documentation assembled by Don Luis Perez das Marinas in justification of his scheme for the conquest of Indochina.

It is a land fertile in foodstuffs and cows and oxen and very healthy in itself. It is not thickly populated and the people are swarthy and heathens. In this kingdom there is no money nor silver with which to sell anything; and in order to buy what they need, they exchange foodstuffs for cotton blankets and other things which they make for the purpose of buying and selling with each other. Nobody is allowed to go shod save only the king, and nobody can be married with more than two wives.

Food and drink

These people do not eat anything properly cooked, but only in raw or putrid condition; and in order to digest these foods, they are great drinkers of very strong spirits, which they drink little by little and very frequently, thinking it no disgrace to fall down from drinking too much.

Seasons

They divide the year into six festivals, during the first of which the vast majority of his vassals pay tribute to the king. The king goes to a field, and there they assemble all these tributes, out of which

they make alms to the souls of the dead and perform great obsequies and funeral rites in their memory.

The second festival also lasts two months and they spend the whole of this time singing to the exclusion of everything else, except when they are actually eating their meals. During these festivals the women, of whatsoever condition they be, have liberty to do what they like for the space of three days, during which they are not asked to account for their behaviour.

During the third festival they go to the seaside, where they stay fishing for another two months. They make merry catching enough fish to last them for the year, pickling it in their jars, with just a little salt, and they eat it putrid in this manner. And they thrive very strong and lusty on this food.

When the king returns to the city, they display lights by night and day, putting on plays and races in public, in which the king participates. This celebration is the fourth of their festivals.

The fifth is when the king goes hunting elephants, of which there are many in this land, taking with him the nobility and their female elephants; and the females go into the place where the wild elephants are, which follow the former into a little space which they have stockaded off for this purpose, and there they keep them for

What is interesting about Funan is the degree to which it provided a model for future states in Southeast Asia. Funan's wealth was built on its links with the sea, and with its ability to exploit maritime trade. The later rulers of Champa, Langkasuka (Malaya), Srivijaya (Sumatra), and Malacca (Malaya) repeated this formula.

Champa (2nd century AD–1720)

In South Vietnam, where the dynastic lords achieved hegemony only in the 18th century, the kingdom of Champa – or Lin-yi as the Chinese called it – was the most significant power. The kingdom evolved in the second century AD and was focused on the narrow ribbon of lowland that runs north-south down the Annamite coast, with its various capitals near the present-day city of Danang. Chinese sources record that in 192 AD a local official, Kiu-lien, rejected Chinese authority and established an independent kingdom. From then on, Champa's history was one of conflict with its neighbour: when Imperial China was powerful, Champa was subservient and sent ambassadors and tributes in homage to the

some days until they are tamed.

The last festival which they celebrate is a tiger-hunt. The tigers come to eat the buffaloes which are tied to a tree in certain places. They place sentinels over them, so that when the tigers approach, the king is informed. And as soon as this news arrives the king gets ready with a great number of Indians and nets, and they do with the tigers what they do with the elephants, surrounding them at once and killing them there and then. It is the custom with these Indians that at the time when they are occupied with this hunt, the king and his wife send out a hundred or more Indians along the roads, with express order that they should not return without filling two gold basins which they give them, full of human gall, which must be from people of their own nation and not foreigners; and these emissaries do as they are told, not sparing anyone they meet, whether of high or low degree. As soon as they can catch a person on the road, they tie him at once to a tree, and there they cut out the gall ... When all this is over the king and his wife bathe and wash with this human gall; and they say that in this way they cleanse themselves of their sins and their faults.

Justice

The justice of this people is peculiar, for they have no fixed criminal code, but only their personal opinions, and when the case is a serious one, they investigate it with two witnesses. Their oaths are made

with fire and boiling oil, and those condemned to death are executed with extreme barbarity. Some are sentenced to be trampled to death by elephants; others are flogged to death; others are tortured for two or three days, during which time bits and pieces are cut out of their bodies with pincers until they die. And for very trifling and common offences, they cut off their feet, hands, arms and ears.

Death

They have another custom invented by the Devil himself, which is that when any leading personage dies, they cremate the body, after it has been kept for eight or 10 days until they have made the necessary preparations in accordance with the quality of the deceased, when they burn it in the field. When such a person dies, they sieze all the household servants and keep them until the same day on which they burn the body of their master, and then they throw them alive into the flames, so that they can serve them therewith in the other ... Another custom which they have, which is a very harsh one for women, is that when the husband dies, they burn the wife with him. They say that this law was made to prevent wives from giving poisonous herbs to their husbands, for there are very great witchcrafts and knaveries in these lands. They say that if the wife realizes that her husband will not live any longer than her, she will take good care of his life and ease, and will not dare to kill him with poison.

Chinese court; when it was weak, the rulers of Champa extended their own influence and ignored the Chinese.

The difficulty for scholars is to decide whether Champa had a single identity or whether it consisted of numerous mini-powers with no dominant centre. The accepted wisdom at the moment is that Champa was more diffuse than previously thought, and that only rarely during its history is it possible to talk of Champa in singular terms. The endless shifting of the capital of Champa is taken to reflect the shifting centres of power that characterized this 'kingdom'.

Like Funan, Champa built its power on its position on the **maritime trading route** through Southeast Asia. During the fourth century, as Champa expanded into previously Funan-controlled lands, they came under the influence of the Indian cultural traditions of the Funanese. These were enthusiastically embraced by Champa's rulers who tacked the suffix '-varman' onto their names (eg Bhadravarman) and adopted the Hindu-Buddhist cosmology. Though a powerful trading kingdom, Champa was geographically poorly endowed. The coastal strip between the Annamite highlands to the west, and the sea to the east, is narrow and

Nguyen Trai

"Our country, Dai Viet, has long been
A land of ancient culture,
With its own rivers and mountains,
*   ways and customs,*
Different from those of the North"
(Opening lines of 'Proclamation of victory
over the invaders')
Nguyen Trai, mandarin, poet and
nationalist rose to prominence as an
adviser to Le Loi during the 10-year
campaign to eject the Ming from Dai Viet.
His famous counsel "better to win hearts
than citadels" (which mirrors similar
advice during a war over five centuries
later) was heeded by Le Loi who aroused
patriotic fervour in his compatriots to

achieve victory on the battlefield. It was
on Nguyen Trai's suggestion that 100,000
defeated Ming troops were given food
and boats to make their way home. After
the war, Nguyen Trai accepted and later
resigned a court post. He was a prolific
composer of verse, which is considered
some of the finest in the national annals.
On an overnight visit to Nguyen Trai,
Emperor Le Thai Tong (Le Loi's son and
heir) died unexpectedly. Scheming
courtiers were able to fix the blame on
Nguyen Trai who in 1442, along with
three generations of his family, were
executed, a punishment known as tru di
tam tôc.

the potential for extensive rice cultivation limited. This may explain why the Champa Empire was never more than a moderate power: it was unable to produce the agricultural surplus necessary to support an extensive court and army, and therefore could not compete with either the Khmers to the south nor with the Viets to the north. But the Cham were able to carve out a niche for themselves between the two, and to many art historians, their art and architecture represent the finest that Vietnam has ever produced (see page 197). Remains litter the central Vietnamese coast from Quang Tri in the north, to Ham Tan 800 kilometres to the south.

For over 1,000 years the Cham resisted the Chinese and the Vietnamese. But by the time Marco Polo wrote of the Cham, their power and prestige were much reduced: "The people are idolators and pay a yearly tribute to the Great Kaan which consists of elephants and nothing but elephants.... In the year of Christ 1285 ... the King had, between sons and daughters, 326 children. There are a very great number of elephants in that country, and they have lignaloes (eagle wood) in great abundance. They have also extensive forests of the wood called Bonús, which is jet black, of which chessmen and pencases are made. But there is nought more to tell, so let us proceed." After 1285, when invading Mongol hoardes were repelled by the valiant Viets, Champa and Dai Viet enjoyed an uneasy peace maintained by the liberal flow of royal princesses South across the Col des Nuages (Hai Van Pass) in exchange for territory. During the peaceful reign of Che A-nan a Franciscan priest, Odoric of Pordenone, reported of Champa "'tis a very fine country, having a great store of victuals and of all good things". Of particular interest, he refers to the practice of suti, writing "When a man dies in this country, they burn his wife with him, for they say that she should live with him in the other world also". Clearly, some of the ancient Indian traditions continued.

Champa saw a late flowering under King Binasuos who led numerous successful campaigns against the Viet, culminating in the sack of Hanoi in 1371. Subsequently, the treachery of a low-ranking officer led to Binasuos' death in 1390 and the military eclipse of the Cham by the Vietnamese. The demographic and economic superiority of the Viet coupled with their gradual drift south contributed most to the waning of the Cham Kingdom, but finally, in 1471 the Cham suffered a terrible defeat at the hands of the Vietnamese. 60,000 of their soldiers were killed and another 36,000 captured and carried into captivity, including the King and 50 members of the royal

Vietnamese dynasties

Dynasty	Dates	Capital (province)
Hong Bang (legendary)	2876-258 BC	Phong Chau (Son Tay)
Thuc	257-208 BC	Loa Thanh (Vinh Phu)
Trieu	207-111 BC	Phien Ngung (South China)
under Chinese domination 111 BC-23 AD		
Trung Sisters	40-43 AD	Me Linh (Son Tay)
under Chinese domination 25-589		
Early Ly	544-602	various (Hanoi)
under Chinese domination 622-938		
Ngo	939-965	Co Loa (Vinh Phuc)
Dinh	968-980	Hoa Lu (Ninh Binh)
Early Le	980-1009	Hoa Lu (Ninh Binh)
Ly	1010-1225	Thang Long (Hanoi)
Tran	1225-1400	Thang Long (Hanoi)
Ho	1400-1407	Dong Do (Hanoi)
Post Tran	1407-1413	
under Chinese domination 1414-1427		
Le	1427-1788	Thang Long (Hanoi)
Mac	1527-1592	
Northern Trinh	1539-1787	Hanoi
Southern Nguyen	1558-1778	Hué
Quang Trung	1787-1792	
Nguyen of Tay Son	1788-1802	Saigon
Nguyen	1802-1945	Hué

NB *From the 16th-18th centuries there were up to four centres of power in Vietnam. For a list of Nguyen Emperors see page 176.*

Background

family. The kingdom shrank to a small territory in the vicinity of Nha Trang which survived until 1720 when surviving members of the royal family and many subjects fled to Cambodia to escape from the advancing Vietnamese.

Le Dynasty and the emergence of Vietnam

During its struggle with the Cham, nascent Dai Viet had to contend with the weight of Ming Chinese oppression from the north, often in concert with their Cham allies. Despite 1,000 years of Chinese domination and centuries of internal dynastic squabbles the Viet retained a strong sense of national identity and were quick to respond to charismatic leadership. As so often in Vietnam's history one man was able to harness nationalistic sentiment and mould the country's discontent into a powerful fighting force: in 1426 it was Le Loi. Together with the brilliant tactician **Nguyen Trai** (see box), Le Loi led a campaign to remove the Chinese from Vietnamese soil. Combining surprise, guerrilla tactics and Nguyen Trai's innovative and famous propaganda, designed to convince defending Ming of the futility of their position, the Viet won a resounding victory which led to the enlightened and artistically distinguished Le period. Le Loi's legendary victory lives on in popular form and is celebrated in the tale of the restored sword in water puppet performances across the country. Following his victory against the Ming he claimed the throne in 1428 and reigned until his death five years later.

Le Loi

Le Thanh Ton With Le Loi's death the Le Dynasty worked its way through a succession of young kings who seemed to hold the throne barely long enough to warm the cushions before they were murdered. It was not until 1460 that a king of substance was to accede: Le Thanh Ton (reigned 1460-1497). His reign was a period of great scholarship and artistic accomplishment. He established the system of rule that was to guide successive Vietnamese emperors for 500 years. He also mounted a series of military campaigns, some as far as Laos to the west.

Le expansion The expansion of the Vietnamese state, under the Le, south from its heartland in the Tonkin Delta, followed the decline of the Cham Kingdom at the end of the 15th century. By the early 18th century the Cham were extinct as an identifiable political and military force and the Vietnamese advanced still further south into the Khmer-controlled territories of the Mekong Delta. This geographical over-extension and the sheer logistical impracticability of ruling from distant Hanoi, disseminating edicts and collecting taxes, led to the disintegration of the – ever tenuous – imperial rule. The old adage 'The edicts of the emperor stop at the village gate' was particularly apt more than 1,000 kilometres from the capital. Noble families, locally dominant, challenged the emperor's authority and the Le Dynasty gradually dissolved into internecine strife and regional fiefdoms, namely Trinh in the north and Nguyen in the south, a pattern that was to reassert itself some 300 years later. But although on paper the Vietnamese – now consisting of two dynastic houses, Trinh and Nguyen – appeared powerful, the people were mired in poverty. There were numerous peasant rebellions in this period, of which the most serious was the **Tay Son rebellion** of 1771 (see page 211). One of the three Tay Son brothers, Nguyen Hue, proclaimed himself **Emperor Quang Trung** in 1788, only to die four years later.

The death of Quang Trung paved the way for the establishment of the **Nguyen Dynasty** – the last Vietnamese dynasty – in 1802 when Emperor Gia Long ascended to the throne in Hué. Despite the fact that this period heralded the arrival of the French – leading to their eventual domination of Vietnam – it is regarded as a golden period in Vietnamese history. During the Nguyen Dynasty, Vietnam was unified as a single state and Hué emerged as the heart of the kingdom.

French colonial troops and a wealthy Vietnamese mandarin flee from a victorious band of nationalist peasant rebels in this 1930's cartoon. The victors are shouting 'Wipe out the gang of imperialists, mandarins, capitalists and big landlords!'
Source: Archives Nationales de France

The colonial period

One of the key motivating factors that encouraged the **French** to undermine the authority of the Vietnamese emperors was their treatment of Roman Catholics. Jesuits had been in the country from as early as the 17th century – one of them, Alexandre-de-Rhodes, converted the Vietnamese writing system from Chinese characters to romanized script (see page 383) – but persecution of Roman Catholics began only in the 1830s. Emperor Minh Mang issued an imperial edict outlawing the dissemination of Christianity as a heterodox creed in 1825. The first European priest to be executed was François Isidore Gagelin who was strangled by six soldiers as he knelt on a scaffold in Hué in 1833. Three days later, having been told that Christians believe they will come to life again, Minh Mang had the body exhumed to confirm the man's death. In 1840 Minh Mang actually read the Old Testament in Chinese translation, declaring it to be 'absurd'.

Yet, Christianity continued to spread as Buddhism declined, and there was a continual stream of priests willing to risk their lives proselytizing. In addition, the economy was in disarray and natural disasters common. Poor Vietnamese saw Christianity as a way to break the shackles of their feudal existence. Fearing a peasants' revolt, the Emperor ordered the execution of 25 European priests, 300 Vietnamese priests, and 30,000 Vietnamese Catholics between 1848 and 1860. Provoked by these killings, the French attacked and took Saigon in 1859. In 1862 **Emperor Tu Duc** signed a treaty ceding the three southern provinces to the French, thereby creating the colony of Cochin China. This treaty of 1862 effectively paved the way for the eventual seizure by the French of the whole kingdom. The French, through weight of arms, also forced the Emperor to end the persecution of Christians in his kingdom. In retrospect, although many Christians did die cruelly, the degree of persecution was not on the scale of similar episodes elsewhere: Minh Mang's successors Thieu Tri (1841-1847) and Tu Duc (1847-1883), though both *fervently* anti-Christian, appreciated French military strength and the fact that they were searching for pretexts to intervene.

The French conquest of the north was motivated by a desire to control trade and the route to what were presumed to be the vast riches of China. In 1883 and 1884, the French forced the Emperor to sign treaties making Vietnam a French protectorate. In August 1883 for example, just after Tu Duc's death, a French fleet appeared off Hué to force concessions. François Harmand, a native affairs official on board one of the ships, threatened the Vietnamese by stating: "Imagine all that is terrible and it will still be less than reality ... the word 'Vietnam' will be erased from history." The emperor called on China for assistance and demanded that provinces resist French rule; but the imperial bidding proved ineffective, and in 1885 the **Treaty of Tientsin** recognized the French protectorates of Tonkin (North Vietnam) and Annam (Central Vietnam), to add to that of Cochin China (South Vietnam).

Resistance to the French: the prelude to revolution

Like other European powers in Southeast Asia, the French managed to achieve military victory with ease, but they failed to stifle Vietnamese nationalism. After 1900, as Chinese translations of the works of Rousseau, Voltaire and social Darwinists such as Herbert Spence began to find their way into the hands of the Vietnamese intelligentsia, so resistance grew. Foremost among these early nationalists were Phan Boi Chau (1867-1940) and Phan Chau Trinh (1871-1926) who wrote tracts calling for the expulsion of the French. But these men and others such as Prince Cuong De (1882-1951) were traditional nationalists, their beliefs rooted in Confucianism rather than revolutionary Marxism. Their efforts and perspectives were essentially in the tradition of the nationalists who had resisted Chinese domination over previous centuries.

Quoc Dan Dang (VNQDD), founded at the end of 1927, was the first nationalist party, while the first significant Communist group was the **Indochina Communist Party (ICP)** established by Ho Chi Minh in 1930 (see profile, page 336). Both the VNQDD and the ICP organized resistance to the French and there were numerous strikes and uprisings, particularly during the harsh years of the Great Depression. The Japanese 'occupation' from August 1940 (Vichy France permitted the Japanese full access to military facilities in exchange for allowing continued French administrative control) saw the creation of the **Viet Minh** to fight for the liberation of Vietnam from Japanese and French control.

The Vietnam War

The First Indochina War (1945-1954)

The Vietnam War started in September 1945 in the south of the country, and in 1946 in the north. These years marked the onset of fighting **between the Viet Minh and the French** and the period is usually referred to as the First Indochina War. The Communists, who had organized against the Japanese, proclaimed the creation of the Democratic Republic of Vietnam (DRV) on 2 September 1945 when Ho Chi Minh read out the Vietnamese **Declaration of Independence** in Hanoi's Ba Dinh Square. Ironically, this document was modelled closely on the American Declaration of Independence. Indeed, the US was favourably disposed towards the Viet Minh and Ho. Operatives of the OSS (the wartime precursor to the CIA) met Ho and supported his efforts during the War, and afterwards Roosevelt's inclination was to prevent France claiming their colony back. Only Churchill's persuasion changed his mind.

The French, although they had always insisted that Vietnam be returned to French rule, were in no position to force the issue. Instead, in the south, it was British troops (mainly Gurkhas) who helped the small force of French against the Viet Minh. Incredibly, the British also ordered the Japanese, who had only just capitulated, to help fight the Vietnamese. When 35,000 French reinforcements arrived, the issue in the south – at least superficially – was all but settled, with Ca Mau at the southern extremity of the country falling on 21 October. From that point, the war in the south became an underground battle of attrition, with the north providing support to their southern comrades.

In the north, the Viet Minh had to deal with 180,000 rampaging Nationalist Chinese troops, while preparing for the imminent arrival of a French force. Unable to confront both at the same time, and deciding that the French were probably the lesser of two evils, Ho Chi Minh decided to negotiate. He is said to have observed in private, that it was preferable to 'sniff French shit for a while than eat China's all our lives'. To make the DRV government more acceptable to the French, Ho proceeded cautiously, only nationalizing a few strategic industries, bringing moderates into the government, and actually dissolving the Indochinese Communist Party (at least on paper) in November 1945. But in the same month Ho also said:

"The French colonialists should know that the Vietnamese people do not wish to spill blood, that it loves peace. But if it must sacrifice millions of combatants, lead a resistance for long years to defend the independence of the country, and preserve its children from slavery, it will do so. It is certain the resistance will win."

In February 1946, the French and Chinese signed a treaty leading to the withdrawal of Chinese forces, and shortly afterwards Ho concluded a treaty with French President de Gaulle's special emissary to Vietnam, Jean Sainteny in which Vietnam was recognized as a 'free' (the Vietnamese word *doc lap* being translated as free, but not yet independent) state within the French Union and the Indochinese Federation.

It is interesting to note that in negotiating with the French, Ho was going against the wishes of most of his supporters who argued for confrontation. But Ho, ever a pragmatist, believed at this stage that the Viet Minh were ill-trained and poorly armed and he appreciated the need for time to consolidate their position. The episode that is usually highlighted as the flashpoint that led to the resumption of hostilities was the French government's decision to open a customs house in Haiphong at the end of 1946. The Viet Minh forces resisted and the rest, as they say, is history. It seems that during the course of 1946 Ho changed his view of the best path to independence. Initially he asked: "Why should we sacrifice 50 or 100,000 men when we can achieve independence within five years through negotiation?", but he later came to the conclusion that it was necessary to fight for independence. The customs house episode might, therefore, be viewed as merely an excuse. The French claimed that 5,000 Vietnamese were killed in the ensuing bombardment, as against five Frenchmen; the Vietnamese put the toll at 20,000.

In a pattern that was to become characteristic of the entire 25 year conflict, while the French controlled the cities, the Viet Minh were dominant in the countryside. By the end of 1949, with the success of the Chinese Revolution and the establishment of the Democratic People's Republic of Korea (North Korea) in 1948, the United States began to offer support to the French in an attempt to stem the 'Red Tide' that seemed to be sweeping across Asia. At this early stage, the odds appeared stacked against the Viet Minh, but Ho was confident that time was on their side. As he remarked to Sainteny "If we have to fight, we will fight. You can kill 10 of my men for every one I kill of yours but even at those odds, I will win and you will lose". It also became increasingly clear that the French were not committed to negotiating a route to independence. A secret French report prepared in 1948 was obtained and then published by the Viet Minh in which the High Commissioner, Monsieur Bollaert wrote: "It is my impression that we must make a concession to Viet-Nam of the term, independence; but I am convinced that this word need never be interpreted in any light other than that of a religious verbalism".

The decisive battle of the First Indochina War was at Dien Bien Phu in the hills of the northwest, close to the border with Laos. At the end of 1953 the French, with American support, parachuted 16,000 men into the area in an attempt to protect Laos from Viet Minh incursions and to tempt them into open battle. The French in fact found themselves trapped, surrounded by Viet Minh and overlooked by artillery. There was some suggestion that the United States might become involved, and even use tactical nuclear weapons, but this was not to be. In May 1954 the French surrendered – the most humiliating of French colonial defeats – effectively marking the end of the French presence in Indochina. In July 1954, in Geneva, the French and Vietnamese agreed to divide the country along the 17th parallel, so creating two states (for a fuller account of the battle see page 112). The border was kept open for 300 days and over that period about 900,000 – mostly Roman Catholic – Vietnamese travelled south. At the same time nearly 90,000 Viet Minh troops along with 43,000 civilians, went north, although many Viet Minh remained in the south to continue the fight there.

Dien Bien Phu (1954)

Background

Ho Chi Minh: 'He who enlightens'

Ho Chi Minh, one of a number of pseudonyms Ho adopted during his life, was born Nguyen Sinh Cung, or possibly Nguyen Van Thanh (Ho did not keep a diary during much of his life, so parts of his life are still a mystery), in Nghe An Province near Vinh on the 19 May 1890, and came from a poor scholar-gentry family. In the village, the family was aristocratic; beyond it they were little more than peasants. His father, though not a revolutionary, was a dissenter and rather than go to Hué to serve the French, he chose to work as a village school teacher. Ho must have been influenced by his father's implacable animosity towards the French, although Ho's early years are obscure. He went to Quoc Hoc College in Hué, and then worked for a while as a teacher in Phan Thiet, a fishing village in South Annam.

In 1911, under the name Nguyen Tat Thanh, he travelled to Saigon and left the country as a messboy on the French ship Amiral Latouche-Tréville. He is said to have used the name 'Ba' so that he would not shame his family by accepting such lowly work. This marked the beginning of three years of travel during which he visited France, England, America (where the skyscrapers of Manhattan both amazed and appalled him) and North Africa. Seeing the colonialists on their own turf and reading such revolutionary literature as the French Communist Party newspaper L'Humanité, he was converted to Communism. In Paris he mixed with leftists,

wrote pamphlets and attended meetings of the French Socialist Party. He also took odd jobs: for a while he worked at the Carlton Hotel in London and became an assistant pastry chef under the legendary French chef Georges Escoffier.

An even more unlikely story emerges from Gavin Young's book A Wavering Grace. In the book he recounts an interview he conducted with Mae West in 1968 shortly after he had returned from reporting the Tet offensive. On hearing of Vietnam, Mae West innocently said that she "used to know someone very, very important there ... His name was Ho ... Ho ... Ho something". At the time she was staying at the Carlton while starring in a London show, Sex. She confided to Young: "There was this waiter, cook, I don't know what he was. I know he had the slinkiest eyes though. We met in the corridor. We – well ..." Young writes that "Her voice trailed off in a husky sigh ..."

Gradually Ho became an ever-more-committed Communist, contributing articles to radical newspapers and working his way into the web of Communist and leftist groups. At the same time he remained, curiously, a French cultural chauvinist, complaining for example about the intrusion of English words like 'le manager' and 'le challenger' (referring to boxing contests) into the French language. He even urged the French Prime Minister to ban foreign words from the French press. In 1923 he

The Second Indochina War (1954-1975)

The Vietnam War, but particularly the American part of that war, is probably the most minutely studied, reported, analysed and recorded in history. Yet, as with all wars, there are still large grey areas and continuing disagreement over important episodes. Most crucially, there is the question of whether the US might have won had their forces been given a free hand and were not forced, as some would have it, to fight with one hand tied behind their backs. This remains the view among many members of the US military.

left France for Moscow and was trained as a Communist activist – effectively a spy. From there, Ho travelled to Canton where he was instrumental in forming the Vietnamese Communist movement. This culminated in the creation of the Indo-China Communist Party in 1930. His movements during these years are scantily documented: he became a Buddhist monk in Siam (Thailand), was arrested in Hong Kong for subversive activities and received a six month sentence, travelled to China several times, and in 1940 even returned to Vietnam for a short period – his first visit for nearly 30 years. Despite his absence from the country, the French had already recognized the threat that he posed and sentenced him to death in absentia in 1930. He did not adopt the pseudonym by which he is now best known – Ho Chi Minh – until the early 1940s.

Ho was a consummate politician and, despite his revolutionary fervour, a great realist. He was also a charming man, and during his stay in France between June and October 1946, he made a great number of friends. Robert Shaplen in his book The Lost Revolution (1965) talks of his "wit, his oriental courtesy, his savoir-faire ... above all his seeming sincerity and simplicity". He talked with farmers and fishermen, and debated with priests; he impressed people wherever he travelled. He died in Hanoi at his house within the former governor's residence in 1969 (see page 79).

Since the demise of communism in the

Ho Chi Minh Pseudonyms

Born 1890:	Nguyen Sinh Cung or Nguyen Van Thanh (Vinh)
1910:	Van Ba (South Vietnam)
1911:	Nguyen Tat Thanh (Saigon)
1913:	Nguyen Tat Thanh (London)
1914:	Nguyen Ai Quoc (Paris)
1924:	Linh (Moscow)
1924:	Ly Thuy (Moscow)
1925:	Wang (Canton)
1927:	Duong (Paris)
1928:	Nguyen Lai, Nam Son, Thau Chin (Siam)
1942:	Ho Chi Minh

former Soviet Union, the Vietnamese leadership have been concerned that secrets about Ho's life might be gleaned from old comintern files in Moscow by nosy journalists. To thwart such an eventuality, they have, reportedly, sent a senior historian to scour the archives. To date, Ho's image remains largely untarnished – making him an exception amongst the tawdry league of former communist leaders. But a Moscow-based reporter has unearthed evidence implying Ho was married, challenging the official hagiography that paints Ho as a celibate who committed his entire life to the revolution. It takes a brave Vietnamese to challenge established 'fact'. In 1991, when the popular Vietnamese Youth or Tuoi Tre newspaper dared to suggest that Ho had married Tang Tuyet Minh in China in 1926, the editor was summarily dismissed from her post.

Ngo Dinh Diem

At the time of the partition of Vietnam along the 17th parallel, the government in the south was chaotic and the Communists could be fairly confident that in a short time their sympathizers would be victorious. This situation was to change with the rise of Ngo Dinh Diem. Born in Hué in 1901 to a Roman Catholic Confucian family, Diem wished to become a priest. He graduated at the top of his class from the French School of Administration and at the age of 32 was appointed to the post of Minister of the Interior at the court of Emperor Bao Dai. Here, according to the political scientist William Turley "he worked with uncommon industry and integrity" only to resign in exasperation at court intrigues and French interference. He withdrew from political activity during the First Indochina War and in 1946 Ho Chi Minh offered him a post in the DRV government – an offer he declined. Turley describes him as a man who was, in many respects, a creature of the past:

Background

"For Diem, the mandarin, political leadership meant rule by example, precept, and paternalism. His Catholic upbringing reinforced rather than replaced the Confucian tendency to base authority on doctrine, morality and hierarchy. Utterly alien to him were the concepts of power-sharing, and popular participation. He was in fact the heir to a dying tradition, member of an élite that had been superbly prepared by birth, training, and experience to lead a Vietnam that no longer existed."

In July 1954 Diem returned from his self-imposed exile at the Maryknoll Seminary in New Jersey to become Premier of South Vietnam. It is usually alleged that the US administration was behind his rise to power, although this has yet to be proved. He held two rigged elections (in October 1955, 450,000 registered voters cast 605,025 votes) which gave some legitimacy to his administration in American eyes. He proceeded to suppress all opposition in the country. His brutal brother, Ngo Dinh Nhu, was appointed to head the security forces and terrorized much of Vietnamese society.

During the period of Diem's premiership, opposition to his rule, particularly in the countryside, increased. This was because the military's campaign against the Viet Minh targeted – both directly and indirectly – many innocent peasants. At the same time, the nepotism and corruption that was endemic within the administration also turned many people into Viet Minh sympathizers. That said, Diem's campaign was successful in undermining the strength of the Communist Party in the south. While there were perhaps 50,000-60,000 Party members in 1954, this figure had declined through widespread arrests and intimidation to only 5,000 by 1959.

The erosion of the Party in the south gradually led, from 1959, to the north changing its strategy towards one of more overt military confrontation. The same year also saw the establishment of Group 559 which was charged with the task of setting up what was to become the Ho Chi Minh Trail, along which supplies and troops were moved from the north to the south (see page 190). But, even at this stage, the Party's forces in the south were kept from open confrontation and many of its leaders were hoping for victory without having to resort to open warfare. There was no call for a 'People's War' and armed resistance was left largely to guerrillas belonging to the Cao Dai (see page 382) and Hoa Hao (Buddhist millenarian) sects. The establishment of the National Liberation Front of Vietnam in 1960 was an important political and organizational development towards creating a credible alternative to Diem – although it did not hold its first congress until 1962.

The escalation of the armed conflict (1959-1963)

Viet Cong The armed conflict began to intensify from the beginning of 1961 when all the armed forces under the Communists' control were unified under the banner of the People's Liberation Armed Forces (PLAF). By this time the Americans were already using the term Viet Cong (or VC) to refer to Communist troops. They reasoned that the victory at Dien Bien Phu had conferred almost heroic status on the name Viet Minh. American psychological warfare specialists therefore invented the term Viet Cong, an abbreviation of *Viet-nam Cong-san* (or Vietnamese Communists), and persuaded the media in Saigon to begin substituting it for Viet Minh from 1956.

The election of **John F Kennedy** to the White House in January 1961 coincided with the Communists' decision to widen the war in the south. In the same year Kennedy dispatched 400 special forces troops and 100 special military advisers to Vietnam – in flagrant contravention of the Geneva Agreement. With the cold war getting colder, and Soviet Premier Nikita Khrushchev confirming his support for wars of 'national liberation', Kennedy could not back down and by the end of 1962 there were 11,000 US personnel in South Vietnam. At the same time the NLF had around 23,000 troops at its disposal. Kennedy was still saying that "In the final analysis, it's their war and they're the ones who have to win or lose it". But just months after the Bay of Pigs débâcle in Cuba, Washington set out on the path that was ultimately to lead to America's first large-scale military defeat.

The bungling and incompetence of the forces of the south, the interference which US advisers and troops had to face, the misreading of the situation by US military commanders, and the skill – both military and political – of the Communists, are most vividly recounted in Neil Sheehan's massive book, *A Bright Shining Lie* (see Recommended reading, page 55). The conflict quickly escalated from 1959. The north infiltrated about 44,000 men and women into the south between then and 1964, while the number recruited in the south was between 60,000 and 100,000. In August 1959, the first consignment of arms was carried down the **Ho Chi Minh Trail** into South Vietnam. Meanwhile, Kennedy began supporting, arming and training the Army of the Republic of Vietnam (ARVN). The US however, shied away from any large-scale, direct confrontation between its forces and the Viet Cong.

An important element in Diem's military strategy at this time was the establishment of '**strategic hamlets**', better known simply as 'hamleting'. This strategy was modelled on British anti-guerrilla warfare during Malaya's Communist insurgency, and aimed to deny the Communists any bases of support in the countryside while at the same time making it more difficult for Communists to infiltrate the villages and 'propagandize' there. The villages which were ringed by barbed-wire were labelled 'concentration camps' by the Communists, and the often brutal, forced relocation that peasants had to endure probably turned even more of them into Communist sympathizers. Of the 7,000-8,000 villages sealed in this way, only a fifth could ever have been considered watertight.

In January 1963 at Ap Bac, not far from the town of My Tho, the Communists scored their first significant victory in the south. Facing 2,000 well armed ARVN troops, a force of just 300-400 PLAF inflicted heavy casualties and downed five helicopters. After this defeat, many American advisers drew the conclusion that if the Communists were to be defeated, it could not be left to the ARVN alone – US troops would have to become directly involved. As John Vann, a key American military adviser, remarked after the débâcle when lambasting South Vietnamese officers: "A miserable fucking performance, just like it always is". In mid-1963 a Buddhist monk from Hué committed suicide by dousing his body with petrol and setting it alight. This was the first of a number of self-immolations, suggesting that even in the early days the Diem régime was not only losing the military war but also the 'hearts and minds' war (see page 262). He responded with characteristic heavy-handedness by ransacking suspect pagodas. On 1 December 1963, Diem and his brother-in-law Nhu were both assassinated during an army coup.

The American war in Vietnam

America's decision to enter the war has been the subject of considerable disagreement. Until recently, the received wisdom was that the US administration had already taken the decision, and manufactured events to justify their later actions. However, the recent publication of numerous State Department, Presidential, CIA, Defence Department and National Security Council files – all dating from 1964 – has shed new light on events leading up to American intervention (these files are contained in the United States Government Printing Office's 1,108 page-long *Vietnam 1964*).

In Roger Warner's *Back Fire* (1995) which deals largely with the CIA's secret war in Laos he recounts a story of a war game commissioned by the Pentagon and played by the Rand Corporation in 1962. They were asked to play a week-long game simulating a 10-year conflict in Vietnam. At the end of the week, having committed 500,000 men, the US forces were bogged down, there was student unrest, and the American population had lost confidence in their leaders and in the conduct of the war. When the game was played a year later but, on the insistence of the US Airforce, with much heavier aerial bombing, the conclusions were much the same. If only, if only …

Vietnam War

By all accounts, **Lyndon Johnson** was a reluctant warrior. In the 1964 presidential campaign he repeatedly said "We don't want our American boys to do the fighting for Asian boys". This was not just for public consumption. The files show that LBJ always doubted the wisdom of intervention. But he also believed that John F Kennedy had made a solemn pledge to help the South Vietnamese people – a pledge that he was morally obliged to keep. In most respects, LBJ was completely in agreement with Congress, together with sections of the American public, who were disquietened by events in South Vietnam. The Buddhist monk's self-immolation, broadcast on prime-time news, did not help matters.

It has usually been argued that the executive manufactured the '**Gulf of Tonkin Incident**' to force Congress and the public to approve an escalation of America's role in the conflict. It was reported that two American destroyers, the *USS Maddox* and *USS C Turner Joy*, were attacked without provocation in international waters on the 2 August 1964 by North Vietnamese patrol craft. The US responded by bombing shore installations while presenting the Gulf of Tonkin Resolution to an outraged Congress for approval. Only two Congressmen voted against the resolution and President Johnson's poll rating jumped from 42 percent to 72 percent. In reality, the *USS Maddox* had been involved in electronic intelligence-gathering while supporting clandestine raids by South Vietnamese mercenaries – well inside North Vietnamese territorial waters. This deception only became apparent in 1971 when the *Pentagon papers*, documenting the circumstances behind the incident, were leaked to the *New York Times* (the Pentagon papers were commissioned by Defense Secretary McNamara in June 1967 and written by 36 Indochina experts).

But these events are not sufficient to argue that the incident was manufactured to allow LBJ to start an undeclared war against North Vietnam. On 4 August, Secretary of State Dean Rusk told the American representative at the United Nations that: "In no sense is this destroyer a pretext to make a big thing out of a little thing". Even as late as the end of 1964, the President was unconvinced by arguments that the US should become more deeply involved. On 31 August, McGeorge Bundy wrote in a memorandum to Johnson: "A still more drastic possibility which no one is discussing is the use of substantial US armed forces in operation against the Viet Cong. I myself believe that before we let this country go we should have a hard look at this grim alternative, and I do not at all think that it is a repetition of Korea".

But events overtook President Johnson, and by 1965 the US was firmly embarked on the road to defeat. In March 1965, he ordered the beginning of the air war against the north perhaps acting on Air Force General Curtis Le May's observation that "we are swatting flies when we should be going after the manure pile". **Operation Rolling Thunder**, the most intense bombing campaign any country had yet experienced, began in March 1965 and ran through to October 1968. In three and a half years, twice the tonnage of bombs was dropped on Vietnam (and

The War in figures

Vietnamese:

Killed (soldiers of the North)	1,100,000
Killed (soldiers of the South)	250,000
Vietnamese civilians	2,000,000

Americans:

Served	3,300,000
Killed	57,605
Captured	766 (651 returned)
Wounded	303,700
MIA	4,993 (121 returned, 4,872 declared dead)

Australians:

Killed	423
Wounded	2,398

At height of the war:

Bombs dropped	1.2 m tonnes/yr
Cost of bombs	US$14bn/yr
Area defoliated	2.2 million ha (1962-71)
US air attacks	400,000/yr
Refugees	585,000/yr
Civilian casualties	130,000/month

☞ *A War glossary*

Agent Orange	*herbicide used to defoliate forests*
APC	*armoured personnel carrier*
ARVN	*Army of the Republic of Vietnam; the army of the South*
Body Count	*the number of dead on a field of battle*
BUFF	*nick-name for the B-52 bomber; stands for Big Ugly Fat Fellow or, more usually, Big Ugly Fat F******
COIN	*counter-insurgency*
DMZ	*de-militarized zone; the border between North and South Vietnam at the 17th parallel*
Dust-off	*medical evacuation helicopter*
DZ	*parachute drop zone*
FAC	*forward air controller, airborne spotter who directed bombers onto the target*
Fire base	*defence fortification for artillery to support Infantry from*
Fragging	*to kill or attempt to kill with a fragmentation grenade; better known as the killing of US officers and NCOs by their own men. In 1970 one study reported 209 fraggings*
Gook	*slang, derogatory term for all Vietnamese*
Grunt	*slang for a US infantryman; the word comes from the 'grunt' emitted when shouldering a heavy pack*
Huey	*most commonly used helicopter, UH1*
LZ	*helicopter landing zone*
Napalm	*jellified fuel, the name derives from two of its constituents, naphthenic and palmitic acids. To be burnt by napalm after an attack was terrible and one of the most famous photo images of the war (taken by Nick Ut) showed a naked local girl (Kim Phuc) running along a road at Trang Bang, northwest of Saigon after being burnt; the girl survived the attack by South Vietnamese aircraft and now lives in Canada*
NLF	*National Liberation Front*
PAVN	*People's Army of Vietnam*
Phoenix	*counter-insurgency programme established by the US after the Tet Offensive of 1968 (see page 347)*
PLAF	*People's Liberation Armed Forces; the army of the Communist North*
POW/MIA	*prisoner of war/missing in action*
Pungi stakes	*sharpened bamboo stakes concealed in VC pits: accounted for 2% of US combat wounds*
Purple Heart	*medal awarded to US troops wounded in action*
R&R	*Rest & Recreation; leave*
ROE	*rules of engagement*
Rome Plow	*20 tonne bulldozer designed to clear forest. Equipped with a curved blade and sharp protruding spike it could split the largest trees*
Tunnel Rats	*US army volunteers who fought VC in the Cu Chi tunnels*
VC, Charlie	*Viet Cong (see page 338); US term for Vietnamese Communist; often shortened to Charlie from the phonetic alphabet, Victor Charlie*
Viet Minh	*Communist troops – later changed to Viet Cong (see above and page 338)*
WP, Willy Pete	*White phosphorous rocket used to mark a target*

Background

Laos) as during the entire Second World War. During its peak in 1967, 12,000 sorties were being flown each month – a total of 108,000 were flown throughout 1967. North Vietnam claimed that 4,000 out of its 5,788 villages were hit. Most terrifying were the B-52s which dropped their bombs from such altitude (17,000 metres) that the attack could not even be heard until the bombs hit their targets. Each aircraft carried 20 tonnes of bombs. By the end of the American war in 1973, 14 million tonnes of all types of munitions had been used in Indochina, an explosive force representing 700 times that of the atomic bomb dropped on Hiroshima. As General Curtis Le May explained on 25 November 1965 – "We should bomb them back into the Stone Age". In the same month that Rolling Thunder commenced, marines landed at Danang to defend its airbase, and by June 1965 there were 74,000 US troops in Vietnam. Despite President Johnson's reluctance to commit the US to the conflict, events forced his hand. He realized that the undisciplined South Vietnamese could not prevent a Communist victory. Adhering to the domino theory, and with his own and the US's reputation at stake, he had no choice. As Johnson is said to have remarked to his press secretary Bill Moyers: "I feel like a hitchhiker caught in a hail storm on a Texas highway. I can't win. I can't hide. And I can't make it stop."

In response to the bombing campaign, industry in the north was decentralized and dispersed to rural areas. Each province was envisaged as a self-sufficient production unit. The economic effect of this strategy was felt at the time in a considerable loss of productivity; a cost judged to be worth paying to protect the north's industrial base. In order to protect the population in the north, they too were relocated to the countryside. By the end of 1967 Hanoi's population was a mere 250,000 essential citizens – about a quarter of the pre-war figure. The same was true of other urban centres. What the primary US objective was in mounting the air war remains unclear. In part, it was designed to destroy the north's industrial base and its ability to wage war; partly to dampen the people's will to fight; partly to sow seeds of discontent; partly to force the leadership in the north to the negotiating table; partly, perhaps, to punish those in the north for supporting their government. By October 1968 the US realized the bombing was having little effect and they called a halt. The legacy of Operation Rolling Thunder, though, would live on. Turley writes:

Dispersal of the North's industry

Background

> "... the bombing had destroyed virtually all industrial, transportation and
> communications facilities built since 1954, blotted out 10 to 15 years' potential
> economic growth, flattened three major cities and 12 of 29 province capitals, and
> triggered a decline in per capita agricultural output".

But, it was not just the bombing campaign which was undermining the north's industrial and agricultural base. Socialist policies in the countryside were labelling small land owners as 'landlords' – in effect traitors to the revolutionary cause – thus alienating many farmers. In the cities, industrial policies were no less short sighted. Though Ho's policies in the battlefield were driven by hard-headed pragmatism, in the field of economic development they were informed – tragically – by revolutionary fervour.

   William Westmoreland, the general appointed to command the American effort, aimed to use the United States' superior firepower and mobility to 'search and destroy' PAVN forces. North Vietnamese bases in the south were to be identified using modern technology, jungle hide-outs revealed by dumping chemical defoliants, and then attacked with shells, bombs, and by helicopter-borne troops. In 'free-fire zones' the army and airforce were permitted to use whatever level of firepower they felt necessary to dislodge the enemy. 'Body counts' became the measure of success and collateral damage – or civilian casualties – was a cost that

The Anzacs in Vietnam

In April 1964, President Johnson called for "more flags" to help defend South Vietnam. Among the countries that responded to his call were Australia and New Zealand. Australia had military advisers in Vietnam from 1962, but in April 1965 sent the 1st Battalion Royal Australian Regiment. Until 1972, there were about 7,000 Australian combat troops in Vietnam, based in the coastal province of Phuoc Tuy, not far from Saigon. There, operating as a self-contained unit in a Viet Cong-controlled zone, and with the support of two batteries of 105 millimetres artillery (one New Zealand), the Australians fought one of the most effective campaigns of the entire war. As General Westmoreland said: "Aggressiveness, quick reaction, good use of firepower, and old-fashioned Australian courage have produced outstanding results."

Of the battles fought by the Australians in Phuoc Tuy, one of the most significant was **Long Tan**, on 18 August 1966. Although caught out by the advance of 4,000 Viet Cong, the Australians successfully responded to inflict heavy casualties: 17 dead against about 250 VC.

Following this they managed to expand control over large areas of the province, and then win the support of the local people. Unlike the Americans who adopted a policy of 'search and destroy', the Australians were more intent on 'hearts and minds' (COIN – counter insurgency). Through various health, education and other civic action programmes, the Australians gained the confidence of many villagers, making it much harder for the VC to infiltrate rural areas of Phuoc Tuy.

This policy of gaining the support of the local population was complemented by the highly effective use of small **Special Air Service** (SAS) teams – who worked closely with the US Special Forces. Many of these men were transferred after fighting in the jungles of Borneo during the Konfrontasi between Malaysia and Indonesia. They came well trained in the art of jungle warfare and ended the war with the highest kill ratio of any similar unit: at least 500 VC dead, against none of their own to hostile fire. The Australians left Phuoc Tuy in late 1971 – having lost 423 men. The ARVN were unable to fill the vacuum, and the Viet Cong quickly regained control of the area.

just had to be borne. As one field commander famously explained: 'We had to destroy the town to save it'. By 1968 the US had more than 500,000 troops in Vietnam, while **South Korean**, **Australian**, **New Zealand**, **Filipino** and **Thai** forces contributed another 90,000. The ARVN officially had 1.5 million men under arms (100,000 or more of these were 'flower' or phantom soldiers, the pay for whom was pocketed by officers in an increasingly corrupt ARVN). Ranged against this vastly superior force were perhaps 400,000 PAVN and National Liberation Front forces.

1964-1968: who was winning?

The leadership in the north tried to allay serious anxieties about their ability to defeat the American-backed south by emphasizing human over physical and material resources. **Desertions** from the ARVN were very high – there were 113,000 from the army in 1965 alone (200,000 in 1975) – and the PAVN did record a number of significant victories. The Communists also had to deal with large numbers of desertions – 28,000 men in 1969. By 1967 world opinion, and even American public opinion, appeared to be swinging against the war. Within the US, **anti-war demonstrations** and 'teach-ins' were spreading, officials were losing confidence in the ability of the US to win the war, and the President's approval rating was sinking fast. As the US Secretary of Defense, Robert McNamara is quoted as saying in the *Pentagon Papers*:

> "... the picture of the world's greatest superpower killing or seriously injuring 1,000 noncombatants a week, while trying to pound a tiny, backward nation into submission on an issue whose merits are hotly disputed, is not a pretty one".

But although the Communists may have been winning the psychological and public opinion wars, they were increasingly hard-pressed to maintain this advantage on the ground. Continual American strikes against their bases, and the social and economic dislocations in the countryside, were making it more difficult for the Communists to recruit supporters. At the same time, the fight against a vastly better equipped enemy was also taking its toll in sheer exhaustion. Despite what is now widely regarded as a generally misguided US military strategy in Vietnam, there were notable US successes (for example the Phoenix Programme, see page 347). American GIs were always sceptical about the 'pacification' programmes which aimed to win the 'hearts and minds' war. GIs were fond of saying, 'If you've got them by the balls, their hearts and minds will follow'. At times, the US military and politicians appeared to view the average Vietnamese as inferior to the average American. This latent racism was reflected in General Westmoreland's remark that Vietnamese "don't think about death the way we do" and in the use by most US servicemen of the derogatory name "gook" to refer to Vietnamese.

At the same time as the Americans were trying to win 'hearts and minds', the Vietnamese were also busy indoctrinating their men and women, and the population in the 'occupied' south. In Bao Ninh's moving *The Sorrow of War* (1994), the main character, Kien, who fights with a scout unit describes the indoctrination that accompanied the soldiers from their barracks to the field:

> "Politics continuously. Politics in the morning, politics in the afternoon, politics again in the evening. 'We won, the enemy lost. The enemy will surely lose. The north had a good harvest, a bumper harvest. The people will rise up and welcome you. Those who don't just lack awareness. The world is divided into three camps.' More politics."

By 1967, the war had entered a period of military (though not political) stalemate. As Robert McNamara writes in his book *In retrospect: the tragedy and lessons of Vietnam*, it was at this stage that he came to believe that Vietnam was "a problem with no solution". In retrospect, he argues that the US should have withdrawn in late 1963, and certainly by late 1967. Massive quantities of US arms and money were preventing the Communists from making much headway in urban areas, while American and ARVN forces were ineffective in the countryside – although incessant bombing and ground assaults wreaked massive destruction. A black market of epic proportions developed in Saigon, as millions of dollars of assistance went astray. American journalist Stanley Karnow once remarked to a US official that "we could probably buy off the Vietcong at US$500 a head". The official replied that they had already calculated the costs, but came to "US$2,500 a head".

The Tet Offensive, 1968: the beginning of the end

By mid-1967, the Communist leadership in the north felt it was time for a further escalation of the war in the south, to regain the initiative. They began to lay the groundwork for what was to become known as the Tet (or New Year) Offensive – perhaps the single most important series of battles during the American War in Vietnam. During the early morning of 1 February 1968, shortly after noisy celebrations had welcomed in the New Year, 84,000 Communist troops – almost all

Patriot games: Vietnamese street names

Like other countries that have experienced a revolution, the Vietnamese authorities have spent considerable time expunging street names that honour men and women who lack the necessary revolutionary credentials. Most obviously, Saigon had its name changed to Ho Chi Minh City following reunification. Most towns have the same street names, and most are in memory of former patriots:

Dien Bien Phu *Site of the Communists' famous victory against the French in 1954 (see page 111).*

Duy Tan *11th Nguyen emperor (1907-16) until exiled to Réunion by the French for his opposition to colonial rule. Killed in an aircrash in Africa in 1945, his remains were interred in Hué in 1987.*

Hai Ba Trung *The renowned Trung sisters who led a rebellion against Chinese overlords in 40 AD (see page 82).*

Ham Nghi *The young emperor who joined the resistance against the French in 1885 at the age of 13 and thus gave it legitimacy.*

Hoang Van Thu *Leader of the Vietnamese Communist Party, executed by the French in 1944.*

Le Duan *Secretary-General of Lao Dong from 1959.*

Le Lai *Brother-in-arms of Emperor Le Loi. Le Lai saved Viet forces by dressing in the Emperor's clothes and drawing away surrounding Chinese troops.*

Le Loi (Le Thai To) *Leader of a revolt which, in 1426, resulted in the liberation of Vietnam from Ming Chinese overlords. Born into a wealthy family he had a life-long concern for the poor. Founder of the Le Dynasty, he ruled 1426-33.*

Le Thanh Ton(g) *A successor to Le Loi, ruled 1460-1498, poet king, and cartographer he established an efficient administration on strict Confucian lines and an enlightened legal code; literature and the arts flourished.*

Ly Thuong Kiet *Military commander who led campaigns against the Chinese and Chams during the 11th century, and gained a reputation as a brilliant strategist. He died at the age of 70 in 1105.*

Viet Cong – simultaneously attacked targets in 105 urban centres. Utterly surprising the US and South Vietnamese, the Tet Offensive had begun.

Preparations for the offensive had been laid over many months. Arms, ammunition and guerrillas were smuggled and infiltrated into urban areas, and detailed planning was undertaken. Central to the strategy was a 'sideshow' at Khe Sanh. By mounting an attack on the marine outpost at **Khe Sanh** (see page 189), the Communists successfully convinced the American and Vietnamese commanders that another Dien Bien Phu was underway. General Westmoreland moved 50,000 US troops away from the cities and suburbs to prevent any such humiliating repetition of the French defeat. But, Khe Sanh was just a diversion; a feint designed to draw attention away from the cities. In this the Communists were successful; for days after the Tet offensive, Westmoreland and the South Vietnamese President Thieu thought Khe Sanh to be the real objective and the attacks in the cities the decoy.

The most interesting aspect of the Tet Offensive was that although it was a strategic victory for the Communists, it was also a considerable tactical defeat. They may have occupied the US embassy in Saigon for a few hours but, except in Hué (see page 176), Communist forces were quickly repulsed by US and ARVN troops. The government in the south did not collapse, nor did the ARVN. Cripplingly high casualties were inflicted on the Communists – cadres at all echelons were killed – morale was undermined and it became clear that the cities would not rise up spontaneously to support the Communists. Tet, in effect, put paid to the VC as an

Nguyen Du (1765-1820) *Ambassador to Peking, courtier and Vietnam's most famous poet, wrote The Tale of Kieu (see page 384).*

Nguyen Hue *Tay Son brother who routed the Chinese at the Battle of Dong Da. Later became Emperor Quang Trung (see below and page 211).*

Nguyen Thai Hoc *Leader of the Vietnam Quoc Dan Dang Party (VNQDD) (see page 334) and the leader of the Yen Bai uprisings; captured by the French and guillotined on 17 June 1930 at the age of 28.*

Nguyen Trai *Emperor Le Loi's advisor and a skilled poet, he advised Le Loi to concentrate on political and moral struggle: "Better to conquer hearts than citadels."*

Nguyen Van Troi *Viet Cong hero who in 1963 tried, unsuccessfully, to assassinate Robert McNamara by blowing up a bridge in Saigon. He was executed.*

Phan Boi Chau *A committed anti-colonialist from the age of 19, he travelled to China and Japan to organize resistance to the French. Captured in Shanghai in 1925 he was extradited to Hanoi and sentenced to life imprisonment. Public pressure led to his amnesty in the same year and he spent the rest of his life in Hué where he died in 1940.*

Quang Trung *Leader of the Tay Son peasant rebellion of 1771; defeated both the Siamese (Thais) and the Chinese (see page 211).*

Ton Duc Thang *Became President of the Socialist Republic of Vietnam; he took part in a mutiny aboard a French ship along with other Vietnamese shipmates in the Black Sea in support of the Russian Revolution.*

Tran Hung Dao *13th century hero who fought and defeated the Yuan Chinese (see page 147). Regarded as one of Vietnam's great military leaders and strategists, also a man of letters writing the classic Binh Thu Yeu Luoc in 1284.*

Tran Nguyen Han *A 15th century general who fought heroically against the Ming Chinese occupiers.*

Tran Phu *The first Secretary General of the Communist Party of Indo-China, killed by the French in 1931 at the age of 27.*

30 Thang 4 Street *Commemorates the fall of Saigon to the Communists on 30 April 1975.*

effective fighting force. The fight now had to be increasingly taken up by the NVA. Walt Rostow wrote in 1995 that "Tet was an utter military and political defeat for the Communists in Vietnam", but adding "yet a political disaster in the United States". But this was not to matter; Westmoreland's request for more troops was turned down, and US public support for the war slumped still further as they heard reported that the US embassy itself had been 'over-run'. Those who for years had been claiming it was only a matter of time before the Communists were defeated appeared to be contradicted by the scale and intensity of the offensive. Even President Johnson was stunned by the VC's successes for he too had believed the US propaganda. As it turned out the VC incursion was by a 20-man unit from Sapper Battalion C-10 – who were all killed in the action. Their mission was not to take the embassy but to 'make a psychological gesture'. In that regard at least, the mission must have exceeded the leadership's wildest expectations.

The Phoenix Programme, established in the wake of the Tet Offensive, aimed to destroy the Communists' political infrastructure in the Mekong Delta. Named after the Vietnamese mythical bird the Phung Hoang, which could fly anywhere, the programme sent CIA-recruited and trained Counter Terror Teams – in effect assassination units – into the countryside. The teams were ordered to try and capture Communist cadres; invariably they fired first and asked questions later. By 1971, it was estimated that the programme had led to the capture of 28,000 members of the VCI (Viet Cong Infrastructure), the death of 20,000, and the defection of a further 17,000. By the early 1970s the countryside in the Mekong

A nation at sea: the boat people

One of the most potent images of Vietnam during the 1970s and 80s was of foundering, overloaded vessels carrying 'boat people' to Hong Kong, Thailand, Malaysia and the Philippines. Beginning in 1976, but becoming a torrent from the late 1970s, these boat people initially fled political persecution. Later, most were 'economic' migrants in search of a better life. Now, the tragedy of the boat people is almost at an end and fast becoming a footnote in history as the last refugees are sent 'home' or onward to what they hope will be a better life.

Escaping the country was not easy. Many prospective boat people were caught by the authorities (often after having already paid the estimated US$500-US$3,000 to secure a place on a boat), and sent to prison or to a re-education camp. Of those who embarked, it has been estimated that at least a third died at sea – from drowning or dehydration, and at the hands of pirates. The boats were usually small and poorly maintained, hardly seaworthy for a voyage across the South China Sea. Captains rarely had charts (some did not even have an experienced sailor on board), and most had never ventured further afield than the coastal waters with which they were familiar.

By 1977, the exodus was so great that some freighters began to stop heaving-to to pick up refugees – a habit which, until then, had been sacrosanct among sailors. Malaysia instructed their coastal patrol vessels to force boats back out to sea – and in the first six months of 1979 they did just that to 267 vessels carrying an

estimated 40,000 refugees. One boat drifted for days off Malaysia, with the passengers drinking their own urine, until they were picked up – but not before two children had died of dehydration. The Singapore and Malaysian governments adopted a policy of allowing boats to replenish their supplies, but not to land – forcing some vessels to sail all the way to Australia before they were assured of a welcome (over 8,000 kilometres). Cannibalism is also reported to have taken place; one boy who had only just survived being killed himself told a journalist: "After the body [of a boy] had been discovered, the boatmaster pulled it up out of the hold. Then he cut up the body. Everyone was issued a piece of meat about two fingers wide".

As numbers rose, so did the incidence of piracy – an age-old problem in the South China Sea. Pirates, mostly Thai, realizing that the boats often carried families with all their possessions (usefully converted into portable gold) began to target the refugee boats. Some commentators have estimated that by the late 1970s, 30 percent of boats were being boarded, and the United Nations High Commissioner for Refugees (UNHCR) in 1981 reported that 81 percent of women had been raped. Sometimes the boats were boarded and plundered, the women raped, all the passengers murdered, and the boats sunk. Despite all these risks, Vietnamese continued to leave in huge numbers: by 1980 there were 350,000 awaiting resettlement in refugee camps in the countries of Southeast Asia and Hong Kong.

Delta was more peaceful than it had been for years; towns which were previously strongholds of the Viet Cong had reverted to the control of the local authorities. Critics have questioned what proportion of those killed, captured and sometimes tortured were Communist cadres, but even Communist documents admit that it seriously undermined their support network in the area. In these terms, the Phoenix Programme was a great success.

The costs The Tet Offensive concentrated American minds. The costs of the war by that time had been vast. The US budget deficit had risen to three percent of Gross National Product by 1968, inflation was accelerating, and thousands of young men had been

Most of these 'illegals' left from the south of Vietnam; identified with the previous régime, they were systematically persecuted – particularly if they also happened to be ethnic Chinese or Hoa (the Chinese 'invasion' of 1979 did not help matters). But as conditions worsened in the north, large numbers also began to sail from Ha Long Bay and Haiphong. Soon the process became semi-official, as local and regional authorities realized that fortunes could be made providing boats and escorts. Large freighters began to carry refugees – the Hai Hong (1,600 tonnes) which finally docked in Malaysia was carrying 2,500 passengers who claimed they had left with the cognizance of the authorities.

The peak period of the crisis spanned the years from 1976-1979, with 270,882 leaving the country in 1979 alone. The flow of refugees slowed during 1980 and 1981 to about 50,000, and until 1988 averaged about 10,000 each year. But in the late 1980s the numbers picked up once again – with most sailing for Hong Kong and leaving from the north. It seems that whereas the majority of those sailing in the first phase (1976-1981) were political refugees, the second phase of the exodus was driven by economic pressures. Daily wage rates in Vietnam at that time were only 3,000 dong (US$0.25) – so it is easy to see the attraction of leaving for healthier economic climes. With more than 40,000 refugees in camps in Hong Kong, the Hong Kong authorities began to forcibly repatriate (euphemistically termed 'orderly return') those screened as economic migrants at the end of 1989 when 51 were flown to Hanoi. Such was the international outcry as critics highlighted fears of persecution, that the programme was suspended. In May 1992, an agreement was reached between the British and Vietnamese governments to repatriate the 55,700 boat people living in camps in Hong Kong and the orderly return programme was quietly restarted. As part of their deal with China, the British government agreed to empty the camps before the hand-over date in 1997 (a target they failed to meet).

Ironically, the evidence is that those repatriated are doing very well – better than those who never left the shores of Vietnam – and there is no convincing evidence of systematic persecution, despite the fears of such groups as Amnesty International. With the European Community and the UN offering assistance to returnees, they have set up businesses, enrolled on training courses and become embroiled in Vietnam's thrust for economic growth.

At the beginning of 1996 there were around 37,000 boat people still living in camps in Hong Kong (mostly), Indonesia, Thailand, the Philippines and Japan. The difficulty is that those who are left are the least attractive to receiving countries. As Jahanshah Assadi of the UNHCR put it at the end of 1994, "Our Nobel Prize winners left a long time ago for the West," adding "What we have now is the bottom of the barrel." Even Vietnam is not enamoured with the idea of receiving ex-citizens who clearly do not wish to be citizens again. For the refugees themselves, they have been wasted years. As the UNHCR's Jean-Noel Wetterwald said in 1996: "Leaving Vietnam was the project of their lives." Now they're going back with nothing to show for the years and the tears.

Background

killed for a cause which, to many, was becoming less clear by the month. Before the end of the year President Johnson had ended the bombing campaign. Negotiations began in Paris in 1969 to try and secure an honourable settlement for the US. Although the last American combat troops were not to leave until March 1973, the Tet Offensive marked the beginning of the end. It was from that date that the Johnson administration began to search seriously for a way out of the conflict. The illegal bombing of Cambodia in 1969, and the resumption of the bombing of the north in 1972 (the most intensive of the entire conflict), were only flurries of action on the way to an inevitable US withdrawal.

··

👉 *Getting our children out of Vietnam: a personal story*

It was 1 April 1975. I was watching the news on television. The North Vietnamese had captured Qui Nhon. From my 26-months experience in the war zone of Vietnam, I knew immediately that South Vietnam was going to fall and we, myself and my Vietnamese wife, had to decide now to go to Vietnam to get our children out or possibly never see them again.

We had not heard from them in over 1 year and did not know if they were still with their grandmother in Luong Phuoc (a village 90 miles northeast of Saigon), whether their village had already been overrun, or if they were already dead. It had been a longer time since we had heard from our son, and believed that he had been killed.

The North Vietnamese had previously moved south and captured Hué and Danang, only to be pushed back. But now they had captured Qui Nhon. They had outflanked the South Vietnamese Army and would now push south to Saigon. The country was lost.

We decided right then to go. In 6 days, we had our passports, shots and visas and were on our way to Saigon. We had been trying to get our girls out of Vietnam for over 3 years. But, government red tape prevented us. Before going, everyone thought that we would not come back alive. So we taped our `last wills' to the kitchen cabinets in our home in Milford

Center, Ohio.

We took as much money as possible – we took out a personal loan for as much as we could from the Farmers and Merchants Bank, emptied our savings and checking accounts, and borrowed whatever we could. On 2 April, we got our shots. On 3 April, we left our 10-month-old daughter, Thao, with my parents in Columbus, Ohio, and went to Washington DC, to get my passport and our visas. Then we flew to San Francisco and on to the Philippines. However, we experienced more delays. First, the flight to Saigon was delayed because the President's Palace in Saigon was being bombed. Then, during the delay, my passport was stolen. We went to the American Embassy in Manila and applied for an `Emergency Passport'. Realizing that Vietnam was about to fall to the North Vietnamese, the Emergency Passport was issued.

Finally, on 10 April 1975, we arrived in Saigon. We got a room in the Embassy Hotel and started to make inquiries about the status of the war. The police in Saigon told us that Luong Phuoc had been evacuated and the villagers were in Vung Tau, a former resort area turned into a refugee camp. Kim Chi went to Vung Tau to find our girls. They were not there and none of the villagers from Luong Phuoc was there. The police had told us the village had been evacuated so they would

··

The Paris Agreement (1972)

US Secretary of State **Henry Kissinger** records the afternoon of 8 October 1972, a Sunday, as the moment when he realized that the Communists were willing to agree a peace treaty. There was a great deal to discuss, particularly whether the treaty would offer the prospect of peaceful reunification, or the continued existence of two states – a Communist north, and non-Communist south. Both sides tried to force the issue: the US mounted further attacks and at the same time strengthened and expanded the ARVN. They also tried to play the 'Madman Nixon' card, arguing that **President Richard Nixon** was such a vehement anti-Communist that he might well resort to the ultimate deterrent, the nuclear bomb. It is true that the PAVN was losing men through desertion and had failed to recover its losses in the Tet Offensive. Bao Ninh in his book *The Sorrow of War about Kinh, a scout with the PAVN*, writes:

not have to go to Luong Phuoc to get the girls.

We had to find someone to go for us. We could not go. I, being an American, and Kim Chi now being too westernized, would both be killed by the Vietcong or stopped by the South Vietnamese Army. We found our cousin, Ty, in Saigon who agreed to go to Luong Phuoc and search for the girls.

Our search for the girls was the main topic of interest at the Embassy Hotel, as none of the other Americans or Vietnamese staying there expected us to ever find them. We had received word that Luong Phuoc was already cut off from Saigon. Ty had to go by boat in order to bypass the Vietcong and arrived at Luong Phuoc to find Kim Chi's mother and the children. They left everything behind. Even then, they were stopped by the South Vietnamese Army and held for over an hour. The village came under attack by the North Vietnamese and Kim Chi's grandmother pushed the girls to the bottom of the boat and lay on top of them, yelling to the boatman to head for the sea. Under fire, they reached the safety of the ocean and headed south.

They reached Vung Tau and the following morning took a bus to Saigon. While waiting for the girls to arrive in Saigon, Kim Chi and I had been processing the papers required for their immigration to the United States. However, on 20 April all that changed. The word had come down that all Vietnamese would be given

'refugee' status if they accompanied an American out of Saigon. You could take anyone you wanted – just as long as you claimed they were a relative. (It really did not matter if they were or not. If an American thought that a Vietnamese should be given refugee status, that was all that mattered.)

We arrived by bus at the Tan San Nhut Airport while the outskirts of the city were being bombed by the North Vietnamese. After several hours, we boarded the Air Force C-141 Transport and flew to the Philippines where we slept on the gymnasium floor of the military base. We were there only 4 days before President Marcos kicked out all the refugees and we had to go to Guam where we were kept in a 'tent city' constructed by the US Navy. Since we did have most of our papers completed for the girls, Mai and Phuong (12 and 7 years old), we were evacuated on 27 April 1975. We arrived in San Francisco on 28 April 1975 – the day that Saigon fell to the North Vietnamese.

Nearly 15 years later, in 1989, Kim Chi returned to Vietnam to visit her mother. In 1995 she bought property near Luong Phuoc where we hope to eventually build a business.
(The above is the personal experience of Ken Thompson and his wife Kim Chi. Ken flew in Vietnam and Laos as a Forward Air Controller (FAC). In Laos he was designated Raven 58.)

Background

"The life of the B3 Infantrymen after the Paris Agreement was a series of long suffering days, followed by months of retreating and months of counter-attacking, withdrawal, then counter-attack. Victory after victory, withdrawal after withdrawal. The path of war seemed endless, desperate, and leading nowhere."

But the Communist leadership knew well that the Americans were committed to withdrawal – the only question was when, so they felt that time was on their side.

By 1972, US troops in the south had declined to 95,000, the bulk of whom were support troops. The north gambled on a massive attack to defeat the ARVN and moved 200,000 men towards the demilitarized zone that marked the border between north and south. On 30 March the PAVN crossed into the south and quickly overran large sections of Quang Tri province. Simultaneous attacks were mounted in the west highlands, at Tay Ninh and in the Mekong Delta. For a while it looked as if the south would fall altogether. The US responded by mounting a succession of intense bombing raids which eventually forced the PAVN to retreat. The spring offensive may have failed, but like Tet, it was strategically important, for it demonstrated that without US support the ARVN was unlikely to be able to withstand a Communist attack.

Both sides, by late 1972, were ready to compromise. Against the wishes of South Vietnam's President Nguyen Van Thieu, the US signed a treaty on 27 January 1973, the ceasefire going into effect on the same day. Before the signing, Nixon ordered the bombing of the north – the so-called Christmas Campaign. It lasted 11 days from 18 December (Christmas Day was a holiday) and was the most intensive of the war. With the ceasefire and President Thieu, however shaky, both in place, the US was finally able to back out of its nightmare and the last combat troops left in March 1973. As J William Fulbright, a highly influential member of the Senate and a strong critic of the US role in Vietnam, observed: "We [the US] have the power to do any damn fool thing we want, and we always seem to do it."

The Final Phase, 1973-1975

The Paris Accord settled nothing – it simply provided a means by which the Americans could withdraw from Vietnam. It was never going to resolve the deep-seated differences between the two régimes and with only a brief lull, the war continued, this time without US troops. Thieu's government was probably in terminal decline even before the peace treaty was signed. Though ARVN forces were at their largest ever and, on paper, considerably stronger than the PAVN, many men were weakly committed to the cause of the south. Corruption was endemic, business was in recession, and political dissent was on the increase. The North's Central Committee formally decided to abandon the Paris Accord in October 1973; by the beginning of 1975 they were ready for the final offensive. It took only until April for the Communists to achieve total victory. ARVN troops deserted in their thousands, and the only serious resistance was offered at Xuan Loc, less than 100 kilometres from Saigon. President Thieu resigned on 27 April. ARVN generals, along with their men, were attempting to flee as the PAVN advanced on Saigon. The end was quick: at 1045 on 30 April a T-54 tank (number 843) crashed its way through the gates of the Presidential Palace, symbolizing the end of the Second Indochina War. For the US, the aftermath of the war would lead to years of soul searching; for Vietnam, to stagnation and isolation. George Ball, a senior State Department figure reflected afterwards that the war was "probably the greatest single error made by America in its history".

Legacy of the Vietnam War

The Vietnam War (or 'American War' to the Vietnamese) is such an enduring feature of the West's experience of the country that most visitors are constantly on the look-out for legacies of the conflict. There is no shortage of physically deformed and crippled Vietnamese. Many men were badly injured during the war, but large numbers also received their injuries while serving in Cambodia (1979-1989). It is tempting to associate deformed children with the enduring effects of the pesticide Agent Orange (1.7 million tonnes had been used by 1973), although this has yet to be proven 'scientifically' – American studies claim that there is no significant difference in congenital malformation. Certainly, local doctors admit that children and babies in the south are smaller today than they were before 1975. But this is more likely to be due to malnutrition than defoliants.

Bomb damage Bomb damage is most obvious from the air: well over five million tonnes of bombs were dropped on the country (north and south) and there are said to be 20 million bomb-craters – the sort of statistic people like to recount, but no one can legitimately verify. Many craters have yet to be filled in and paddy fields are still pockmarked. Some farmers have used these holes in the ground to farm fish and to use as small reservoirs to irrigate vegetable plots; they may also be partially to blame for the dramatic increase in the incidence of malaria. War scrap was one of the country's most valuable exports and PSS (perforated steel sheeting) and other remnants can be seen piled high by roadsides – although even Vietnam is running out of accessible scrap. The cities in the north are surprisingly devoid of obvious signs of the bombing campaigns – Hanoi remains remarkably intact. Hué however, formerly Vietnam's greatest historical treasure, is a tragic sight. The Citadel and Forbidden Palace were extensively damaged during the Tet offensive in 1968 and are still being repaired (see page 179). In response to the American bombing campaign, the North Vietnamese leadership ordered the dispersal of industrial activities to the countryside. Though effective in protecting some of the north's limited industrial base, this strategy created an inefficient pattern of production – a factor which even today hinders the north's efforts at promoting growth.

Even harder to measure, is the effect of the war on the Vietnamese psyche. Bao Ninh in *The Sorrow of War* writes of a driver with the PAVN who, talking with Kien the book's main character, observes: "I'm simply a soldier like you who'll now have to live with broken dreams and with pain. But, my friend, our era is finished. After this hard-won victory fighters like you, Kien, will never be normal again. You won't even speak with your normal voice, in the normal way again." Later in the book, Kien muses about the opportunities that the war has extinguished. Although the book is a fictional story, the underlying tale is one of truth:

Psycological effect of the war

> "Still, even in the midst of my reminiscences I can't avoid admitting there seems little left for me to hope for. From my life before soldiering there remains sadly little. ... Those who survived continue to live. But that will has gone, that burning will which was once Vietnam's salvation. Where is the reward of enlightenment due to us for attaining our sacred war goals? Our history-making efforts for the next generations have been to no avail."

The Vietnamese Communist Party leadership still seem to be preoccupied by the conflict, and school children are routinely shown War Crimes Museums, War Museums and Ho Chi Minh Memorials. But despite the continuing propaganda offensive, people harbour surprisingly little animosity towards America or the West. Indeed, of all Westerners, it is often Americans who are most warmly welcomed, even in the north. During the Gulf conflict of 1991 young Vietnamese were rooting for the Americans and their allies, not for Saddam Hussein. But it must be remembered that about 60 percent of Vietnam's population has been born since the US left in 1973, so have no memory of the American occupation.

The deeper source of antagonism is the continuing divide between the north and south. It was to be expected that the forces of the north would exact their revenge on their foes in the south – and many were relieved that the predicted blood bath did not materialize. But few would have thought that this revenge would be so long-lasting. The quarter of a million southern dead are not mourned or honoured, or even acknowledged. Former soldiers are denied jobs, and the government does not seem to accept any need for national reconciliation.

This is the multiple legacy of the War on Vietnam and the Vietnamese. The legacy on the US and Americans is more widely appreciated. The key question which still occupies the minds of many, though, is, was it worth it? Walt Rostow, Lee Kuan Yew and others would probably answer 'yes'. If the US had not intervened, Communism would have spread farther in Southeast Asia; more dominoes, in their view, would have fallen. In 1973, when US withdrawal was agreed, Lee Kuan Yew observed that the countries of Southeast Asia were much more resilient and resistant to Communism than they had been, say, at the time of the Tet offensive in 1968. The US presence in Vietnam allowed them to reach this state of affairs. Yet Robert McNamara in his book *In Retrospect: the tragedy and lessons of Vietnam*, and one of the architects of US policy, writes:

> *"Although we sought to do the right thing – and believed we were doing the right thing – in my judgment, hindsight proves us wrong. We both overestimated the effects of South Vietnam's loss on the security of the West and failed to adhere to the fundamental principle that, in the final analysis, if the South Vietnamese were to be saved, they had to win the war themselves."*

Land and environment

The Regions of Vietnam

The name Vietnam is derived from that adopted in 1802 by Emperor Gia Long: Nam Viet. This means, literally, the Viet (the largest ethnic group) of the south (Nam), and substituted for the country's previous name, Annam. The country is 'S' shaped, covers a land area of 329,600 square kilometres and has a coastline of 3,000 kilometres. The most important economic zones, containing the main concentrations of population, are focused on two large deltaic areas. In the north, there are the ancient rice fields and settlements of the Red River, and in the south, the fertile alluvial plain of the Mekong. In between, the country narrows to less than 50 kilometres wide, with only a thin ribbon of fertile lowland suited to intensive agriculture. Much of the interior, away from the coastal belt and the deltas, is mountainous. Here minority hilltribes (Montagnards), along with some lowland Vietnamese resettled in so-called New Economic Zones since 1975, eke out a living on thin and unproductive soils. The rugged terrain means that only a quarter of the land is actually cultivated. Of the remainder, somewhere between about 20 percent and 25 percent is forested and some of this is heavily degraded.

Geography

Vietnam consists of five major geographical zones. In the far north are the northern highlands which ring the Red River Delta and form a natural barrier with the People's Republic of China. The rugged mountains on the west border of this region – the Hoang Lien Son – exceed 3,000 metres in places. The tributaries of the Red River have cut deep, steep-sided gorges through the Hoang Lien Son, which are navigable by small boats and are important arteries of communication. The eastern portion of this region, bordering the Gulf of Tonkin, is far less imposing; the mountain peaks of the west have diminished into foothills, allowing easy access to China. It was across these hills that the Chinese mounted their successive invasions of Vietnam, the last of which occurred as recently as 1979.

Northern highlands

The second region lies in the embrace of the hills of the north. This, the Red River Delta, can legitimately claim to be the cultural and historical heart of the Viet nation. Hanoi lies at its core and it was here that the first truly independent Vietnamese polity was established in 939 AD by Ngo Quyen. The delta covers almost 15,000 square kilometres and extends 240 kilometres inland from the coast. Rice has been grown on the alluvial soils of the Red River for thousands of years. Yet despite the intricate web of canals, dykes and embankments, the Vietnamese have never been able to completely tame the river, and the delta is the victim of frequent and sometimes devastating floods. The area is very low-lying, rarely more than three metres above sea level, and often less than one metre. The high water mark is nearly

Red River Delta

The Mekong: mother river of Southeast Asia

The Mekong River is one of the 12 great rivers of the world. It stretches 4,500 kilometres from its source on the Tibet Plateau in China to its mouth (or mouths) in the Mekong Delta of Vietnam. (On 11 April 1995 a Franco-British expedition announced that they had discovered the source of the Mekong – 5,000 metres high, at the head of the Rup-Sa Pass, and miles from anywhere.) Each year, the river empties 475 billion m3 of water into the South China Sea. Along its course it flows through Burma, Laos, Thailand, Cambodia and Vietnam – all of the countries that constitute mainland Southeast Asia – as well as China. In both a symbolic and a physical sense then, it links the region. Bringing fertile silt to the land along its banks, but particularly to the Mekong Delta, the river contributes to Southeast Asia's agricultural wealth. In former times, a tributary of the Mekong which drains the Tonlé Sap (the Great Lake of Cambodia), provided the rice surplus on which the fabulous Angkor empire was founded. The Tonlé Sap acts like a great regulator, storing water in time of flood and then releasing it when levels recede.

The first European to explore the Mekong River was the French naval officer Francis Garnier. His Mekong Expedition (1866-1868), followed the great river upstream from its delta in Cochin China (southern Vietnam). Of the 9,960 kilometres that the expedition covered, 5,060 kilometres were 'discovered' for the first time. The motivation for the trip was to find a southern route into the Heavenly Kingdom – China. But they failed. The river is navigable only as far as the Lao-Cambodian border where the Khone rapids make it impassable. Nonetheless, the report of the expedition is one of the finest of its genre.

Today the Mekong itself is perceived as a source of potential economic wealth – not just as a path to riches. The Mekong Secretariat was established in 1957 to harness the waters of the river for hydropower and irrigation. The Secretariat devised a grandiose plan incorporating a succession of seven huge dams which would store 142 billion m^3 of water, irrigate 4.3 million hectares of riceland, and generate 24,200MW of power. But the Vietnam War intervened to disrupt construction. Only Laos' Nam Ngum Dam on a tributary of the Mekong was ever built – and even though this generates just 150MW of power, electricity exports to Thailand are one of Laos' largest export earners. Now that the countries of mainland Southeast Asia are on friendly terms once more, the Secretariat and its scheme have been given a new lease of life. But in the intervening years, fears about the environmental consequences of big dams have raised new questions. The Mekong Secretariat has moderated its plans and is now looking at less ambitious, and less contentious, ways to harness the Mekong River.

eight metres above the level of the land in some places. During the monsoon season, the tributaries of the Red River quickly become torrents rushing through the narrow gorges of the Hoang Lien Son, before emptying into the main channel which then bursts its banks. Although the region supports one of the highest agricultural population densities in the world, the inhabitants have frequently had to endure famines – most recently in 1989.

South of the Red River Delta South of the Red River Delta region lie the central lowlands and the mountains of the Annamite Chain. The **Annam Highlands**, now known as the **Truong Son Mountain Range**, form an important cultural divide between the Indianized nations of the west and the Sinicized cultures of the east. Its northern rugged extremity is in Thanh Hoa Province. From here the Truong Son stretches over 1,200 kilometres south, to peter out 80 kilometres north of Saigon. The highest peak is Ngoc Linh Mountain in Kon Tum Province at 2,598 metres. The Central Highlands form an upland plateau on which the hill resorts of **Buon Ma Thuot and Dalat** are situated. On the plateau, plantation agriculture and hill farms are interspersed with stands of bamboo and tropical forests. Once rich in wildlife, the plateau was a popular hunting ground during the colonial period.

To the east, the Annamite Chain falls off steeply, leaving only a narrow and fragmented band of lowland suitable for settlement – the central coastal strip. In places the mountains advance all the way to the coast, plunging into the sea as dramatic rockfaces and making north-south communication difficult. At no point does the region extend more than 64 kilometres inland, and in total it covers only 6,750 square kilometres. The soils are often rocky or saline, and irrigation is seldom possible. Nonetheless, the inhabitants have a history of sophisticated rice culture and it was here that the Champa Kingdom was established in the early centuries of the Christian era. These coastal lowlands have also formed a conduit along which people have historically moved. Even today, the main road and rail routes between the north and south cut through the coastal lowlands.

Central coastal strip

Finally, there is the Mekong Delta. Unlike the Red River Delta this region is not so prone to flooding, and consequently rice production is more stable. The reason why flooding is less severe lies in the regulating effect of the Great Lake of Cambodia, the TonlÕ Sap. During the rainy season, when the water flowing into the Mekong becomes too great for even this mighty river to absorb, rather than overflowing its banks, the water backs up into the TonlÕ Sap, which quadruples in area. The Mekong Delta covers 67,000 square kilometres and is drained by five branches of the Mekong, which divides as it flows towards the sea. The vast delta is one of the great rice bowls of Asia producing nearly half of the country's rice, and over the years has been cut into a patchwork by the canals that have been dug to expand irrigation and rice cultivation. Largely forested until the late 19th century, the French supported the settlement of the area by Vietnamese peasants, recognizing that it could become enormously productive. The deposition of silt by the rivers that cut through the delta, means that the shoreline is continually advancing – by up to 80 metres each year in some places. To the north of the delta lies **Saigon** or **Ho Chi Minh City**.

Mekong Delta

Background

The French sub-divided Vietnam into three regions, administering each separately: *Tonkin* or **Bac Ky** (the north region), *Annam* or **Trung Ky** (the central region) and *Cochin China* or **Nam Ky** (the south region). Although these administrative divisions have been abolished, the Vietnamese still recognize their country as consisting of three regions, distinct in terms of geography, history and culture. Their new names are **Bac Bo** (north), **Trung Bo** (centre) and **Nam Bo** (south).

The three regions

Climate

Vietnam stretches over 1,800 kilometres from north to south and the weather patterns in the two principal cities, Hanoi in the north and Saigon in the south, are very different (for best time to visit, see page 19). Average temperatures tend to rise the further south one ventures, while the seasonal variation in temperature decreases. The exceptions to this general rule of thumb are in the interior highland areas where the altitude means it is considerably colder.

Temperature and rainfall: selected towns

	Annual Rainfall (mm)	Mean Annual Temp (°C)	Mean Annual Variation (°C)
Hanoi	1,680	23.4	12.4
Hu	3,250	25.1	9.0
Danang	2,130	25.4	7.8
Nha Trang	1,562	26.4	4.2
Dalat	1,600	19.1	3.4
Saigon	1,980	26.9	3.1
Sapa	2,750	13.0	10.0

North Vietnam The seasons in the north are similar to those of South China. The winter stretches from November to April, with temperatures averaging 16°C, and little rainfall. The summer begins in May and lasts until October. During these months it can be very hot indeed, with an average temperature of 30°C, along with heavy rainfall and the occasional violent typhoon.

Central Vietnam Central Vietnam experiences a transitional climate, half way between that in the south and in the north. Hué has a reputation for particularly poor weather: it is often overcast, and an umbrella is needed whatever the month – even during the short 'dry' season between February and April. The annual rainfall in Hué is 3,250 millimetres (see page 176 for best time to visit).

South Vietnam Temperatures in the south are fairly constant through the year (25°C-30°C) and the seasons are determined by the rains. The dry season runs from November to April (when there is virtually no rain whatsoever) and the wet season from May to October. The hottest period is during March and April, before the rains have broken. Typhoons are quite common in coastal areas between July and November.

Highland Areas In the hill resorts of Dalat (1,500 metres), Buon Ma Thuot and Sapa nights are cool throughout the year, and in the 'winter' months between October to March it can be distinctly chilly with temperatures falling to 4°C. Even in the hottest months of March and April the temperature rarely exceeds 26°C.

Flora and fauna

The Vietnam War not only killed many people, but also decimated the country's flora and fauna. Communist soldiers killed game for food, while the American bombing campaign and the extensive use of defoliants – over 72 million litres – destroyed huge swathes of forest. Such was the degree of destruction that studies talk of 'ecocide'. With over 20 million bomb craters and the loss of 2.2 million hectares of forest, it is easy to see why. In 1943, 44 percent of the country was forested. In 1990 the figure was about 19 percent. Although there can be no doubt that the Vietnam War did massive damage to the country, it also, in a strange sense, protected Vietnam's environment. For 50 years, people were usually too concerned with fighting to pollute and ravage the environment, and the more remote and wild areas of the country were simply out of bounds to all but the foolhardy or those in uniforms. But the government has been in no position to direct funds towards maintaining the integrity of the country's national parks and little is known about the status of many rarer animals and birds.

Fields in the forest – shifting cultivation

Shifting cultivation, also known as slash-and-burn agriculture or swiddening, as well as by a variety of local terms, is one of the characteristic farming systems of Southeast Asia. It is a low-intensity form of agriculture, in which land is cleared from the forest through burning, cultivated for a few years, and then left to regenerate over 10-30 years. It takes many forms, but an important distinction can be made between shifting field systems where fields are rotated but the settlement remains permanently sited, and migratory systems where the shifting cultivators shift both field (swidden) and settlement. The land is usually only rudimentarily cleared, tree stumps being left in the ground, and seeds sown in holes made by punching the soil with a dibble stick. In Vietnam shifting cultivation is confined to the upland areas and practised by tribal minorities thus adding an ethnic and political dimension to the shifting versus sedentary farming debate.

For many years, shifting cultivators were regarded as 'primitives' who followed an essentially primitive form of agriculture and their methods were contrasted unfavourably with 'advanced' settled rice farmers. There are still many government officials in Vietnam and in the wider Southeast Asian region who continue to adhere to this mistaken belief, and further argue that shifting cultivators are the
principal cause of forest loss and soil erosion. They are, therefore, painted as the villains in the region's environmental crisis, neatly sidestepping the considerably more detrimental impact that commercial logging has had on Southeast Asia's forest resources.

Shifting cultivators have an intimate knowledge of the land, plants and animals on which they depend. One study of a Dayak tribe, the Kantu' of Kalimantan (Borneo), discovered that households were cultivating an average of 17 rice varieties and 21 other food crops each year in a highly complex system. Even more remarkably, Harold Conklin's classic 1957 study of the Hanunóo of the Philippines – a study which is a benchmark for such work even today – found that the Hanunóo identified 40 types and subtypes of rocks and minerals when classifying different soils. The shifting agricultural systems are usually also highly productive in labour terms, allowing far more leisure time than farmers using permanent field systems.

But shifting cultivation contains the seeds of its own extinction. Extensive, and geared to low population densities and abundant land, it is coming under pressure in a region where land is becoming an increasingly scarce resource, where patterns of life are dictated by an urban-based élite, and where populations are pressing on the means of subsistence.

Background

The **Javan rhinoceros** is one of the rarest large mammals in the world and until recently was thought only to survive in the Ujung Kulon National Park in West Java, Indonesia. However in November 1988 it was reported that a Stieng tribesman had shot a female Javan rhino near the Dong Nai River around 130 kilometres northeast of Saigon. When he tried to sell the horn and hide he was arrested and this set in train a search to discover if there were any more of the animals in the area. Researchers discovered that Viet Cong soldiers operating in the area during the war saw – and killed – a number of animals. One former revolutionary, Tran Ngoc Khanh, reported that he once saw a herd of 20 animals and that between 1952 and 1976 some 17 animals were shot by the soldiers. With the Viet Cong shooting the beasts whenever they chanced upon them, and the Americans 'spraying' tonnes of defoliant on the area, it is a wonder than any survived through to the end of the war. However, a study by George Schaller and three Vietnamese colleagues in 1989 found tracks, also near the Dong Nai River, and estimated that a population of 10-15 animals probably still survived in a 750 square kilometres area of bamboo and dipterocarp forest close to and including the Nam Cat Tien National Park.

The cycle of wet rice cultivation

There are an estimated 120,000 rice varieties. Rice seed – either selected from the previous harvest or, more commonly, purchased from a dealer or agricultural extension office – is soaked overnight before being sown into a carefully prepared nursery bed. Today farmers are likely to plant one of the Modern Varieties or MVs bred for their high yields.

The nursery bed into which the seeds are broadcast (scattered) is often a farmer's best land, with the most stable water supply. After a month the seedlings are uprooted and taken out to the paddy fields. The fields will also have been ploughed, puddled and harrowed, turning the heavy clay soil into a saturated slime. Traditionally, buffalo and cattle would have performed the task and although today rotavators, and even tractors are sometimes used the sight of men and boys ploughing with a buffalo is an unmistakable feature of the Vietnamese landscape. The seedlings are transplanted into the mud in clumps. Before transplanting the tops of the seedlings are twisted off (this helps to increase yield) and then they are pushed in to the soil in neat rows. The work is back-breaking and it is not unusual to find labourers – both men and women – receiving a premium – either a bonus on top of the usual daily wage or a free meal at midday, to which marijuana is sometimes added to ease the pain.

After transplanting, it is essential that the water supply is carefully controlled. The key to high yields is a constant flow of water, regulated to take account of the growth of the rice plant. In 'rain-fed' systems where the farmer relies on rainfall to water the crop, he has to hope that it will be neither too much nor too little. Elaborate ceremonies are performed to appease the rice spirits and to ensure bountiful rainfall.

In areas where rice is grown in irrigated conditions, farmers need not concern themselves with the day-to-day pattern of rainfall, and in such areas two or even three crops can be grown each year. But such systems need to be carefully managed, and it is usual for one man (very rarely, woman) to be in charge of irrigation. He decides when water should be released, organizes labour to repair dykes and dams and to clear channels, and decides which fields should receive the water first.

Traditionally, while waiting for the rice to mature, a farmer would do little except weed the crop from time to time. He and his family might move out of the village and live in a field hut to keep a close eye on the maturing rice. (A good harvest, after all, is a matter of life and death.) Today, farmers also apply chemical fertilizers and pesticides to protect the crop and ensure maximum yield. After 90-130 days, the crop should be ready for harvesting.

Harvesting also demands intensive labour. Traditionally, farmers in a village would secure their harvesters through systems of reciprocal labour exchange. Today, wage labouring is more common. After harvesting, the rice is threshed, sometimes out in the field, and then brought back to the village to be stored in a rice barn, or sold. It is only at the end of the harvest, with the rice safely stored in the barn, that the festivals begin.

This remarkable find was followed by, if anything, an even more astonishing discovery: of two completely new species of mammal. In 1992 British scientist Dr John MacKinnon discovered the skeleton of an animal now known as the **Vu Quang ox** (*Pseudoryx nghetinhensis*) but known to locals as *sao la*. The Vu Quang ox was the first new large mammal species to be found in 50 years; scientists were amazed that a large mammal could exist on this crowded planet without their knowledge. In June 1994 the first live specimen (a young calf) was captured and shortly afterwards a second *sao la* was caught and taken to the Forestry Institute in Hanoi. Sadly, both died in captivity but in early 1995 a third was brought in alive. The

Farmers versus forests

In an attempt to conserve what is left of Vietnam's forest cover the government is encouraging swidden or shifting cultivators (see page 359) to practise sedentary (settled) farming. Since 1968 a total of 1.9 million ethnic minority people have been resettled as part of this expensive and culturally disruptive programme. Commentators seem undecided whether this is a fair response to the problem of disappearing forest land or just another reprehensible expression of ethnic rivalry and Kinh domination. The United Nations Food and Agriculture Organisation would appear to support the government; it has said that pressure on the highlands is so intense that shifting cultivation is no longer a sustainable agricultural system. Fallow periods, which allow the soil to recover and forest to regrow, are too short. Consequently the soil is degraded and eroded and the forests do not get the opportunity to regenerate. In Lao Cai province, for example, forest cover has fallen from 240,000 hectares 15 years ago to 123,000 hectares today; three quarters of this loss is attributed to hill farmers. In an attempt to reduce forest cover by logging, the government, in early 1992, introduced a ban on the export of raw logs and sawn timber. Unfortunately, the vested interests of local officials make it likely that the timber export ban will be less rigidly enforced than measures against minority farmers.

animals look anything but ox-like, and have the appearance, grace and manner of a small deer. The government responded to the discovery by extending the Vu Quang Nature Reserve and banning hunting of *sao la*. Local hilltribes, who have long regarded *sao la* as a tasty and not uncommon beast, have therefore lost a valued source of food and no longer have a vested interest in the animal's survival. *Sao la* must rue the day they were 'discovered'. In 1993 a new species of deer which has been named the **giant muntjac** was also found in the Vu Quang Nature Reserve. The scientists have yet to see the beast alive but villagers prize its meat and are reported to trap it in quite large numbers.

Large rare mammals are confined to isolated pockets where the government does its best to protect them from hunters. On Cat Ba Island, the national park is home to the world's last wild troops of white-headed langur. In North Vietnam tigers have been hunted close to extinction and further south territorial battles rage between elephants and farmers. Rampaging elephants sometimes cause loss of life and are in turn decimated by enraged villagers.

Among the **larger mammals**, there are small numbers of tiger, leopard, clouded leopard, Indian elephant, Malayan sun bear, Himalayan black bear, sambar deer, gibbon and gaur (wild buffalo). These are rarely seen, except in zoos, although many of the minorities in the Central Highlands capture and train elephants for domestic use. There are frequent news reports of farmers maiming or killing elephants after their crops have been trampled or their huts flattened. The larger reptiles include two species of crocodile, the estuarine (*Crocodilus porosus*) and Siamese (*Crocodilus siamensis*). The former grows to a length of five metres and has been reported to have killed and eaten humans. Among the larger snakes are the reticulated python (*Python reticulatus*) and the smaller Indian python (*Python molurus*), both non-venomous constrictors. Venomous snakes include two species of cobra (the king cobra and common cobra), two species of krait, and six species of pit viper.

Given the difficulty of getting to Vietnam's more remote areas, the country is hardly a haven for amateur naturalists. Professional photographers and naturalists have been escorted to the country's wild areas, but this is not an option for the average visitor. Getting there requires time and contacts. A wander around the markets of Vietnam reveals the variety and number of animals that end up in the

Background

cooking pot: deer, bear, snakes, monkeys, turtles etc. The Chinese penchant for exotic foods (such gastronomic wonders as tigers' testicles and bear's foot) has also become a predilection of the Vietnamese, and most animals are fair game.

The Greening of Vietnam

However, the picture should not be entirely shaded in sombre tones. In particular, there is some evidence that the birth, or arguably rebirth, of environmentalism in other countries in Southeast Asia, most notably Thailand, is also emerging in Vietnam.

Together with overseas conservation agencies such as the Worldwide Fund for Nature, Vietnamese scientists have, in recent years, been enumerating and protecting their fauna and flora. The establishment of nature reserves began in 1962 with the gazetting of the Cuc Phuong National Park. Today there are a total of 87 reserves covering 3.3 percent of Vietnam's land area. However, some of them are too small to sustain sufficiently large breeding populations of endangered species and many parks are quite heavily populated. For instance 80,000 people live, farm and hunt within the 22,000 hectares Bach Ma National Park.

The country's environmental 'crisis' has spilled out onto the international arena. Plans to build a dam on the Black River in Son La province to the northwest of Hanoi, for example, have provoked considerable controversy. The dam is intended to provide power for Vietnam's industrialization, but it will also displace an estimated 130,000 Thai Den – the Black Thai, one of Vietnam's minorities – and flood large areas of their ancestral lands. The Tai Solidarity International, a group comprising mainly foreign resident ethnic Tai, is campaigning against the dam, claiming that it will be an environmental disaster and a human and cultural tragedy.

Birds have, in general, suffered rather less than mammals from over-hunting and the effects of the war. There have been some casualties however: the eastern sarus crane of the Mekong Delta – a symbol of fidelity, longevity and good luck – disappeared entirely during the war. However, in 1985 a farmer reported seeing a single bird, and by 1990 there were over 500 pairs breeding on the now pacified former battlefields. A sarus crane reserve has been established in Dong Thap Province. Among the more unusual birds are the snake bird (named after its habit of swimming with its body submerged and only its snake-like neck and head above the surface), the argus pheasant, which the Japanese believe to be the mythical phoenix, the little bastard quail of which the male hatches and rears the young, three species of vulture, the osprey (sea eagle), and two species of hornbill (the pied and great Indian). Vietnam also has colonies of the endangered white-winged wood duck, one of the symbols of the world conservation movement. The Vietnamese, or Vo Quy, pheasant which was thought to be extinct was recently rediscovered in the wild and two males are now held in captivity in Hanoi zoo.

Art and architecture

Art

The first flourishing of Vietnamese art occurred with the emergence of the Dongson culture (named after a small town near Thanh Hoa where early excavations were focused) on the coast of Annam and Tonkin between 500 and 200 BC. The inspiration for the magnificent bronzes produced by the artists of Dongson originated from China: the decorative motifs have clear affinities with earlier Chinese bronzes. At the same time, the exceptional skill of production and decoration argues that these pieces represent among the first, and finest, of Southeast Asian works of art. This is most clearly evident in the huge and glorious **bronze drums** which can be seen in museums in both Hanoi and Saigon (see box, page 369).

Dongson culture

If there was ever a 'golden' period in Vietnamese art and architecture, it was that of the former central Vietnamese **kingdom of Champa**, centred on the Annamite coast, which flowered in the 10th and 11th centuries. Tragically however, many of the 250 sites recorded in historical records have been pillaged or damaged and only 20 have survived the intervening centuries in a reasonable state of repair. Most famous are the sites of My Son and Dong Duong, south of Danang (see page 201). Many of the finest works have been spirited out of the country to private collections and foreign museums; others destroyed by bombing and artillery fire during the Vietnam War. Nonetheless, the world's finest collection – with some breathtakingly beautiful work – is to be found in Danang's Cham Museum (see page 198).

Cham art

The earliest Cham art belongs to the Mi Son E1 period (early eighth century). It shows stylistic similarities with Indian Sanchi and Gupta works, although even at this early stage in its development Cham art incorporated distinctive indigenous elements, most clearly seen in the naturalistic interpretation of human form. By the Dong Duong period (late ninth century), the Cham had developed a unique style of their own. Archaeologists recognize six periods of Cham art:

Mi Son E1	early eighth century
Hoa Lai	early ninth century
Dong Duong	late ninth century
Tra Kieu	late ninth-early 10th century
Thap Mam	12th-13th century
Po Klaung Garai	13th-16th century

The Cham Kingdom was ethnically and linguistically distinct, but was overrun by the Vietnamese in the 15th century. It might be argued, then, that their monuments and sculptures have little to do with 'Vietnam' per se, but with a preceding dynasty.

Background

Modern Vietnamese art

Contemporary art in Vietnam, as elsewhere in Southeast Asia, has recently benefited from an upsurge in interest from young Asian collectors with plenty of money and a preference for arts oriental to arts occidental. Exhibitions in New York, Paris and London have helped bring contemporary Vietnamese art to a wider public. Galleries have opened in all the major cities of Vietnam and although much of the work displayed is purely commercial, artists now have an opportunity to exhibit pictures which until recently were considered subversive. Vietnam has three art colleges, in Saigon, Hué and the School of Fine Arts in Hanoi, which was founded by the French in 1925.

Although most Vietnamese painting is still conservative in subject, idiom and medium, some painters of the younger generation, including Dao Hai Phong, Tran Trong Vu and Truong Tan, are experimenting with more abstract ideas and, in the more liberal artistic clime of the 1990s, their work is more expressive and less clichéd than that of 10 or 20 years ago. Even established artists such as Ly Quy Chung, Tran Luu Hau and Mai Long are taking advantage of their newly found artistic freedom to produce exciting experimental work; Trinh Cung and Tran Trong Vu are noted for their abstract paintings. Among the most respected artists of the older generation are Professor Nguyen Thu, Colonel Quang Tho and Diep Minh Chau, whose work draws heavily on traditional Vietnamese themes, particularly rural landscapes, but also episodes from recent history: the battle of Dien Bien Phu, life under American occupation and pencil sketches of Ho Chi Minh. Such traditional art forms as watercolour paintings on silk and lacquerwork are still popular.

Hué architecture   More characteristic of Vietnamese art and architecture are **the pagodas and palaces at Hué** (see page 175) and in and around Hanoi (page 71). But even this art and architecture is not really 'Vietnamese', as it is highly derivative, drawing heavily on Chinese prototypes. Certainly there are some features which are peculiarly Vietnamese, but unlike the other countries of mainland Southeast Asia, the Vietnamese artistic tradition is far less distinct. Vietnamese artistic endeavour was directed more towards literature than the plastic arts. In his art history of Indochina, French art historian Bernard Groslier – better known for his work on Angkor – writes, rather condescendingly:

> 'From 1428 to 1769 Vietnamese art is bogged down in formulas. Despite the absorption of Champa, no foreign influence, save that of China, affected them. However, execution and technique greatly improved, so that some of the works take an honourable place among Chinese provincial products' (1962: 227).

Contemporary Vietnamese art   The beginnings of contemporary or modern Vietnamese art can be traced back to the creation of the **Ecole de Beaux Arts Indochine** in Hanoi in 1925. By this time there was an emerging Westernized intelligentsia in Vietnam who had been schooled in French ways and taught to identify, at least in part, with French culture. Much of the early painting produced by students taught at the Ecole de Beaux Arts Indochine was romantic, portraying an idyllic picture of Vietnamese life and landscape. It was also weak. However by the 1930s a Vietnamese nationalist tone began to be expressed both in terms of subject matter and technique. For example, paintings on silk and lacquer became popular around this time.

In 1945, with the Declaration of Independence, the Ecole de Beaux Arts Indochine closed, and art for art's sake came to an end. From this point, artists were strongly encouraged to join in the revolutionary project and, for example, paint posters of heroic workers, stoic peasants and brave soldiers. Painting landscapes or bucolic pictures of rural life was no longer on the agenda.

In 1950 a new **School of Fine Art** was established in Viet Bac with the sole remit of training revolutionary artists. Central control of art and artists became even more stringent after 1954 when many artists were sent away to re-education camps. Established artists like Bui Xuan Phai, for example, were no longer permitted either to exhibit or to teach were they so lacking were they in revolutionary credentials.

In 1957 a new premier art school was created in the capital – the **Hanoi School of Fine Arts**. Students here were schooled in the methods and meanings of socialist-realism and western art became, by definition, capitalist and decadent. But while the State saw to it that artists kept to the revolutionary line, fine art in North Vietnam never became so harsh and uncompromising as in China or the Soviet Union; there was always a romantic streak. In addition, the first director of the Hanoi School of Fine Arts, Nguyen Do Cung, encouraged his students to search for inspiration in traditional Vietnamese arts and crafts, in simple village designs, and in archaeological artefacts. Old woodblock prints, for example, strongly influenced the artists of this period.

With *doi moi* – economic reform – has come a greater degree of artistic freedom. Nguyen Van Linh, the secretary-general of the Vietnamese Communist Party, has talked of 'untying the strings', to give artists greater freedom of individual expression. Today there are numerous art galleries in Hanoi and Saigon and while artists must still paint within limits set by the Communist Party, these limits have been considerably loosened. The first exhibition of abstract art in Vietnam was held in 1992.

The Vietnamese Pagoda

The pagoda or *chua* is a Buddhist temple, and shows clear affinities with its Chinese equivalent (see page 378 for a background to Vietnamese Buddhism). A Vietnamese pagoda is not a many-tiered tower – it is usually a single-storeyed structure. But some pagodas do have a tower (*thap*) which in most cases was erected as a memorial to the founder of the pagoda. Most will have a sacred pond (often with sacred turtles), bell tower, and yard. The main building – the pagoda itself – usually consists of a number of rooms. At the front are three main doors which are opened only for special festivals. Behind these doors are the front hall, outer hall and the inner or main altar hall, the former being at the lowest level, the altar hall at the highest. There will be Buddha statues, sometimes three, past, present and future. At the back of the pagoda are living quarters for monks and nuns, as well as gardens

Background

Vietnamese Pagoda

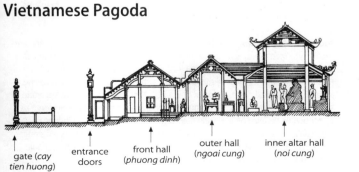

gate (*cay tien huong*)

entrance doors

front hall (*phuong dinh*)

outer hall (*ngoai cung*)

inner altar hall (*noi cung*)

Adapted from Bezacier, Louis (1959) *Relevés des monuments anciens du Nord Viet-nam*, Ecole Française D'Extrême-Orient: Paris

and other secular structures. Monks and nuns never serve in the same pagoda. While a temple may be dedicated to a hero, a mythical character or holy animal a pagoda is an exclusively Buddhist place of worship.

Common pagoda characters and iconography

Avalokitesvara or Ti-Ts'ang Wang: the compassionate male Boddhisattva, usually depicted in an attitude of meditation with his attributes, a water flask and lotus. The figure is sometimes represented with four arms, in which case his attributes are a rosary and book, as well as the lotus and water flask. He is merciful and offers help and solace to those suffering the torments of hell.

Bodhisattvas: enlightened beings or future Buddhas who have renounced nirvana to remain on earth. They are in theory countless, although just a handful are usually represented, most easily recognizable to the devotee. Bodhisattvas are usually depicted as princes with rich robes and a crown or head-dress.

Buddha (Sakyamuni): the Buddha, or the historic Buddha; usually depicted seated on a throne or thrones (often a lotus) in one of the mudras or 'attitudes' of the Buddha, and clothed in the simple dress of an ascetic. Among the Buddha's features are elongated ear lobes, the *urna* or third 'eye' in the centre of the forehead, and tightly curled hair.

Buddha of the Past (Amitabha): central to the Pure Land faith. Adherents chant the Amitabha sutra, and on their death are transported to the Western Paradise where they are guided to nirvana. The Amitabha Buddha is merciful and wise. Recent interpretations can sometimes be identified by a very long right arm – so carved so that the Buddha can embrace all of humanity, and bring salvation to everyone.

Ch'eng-huang Yeh (City God): each town will have its own deity who controls the behaviour of the population. He also keeps the records of the dead, and sends out his henchmen to collect people when their due date has arrived. He is therefore greatly feared. More generally, he controls the demons and therefore has some power over natural disasters like flood and pestilence.

Dragon (long/rong): not the evil destructive creature of Western mythology but divine and beneficial. Often associated with the emperor.

Fertility Goddesses: there are lots of these, of which the most famous is Quan Am. Other popular fertility goddesses can usually be identified by the children that they hold in their laps. Sometimes they are surrounded by attendants who hold infants, or are shown breast-feeding, teaching or playing with them.

Judges or Magistrates: these 10 men run the Ten Courts of the Afterworld and are usually arranged in two rows of five (often on either side of the hall). Their mission is to sentence the dead according to their role and life on earth. Each Judge is responsible for a different sin – murder, unfilial acts, arson, and so on – and having judged an individual passes them on to the next Judge. But just like the real world, sinners can have their sentences lightened by handing over money (Hell Money), so corruption works even here! Having passed through the hands of 10 Judges, the poor soul then arrives at the feet of **Mother Meng**. She gives the extirpated sinner the Soup of Oblivion, whereupon he or she forgets everything and is in a suitable state to be re-born in the real world.

Ong Tao: ascends to heaven at the end of the old year to inform God of the family's conduct during the previous 12 months. He is, therefore, fêted and petitioned for days before.

Patron deities: this includes a large number of deities that look after the interests of particular groups of people – fishermen (see Thien Hau), actors, policemen, farmers, and so on.

Quan Am (Kuan-yin): Chinese Goddess of Mercy (Kuan-yin), often all-white, and usually depicted holding her adopted son in one arm and standing on a lotus leaf (the symbol of purity). Quan Am's husband is occasionally depicted as a parakeet (see page 77). Quan Am is sometimes represented as a man, and as a Bodhisattva – Avalokitesvara – the two are fused in a single representation.

Quan Cong and companions: usually red-faced and green-cloaked and accompanied by his two trusty companions, General Chau Xuong and the Mandarin Quan Binh, and sometimes also with his horse and groom.

Swastika: running either left to right or vice versa, it is often complicated by various additions. The motif symbolizes the 'heart of the Buddha', 'long life' and 'ten thousand'. In Buddhist and Cao Dai temples, swastikas run in opposite directions. Cao Dai believers argue that 'their' direction is in harmony with the movement of the universe.

Thien Hau Thanh Mau (also Ma Tsu): goddess of the sea and protector of sailors. She first appeared, so to speak, in Fukien province in China during the 11th century. Folklore has it that she was the daughter of a fisherman named Lin and that she died while a virgin. She appears to fishermen in times of extreme peril and saves their lives. Thien Hau Thanh Mau is usually represented seated, with a flattened crown. But the real giveaway are her two companions, who go by the great names of **Thousand-mile Eye** and **Follow the Wind Ear**. These are both tamed demons who the goddess uses to provide long range weather forecasts to fishermen. Thousand-mile Eye is red-skinned and peers towards the horizon, hand shading his eyes; Follow the Wind Ear is green-skinned and is usually depicted cupping his hand to his ear as he listens for minor climatic changes. The three of them are usually seen, unsurprisingly, in coastal towns.

T'u-ti Kung or Fu-te Cheng-shen (Earth God): the Lord of the Earth is effectively a petty official and not to be greatly feared as he merely does the work of much more powerful gods. He keeps track of birth, deaths and marriages – as headmen do in real life. He is usually represented as an old man.

Yin-yang symbol: the Taoist symbol, a circle divided by an 'S' line, splitting the circle into dark and light halves and symbolizing the dualism of the world (see page 380).

Background

Culture

People

Vietnam is home to a total of 54 ethnic groups including the Vietnamese themselves. The ethnic minorities vary in size from the Tày, with a population of about 1.3 million, to the O-du who number only 100 individuals. Life has been hard for many of the minorities who have had to fight not only the French and Vietnamese but often each other in order to retain their territory and cultural identity. Traditions and customs have been eroded by outside influences such as Catholicism and Communism although some of the less alien ideas have been successfully accommodated. Centuries of Viet population growth and decades of warfare have taken a heavy toll on minorities and their territories; increasingly, population pressure from the minority groups themselves poses a threat to their way of life.

Highland peoples: the Montagnards of Vietnam

The highland areas of Vietnam are among the most linguistically and culturally diverse in the world. In total, the highland peoples number six to eight million. As elsewhere in Southeast Asia, a broad distinction can be drawn in Vietnam between the peoples of the lowlands and valleys, and the peoples of the uplands. The former tend to be settled, cultivate wet rice, and are fairly tightly integrated into the wider Vietnamese state: in most instances they are Viet. The latter are often migratory, they cultivate upland crops often using systems of shifting cultivation (see page 359), and are comparatively isolated from the state. The generic term for these diverse peoples of the highlands is Montagnard (from the French, 'Mountain People'), in Vietnamese *nguoi thuong* ('highland citizen') or, rather less politely, *moi* ('savage' or 'slave'). As far as the highland peoples themselves are concerned, they identify with their village and 'tribal' group, not as part of a wider 'highland citizens' grouping.

The French attitude towards the Montagnards was often inconsistent. The authorities wanted to control them and sometimes succumbed to the pressure from French commercial interests to conscript them into the labour force, particularly on the plantations. But some officials were positively protective, one, Monsieur Sebatier refused missionaries access to the territory under his control, destroyed bridges to prevent access, and had three tribal wives. He recommended total withdrawal from their lands in order to protect their cultural integrity. In *A Dragon Apparent*, Norman Lewis provides a wonderful account of the Montagnards and their way of life, and perceptively examines the relationship between them and the French.

Relations between the minorities and the Viet have not always been as good as they are officially portrayed. Recognizing and exploiting this mutual distrust and animosity, both the French and American armies recruited from among the minorities. In 1961 US Special Forces began organizing Montagnards into defence groups to prevent Communist infiltration into the Central Highlands from the north. Since 1975 relations between minorities and Viet have improved but there is still hostility, particularly in areas of heavy logging. Official publications paint a touching

Brilliance in Bronze: rain drums of Dongson

Of the artefacts associated with the Dongson culture, none is more technologically or artistically impressive than the huge bronze kettle drums that have been unearthed. Vietnamese archaeologists, understandably, have been keen to stress the 'Vietnamese-ness' of these objects, rejecting many of the suggestions made by Western scholars that they are of Chinese or Indian inspiration. As Professor Pham Huy Thong of the Academy of Sciences writes, Western studies are "marked by insufficient source material, prejudices and mere deductions", and that their "achievements [in understanding the drums] remain insignificant". He supports the view that these magnificent objects were products of the forebears of the Viet people. The jury on the issue remains out.

The squat, waisted, bronze Dongson drums show their makers to have been master casters of the first order. They can measure over one metre in height and width and consist of a decorated tympanum, a convex upper section, waisted middle, and expanding lower section. Decoration is both geometric and naturalistic, most notably on the finely incised drum head. An area of continuing debate concerns the function of the drums. They have usually been found associated with human remains and other precious objects, leading archaeologists to argue that they symbolized power and prestige, and were treasured objects in the community. Also known as 'rain drums', they are sometimes surmounted with bronze figures of frogs (or toads). It is thought that the drums were used as magical instruments to summon rain – frogs being associated with rain. Other decorative motifs include dancers (again, possibly part of rain-making rites) and boats with feather-crowned passengers (perhaps taking the deceased to the Kingdom of the Dead). Other Dongson drums have been found as far east as the island of Alor in Nusa Tenggara, Indonesia, indicating trade links between northern Vietnam and the archipelago.

As if to emphasize the nationalist symbolism of the drums an image of an ornate tympanum is used as an icon by Vietnamese television, and Vietnam Airlines prints the motif on their tickets.

Background

---

picture portraying the relationship between Viet and minority peoples: thus we read "successive generations of Vietnamese, belonging to 54 ethnic groups, members of the great national community of Vietnam, have always stood side by side with one another, sharing weal and woe, shedding sweat and blood to defend and build up their homeland ...". The government is keen to stress its role in eradicating poverty and introducing a settled rather than a nomadic existence among the minorities but ignores the consequences, namely the narrowing, blunting and elimination of cultural differences. In recent years the government has come to regard the minorities as useful 'tourist fodder' – with a splash of colour, primitive villages and ethnic dances, they provide a taste of the 'mystical East' which much of the country otherwise lacks.

Potentially tourism is a more serious and insidious threat to the minorities' way of life than any they have yet had to face. A great deal has been written about cultural erosion by tourism and any visitor to a minority village should be aware of the extent to which he or she contributes to this process. Traditional means of livelihood are quickly abandoned when a higher living standard for less effort can be obtained from the tourist dollar. Long-standing societal and kinship ties are weakened by the intrusion of outsiders. Young people may question their society's values and traditions which may seem archaic, anachronistic and risible by comparison with those of the modern, sophisticated tourist. And dress and music lose all cultural significance and symbolism if they are allowed to become mere tourist attractions.

Nevertheless, this is an unavoidable consequence of Vietnam's decision to admit tourists to the highland areas. Perhaps fortunately, however, for the time being at least, many of the minorities are pretty inaccessible to the average traveller. Visitors can minimize their impact by acting in a sensitive way (it is, for example, perfectly obvious when someone does not want their photograph taken). (See box for general advice on visiting minority villages.)

But the minority areas of Vietnam are fascinating places and the immense variety of colours and styles of dress add greatly to the visitor's enjoyment.

The peoples of the hills

Ba-na (Bahnar) A Mon-Khmer-speaking minority group concentrated in the central highland provinces of Gia Lai-Kon Tum and numbering about 150,000. Locally powerful from the 15th-18th centuries, they were virtually annihilated by neighbouring groups during the 19th century. Roman Catholic missionaries influenced the Ba-na greatly and they came to identify closely with the French. Some conversions to Catholicism were made but Christianity, where it remains, is usually just an adjunct to Ba-na

Dongson drum and mantle, bronze (79cm in width, 63cm high).
Unearthed, Northern Vietnam 1893-94.

Visiting the minorities: house rules

Etiquette and customs vary between the minorities. However, the following are general rules of good behaviour that should be adhered to whenever possible.
1. Dress modestly and avoid undressing/changing in public.
2. Ask permission before photographing anyone (old people, pregnant women and mothers with babies often object to having their photograph taken).
3. Only enter a house if invited.
4. Do not touch or photograph village shrines.

5. Do not smoke opium.
6. Avoid sitting or stepping on door sills.
7. Avoid excessive displays of wealth and be sensitive when giving gifts (for children, pens are better than sweets).
8. Avoid introducing Western medicines.
9. Do not sit with the soles of your feet pointing at other people (ie sit cross-legged).
10. If offered a cup of rice wine it is polite to down the first cup in one (what the Vietnamese call tram phan tram – 100%).

animism. Ba-na houses are built on stilts and in each village is a communal house, or *rông*, which is the focus of social life. When a baby reaches his first full month he has his ears pierced in a village ceremony equivalent to the Vietnamese *day thang* (see box 'Rite of passage', page 372); only then is a child considered a full member of the community. Their society gives men and women relatively equal status. Male and female heirs inherit wealth, and marriage can be arranged by the families of either husband or wife. Ba-na practise both settled and shifting cultivation.

Co-ho

(Also Kohor, with small local groups the **Xre, Chil** and **Nop**) Primarily found on the Lam Dong Plateau in Lam Dong Province (Dalat) with a population of about 100,000. Extended family groups live in longhouses or *buon*, sometimes up to 30 metres long. Unusually, society is matrilineal and newly-married men live with their wives' families. The children take their mother's name; if the wife dies young her smaller sister will take her place. Women wear tight-fitting blouses and skirts. Traditional shifting cultivation is giving way to settled agriculture.

Dao
(also Mán)

The Dao live in northern Vietnam in the provinces bordering China particularly Lao Cai and Ha Giang. They number, perhaps, half a million in all and include several sub-groupings notably the Dao Quan Chet (Tight Trouser Dao), the Dao Tien (Money Dao) and the Dao Ao Dai (Long Dress Dao). As these names suggest, Dao people wear highly distinctive clothing although sometimes only on their wedding day. The **Dao Tièn** or Money Dao of Hoa Binh and Son La provinces are unique among the Dao in that the women wear black skirts and leggings rather than trousers. A black jacket with red embroidered collar and cuffs, decorated at the back with coins (hence the name) together with a black red-tassled turban and silver jewellery are also worn. By contrast the male of the species is rather plain in black jacket and trousers. Head gear tends to be elaborate and includes a range of shapes (from square to conical), fabrics (waxed hair to dried pumpkin fibres) and colours.

The women of many branches of Dao shave off their eyebrows and shave back their hair to the top of their head before putting on the turban – a hairless face and high forehead are traditionally regarded as attributes of feminine beauty.

Dao wedding customs are as complex as Dao clothing and vary with group. Apart from parental consent, intending marriage partners must have compatible birthdays, and the groom has to provide the bride's family with gifts worthy of their daughter. If he is unable to do this a temporary marriage can take place but the outstanding presents must be produced and a permanent wedding celebrated before *their* daughter can marry.

Background

👉 *Rite of passage: from baby to infant*

In a poor country like Vietnam staying alive for long enough to see one's own first birthday has not always been easy. Fortunately, infant mortality levels have fallen dramatically (from 156/1,000 in 1960 to 33/1,000 in 1996) but remain high by Western standards. Perhaps not surprisingly therefore, Vietnamese families celebrate two important milestones in the early lives of their children.

Day thang, or full month, is celebrated exactly 1 month after birth. Traditionally, the mother remained in bed with her heavily-swaddled baby for the first month keeping him or her away from sun, rain and demon spirits. At 1 month the child is beyond the hazardous neo-natal stage and the mother would leave her bed and go out of the house to introduce her baby

to the village. Today, the parents hold a small party for friends and neighbours.

Thoi noi is celebrated at the end of the first year; it marks the time the baby stops sleeping in the cot and, having reached a full year, it is also a thanksgiving that the child has reached the end of the most dangerous year of life. At the party the baby is presented with a tray on which are various items such as a pen, a mirror, scissors, some soil and food; whichever the baby takes first indicates its character and likely job: scissors for a tailor, pen for a teacher, soil for a farmer and so on. Babies are normally weaned at about this time: some Vietnamese mothers use remarkably unsubtle but effective means for turning the baby from the breast, smearing the nipple with charcoal dust or Tiger Balm!

The Dao live chiefly by farming: those in higher altitudes are swidden cultivators growing maize, cassava and rye. In the middle zone shifting methods are again used to produce rice and maize, and on the valley floors sedentary farmers grow irrigated rice and rear livestock.

Spiritually the Dao have also opted for diversity: they worship *Ban Vuong*, their mythical progenitor as well as their more immediate and real ancestors. The Dao also find room for elements of Taoism, and in some cases Buddhism and Confucianism, in their elaborate metaphysical lives. Never enter a Dao house unless invited, if tree branches are suspended above the gate to a village, guests are not welcome – reasons might include a post-natal but pre-naming period, sickness, death or special ceremony. Since the Dao worship the kitchen god guests should not sit or stand immediately in front of the stove.

E-de (also Rhade) Primarily concentrated in the Central Highlands province of Dac Lac and numbering nearly 200,000, they came into early contact with the French and are regarded as one of the more 'progressive' groups, adapting to modern life with relative ease. Traditionally the E-de live in longhouses on stilts; accommodated under one roof is the matrilineal extended family or commune. The commune falls under the authority of an elderly, respected woman known as the *khoa sang* who is responsible for communal property, especially the gongs and jars, which feature in important festivals. In E-de society it is the girl's family that selects a husband, who then comes to live with her (ie society is matrilocal). As part of the wedding festivities the two families solemnly agree that if one of the partners should break the wedding vow they will forfeit a minimum of one buffalo, a maximum of a set of gongs. Wealth and property are inherited solely by daughters. Shifting cultivation is the traditional subsistence system, although this has given way in most areas to settled wet rice agriculture. Spiritually the E-de are polytheist: they number animism (recognizing the spirits of rice, soil, fire and water especially) and Christianity among their beliefs.

Primarily found in Gia Lai and Kon Tum provinces (especially near Play Ku) and numbering 260,000, they are the largest group in the Central Highlands. They are settled cultivators and live in houses on stilts in villages called ploi or bon. The Gia-rai are animist and recognize the spiritual dimension of nature; ever since the seventh century they have had a flesh and blood King of Fire and King of Water whose spirit is invoked in rain ceremonies.

Gia rai (also Zrai)

Widely spread across the highland areas of the country, but particularly near the Chinese border down to the 18th parallel. The Hmông number about 750,000 (over one percent of Vietnam's population) and live at higher altitudes than all other hill people – above 1,500 metres. Comparatively recent migrants to Vietnam, the Hmông began to settle in the country during the 19th century, after moving south from China. The Hmông language in its various dialects remained oral until the 1930s when a French priest attempted to romanize it with a view to translating the Bible. A more sucessful attempt to create a written Hmông language was made in 1961 but has since fallen into disuse. Nevertheless – or perhaps because of this failure – the Hmông still preserve an extraordinarily rich oral tradition of legends, stories and histories. Hmông people are renowned for their beautiful folk songs. Each branch of the Hmông people preserves its own corpus of love songs, work songs and festival songs which are sung unaccompanied or with the accompaniment of the *khène*, a small bamboo pipe organ, a two stringed violin, flutes, drums, gongs and jew's harps. Numerous Hmông dances also exist to celebrate various dates in the social calendar and to propitiate animist spirits.

Hmông (also Mèo, Mieu, Miao)

They have played an important role in resisting both the French and the Vietnamese. Living at such high altitudes they tend to be one of the most isolated of all the hill people. Their way of life does not normally bring them into contact with the outside world which suits them well – the Hmông traders at Sapa are an exception (see page 121). High in the hills, flooding is not a problem so their houses are built on the ground, not raised up on stilts. Hmông villages are now increasingly found along the river valleys and roads as the government resettlement schemes aim to introduce them to a more sedentary form of agriculture. The Hmông practice slash and burn cultivation growing maize and dry rice. Traditionally opium has been a valuable cash crop. Although fields are often cleared on very steep and rocky slopes, the land is not terraced. There are a number of different groups among the Hmông including the White, Black, Red and Flower Hmông which are distinguishable by the colour of the women's clothes. Black Hmông wear almost entirely black clothing with remarkable pointed black turbans. White Hmông women wear white skirts and the Red Hmông tie their heads in a red scarf while the Flower Hmông wrap their hair (with hair extensions) around their head like a broad-brimmed hat. However, such numerous regional variations occur that even experts on ethnic minority cultures sometimes have problems trying to identify which branch of Hmông they have encountered. Serious social problems have occurred among the Hmông owing to opium addiction; with over 30 percent of the male population of some Hmông villages addicted the drug has rendered many incapable of work causing misery and malnutrition for their families, and with the drug finding its way on to the streets of Vietnam's cities, the authorities have resolved to clamp down hard on opium production and in 1995 destroyed 4,500 hectares of opium fields. This has had tragic consequences when the Hmông have tried to protect their livelihoods. In 1993 12 Hmông villagers in Son La Province killed a local party official in protest at opium clearances, then burnt themselves to death.

Numbering almost one million the Muong are the fourth largest ethnic minority in Vietnam. They live in the area between northern Thanh Hoa Province and Yen Bai

Mùòng (also Mol)

Background

but predominantly in Hoa Binh Province. It is thought that the Muòng are descended from the same stock as the Viets: their languages are similar, and there are also close similarities in culture and religion. But whereas the Vietnamese came under strong Chinese cultural influence from the early centuries of the Christian era, the Muòng did not. The Muòng belong to the Viet-Muòng language group, their language is closest to Vietnamese of all the ethnic minority languages. It once had its own script but all the original literary works have been lost and today there is no trace. Muòng practise wet and dry rice cultivation where possible, supplementing their income with cash crops such as manioc, tobacco and cotton. Weaving is still practised, items produced including pillowcases and blankets. Culturally the Muòng are akin to the Thai and live in stilt houses in small villages called quel; groupings of from three to 30 quel form a unit called a *muong*. Muòng society is feudal in nature with each *muong* coming under the protection of a noble family (*lang*). The common people are not deemed worthy of family names so are all called Bui. Each year the members of a *muong* are required to labour for one day in fields belonging to the *lang*.

Marriages are arranged: girls, in particular, have no choice of spouse. Muòng cultural life is rich, literature has been translated into Vietnamese and their legends, poems and songs are considered particularly fine.

Nung Concentrated in Cao Bang and Lang Son provinces, adjacent to the Chinese border, the Nung number approximately one million. They are strongly influenced by the Chinese and most are Buddhist, but like both Vietnamese and Chinese the Nung practise ancestor worship too. In Nung houses a Buddhist altar is placed above the ancestor altar and, in deference to Buddhist teaching, they refrain from eating most types of meat. The Nung are settled agriculturalists and, where conditions permit, produce wet rice; all houses have their own garden in which fruit and vegetables are grown.

Tày (also Tho) The Tày are the most populous ethnic minority in Vietnam; they number about 1.3 million and are found in the provinces of northwest Vietnam stretching from Quang Ninh east to Lao Cai. Tày society was traditionally feudal with powerful lords able to extract from the free and semi-free serfs' obligations such as *droit de seigneur*. Today Tày society is male dominated with important decisions being taken by men and eldest sons inheriting the bulk of the family's wealth.

Economically the Tày survive by farming and are highly regarded as wet rice cultivationists, they are also noted for the production of fruits (pears, peaches, apricots and tangerines), herbs and spices. Diet is supplemented by animal and fish rearing and cash is raised by the production of handicrafts. The Tày live in houses on stilts, located in the river valleys. Tày architecture is quite similar in design to that of the Black Thái, but important differences may be identified, most notably the larger size of the Tày house, the deeper overhang of the thatched or (amongst more affluent Tày communities) tiled roof and the extent of the railed balcony which often encircles the entire house.

Like the Thái, Tày ancestors migrated south from southern China contemporaneously with those of the Thái and they follow the three main religions of Buddhism, Confucianism and Taoism in addition to ancestor worship and animist beliefs. Whilst Tày people have lived in close proximity to the Viet majority over a period of many centuries, their own language continues to be their primary means of communication. They hail from the Austro-Asian language family and specifically the Thai-Kadai language group. Tày literature has a long and distinguished history and much has been translated into Vietnamese. During the French colonial period missionaries romanized Tày script.

Numbering over one million this is the second largest ethnic minority in Vietnam and ethnically distinct from the Thais of modern-day Thailand. There are two main sub-groups, the Black (Thái Den), who are settled mainly in Son La, Lai Chan, Lao Cai and Yen Bai provinces, and the White Thái (Thái Don), who are found predominantly in Hoa Binh, Son La, Thanh Hoa and Vinh Phu provinces, as well as many others, including the Red Thái (Thái Do). The use of these colour-based classifications has usually been linked to the colour of their clothes, particularly the colour of women's shirts. However there has been some confusion over the origins of the terms and there is every reason to believe that it has nothing to do with the colour of their attire, and is possibly linked to the distribution of the sub-groups near the Red and Black rivers. The confusion of names becomes even more perplexing when the Vietnamese names for the sub-groups of Thái people are translated into Thái. Some scholars have taken Thái Den (Black Thái) to be Thái Daeng – *daeng* being the Thái word for red, thereby muddling up the two groups. With the notable exception of the White Thái communities of Hoa Binh traditional costume for the women of both the Black and White Thái generally features a coloured blouse with a row of silver buttons down the front, a long black skirt, a coloured waist sash and a black head-scarf embroidered with intricate, predominantly red and yellow designs.

The traditional costume of the White Thái women of Hoa Binh comprises a long black skirt with fitted waistband embroidered with either a dragon or chicken motif together with a plain pastel coloured blouse and gold and maroon sash.

Being so numerous the Thái cover a large part of northwest Vietnam, in particular the valleys of the Red River and the Da and the Ma rivers, spilling over into Laos and Thailand. They arrived in Vietnam between the fourth and 11th centuries from southern China and linguistically they are part of the wider Thái-Kadai linguistic grouping. Residents of Lac village in Mai Chau claim to have communicated with visitors from Thailand by means of this shared heritage.

The Thái tend to occupy lowland areas and they compete directly with the Kinh (ethnic Vietnamese) for good quality, irrigable farmland. They are masters of wet rice cultivation producing high yields and often two harvests each year. Their irrigation works are ingenious and incorporate numerous labour-saving devices including river-powered water wheels that can raise water several metres. Thái villages (*ban*) consist of 40-50 houses on stilts; they are architecturally attractive, shaded by fruit trees and surrounded by verdant paddy fields. Being, as they so often are, located by rivers one of the highlights of a Thái village is its suspension footbridge. The Thái are excellent custodians of the land (particularly by comparison with some other minority peoples) and their landscapes and villages are invariably most scenic.

Owing to their geographical proximity and agricultural similarities with the Kinh it is not surprising to see cultural assimilation – sometimes via marriage – and most Thái speak Vietnamese. Equally it is interesting to note the extent to which the Thái retain a distinctive cultural identity, visibly most noticeable in their dress.

When a Thái woman marries, her parents-in-law give her a hair extension (*can song*) and a silver hair pin (*khat pom*) which she is expected to wear (even in bed) for the duration of the marriage. There are two wedding ceremonies, the first at the bride's house where the couple live for one to three years, followed by a second when they move to the husband's house.

Concentrated in Gia Lai and Kon Tum provinces and numbering about 100,000, the Xo-dang live in extended family longhouses and society is patriarchal. The Xo-dang practise both shifting agriculture and the cultivation of wet rice. A highly war-like people, they almost wiped out the Ba-na in the 19th century. Xo-dang thought nothing of kidnapping neighbouring tribesmen to sacrifice to the spirits; indeed the practice of kidnapping was subsequently put to commercial use and formed the basis of a slave trade with Siam (Thailand). Xo-dang villages, or *ploi*, are usually well

Thai (also Táy and T'ai)

Xo-dang

Background

defended (presumably for fear of reprisal) and are surrounded by thorn hedges supplemented with spears and stakes. Complex rules designed to prevent in-breeding limit the number of available marriage partners which sometimes results in late marriages.

Other Groups (with populations of over 50,000 population) *Hre* – Quang Ngai and Binh Dinh provinces, 94,000. *Mnong* – Dac Lac and Lam Dong provinces, 65,000. *Xtieng* – Song Be province 50,000.

Kinh The 1989 census revealed that 87 percent of Vietnam's population were ethnic
(also Viet) Vietnamese. But with a well-run family planning campaign beginning to take effect in urban areas and higher fertility rates among the ethnic minorities it is likely that this figure will fall. The history of the Kinh is marked by a steady southwards progression from the Red River basin to the southern plains and Mekong Delta. Today the Kinh are concentrated into the two great river deltas, the coastal plains and the main cities. Only in the central and northern highland regions are they outnumbered by ethnic minorities. Kinh social cohesion and mastery of intensive wet rice cultivation has led to their numerical, and subsequently political and economic dominance of the country. Ethnic Vietnamese are also found in Cambodia where some have been settled for generations; recent Khmer Rouge attacks on Vietnamese villages have, however, caused many to flee to Vietnam.

Cham With the over-running of Champa in 1471 (see page 328) Cham cultural and ethnic identity was diluted by the more numerous ethnic Vietnamese. The Cham were dispossessed of the more productive lands and found themselves in increasingly marginal territory. Economically eclipsed and strangers in their own land, Cham artistic creativity atrophied, their sculptural and architectural skills, once the glory of Vietnam, faded and decayed like so many Cham temples and towers. It is estimated that there are, today, 99,000 Cham people in Vietnam chiefly in central and southern Vietnam in the coastal provinces extending south from Qui Nhon. Small communities are to be found in Ho Chi Minh City. They are artistically the poor relations of their forebears but skills in weaving and music live on.

The Cham of the south are typically engaged in fishing, weaving and other small scale commercial activities; urban Cham are poor and live in slum neighbourhoods. Further north the Cham are wet or dry rice farmers according to local topography; they are noted for their skill in wet rice farming and small scale hydraulic engineering.

In southern Vietnam the majority of Cham are Muslim, a comparatively newly acquired religion although familiar from earlier centuries when many became acquainted with Islamic tenets through traders from India and the Indonesian isles. In central Vietnam most Cham are Brahminist and the cult of the linga remains an important feature of spiritual life. In these provinces, away from the influence of Islam, vestiges of matriliny remain.

The Hoa: ethnic Chinese

There are nearly one million **ethnic Chinese** or *Hoa* in Vietnam, 80 percent living in the south of the country. Before reunification in 1975 there were even more: persecution by the authorities and the lack of economic opportunities since the process of socialist transformation was initiated, encouraged hundreds of thousands to leave. There are now large Vietnamese communities abroad, particularly in Australia, on the west coast of the US, and France. It has been estimated that the total Viet-kieu population numbers some two million.

With the reforms of the 1980s, the authorities' view of the Chinese has changed – they now appreciate the crucial role they played, and could continue to play, in the economy. Before 1975, the *Hoa* controlled 80 percent of industry in the south and 50 percent of banking and finance. Today, ethnic Chinese in Vietnam can own and operate businesses and are once again allowed to join the Communist Party (although only 1,000 out of two million are members), the army, and to enter university. The dark days of the mid to late 1970s seem to be over.

The Viet Kieu: Overseas Vietnamese

Since 1988, **Overseas Vietnamese** or *Viet Kieu* (most of whom are of Chinese extraction) have been allowed back to visit their relatives, in some cases helping to spread stories of untold wealth in the US, Australia and elsewhere. The largest community of overseas Vietnamese live in the US, about 1.4 million. The next largest populations are resident in France (250,000) and Australia (160,000), with much smaller numbers in a host of other countries. In 1990, 40,000 returned to visit; in 1995, 265,000 returned 'home'.

Many Viet Kieu are former boat people, while others left the country as part of the UN-administered Orderly Departure Programme which began in earnest in the late 1980s. The Viet Kieu have often shown, in the adopted homes, enormous perserverance and grit. Take the small Texan shrimping town of Palacios. Today there are around 300 Americans of Vietnamese extraction, mostly Catholics, living in and around Palacios. When the first settlers arrived in 1976 escaping from the defeated South, most had nothing. Many faced bigotry from racist elements in the local community who feared competition from 'foreigners'. But they worked and saved and by the early 1980s some families had managed to buy shrimping boats for themselves. Another 10 years on and the most successful boats were owned and operated by Vietnamese. By that time, many of their children had been born and raised in the local community, they had gone through local schools (often winning the top scholastic prizes) and few questioned their credentials to be counted as Americans. As *The Economist* put it, locals 'say the Vietnamese remind them of traditional American virtues family, community, God, a Herculean work effort, and a passionate hatred of communism' (1st August 1998).

Having discovered some measure of prosperity in the West, the Vietnamese government is anxious to welcome them back – or rather, welcome their money. So far, however, flows of investment have been rather disappointing and largely concentrated in the service sector – particularly hotels and restaurants. Part of the problem is that many Viet Kieu were escaping from persecution in Vietnam and of all people continue to harbour doubts about a government which is, in essence, the same as the one they fled. On the government's side, they worry that the Viet Kieu may be a destabilizing influence, perhaps even a Fifth Column intent on undermining the supremacy of the Communist Party. Again the leadership have cause for concern as the most vocal opponents of the US policy of rapprochement have been Viet Kieu. They have also been the main source of funds for (the admittedly ineffectual) groups trying to overthrow the government. Nor are the Overseas Vietnamese quite as rich as their ostentatious displays of wealth on the streets of Saigon and Hanoi would indicate. They do not have the economic muscle of the Overseas Chinese, for example, and in most cases have only been out of the country for less than 20 years, many having lost everything in their attempt to escape. Many young Viet Kieu have, however, equipped themselves with qualifications and skills while overseas and can find lucrative employment back in Vietnam.

Background

Religion

Vietnam supports adherents of all the major world 'religions', as well as followers of religions that are peculiarly Vietnamese: Theravada and Mahayana Buddhism, Protestant and Catholic Christianity, Taoism, Confucianism, Islam, Cao Daism, Hoa Hao and Hinduism. In addition, spirit and ancestor worship (*To Tien*) are also practised. Confucianism, although not a formal religion, is probably the most pervasive doctrine of all. Nominal Christians and Buddhists will still pay attention to the moral and philosophic principles of Confucianism and it continues to play a central role in Vietnamese life.

Following the Communist victory in 1975, the authorities moved quickly to curtail the influence of the various religions. Schools, hospitals and other institutions run by religious organizations were taken over by the state and many clergy either imprisoned and/or sent to re-education camps. The religious hierarchies were institutionalized, and proselytizing severely curtailed.

During the late 1980s and into the early 1990s some analysts identified an easing of the government's previously highly restrictive policies towards religious organizations. At the beginning of 1993, former General Secretary of the Vietnamese Communist Party, Do Muoi, even went so far as to make a pair of official visits to a Buddhist monastery and a Catholic church. However it is clear that the Communist hierarchy is highly suspicious of priests and monks. They are well aware of the prominent role they played in South Vietnamese political dissension and are quick to crack down on any religious leader or organization that becomes involved in politics.

There is no question that more people today are attending Buddhist pagodas, Christian churches and Cao Dai temples. However, whether this rise in attendance at temples and churches actually means some sort of religious re-birth is questionable. Dang Nghiem Van, head of Hanoi's Institute of Religious Studies, interviewed in 1996, poured scorn on the notion that young people are finding religion. They "are not religious", he said, "just superstitious. This isn't religion. It's decadence".

Mahayana Buddhism

Although there are both Theravada (also known as Hinayana) and Mahayana Buddhists in Vietnam, the latter are by far the more numerous. Buddhism was introduced into Vietnam in the second century AD: Indian pilgrims came by boat and brought the teachings of Theravada Buddhism, while Chinese monks came by land and introduced Mahayana Buddhism. In particular, the Chinese monk Mau Tu is credited with being the first person to introduce Mahayana Buddhism in 194/195 AD.

Initially, Buddhism was very much the religion of the élite, and did not impinge upon the common Vietnamese man or woman. It was not until the reign of Emperor Ly Anh Tong (1138-1175) that Buddhism was promoted as the State Religion – nearly 1,000 years after Mau Tu had arrived from China to spread the teachings of the Buddha. By that time it had begun to filter down to the village level, but as it did so it became increasingly syncretic: Buddhism became enmeshed with Confucianism, Taoism, spirituality, mysticism and animism. In the 15th century it also began to lose its position to Confucianism as the dominant religion of the court.

There has been a resurgence of Buddhism since the 1920s. It was the self-immolation of Buddhist monks in the 1960s which provided a focus of discontent against the government in the south (see page 262), and since the Communist victory in 1975, monks have remained an important focus of dissent – hence the persecution of Buddhists during the early years following reunification.

In Siddhartha's footsteps: a short history of Buddhism

Buddhism was founded by Siddhartha Gautama, a prince of the Sakya tribe of Nepal, who probably lived between 563 and 483 BC. He achieved enlightenment and the word buddha means 'fully enlightened one', or 'one who has woken up'. Siddhartha Gautama is known by a number of titles. In the west, he is usually referred to as The Buddha, ie the historic Buddha (but not just Buddha); more common in Southeast Asia is the title Sakyamuni, or Sage of the Sakyas (referring to his tribal origins).

Over the centuries, the life of the Buddha has become part legend, and the Jataka tales which recount his various lives are colourful and convoluted. But, central to any Buddhist's belief is that he was born under a sal tree, that he achieved enlightenment under a bodhi tree in the Bodh Gaya Gardens, that he preached the First Sermon at Sarnath, and that he died at Kusinagara (all in India or Nepal).

The Buddha was born at Lumbini (in present-day Nepal), as Queen Maya was on her way to her parents' home. She had had a very auspicious dream before the child's birth of being impregnated by an elephant, whereupon a sage prophesied that Siddhartha would become either a great king or a great spiritual leader. His father, being keen that the first option of the prophesy be fulfilled, brought him up in all the princely skills – at which Siddhartha excelled – and ensured that he only saw beautiful things, not the harsher elements of life.

Despite his father's efforts Siddhartha saw four things while travelling between palaces – a helpless old man, a very sick man, a corpse being carried by lamenting relatives, and an ascetic, calm and serene as he begged for food. The young prince renounced his princely origins and left home to study under a series of spiritual teachers. He finally discovered the path to enlightenment at the Bodh Gaya Gardens in India. He then proclaimed his thoughts to a small group of disciples at Sarnath, near Benares, and continued to preach

and attract followers until he died at the age of 81 at Kusinagara.

In the First Sermon at the deer park in Sarnath, the Buddha preached the Four Truths, which are still considered the root of Buddhist belief and practical experience: suffering exists; there is a cause of suffering; suffering can be ended; and to end suffering it is necessary to follow the 'Noble Eightfold Path' – namely, right speech, livelihood, action, effort, mindfulness, concentration, opinion and intention.

Soon after the Buddha began preaching, a monastic order – the Sangha – was established. As the monkhood evolved in India, it also began to fragment into different sects. An important change was the belief that the Buddha was transcendent: he had never been born, nor had he died; he had always existed and his life on earth had been mere illusion. The emergence of these new concepts helped to turn what up until then was an ethical code of conduct, into a religion. It eventually led to the appearance of a new Buddhist movement, Mahayana Buddhism which split from the more traditional Theravada 'sect'.

Despite the division of Buddhism into two sects, the central tenets of the religion are common to both. Specifically, the principles pertaining to the Four Noble Truths, the Noble Eightfold Path, the Dependent Origination, the Law of Karma, and nirvana. In addition, the principles of non-violence and tolerance are also embraced by both sects. In essence, the differences between the two are of emphasis and interpretation. Theravada Buddhism is strictly based on the original Pali Canon, while the Mahayana tradition stems from later Sanskrit texts. Mahayana Buddhism also allows a broader and more varied interpretation of the doctrine. Other important differences are that while the Thervada tradition is more 'intellectual' and self-obsessed, with an emphasis upon the attaining of wisdom and insight for oneself, Mahayana Buddhism stresses devotion and compassion towards others.

Background

Mahayana Buddhists are concentrated in the centre and north of the country, and the dominant sect is the Thien (Zen) meditation sect. Of the relatively small numbers of Theravada Buddhists, the majority are of Cambodian stock and are concentrated in the Mekong Delta. In Vietnam, Buddhism is intertwined with Confucianism and Taoism.

Confucianism

Although Confucianism is not strictly a religion, the teachings of the Chinese sage and philosopher Confucius (551-479 BC) form the basis on which Vietnamese life and government were based for much of the historic period. Even today, Confucianist perspectives are, possibly, more strongly in evidence than Communist ones. Confucianism was introduced from China during the Bac Thuoc Period (111 BC-938 AD) when the Chinese dominated the country. The 'religion' enshrined the concept of imperial rule by the mandate of heaven, effectively constraining social and political change.

In essence, Confucianism stresses the importance of family and lineage, and the worship of ancestors. Men and women in positions of authority were required to provide role models for the 'ignorant', while the state, epitomized in the emperor, was likewise required to set an example and to provide conditions of stability and fairness for his people. Crucially, children had to observe filial piety. This set of norms, which were drawn from the experience of the human encounter at the practical level, were enshrined in the Forty-seven Rules for Teaching and Changing first issued in 1663. A key element of Confucianist thought is the Three Bonds (*tam cuong*) – the loyalty of ministers to the emperor, the obedience of children to their parents, and the submission of wives to their husbands. Added to these are mutual reciprocity among friends, and benevolence towards strangers. Not surprisingly the Communists are antipathetic to such a hierarchical view of society although ironically Confucianism which inculcates respect for the elderly and authority unwittingly lends support to a politburo occupied by old men. In an essay entitled 'Confucianism and Marxism', Vietnamese scholar Nguyen Khac Vien explains why Marxism proved an acceptable doctrine to those accustomed to Confucian values: "Marxism was not baffling to Confucians in that it concentrated man's thoughts on political and social problems. By defining man as the total of his social relationships, Marxism hardly came as a shock to the Confucian scholar who had always considered the highest aim of man to be the fulfilment of his social obligations ... Bourgeois individualism, which puts personal interests ahead of those of society and petty bourgeois anarchism, which allows no social discipline whatsoever, are alien to both Confucianism and Marxism."

Taoism

Taoism was introduced from China into Vietnam at about the same time as Confucianism. It is based on the works of the Chinese philosophers Lao Tzu (circa sixth-fifth centuries BC) and Chuang Tzu (fourth century BC). Although not strictly a formal religion, it has had a significant influence on Buddhism (as it is practised in Vietnam) and on Confucianism. In reality, Taoism and Confucianism are two sides of the same coin: the Taoist side is poetry and spirituality; the Confucianist side, social ethics and the order of the world. Together they form a unity. Like Confucianism, it is not possible to give a figure to the number of adherents of Taoism in Vietnam: it functions in conjunction with Confucianism and Buddhism, and also often with Christianity, Cao Daism and Hoa Hao.

Of all the world's religions, Taoism is perhaps the hardest to pin down. It has no formal code, no teachings, and no creed. It is a cosmic religion. Even the word Tao is usually left untranslated – or merely translated as "The Way". The inscrutability of it all is summed up in the writings of the Chinese poet Po Chu-i:

> *'Those who speak know nothing,*
> *Those who know keep silence.'*
> *These words, as I am told,*
> *Were spoken by Lao Tzu.*
> *But if we are to believe that Lao Tzu*
> *Was himself one who knew,*
> *How comes it that he wrote a book*
> *Of five thousand words?*

Or to quote Chuang Tzu, and even more inscrutably: "Tao is beyond material existence ... it may be transmitted, but it cannot be received [posessed]. It may be attained, but cannot be seen. It exists prior to Heaven and Earth, and, indeed, for all eternity ... it is above the Zenith, but is not high; it is beneath the Nadir, but it is not low. It is prior to Heaven and Earth, but it is not ancient. It is older than the most ancient, but it is not old."

Central to Taoist belief is a world view based upon *yin* and *yang*, two primordial forces on which the creation and functioning of the world are based. The yin-yang is not specifically Taoist or Confucianist, but predates both and is associated with the first recorded Chinese ruler, Fu-hsi (2852-2738 BC). The well-known *yin-yang* symbol symbolizes the balance and equality between the great dualistic forces in the universe: dark and light, negative and positive, male and female. JC Cooper explains in *Taoism: the Way of the Mystic* the symbolism of the black and white dots: "There is a point, or embryo, of black in the white and white in the black. This ... is essential to the symbolism since there is no being which does not contain within itself the germ of its opposite. There is no male wholly without feminine characteristics and no female without its masculine attributes." Thus the dualism of the *yin-yang* is not absolute, but permeable.

To maintain balance and harmony in life it is necessary that a proper balance be maintained between *yin* (female) and *yang* (male). This is believed to be true both at the scale of the world and the nation, and also for an individual – for the human body is the world in microcosm. The root cause of illness is imbalance between the forces of *yin* and *yang*. Even foods have characters: 'hot' foods are *yang*, 'cold', *yin*. Implicit in this is the belief that there is a natural law underpinning all of life, a law upon which harmony ultimately rests. Taoism attempts to maintain this balance, and thereby harmony. In this way, Taoism is a force promoting inertia, maintaining the status quo. Traditional relationships between fathers and sons, between siblings, within villages, and between the rulers and the ruled, are all rationalized in terms of maintaining balance and harmony. Forces for change – like Communism and democracy – are resisted on the basis that they upset this balance.

Christianity

Christianity was first introduced into Vietnam in the 16th century by Roman Catholic missionaries from Portugal, Spain and France. The first Bishop of Vietnam was appointed in 1659, and by 1685 there were estimated to be 800,000 Roman Catholics in the country. For several centuries Christianity was discouraged, and at times, outlawed. Many Christians were executed and one of the reasons that the French gave for annexing the country in the late 19th century was religious persecution (see page 333). Today, eight to 10 percent of the population are thought to be Catholic, some six million people; less than one percent are Protestant. This Christian population is served by around 2,000 priests.

Following reunification in 1975, many Catholics in the former south were sent to re-education camps. They were perceived to be both staunchly pro-American and anti-Communist, and it was not until 1988 that many were returned to normal life. Today, Catholics are still viewed with suspicion by the state and priests felt to be drifting from purely religious concerns into any criticism of the state are detained. Indicative of this 'fear' of Christianity is the fact that the last Archbishop of Hanoi died in 1989 and the church is still waiting for permission to appoint a replacement. Similarly the Vatican is awaiting government permission to appoint a prelate of Hué, a post viewed with distaste by the authorities as it was last held by the worldly brother of former president Ngo Dinh Diem. More generally, the authorities have been slow to permit Vietnamese men to become ordained, and they have limited the production and flow of religious literature.

Islam and Hinduism

The only centres of Islam and Hinduism are among the Cham of the central coastal plain and Chau Doc, a province in the Mekong Delta. The Cham were converted to Islam by Muslim traders. There are several mosques in Saigon and Cholon – some of them built by Indians from Kerala.

Cao Daism

Cao Dai took root in southern Vietnam during the 1920s after Ngo Van Chieu, a civil servant, was visited by 'Cao Dai' or the 'Supreme Being' and was given the tenets of a new religion. Ngo received this spiritual visitation in 1919 on Phu Quoc Island. The Cao Dai later told Ngo in a seance that he was to be symbolized by a giant eye. The religion quickly gained the support of a large following of dispossessed peasants. It was both a religion and a nationalist movement. In terms of the former, it claimed to be a synthesis of Buddhism, Christianity, Taoism, Confucianism and Islam. Cao Dai 'saints' include Joan of Arc, the French writer Victor Hugo, Sir Winston Churchill, Sun Yat Sen, Moses and Brahma.

Debates over doctrine are mediated through the spirits who are contacted on a regular basis through a strange wooden contraption called a *corbeille-à-bec* or planchette. The five Cao Dai commandments are: do not kill any living creature; do not covet; do not practise high living; do not be tempted; and do not slander by word. But, as well as being a religion, the movement also claimed that it would restore traditional Vietnamese attitudes, and was anti-colonial and modestly subversive. Opportunist to a fault, Cao Dai followers sought the aid of the Japanese against the French, the Americans against the Viet Minh, and the Viet Minh against the south. Following reunification in 1975, all Cao Dai lands were confiscated and their leadership emasculated. The centre of Cao Daism remains the Mekong Delta where – and despite the efforts of the Communists – there are thought to be perhaps two million adherents and perhaps 1,000 Cao Dai temples. The Cao Dai Cathedral or Great Temple is in the town of Tay Ninh, 100 kilometres from Saigon (see page 270).

Hoa Hao

Hoa Hao is another Vietnamese religion which emerged in the Mekong Delta. It was founded by Huynh Phu So in 1939, a resident of Hoa Hao village in the province of Chau Doc. Effectively a schism of Buddhism, the sect discourages temple-building and worship, maintaining that simplicity of worship is the key to better contact with God. There are thought to be perhaps one to 1.5 million adherents of Hoa Hao, predominantly in the Chau Doc area.

Background

Language

The Vietnamese language has a reputation for being fiendishly difficult to master. Its origins are still the subject of dispute – at one time thought to be a Sino-Tibetan language (because it is tonal), it is now believed to be Austro-Asiatic and related to Mon-Khmer. Sometime after the ninth century, when Vietnam was under Chinese domination, Chinese ideograms were adapted for use with the Vietnamese language. This script – *chu nho* ('scholars script') was used in all official correspondence and in literature right through to the early part of the 20th century. Whether this replaced an earlier writing system is not known. As early Vietnamese nationalists tried to break away from Chinese cultural hegemony in the late 13th century, they devised their own script, based on Chinese ideograms but adapted to meet Vietnamese language needs. This became known as *chu nom* or 'vulgar script'. So, while Chinese words formed the learned vocabulary of the intelligentsia – largely inaccessible to the man on the street or in the paddy field – non-Chinese words made up a parallel popular vocabulary.

Finally, in the 17th century, European missionaries under the tutelage of Father Alexandre-de-Rhodes, created a system of romanized writing – *quoc ngu* or 'national language'. It is said that Rhodes initially thought Vietnamese sounded like the 'twittering of birds' (a view interestingly echoed by Graham Greene in *The Quiet American*: "To take an Annamite to bed with you is like taking a bird: they twitter and sing on your pillow") but had mastered the language in six months. The first quoc ngu dictionary (Vietnamese-Portuguese-Latin), *Dictionarium Annamiticum Lusitanum et Latinum*, was published in 1651. Quoc ngu uses marks – so-called diacritical marks – to indicate tonal differences. Initially it was ignored by the educated unless they were Catholic, and it was not until the early 20th century that its use became a mark of modernity among a broad spectrum of Vietnamese. Even then, engravings in the mausolea and palaces of the royal family continued to use Chinese characters. It seems that the move from chu nom to quoc ngu, despite the fact that it was imposed by an occupying country, occurred as people realized how much easier it was to master. The first quoc ngu newspaper, *Gia Dinh Bao* (Gia Dinh Gazette), was published in 1865 and quoc ngu was adopted as the national script in 1920.

'Standard Vietnamese' is based on the language spoken by an educated person living in the vicinity of Hanoi. This has become, so to speak, Vietnam's equivalent of BBC English. There are also important regional dialects in the centre and south of the country, and these differ from Standard Vietnamese in terms of tone and vocabulary, but use the same system of grammar.

For some useful Vietnamese words and phrases, see the back inside covers of the book and the food and drink and shopping boxes on pages 39 and 41 respectively.

Literature

In ancient Vietnam, texts were reproduced laboriously, by scribes, on paper made from the bark of the mulberry tree (*giay ban*). Examples exist in Saigon, Paris, Hanoi and Hué. Printing technology was introduced in the late 13th century, but unfortunately, because of the hot and humid climate no early examples exist.

Vietnam has a rich folk literature of **fables**, **legends**, **proverbs** and **songs**, most of which were transmitted by word of mouth. In the 17th and 18th centuries,

··

 Kieu: oriental Juliet or prototype Miss Saigon?

The Tale of Kieu is a story of pure love corrupted by greed and power. It also offers a fascinating glimpse into the Vietnamese mind and Vietnamese sexual mores. Kieu is in love with the young scholar Kim and early on in the story she displays her physical and moral qualities:

> "A fragrant rose, she sparkled in full bloom,
> bemused his eyes, and kindled his desire.
> When waves of lust had seemed to sweep him off,
> his wooing turned to wanton liberties.
> She said: 'Treat not our love as just a game –
> please stay away from me and let me speak.
> What is a mere peach blossom that one should
> fence off the garden, thwart the bluebird's quest?
> But you've named me your bride – to serve her man,
> she must place chastity above all else.'"

But the overriding theme of the story is the ill-treatment of an innocent girl by a duplicitous and wicked world unopposed by Heaven. Unmoved by Kieu's sale into prostitution the fates actively oppose her wishes by keeping her alive when she attempts to kill herself.

Any respite in her tale of woe proves short-lived and joy turns quickly to pain. The story illustrates the hopelessness of women in a Confucianist, male-dominated world: Kieu likens herself to a raindrop with no control over where she will land. Early on in the story when Kim is away attending to family matters Kieu has to choose between Kim, to whom she has pledged herself, and her family. Such is the strength of family ties that she offers herself to be sold in marriage to raise money for her kith and kin:

> "By what means could she save her flesh and blood?
> When evil strikes you bow to circumstance.
> As you must weigh and choose between your love
> and filial duty, which will turn the scale?
> She put aside all vows of love and troth –
> a child first pays the debts of birth and care."

Kieu gets married off to an elderly 'scholar' called Ma who is in fact a brothel keeper; but so as not to arouse Kieu's suspicion before removing her from her family he deflowers her. Kieu is now commercially less valuable but Ma believes he can remedy this:

> "One smile of hers is worth pure gold – it's true.
> When she gets there, to pluck the maiden bud,
> princes and gentlefolk will push and shove.
> She'll bring at least three hundred liang, about
> what I have paid – net profit after that.
> A morsel dangles at my mouth – what God
> serves up I crave, yet money hate to lose.
> A heavenly peach within a mortal's grasp:
> I'll bend the branch, pick it, and quench my thirst.
> How many flower-fanciers on Earth
> can really tell one flower from the next?
> Juice from pomegranite skin and cockscomb blood
> will heal it up and lend the virgin look.
> In dim half-light some yokel will be fooled:
> she'll fetch that much, and not one penny less."

··

*Kieu's sorrows deepen; she becomes a concubine of a married brothel patron, Thuc. After a year
of happiness together with Thuc his spurned wife, Hoan, decides to spoil the fun. Kieu ends up as
a slave serving Thuc and Hoan. She laments her fate knowing full well the reason for it:*

> "I've had an ample share of life's foul dust,
> and now this swamp of mud proves twice as vile.
> Will fortune never let its victims go
> but in its snares and toils hold fast a rose?
> I sinned in some past life and have to pay:
> I'll pay as flowers must fade and jade must break."

*She later commits her only earthly crime stealing a golden bell and silver gong from the shrine
she is charged with keeping, and flees to seek sanctuary in a Buddhist temple. But when her
crime comes to light she is sent to live with the Bac family which, again on the pretext of
marriage, sells her to another brothel. This time she meets a free-spirited warlord Tu Hai:*

> "A towering hero, he outfought all foes
> with club or fist and knew all arts of war.
> Between the earth and heaven he lived free...."

*who rescues her from the brothel. They become soul- and bed-mates until, after 6 months,
Tu Hai's wanderlust and urge to fight take him away from her. He returns a year later
victorious in battle. At this stage the story reaches a happy (and false) ending; Tu Hai sends
his Captains out to round up all those who have crossed Kieu's path.*

> "Awesome is Heaven's law of recompense –
> one haul and all were caught, brought back to camp.
> Under a tent erected in the midst,
> Lord Tu and his fair lady took their seats.
> No sooner had the drumroll died away
> than guards checked names, led captives to the gate.
> 'Whether they have used you well or ill,' he said,
> 'pronounce yourself upon their just deserts.'"

*Those who have shown Kieu kindness are rewarded while those who have harmed her are
tortured horribly. The only exception is Hoan who, cruel though she was, Kieu releases (after
torture, of course) in a show of mercy following Hoan's plea "I have a woman's mind, a
petty soul, and jealousy's a trait all humans share" – Kieu had, after all, been living with
Hoan's husband for a year.*

*All is well for 5 years until another warlord, Lord Ho, flatters Kieu encouraging her to
persuade Tu to put down his sword and make peace with the emperor. Guileless Kieu does
so and "Lord Tu lets flags hang loose, watch-drums go dead. He slackened all defence –
imperial spies / observed his camp and learned of its true state." All is lost: Tu is killed, Kieu
has betrayed her hero and she is married off to a tribal chief. She throws herself into a river
but yet again fails to die. Eventually Kieu, is reunited with Kim and her family:*

> "She glanced and saw her folks – they all were here:
> Father looked quite strong, and Mother spry;
> both sister Van and brother Quan grown up;
> and over there was Kim her love of yore."

*Kieu and Kim hold a wedding feast and share a house but not a bed; Kim has sons by
Van, Kieu's sister, and they all settle down to an untroubled life overseen by a more
benevolent Heaven.*

*Huynh Sang Thong's translation (see recommended reading) is considered the finest
and is accompanied by excellent notes which explain the Vietnamese phrasing of the
original and which set the story in context. Translation and commentary will bring
Truyen Kieu to a wider and, one hopes, appreciative audience and help shed some light
on what many Vietnamese regard as their most important cultural statement.*

Background

satirical poems and, importantly, verse novels (*truyen*) appeared. These were memorized and recited by itinerant story-tellers as they travelled from village to village.

Like much Vietnamese art, Vietnamese literature also owes a debt to China. Chinese characters and literary styles were duplicated and although a tradition of *nom* literature did evolve (nom being a hybrid script developed in the 13th century), Vietnamese efforts remained largely derivative. One exception was the scholarly **Nguyen Trai** (see box on page 330) who bridged the gap; he excelled in classical Chinese chu nho as well as producing some of the earliest surviving, and very fine, poetry and prose in the new chu nom script. An important distinction is between the literature of the intelligentsia (essentially Chinese) and that of the people (more individualistic). These latter nom works, dating from the 15th century onwards, were simpler and concerned with immediate problems and grievances. They can be viewed as the most Vietnamese of literary works and include *Chinh Phu Ngam* (Lament of a Soldier's Wife), an anti-war poem by Phan Huy Ich (1750-1822). The greatest Vietnamese literature was produced during the social and political upheavals of the 19th century – *Truyen Kieu* (The Tale of Kieu) written by Nguyen Du (1765-1820) is a classic of the period. This 3,254-line story is regarded by most Vietnamese as their cultural statement *par excellence* (see the box on page 384 for a taster). Nguyen Du was one of the most skilled and learned mandarins of his time, and was posted to China as Vietnam's Ambassador to the Middle Kingdom. On his return, Nguyen Du wrote the *Truyen Kieu* (or *Kim Van Kieu*), a celebration of Vietnamese culture, in the lines of which can be traced the essence of Vietnamese-ness.

French influence, and the spread of the Romanized Vietnamese script, led to the end of the Chinese literary tradition by the 1930s and its replacement by a far starker, freer, Western-derived style. Poetry of this period is known as *Tho Moi* (New Poetry). The Communist period has seen restrictions on literary freedom, and in recent years there have been numerous cases of authors and poets, together with journalists, being imprisoned owing to the critical nature of their work. Much of Vietnam's literature is allegorical (which the people readily understand); this reflects a centuries old intolerance of criticism by the mandarinate and royal family. Although the Communist party might be expected to approve of anti-royal sentiment in literature it seldom does, fearing that the Party itself is the true object of the writer's scorn.

A Vietnamese account of the 'American' War

Most visitors to Vietnam, if they were not involved in the war themselves, gain their views from literature and films made by Westerners, for Westerners. It is rare for people to have access to Vietnamese literary perspectives on the war, partly because most that do exist are untranslated and because, in comparison to the torrent of especially American accounts, there have been comparatively few written by Vietnamese. One of these few is Bao Ninh's moving and poetic *The Sorrow of War* which was first published in Vietnamese in 1991 under the title *Thân Phân Cua Tinh Yêu*. In Vietnam it was a huge success, no doubt prompting its translation into English by Frank Palmos. The English edition was published in 1994 and it is now available in paperback (in the UK under the Minerva imprint). This is not a romantic vision of war; nor a macho account relishing the fight; nor once revelling in victory. It is a deeply sad and melancholic book. Perhaps this is because Bao Ninh is recounting his story from the position of one who was there. He served with the Glorious 27th Youth Brigade, joining-up in 1969 at the age of 17. Of the 500 who went to war with the Glorious 27th, he was one of just 10 to survive the conflict. For those who want an alternative perspective, the book is highly recommended.

Drama

Classical Vietnamese theatre, known as *hat boi* (hat = to sing; boi = gesture, pose), shows close links with the classical theatre of China. Emperor Tu Duc had a troupe of 150 female artists and employed stars from China via a series of extravagant productions. Since the partition of the country in 1954, there has developed what might be termed 'revolutionary realist' theatre and classical Vietnamese theatre is today almost defunct. However, the most original theatrical art form in Vietnam is *mua roi nuoc* or **water puppet theatre**. This seems to have originated in Northern Vietnam during the early years of this millennium when it was associated with the harvest festival (at one time scholars thought water puppet theatre originated in China before being adopted in Vietnam). An inscription in Nam Ha province mentions a show put on in honour of King Ly Nhan Ton in 1121. By the time the French began to colonize Vietnam at the end of the 19th century it had spread to all of the major towns of the country.

As the name suggests, this form of theatre uses the surface of the water as the stage. Puppeteers, concealed behind a bamboo screen symbolizing an ancient village communal house, manipulate the characters while standing in a metre of water. The puppets – some over half a metre tall – are carved from water resistant *sung* wood which is also very lightweight and then painted in bright colours. Most need one puppeteer to manipulate them, but some require three or four. Plays are based on historical and religious themes: the origins of the Viet nation, legends, village life, and acts of heroism. Some include the use of fireworks – especially during battle scenes – while all performances are accompanied by folk opera singers and traditional instruments. Performances usually begin with the clown, Teu, taking the stage and he acts as a linking character between the various scenes.

The most famous and active troupe is based in Hanoi (see page 96), although in total there are about a dozen groups. Since the 1980s Vietnamese writers have turned their attention from revolutionary heroes to commentary on political and social issues of the day. Consequently, many plays have failed to see the light of day and those that have, have often been badly mauled by the censoring committee's scissors; references to corrupt officials and policemen seldom make the transition from page to stage.

Background

buffalo teeth

prickles

jaw bone of the cricket

kapok

spines

toucan's beak

rice pounder patterns

bird's feathers

Vietnam War textile patterns

Montagnard textile patterns
(after Dournes, Boulbert, Huard and Maurice and France Asie.)

Crafts

True Vietnamese influence is best seen in the 'lower' arts – the crafts.

Lacquerware The art of making lacquerware is said to have been introduced into Vietnam after
(son mai) Emperor Le Thanh Ton (1443-1459) sent an emissary to the Chinese court to
investigate the process. Lacquer is a resin from the son tree (*Rhus succedanea or R
vernicifera*) which is then applied in numerous coats (usually 11) to wood
(traditionally teak), leather, metal or porcelain. Prior to lacquering, the article must be
sanded and coated with a fixative. The final coat is highly polished with coal powder.
The piece may then be decorated with an incised design, painted, or inset with
mother-of-pearl. If mother-of-pearl is to be used, appropriately shaped pieces of
lacquer are chiselled out and the mother-of-pearl inset. This method is similar to
that used in China, but different from Thailand and Burma. The designs in the north
show Japanese influences, apparently because Japanese artists were employed as
teachers at the École des Beaux Arts in Hanoi in the 1930s.

Non la This cone-shaped hat is one of the most common and evocative sights in Vietnam's
conical hat countryside. Worn by women (and occasionally men), it is usually woven from
latania leaves. The poem hats of Hué are the best known examples (see page 194).

Ao dai The garment that exhibits more conspicuously what it was intended to hide.
National women's costume of Vietnam, literally, but prosaically, 'long dress'. *Ao dai*
consists of a long flowing tunic of diaphanous fabric worn over a pair of
loose-fitting white pants; the front and rear sections of the tunic are split from the
waist down. The modern design was created by a literary group called the *Tu Luc
Van Doan* in 1932 based on ancient court costumes and Chinese dresses such as the
chong san. In traditional society, decoration and complexity of design indicated the
status of the wearer (eg gold brocade and dragons were for the sole use of the
emperor; purple for higher-ranked mandarins). The ao dai's popularity has spread
worldwide and the annual *Miss Ao Dai* pageant at Long Beach attracts entrants from
all over the US. Today *ao dai* is uniform for hotel receptionists and many office
workers, particularly in Saigon but less so in cooler Hanoi. French designer Elian Lille:
"The first thing most people see when they come to Vietnam is the young students
wearing a white ao dai, with their long hair clipped back and sitting very straight on
their bicycles. It is exquisite."

Montagnard There are over 50 different hill peoples, so their crafts are highly diverse. Textiles,
crafts jewellery and basketwork are the most widely available. The finely worked clothing
of the Muong (with Dongson-derived motifs) and indigo-dyed cloth of the Ba-na
are two examples of Montagnard crafts.

Modern Vietnam

Politics

Political stability versus economic reform

The Vietnamese Communist Party (VCP) was established in Hong Kong in 1930 by Ho Chi Minh, and arguably has been more successful than any other such party in Asia in mobilizing and then maintaining support. While others have fallen, the VCP has managed to stay firmly in control and in 1998 had a total of 2.3 million members. In 1986 at the sixth party congress the VCP launched its economic reform programme known as *doi moi* – a momentous step in ideological terms (see below). However, although the programme has done much to free up the economy, the party has ensured that it retains ultimate political power. Marxism-Leninism and Ho Chi Minh thought are still taught to Vietnamese school children and even so-called 'reformers' in the leadership are not permitted to diverge from the party line. In this sense, while economic reforms have made considerable progress (but see below) – particularly in the south – there is a very definite sense that the limits of political reform have been reached, at least for the time being.

The last couple of years has seen a number of arrests and trials of dissidents charged with what might appear to be fairly innocuous crimes (see the section below, 'The future of Communism in Vietnam') and although the economic reform enacted since the mid-1980s are still in place there is very little support within the party for any moves towards greater political pluralism. As the *Far Eastern Economic Review* argued after the 1996 Party Congress, for Vietnamese Communists the collapse of the Soviet Union and the Communist states of Eastern Europe did not reflect a failure of ideas, just a failure of management. There is not a single department of political science in any of Vietnam's universities reflecting a widespread belief in the hierarchy that there are no (better) alternatives to the present political system.

At the end of 1997 the recently elected 10th National Assembly selected a phalanx of leaders to take Vietnam into the millennium. As was the case in the weeks leading up to the eighth Communist Party Congress of June 1996, analysts had been waiting, moist with excitement, to see what the elections would reveal about the inner workings of the Party. Would there be an infusion of young blood? Would the conservatives or the reformists win the day? As always seems to be the case in these things, the evidence was mixed. Tran Duc Luong, a conservative technocrat, replaced Le Duc Anh as President; Phan Van Khai, a reformist, filled Vo Van Kiet's shoes as Prime Minister; and Le Kha Phieu, another so-styled conservative, replaced Du Muoi as Party General Secretary. While they are younger than the outgoing members at 63, 60 and 66 (Mr Anh and Mr Kiet were both septuagenarians and Mr Muoi an octogenarian when they retired from their posts) they don't represent an infusion of new blood and ideas. Mr Phieu's public statements certainly don't give the impression that here is a man who is at ease with market forces. In 1997 he argued that capitalism would ultimately fail because "it is backward in satisfying people's desire for happiness". He also has a habit of warning airily against 'hostile forces'. Shortly after these elections the new **politburo standing board** was selected. While both so-styled reformists and conservatives gained seats on the board, the overall impression is of some advance for the conservative wing of the party.

To many Westerners the pronouncements of the leadership may seem contradictory. But to most Vietnamese there is nothing strange about, for example, former general-secretary Do Muoi's comment that economic reform is the keystone of party policy while the party remains unshakably determined to follow the path of socialism. The new constitution approved in April 1992 merely re-emphasizes this point by bluntly stating that the VCP will continue to be the only political player in the country.

How long the VCP can maintain the charade, along with China, while other Communist governments have long since fallen (with the hardly edifying exceptions of Cuba and North Korea) , is a key question. Despite the reforms, the leadership is still divided over the road ahead. It is common to hear and read of 'conservatives' and 'reformists' or 'pragmatists'. The labels themselves probably mean little – indeed they simplify what is a complex debate between people with multiple stances by reducing the question to a binary one of yes/no, black/white, conservative/reformist. But the fact that debate is continuing, sometimes openly, suggests that there is continuing disagreement over the necessity for political reform, and the degree of economic reform that should be encouraged.

The crux is, how long will the population of Vietnam continue to accept a standard of living among the lowest in the world? One economist, referring to the momentum that is built into the process of economic reform, tartly observed in 1996 that "Life is stronger than dogma". This will become even more pertinent as *doi moi* brings wealth to a few, but leaves most people living in poverty. This has preoccupied Vietnam's leaders in recent years. In January 1992, the reformist Premier Vo Van Kiet who retired in 1997 said in an interview in the party daily *Nhan Dan* that the "confrontation between luxury and misery, between cities and country" could cause problems and talked of the need to "establish a new order of sharing" (see box "The bottom of the pile", page 399). As former Party General Secretary Do Muoi put it with great understatement at the Special Party Conference held at the beginning of 1994, there are "complicated factors" with which the leadership will have to contend.

The political tensions that are bubbling just beneath the surface of Vietnamese society broke the surface in 1997 when it became clear that there had been **serious disturbances** in the poor coastal northern province of Thai Binh, 80 kilometres south-east of Hanoi. In May, 3,000 local farmers began to stage demonstrations in the provincial capital, complaining of corruption and excessive taxation. There were reports of rioting and some deaths – strenuously denied, at least at first, by officials. However a lengthy report appeared in the army newspaper *Quan Doi Nhan Dan* in September detailing moral decline and corruption in the Party in the province. For people in Thai Binh, and many others living in rural areas, the reforms of the 1980s and 1990s have brought little benefit. People living in Saigon may tout mobile phones and drive cars and motorbikes, but in much of the rest of the country average incomes are around US$50. The Party's greatest fear is that ordinary people might lose confidence in the leadership and in the system. The fact that many of those who demonstrated in Thai Binh were, apparently, war veterans didn't help either. Nor can the leadership have failed to remember that Thai Binh was at the centre of peasant disturbances against the French. A few months later riots broke out in prosperous and staunchly Roman Catholic Dong Nai, just north of Saigon. The catalyst to these disturbances was the seizure of church land by a corrupt Chairman of the People's Committee. The mob razed the Chairman's house and stoned the fire brigade. Clearly, pent up frustrations were seething beneath the surface for Highway

1 had to be closed for several days while the unrest continued. While the Dong Nai troubles went wholly unreported in Vietnam a Voice of Vietnam broadcast admitted to them and went on to catalogue a list of previous civil disturbances, none of which was known to the outside world; it appears the purpose was to advise Western journalists that this was just another little local difficulty and not the beginning of the end of Communist rule.

At around the same time that peasants were demonstrating in Thai Binh, around 12,000 kilometres away the last link with Vietnam's imperial past was extinguished with the **death of Bao Dai** in Paris at the age of 83, the 13th and last emperor of the Nguyen dynasty. Bao Dai, 'Keeper of Greatness', ascended to the throne in Hué in 1925 and abdicated in 1945 after Ho Chi Minh had declared the creation of the Republic of Vietnam. He served for a short time as a special advisor in Ho's government and then fled to Hong Kong before returning under French protection in 1949 to become ruler of the State of Vietnam. Bao Dai was deposed in 1954 following the defeat of the French at Dien Bien Phu, and lived the last four decades of his life in exile in France. There, he gained a name for himself as a bon viveur, gambling with passion and living in a 20 room chateau near Cannes surrounded by fast cars and a retinue of servants. Bao Dai was, it is said, more French than Vietnamese. He dressed in Western clothes, was more comfortable speaking French than Vietnamese, preferred French cuisine to that of his homeland – and converted from Buddhism to Roman Catholicism.

Recent sentences handed down to political activists

August 1995
Nine political activists sentenced to prison for between four to15 years for trying to organize a pro-democracy conference in Saigon in 1993.

August 1995
Five Buddhists given custodial sentences of up to five years for 'undermining the policy of unity'.

November 1995
Two former Party members sentenced to two years in jail for 'abusing the rights of freedom and democracy to damage national security'.

December 1995
Two government critics, one a dissident and the other a senior government official arrested for questioning the authority of the Party.

September 1997
Dissident Pham Duc Kham released after serving seven years of a 12-year prison sentence. Given entry visa to US.

Economic reform versus social degradation

Another theme that has become popular among Party leaders is the fear of social degradation and malaise. In 1996 former general-secretary Do Muoi warned that Saigon had become a 'fertile ground for hostile forces', and talked of 'cultural pollution', 'political destabilization' and 'economic sabotage'. The Party also refers, as if it is a poisonous cloud, to the 'intrusion of noxious cultures', another reference to the social changes presumed to have been brought about by Vietnam's opening-up process.

For the majority of the Communist leadership, the developments to which Do Muoi referred are intimately associated with the economic reform process and the inflow of foreign investment, foreign goods, foreign ideas, and foreigners. In other words, Westernization. 'Social evils' has become a stock phrase and older people talk with worry and disgust about the growing number of young troublemakers on the streets of the country's larger cities. The government has begun to try and root out what it regards as these malignant influences.

Background

To a foreigner, perhaps the crassest policy has been the one to 'indigenize' hoardings and other advertisements, as if doing this will somehow stamp out social ills. In early 1996, Chase Manhattan Bank, that cesspool of degeneration and social evil, found that it had to pull down its sign because pride of place was given to a foreign language. The same went for Kodak and Pepsi, even western law firms with offices in Vietnam. To the despair of reformers and overseas investors, police in Hanoi openly stoned the petrol station hoardings of western oil companies. Shops and offices were forced to cover their names and advertising displays with sheets of plastic – effective by day but less so at night when lit up!

The fear in some quarters is that growing social ills will be used as a reason to backtrack on the economic reforms. Given the Asian economic crisis, which some have characterized as a failure of capitalism, even the apparently superior ability of the market system to put rice in bowls and money in pockets is open to question. Party leaders are fond of quoting Ho Chi Minh's axiom that 'Individualism is the cruel enemy of socialism'.

But not everyone sees the problem as lying only – or even mostly – with the market system; some point the finger of blame at the Party itself. At the beginning of 1997, six people were sentenced to death for corruption after a trial in Ho Chi Minh City. Shortly afterwards, the Party adopted new ethical guidelines to stem the spread of corruption in the party, the military, and in government and administration. The crack-down on corruption in the Party continued into 1998 and in March it was announced that 'thousands' had been expelled, 18,000 disciplined and 469 sentenced to terms of imprisonment.

International relations

In terms of international relations, Vietnam's relationship with the countries of the **Association of Southeast Asian Nations (Asean)** have warmed markedly since the dark days of the early and mid-1980s and in mid-1995 Vietnam became the Association's seventh – and first Communist – member. No longer is there a deep schism between the capitalist and Communist countries of the region, either in terms of ideology or management. The main potential flashpoint concerns Vietnam's long-term historical enemy – China. The enmity and suspicion which underlies the relationship between the world's last two real Communist powers stretches back over 2,000 years. Indeed, one of the great attractions to Vietnam of joining Asean has been the bulwark that it creates against a potentially aggressive China.

China and Vietnam, along with Malaysia, Taiwan, Brunei and the Philippines all claim part (or all) of the South China Sea's **Spratly Islands**. These tiny islands, many no more than coral atolls, would have caused scarcely an international relations ripple, were it not for the fact that they are thought to sit above huge oil reserves. He who claims the islands, so to speak, lays claim to this undersea wealth. Over the last decade China has been using its developing blue water navy to project its power southwards. This has led to skirmishes between Vietnamese and Chinese forces, and to diplomatic confrontation between China and just about all the other claimants. Although the parties are committed to settling the dispute without resort to force, most experts see the Spratly Islands as the key potential 'flashpoint' in Southeast Asia – and one in which Vietnam is seen to be a central player. The **Paracel Islands** further north are similarly disputed by Vietnam and China.

Rapprochement with the United States

One of the keys to a lasting economic recovery (see below) was a normalization of relations with the US. From 1975 until early 1994 the US made it largely illegal for any American or American company to have business relations with Vietnam. The US, with the support of Japan and other Western nations, also black-balled attempts by Vietnam to gain membership to the IMF, World Bank and Asian Development Bank, thus cutting off access to the largest source of cheap credit. In the past, it has been the former Soviet Union and the countries of the Eastern Bloc which have filled the gap, providing billions of dollars of aid (US$6 billion during the period 1986-1990), training, and technical expertise. But in 1990 the Soviet Union halved its assistance to Vietnam, making it imperative that the government look to improving relations with the West and particularly the US.

In April 1991 the US opened an official office in Hanoi (to assist in the search for MIAs), the first such move since the end of the war, and in December 1992 allowed US companies to sign contracts to be implemented after the US trade embargo had been lifted. In 1992, both Australia and Japan lifted their embargoes on aid to Vietnam, and the US also eased restrictions on humanitarian assistance. Support for a **full normalization of relations** was provided by French President Mitterand during his visit in February 1993 – the first by a Western leader since the end of the war. He said that the US veto on IMF and World Bank assistance had "no reason for being there", and applauded Vietnam's economic reforms. He also pointed out to his hosts that respect for human rights was now a universal obligation – which did not go down quite so well. Nonetheless he saw his visit as marking the end of one chapter, and the beginning of another.

This inexorable process towards normalization continued with the full lifting of the trade embargo on 4 February 1994 when President Bill Clinton announced the normalization of trade relations. Finally, on 11 July 1995 Bill Clinton announced the full normalization of relations between the two countries, and a month later Secretary of State Warren Christopher opened the new American embassy in Hanoi. On 9 May 1997 Douglas 'Pete' Peterson, the first 'post-war' American ambassador to Vietnam – and a former POW who spent six years of the war in the infamous 'Hanoi Hilton' – took up his post in capital.

The progress towards normalization was so slow because many Americans still harbour painful memories of the war. With large numbers of ordinary people continuing to believe that servicemen shot down and captured during the war and listed as **Missing in Action** (MIAs) were still languishing in jungle gaols, presidents Bush and Clinton had to tread exceedingly carefully. In a sense, it was recognized long ago that the embargo no longer served American interests; it was just that the public were not yet ready to forgive and forget.

Even though the embargo is now a thing of the past, there are still the families of over 2,000 American servicemen listed as Missing in Action who continue to hope that the remains of their loved ones might, some day, make their way back to the United States. (The fact there are still an estimated 300,000 Vietnamese MIAs is, of course, of scant interest to the American media.) It was this, among other legacies of the war, which made progress towards a full normalization of diplomatic and commercial relations such a drawn-out business. It was only at the beginning of 1995 that Washington opened a 'liaison' office in Hanoi, and even then, in a very un-American show of modesty, there was no US flag flying from the building. As one American diplomat explained to a journalist from *The Economist* at the time, "Washington would very much like this to be an invisible office". This diplomacy-at-a-snail's-pace frustrated many American businessmen who were clamouring for fanfare and celebration, not the slightly embarrassed shuffling of diplomats.

Background

The future of Communism in Vietnam

In his book *Vietnam at the Crossroads*, BBC World Service commentator Michael Williams asks the question: "Does communism have a future in Vietnam?". He answers that "the short answer must be no, if one means by communism the classical Leninist doctrines and central planning". Instead some bastard form of Communism has been in the process of evolving. As Williams adds, "Even party leaders no longer appear able to distinguish between communism and capitalism ...".

There is certainly **political opposition** and disenchantment in Vietnam. At present this is unfocused and dispersed. Poor people in the countryside, especially in the north, resent the economic gains in the cities, particularly those of the south (see the paragraph above on peasant demonstrations in Thai Binh). But this rump of latent discontent has little in common with those intellectual and middle class Vietnamese itching for more political freedoms; or those motivated entrepreneurs pressing for accelerated economic reforms; or those Buddhist monks and Christians demanding freedom of expression and respect for human rights; or the various groups of 'freedom' fighters operating (sporadically) from bases in Cambodia. Unless and until this loose broth of opposition groups coalesces, it is hard to see a coherent opposition movement evolving.

Nonetheless, each year a small number of brave, foolhardy or committed individuals challenge the authorities. Most are then arrested, tried, and imprisoned for various loosely defined crimes (see box). There is always the possibility that cataclysmic, and unpredictable, political change will occur. As one veteran, but anonymous, Central Committee member said in an interview at the end of 1991: "If the CPSU [Communist Party of the Soviet Union], which had been in power for 74 years, can fall to pieces in 72 hours, we have at least to raise that possibility in Vietnam". Major General Tran Cong Man highlighted these fears when he remarked that:

> "the collapse of the Soviet Union was a devastating blow for [Vietnam] ... [It] was our support, ideologically and psychologically, also militarily and economically. It was our unique model. Now we find it was a false model."

The tensions between reform and control were evident in the run-up to the special mid-term Conference of the Vietnamese Communist Party held at the end of January 1994. Intellectuals mounted attacks on the tenets of Marxist-Leninism in Vietnam and even questioned the role and ideals of Ho Chi Minh. Lu Phuong, a southern intellectual, authored a pamphlet which was unofficially circulated, but never published, in which he wrote that Ho had "borrowed Leninism as a tool" and never imagined that it would "turn intelligent people into foolish ones, turn people with ideals into degenerate ones and bog down the nation in stagnation." Other tracts echoed similar sentiments. The leadership silenced these questioning minds, and a **press law** which came into effect in mid-1993 prohibits the publication of works "hostile to the socialist homeland, divulging state or [Communist] party secrets, falsifying history or denying the gains of the revolution". Ly Quy Chung, a newspaper editor in Saigon, described the Vietnamese responding to the economic reforms "like animals being let out of their cage". But, he added, alluding to the tight control the VCP maintains over political debate, "Now we are free to graze around, but only inside the fences". The Party's attempts to control debate and the flow of information extend to the internet. In 1997 a National Internet Control Board was established and all internet and email usage is strictly monitored. The authorities attempt to fire-wall topics relating to Vietnam in a hopeless attempt to censor incoming information.

Economy

Partition and socialist reconstruction 1955-1975

When the French left North Vietnam in 1954 they abandoned a country with scarcely any industry. The north remained predominantly an agrarian society, and just 1.5 percent of 'material output' (the Socialist equivalent of Gross Domestic Product) was accounted for by modern industries. These employed a few thousand workers out of a population of about 13 million. The French added to the pitiful state of the industrial sector by dismantling many of the (mostly textile) factories that did exist, shipping the machinery back to France.

With **independence**, the government in the north embraced a socialist strategy of reconstruction and development. In the countryside, agricultural production was collectivized. Adopting Maoist policies, land reform proceeded apace. Revolutionary cadres were trained to spot 'greedy, cruel and imperialist landlords', farmers of above average wealth who might themselves have owned tiny plots. Leaders of land reform brigades applied Chinese-inspired rules through people's tribunals and summary justice. An estimated 10,000 people died; Ho Chi Minh was opposed to the worst excesses and, although he failed to curb the zealots, land reform in Vietnam was a much less bloody affair than it was in China. In industry, likewise, the means of production were nationalized, cooperatives were formed, and planning was directed from the centre. Although evidence is hard to come by, it seems that even as early as the mid-1960s both the agricultural and industrial sectors were experiencing shortages of key inputs and were suffering from poor planning and mismanagement. The various sectors of the economy were inadequately linked, and the need for consumer goods was largely met by imports from China. But it was just at this time that the US bombing campaign 'Rolling Thunder' began in earnest (see page 341), and this served to obscure these economic difficulties. It was not until the late 1970s that the desperate need to introduce reforms became apparent. The bombing campaign also led to massive destruction and caused the government in the north to decentralize activity to the countryside in order to protect what little industry there was from the American attacks.

Reunification and a stab at socialist reconstruction (1975-1979)

With the reunification of Vietnam in 1975, it seems that most leaders in the north thought that the re-integration of the two economies, as well as their re-invigoration, would be a fairly straightforward affair. As one of the Party leadership tellingly said during the Sixth Plenum at the end of 1979: "In the euphoria of victory which came so unexpectedly, we ... somewhat lost sight of realities; everything seemed possible to achieve, and quickly". This is understandable when it is considered that the north had just defeated the most powerful nation on earth. But the war disguised two economies that were both chronically inefficient and poorly managed, albeit for different reasons and in different ways. The tragedy was that just as this fact was becoming clear, the Vietnamese government embarked on another military adventure – this time the invasion and subsequent occupation of Cambodia in December 1978. Shortly afterwards, Hanoi had to deploy troops again to counter the Chinese 'invasion' in 1979. As a result, the authorities never had the opportunity of diverting resources from the military to the civilian sectors.

Conditions in the south were no better than in the north. The US had been supporting levels of consumption far above those which domestic production

....

Top investors cumulative investment, 1988 – end 1997

	US$ billion
1. Singapore	5.3
2. Taiwan	4.1
3. Hong Kong	3.7
4. Japan	3.5
5. South Korea	3.1
6. Britain	1.6
7. France	1.4
8. Malaysia	1.3
9. United States	1.2
10. Australia	0.7
11. Netherlands	0.4

....

could match, the shortfall being met through massive injections of aid. Following the Communists' victory, this support was ended – overnight. The Americans left behind an economy and society deeply scarred by the war: three million unemployed, 500,000 prostitutes, 100,000 drug addicts, 400,000 amputees and 800,000 orphans. Nor did many in the south welcome their 'liberation'. The programme of socialist transition which began after 1975 was strongly resisted by large sections of the population, and never achieved its aims. As resistance grew, so the government became more repressive, thus leading to the exodus of hundreds of thousands of 'boat people' (see page 348). Even as late as 1978, with the economy close to crisis, sections of the leadership were still maintaining that the problems were due to poor implementation, not to the fact that the policies were fundamentally flawed. The key problem was the characteristic of 'bureaucratic centralism': if a factory wished to transport umbrellas from Tay Ninh to Saigon, less than 100 kilometres, it was required to go through 17 agencies, obtain 15 seals, sign five contracts, and pay numerous taxes.

The roots of economic reform (1979-1986)

In a bid to re-invigorate the economy, the Vietnamese government – like others throughout the Communist and former Communist world – has been introducing economic reforms. These date back to 1979 when a process of administrative decentralization was set in train. Farmers signed contracts with their collectives to deliver produce in return for access to land and inputs like fertilizers and pesticides, thereby returning many aspects of decision making to the farm level. Surplus production could be sold privately. Factories were made self-accounting, and workers' pay was linked to productivity. The reforms of 1979 also accepted a greater role for the private sector in marketing, agriculture and small-scale industry.

Unfortunately these reforms were generally unsuccessful in stimulating Vietnam's moribund economy. Agriculture performed reasonably, but industry continued to decline. Cadres at the regional and local levels often ignored directives from the centre, and critical inputs needed to fuel growth were usually unavailable. Both national income and per capita incomes continued to shrink. The reform process is referred to as *doi moi* or 'renovation', the Vietnamese equivalent of Soviet perestroika. Implementation of *doi moi* has not been easy. In Neil Sheehan's book *Two Cities: Hanoi and Saigon* he asked one manager of a state enterprise: "What was worse ... fighting the French in Interzone Five ... or directing a state factory during doi moi?" The answer: "It was easier in Interzone Five."

Some commentators have argued that the economic reforms of 1979 demonstrated that the Vietnamese government was forward-looking and prescient. However there is also considerable evidence to show that the pressure for reform was coming as much from the bottom, as from the top. Farm households and agricultural cooperatives, it seems, were engaged in what became known as 'fence-breaking', by-passing the state planning system. The Communist Party, to some degree, was forced to follow where peasants had already gone. This raises the questions of how far Vietnam's 'command' economy was truly commanding.

Vietnam: selected economic reforms, 1979-1998

1975
April: *end of the Vietnam War*
1978
December: *Vietnamese forces invade Cambodia.*
1979
September: *Resolution No 6 issued by the Sixth Plenum of the VCP calls for reforms in industry and agriculture, including a loosening of State control.*
1981
April: *Directive 100/CT (Contract 100), introduces the first stage of agricultural decollectivization.*
1986
December: **Doi moi** *– 'new change' or 'renovation' – officially endorsed at the Sixth Party Congress.*
1987
December: *liberal foreign investment law promulgated to attract foreign investment.*
1988
April: *Resolution No 10 (Contract 10), makes individual households the basis of agricultural production. Banking reforms introduced separating the roles of the Central Bank and commercial banks. Exchange rate unified.*
1989
January: *fiscal policy tightened and positive real interest rates introduced. Subsidies to state-operated industries sharply reduced.* **March**: *price reforms introduced; price subsidies are gradually abolished for most goods.*
1992
`Equitization programme' introduced in which a handful of small state-owned enterprises are sold off to employees and others. **June and August**: *vague reference in revised Land Law to mortgaging and renting of land.*
1993
June: *granting of long-term use of agricultural land to peasant families.* **July**: *new Land Law passed. Households and individuals are allocated land according to household size and given the right to exchange, transfer, lease, inherit and mortgage land use rights.*
1994
New bankruptcy law passed making it possible for banks to seize the assets of state-owned enterprises.
February: *normalization of trade relations with the US.*
May: *new labour legislation enacted giving workers the right to strike.*
1995
April: *National Assembly considers new law partially or fully ending the state monopoly in selected sectors.*
1996
Third Amendment to Foreign Investment Law.
1998
February: *new foreign investment decree introduced to increase foreign direct investment.*

Sources: *Rigg, Jonathan (1997) Southeast Asia: the human landscape of modernization and development, London: Routledge; and Keesing's Record of World Events.*

Background

Benedict Kerkvliet, for example, argues that "Even at the height of state economic planning and control, there were social, economic, and political activities in Vietnam that the state did not authorize. ... 'Pluralism' ... has been around in Vietnam for some time". Peasants in Vietnam devoted enormous efforts in time and energy to the cultivation of their small private plots and tried to bypass the collective system through what became known as *khóan chui* or 'sneaky contracts'.

Doi moi: the reform economy (1986-present)

Recognizing that the limited reforms of 1979 were failing to have the desired effect, the VCP leadership embraced a further raft of changes following the **Sixth Congress in 1986**. At the time, the Party daily, *Nhan Dan* wrote that never had

Tourism in Vietnam

The Vietnamese government nominated 1990 'Visit Vietnam Year'. Although it did not have the razzmatazz of the Visit Thailand (1989), Malaysia (1990) or Indonesia (1991) years, the authorities hope that tourism will become a significant foreign exchange earner in the future. In 1989, 60,000 tourists visited the country, of which a quarter were overseas Vietnamese and a further 10 percent were from former Eastern Bloc countries. In 1990 the figure was 187,000, of whom 40,000 were overseas Vietnamese, and in 1993, 670,000 tourists visited the country. The target is now 3 million visitors by the year 2000. Clearly, the authorities have identified tourism as a lucrative money spinner for a country short of dollars.

Despite the high hopes and euphoria of the early 1990s tourism in Vietnam is facing serious reverses. The relative paucity of interesting sights (compared with Cambodia or Thailand) has resulted in a low rate of return visits particularly in the higher cost package market. Poor service and high prices have resulted in short stays and dramatic falls in the number of overseas visitors. Numbers visiting Hué were down by 40 percent in 1998. The Director of Hué's tourism service attributes this to high admission fees (foreigners pay 11 times more than Vietnamese) and poor service in the hotels where "The best hotel

in the old imperial city serves tepid coffee as dark as India ink, and any hope of a restful snooze in the morning is shattered by the banging and scraping that begins at 0700 – that or the urgent need to check on the use of the mini bar".

Hanoi has fared no better. In 1998 occupancy rates in state-run hotels were averaging 30-40 percent and joint venture hotels counted themselves lucky to creep over 50 percent.

Complaints centre around the high cost and poor value of Vietnam. The problem begins at the top with dual charging structures for internal air and train tickets with foreigners paying two to three times more than Vietnamese. Never slow to follow any money-making scheme, enterprising hoteliers, restaurateurs, cyclo drivers and everyone else with a product to sell have jumped on the bandwagon. One visitor lamented, 'accommodation everywhere was much more expensive than we imagined ... we were mercilessly overcharged in local restaurants, especially Nha Trang.'

Tourism authorities are belatedly beginning to realize that tourists can and do vote with their feet. There is now a sense of realization that Vietnam will have to compete for visitors with other countries in the region and at last there is a hint of more realistic prices and slightly better service.

"morale been so eroded, confidence been so low or justice been so abused". Subsidies on consumer goods were reduced and wages increased partially to compensate. There was also limited monetary reform, although prices were still centrally controlled. In late 1987 the central planning system was reformed. The net effect of these changes was to fuel inflation which remained high from 1986-1988 – in 1988 it was running at well over 100 percent.

Again, appreciating that the reforms were not having the desired effect, and with the advice of the IMF, a third series of changes were introduced in 1988 and 1989. The market mechanism was to be fully employed to determine wages, output and prices for the great majority of goods. The domestic currency, the dong, was further devalued to bring it into line with the black market rate and foreign investment actively encouraged.

But, with each series of reform measures disquiet in some sections of the Party grows. For example, in 1993 government salary differentials were widened to better reflect responsibilities. Whereas under the old system the differential between the highest and lowest paid workers was only 3.5 to one, the gap under the new system

The bottom of the pile: poverty and inequality

Except in the sense that a starving person is poor wherever he or she happens to live, poverty is relative. With an average per capita income of barely US$230 most Vietnamese, by Western standards, are poor. But over a decade of serious economic reform have already created deep divisions between the haves and have-nots. In Thanh Hoa Province in the north, foreign relief agencies estimate that well over a third of children under three years old are malnourished, and this is probably also true over large swathes of the country. Luong Xuan Hoang, a farmer from Quang Trang Province was quoted in the Far Eastern Economic Review as saying "Our lives haven't improved much under renovation" and his son had to drop out of school because the family couldn't pay the fees of 5-6,000 dong per month (about US$0.50). The bicycles, restaurants and electronic goods of Hanoi and Saigon are a world away from the grinding poverty of the countryside, and that world seems to be drifting further and further from the grasp of most farmers. Vietnam's leaders have already acknowledged that

the 'politics of envy' is a cause for concern – both political and moral.

The preliminary results of Vietnam's first substantive poverty survey show what might have been guessed: that incomes in Saigon and its surrounds are 2.7 times higher than the national average; that nine-tenths of the poor live in the countryside; that two-thirds of the richest are city dwellers; and that incomes in the Red River Delta are half those in the Mekong Delta. A World Bank study released in 1995 told the same story: rural poverty running at 57 percent, urban poverty at 27 percent. The question is what to do about it. The pressure to continue the process of reform and to make the country attractive to foreign investors will almost certainly cause inequalities to widen further in the short to medium term. Hoang, like poor people the world over, strives for his children rather than for himself: "I hope the lives of my children will be different from my life. I want their futures to be the same as those of rich families' children," he explains. His son is not well placed to achieve this wish.

is 13 to one. This may make good sense to World Bank economists, but it is hard to swallow for a Party and leadership who have been raised on ideals of equality.

Until the Asian crisis was heralded with the collapse of the Thai baht at the beginning of July 1997, the Vietnamese economy had done well to ride some pretty serious **external shocks**. With the collapse of communism in Eastern Europe, around 200,000 migrant workers returned to the country and had to be reintegrated. The decline in aid and assistance from the former Soviet Union (which was only partially compensated by aid from Russia) and the corresponding precipitous decline in trade from US$1.8 billion (admittedly at the then unrealistic rouble exchange rate) in 1990 to US$85 million in 1991, illustrates the extent to which Vietnam had to re-orientate its economy in the face of global political and economic change. No longer able to rely on the Soviet Union to bail it out (although even before then the Vietnamese would lament that the Soviets were 'Americans without dollars'), the Vietnamese government took the drastic step of banning the import of all luxury consumer goods in October 1991 in an attempt to save valuable foreign exchange.

Japan – not the Soviet Union – is now Vietnam's largest trading partner, and **foreign interest and investment** has grown considerably since the country began to open up to foreigners in the mid-1980s. By the end of 1997, cumulative authorized foreign investment since 1988 totalled over US$30 billion and over the period the investment trend – overall – has been upwards. However, while on paper it may be possible to give Vietnam a favourable report, there are numerous problems still to be overcome and over the last two years foreign investment has

Background

Waste not, want not

Men fashioning spare parts from scrap metal, boys busily collecting tins and cans, women sewing sandals from car tyres, mechanics cannibalizing cars; these are some of the most potent images of Vietnam to Western visitors. In a country where labour is abundant, time is cheap, and where resources are scarce, almost all scrap has value. Michael DiGregorio of the East-West Center in Hawaii estimates that in Hanoi 6,000 people earn a living scavenging for scrap, feeding 250 tonnes of 'garbage' from the waste economy back into the productive economy every day, constituting over a third of the 830 tonnes of refuse produced daily in the capital. This informal process of recycling reduces waste, helps to limit environmental degradation, and provides a living for the poor.

faltered. In 1996 the number of approved projects fell from the year earlier, in 1997 the actual value of investment shrunk – and 1998 looks like being even worse. In addition, it is worth remembering that Vietnam has one of the worst records when it comes to 'realizing' approved investment – it is estimated that only about one-third actually finds its way into the country.

Vietnam and the Asian crisis

While Vietnam may have weathered the collapse of the Soviet Union, it has not been immune from the effects of the economic crisis in Asia. The expected rate of economic growth for 1998 has been progressively cut from nine percent to seven percent to six percent (and even the latter figures looks over-optimistic – at the end of 1998 the World Bank was forecasting three percent growth) , the international credit rating agency Moody's has downgraded the status of Vietnam's bonds and bank deposits, projected export growth for 1998 has been more than halved, and the dong was de facto devalued in October 1997 as the authorities widened the trading band. There seems little doubt that the Asian crisis has created tensions in the Vietnamese leadership. In January 1998 Prime Minister Phan Van Khai talked of 'two camps of thought' and 'second thoughts about *doi moi*'. There are many more in the leadership and in the Party who wonder about the wisdom of taking the market road.

The Asian crisis has exposed serious weaknesses in Vietnam's leadership and its ability to run an economy. During the early to mid-nineties no political skill or economic management was required; foreign investment just came pouring in. With the drying up of overseas funds the government has had to take a lead. In one of the nicest of ironies, Vietnam's biggest problem has been the US dollar: arguably the US dollar has wreaked more harm on the Vietnamese economy than US bombs ever did. The total lack of confidence in the dong (chiefly on the part of Vietnamese) has meant that the dollar has remained the basic unit of account in Vietnam. Almost all businesses, small and large, and every landlord reckons in dollars. Even the government lacks faith in its own currency and virtually every state-run operation (from Vietnam Airlines to the railways, from Post and Telecoms to the airport tax department) charges in dollars. Therefore, as Asian currencies devalued and Thailand, Malaysia and Indonesia became cheaper Vietnam became increasingly expensive compared with its main competitors. Time and time again the Vietnamese Prime Minister and Party officials have underlined the law: foreign companies must fix the salaries of Vietnamese workers in dollars. Vietnam's supposed advantage, cheap labour, is a fallacy. A Senior Partner in one of the big accountancy firms recently said "it is cheaper for me to bring in an ex-pat than to employ an experienced Vietnamese". And with income tax rates of 80 percent for Vietnamese staff it is easy to see why.

Looking back on 20 Years of Peace

The 20th anniversary of the end of the Vietnam War fell on the 30 April 1995. The celebrations in Saigon raised the issue of whether political reunification had served merely to disguise a continuing sharp divide between the North and the South. Many southerners resent the fact that their graves go unmarked, their losses of 225,000 unacknowledged, and their former lives demeaned. Many find jobs hard to come by, and veterans – unlike those from the army of the former North – receive no pensions.

At the end of the war, 200,000 former southern politicians, soldiers and functionaries were sent to re-education camps – many never returned. One senior northerner remarked to Nayan Chanda, who was himself in Saigon during the final days of the war, that "After 20 years there is no sign of reconciliation ... Our press is still celebrating victory over the Saigon army. Mothers of northern heroes have been decorated and given rewards but mothers of Saigon troops have only humiliation." Despite the attempt to play down the victory for American consumption – who need to be placated for their dollars – in Vietnam the chasm

between the two regions remains.

Nor is it clear, to some at least, from what it was that the former South was liberated. James Webb, a Marine in Vietnam, author of Fields of Fire, *and an apologist for the American presence in the country, wrote on the occasion of the 20th anniversary that "Oddly, Vietnam seems to be emerging into what might have occurred if the war had indeed ended in a negotiated stalemate: an authoritarian, Western-oriented, market economy." These sentiments are echoed by Gabriel Kolko, an anti-war activist and a man with very different views from those of Webb, and with a very different agenda. He wrote, also on the anniversary of the end of the war:*

"The irony of Vietnam today is that those who gave and suffered the most, and were promised the greatest benefits, have gained the least. The Communists are abandoning them to the inherently precarious future of a market economy which increasingly resembles the system the US supported during the war. For the majority of Vietnam's peasants, veterans, and genuine idealists, the war was a monumental tragedy – and a vain sacrifice."

Economic challenges

The fact that Vietnam survived relatively unscathed the economic and political collapse of the former Soviet Union, has led some commentators to argue that the economy is more resilient than it looks. Although in terms of per capita income the country may be one of the 12 poorest in the world, Vietnam does have a well-educated population, good access to world markets and, as former Singapore Prime Minister Lee Kuan Yew put it, that "vital intangible" necessary for Newly Industrailizing Country-style rapid economic growth.

Up until 1997 it seemed to be taken for granted that Vietnam was destined for Asian-style rates of economic growth – apparently for the simple reason that it occupies a piece of Asian geographical space. Not only has the regional crisis put talk of Tiger economies on the back burner for the time being, but even before the crisis there were voices of caution. The gloss of the immediate post-*doi moi* years has dulled, and people now accept that reforms will need to be both deeper and wider. As Bradley Babson, the World Bank's representative in Hanoi said at the end of 1996, "It's been a painful process but it's better to be in a more realistic environment".

For a start, many of the reforms apparently in place are not being implemented in the expected manner. Take the process of privatization introduced in 1993. By

Background

1998, out of 5,800 state-owned enterprises only 29 had been partially sold off. Foreign investors, who initially piled into the country thinking there was money to be made, are now shying away, daunted by the red tape, infuriated by the bureaucratic inertia, and fed up with the corruption. A related problem is that while there are technocrats who are skilled and knowledgeable about the demands of building a market economy, the Party leadership have very little understanding of what it takes – and it is the Party which ultimately calls the shots. In 1996 the Party Congress reaffirmed the state sector's 'leading role' in building the economy, granting just a supporting role to the private sector.

But Vietnam's problems do not begin and end with the reform programme. There are also many more rather more familiar challenges.

The population is growing rapidly in a country where there are 900 people for every square kilometres of agricultural land. As the World Bank has pointed out, this means "the country will have to develop on the basis of **human resources** rather than natural resources." But the human resources themselves need substantial 'upgrading': malnutrition is widespread and poverty in the countryside over large areas of the north and interior uplands, the norm rather than the exception (see box "The bottom of the pile"). Education and health facilities also require massive investment, not to mention the physical infrastructure including roads and power. **Strikes** are also becoming more common. Officially, there were over 200 between 1990 and 1996, although most believe that the true figure is considerably higher.

In addition, and despite the much publicized reforms, there is still an extremely large, inefficient and unprofitable **state sector**. As in China, what to do about this part of the economy is proving the most intractable of the government's challenges. In 1996 there were still over 6,000 state-owned enterprises employing 1.5 million workers – admittedly down from 12,000 and some 2.5 million workers in 1990. But the 6,000 that have been closed down or sold off have been the smaller and/or more profitable firms – the big enterprises remain in place, sapping scarce funds. It has been estimated that just a third of these 6,000 enterprises are profitable. Managers and workers in state-owned enterprises are often resistant to changes, fearing the consequences of market 'discipline'. Workers expect to have a 'job for life', irrespective of profitability. The social consequences of the government forcing a change in this assumption are too great to contemplate, so instead state enterprises are being allowed to engage in joint ventures with foreign companies in the forlorn hope that either the problem will simply go away, or become less significant as other parts of the economy grow. The failure – or the unwillingness – of the government to dismantle the state sector is a particular bugbear of the World Bank which in most other respects awards the Vietnamese high marks.

The numbers of **unemployed** are also being boosted by the reduction in the size of the army – which celebrated its 50th anniversary in 1995. By late 1997 the country's standing army had been cut by two-thirds from its strength in 1989, to 500,000. Preparation for civvy life for the hundreds of thousands demobilized seems perfunctory to say the least. As one former soldier, now a cyclo driver, recounted to a journalist from *The Economist*, "When I joined, I was told they would help me find a job later. But when I left, all they gave me was a set of clothes, a piece of cloth and a paper that said that I had fulfilled my requirements."

Foreign investors also worry about the **lack of legal, banking and accounting systems**, and are put off by the **archaic physical infrastructure** when compared to such other Southeast Asian countries as the Philippines and Indonesia. The fact that, for example, nearly three-quarters of law students were sent to the former Soviet Union and Eastern Europe for their training, explains the lack of expertise in some crucial areas. At the end of 1994, Le Dang Doanh of Hanoi's Central Institute of Economic Management plainly stated that many of the new laws introduced since the late 1980s to deal with the economic reforms 'are words, not really laws'.

From Cold War to Cola War

The lifting of the US trade embargo at the beginning of February 1994 marked the full and final end of the Vietnam War but heralded the start of another war: the Cola War. PepsiCo erected a giant Pepsi can outside Reunification Palace in Saigon to celebrate the end of the embargo and had their bottles rattling off the production line the same evening, while rival Coca-Cola replied by inflating two outsized Coke bottles outside the Opera House in Hanoi. These brazen and somewhat insensitive stunts made longtime US residents shrink with embarrassment.

The rivalry is intense and unmissable: one of the first things visitors will notice on arrival in Vietnam, whether Hanoi or Saigon, are the Pepsi-Cola airport buses which ferry passengers from aircraft to terminal. At the end of the second year Pepsi had its nose in front, claiming a 55 percent share of the market to Coca-Cola's 39 percent. Coke has faced a series of problems; licensing its bottling factory was one. But the launch of their new 300 millilitre bottle – "that's 50 percent more great Coca-Cola taste without increasing the price" – looked set to narrow the gap: the war was hotting up.

Commercial law, for instance, barely exists in Vietnam, and some foreign companies are unwilling to throw money into a country which is, in legal terms, the equivalent of a black hole.

Investors arriving in Vietnam for the first time often imagine that, being communist, Vietnam will be centrally controlled. Nothing could be further from the truth. Every province is a law unto itself. A valuable piece of advice to potential investors in Vietnam is to regard the country as a federation. While official backing from Hanoi is very welcome the most important body to win over is the province People's Committee. Indeed senior government officials are frequently reduced to impotence when minor functionaries from Central Highland or Mekong Delta provinces calmly disregard their decrees. As they used to say, 'the writ of the emperor ends at the village gate'. In a modern context the same is true today. It is no use appealing to the Finance Ministry in Hanoi because the Lam Dong tax department is charging double what the ministry has decreed it should; the Lam Dong tax department charges whatever the Lam Dong tax department feels like charging.

The country's **export base** is also still comparatively narrow: oil, coal, rice, marine products and garments are the country's key exports. It has been estimated that just to double incomes from their current derisory US$230 per head by the year 2000 will require US$20 billion in external funding.

In addition, the economic growth of the nineties has brought its own problems – in the same way that has occurred in China. **Inequalities**, both spatial and personal, are widening as some areas and people benefit, while others do not. Growth in agriculture is down to three to four percent, while industry is expanding at an annual rate of 12 percent. So, while the economies of Hanoi and Saigon have been growing at an annual rate of about 20 percent, the countryside is stagnating or, at best, growing slowly. Nationally, the World Bank estimates that 51 percent of the population live in poverty; in the cities the figure is 27 percent. This is drawing people in from the countryside, creating urban problems of both a social (for instance, unemployed people living in poor conditions and a lack of educational facilities) and economic (such as strains on the physical infrastructure) nature. These inequalities are likely to widen further in the short to medium term with the on-going process of reform.

Background

Widening inequalities are also raising political challenges. Local and provincial governments in wealthy areas are beginning to resent financing poorer parts of the country, and are showing a greater inclination to 'go it alone', ignoring directives from Hanoi. This feeds back to foreign investors who find that they have to deal with different sets of regulations in different parts of the country.

Footnotes

Footnotes

Fares and timetables

Vietnam Airlines Summary Timetable

	Flight No	Day	Depart	Arrive
From Hanoi				
To Danang	VN311	Daily	0750	0900
	VN315	M,Tu,Th,F,Su	1645	1755
To Dien Bien Phu	VN492	Tu, Th,Sa,Su	1000	1100
To Saigon	VN741	Daily	0720	1920
	VN217	M,Tu,W, F, Sa	1210	1410
	VN223	Daily	1430	1630
	VN229	Daily x M	1710	1910
	VN233	Daily	1930	2130
To Hué	VN247	Daily	0630	1740
To Nha Trang	VN267	Daily	1330	1610
From Saigon				
To Ban Me Thuot	VN338	M,Tu,Th,Sa,Su	0620	0715
	VN440	W,F	1300	1355
To Dalat	VN464	M	0720	0810
	VN464	Daily x M	1010	1100
To Danang	VN320	Tu,F	0630	0740
	VN320	M,W,Th,Sa,Su	0710	0820
	VN322	Daily x F	1500	1610
	VN324	Tu,W,F,Su	1730	1840
To Hanoi	VN210	Daily	0700	0900
	VN212	M,Th,Sa,Su	0800	1000
	VN220	Daily	1130	1330
	VN222	W,F,Su	1220	1420
	VN224	M,Tu,Th,Sa	1330	1530
	VN226	Daily	1510	1710
	VN740	Daily	1640	1840
	VN232	M,Tu,Th,Sa,Su	1800	2000
	VN236	Daily	1945	2145
To Haiphong	VN282	Tu,W,Th,Sa,Su	0705	0905
To Hué	VN252	Daily	0620	0750
	VN254	Th,F,Sa	1050	1220
	VN254	M,W	1400	1550
To Nha Trang	VN334	Tu, Th, Su	0620	0730
	VN450	M, W, F, Sa	0730	0840
	VN454	Daily	1450	1600
To Phu Quoc	VN483	M,W,F,Su	0640	0740
	VN481	Th,Sa	0655	0755
To Play Ku	VN342	Daily x Tu	0625	0740
	VN446	Tu	1345	1500

Footnotes

	Flight No	Day	Depart	Arrive
To Quy Nhon	VN458	M,W	1105	1205
	VN458	F	1320	1435
	VN458	Su	1345	1500
To Rach Gia	VN483	M,W,F	0640	0905

From Hué

To Hanoi	VN246	Daily	0825	0935
	VN248	Tu,Su	1215	1345
	VN248	M,W,F,Sa	1305	1415
To Saigon	VN253	Daily	0835	1005
	VN255	Th,Sa	1310	1440
	VN255	M,Tu,W,F,Su	1640	1830

From Dalat

To Saigon	VN465	M	0855	0945
	VN465	Daily x M	1145	1235
	VN467	F,Sa,Su	1630	1720

From Ban Me Thuot

To Danang	VN338	M,Tu,Th,Sa,Su	0800	0910
To Saigon	VN339	M,Tu,Th,Sa,Su	1205	1300
	VN441	W,F	1440	1535

From Danang

To Ban Me Thuot	VN339	M,Tu,Th,Sa,Su	1010	1120
To Hanoi	VN310	Daily	1010	1120
	VN312	W,Sa	1715	1825
	VN314	M,Tu,Th,F,Su	1845	1955
To Saigon	VN321	Tu,F	0830	0940
	VN321	M,W,Th,Sa,Su	0910	1020
	VN323	Daily x F	1700	1810
	VN325	Daily	1930	2040
To Nha Trang	VN335	Tu, Th, Su	1030	1145
	VN335	M,Sa	1430	1545
To Play Ku	VN343	Th,F	1015	1105
	VN	M,W,Sa	1410	1500
To Vinh	VN370	M, W, Sa	1015	1125

From Dien Bien Phu

To Hanoi	VN493	Tu, Th, Sa, Su	1145	1245

From Haiphong

To Saigon	VN283	Tu,W,Th,Sa,Su	1030	1230

From Nha Trang

To Danang	VN334	Tu,Th, Su	0815	0930
	VN334	M,Sa	1225	1340
To Hanoi	VN266	Daily	1655	1935
To Saigon	VN451	M, W, F, Sa	0925	1025
	VN453	W,F	1135	1235
	VN335	Tu,Th,Su	1230	1330
	VN455	Daily	1645	1745

From Phu Quoc

To Saigon	VN480	Th,Sa,Su	0825	0925
	VN482	M,W,F	1115	1215

From Play Ku

To Danang	VN342	M,W,Th,F,Sa	0825	0915
To Saigon	VN343	Th,F 1150	1300	
	VN343	M,W,Sa	1545	1655

From Quy Nhon

To Saigon	VN459	M,W 1250	1350	
	VN459	F,Su 1520	1640	

From Vinh

To Danang	VN371	M,W,Sa	1210	1320

Trains from Hanoi

From Hanoi to Haiphong
Daily

Depart	Arrive
0600	0800 Depart from Tran Qui Cap St Station
0820*	1050
0955*	1235
1455*	1740
1710*	1950

*Dept from Long Bien station, Hanoi-Haiphong : 52,000d

From Hanoi to Dong Dang and Peking (50 hours)
Tuesday and Friday

Depart	Arrive	Depart	Arrive	Arrive
Hanoi	Dong Dang	Dong Dang	Nanning	Peking
1400	2000	2300	0710	1720

Hanoi-Dong Dang = 140,500d, soft sleeper, a/c
　　　　　　　　 = 75,000d, normal seat
Hanoi-Peking　　 = 1,500,000d, soft sleeper, a/c

From Hanoi to Lao Cai
Daily

Depart	Arrive
Hanoi	Lao Cai
0510	1630
2145	0745

Hanoi-Lao Cai = 207,500d, hard sleeper; 125,000d normal seat

From Hanoi to Hué, Danang, Nha Trang and Saigon

Train No	Depart	Depart	Depart	Depart	Depart	Arrive
	Hanoi	Vinh	Hué	Danang	Nha Trang	Saigon
S1	1930	****	0833	1126	2131	0530
S3	2000	0210	1030	1348	0100	1030
S5	1035	1705	0211	0535	1723	0335

S1 = Daily, S3 = Daily, S5 = Daily

Prices on Train S1

To	soft seat	hard sleeper (middle berth)	soft sleeper (a/c)
Hué	293,000	444,000	665,000
Danang	335,000	509,000	762,000
Nha Trang	601,000	917,000	1,377,000
Saigon	719,000	1,098,000	1,651,000

Prices on Train S5

To	hard seat	soft seat	hard sleeper (middle berth)	soft sleeper (fan)
Vinh	107,000	115,000	177,000	201,000
Hué	217,000	235,000	369,000	420,000
Danang	248,000	268,000	422,000	482,000
Nha Trang	442,000	478,000	759,000	867,000
Saigon	529,000	572,000	929,000	1,038,000

Prices quoted are 'foreigner prices' in dong

Trains to Hanoi

From Haiphong to Hanoi: 52,000d (daily)

Depart	Arrive
0640	0915*
1025	1305*
1400	1630*
1610	1840*
1845	2045

*Arr Long Bien station

From Peking and Dong Dang to Hanoi
Monday and Friday

Departt	Depart	Arrive
Peking	Dong Dang	Hanoi
1050	0330	1130

From Lao Cai to Hanoi (daily)

Depart	Arrive
Lao Cai	Hanoi
1000	2010
1830	0450

Lao Cai-Hanoi = Normal seat 125,000d; hard sleeper 207,500d

From Saigon, Nha Trang, Danang and Hué to Hanoi

Train No	Depart Saigon	Depart Nha Trang	Depart Danang	Depart Hué	Depart Vinh	Arrive Hanoi
S2	1930	0308	1252	1558	****	0530
S4	2000	0410	1521	1854	0326	1030
S6	2100	0617	1837	2223	0730	1430

S2 = Daily, S4 = Daily, S6 = Daily

Glossary

A

Amitabha
the Buddha of the Past (see Avalokitsvara)

Amulet
protective medallion

Arhat
a person who has perfected himself; images of former monks are sometimes carved into arhat

Avadana
Buddhist narrative, telling of the deeds of saintly souls

Avalokitsvara
also known as Amitabha and Lokeshvara, the name literally means `World Lord'; he is the compassionate male Bodhisattva, the saviour of Mahayana Buddhism and represents the central force of creation in the universe; usually portrayed with a lotus and water flask

B

Bai sema
boundary stones marking consecrated ground around a Buddhist bot

Batik
a form of resist dyeing

Ben Xe
bus station

Bhikku
Buddhist monk

Bodhi
the tree under which the Buddha achieved enlightenment (*Ficus religiosa*)

Bodhisattva
a future Buddha. In Mahayana Buddhism, someone who has attained enlightenment, but who postpones nirvana to help others reach it.

Boun
Lao festival

Brahma
the Creator, one of the gods of the Hindu trinity, usually represented with four faces, and often mounted on a hamsa

Brahmin
a Hindu priest

Bun
to make merit

C

Cao Dai
composite religion of south Vietnam (see page 382)

Caryatid
elephants, often used as buttressing decorations

Champa
rival empire of the Khmers, of Hindu culture, based in present day Vietnam (see page 328)

Chao
title for Lao kings

Charn
animist priest who conducts the basi ceremony in Laos

Chat
honorific umbrella or royal multi-tiered parasol

Chedi
from the Sanskrit *cetiya* (Pali, *caitya*) meaning memorial. Usually a religious monument (often bell-shaped) containing relics of the Buddha or other holy remains. Used interchangeably with stupa

Chenla
Chinese name for Cambodia before the Khmer era

Chua
pagoda (see page 365)

Cyclo
bicycle trishaw

D

Deva
a Hindu-derived male god

Devata
a Hindu-derived goddess

Dharma
the Buddhist law

Dipterocarp
family of trees (*Dipterocarpaceae*) characteristic of Southeast Asia's forests

Doi moi
`renovation', Vietnamese perestroika

Dok sofa
literally, `bucket of flowers'. A frond-like construction which surmounts temple roofs in Laos. Over 10 flowers signifies the wat was built by a king

Dtin sin
Lao decorative border on a tubular skirt

Dvarapala
guardian figure, usually placed at the entrance to a temple

Funan
the oldest Indianised state of Indochina and precursor to Chenla

Ganesh
elephant-headed son of Siva

Garuda
mythical divine bird, with predatory beak and claws, and human body; the king of birds, enemy of naga and mount of Vishnu

Gautama
the historic Buddha

Geomancy
the art of divination by lines and figures

Gopura
crowned or covered gate, entrance to a religious area

Hamsa
sacred goose, Brahma's mount; in Buddhism it represents the flight of the doctrine

Hinayana
`Lesser Vehicle', major Buddhist sect in Southeast Asia, usually termed Theravada Buddhism (see page 378)

Honda om
motorcycle taxi (*om* means `to cuddle')

Hor latsalot
chapel of the funeral cart in a Lao temple

Hor song phra
secondary chapel in a Lao temple

Hor tray/trai
library where manuscripts are stored in a Lao or Thai temple

Hor vay
offering temple in a Lao temple complex

Ikat
tie-dyeing method of patterning cloth

Indra
the Vedic god of the heavens, weather and war; usually mounted on a 3 headed elephant

Jataka(s)
the birth stories of the Buddha; they normally number 547, although an additional 3 were added in Burma for reasons of symmetry in mural painting and sculpture; the last ten are the most important

Kala (makara)
literally, `death' or `black'; a demon ordered to consume itself; often sculpted with grinning face and bulging eyes over entranceways to act as a door guardian; also known as kirtamukha

Kathin/krathin
a one month period during the eighth lunar month when lay people present new robes and other gifts to monks

Ketumula
flame-like motif above the Buddha head

Kinaree
half-human, half-bird, usually depicted as a heavenly musician

Kirtamukha
see kala

Koutdi
see kuti

Krishna
incarnation of Vishnu

Lambro
small three-wheeled motorised van

Laterite

bright red tropical soil/stone commonly used in construction of Khmer monuments

Linga
phallic symbol and one of the forms of Siva. Embedded in a pedastal shaped to allow drainage of lustral water poured over it, the linga typically has a succession of cross sections: from square at the base through octagonal to round. These symbolise, in order, the trinity of Brahma, Vishnu and Siva

Lintel
a load-bearing stone spanning a doorway; often heavily carved

Lokeshvara
see Avalokitsvara

Mahabharata
a Hindu epic text written about 2,000 years ago

Mahayana
`Greater Vehicle', major Buddhist sect (see page 378)

Maitreya
the future Buddha

Makara
a mythological aquatic reptile, somewhat like a crocodile and sometimes with an elephant's trunk; often found along with the kala framing doorways

Mandala
a focus for meditation; a representation of the cosmos

Mara
personification of evil and tempter of the Buddha

Matmii
Northeastern Thai and Lao cotton ikat

Mat mi
see matmii

Meru
sacred or cosmic mountain at the centre of the world in Hindu-Buddhist cosmology; home of the gods

Mondop
from the sanskrit, *mandapa*. A cube-shaped building, often topped with a cone-like structure, used to contain an object of worship like a footprint of the Buddha

Montagnard
`hill people', from the French (see page 368)

Mudra
symbolic gesture of the hands of the Buddha

Nak
Lao river dragon, a mythical guardian creature (see naga)

Naga
benevolent mythical water serpent, enemy of Garuda

Naga makara
fusion of naga and makara

Nalagiri
the elephant let loose to attack the Buddha, who calmed him

Nandi/nandin
bull, mount of Siva

Nirvana
release from the cycle of suffering in Buddhist belief; `enlightenment'

Pa kama
Lao men's all purpose cloth usually woven with checked pattern

paddy/padi
unhulled rice

Pagoda
a Mahayana Buddhist temple

Pali
the sacred language of Theravada Buddhism

Parvati
consort of Siva

Pathet Lao
Communist party based in the north-eastern provinces of Laos until they came to power in 1975

Pha biang
shawl worn by women in Laos

Phi
spirit

Phra sinh
see pha sin

Pra Lam
Lao version of the Ramayana (see Ramakien)

Pradaksina
pilgrims' clockwise circumambulation of holy structure

Prah
Sacred

Prang
form of stupa built in Khmer style, shaped like a corncob

Prasada
stepped pyramid (see prasat)

Prasat
residence of a king or of the gods (sanctuary tower), from the Indian prasada

Quan Am
Chinese goddess (Kuan-yin) of mercy (see page 77)

Rama
incarnation of Vishnu, hero of the Indian epic, the *Ramayana*

Ramakien
Lao version of the *Ramayana*

Sakyamuni
the historic Buddha

Sal
the Indian sal tree (*Shorea robusta*), under which the historic Buddha was born

Sangha
the Buddhist order of monks

Singha
mythical guardian lion

Siva
the Destroyer, one of the three gods of the Hindu trinity; the sacred linga was worshipped as a symbol of Siva

Sofa
see dok sofa

Sravasti
the miracle at Sravasti when the Buddha subdues the heretics in front of a mango tree

Stele
inscribed stone panel

Stucco
plaster, often heavily moulded

Stupa

Tam bun
see bun

Taoism
Chinese religion (see page 380)

Tavatimsa
heaven of the 33 gods at the summit of Mount Meru

Theravada
`Way of the Elders'; major Buddhist sect also known as Hinayana Buddhism (`Lesser Vehicle') (see page 378)

Traiphum
the three worlds of Buddhist cosmology – heaven, hell and earth

Trimurti
the Hindu trinity of gods: Brahma, the Creator, Vishnu the Preserver and Siva the Destroyer

Tripitaka
Theravada Buddhism's Pali canon

Ubosoth
see bot

Urna
the dot or curl on the Buddha's forehead, one of the distinctive physical marks of the Enlightened One

Usnisa
the Buddha's top knot or `wisdom bump', one of the physical marks of the Enlightened One

Vahana
`vehicle', a mythical beast, upon which a deva or god rides

Viet Cong
Vietnamese Communist troops (see page 338)

Viet Minh
Vietnamese Communist troops (see page 334)

Viharn
from Sanskrit *vihara*, an assembly hall in a Buddhist monastery; may contain Buddha images and is similar in style to the bot

Vishnu
the Protector, one of the gods of the Hindu trinity, generally with four arms holding a disc, conch shell, ball and club

Shorts

Index

Note: grid references to the colour maps are shown in italics after place names. So 'Danang *M3A5*' can be found on Map 3, square A5.

Map index

Footnotes

Complete listing

Latin America
Argentina Handbook 1st
1 900949 10 5 £11.99
Bolivia Handbook 1st
1 900949 09 1 £11.99
Bolivia Handbook 2nd
1 900949 49 0 £12.99
Brazil Handbook 1st
0 900751 84 3 £12.99
Brazil Handbook 2nd
1 900949 50 4 £13.99
Caribbean Islands Handbook 2000
1 900949 40 7 £14.99
Chile Handbook 2nd
1 900949 28 8 £11.99
Colombia Handbook 1st
1 900949 11 3 £10.99
Cuba Handbook 1st
1 900949 12 1 £10.99
Cuba Handbook 2nd
1 900949 54 7 £10.99
Ecuador & Galápagos Handbook 2nd
1 900949 29 6 £11.99
Mexico Handbook 1st
1 900949 53 9 £13.99
**Mexico & Central America
Handbook 2000**
1 900949 39 3 £15.99
Peru Handbook 2nd
1 900949 31 8 £11.99
South American Handbook 2000
1 900949 38 5 £19.99
Venezuela Handbook 1st
1 900949 13 X £10.99
Venezuela Handbook 2nd
1 900949 58 X £11.99

Africa
East Africa Handbook 2000
1 900949 42 3 £14.99
Morocco Handbook 2nd
1 900949 35 0 £11.99
Namibia Handbook 2nd
1 900949 30 X £10.99
South Africa Handbook 2000
1 900949 43 1 £14.99
Tunisia Handbook 2nd
1 900949 34 2 £10.99
Zimbabwe Handbook 1st
0 900751 93 2 £11.99

Wexas
Traveller's Handbook
0 905802 08 X £14.99
Traveller's Healthbook
0 905802 09 8 £9.99

Asia
Cambodia Handbook 2nd
1 900949 47 4 £9.99
Goa Handbook 1st
1 900949 17 2 £9.99
Goa Handbook 2nd
1 900949 45 8 £9.99
India Handbook 2000
1 900949 41 5 £15.99
Indonesia Handbook 2nd
1 900949 15 6 £14.99
Indonesia Handbook 3rd
1 900949 51 2 £15.99
Laos Handbook 2nd
1 900949 46 6 £9.99
Malaysia & Singapore Handbook 2nd
1 900949 16 4 £12.99
Malaysia Handbook 3rd
1 900949 52 0 £12.99
Myanmar (Burma) Handbook 1st
0 900751 87 8 £9.99
Nepal Handbook 2nd
1 900949 44 X £11.99
Pakistan Handbook 2nd
1 900949 37 7 £12.99
Singapore Handbook 1st
1 900949 19 9 £9.99
Sri Lanka Handbook 2nd
1 900949 18 0 £11.99
Sumatra Handbook 1st
1 900949 59 8 £9.99
Thailand Handbook 2nd
1 900949 32 6 £12.99
Tibet Handbook 2nd
1 900949 33 4 £12.99
Vietnam Handbook 2nd
1 900949 36 9 £10.99

Europe
Andalucía Handbook 2nd
1 900949 27 X £9.99
Ireland Handbook 1st
1 900949 55 5 £11.99
Scotland Handbook 1st
1 900949 56 3 £10.99

Middle East
Egypt Handbook 2nd
1 900949 20 2 £12.99
Israel Handbook 2nd
1 900949 48 2 £12.99
Jordan, Syria & Lebanon Handbook 1st
1 900949 14 8 £12.99

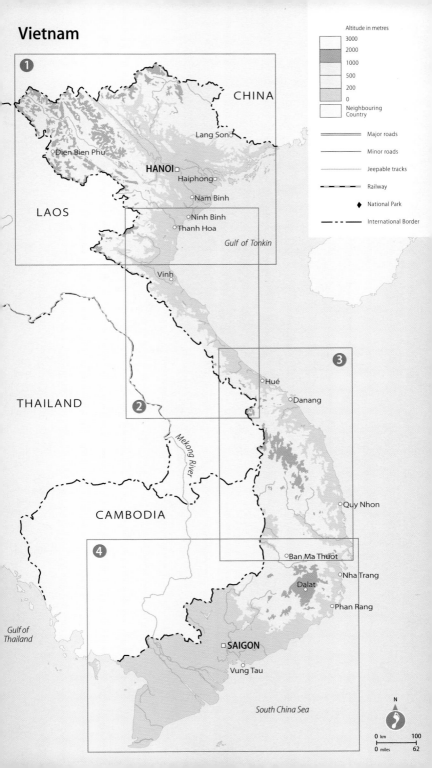

MAP 2

Gia River

Hoa Lu
Ninh Binh
Bich Dong

*Cuc Phuong
National Park* ◆

Gulf of Tonkin

Ⓐ

Ca River

Thanh Hoa
Sam Son ○

⬆ Map 1

rain Range

Cua Lo ○
Vinh

▲ *Ong Mountain
(1,587m)*

Ha Tinh ○

Ⓑ

*Phong Nha
Cave* ○

*Da Mao
Mountain
(665m)* ▲   Dong Hoi

*Len Mu
Mountain
(918m)* ▲

L A O S

*Voi Mep
Mountain
(1,701m)* ▲   Dong Ha
Quang

Khe Sanh
Lao Bao ○

➡ Map 3

Ⓒ

N

0 km ———— 50
0 miles ———— 31

①   **②**   **③**

MAP 3

Dong Ha

Quang Tri

Hué

Cau Hai Lagoon

Lan Co

Hai Van Pass

Bana○

Danang

Hoi An

My Son

Tam Ky

Quang Ngai

Ngoc Linh (2,598m)

Hoai Nhon

Kontum

Kontum Plateau

Play Ku

Ba Mountain (892m)

Quy Nhon

Song Cau

Ba River

Tuy Hoa

Da Rang River

Dac Lac Plateau

Buon Ma Thuot

A

B

C

ap 2

ap 4

N

50

31

4

5

6

MAP 4

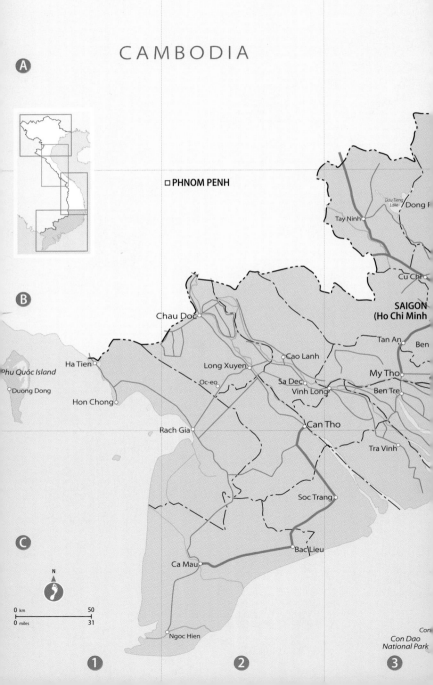

CAMBODIA

□ PHNOM PENH

Dau Tieng Lake

Dong F

Tay Ninh

Cu Chi

SAIGON
(Ho Chi Minh

Chau Doc

Tan An

Ben

Ha Tien

Cao Lanh

Long Xuyen

My Tho

Phu Quoc Island

Oc-eo

Sa Dec

Ben Tre

Duong Dong

Vinh Long

Hon Chong

Rach Gia

Can Tho

Tra Vinh

Soc Trang

Bac Lieu

Ca Mau

Con
Con Dao
National Park

Ngoc Hien

N

0 km   50
0 miles   31

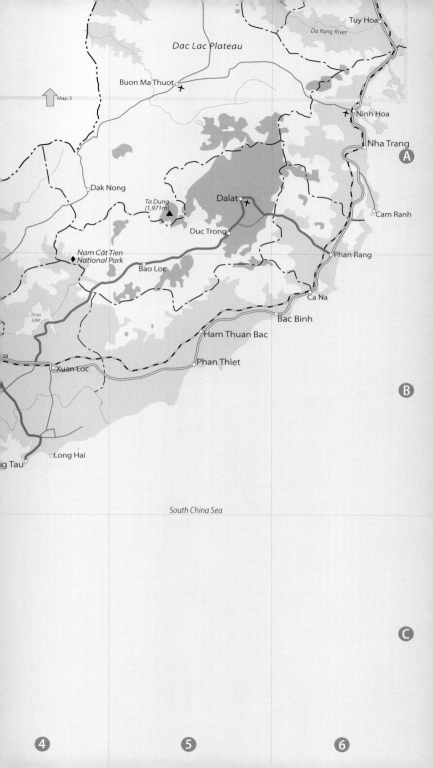

What the papers say

"*I carried the South American Handbook in my bag from Cape Horn to Cartagena and consulted it every night for two and a half months. And I wouldn't do that for anything else except my hip flask.*"

Michael Palin

"*Footprint's India Handbook told me everything from the history of the region to where to get the best curry*"

Jennie Bond, BBC correspondent

"*Of all the main guidebook series this is genuinely the only one we have never received a complaint about.*"

The Bookseller

"*All in all, the Footprint Handbook series is the best thing that has happened to travel guidebooks in years. They are different and take you off the beaten track away from all the others clutching the competitors' guidebooks.*"

The Business Times, Singapore

Mail order
Available worldwide in good bookstores, Footprint Handbooks can also be ordered directly from us in Bath, via our website or from the address on the back cover.

Website
www.footprintbooks.com
Take a look for the latest news, to order a book or to join our mailing list.

Acknowledgements

Thanks in particular to Tim Doling for his meticulous work on the north of Vietnam and for unearthing so much of historical interest; to Simon Boas for his research, conducted from the back of a Minsk, in the Central Highlands and the Mekong Delta; to Craig O'Hara who lost his glasses and his girlfriend while updating the southern coastal areas on his Minsk; yet again to Tran Quoc Cong for his contributions from Danang, Hoi An and surrounds, and to Chau for her painstaking work compiling data for many of the maps and the Saigon listings. Peter Murray's detailed knowledge of North East Vietnam was of enormous value in updating the travelling text.

Thanks also to: Giles Watkins, Saigon; Thomas Hege, Hinterkappelen, Switzerland; Anastasia von Seibold, Hanoi and Abingdon; Ivan Wainewright, London; Tanya Hines, London; Hanne Olsen, London; François and Anne-Marie Boller, Paris; Andy Dong, California.